What the critics said about
DAVID KEREKES & DAVID SLATE[illegible]
previous book

KILLING FOR C[illegible]

"Utterly un[illegible]
Melody[illegible]

"The undisputed film book of th[illegible] die."
Fatal Visions

"Refreshing. Stands as a defi[illegible]e study."
Sight and Sound

"Exhaustive and definitive study of the phenomenon."
Manchester Evening News

"Meticulously researched, comprehensive, well-written and intellectually fertile."
Eros Digest

"One of the most bizarre books you're ever going to come across."
Metal Hammer

"A must have."
Film Threat Video Guide

"A fascinating read. Worryingly so."
The List

"Yeeuch."
The Sunday Times

"The definitive guide."
Empire

"A truly vital and genuinely unique book."
Samhain

"Not a work to be taken lightly . . . Compulsive."
Flesh & Blood

"Sensible . . . Informed . . . Necessary."
The Dark Side

"The tome of choice for those fascinated with the marginalia."
Tower Pulse!

"A sane and rational voice . . . the authoritative guide."
Compulsion

"A captivating read . . . cleverly structured, well-researched and lucidly written."
Shivers

"A beautiful book."
Shock Cinema

A Critical Vision Book
Published in 2000
by Headpress

Critical Vision
PO Box 26
Manchester
M26 1PQ
Great Britain
fax: +44 (0)161 796 1935
email: david.headpress@zen.co.uk
http://www.headpress.com/

See No Evil: Banned Films and Video Controversy

Book layout & design: Walt Meaties
Front cover: Design based on 'The Toolbox Murders' Hokushin videobox art.
Back cover: Design based on a German lobby card for 'Scanners.'
Proof reading: Sun Paige

The publisher welcomes letters of comment, suggestions and possible amendments for future editions of this book. However, please do not write for details and availability of any films that are discussed.

British Library Cataloguing in Publication Data
A catalogue record for this book is available from the British Library.

ISBN 1 900486 10 5

SEE NO EVIL

Banned Films and Video Controversy

David Kerekes & David Slater

CRITICAL VISION
is an imprint of HEADPRESS

CONTENTS

"The more you try to ban it the more it grows"
—James Ferman, director of the BBFC 1975-1998

"Something huge, like an elephant"
—James C Wasson, Night of the Demon

INTRODUCTION

This book isn't intended to be an encyclopaedia of contentious films, nor have the authors set out to isolate and discuss every video that has had a run-in with the law or the British Board of Film Classification. *See No Evil* is primarily a chronicle of video culture in Britain, and of political anti-film propaganda from the late-seventies to the present. A substantial part of the book deals, naturally, with the Video Recordings Act 1984 and the so-called 'video nasties.' It was during this turbulent era — to quote the little boy in *Shogun Assassin* — that "everything changed, forever."

Extended thanks and gratitude go to Stefan Jaworzyn for the loan of illustrations, and for his support and help, and to David Kenny for allowing us access to his interview with James Ferman, which was to become part of the back bone to his documentary *Fear, Panic & Censorship* (A ShashMedia Production for Channel 4). For contributions to the text and for interviews, we would like to thank William Black, Mikita Brottman, Steve Ellison, Carl Daft (Exploited), Richard King (Screen Edge) and Christopher Glazebrook.

We are also grateful to the following people for assistance and/or the forwarding of newspaper clippings, assorted ephemera and information: Gerard Alexander, Douglas Baptie, Bruce Barnard, David Barraclough, KA Beer, Anton Black, Ray Brady, Paul Brown, Tim Buggie, Simon Collins, Jonathan Davies, David Greenall, David Gregory, Marie-Luce Giordani, Adrian Horrocks, David Huxley, David Hyman, Martin Jones, Lesley Kerekes, Paul Kevern, Chris Mikul, David Monaghan, Carl Nolan, Sun Paige, Steve Puchalski, Roger Sabin, Salvation Films (Chris Charlston, Marc Morris, Louise Ross), Mark Slater, David Lass, Shaun Kimber and Tristan Thompson.

There are many other people to whom we owe a debt of gratitude, but who for obvious reasons prefer to remain anonymous (some of them can be found under pseudonyms in the chapter BLACK MARKET & PIRATES).

A NOTE ON THE TEXT: Titles commonly attributed to the video nasties are quite often not the same as the title that appears on the actual print of the film itself, i.e. the box may say *Late Night Trains* but the print says *Night Train Murders*. For the sake of clarity and continuity we have listed video nasties under the titles to which they are most commonly referred — i.e. the title appearing on the videobox and used by the DPP in compiling their list of films liable to be prosecuted under the Obscene Publications Act 1959.

Actual titles as they appear on the prints themselves can be found in the sidebars of the VIDEO NASTIES chapter.

A Jaguar Video Release
4½ HOURS OF UNRELENTING
TERROR
WITH THESE 3 GREAT JAGUAR VIDEO CASSETTES
THE HILLS HAVE EYES
THE LUCKY ONES DIED FIRST....
Just keep telling yourself it's only a film it's only a film...
RUN - if you must
HIDE - if you can
SCREAM
but...
DON'T ANSWER THE PHONE!
X
....He'll Know You're Alone!
Starring JAMES WESTMORELAND · FLO GERRISH · Directed by ROBERT HAMMER
A JOURNEY INTO TERROR AND
HUMAN EXPERIMENTS
HUMAN EXPERIMENTS
Exclusive distribution by
WORLD OF VIDEO 2000 LTD
Tomorrow's world of video entertainment today
MAINE HOUSE, 15 LYON ROAD
LONDON SW19 2SB TEL: (01) 540 88

'Time marches on!'

BEGINNINGS

"Time marches on!" — This was a pronouncement made by the *International Film Guide* of 1982 in relation to the rapid encroachment of video in the film collector's marketplace, once the bastion of Super-8 and, to a lesser extent, 16mm. So swift was its encroachment in fact, that by the time the article appeared in print many cine specialists had folded or already switched to a dedicated video dealership. The reasons for this transition were numerous. On the face of it, escalating increases in the price of raw stock and labour intensive laboratory costs, meant that Super-8 was unable to compete financially with pre-recorded videocassettes.[1] Video also served to better domesticate home entertainment, with complete films in a single manageable cartridge as opposed to the 'digest' versions of movies or 'extracts' generally offered for Super-8 consumption.[2] The new technology was more user-friendly, eliminating the necessity for darkened rooms and the assemblage of extraneous equipment like screens and projectors prior to viewing.

As interest rose dramatically through the early eighties, video ceased to be the reserve of film buffs, and by 1983 close on six million video machines had found their way into homes across Britain. Fresh distribution outlets for films appeared with unerring regularity. Major film studios struggled to keep pace as upstart independents with little to lose and a lot to gain took the initiative and forced the market to expand.

With film and distribution companies barely able to meet the demand for new product, all manner of diverse material found its way onto magnetic tape. Any topic it seemed, no matter how esoteric or specialist, was guaranteed a sizeable audience amongst video viewers. Documentaries on surrealist painters (*Monsieur Rene Magritte*), experimental graphics set to music (*Music-Image Odyssey*), home help guides (*Bar-B-Q*) and tutorials for everyone from Rubik's cube enthusiasts (*You Too Can Do the Cube*) to budding guitarists were promoted as major acquisitions in the early video catalogues. Even something as mundane as *The Entertaining*

Electron, a practical insight into the way in which television programmes were made and broadcast, and the 156-minute *The Mighty Micro*, had commercial potential thanks to video. British Home Video was a company specialising in teach-yourself home courses, with a selection of three-hour videocassettes devoted to subjects as diverse as motor mechanics, kung fu, medical advice and even video maintenance (which answered the question "What is a tracking fault?"). With the country in the grip of royal wedding fever, following the announcement in February 1981 of Prince Charles' marriage to Lady Diana Spencer,[3] video wasn't left out of the souvenir cash-in stakes. Michael Barratt Home Video Programmes offered "exclusive new sequences and intimate glimpses" in *Princess*,[4] while their companion release *The Story of Prince Charles and Lady Diana* traced the couple's "parallel life stories from birth up to the day of their engagement." *The Glittering Crowns* was The Electronic Publishing Company's first production for videocassette and featured the story of the monarchy in the twentieth century. Another company, World of Video, simply offered buyers of their thirty minute guide to London landmarks an optional second sleeve depicting the royal couple.

The demand for video meant that even promotional films — 'infomercials' by any other name — could be sold to the public, as in the case of Pedigree Petfood's *All You Need To Know About Dogs* and practical painting advice with *The Dulux Videoguide To Colouring Your Home*.

Narration by such TV favourites as Edward Fox, Sir Huw Wheldon, Leslie Judd, and Johnny Ball gave many of the above tapes a familiar, friendly feel.

Another aspect of the market came in the guise of the video magazine programme, which for all intents was a compilation of material in the manner of a television variety show, but with a twist of the alternative in keeping with the cutting edge medium on which it now played. Indeed one of the first, a one-hour programme entitled *The Mad Tape* — containing a juggler of meat, a Wild West shootout, and a singing jukebox — was made primarily for TV but never broadcast. Another one-hour video magazine programme, *Red Tape*, hosted by "zany" comedian Keith Allen, promoted itself as "alternative television for the eighties." Amongst its line-up was an X-rated cartoon, a look at hang-gliding, *Star Trek* bloopers, and a bevy of topless girls. Along the same lines was *Rewind*, which Catalyst Video purported hit sales of almost 40,000. Quick to follow was *Rewind 2*, a one-hour programme which came on a three-hour tape, the incentive being that the purchaser would not only be getting an hour's entertainment but also two-hour's worth of blank tape. The fact the programme's running time was taken up with trailers for EMI movies lasting almost twenty minutes couldn't have impressed viewers much, however.

Disc jockey and popular entertainer Kenny Everett was the host and star of *The Kenny Everett Naughty Joke Box*, a live show recorded exclusively for release on video whose content — famous comedians telling blue jokes, with some scantily clad ladies running about — was promoted by VideoSpace as going beyond the limit of broadcast television acceptability.

Everett had found success in television (reaching the audience that had so eluded his earlier small screen ventures) when he launched *The Kenny Everett Video Show* in 1978. Not only did it utilise state of the art video effects trickery to bring the comedian's many grotesque characters to life, but also piqued interest with a title that incorporated the new buzz word.

With *Electric Blue*, the Electric Video company developed and specialised what they billed as "the world's first and original men's magazine on a videocassette." This "Electronic Sex for the eighties" was a series of highly successful video programmes[5] — whose features included nude wives, centrefolds, film clips (several starring Traci Lords) and sporting mishaps.[6] In spite of a slow-motion replay of Erica Rowe streaking across a Twickenham rugby pitch, and a variety of women riding a mechanical bull in the nude, the highlight of *Electric Blue* volume eight was "The World's First 3-D Centrefold." Coming with a free pair of 3-D glasses, this special seven minute segment — filmed in Los Angeles and utilising new technology — was described by *Continental Film and Video Review*[7] as working "quite effectively at the press launch."[8]

The *Electric Blue* tapes inspired imitators, notably *Mirage* and *Shades of Blue*, "the 'All-American Video Magazine' aimed at the man who still likes his fruit ripe!" Inspired by the Miss Nude Europe pageant held in Paris, a British model agent hit upon the idea for *Miss Nude UK* — a series of five video tapes of one-hour duration, each of which depicted four girls going about their daily routines, their pastime pursuits and, of course, stripping off for the camera. Viewers were invited to vote for a girl from each tape and ultimately select Miss Nude UK.

Crest Films tried a different tack with their *Stag & Hen Night*, which attempted to redress the bias of the "girlie video magazines," and reach an audience of both sexes with the crossover implied in its title. Shot live (with psychedelic effects) and featuring two male strippers, two female strippers, a female impersonator and a comedian, *Stag & Hen Night* encouraged the home viewer to "find out what the other half gets up to"...

Aerobicise,[9] the first original production from CIC Video and one that was to establish a trend for glamorous aerobic workout tapes for years to come, promised to be desirable to the passive hot-blooded male viewer as well as the keep-fit enthusiast.

Such was its popularity and influence that the eighties saw a rash of diverse video tie-ins, many of which fell from public view almost as swiftly as they had materialised. Interactive video games were a fad resurrected on a number of different occasions which met with continued public indifference. Waddington turned their famous detective board game Cluedo into a not-so-famous video game (which required that players gather facts from the tape), while Tevele tried their luck with *Travel Bug* and *The Great Australian Horse Racing Game*. Using Fast Forward and Rewind, players of the former were required to complete a journey by air — courtesy of playing cards, a score sheet and video footage especially shot by a wildlife photographer; the latter game necessitated randomly stopping the video tape on one of a

number of pre-recorded horse races, placing a bet and then running the race to determine the winner.

Some years later Scotch videocassettes ran a promotion in which they gave away a free £1 Ladbrokes betting voucher on selected blank tapes. "It costs the consumer nothing extra," said a spokesperson for Scotch, "and it provides a chance to have a bit of fun and — who knows? — win back the price of the cassette and a bit more besides." Other companies, notably those in tobacco and alcohol, saw a promotional opportunity in video no longer open to them elsewhere. Given the ban on commercials for cigarettes and drink, video was for a time the only way these manufacturers could get their products on domestic TV screens. Holiday Video Brochures — a concept developed by Pebblebond International on behalf of the leading holiday tour operators — were the first tapes in the UK to feature such commercials. Stocked by travel agents and available to potential holiday goers on a free-of-charge rental basis, the overheads for Video Brochures were met with the use of outside advertising. Not a fact lost on Viewpoint Ltd, a new company who announced to the press in late 1982 its plans to introduce advertising spots on pre-recorded cassettes, located before or after the tape's main feature.[10] Such a move was seen as an opportunity to keep rental costs down for consumers and help suppliers generate revenue for more and better films.[11]

Music and video was an obvious natural amalgamation, given that pop musicians were turning to ever more elaborate and controversial 'featurettes' in which to promote their record releases (or, in the case of Buggles and 'Video Killed The Radio Star,' lamenting the fact). *The Making of Michael Jackson's Thriller* was one of video's first success stories, selling 800,000 copies in the first two months of sale. But not all music/video pairings struck a chord: the world wasn't quite ready to switch vinyl for the 'video single', for instance, nor particularly interested in simultaneous LP and video releases, as in the case of Toni Basil's *Word of Mouth* album (£29.95 on video and £3.99 on vinyl). The fad that was the video jukebox served to distract patrons in pubs across the land with an esoteric selection of audio-visual numbers.[12] The Camelot song-and-dance sketch from *Monty Python and the Holy Grail* can't sustain interest indefinitely however, and in spite of its high public profile the plug was pulled on the 'VJB.'

At least one vicar in Britain considered that the screening of video films would help brighten up church services and turn around the steady decline in attendances. But families stayed away, no doubt glued to the home movies they had recently converted to video tape, an inspiration derived in part by *Middle Age Crazy*. This Canadian movie starred Ann-Margret as a woman who presents her husband with a video-biography of his life. Its screening on ITV in 1981 prompted one critic to comment: "Video is now starting to infiltrate even the traditional arts" — a viewpoint more suited perhaps to the idea of selling videocassettes of stage shows to theatre audiences, which Carnaby Video had proposed to the Apollo chain of theatres earlier in the year. In principle, each show's performance would be recorded and the videos then offered for sale in the foyer. The negotiations between the two companies came to nothing, but the concept did find favour with The New Theatre in Oxford, who didn't offer original recordings as such but rather existing productions on video of shows featured in their own repertoire (such as *Oh Calcutta*, *The Mikado* and *HMS Pinafore*). Competitors in the 1982 Gillette London Marathon had the opportunity to buy the BBC's rush video release — which incorporated highlights from the previous year's race — at a special discounted price. The idea met with greater success when cinemas took to offering their patrons videocassettes — albeit not necessarily of the movies currently playing. Alongside soft drink machines, the Odeon group installed dispensers in their foyers from which video tapes could be obtained. With a capacity to hold 270 videocassettes these dispensers from The UK Video Vending Corporation, directed at the "places where the public regularly visit," were operated via a special charge card. Although such units weren't that common a sight and were only in circulation for a limited period, following their use at least one Odeon cinema (Manchester) refurbished their foyer in order to accommodate a dedicated video store.

How much of an impact video would have on cinema attendance remained a concern for many years.[13] But as early as 1981 — four years after the first domestic recorders had gone on sale in Britain — the threat that 'legitimate' cinema might be effectively wiped out was no longer an issue. Cinema attendance varied across Europe, fluctuating as it always did, with West Germany seeing a slump in 1981, while France enjoyed something of a boom. A survey carried out in Britain suggested that the availability on video of films like *The Exorcist* and *Every Which Way But Loose* had no adverse effect on audience attendance when the same films played the cinemas. Studios started to consider video a means to augment a film's revenue beyond its theatrical life, often making up for poor box office returns. And a relatively cost-effective means too, considering that the audience for a film on video was pre-sold via publicity from theatrical advertising campaigns.

TV advertisements for video releases started to appear in the Spring of 1981.

As proprietor of Phoenix Home Leisure in the north of England — formerly Phoenix Film Services, one of the biggest 8mm libraries in the country — Steve Ellison recalls the formative years of video.

We were an established Super-8 library and did a lot of mail order and rental. What happened was that Intervision — who were distributors of Super-8 movies, and our suppliers — started renting videos through some of their retail outlets in London. Then they spread their wings throughout the country, going first to all the 8mm film libraries. I think I may have been the first video library in the country outside London because my Intervision account number was '001.'

Other Super-8 suppliers got on the bandwagon, like Mountain Films, Derann and Iver.

A lot of the stuff that they had rights for on Super 8, they transferred to video. There was a bit of a grey area about the rights, the films were vaguely public domain stuff, but that was what happened.

And it sort of caught on with people who were hiring films on Super-8, you know, and it kind of caught on a little bit with people who were buying equipment at the hardware places. But it was a few years before it really caught on big. Most people weren't in the habit of renting a film to watch at home. It was a whole new concept for movies — people watched television at home. It was probably 1979 or 1980 before it really started taking off. And then of course the whole thing exploded. Then we were very busy.

Although the idea of a technological revolution had been anticipated for some years before the boom of the eighties, video itself has a lineage dating back to 1956, when the Ampex corporation in the USA developed the forerunner of the domestic video recorder (of which 'VTR' – Video Tape Recorder – was originally a trademark). The system was a costly and complex piece of hardware directed primarily toward use by television networks. Ampex were quick to realise the potential that a cheaper and more compact system might have on the consumer market, as did other manufacturers in Europe and Japan, eager to capitalise on a possible successor to the lucrative colour TV market[14] – which, in the 1960s, showed little signs of waning.

The result of all these different manufacturers working independently from one another was to be a series of different, incompatible recording formats. When the much-vaunted Videocassette Revolution seemed imminent in 1970, American backers sunk money into what was heralded as the system leader in the projected marketplace. Unfortunately, the system thought by many as most-likely-to-succeed was Cartrivision, a cumbersome machine that came with its own integral TV set. Endorsed by Columbia film studios, Cartrivision carried a certain prestige. But with poor picture quality playback, cartridges that quickly perished, and predicted sales figures that failed to materialise, backers pulled out.

Cartrivision was by no means the only system to suffer and, come 1973, the Videocassette Revolution was being dismissed as "The Great Videocassette Fiasco."

The fortunes that had been invested and lost in these few short years didn't deter all manufacturers however, and while many companies abandoned video development, many more persevered, adamant that a multi-billion pound industry lay within reach.

By the mid-seventies, technology had overcome the practical problems that had prevented mass production of video recorders, and the second video wave got underway. The consumer now had a choice between several fresh and relatively reliable systems, notably Sony's Betamax format (launched in 1975) and Japan Victor Company's (JVC) Video Home System (VHS; launched the following year, and again a trade name which has been assimilated as a common term). Other formats, which included Video 2000, Micro Video and CED, found a market but lacked the commercial support to make much of a lasting impact and soon fell by the wayside — as ultimately would Betamax, leaving the arguably inferior VHS to dominate by the latter half of the 1980s.[15]

If technological advances brought renewed interest to video, it was the volatile political climate which helped crystallise its success in the late-seventies. The world was in the midst of a new economic recession. In Britain, the Conservatives had come into power with Margaret Thatcher as the country's first female Prime Minister. Strikes were common as workers fought for better pay and working conditions, and ultimately their jobs. The process of economic deregulation championed by Thatcher, President Reagan in the US and other western leaders had begun to change the powers of big business, trade unions and even the established church.

As cinema had done in America during the Great Depression of the 1930s, video formed an escape valve for the troubled times. And, for families and groups of friends, hiring a videocassette offered a cheaper alternative to paying for cinema seats.

Another factor which helped to elevate interest in video was hardcore pornography, which couldn't be accessed via conventional broadcast media in the United States and was banned outright in Britain. Courtesy of a network of underground dealers (with exotic sounding names like Emerald Nederland and J Svenson) who were accessed typically via a Dutch postal address, hardcore movies in the Super-8 format had been available illegally for years in

Adult comedy & drama. Let it roll with IFS

Available on VHS V2000

The Professionals at Pinewood

Intervision TOP 20

TOP RENTAL

1. BLACK DEEP THROAT
2. THE REAL BRUCE LEE
3. UPS AND DOWNS OF A HANDYMAN
4. HARDWARE
5. CONFESSIONS OF A SEX KITTEN
6. MAID IN SWEDEN
7. NORTHVILLE CEMETRAY MASSACRE
8. TAKE TIME TO SMELL THE FLOWERS
9. PETS
10. SUPERKNIGHT
11. No. 1. OF THE SECRET SERVICE
12. FALL OF THE ROMAN EMPIRE
13. EL CID
14. HARDCORE
15. EXPOSE
16. LETS GET LAID
17. LOVE BUTCHER
18. DEVIL x FIVE
19. HAPPY HOOKER
20. 55 DAYS TO PEKING

Intervision's Top 20 charts are compiled from dealers returns for rental and retail each month.

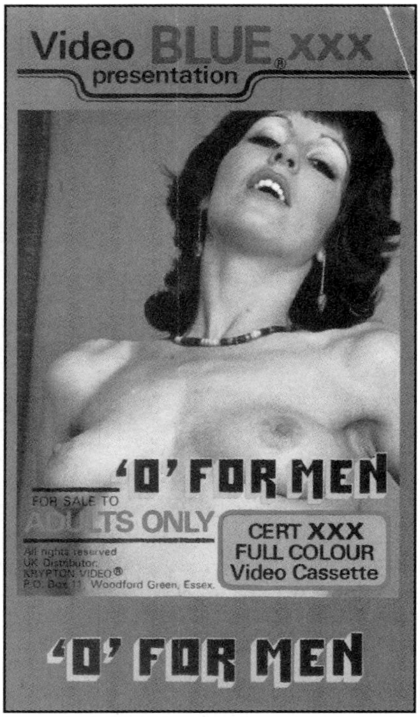

the UK. The alternative was the members-only film club and, in the US, XXX theatres, neither of which were safe from impromptu visits by the local vice squad. As noted at the beginning of this chapter, cumbersome Super-8 was rendered obsolete virtually overnight by the arrival of video — and why risk a film club or theatre when the same films could be seen in the privacy of one's own home, not only feature-length (complete with sound and in colour), but 'interactive' as well (thanks to Fast Forward, Rewind and Pause facilities)? None of this was lost on the commercial sectors, who had bought up the video rights to blue movies virtually ad hoc back in the early seventies, transferring in the region of 10,000 films to video by the mid-eighties.

Indeed, European porn giant Rodox Trading, manufacturers of the Color Climax line, met some of the cost of their sophisticated video editing and copying facilities in Denmark by reproducing under licence Hollywood blockbusters like *First Blood*, *Police Academy* and — shifting 80,000 videocassettes in just five weeks in the UK alone — *Raiders of the Lost Ark*.

But the fact that an estimated sixty per cent of all the pre-recorded videocassettes sold in 1978 were pornographic in nature wasn't so much down to this being the material most favoured by the general public, but more to do with there being little other product available. This imbalance was gradually redressed in Britain, courtesy of film companies Rank and EMI and the publishing group IPC, who had started to issue sport and documentary features through their newly formed video auxiliary.

The video software of this time didn't consist of any notable movie releases. Even Rank and EMI's video catalogue excluded their own best product, concentrating instead on early feature films already available to TV companies.

At a time when the majority of video releases were cartoon programmes for children, music or documentary related ("special interest" being the favoured expression), companies starved of anything fresh tried desperately to make old movies sound new and exciting. Take, for instance, *The Big Cat*, a feature film of indeterminate origin which was advertised by Krypton Video as being

> More terrifying than *Jaws*!!! Great entertainment for all the family. Made among the stunning canyons and landscapes of Utah. This film is a story similar to *Jaws* except that instead of a shark the actors are terrorised by a deadly mountain lion, preying on people and cattle. It is even more terrifying than *Jaws*. This film will keep you on the edge of your seat.

Kingston Video of London offered two creaky b&w movies for the price of a single pre-recorded videocassette (£39.95), when they relaunched the 'double-bill' using "the latest video technology." The ingenious idea was to recreate in the home the glory days of cinema-going, when a main feature was always preceded by a B-picture, news bulletins and perhaps even a cartoon. A sampling of their double-bill tapes includes *Second Chance* with *Great Day in the Morning*, *The Sky's the Limit* with *Step Lively*, and *Berlin Express* with *Isle of the Dead* — for the most part films dating back to the Forties.

Says Steve Ellison of the movies available at the time video started to take-off:

> There wasn't a lot of top stuff available. It was a bit like, "My God, there's a feature film!" A lot of the stuff was what you'd regard as run of the mill, mostly B-movies. Or very bad movies that someone had bought rights for very cheaply. You've got to remember that the film companies were a little bit wary of video. They didn't really want their product getting into people's homes that easily.

It was this state of affairs that enabled Brent-Walker to score a huge all-round hit with two decidedly average — but *recent* — movies, releasing both *The Bitch* and *The Stud* to video hot on the heels of their theatrical run. "Popular by default," as Ellison puts it, because they were the few big movies available. And popular enough to make something of a video superstar out of actress Joan Collins, described affectionately as a "heavy video user" in one industry newsletter. "When I get home from a performance at the Cambridge Theatre," Joan is quoted as saying, "there is nothing I like better than sitting down before a warm fire with my video recorder."

There could be no doubting that a video explosion was imminent, but what its long term effects might be on an entertainment industry grounded in traditional media was open to conjecture. When Magnetic Video — who would later become Twentieth Century-Fox Video — began to distribute film classics and recent Hollywood blockbusters, other companies were forced to sit up and acknowledge that video might not merely be a slight return of the fad of the early seventies. The prospect of being left behind didn't appeal to any one, but at the

"My God, there's a feature film!"

THIS PAGE AND NEXT: Obscure movies on obscure video labels – amongst them Oscar Video, Ultramodern, BB Home Video, Archer, CID, Portland Films, KTC, Cable Communications, Temple and Mountain.

same time the major studios were hesitant make a move which might have an adverse affect on their product.

Gulf & Western — the parent company of Paramount Motion Pictures — employed a marketing research and consulting firm to determine whether they should diversify into video. The consequence being they did, with an announcement to the media that

> By being a part of potential threats, Paramount will not only be protecting itself against an uncertain future, but could be getting itself involved in a lucrative industry. Video is likely to be as popular in the next decade as television was in the fifties.

The future of the movie industry was seen as unpredictable because of video, but there was no way around it. Following the acquiescence of Paramount, together with other major studios United Artists, Universal, and Warner Brothers, and the launch of Lord Grade's ITC, so it was that video entered a period of sudden and rapid growth.

At the end of 1980, there were a modest 600 pre-recorded videocassette titles available in Britain, sales of which notched up $15 million. By 1981 the choice had more than doubled, creating sales of £36 million[16] — a figure which is increased when the revenue generated by rental is taken into consideration.

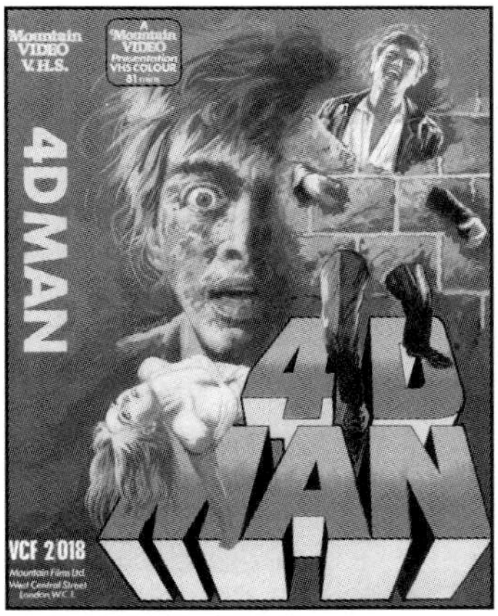

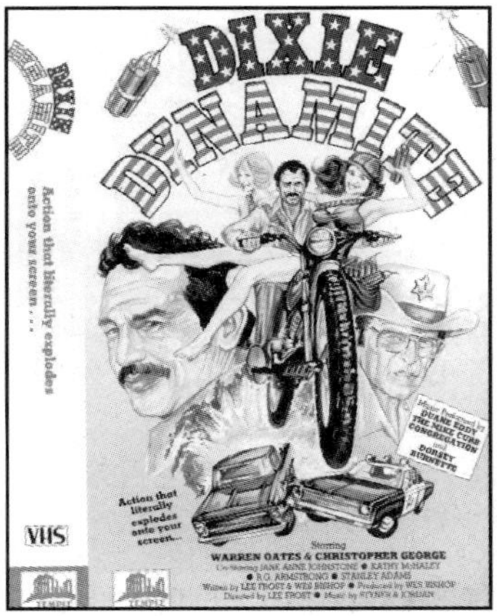

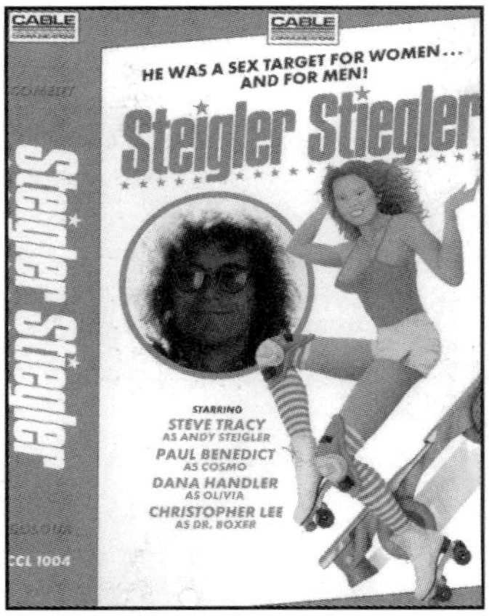

Some of the trepidation felt by the film companies, however, was shared by other parties and manifested itself in high videocassette prices, as well as in a series of conflicting and unnecessary restrictions placed on the consumer faced with no choice but to rent tapes.

Obtaining videogram clearing rights was a nightmare for film companies, as nobody wanted to miss out on the profits not even anticipated a year-or-so earlier. Film directors, producers, actors, music publishers, distributors and studios hammered it out, one result being that Thorn EMI got taken to court over a dispute pertaining to royalties on six films they released to video — including *Stardust* and *That'll Be The Day* — which they were forced to withdraw. Matters like this also caused consternation for the TV networks, particularly the BBC whose launch into video was delayed for a year pending a satisfactory agreement with the various unions. Despite a back catalogue renowned as being the largest of any broadcasting organisation, BBC Video wasn't launched until the latter months of 1981 and for a long time comprised a tentative eighteen titles (*Play Golf*, *Toyah at the Rainbow* and *The Story of English Furniture* being among them).

As with the film companies, video dealers were advancing into uncharted territory. There were no guidelines or rules as such, and anyone with a little collateral who was prepared to take a chance stood to make a fair amount of money. Video clubs were predominantly mail order to begin with. Notching up a self-proclaimed 500 new members a week, the biggest of these was perhaps Video Club, which sold its membership kits in selected high street TV rental and department stores, as well as through magazine advertisements and leisure centres.[17] Mail order generally offered the consumer a wider selection of titles than could be obtained on the high street, where a stock of 100 different tapes was considered expansive. But this was to change, due in part to the stores getting wise and devoting more shelf space to video software, and mail order consumers getting burned by cowboy outfits failing to deliver what they promised or, in some instances, cashing cheques and not delivering anything at all. The most significant turnaround, however, came when record wholesalers moved into video distribution and utilised their sophisticated supply networks for films from the major studios.[18] (A move which would ultimately have a devastating effect on independent wholesalers, as will be seen later.) Department stores, record stores, newsagents, pharmaceutical chains and supermarkets all became stockists of video software.

The Bellford Service Station near Guildford became one of the first garages in the country to offer videos, the scheme proving so popular with motorists that they had to switch the video operation from their forecourt accessory shop to new custom built premises. Super-8 specialists, with an established customer base and often the support of a familiar stockist — such as Fletcher and Intervision, who had also moved on from Super-8 to video — were ideally equipped for the formative marketplace. Even some ice-cream vans are known to have carried a small stock of videocassettes on their rounds.

Video was open to anybody, and a new outlet had as much chance of originating from the redundancy money of those hit by recession as it did from companies established in other fields who chose to diversify. Market stalls trading in videos opened up. Vacant high street properties on the cheaper outskirts of town were bought and turned into dedicated video stores. A more personal touch came from video dealers who operated out of a car boot, bringing a videocassette direct to the customer's door and exchanging it for another from their list of titles on a designated return trip. Expanding upon this concept were mobile video libraries, walk-through vans equipped with a selection of tapes, travelling from district to district on a weekly basis.

(The antithesis of this concept were the stand-alone automated rental booths for use on high streets announced in January 1987. Called Movie Machines, this American import was operated with the use of a credit card. Offered a choice of 374 videocassettes, the customer would rent a title and return the tape after use, whereupon the machine would issue a receipt and debit the customer's card accordingly. It isn't believed that Movie Machines ever saw commercial use on the streets of Britain, although, as already noted, automated video dispensers did become a reality in cinemas for a brief period.)

"Video was a growth market," recollects Christopher Glazebrook, a TV and Radio Section Supervisor selling televisions, video recorders and other electrical equipment in a department store in the late-seventies. "Deciding to stock the software, as well as the hardware, was a natural progression to aid sales."

> It must have been about 1980 when I first became involved with videocassettes. Initially my job was to purchase the tapes and oversee the running of the library. As the business expanded I was appointed the Video Libraries Manager responsible for seven outlets.
>
> At this early stage there was only one other retailer in the vicinity dealing in videocassettes. As the popularity of video grew, several more soon sprang up, but mainly on the outskirts of town, too far away to have any effect on our trade.
>
> Reps would call once a month. Demand was very high for anything available, both on VHS and Betamax, and we would order all the new feature films released.

One of the independent retailers on the 'outskirts of town' was Phoenix Home Leisure, whose operation was soon expanded into wholesale distribution and the supply of videos to other retailers. Steve Ellison gives an insight into the unexpected quarters from which a video competitor was likely to originate:

I had a competition at the time with another wholesaler who, strangely enough, used to be my accountant. By virtue of being my accountant, of course, he got all the names and addresses of all the film distributors and suddenly announced he was leaving accountancy and becoming a video wholesaler. And he really got serious about it and supplied all his reps with the new Escort XR3, these fast cars so they would whiz down to London, pick up films, and guarantee to have them back in the shops the same day of release. There was always a bit of a bone of contention because London shops would get the films, and it would be a couple of days by the time the carrier got them up to the North. In actual fact, three reps — not his reps — were killed on the M6 and the M1 during this short period of time, because of all the dashing around with films.

There was little uniformity running through the various video clubs springing up, and membership protocol and customer schemes were essentially down to whatever it was the individual dealer chose to implement: rental, straight sale, exchange, or a combination thereof. However, there were certain conditions imposed on the dealers by distributors and film companies, which became increasingly convoluting as the market expanded and the impetus shifted away from mail order onto the high street.

Exchange schemes had been the preference for mail order companies, who generally required that a customer first become a member, then purchase one videocassette outright, which could be exchanged for another — of the same price range — for a small fee and the price of postage.

For a membership fee of £40, Video Unlimited of Bournemouth ran a tape exchange scheme at a cost of £6 per tape (or, if payment was made in advance, £60 for twenty exchanges). Relocating to prestigious quayside premises in Dorset after eighteen months of trading, the company became something of a video superstore in 1981 with a stock of 3,000 different film titles; the largest of its kind in Britain, if not Europe.

Some dealers offered lifelong membership and free tape-exchange for a one-off fee of £150 (Cathedral Films of Worcester), while others required no membership at all but the purchase of one tape and £2.95 per exchange thereafter (Caramel Video of Devon). The concept of the videocassette exchange scheme, however, was intrinsically a straightforward one and not regarded as a breach of copyright or suppliers' trading terms. The same cannot be said for the options that came to dominate as mail order and exchange schemes waned.[19]

Almost every source company — be it videocassette distributor or major film studio — had their own idea of how best to bring their product into the hands of the consumer. Retailers were often faced with a boggling array of paperwork when they stocked films by different

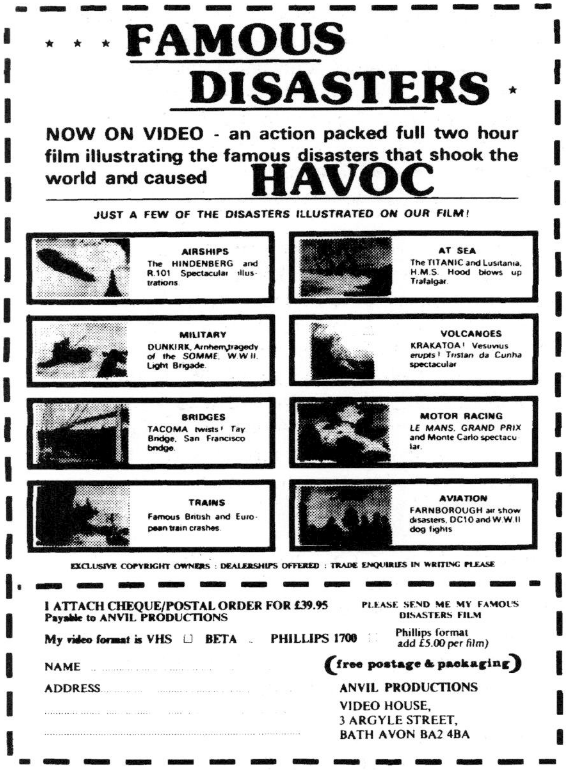
FAMOUS
DISASTERS
NOW ON VIDEO - an action packed full two hour film illustrating the famous disasters that shook the world and caused
HAVOC
JUST A FEW OF THE DISASTERS ILLUSTRATED ON OUR FILM!
AIRSHIPS
The HINDENBERG and R.101 Spectacular illustrations.
AT SEA
The TITANIC and Lusitania, H.M.S. Hood blows up Trafalgar.
MILITARY
DUNKIRK, Arnhem tragedy of the SOMME. W.W.II. Light Brigade.
VOLCANOES
KRAKATOA! Vesuvius erupts! Tristan da Cunha spectacular
BRIDGES
TACOMA twists! Tay Bridge, San Francisco bridge.
MOTOR RACING
LE MANS, GRAND PRIX and Monte Carlo spectacular.
TRAINS
Famous British and European train crashes.
AVIATION
FARNBOROUGH air show disasters, DC10 and W.W.II dog fights
EXCLUSIVE COPYRIGHT OWNERS : DEALERSHIPS OFFERED : TRADE ENQUIRIES IN WRITING PLEASE
I ATTACH CHEQUE/POSTAL ORDER FOR £39.95
Payable to ANVIL PRODUCTIONS
PLEASE SEND ME MY FAMOUS DISASTERS FILM
My video format is VHS BETA PHILLIPS 1700
Phillips format add £5.00 per film)
NAME
ADDRESS
(free postage & packaging)
ANVIL PRODUCTIONS
VIDEO HOUSE,
3 ARGYLE STREET,
BATH AVON BA2 4BA

studios, each with different conditions and rates as a result of the royalty agreements they had anxiously established with the various copyright holders of material. United Artists and Guild Home Video were among the companies operating a 'rental only' policy on their titles. Warner Home Video and IPC on the other hand, were among those stipulating 'straight sale' only. In time the companies adhering to the latter system were forced to reconsider, as the choice of rental titles increased and consumers were less willing to pay the high asking price for outright sales. Magnetic Video — holding out until 1982 — was the last company to switch to the rental idea.

Rental wasn't necessarily a straight cut alternative, however, with club membership fees, deposits, hire charges and forms to be filled out by both dealer and customer for every rental transaction undertaken. In the case of Warner Home Video, the lease scheme with which they chose to replace their 'sales only' policy was such that many wholesalers refused to participate anyway. (The retailer was required to pay Warners £12 a month for their films, and take a minimum of twenty titles.) Rank and Precision Video both stipulated that their rental tapes had to be rented for a three-day minimum period. Because many of the major video companies had negotiated special deals with the larger retail outlets, many independent dealers wishing to stock films by these companies had to do so via other suppliers. In the case of Thorn EMI's product this was Intervision, who were one of the earliest independent suppliers of videocassettes and required more paperwork than anyone else — indeed different forms for different titles. Intervision also required that the dealer lodge a sizeable cash bond for Thorn EMI's tapes, which could take up to a year to recover should the deal be cancelled.

Steve Ellison recalls the tumultuous business of video retailing.

> Intervision had a whole rack of feature films and a rental system whereby you sign the contract with them, and were charged, I think, £5.95 for three days hire or £7.95 for a week — you kept the odd £1.95 or £2.95 and sent the rest to them. They invoiced you and you sent all the copies of the forms to them. It was very complicated and long-winded. Then very quickly a lot of people just started buying the videos and hiring them out even though they weren't supposed to. The first big controversy in video was tapes that were supposed to be for 'sale only' being hired out. Magnetic Video came on the scene with a whole string of Twentieth Century-Fox stuff that was supposed to be for sale only at £39.95. But what was happening was people were buying piles of this stuff and renting it for £1.50 or £2.00 a night. The only stuff that should have been rented was the Intervision stuff. The rest of it was purely and simply for sale. It actually said on the box 'For Sale'. That was the first thing in video that caused some bones of contention. But eventually, like most of these things, people just ignored the law anyway. And to get anywhere you had to start renting when everyone else was renting anyway.

Dealers simply refused to adhere to the sales and lease guidelines stipulated by film companies and suppliers, which they saw as unnecessarily restrictive and convoluting. Intervision urged dealers to play ball with a motto that threatened "Reckless Exploitation of Copyright Programme Material Can Seriously Damage Your Business," and even incorporated a spoken warning on their actual tapes — the remonstrative tones of actor Patrick Allen[20] — whose pre-feature announcement hammered home the importance of filling in the correct rental documentation. Viewers who experienced any irregularity in their rental agreement were urged to contact Intervision, receiving a free blank videocassette should their claim be justified.

But independent companies were finding it increasingly difficult to stay afloat as the major film companies got a grip on the market, no longer looking to the likes of Intervision to distribute their product. The sparse landscape they had once monopolised was by 1981 rapidly changed, and the independents were forced to invest large sums of money in exclusive distribution deals, or go under. As a result VCL — who had a penchant for music videos — signed a deal with GTO Films for the likes of *Phantasm*, *Scum* and *Breaking Glass*. Intervision sought to raise $2.5 million for the rights to a number of films from United Artists, a company who wanted to break the British market without having to set up their own subsidiary.

Phoenix Home Leisure was one of the many independents forced into closure. "I was wholesaling mostly the second rate stuff," says Steve Ellison, "because the 'big boys' wouldn't let us have wholesale terms." He explains:

> I liquidated in 1982. By 1982, all the big companies like Warner Brothers, EMI, Fox, RCA, Columbia, had got their own national capability for distribution so they didn't need local wholesalers any more. They just cut us up for price. They had their own reps on the road and they just started going straight to the shops. The same kind of thing that had happened previously with the long playing record business was happening with video. With records, Music For Pleasure had come along and put racks into newsagents and everywhere else, and it killed these local little wholesalers.
>
> When I liquidated I owed EMI £18,000 for blank tape. And in those days, a blank three-hour tape retailed for round about £8. We were invoiced by EMI at a distributor price of £5 a tape, to sell to the shops at £6. I had something like 10,000 tapes at this price. I was walking round the wholesalers in Eccles the next week and saw that they were selling tapes at the same price I was paying. I rang EMI and they told me, "Oh, the price has gone down." I asked them to send me a credit note for the difference. "We can't do that," they replied. "It's not our fault if the market fluctuates."
>
> We got left with a lot of blank tape which we ended up trading off to Surrey Video or something. A lot of local wholesalers did go under, because national wholesalers took over.

While leasing obligations were blatantly ignored by some retailers, the 1959 Copyright Act — which had yet to catch up with video — allowed many other dealers to happily operate in a legal twilight. There was no High Court test case on which video suppliers and film companies could fall back and until there was, no dealer was technically breaking any copyright law. Still, it seems inconceivable today that legitimate companies — like Video Exchange in Bath — could ever have entertained such copyright-scamming notions as trading programmes taped off-air, actively encouraging customers to send in their unwanted 'time-shift' recordings. Even Palace Video, celebrated distributors of award winning arthouse and cult movies, decided in their inaugural first months to introduce a scheme which seems nothing short of a legal time bomb. As a means of reducing the cost of films to their customers, Palace provided an opportunity to buy selected titles at a discount price of £13.50 if a blank tape was provided on which to have them copied. *Pink Flamingos*, *Eraserhead* and *The Enigma of Kaspar Hauser* were amongst those films requiring a two-hour blank tape, while *Mephisto* and *Aguirre, Wrath of God* (a double-bill of both German and English language versions) required the purchaser to provide a three-hour tape. The idea was enough of a success to warrant Palace repeating the scheme with a concert film of Gary Numan at Wembley Arena, called *Micromusic*

(a title that probably derived from the fact the film was also available in Technicolor's innovative micro videocassette format).

Legal problems surrounding video software were the subject of a major conference in the UK in October 1980. The following month, the British Videogram Association (BVA) came into existence to create a "healthy environment for business" — as stipulated in their remit — tackling copyright issues such as unauthorised home copying and off-air taping.[21] A levy on blank videocassettes and possibly even hardware was seen as the best solution to the problem,[22] but this threat — a proposed ten per cent of the cost of a videocassette — was ultimately dropped, leaving the contentious issue of home-taping unresolved.[23]

As video wholesalers sought to protect themselves against the major studios, their movie catalogues expanded with product from a growing selection of sources. Material had as much chance of coming from a supplier who had sought out the proper film rights, as it had from someone offering "vaguely public domain" films. Other suppliers simply transferred material to video tape with no licensing agreement whatsoever, hoping that nobody would notice.

Recalls Ellison:

> The very first year we were wholesaling we were offered a stand at a video trade exhibition organised by *Video Trade Weekly*, because someone had pulled out. I was this little wholesaler in Wigan. I said "How much is it?" and they said "Well what can you offer?" I actually offered them a crate of wine. We got use of this exhibition for a crate of wine! I was also tied in with Fletcher Video as their northern agent at the time, so I rang Fletchers and said, "You know

this exhibition that starts next week? I've got a stand there but I've nothing to put on it." And they gave me a whole pile of cartoons that had just come in from Techno in Italy — plastic-cased cartoons, Bugs Bunny, Daffy Duck and all that. They were old, pre-war and early fifties cartoons that Warners Brothers had originally hired down to a company called AAP — an American firm, I think, who were pretty big in 8mm. All this stuff had been on 8mm. In Italy Bugs Bunny is called just "Bunny". Well, our stand turned out to be right by the entrance opposite Twentieth Century-Fox with Magnetic Video, who had built a replica of the space-ship from *Alien* as their stand. And next to them was Warner Home Video and the guy from Warner Brothers was looking over at our stand, at all our cartoons, and he comes over saying "That's Bugs Bunny". I'm saying, "No, it's not, it's '*Bunny*.' If you look at it closely, the ears are shorter."[24]

And, in another case:

Hokushin put a few videos out. Basically Hokushin was a company that supplied 16mm projectors — there's a Hokushin 16mm projector that was made in the seventies — and they brought over some American tapes from Magnetic Video and transferred them to the PAL system. They got into trouble quite quickly with Twentieth Century-Fox and had to stop it, but by then they'd got hold of the rights for *The Playbirds* and *Come Play With Me*, the Mary Millington films, and were able to put those out.

Ellison remembers there being a "clearing house for video rights" based in Paris where some early distributors in Britain got their films, Intervision among them. Fletcher Video, however, were a company importing films ad hoc, boxed up and ready for sale. They literally had a container full of films flown in, with the briefest of advance notification from the Italian suppliers of what to expect. Once off the plane, the tapes were taken to Fletcher's Space Way warehouse near Heathrow airport, and from there were distributed around Britain.

There was little chance of beating the major studios in terms of big name blockbusters. But with the influx of cheap, exploitative features and plenty of hard-nosed promotion, the territory formally dominated by the majors came under considerable pressure.

CAPTURED BY
FLESH-EATING
SAVAGES..!
SAVAGE
TERROR
GO VIDEO,
PO Box 4BT, 35-37 Wardour Street, London W1A 4B
Telephone: 01-734 7195/6

'An orgy of commercialism'

UNEASE

There was no such thing as all-night television.

When video arrived, television networks in Britain were in the habit of closing down broadcasts at around midnight. As had been the tradition in cinemas for many years, the BBC signed off with the National Anthem.

Video helped to eradicate such scheduling constraints and gave people the opportunity to watch what they wanted when they wanted. The growing likelihood that cable and satellite television would soon take-off didn't seem to hinder sales of video recorders. Instead these technologies were seen to offer the video public an even greater choice for time-shift taping — which remained the most common use for video up until the middle of 1981 when the upsurge in pre-recorded titles began. A glut of faddish gadgetry and paraphernalia arrived on the market to assist the video owner in their hectic video recording schedule. These included the Videolog, Video Organiser, Videoplanner and write'n'wipe label kits. The hopeless enthusiast could even attire themselves in a "Video Freak" or "I Love Video" T-shirt (£5.99 each from BBS in North Humberside).

Video didn't become a substitute for TV viewing, but more a reason to watch for longer. As noted by Laurie Taylor and Bob Mullan in their book *Uninvited Guests*, "Extra time has to be found to accommodate the extra viewing."

For many, playing tapes deep into the night provided the answer — a habit which often drew unwelcome attention from opportunist crooks, trawling the darkened streets for the give-away flicker of an 'after hours' TV screen. Protection from the thieves — poised outside, awaiting the cathode glow to terminate and make their move[1] — could be obtained in the guise of VCR alarm systems.

"In Coventry, about fifteen video recorders are stolen each week," the Midlands based manufacturer of Videoalert told the *Sunday Times* in May 1983. With advance orders for

A Clockwork Orange.

300, it was estimated that annual sales of Videoalert — which attached to the outside of the VCR, emitting a ninety-eight decibel shriek should the unit be moved or lifted — would hit a rather optimistic 25,000 mark. A window sticker served to ward off the crooks.

Another concern came from a different quarter entirely. It was feared that people were becoming *addicted* to watching videos, especially late at night. Without the discipline of television's midnight termination, it was believed that video would wean a nation of insomniacs. At the height of the video boom, counselling was even established in some areas to help these "videoholics."

"There was certainly one lady who could be described as a videoholic," recalls Chris Glazebrook of his days as Video Libraries Manager in a department store. "She would work out how long the tapes lasted on a piece of paper, and decide when the family could have dinner."

At a Methodist Conference held in Portsmouth, a Reverend Pat Brown attacked the National Children's Home (NCH) for its association with what he perceived as "a tainted industry."[2] The Video Charity Day, held in May 1987 and organised by the BVA with the support of the whole industry, managed to raise £150,000 from donations, proceeds of videocassette rentals and a series of fund-raising events across the country. The Reverend Brown accused the charity of accepting "blood money."

With a turnover in 1987 of around half-a-billion pounds, the video industry had reached a peak. However, its swift ascendance had not come without a price, and a backlash that started at the beginning of the eighties was to have a lasting effect on the medium, shaping irrevocably its image in the public mind. Mounting pressure from lobby groups and the media led to the creation of the 1984 Video Recordings Act, which resulted in many films on videocassette being outlawed. Renewed concern came in 1987, when the press laid the cause of a massacre in the small English town of Hungerford almost exclusively on the influence of video. (See THE BIG INFLUENCE.)

The appearance of lurid advertisements for video films in the early months of 1982 sparked off criticism from members of the public and the BVA. In their monthly case report for May 1982, the Advertising Standards Authority (ASA) upheld complaints against three of the advertisements forwarded to them, and condemned editors who were

> prepared to publish advertisements in which, increasingly, films of a violent or sexually perverted character were described in terms, which, like the films themselves, were calculated to appeal only to the most degraded tastes, and which unnecessarily caused offence to many readers.

The three ads in question pertained to *Cannibal Holocaust*, *The Driller Killer* and *SS Experiment Camp*. The latter — with its depiction of a semi-naked woman tied upside down to a cross with a swastika hanging from her wrist — was singled out by the authority as being particularly vile.

In response, a meeting took place between the magazine editors who shared the ASA's concern and agreed to carry out "much more careful vetting in future." From now on, went the theory, there would be consultation between the publishers, and any advertisement deemed objectionable would be collectively rejected — although the contentious ad for *SS Experiment Camp* continued to appear through June 1982.[3]

The backlash against video started as these things often do: relatively innocuously. The general anxiety that comes with any innovative technology manifested itself in public fears of burglary and addiction, while the various pressure groups — who had doggedly rallied against permissiveness for many years — found in video a brand new menace.

Possibly most vociferous of these groups was the National Viewers and Listeners Association (NVALA[4]), which was founded in the early sixties by a sanctimonious schoolteacher from Shropshire called Mary Whitehouse and her friend, Norah Buckland. These two middle-aged Englishwomen became appalled at the shape of cultural change about them and the shift away from middle-class Christian principles — a change personified in the BBC's growing penchant for gutsy 'kitchen sink' dramas, scathing satire and current affairs programmes. In 1964, and after rallying for support in a highly publicised meeting at Birmingham's Town Hall, the Clean Up TV campaign was the first action proper of what was to become the NVALA.

Not only was she the single most influential figure in the NVALA, but following a hotly debated BBC panel show in October 1967, Mary Whitehouse became its public face as well.[5] According to Whitehouse, television was in such a state that even BBC personnel, "so deeply troubled about the kind of material [they were] expected to transmit,"[6] were anonymously turning to the NVALA. Come the following year and the resignation of the BBC's Director General (Whitehouse's arch enemy Sir Hugh Greene), the Association moved its emphasis away from television and more toward the notion of pornography in general. Indeed, the NVALA doesn't identify any distinct group to which it is opposed, but rather lumps them all together as one nebulous, ungodly whole.

"Radicalism is the keynote to the NVALA's work," state the authors of a study that appears in *Censorship and Obscenity*. "Theirs is a total disenchantment with, and critique of, the existing social world... the complex and disturbed world 'out there' which they see as more and more likely to engulf their own world of Christian truths."

Wrote a reporter of Whitehouse in *The Observer*: "The real trouble is that she doesn't seem to be able to tell the difference between a sensitive documentary about being a homosexual... and someone saying 'git' in *Till Death Do Us Part*."

Regarded as something of a crank and prudish busybody by the majority of people, Whitehouse was nevertheless persistent enough to succeed in getting TV programmes dropped, and landing stage plays and periodicals in the dock with alarming regularity. *The Little Red Schoolbook* and the School Kids' *Oz* were two of the items brought to trial and successfully prosecuted as a result of her campaigning. These particular items Whitehouse took to Italy to show the Pope (whereupon they were deposited in the Vatican archives, supposedly comprising the finest collection of erotica in the world). Hers wasn't the voice of reason, but a voice that rarely faced any opposition.

The NVALA claimed to gain its strength by

> providing timely information to the Prime Minister, the Secretary of State for National Heritage, the Home Secretary and other members of HM Government; also lobbying Members of Parliament

but more than anything, public apathy fuelled their campaign and brought a disproportionate impression of controversy to those things it deemed objectionable.[7]

With support from the Prince of Wales and political factions who saw her cause as an opportunity to win votes, Mary Whitehouse — later to be made a CBE[8] by the Queen — was able to posit herself as a matriarch for the nation.

The moral standards dictated by the NVALA are those decided upon by the association's founders. Everyone else is expected to accept unquestioningly their definition of what is acceptable. Although statistics indicate that the NVALA activity is tremendously unpopular, the organisation still insists it functions for the majority. But few who sign up to the NVALA's philosophy are aware of how deep the protective knife cuts into personal and public freedom of choice.[9] They claim to be *opposed to* any form of Government censorship, yet stress that a tightening of the Obscene Publications Act is long overdue. (What is the Obscene Publications Act if not Government censorship?) Instead of censorship they advocate self-restraint, but of course the NVALA wish to set the benchmarks of that restraint.[10] When the NVALA publish their propaganda it is riddled with references of criminal acts as reported in the media. A report on television violence will be interspersed with snippets from the press relating to rape, murder, robberies and other acts of violence. The intention is to bamboozle the reader into thinking that all real-life violent crimes are a direct result of acts of violence portrayed on television. (See also THE BIG INFLUENCE.)

Whitehouse is considered a goodly person yet on more than one occasion has implied that those who break the 'moral code' should be put to death. In *The Little Red Schoolbook* trial, she quoted from the scriptures and warned a defence witness that "it were better for him that a millstone were hanged about his neck, and he were cast into the sea."[11] Sociologist Howard Becker described such fervent campaigners as "moral entrepreneurs," whom he effectively epitomises in the following statement:

> The existing rules do not satisfy him because there is some evil which profoundly disturbs him. He feels that nothing can be right in the world until rules are made to correct it. He operates with an absolute ethic; what he sees is truly and absolutely evil with no qualification. Any means is justified to do away with it. The crusader is fervent and righteous, often self-righteous.[12]

He concluded that if the crusade shows any signs of success it may encourage the entrepreneur to become a professional rule creator. Becker's theories were published in 1963. The following year the NVALA took its first steps.

Other groups for moral rearmament followed in the wake of the NVALA, notably the Nationwide Festival of Light (NFOL) and more recently the Community Standards Association (CSA),

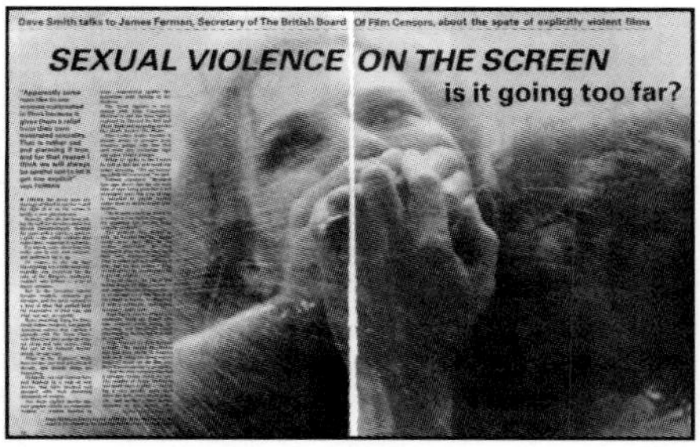
Dave Smith talks to James Ferman, Secretary of The British Board Of Film Censors, about the spate of explicitly violent films

SEXUAL VIOLENCE ON THE SCREEN
is it going too far?

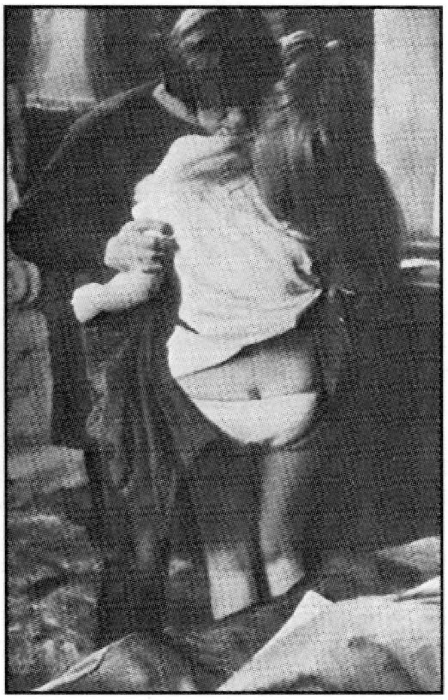

ABOVE: *The Texas Chain Saw Massacre.*
RIGHT, TOP: *Photoplay*, January 1981. BOTTOM: Susan George is raped in *Straw Dogs*.

all of whom had a representative in Whitehouse.

The Nationwide Festival of Light was launched in September 1971 with a series of meetings and processions taking place throughout the country. Sponsored by Christians, but open to anyone concerned about love, purity and family life, the gathering of some 30,000[13] people in Trafalgar Square on the twenty-fifth of that month was the hub of the Festival. It was from this gathering that the NFOL made their "Proclamation to the Government" with regard to media representations of sex, drugs and violence:

> The present trafficking in sadistic and obscene material and the ridiculing of purity and family life are placing in peril the innocence of children, the dignity and equality of women, and the true fulfillment of human personality. The health of society is now endangered, and those in authority in national and local government must act at once.[14]

The group followed this with Operation Newsagent, a scheme requesting that people boycott ordinary newsagents who sold pornographic magazines (years later, the CSA were to award a "Family Seal of Approval" to those shops that forfeited their pin-up magazines). At the annual meeting of the Wales and Monmouth Advisory Committee of Llandrindod, the Government was urged to promote moral values by every means possible. Mrs Madge Westmoreland spoke also of the press pandering "to the baser instincts of the 'sick' minority"

and added, "I don't want to see photographs of unmarried mothers with their babies or to read of the love life of a hippie, or how families started wife-swapping."

Another spokesperson said that foreigners should be stopped from having abortions in Britain.

Films like *The Devils*, *Straw Dogs* and *A Clockwork Orange* played amidst persistent cries of outrage and, in the case of *Flesh*, earned a fine for its exhibitors the Open Space Theatre. The 'health of society' may have been at risk, but concern over the issue of pornography was becoming obsessive.[15] Into this flurry of protest and police raids came the Earl of Longford, teacher, politician, journalist, author, Labour convert, Roman Catholic peer and amateur missionary. On April 21, 1971, Longford initiated a debate in the House of Lords on pornography, and proposed that the Government might care to set up a far-reaching inquiry whilst volunteering an immediate unofficial inquiry of his own. Sixteen months of work resulted in the publication of *Pornography: The Longford Report*, a 500-page paperback book published by Coronet, a London-based firm in which Longford had an interest. The fanfare that surrounded the investigation led many to believe it was nothing more than an exercise in self-promotion on Longford's part. "Lord Porn" — as he came to be known in the pages of *Private Eye* — delighted the tabloid press with research that took him and his entourage to the seedy shops and sex clubs of Soho and Copenhagen (Customs allowed him to keep the twelve sex mags in his possession on his return to Britain). In one establishment, having declined to flagellate a semi-naked girl whose whip had become tangled around his neck, he informed awaiting news hounds, "I have seen enough for science and more than enough for entertainment."

That the book became a best-seller was no surprise, given its subject matter,[16] the publicity which surrounded its writing and the profile afforded it by some of its celebrity committee members, such as Kingsley Amis, Jimmy Saville and "the pious pop star"[17] Cliff Richard. Mary Whitehouse attributed its success to the fact that the majority of people in Britain — "four-fifths" of the population to be exact — objected to the rising tide of pornography. But remained blissfully ignorant to the conundrum this created or indeed why the book should be such a hit in the very porn shops it vilified.

But while the report's "Christian approach," findings and recommendations were applauded by the NVALA and NFOL, Longford was at pains to distance himself professionally from Whitehouse *et al* should the association tarnish the credibility of his report. In the end it didn't seem to matter. Most critics dismissed the work as ineffectual, claiming it offered no basis for legal reform. *The Times* thought it a piece of "good campaigning," *The Spectator* regarded it as "funny," while Robert Robinson in a Radio 4 interview programme called it the "lost cause of the year" and even managed to extract an apology from Longford for being rude. Having no direct impact on parliament, the reactionary report did however exert an influence, no less upon the police who went on a raiding campaign following its publication. The police netted 150 tons of Paul Raymond's *Club International* and *Men Only*, two magazines to which Longford had paid particular attention, commenting that a crude cartoon strip in the latter was "a clear attraction to young children." An unexpected twist came when journalists at the *Sunday People* and *News of the World* embarked on an exposé of the smut trade, and unearthed corrupt dealings between the porn barons of Soho and members of Scotland Yard's Obscene Publication Squad. Pornography — in Soho at least — was flourishing on account of deals made with bent coppers stretching back twenty years.[18]

Moral crusaders also found support from within 'enemy' ranks when Women's Lib and Gay Lib — two groups who would do their utmost to disrupt the Nationwide Festival of Light in Trafalgar Square before the year was out — attacked the Underground press for having "a sexist viewpoint" and carrying ads for "pornography and those which offer jobs posing in it." One leaflet protested that "Lately, porn has been mistakenly associated with sexual freedom."

Demanding the right to walk the streets free of abuse and assault, women in the north of Britain entered the 1980s with a series of protests, ranging from sloganeering and the defacement of posters through to city centre marches and attacks on men. Such acts were an angry response to the reign of terror created by the "Yorkshire Ripper" — the killer of at least thirteen women — and the fact that he still eluded the police after five

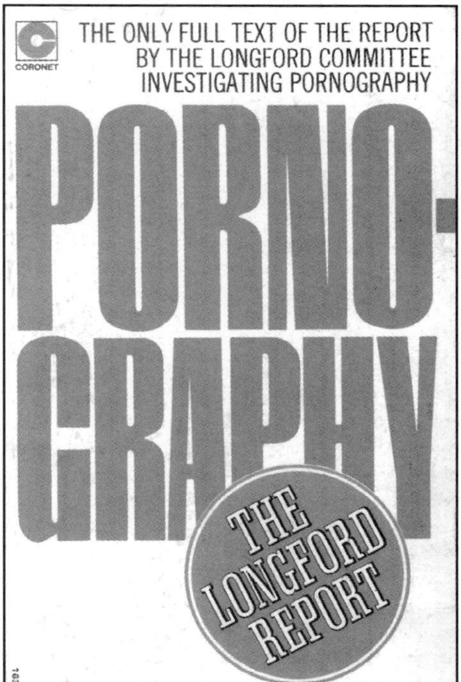

PREVIOUS PAGE: School kids' *Oz*.
THIS PAGE, TOP: Teaser advertisement for *The Devils*.
THIS PAGE, ABOVE: With a sensationalistic cover like this, it was little wonder that the Longford committee's anti-porn tract could be found in Soho sex shops.

THIS PAGE: A couple of older moral panics...
Comic books (LEFT): Jack Cole's strip 'Murder, Morphine and Me!' from *True Crime Comics* May 1947 was regarded as typically lurid and objectionable.
Penny Dreadfuls (ABOVE): Boy Savages from Percival Wolfe's *Red Ralph, or The Daughter of the Night*, 1860.

NEXT PAGE, LEFT: Sixteen-year-old Danny Logan is driven to kill because of the "brutality and unending murders flashed across the screen" in *Telekiller* (pub: NEL, 1978), a novel cashing in on the cause-and-effect argument raging in the media.
NEXT PAGE, RIGHT: *The Sun*, December 17, 1976.

years. It was the murder of twenty-year-old Jacqueline Hill, a student at Leeds University, that galvanised women across the country into fresh action. Some of their principal objections included men being on the streets after dark,[19] and films considered to be pornographic or containing violence against women.

Video was an obvious target for the lobby groups who had doggedly rallied against permissiveness since the early seventies. Fuelled by the media, who perhaps saw video as a refreshing twist on a rather tired argument, moral crusaders reiterated their arguments concerning pornography, and reservedly supported the women's groups who embraced a more direct form of protest. More was gained when into the equation came the notion of *sadistic* pornography and the insidious effect it might be having on children.

The cry was for censorship and the 'banning' of videos.

Film distributors who had to attain a certificate prior to releasing a film theatrically had no such obligation when it came to video. And feature films that had been cut for the cinemas — or, in some instances, rejected outright — often appeared on video intact. As a consequence, the video market quickly expanded with movies of all kinds, as an increasing number of distributors trawled for fresh and exclusive product. As there was no legal requirement to submit videos for classification, companies could put out a film relatively cheaply — a set-up that led to the influx of obscure exploitation vehicles on some equally obscure video labels. These were films made in less censorial climes, like Italy, or films that played the drive-in circuits of America — the sleazy crowd-pleasing content of which would undoubtedly have caused consternation with the British Board of Film Censors if presented for a theatrical

release.

Before the advent of video, films like this were nigh on impossible to see in Britain (unless they were considered a genre classic, in which case there was a slim possibility they might turn up at a film society screening someplace). But that isn't to say video created a market for them. The following letter, printed in the American magazine *Midnight Marquee*,[20] identifies the mood of frustration felt by some fans of horror films living in Britain:

> I was particularly pleased to find that you have changed to 'capsule comment' style reviews: I do not mean that to sound as if I did not enjoy your full reviews, but this change does mean that you can now review low-budget minor films (*I Spit On Your Grave, Final Exam* and *Student Bodies*) which, since they are unlikely to be released theatrically in England, we do not hear about normally.

The 'moral panic' that led to the crusade against so-called 'video nasties' was a cyclic one, fitting a pattern that can be traced back through campaigns against comics books and cheap paperbacks in the 1950s, Hollywood gangster and horror films in the 1930s, and the Penny Dreadfuls and Penny Theatres of the Victorian era. Each of these inspired a clampdown of some form or a complete ban, the primary motivation of which was always cited as being the protection of juveniles. More recent concerns have included the 'freedom' press of the Underground in the sixties and seventies, violence on TV, Gangsta-Rap, computer games and the Internet.

"The technical and cultural competence young people gain as spin-offs of media use," states John Springhall in his book *Youth, Popular Culture and Moral Panics*, "pose a potential threat to existing power relations within society."

The panic that accompanies any burgeoning popular culture or new technology occurs when the parental generation, suddenly insecure, feel they want to be back in charge. In contrast to the Victorian era, with video the threat was no longer perceived as exclusively the domain of the working class.

FEAR . . . for Colleen Dewhurst in When a Stranger Calls

FEAR: He Knows You're Alone

FEAR of a razor . . . in the controversial murder movie Dressed to Kill

FEAR of a maniac husband . . . in Jack Nicholson's film The Shining

SPECIAL REPORT By LIZ GILL

SCANDAL OF THE X-CERT RIPPERS

"The idea is to make women afraid and vulnerable"

CONSIDER these four horrific stories.

- An attractive middle-aged woman is slashed to death by a maniac wielding a razor.
- A pretty teenager is sexually assaulted and so badly battered that her body is identifiable only by her jewellery.
- Another teenager soon to be a bridesmaid for her best friend is found brutally murdered, her head has been severed from her body.
- A young girl student is viciously killed as she walks home alone. Her body is grotesquely mutilated.

SINISTER

Real-life victims

TERROR

VIOLENCE

PUNISHED

"I think this is the trouble with video. It changes the times of everything." So said a parent in *Uninvited Guests* with regard to time-shift recordings she had made of *The Young Ones* at the behest of her children, only to be shocked by the programme's content when she finally sat down to watch an episode. The parent implies that the problem lies not in the fact she allowed her children to watch material typically broadcast after their bed time, but with the innovative technology that she utilised in order that they could do so. Elsewhere in the book, another parent expresses a similar fear:

> There was a time when I videoed various things and then I realised my six-year-old could work it himself. He'd take it out, put it in, and I'd find him watching *The A-Team*.

A report published in May 1983 by the National Association of Head Teachers outlined concerns over the amount of time children spent watching television, as well as the easy access many children had to video films of a violent and pornographic nature. At a conference in Harrogate the following month, head teachers spoke of the "orgy of commercialism" which allowed the availability of such videos to go unchecked. Peter Roberts, headmaster of a school in Suffolk, suggested that youngsters were pooling their cash to hire films clearly not suited for them. He feared they would ape the behaviour they saw on the screen, or possibly become desensitised to it.

(Aside from protecting children from films of sex and violence, the conference demanded greater protection for head teachers, who were said to risk suspension following "mischievous" allegations made by children.)

Turning the clock back some 150 years, Springhall in *Youth, Popular Culture and Moral Panics* reflects on the newspaper reports pertaining to penny theatres in the mid- to late-1800s, and the general belief that such popular, unlicensed entertainment was responsible for the apparent rise in juvenile crime. Featuring comedy acts, magic tricks, melodramas, farces and dancers, the penny theatre — or "gaff" — was staged primarily for working class children and adolescents who could not afford entrance to the 'legitimate' theatres and music halls around the country. But the idea of an autonomous youth subculture didn't sit well with the establishment, and with the introduction of controls such as the 1843 Theatres Act, there followed a crackdown during which the gaffs were banned from showing performances of a theatrical or musical nature without a licence.

As Springhall points out, in a statement as pertinent to the rising video culture as it was to the penny theatres:

> Whenever the introduction of a new mass medium is defined as a threat to the young, we can expect a campaign by adults to follow.

"It used to be drink, smoking and drugs," said Detective Superintendent Peter Kruger, head of Scotland Yard's Obscene Publications Squad. "Then there was a fourth thing, porn, and now there's a fifth, horror."

Kruger was reflecting on the changing face of the nation's leisure pursuits, specifically the increase in complaints that police were receiving from people who had been shown videos at parties, or whose children had been shown videos. From 1979 through to March of 1982, the police seized in excess of 22,300 videocassettes of a pornographic nature.[21] Although the interview with Kruger in the *Sunday Times* dated May 30, 1982, makes no mention of the fact, all the confiscated material comprised of hardcore pornography available only under-the-counter or from sex shops, as opposed to being material openly available in the high street. (See chapter on BLACK MARKET & PIRATES.)

The arrival of video had caught the legislative bodies off-guard, and its explosive growth created a whole new industry to which few of the existing rules and regulations applied. One apparent exception was the Obscene Publications Act (OPA), whose ethereal test for obscenity — defined by law as "having a tendency to deprave and corrupt" — could be brought against horror comics and contemporary literature, as much as it could be brought against images of a sexual nature. It was under this act that police seized the many thousands of pornographic videocassettes noted above and — with growing outrage directed at the high street — it was with the OPA that police sought to prosecute material of a different type: horror and terror videos.

"The horror videos are a new concept," Kruger told the *Sunday Times*, "and I think we are going to get involved with them more and more."

So it was that the video backlash started in earnest and a new moral panic was created.

May of 1982 was the month in which the Advertising Standards Authority announced it had upheld complaints against advertisements for *Cannibal Holocaust*, *The Driller Killer* and *SS Experiment Camp*, and it was the month that a working party was mobilised to try and deal with the videos issue. It was also the month that police seized copies of *SS Experiment Camp*, the first horror video taken with a view to prosecution.

"Some small companies seem to be cashing in on a minor boom in violence on video," reported the *Daily Mail* on May 20, 1982, "But sometimes what's on the packaging may not represent what's actually on the tape."

This adroit observation was in response to the ASA's ruling with regard to offensive advertisements. A rather more emotive full-page article had appeared a week earlier, on May 12, in the section of the newspaper devoted to mums. "Could these be your children... and this your home?" ran the header. The report centred upon a survey by a careers teacher, which revealed that the top ten video films amongst youngsters comprised of titles like *Scum*, *Zombie Flesh-Eaters*, *The Exorcist*, *Flesh Gordon* and *The Texas Chain Saw Massacre* — "all films they were far too young to see in the local cinema."

Parents not owning video players, the article determined, shouldn't necessarily feel that their children were safe as there was every likelihood they would be watching videos at a friend's house.

Although the *Mail* would play a major part in forcing parliament to take a stand on video software, their campaign to "Ban the Video Nasties" was still a year away, and it was a series of reports by Peter Chippindale in the *Sunday Times* that fanned the flames of dissent. Reproducing images that the ASA had condemned, the first of these reports, "How High Street Horror is Invading the Home," dated May 23, 1982, warned that

> Uncensored horror videocassettes, available to anybody of any age, have arrived in Britain's High Streets. The videos — called 'nasties' in the trade — are freely available for hire or sale off the shelves of hundreds of shops catering for the video boom. They cost as little as £2 to hire for up to four nights. They exploit extremes of violence, and are rapidly replacing sexual pornography as the video trade's biggest moneyspinner.

Whether the term 'nasties' was a colloquialism banded around by those 'in the trade' isn't known, but its first appearance in print in connection to videocassettes dates back to the *Sunday People* in December 1981, where it was used to describe a tape of pornographic content. Following Chippindale's report the term came to identify a strain of horror films far removed from the traditional concept of horror, and which were a by-product of the inherently dangerous new medium of video.

> Video viewers use the freeze-frame, slow-motion and rewind buttons on their recorders to revel in the gory bits as often as they like.

Naturally, the people who peddled these 'nasties' were portrayed as an unscrupulous lot and not a little smug, as per the flippant remarks they made to Chippindale concerning films like *Snuff* and *The Driller Killer*. Said Mike Behr, managing director of Astra Video: "There's no censorship laws on video at all. What can they do about it?" A spokesperson for Vipco admitted:

> We are feeding a demand, not creating it. People want to see this sort of stuff, and we are giving them what they want... I agree that there's a lot of violence, and that is probably bad. But who are we to decide?

A survey in 1983 put it into figures: two percent of people who bought videocassettes and fifteen percent of those who rented "chose 'horror' titles, a category that included 'nasties' but also covered the traditional horror film."[22] The ethereal 'other horror' that was the 'nasty' slowly manifested over the coming months into a quantifiable enemy — the unacceptable face of the phenomenon that was video. These 'video nasties' became the subject of much concern in the media over the next few years. This served to exaggerate the issue and prevented public interest in predominantly cheap horror movies from running its natural course. (Indeed it increased it, as shall be seen in the chapter to come.) "Many people, including many MPs, do not seem to appreciate how violent, brutal and sadistic these sort of films are," said Conservative MP Peter Lloyd.

> My girl raped! Two seventeen-year-olds. Said they thought girls enjoyed it after watching videos. Yes, I think that kids "grow up thinking this is the way it is" — how can they think any different when they've had no other experience?
> Who do I blame? I blame shit-holes like you who don't know the difference between sexual liberation and pornography. So you think that "nasties" don't affect people? "Nasties" affected two young lads, giving them a distorted view of reality. "Nasties" affected my girl, who's mentally dead for the rest of her life. "Nasties" affected me. Yes, me! And I've never even watched one. Yes, it's changed me because now I hate! I just hate! I fucking hate!
>
> *—Letter from 'Anon,' NME, March 31, 1985*

'Video nasties' were used by some law-breakers to try and vindicate themselves of their crimes via the negative publicity already given to video. In April 1983, a sixteen-year-old boy admitted to the charge of burglary with intent to rape and claimed that *Confessions of a*

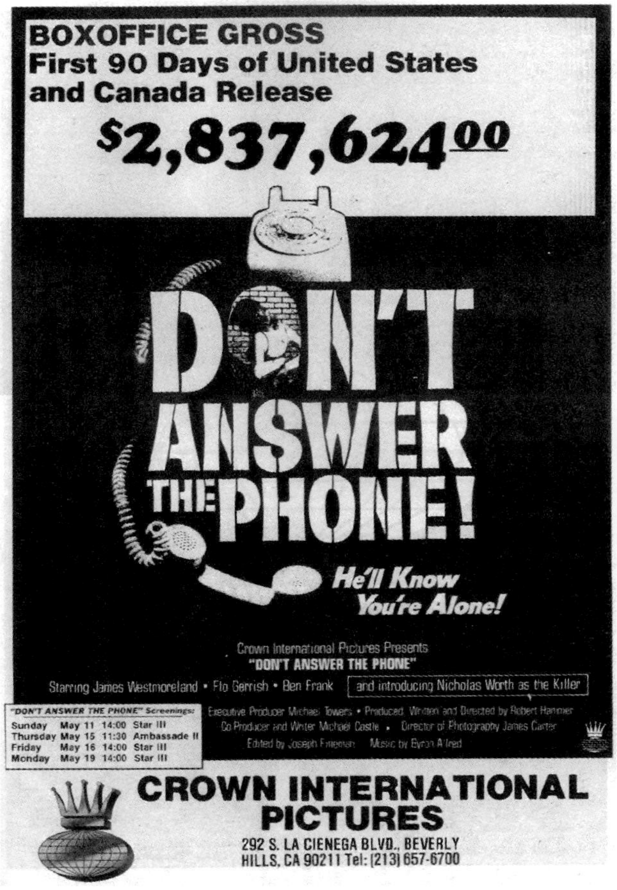

BOXOFFICE GROSS
First 90 Days of United States
and Canada Release
$2,837,624.00
DON'T ANSWER THE PHONE!
He'll Know You're Alone!
Crown International Pictures Presents
"DON'T ANSWER THE PHONE"
Starring James Westmoreland • Flo Gerrish • Ben Frank
and introducing Nicholas Worth as the Killer
"DON'T ANSWER THE PHONE" Screenings:
Sunday May 11 14:00 Star III
Thursday May 15 11:30 Ambassade II
Friday May 16 14:00 Star III
Monday May 19 14:00 Star III
Executive Producer Michael Towers • Produced, Written and Directed by Robert Hammer
Co Producer and Writer Michael Castle • Director of Photography James Carter
CROWN INTERNATIONAL PICTURES
292 S. LA CIENEGA BLVD., BEVERLY HILLS, CA 90211 Tel: (213) 657-6700

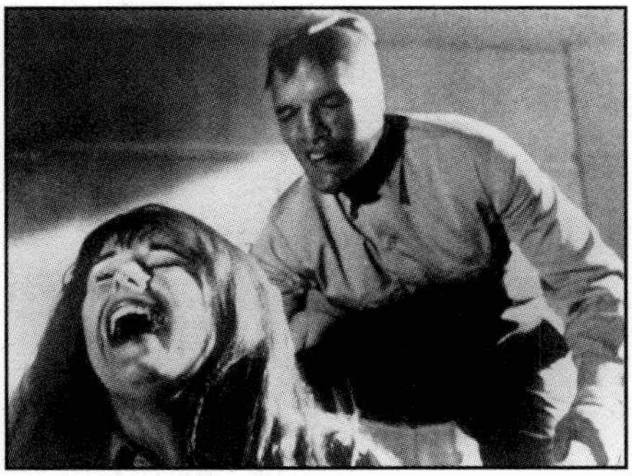

LEFT AND RIGHT, TOP: A couple of stalk-and-slash films that upset feminists – *Don't Answer the Phone!* and *Prom Night*. **ABOVE:** Robert Vincent O'Neil's *Psycho Killer*, a proto example of the genre, made in 1969, released in Britain in 1972.

Window Cleaner — a British sex comedy in the mould of the *Carry On* films — had made him do it. "I watched the film and then went out because I wanted to have sex with a girl," the boy said. *The Times* reported the incident as "Youth Tried Rape After Seeing Video." Soon to follow was the case of eighteen-year-old Martin Austin, found guilty on June 27, 1983, of two counts of rape and seven charges of burglary. The unemployed youth, emotionally immature with a low IQ, was described by the press as a habitual glue-sniffer who lived in a fantasy world ruled by a daily diet of films like *I Spit On Your Grave*. "I got the ideas for the rapes from a so-called video nasty," Austin told the police, before receiving six years in youth custody.

Ignorant to the fact that her son was hiring such films and watching them at home, Mrs Joan Austin told the press, "These films have helped destroy my son's life. They must be banned before another boy's mind is infected by them."

The case acted as a catalyst. The *Daily Mail* responded with the front page headline "Fury Over The Video Rapist," and reported how Austin — whose "moral values had been obliterated by the video films" — had intended only to burgle on the two nights he committed rape. Their editorial comment[23] queried "How many more women will be savaged and defiled by youths weaned on a diet of rape videos...?" Pulling out all the emotive stops, the *Mail* accused the Government of dithering while

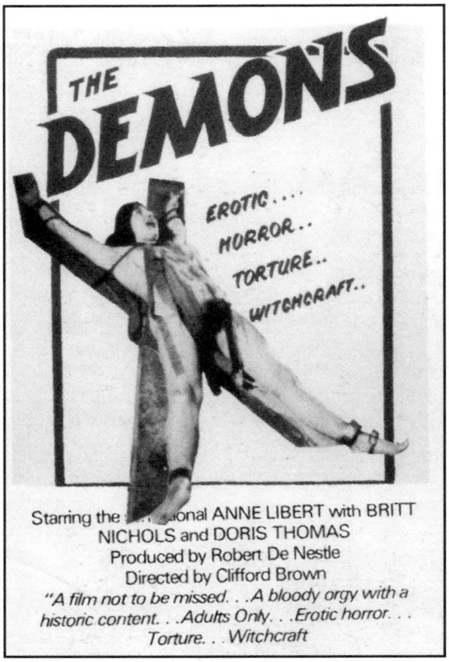

LEFT: A typically arresting advertisement from Go Video for the release of *The Demons*.
RIGHT: Following the complaints upheld against lurid advertisements for horror videos, Go Video returned with a full-page ad for the same release – arguably more lurid thanks to the impromptu penned warning.

> our children can continue to buy sadism from the video-pusher as easily — and as cheaply — as they can buy fruit gums from the sweetie shop…

In reference to *SS Experiment Camp*, seized by police some months previously, the *Mail* lambasted depictions of Nazi atrocities which were "complete with the screams of the Jewish girl victims, played for kicks. And rape, rape, rape."

> Britain had fought the last World War against Hitler to defeat a creed so perverted that it spawned such horrors in awful truth. Now the nation allows our own children to be nurtured on these perverted horrors and on any permutation of them under the guise of entertainment.
>
> Are we insane? Are we bent on rotting our own society from within?

Two months later the "soul-soilers that deaden decency and encourage depravity" struck again in the guise of Christopher Meah, aged thirty, who received two life sentences for separate counts of sexual assault and rape, and for using a knife with intent to cause grievous bodily harm. Having suffered brain damage in a car accident some years earlier, the defendant was said to have been driven completely out of his head by drugs, drink and video films "of the most vile kind." The court heard how Meah acted as if "he was looking at himself playing a video nasty film role." Mrs Christine Meah claimed that her husband "was loving, kind and considerate until he became addicted to watching an endless string of horrifying video films containing detailed scenes of the most depraved and vicious kind."

She added:

> When my husband first began watching these videos, we treated them as a bit of a sick joke. Now I am convinced that they changed his personality and that they should be banned... He began watching them day and night and they obviously turned him into a Jekyll and Hyde. Things got so bad that our daughters were waking up in the early hours and switching the video on.

The furore surrounding 'sadistic' videos in the early eighties was one that had surrounded 'sadistic' films throughout the seventies. In December 1976, *The Sun* newspaper ruminated on some recent cinema releases — including *Marathon Man*, *Rolling Thunder* and *The Texas Chain Saw Massacre* — and asked, "Will you ever dare go to the pictures?" The report states how Dr Malcolm Carruthers, a consultant clinical pathologist of The Maudsley Hospital in London, took a dozen volunteers to see *A Clockwork Orange* and *Soldier Blue*. Measuring heart rate and testing urine, he recorded that the volunteers[24] "got very, very excited at the violent scenes... They were also revolted. Their heart beats slowed down. In any person there are always these two divided reactions — excitement and revulsion." Despite the apparent normality of his findings, the doctor was able to deduce that audiences are becoming "blasé about violence... And if youngsters in particular turn to violence how can we blame them?"

In the early eighties there was concern over a cycle of horror films whose plots revolved exclusively around a lone killer hunting down and butchering the other characters. These films earned themselves the epithet 'stalk-and-slash,' and created controversy on both sides of the Atlantic when accused of signifying a trend for misogynist violence. In Britain, the likes of *He Knows You're Alone* and *When A Stranger Calls* were released amidst the anxiety of the Yorkshire Ripper murders.[25] "The idea," wrote Liz Gill in the *Daily Express*, "is

Daily Mail

18p

SUPER SNOOKER

Boy, 18, attacked women after seeing films

FURY OVER THE VIDEO RAPIST

By TIM MILES

DEMANDS for action on video 'nasties' mounted last night following the case of a teenage rapist who struck after watching pornographic films.

An Old Bailey judge was told that 18-year-old Martin Austin, emotionally

Virginia wins but it all goes wrong for Jimbo

Your chance to get in on the £1·7m game

High Street "nasties": three films that are helping the video boom in Britain

How High Street horror is invading the home

by Peter Chippindale

UNCENSORED horror video cassettes, available to anybody of any age, have arrived in Britain's High Streets. The videos—called "nasties" in the trade—are freely available for hire or sale off the shelves of hundreds of shops catering for the video boom. They cost as little as £2 to hire for up to four nights. They exploit extremes of violence, and are rapidly replacing sexual pornography as the video trade's biggest moneyspinner.

The "nasties" are far removed from the suspense of the traditional horror film. They dwell on murder, multiple rape, butchery, sado-masochism, mutilation of women, cannibalism and Nazi atrocities. The films have such titles as The Driller Killer—the cassette box of which carries a colour photograph of a man screaming while an electric drill is driven through his forehead. Then there is SS Experiment Camp, which features experiments on women in a Nazi concentration camp. Other titles are Cannibal Terror, Cannibal Holocaust, Blood Feast and I Spit on Your Grave.

Great adv... in special effects have ... that realism

the reports were true or merely a sensational sales ploy, the product is horrifyingly convincing—and can now be viewed at home by anyone with a video recorder. The cassette's cover pushes the ambiguity. It reads: "Are the killings in the film for real? You are the judge."

Despite the US ban on Snuff, Mike Behr, the managing director of its British distributor, Astra Video of Croydon, says he is not worried about it being stopped here. "There's no censorship laws on video at all. What can they do about it?"

A Home Office official said last week that video cassettes

about £2 for the hire of one video cassette for between one and four nights.

A spokesman for VIPCO, the London company that distributes The Driller Killer, among other videos, said: "We are feeding a demand, not creating it. People want to see this sort of stuff, and we are giving them what they want.

"I agree that there's a lot of violence, and that is probably bad. But who are we to decide? Ideally there ought to be a line drawn somewhere — but there isn't."

This new phenomenon of video violence sparked off by technological change which has brought a huge boom in video recorders and cassettes in Britain, has left the law far behind. The Williams Committee on Obscenity and Film Censorship, which reported in 1979, did not even mention video.

Peter Lloyd, Conservative MP for Fareham, whose Cinematograph Bill is now before the House of Lords, said that his private member's bill did not even begin to touch the problem of video at home. "What worries me is not so much the pornography but the really harmful ...

Unease gives way to panic and a clampdown.

TOP: *Daily Mail* headlines, June 28, 1983.
ABOVE: *The Sunday Times*, May 23, 1982.

to make women afraid and vulnerable."

She asked the reader to "consider these four horrific stories":

- An attractive middle-aged woman is slashed to death by a maniac wielding a razor.
- A pretty teenager is sexually assaulted and so badly battered that her body is identifiable only by her jewellery.
- Another teenager soon to be a bridesmaid for her best friend is found brutally murdered, her head has been severed from her body.
- A young girl student is viciously killed as she walks home alone. Her body is grotesquely mutilated.

Stories two and four actually happened, stated Gill, while the first and third were episodes from films on release in Britain at the time. A caption beneath pictures showing two women recently murdered (one of whom was Ripper victim Jacqueline Hill), reflects "Could their killers have been aroused by horror films?"

The film most often criticised for its portrayal of sex and graphic violence was Brian de Palma's *Dressed To Kill*, a stylish remodelling of *Psycho* — a film which Gill applauded — starring Angie Dickinson and Michael Caine. Critics, care workers, former sex symbols and film directors were unanimous in their outrage. James Ferman, secretary of the BBFC, on the other hand offered that it was wrong to make any one film pay the price of a whole genre and claimed that generally films had become less violent over the years. "As far as violence is concerned," he told *Photoplay* in January 1981,

> I don't think we're getting the same kind. We had an awful lot of very, very violent Hong Kong and Italian movies in the mid-seventies; blood everywhere, loads of rape scenes... from America too, like *The Texas Chain Saw Massacre*, a film we've never given a certificate to.

Unfortunately for Ferman, both the violence of the mid-seventies and the films to which he never gave a certificate were about to return on video. And, for the women who had attacked cinemas and hurled red paint and bad eggs at screens on which played *Dressed To Kill*, so arrived a new target in the form of any video shop that carried X-rated material.[26]

Staging protests outside shops selling violent and X-rated videocassettes in December 1982, fifty women took part in a two-hour protest at the Video Centre on the Tottenham Court Road in London, resulting in three arrests for obstruction. In Liverpool seven women who sat down in the doorway of Cut Price Records were dragged on to the pavement by shop assistants. The following month, a group calling itself Angry Women launched attacks on video shops in West Yorkshire, breaking windows and lighting fires. Other shops were spray-painted with slogans.

The *Daily Mail*'s "Fury Over The Video Rapist" headline coincided with the announcement that a damning report on the police handling of the Yorkshire Ripper investigation was to be made public.

The video trade was preparing itself for a police purge on 'nasties' following the successful prosecution of *The Driller Killer* and *Death Trap* at Willesden Magistrates Court at the end of August 1982, and *I Spit On Your Grave* in Croydon the following month. These were the first films found obscene for content of "ultra-sadistic horror and terror, rather than straightforward sexual pornography."[27] The Director of Public Prosecutions (DPP) brought charges under Section Three of the Obscene Publications Act, which meant forfeiture and destruction of the videocassettes under a magistrate's warrant. (In the case of *I Spit On Your Grave*, this meant a total of 234 tapes that had been removed by police from the offices of Astra Video.)

A far more serious ruling would have been a Section Two prosecution, which requires the publisher of an obscene article to face a full criminal trial, and the prospect of a jail sentence of up to three years.[28]

The leniency in this instance was based on the case having no precedent, and the fact that the distributors willingly handed the master tapes over to the police. Also to be considered was that under Section Two the case may have taken several months to hear, and the DPP were anxious to be seen to make a move. Mary Whitehouse, however, thought the leniency to be a public scandal, and accused the DPP of protecting the interests of the video nasty distributors.

But the illogical notion that 'nasties' were "a tangible concrete genre removed from other forms of video,"[29] did little to help traders determine what films to look out for in future. There existed no official set of guidelines. Following the ruling against *The Driller Killer* and *Death Trap*, the Video Trade Association — who represented the owners of rental shops — informed its members and the press

> We now believe that a lot of police forces will be keen to take action, often spurred by complaints by members of the public. We have had a lot of calls from traders who are very worried. Half are concerned that they might be doing something illegal, and the others are worried about a substantial loss of profit if they withdraw the nasties.
> We are advising them to take the two titles which have already been through the courts off the shelves immediately, but we are also warning them that any film which exploits gratuitous violence may now be open to the same sort of prosecution as pornography. There are probably lots of other uncensored films around as bad as the ones which have been convicted and they may be liable under the act.[30]

Indeed there were, as witnessed in the many thousands of horror film videocassettes seized over the coming year and a rapidly expanding list of blacklisted titles. But what exactly constituted "unnecessary violence," one of the damning allegations often levelled at the nasties? And by what comparative scale were such scenes and these films being measured? No one knew, least of all the police who were seizing them.

"The forthcoming election and the threat of video nasties has given a new impetus to our campaign." Speaking for the NVALA in the run up to the June 1983 General Election, Mary Whitehouse warned the political parties of the perils they faced should they ignore the issue of video legislation. Not one to take the ex-school teacher's views lightly, Margaret Thatcher, soon to win a second term as Prime Minister, pledged in her Election Manifesto to protect the young against video pornography and horror.

Video's golden age was fast becoming a twilight zone.

HORRIFYING EXPERIMENTS
......In pursuit of the Master Race
GO VIDEO
SS
Experiment Camp
Available at all good VIDEO dealers
GO VIDEO,
PO Box 4BT, 35-37 Wardour Street, London W1A 4BT.

'Privately funded by individuals and churches'

CLAMPDOWN

It doesn't take an awful lot to trigger the machinations of the Obscene Publications Act. A police constable may apply for a warrant to search any premises in which he has 'reasonable cause' to suspect obscene articles are being kept for gain. This reasonable cause may be an unverified complaint from a member of the public or 'observations' the police themselves have made. Under the original 1857 Act, a magistrate would require some evidence of sale in order to issue a warrant, but with the reformed 1959 Act, the police could base their action on a mere suspicion.

Suspicion in the case of the video nasties arose from an article published in a Sunday newspaper. In exposing the violent films that were supposedly "replacing sexual pornography as the video trade's biggest moneyspinner," the *Sunday Times* dated May 23, 1982,[1] provided the police with reasonable enough cause for action. More than that however, it put them in a position whereby they couldn't be seen *not* to act. Playing Devil's Advocate, the article had video distributors claiming they were effectively above the law, while its author pressed the Home Office for comment. As a consequence, Scotland Yard's Obscene Publications Squad secured a warrant and raided the offices of Astra Video, removing copies of *SS Experiment Camp*, one of the films cited in the report. As Detective Superintendent Peter Kruger was to speculate in the pages of the *Sunday Times* the following week, this was undoubtedly just the first in a line of video horror films deserving of police attention.

It was, but little did the detective realise quite how far that line of videos stretched or the ramifications of trying to police it. Two years of police raids and questionable charges under the Obscene Publications Act would come to a head in 1984, with the formation of a highly controversial parliamentary bill known as the Video Recordings Act. This legislation marked the official end for many video titles, not all of them nasty.

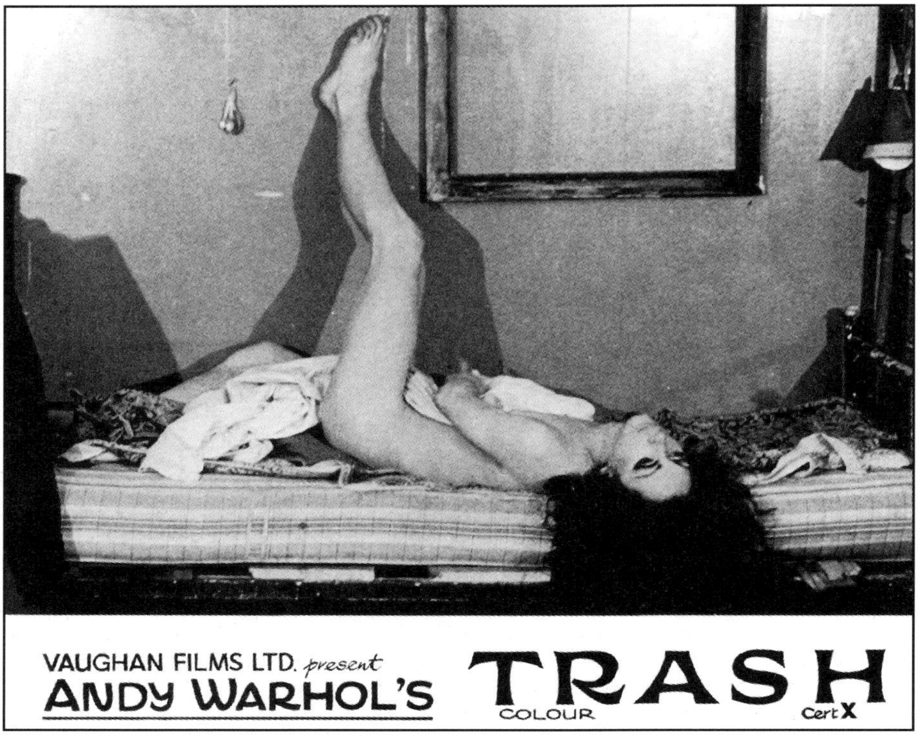

Charges of obscenity against written text[2] were effectively abandoned in January 1976 following the acquittal of *Inside Linda Lovelace*, a book in which the star of *Deep Throat* revealed how to suck cock and perform anal sex. In his summing up, the judge lamented "If this book is not obscene within the definition of the [Obscene Publications] Act it might well be difficult to imagine anything that would fall into that category." (Not unreasonably, given publicity of this calibre, the circulation of the book rose from 20,000 to 600,000 within the space of three weeks.)

From here on, it was the pictorial depiction of the labia and the erect penis that were considered the main taboo subjects, so too any depiction of anal, oral, animal or group sex. (Child sex was covered by the Protection of Children Act 1978.) This became the 'rule of thumb' by which the police gauged obscenity, and such subject matter invariably stood to be charged. But things were rarely that clear-cut, particularly if the contentious material didn't originate from a sex shop.

British obscenity law is decidedly vague and elastic. What constitutes an obscene article in one part of the country may be freely available in another part. This is a criteria that has as much to do with, say, the religious beliefs of the area's Chief Constable as it does the manpower available.[3]

A confidential memorandum issued by Scotland Yard's Assistant Commissioner (Crime) in March 1970 highlighted the difficulties in policing pornography and obscenity. Raids on "dirty bookshops" resulted in no real protest, and it was a relatively simple matter "to assert that the seized articles [were] 'filth for filth's sake'..." However, the report continued, there was a level of pornography designated "exceptionally delicate, where any police action will obviously attract much publicity, subsequent analysis and criticism." Pornography of this latter type was said to comprise

(a) Displays in recognised galleries and books expensively published.
(b) Works of alleged or real masters.
(c) Exhibitions of famous, infamous or notorious individuals.
(d) Films at private clubs and associations, etc.

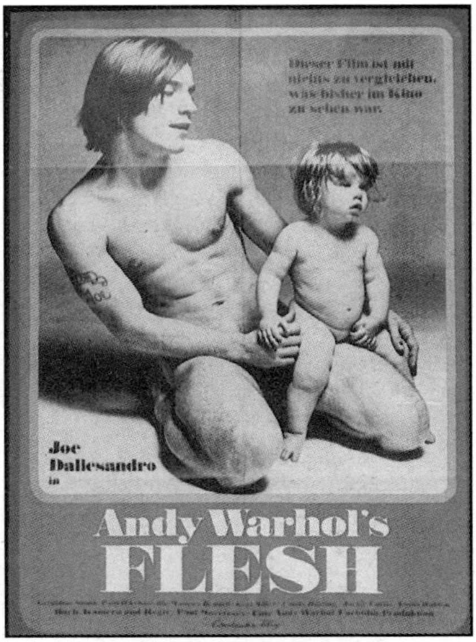

PREVIOUS PAGE AND ABOVE: The films of Paul Morrissey and Andy Warhol – championed by the BBFC; disliked by the police.

The memorandum appears to have been influenced by *Flesh*, a film from the Andy Warhol stable, containing nudity, sex and swear words. Or rather, influenced by media reaction following a screening[4] which was halted after no less than thirty-two policemen descended on the theatre. Not only did the invading officers take the print, but also the projector, screen, and name and address of everybody in attendance. *Flesh* was a critically acclaimed film, and the Open Space Theatre in which the screening was taking place was a "reputable theatre club, supported by the Arts Council, with a membership of intellectuals."[5] The incident made headline news, with most newspapers showing support for the theatre.[6] Questions were even raised in the House of Commons. Ultimately, the owners of the Open Space Theatre were not prosecuted for obscenity, but did plead guilty to failing to uphold a members-only policy on the door. It may have been a conviction – granted not the one envisaged – but the police weren't entirely off the hook. In a publicity masterstroke,[7] Andy Warhol flew in and paid the fines imposed on the theatre owners, telling reporters that it "was the least he could do to fight against censorship in Britain."

Despite the *Flesh* debacle, the police were to spend a good deal of the 1970s seizing material of an "exceptionally delicate" nature. The upshot being, as per the cautionary advice from the Assistant Commissioner, "much publicity, subsequent analysis and criticism." Throughout the decade, the underground press was a prime target because of their use of pornography for political ends. The trials of *International Times*, *The Little Red Schoolbook*, *Nasty Tales*, *Libertine* and *Oz*[8] all took place amidst a blaze of publicity and critical disdain. In the *Oz* case – at twenty-seven working days, the longest obscenity trial in British history – the resultant guilty verdicts brought riotous crowds outside the Old Bailey, and saw the presiding judge burned in effigy. On appeal the charges of obscenity that had landed the publishers in jail were quashed, and at a cost of some £100,000, the press were unanimous in condemning the trial a disaster.

The Obscene Publications Act was capricious and unreliable, liable to swing either way. Unlike the material which fell within the ridiculous criterion of "filth for filth's sake" – constituting the sexshop smut seized by police with little ado or objection – almost everything else brought with it defence lawyers and expert witnesses willing to testify in its favour.

When material is seized by the police, it is examined by the Crown Prosecution Service (formerly police lawyers) and the Director of Public Prosecutions (DPP), whose office will then decide on what action to take. If the decision is made that the material is obscene and liable to have a corrupting influence, its publisher faces proceedings under one of two statutory alternatives. As noted in the previous chapter, these consist of either a prosecution for a criminal offence under Section Two of the 1959 Obscene Publications Act, or a civil forfeiture hearing under Section Three.[9]

Not all material has to go through police hands to reach the DPP. Outraged members of the public are entitled to submit works they consider to be obscene directly to the department themselves. "Custodian of public morals" — as Geoffrey Robertson labels the DPP in his book, *Obscenity* — is not a role that many Directors would like to project however, particularly when in prosecuting they are forced to act as censor. Director Sir Theobald Matthew said of the Obscene Publications Bill in 1957, "I do not know, and I do not suppose anybody else knows, what corrupts." His successor, Sir Norman Skelhorn, stated in 1973:

> The DPP is not acting as a censor, he is not judging the moral standards of the day. All we try to do is predict what a jury is likely to do. We try to assess the prospects of conviction if we prosecute. Of course, it is not easy to predict what a jury is likely to do, but one is guided by the statutory definition of obscenity and one's experience of how the courts have reacted in previous cases.

But court cases are hardly consistent and the statutory definition of obscenity offers little guidance. Indeed the Test of Obscenity — the tendency to deprave and corrupt — is ambiguous to the point of meaninglessness. (In the case of the *Oz* trial, the judge decided to broaden the scope of the Act by incorporating the literal meaning of the word 'obscene.'[10] It was this serious misdirection that helped to overturn the charges on appeal.) It comes as no surprise therefore that the law is unwilling to pre-empt what might constitute an obscene item prior to it being published. Indeed, when the firm of Calder & Boyars took the precaution of contacting the DPP for just such advice in the matter of *Last Exit to Brooklyn*, the response was apologetic:

> If you find — as I am afraid you will — that this is a most unhelpful letter, it is not because I wish to be unhelpful but because I get no help from the Acts.

Hubert Selby Jr's *Last Exit to Brooklyn* was published in the UK in January 1966. The following August a search warrant was issued for copies to be seized from bookshops, and in November, under Section Three of the Obscene Publications Act, the book was ordered to be destroyed. As one reporter put it, Britain once again had "made herself the laughing stock of the civilised world." These were proceedings which had been launched, not by the DPP who hadn't considered the book to be obscene, but a private individual who believed the book was.[11] The destruction order given in court obliged the DPP to change its mind.[12]

If the 1959 Obscene Publications Act was vague and uncertain when it came to differentiating serious literature from pulp pornography (the purpose for which it was intended), its application to videocassettes in the 1980s was to prove even more problematic.

"Videos are difficult to deal with because you cannot flip through them like a publication," was one of the obvious drawbacks of policing video obscenity, as voiced by Peter Lloyd MP. A bigger pitfall however, was that over the course of the next few years, more than ever the police would be working as arbiters of public taste. And in so doing would try to contain a phenomenon on a nation-wide scale with a law that was anything but consistent.

Indeed, the first obscenity case with regard to video resulted in the court deciding that the medium fell outside the scope of the Obscene Publications Act. Film club owner Tom Hays and two of his employees were charged with showing a sexually explicit videotape in a Soho basement cinema. Defending the case at Knightsbridge Crown Court was Geoffrey Robertson QC who argued that a videotape was not a film or "article" as defined by the Act,[13] but a "piece of plastic storing invisible electrical impulses capable of being converted into audio-visual signals."[14] This was a fact supported by a BBC TV engineer, called in as an expert witness. Hays was acquitted in July 1980 and the offending tape — which comprised of material copied from 8mm film — was returned to him. "As it stands," Hays optimistically told the press, "I could, if I wanted to, show whatever I liked on video."

With some urgency this matter was redressed. In September 1980, the Court of Appeal ruled that obscene displays from videotape were "indistinguishable to the watcher from conventional film shows" and therefore were to be covered by the Obscene Publications Act.

The police wasted no time in clearing shelves of anything they thought would be suitable for prosecution. When it came to video nasties quite often titles were seized by mistake, while other titles would be acquitted but then seized again. What's more, as had happened with other media, the zeal with which the police undertook their purge on video varied considerably from one force to the next.

Armed with search warrants, copies of Francis Ford Coppola's *Apocalypse Now* would be taken by police — for no other reason than it sounded like the cheap Italian horror movie *Cannibal Apocalypse*, which they already considered as suitable for prosecution. In another incident, police took away a copy of Vernon Sewell's *The Blood Beast Terror*, a 1967 Tigon film starring Peter Cushing which continues to regularly air on television. The film was eventually returned to the shop, and placed by the owner in the 'for sale' section so as to avoid it being seized again.

Copies of *The Best Little Whorehouse in Texas* were also netted, an innocuous musical comedy starring Burt Reynolds and Dolly Parton, but whose box blurb determined "This much fun couldn't be legal."

The Evil Dead, having already enjoyed a successful run in cinemas, was a horror film that seemed to galvanise forces across the country in a video raiding frenzy. When a Leeds based video firm was finally acquitted of obscenity in June 1984 for having stocked the film, its distributors asked the DPP for no less than forty-seven other cases pending *The Evil Dead* to be dropped.

The truth of the matter was that the video nasty wasn't a quantifiable entity; they weren't a definable genre next to the Western, Thriller or Science Fiction. The British Videogram Association (BVA), unable to get the DPP to disclose details of the guidelines for judging them, shrewdly noted that 'video nasty' quite simply, was

> A phrase coined by the press that generally refers to material that can include disembowelling, castration, cannibalism, and humiliation.

Pressured by the industry, and seeking to help police with some semblance of a directive for their many raids, a Parliamentary Question on July 23, 1984, finally led the DPP to draw up a set of guidelines. Although maintaining that it was for the court to decide what was and wasn't obscene, the department recommended that a video work

> is likely to be regarded as obscene if it portrays violence to such a degree and so explicitly that its appeal can only be to those who are disposed to derive positive enjoyment from seeing such violence.
>
> Other factors may include:
> violence perpetrated by children;
> self-mutilation;
> violent abuse of women or children;
> cannibalism;
> use of vicious weapons (e.g. broken bottle);
> use of everyday implements (e.g. screwdriver, shears, electric drill);
> violence in a sexual context.

Style was also acknowledged as being important. "The more convincing the depictions of violence," stated the DPP, "the more harmful it is likely to be."

> Who is the perpetrator of the violence, and what is his reaction to it?
> Who is the victim, and what is his reaction?
> How is the violence inflicted, and in what circumstances?
> How explicit is the description of the wounds, mutilation or death? How prolonged? How realistic?
> Is the violence justifiable in narrative terms?

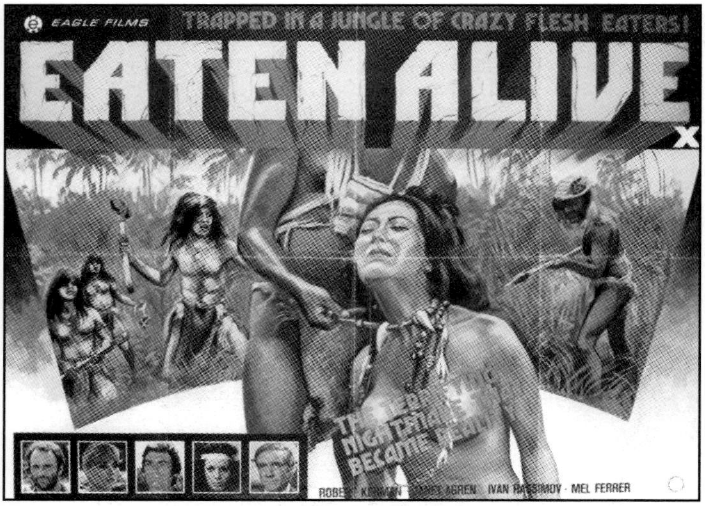

LEFT, AND NEXT PAGE: *Eaten Alive* and *Cannibal* – likely contenders for the DPP list but never included. On the other hand... RIGHT: Dolly Parton and Burt Reynolds' *The Best Little Whorehouse in Texas* – seized by police as liable to prosecution.

These signposts didn't really benefit anyone much at all. They could be interpreted in a broad variety of ways, and just as easily absolve those very films they sought to identify. (For instance, the rape victim in *I Spit On Your Grave* avenges herself by gruesomely murdering her assailants in a series of violent acts that few viewers would deny was justifiable.) The guidelines certainly didn't enable the police to narrow down their scale of operations, and they continued to raid indiscriminately. An exasperated Alf Morton, president of the Greater Manchester Retail Video Association, couldn't understand it. "They are spending an awful lot of money on raids," said Morton about the police. "If they would just give us the information about films which are likely to bring prosecutions they could be taken out of the shops almost overnight."

It was a sentiment shared by virtually every retailer in the country who lobbied Sir Thomas Hetherington, then Director of Public Prosecutions, to do something about it.[15] As a result, Scotland Yard compiled a list of titles that had been prosecuted under the Obscene Publications Act, or were considered as being suitable for prosecution. This list — which came to be known as the DPP list, as well as the 'video nasties' and 'banned' list — initially comprised of thirty-nine titles. With monthly updates the number of titles fluctuated, reaching in excess of sixty different titles before tailing off again. This rise was attributable to the police finding fresh titles they considered to be obscene, while the drop came when films were acquitted in court or examined by the DPP who decided not to launch proceedings. Needless to say, there was some ambiguity involved. For instance, early incarnations of the list didn't include *Death Trap*, prosecuted back in August 1982, but did include *Snuff*, a film supposedly pulled by its distributor and never officially released in Britain. (See VIDEO NASTIES.) Scotland Yard evidently didn't agree with some of the verdicts returned on the more notorious videocassettes. *The Evil Dead* was begrudgingly dropped from the list several months after being cleared of obscenity, while other titles never left the list at all. These included *I Spit On Your Grave*, *Cannibal Apocalypse*, *SS Experiment Camp* and *The Last House on the Left*, for which a London-based video shop owner was acquitted in April 1985.[16] (The full content of the list will be discussed in detail in VIDEO NASTIES.)

Knowledge of the list for most people came via the film magazines that reproduced it, specifically those publications devoted to horror and fantasy. Indeed, few people during the video clampdown of the eighties recall ever having seen or been given a copy of the list, a facet which has led some traders to erroneously surmise that it never existed in the first place.

"There was never an official list," states Steve Ellison, proprietor of Phoenix Home Leisure, adding

> There was a list that each Chief Superintendent of each constabulary probably had in his head and wrote down, but there was never an official list; nothing that the DPP put out to constabularies and said 'these are the films to seize.'

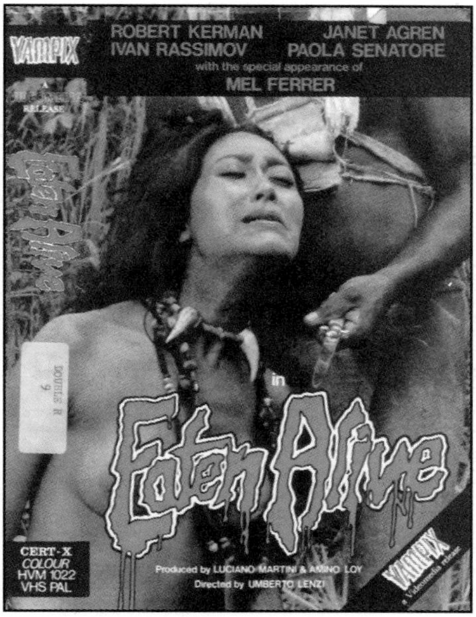

It's a view shared by Chris Glazebrook, buyer of video films for a chain of department stores. "I think the list is something of a myth. I never saw or heard of an official list."

The fact that there did exist a DPP list however is irrefutable: after much searching the authors of this book managed to secure a copy of it from a reliable source. But the confusion which surrounds it is understandable, deriving from the fact that to see it one had to seek it out, and to seek it out one had to know that it existed in the first place. It was never officially made public, nor was it offered to those people one assumes needed it the most: the retailers.

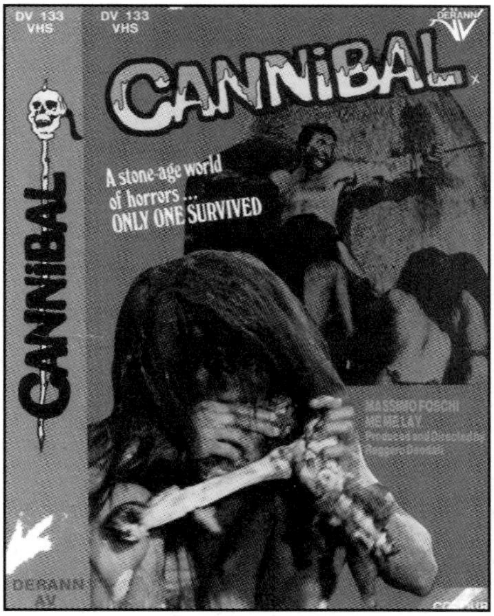

In theory, Scotland Yard's Vice Squad would distribute each new list to police authorities around the country. From here it would have been available to anyone who requested a copy. Many dealers had hoped that given a list they could work with the police in identifying the nasties, remove them from their shelves and thereby safeguard themselves against a raid. But plenty of local forces either remained ignorant, denying all knowledge of a blacklist,[17] or were unwilling to work with the retailers. Either way the raids continued.

On February 3, 1984, three men were found guilty of possessing obscene articles for publication and gain. These comprised 212 videocassettes of *Nightmares in a Damaged Brain* which had been seized by police in October 1982 following raids on premises in London and Leeds. The men were sentenced under Section Two of the Obscene Publications Act. Malcolm Fancey and Roger Morley both received suspended sentences and fines, while company secretary David Hamilton-Grant was jailed for six months.[18] This effectively marked the end of the grace afforded the video industry, as until now no one had actually gone to prison for handling video nasties. Defending the case had been the distinguished Geoffrey Robertson, who several years earlier had rankled the courts in arguing that video was not covered by the Obscene Publications

HORROR VIDEO CASSETTES

Following the Attorney General's Statement in the House of Commons on 23 July 1984 a list of titles of video cassettes of the horror variety which have been the subject of prosecution under Section 2 of the Obscene Publications Act, 1959 or advised as suitable for such prosecution is as follows:-

HORROR

ABSURD (Uncut)
ANTHROPOPHAGEOUS BEAST
AXE
BEAST IN HEAT
BLOOD BATH
BLOOD FEAST
BLOOD RITES
BLOODY MOON
BURNING, THE (Uncut)
CANNIBAL APOCALYPSE
CANNIBAL FEROX (Uncut)
CANNIBAL HOLOCAUST
CANNIBAL MAN
DEVIL HUNTER
DON'T GO IN THE WOODS ALONE
DRILLER KILLER
EVIL SPEAK (Uncut)
EXPOSE
FACES OF DEATH
FIGHT FOR YOUR LIFE
FOREST OF FEAR
FRANKENSTIEN (BY ANDY WARHOL)
GESTAPO'S LAST ORGY
HOUSE BY THE CEMETARY
HOUSE ON THE EDGE OF THE PARK
I SPIT ON YOUR GRAVE
ISLAND OF DEATH (NICO MASTORAKIS VERSION)
LAST HOUSE ON THE LEFT
LOVE CAMP 7
MADHOUSE
MARDI GRAS MASSACRE
NIGHTMARES IN A DAMAGED BRAIN
NIGHT OF THE BLOODY APES
NIGHT OF THE DEMON
SNUFF
SS EXPERIMENT CAMP
TENEBRAE
WEREWOLF AND THE YETI
ZOMBIE FLESH EATERS (Uncut)

All correspondence must be addressed to the Chief Constable

P O Box 22 (S. West PDO)
Chester House
Boyer Street
Manchester M16 0RE
Telephone 061 855 2806

Your reference
Our reference X/RB/ET
Date 4th April, 1984

D. Kerekes, Esq.,

Dear Sir,

I have been asked by the Chief Constable to acknowledge receipt of your letter of 29th March, 1984, the contents of which have been noted, and I thank you for your interest.

I cannot comment on the procedures of other Forces, but I can tell you that the Greater Manchester Police do not publish a similar list.

Yours faithfully,

Chief Superintendent

TOP: Actual copy of perhaps the first list of videocassettes liable to prosecution as issued by the DPP – a total of thirty-nine titles. ABOVE: The police reply to co-author David Kerekes' enquiry concerning the existence of a DPP list in April 1984.

Act.[19] The expert witnesses included film critics Derek Malcolm and Marjorie Bilbow. It was while giving evidence on the film's competent camerawork that Malcolm was famously interrupted by Judge Christopher Beaumont, who unwittingly quantified the inanity of the whole nasties debate in his remark: "How is this relevant to the jury in deciding the case? You might say the German tank invasion of Poland was well executed. Does excellence and camerawork help the jury to come to a conclusion in the case?"[20]

In what may or may not have been a premeditated reversal on the corruption of minors argument, the critic defended *Nightmares in a Damaged Brain* as one concerned with the likely perversion of children by the excesses of the adult world. A bloody decapitation scene at the end, Malcolm deduced, was the film's "least memorable part." (See VIDEO NASTIES for synopsis.) Marjorie Bilbow agreed, believing that while the film showed promise and was on a par with "early Hitchcock", its bloodshed was over-the-top albeit "commercially important."

After watching the film, the jury of three women and nine men decided that it was likely to deprave and corrupt. "People who make money out of this sort of obscenity," concurred Judge Beaumont, "have got to be punished."

For April Electronics — distributing the film through their subsidiary label, World of Video 2000 — the verdict meant going into liquidation. Although the severity of the sentencing set a precedent, the trial of *Nightmares in a Damaged Brain* wasn't the first instance of a successful Section Two prosecution. That dubious honour fell to a video dealer in Leeds called Stephen Taylor, who in 1983 had received a fine of £600 for dealing in nasties. Although he considered the sum to be excessive, Taylor was mindful that things could have been much worse had this not been the first prosecution. "If I had been the second, I might have got six months' imprisonment."

Taylor was interviewed for a Channel 4 documentary entitled *A Gentleman's Agreement?*, which investigated the idea of voluntary code of practice within the video industry. Driving around in his van and delivering videos to his clients — amongst them "the Speights and their five children", about to take receipt of *Nightmares in a Damaged Brain* — he told the film makers that he often inquired as to what customers really thought about the video nasties. "Not one of them objected," he said. This was the attitude of a good deal of the video viewing public. Asked whether he had ever received complaints as to a film's content during his years working in video software, Chris Glazebrook told the authors of this book:

> The only film we ever had any complaints about was *Monty Python's Life of Brian*, on the grounds that it was blasphemous. No one ever complained about violence or bad language.

Of course, this runs contrary to the outrage being expressed in the media and with lobby groups and MPs, intent on demonising video to their own ends. So fired up on the subject of horror films were some that even a debate on the topic was out of the question — as very nearly was the television documentary *A Gentleman's Agreement?*, whose title derived from a statement made by Gareth Wardell MP. Withdrawing from Parliament a Private Member's Bill aimed at legislating against the nasties, Wardell made it clear that he thought it unlikely the industry would be able to control itself, as suggested by the BVA. The profits were just too large, he lamented. How could a gentleman's agreement be expected of "people who basically are not gentlemen"?

The documentary was scheduled for broadcast on June 8, 1983. The 8:30 time slot was moved back to 10:30 PM on account of the inclusion of scenes taken from video films containing "extreme violence,"[21] notably *I Spit on your Grave* and *SS Experiment Camp* which had been found obscene the previous September. But the Independent Broadcasting Authority's decision to allow the documentary to be broadcast at all riled Mary Whitehouse, who requested that the DPP intervene and stop the screening. Mrs Whitehouse told *The Times* newspaper that she had not actually viewed the documentary, nor the scenes to which she objected. "It really would not have made the slightest difference," she asserted, "because I know very well what they are — we were responsible for bringing them before the courts."

Police were also said to be alarmed that extracts from obscene material would be aired. The DPP pointed out that it wasn't an offence under the Obscene Publications Act to transmit the scenes, so the broadcast went ahead.

The following month, July 1983, it was reported that of the 5,000 accredited video shop owners in Britain,[22] almost half were in support of government legislation to control the video nasties. Responding to the question "Would you prefer a clear law to govern what videocassettes you should stock rather than a voluntary certification system?", forty-five per cent said yes, fifty-three per cent said no, and two per cent of the dealers didn't know.

This shift of opinion away from the voluntary self-regulation volunteered by the BVA, reflected the concern dealers felt with regard to the increasing negative press and prospect of a police raid. But the premature death knell for self-regulation was to come from outside the industry. Still smarting over the DPP's refusal to stop at her behest the screening of *A Gentleman's Agreement?*, Mary Whitehouse attacked the video medium with renewed vigour. In 1980 she had sent a letter to the Home Secretary citing video as being "the biggest threat to the quality of life in Britain." In 1983, along with the NVALA, she held special fringe meetings at the Conservative Party conference, showing excerpts from several video nasties (outraged by the excerpts in Channel 4's documentary, this presentation however posed no dilemma to Whitehouse). These screenings led to a meeting at Conservative Party Offices with Graham Bright MP for Luton South, who was to take heed of Whitehouse's concerns over video.

The Prime Minister told the House of Commons that the Home Secretary was considering the introduction of a new law to curb video nasties. Only a few weeks had passed since a Private Member's Bill from the opposition was withdrawn in order to give the industry a chance to establish its own code of practice. Now came a sudden and complete reversal as the Commons prepared to debate a Private Member's Bill from Bright, which sought "to outlaw pornographic, obscene and horror video tapes." Come November 1983, the month in which it was given its second reading in the Commons, the MP had resigned from his minor position at the Home Office in order to dedicate more time to his 'Bright Bill.' Soon to become the Video Recordings Bill, this badly drafted piece of legislation would go beyond forever changing the culture of video in Britain to launch a black-market industry whose revenue remains inestimable. (See BLACK MARKET & PIRATES.)

On November 1, 1983, a few days before his Bill was to get a second reading, Bright gave Members of Parliament "the experience of seeing a video nasty." In a Commons committee room, attended by about 100 MPs, a film of twenty-two minutes duration was screened comprising of scenes from videotapes confiscated by Scotland Yard. With entrepreneurial aplomb, Bright had warned his audience of what to expect — rape, gang rape, sexual killings and a monkey having its head bashed in — and that nobody should feel ashamed if they were unable to sit through the horror and had to leave. Reaction to the film was suitably galvanised. After the screening, one MP told *The Times* newspaper:

> Some people think that the sight of two or three people making love is aesthetic, but there cannot be two conflicting views about seeing a girl chopped up and her entrails ripped out and eaten.

Another MP lamented

> What we have just seen is bestial and horrific. To show this to youngsters would be deplorable.

Jeremy Hanley, Conservative MP for Richmond and Barnes, couldn't sit through the whole thing. He told the reporter:

> Many people did not want the showing to continue they were so horrified by what they saw. I am still shaken now by what I saw. I am not a believer in total censorship, but I am afraid I think I have just seen where the limit lies.

Is that what Bright's bill entailed? Total censorship? On November 16, Bright took the film to Strasbourg in order to find European support. Euro-MPs, parliament staff and journalists were amongst those who viewed the compilation tape. "Nasty is too weak a word for it," noted the reporter for *The Times*. "One girl had to rush from the viewing room to be sick and more than one journalist will be unable to give a full account of what happened."[23] Ironically, one of the arguments frequently used against video is that the technology allows violent or sadistic scenes to be played out of context. This is exactly what Bright was presenting in his showreel — violent and sadistic scenes taken out of context – despite guidelines indicating that films should be assessed as a whole.[24]

The British Videogram Association commissioned a MORI poll. Two million questionnaires were sent to video dealers for distribution amongst customers, the intention being to help "bring to the attention of both Government and Parliament the views of the video public." It was an obvious ploy to alert people to the ramifications of Government legislation, and avert the clampdown threatened by the Bright bill.

The confidential survey asked four questions of the public:

1. Do you believe that the video films which you watch at home should be more censored than the cinema, the same as the cinema or less censored than the cinema?
2. Do you believe that any film which is considered not to be obscene should be available to adults from their video library?
3. Do you believe that parents have the final responsibility as to what their children should or should not watch?

4. Do you believe there should be censorship on video films which are watched in the privacy of the home?

The resultant figures reflected that sixty-five per cent of the British public were against video censorship. And while in favour of a categorisation system, the general opinion was that the Government shouldn't determine what videos people be allowed to watch in their homes. However, another unrelated survey was already in progress, one which was predestined to have a far greater impact when its findings were presented to Government. Published under the title *Video Violence and Children*, this was a survey conducted amongst schoolchildren across the country, of ages seven to 16 years. Given the Working Party involved in the enquiry, it could come as no surprise that its findings fully supported Graham Bright. (The results were, in the words of one associated with the Party, "exactly what we wanted.")

The topic was video and its effect on children, already the staple of news panics dating back to 1982 and the subject of an all-party Parliamentary committee led by anti-porn crusader Jill Knight MP earlier in the year. Having been postponed from its initial date in May, the Parliamentary Group Video Enquiry was formed following a meeting that took place in a room at the House of Lords on June 27, 1983. Its chairman was Lord Nugent of Guildford, a supporter of moral legislation in the Lords, and in attendance were representatives of the political parties and senior members of many Churches.[25]

Given the job of leading the Enquiry was Dr Clifford Hill, who ran an evangelical mission in London.[26] Raymond Johnston, with whom Hill was to produce an outline of research proposals, was the director of CARE (Christian Action Research and Education), formerly the Nationwide Festival of Light. Johnston had told the assembly that children were "regularly hiring violent, pornographic and occult horror videos", and that he considered the Obscene Publications Act to be a "flawed instrument" that needed to be strengthened.

The Working Party's directive, which concerned "the phenomenon of violence not pornography", was to provide Members of Parliament, the media and the public with (a) an overview of the current social, commercial and legal situation in Britain with regard to video films depicting scenes of explicit violence, (b) evidence of children's viewing patterns in relation to the suitability of the films seen, and (c) deal with the effects upon children of viewing scenes of violence in video films.

Data for the Enquiry was amassed from 7,000 questionnaires given to children and parents. These were completed during school time, with children working independently from one another. Following this, children were encouraged to divulge their video viewing habits in a class discussion, and on occasion a member of the Working Party would attend to conduct taped interviews.

Director Clifford Hill stressed that "checks upon the honesty and reliability of the children's answers were carried out", but it became common knowledge that the Report was rushed to completion in order to influence the latter stages of the Video Recordings Bill. Indeed, the Commons had been influenced right from the beginning when, at the request of the sponsors, the Working Party produced an interim Report to coincide with the early stages of the Bill. This interim Report was published in spite of it comprising, in Hill's own words, "incomplete figures which made it vulnerable to misinterpretation." That there were any figures at all — let alone assertions, conclusions and recommendations — was something of a mystery, as less than a fortnight earlier Hill was admitting that "the analysis of data had not yet begun."

Nevertheless, the inconclusive and misrepresentative statistics made good copy. Britain's schoolchildren on a daily diet of violent and horrific films — in excess of anything that cinema-going adults could legally see — was a topic the media lapped up. Newspapers, TV and radio revelled in proclaiming that "nearly half" of the nation's youngsters had seen a video nasty (a third by the time they were eight).

Many people were supportive of any Bill that sought to protect kids from the corruption that was the video nasty. But there were some who voiced their concern over the legal control of video films and the makeup of the Enquiry's research. These included Brian Brown, whose name and research unit at Oxford Polytechnic were attached to the Report, but who ultimately repudiated its "framework, context and conclusions." Part of Brown's concern originated from the fact that Dr Hill was using material whose source was unknown to anybody else. This challenge resulted in Hill unexpectedly, and in Brown's absence, raiding the unit at Oxford Polytechnic and removing all questionnaires, material and data pertaining to the Report. Even computer tapes were wiped.[27] When *Video Violence and Children* was finally published on March 7, 1984, delegates for the Methodist and Roman Catholic Churches had already formally withdrawn from the Enquiry, sceptical about its alarming findings. In response to the claims that forty-five per cent of British schoolchildren had seen at least one violent video film, the Methodists told the press that more important social issues than videos faced children, such as alcohol abuse and glue sniffing.[28] Brian Brown and his team suspected these figures to be a gross exaggeration anyway, but of course were unable to follow up their suspicions on account of Hill having confiscated the research data.[29] Even Graham Bright himself appeared on TV and aired some doubts. "I do question the validity of the research," he told the BBC. "It points at the problem, but I don't think one can take that as concrete evidence."[30]

The validity of the evidence however, didn't deter the press from proclaiming that young people were addicted to violence like drugs. "The wave of video filth that has swept through Britain's homes," stated the educational correspondent for the *Daily Express*, was partly responsible for the increase in "child abuse, brutal sexual attacks, violent assaults and street rioting."

Palace Video prepared libel actions against the Hill Report for prejudicing legal hearings against their film *The Evil Dead* and "influencing the press into mistakenly categorising it as a video nasty."[31] Several other distributors complained that the Parliamentary Group was in contempt of Court, given that the Report detailed the synopses for several video films currently embroiled in legal proceedings. These allegations were rejected and no action was taken. Neither were they made public. This was because the Sponsors of the Enquiry, according to Hill, "did not want any publicity that might have detracted from the main issues."

Contrary to what many believed, the Video Enquiry was not an official parliamentary investigation but a privately funded one ("funded by individuals and Churches" was Hill's vague declaration). Its political significance however, was never in doubt, and the Prime Minister herself took a personal interest in its development. Less than a week after *Video Violence and Children* was published, Graham Bright's Bill was well on its way through Parliament. On July 12, with only two Tory MPs and one Labour peer dissenting, the Video Recordings Act 1984 reached the Statute Book.

Its official stamp being to "make provision for regulating the distribution of video recordings and for connected purposes", the Act was a major piece of legislation adopted at the height of a moral panic. Agitated by the press and the findings of the Video Enquiry, public concern over video nasties so great that the Bill met with only muted, belated protest. When it became clear that its implications went far beyond the censorship of mere video nasties, the rapidity with which the Bill had moved through parliament meant that any opposition to it would invariably be too late. The same few titles were exploited in the media as being excessively violent and brutal. Yet, on the back of this handful of videocassettes a wide-reaching law was hurriedly shaped and introduced. There arose stirrings of an industry outcry. With the Act only weeks away from the Statute Book, the Directors Guild of Great Britain claimed it posed "an infringement on the freedom of artistic expression." This was a concern shared by the Advertising Standards Authority, who had been instrumental in kick-starting the media interest in nasties when they upheld complaints against advertisements back in May 1982 (see previous chapter). The ASA feared that the country was moving into a period of creeping censorship.

For the British Council of Churches, the law had to "strike delicate balance between public good and the freedom of the individual." Protection of children, the Council insisted, lay foremost with parents and guardians.

Of the formative days of the Video Recordings Act, Steve Ellison recalls that

Fears grow at threat of increased cinema censorship

INDUSTRY OUTCRY OVER VIDEO BILL

THE GROWING outcry from the UK film and video industries over the implications of the Video Recordings Bill reached a peak this week as the Bill passed unopposed through the House of Lords on Monday (April 2).

By Alex Sutherland

The UK film industry fears that the Bill, designed to ban so-called "video nasties" and introduce a system of classification for all cassettes shown in the home, will result in increased censorship of films in cinemas.

The Directors Guild of Great Britain, representing over 500 film, television and theatre directors, described the Bill as "an infringement on the freedom of artistic expression", and believes the terms "go dangerously far beyond (the Bill's) declared purpose of controlling socially and morally unacceptable material".

"We now face a period of even stricter censorship in films from the British Board of Film Censors, who have already permitted films in Britain to be censored more heavily than in any other country in the free world," the Guild's chairman

• **Continued on page 2**

As a member of the Video Trade Association I was invited down to London to Westminster Hall to a couple of the meetings with Graham Bright. Dear old Mary Whitehouse was there, and a few other people. I was there in a couple of the meetings when the actual terms of the Act were thrashed out. I remember saying at one of the meetings, "Why don't they make every film that was produced before 1940 exempt?" And Graham Bright said, "No. They were making pornographic movies in 1915." That was the problem. He was a bigger problem than Mary Whitehouse ever was. Mary got the stick in the press because she was very outspoken. Really, what she wanted to do was to protect the kids. I remember standing on the steps at Whitehall and saying, "Come on, Mary. What would happen if I told you a dirty joke?" She looked around and said, "Well, there are no kids around — I'd probably laugh." She wasn't the matriarch that people make her out to be — she was actually quite a normal, warm human being. But Bright was difficult to deal with.

Bright Bill likely to restructure BBFC

MAJOR CHANGES to the structure of the British Board of Film Censors (BBFC) seem likely if Graham Bright's Video Recordings Bill becomes law, **writes Sue Newson-Smith.**

Home Secretary Leon Brittan has already made it clear that he favours the BBFC as the classifying authority for video cassettes.

However, this proposal has been questioned by several MPs, discussing the Bill at committee stage.

At the committee's last meeting (Jan 18), Home Office Under Secretary David Mellor announced four new proposals in an attempt to ward off ... criti...

Bill that the Home Secretary should himself name the four without anyone else having a say. The Government proposes to formalise the present informal arrangement by which the president and secretary are nominated by the cinematogaph industry with the tradition of their names being acceptable to the Home Secretary.

2) *Examiners*. At present there are 12 part-time examiners. This number will be greatly expanded and there will be a clear and definite need for their range of experience to be greater than at present.

3) *Accountability*: The ... see an ...

Video Bill completed

THE Bill banning video nasties has finally completed its proceedings in Parliament and will soon become law.

By Sue Newson-Smith

It outlaws video recordings portraying explicit sex and excessive violence, and gives guidance to retailers, customers and parents on the suitability of other videos for particular age groups.

Welcoming the Video Recordings Bill's completion, Home Secretary Leon Brittan told MPs, "Parliament has acted speedily to deal with this new and evil trade. I am sure that it has done so with very widespread public support."

The Bill was sponsored by Conservative MP Graham ...

Screen International documents the Video Bill.

FROM TOP: April 7-14; January 28-February 4; July 14-21, 1984.

Conan Le Cilaire's documentary film *Faces of Death* was available in Britain in the early days of video, but quickly found itself on the DPP's list of 'banned' films once the clampdown got under way. (An excerpt from it — in which diners at a Turkish restaurant supposedly feed on fresh monkey brains — had been included in Graham Bright's inflammatory showreel shown in Parliament.[32]) During the brief hiatus in which the film was legitimately available for rental, access to this "particularly offensive and revolting" film[33] was hindered only by extraneous factors like limited distribution and the reluctance of rental outlets to give shelf space to a supposed documentary feature. There was no regulation on the actual content of the film or restrictions as to who should and shouldn't be allowed to see it. Indeed, as noted earlier, there was nothing to stop any enterprising businessman from putting any old thing out on video. The result: video shelves crammed with all manner of diverse product from around the world. And wherever quality was lacking in a film's production, the promise of sex and violence was always a workable substitute.

The blurb on the reverse of the *Faces of Death* box sleeve concluded with the following statement:

> Scenes in this video film are of explicit and shocking nature [sic]. They should not be viewed by young persons, or those of a nervous disposition. In the opinion of the distributors many of the scenes contained herein would not pass the British Board of Film Censors.

A shrewd observation, if a little presumptuous. At the hands of the British Board of Film Censors (BBFC) the film would undoubtedly have suffered cuts or perhaps rejected outright. But *Faces of Death* was never submitted to the Board for the simple reason that prior to the Video Recording Act 1984 it didn't need to be. Material destined for theatrical release required examination by the BBFC and a certificate (although local councils could overrule any of the Board's decisions on appeal), while distributors of video had no such obligation,[34] the medium falling outside the parameters of existing Home Office guidelines.[35]

By default the BBFC landed the job of videocassette classification. They were, in the words of Graham Bright, "the only classifying board in operation at the moment."

The BBFC is an independent, non-profit making body that derives almost all its income from the examination fees it charges. With the exception of some works that qualify as exempt, this includes all feature films, short films, trailers and advertisements.

Formed in 1912 under the aegis of the Incorporated Association of Kinematograph Manufacturers — a trade collective representing manufacturers of cinema equipment and film processors — the BBFC provided a uniform, national alternative to the various local authorities who were imposing their own disparate forms of censorship on films.

The Cinematograph Act had been introduced in 1909 and required that all cinemas carry a license issued by the local council. Primarily concerned with safety of the public, the Act brought cinemas into line with similar regulations which were already applicable to music halls and pubs. But a wider ruling shortly after — which ostensibly sought to restrict the showing of films on Sundays — was interpreted as giving local authorities the power to censor films.[36] Film companies were unhappy with this and approached Parliament with a view to establishing a recognised central censorial board. Initially viewed with some suspicion by the local authorities, the BBFC was eventually adopted as the unofficial body that would classify, cut or reject the films destined for the nation's cinema screens.[37]

Not until the Cinematograph Act 1952 — which sought to prohibit children from gaining admittance to works designated as unsuitable — did Parliament formally acknowledge the BBFC, however.[38]

Two major pieces of legislation were to have a direct impact on the Board in the 1980s. These were the Cinematograph Act 1982[39] and the Video Recordings Act 1984. Both incorporated recommendations made some years earlier by the Committee on Obscenity and Film Censorship, which had been chaired by the philosopher Bernard Williams.[40] Appointed by the Labour Government in July 1977 with the charge of reviewing the obscenity laws, Williams had been an expert witness in the defence of *Last Exit to Brooklyn* a decade earlier. His choice as head of the Committee angered the Festival of Light and many other moral crusaders, who regarded the appointment of a non-Christian as prejudicial. Indeed, the Committee favoured a rational approach as opposed to a moral one, deducing that pornography was an effect of the new permissiveness, not a cause, and posed no threat. "Terms such as 'obscene', 'indecent' and 'deprave and corrupt' should be abandoned as having outlived their usefulness," was one of their common sense proposals.

Upon its presentation in 1979, Mary Whitehouse demanded that the Government reject

the Report, as did politicians and many newspapers.[41] But while its findings were to have no immediate impact, certain recommendations were to be incorporated into fresh legislation over the coming years. In the case of the Cinematograph Act 1982, this meant tighter control over bogus cinema clubs and the introduction of a new film category, the troubled R18 rating (which the BBFC designated "for restricted distribution only, through specially licensed cinemas or sex shops to which no one under 18 is admitted"[42]). With regard to the Video Recordings Act 1984 – despite there being no provision for video in the Report itself – an updated set of classification categories were among the proposals adopted, whose display in the form of an inclosed symbol would appear on all screenings and advertisements for a film.

Interestingly, the Williams Committee also suggested that a statutory body be introduced to take over the censorship powers of local authorities, and proposed this authority be called the Film Examining Board. Under the Video Recordings Act, the BBFC found itself exercising a statutory function on behalf of central government. Although they didn't become the Film Examining Board as a result, they did undergo a change of name, from the British Board of Film Censors to the less draconian, but hardly more accurate, British Board of Film Classification.[43]

The Video Recordings Act 1984 was a means to outlaw the video nasties, and classify all video material as to its suitability for viewing in the home. This latter test was the remit under which the whole Act balanced, and the factor that necessitated a film destined for video would be subject to greater scrutiny than one destined for a theatrical release (what might be a 15 certificate film in the cinema may carry a more strict 18 rating on video, or even require cuts). A film which was refused a certificate could still play at a cinema if the local authority authorised it, whereas on video – although there existed a Video Appeals Committee – such a refusal invariably represented a legal ban.

The Bill was devised to eliminate the element of chance that accompanied any prosecution under the Obscene Publications Act (which required proof that material seized, if taken as a whole, was liable to deprave and corrupt). Now, with a classification system supported by the state, video was a quantifiable commodity and the industry bound by clear-cut legislation: anyone supplying for gain material that hadn't been classified as suitable for viewing in the home, was a transgressor of the law. As indeed was anyone found supplying material to persons below the age stipulated in the packaging, or supplying an R18 video on premises other than a licensed sex shop. The penalty stood as high as £20,000.[44]

The government was under pressure to implement the Act – *any* Act, it seemed, in light of MPs sickened by Graham Bright's showreel, the media blitz, and lobby groups baying for an end to the video nasties. "Why was the Act delayed for more than a year?" queried the *Daily Express* in October 1985. No better reason, determined the newspaper, than because "Whitehall civil servants were busy reworking such peripheral details as labelling regulations and details of consumer protection... meanwhile, children were without the protection of the new law."

Even as the Bill was making its way through Parliament, the vocal Mary Whitehouse was picking holes in it. She spent an hour in discussion with the Home Secretary, Leon Brittan, whose later Parliamentary statement with regard to "this new and evil trade" was uncannily adjoined to the feeling and phraseology of the moral reformist. Whitehouse believed the BBFC were the wrong body for the job of classifying videocassettes, and explained to the *New Video Viewer* in November 1983 that, "Inevitably, when a group is dealing with the kind of material which over the years [the BBFC] have seen, their judgement becomes de-sensitised."

BRITISH BOARD OF FILM CLASSIFICATION

VIDEO RECORDINGS ACT 1984

Tariff of Fees

July 1985

Type of work	Fee
Video works not previously examined in any form	
Works in which the spoken language is predominantly English (standard rate)	£4.60 per minute to 2 hours £3.45 per minute thereafter
Minimum charge	trailers/shorts up to 10 minutes: £46.00
Sub-titled works in a spoken language which is predominantly other than English	£3.45 per minute to 2 hours £2.30 per minute thereafter
Minimum charge	trailers/shorts up to 10 minutes: £34.50
Untranslated works in a spoken language predominantly other than English	£2.30 per minute to 2 hours £1.15 per minute thereafter
Minimum charge	trailers/shorts up to 10 minutes: £23.00
Charities and non-profit-making organisations are invited to apply for a reduced fee chargeable at the Board's discretion for works which are not to be distributed for private gain.	£1.15 per minute
Minimum charge	trailers/shorts up to 10 minutes: £11.50
Video works previously certificated as films or broadcast as British television programmes	£2.30 per minute to 4 hours £1.15 per minute thereafter
Minimum charge	trailers/shorts up to 10 minutes: £23.00

(For this purpose, television serials will be charged as one complete work, although episodes of a series which may be supplied and viewed independently will be charged as separate works.)

The above charges are subject to VAT at the prevailing rate.

CUTS

THE THRILL KILLERS (Video Feature) Palace Video 14 10 88 '18'

The title is likely to prove unacceptable for this video even if it is successfully cut, as follows:

At 16½ mins Reduce sadistic killing in bedroom by removing entire humilation by threat and slapping to woman, cutting from killer advancing with scissors saying "I'm going to kill you" (TC 13:26:32:21) to shot of her trying to reach door for second time (TC 13:27:15:16).

At 32 mins Reduce sequence of maniacs taunting woman by removing suggestion of rape, cutting away after frightened woman says "Oh, no..." (TC 13:41:53:00) and resuming on group shot (TC 13:42:20:00) just before man runs across to grab her.

At 32½ mins Then reduce assault on woman and maniacal laughter by cutting from face of husband being held down on floor (TC 13:42:30:12) to shot of struggle in middle of room (TC 13:42:53:01) shortly before woman is rescued.

At 33½ mins After husband is punched at door, remove second assault on him by cutting from man crouching in corner before he says "hit him" (TC 13:43:23:18) to shot of man hitting floor with head at bottom of screen (TC 13:43:30:00).

At 33½ mins Immediately after close-up of worried wife, remove shot of man picking up axe (TC 13:43:33:13) resuming on man in corner after axe is pushed across room (TC 13:43:39:05).

At 36½ mins After woman escapes from house, reduce chase and taunting with axe and gun by removing whole sequence round van, cutting from end of tilted shot of man chasing her round house and past camera (TC 13:46:19:23) to shot of her entering room (TC 13:47:11:03).

At 37½ mins Reduce final chase and exhilaration of killers by cutting away after men chase woman up staircase past camera (TC 13:47:46:06), resuming on mid shot of man sitting against wall taking off glasses (TC 13:47:56:15), then cutting (TC 13:48:02:09) to long shot of axeman rushing forward for kill (TC 13:48:06:16).

At 47½ mins After blonde woman in close-up says, "You're awfully brave with a gun in your hand," remove threat to her with axe (TC 13:57:10:21), together with threat to others by hysterical axeman and sight of man taunted with gun in neck, face and eye, resuming on man with gun saying "OK, coffee..." (TC 13:57:34:01).

Resubmit.

Further cuts may be required.

LEFT: BBFC tariff of fees for video at the implementation of the VRA 1984.
RIGHT: A typical BBFC cuts sheet.

(Whitehouse doesn't volunteer who she considers better suited to the job, but one suspect she'd be happiest doing it herself.)

However stringent the Video Recordings Act was likely to be, it evidently wasn't stringent enough for Whitehouse. "Whatever goes on to videotape," was her portentous message, "children will inevitably see it. There's no way you can be sure of protecting them."

> The degree of corruption and fear and terror in those films wouldn't be allowed by any society in its right mind. It would ensure that the legislation was such that the children were protected. If that meant that adults who have a weakness for corrupting and violent material of that kind couldn't see it, so be it.

The Act took effect on September 1, 1985, after which date all new video releases required a BBFC certificate and appropriate labelling prior to release. Of the video titles already in circulation, the Board was given until September 1988 — an additional three years — to clear the backlog. (This it was required to do incrementally: an English language title theatrically distributed in 1980 would need to be certified by March 1987; an English language title theatrically distributed between 1975 and 1979 would need to be certified by September 1987; all foreign language material would be due for classification by September 1988, and so on.) Three years to examine, impose cuts, classify or reject some 10,000 videocassettes already on the market. As we shall see later, many films were never submitted — for economic reasons, companies going bust, and so forth — so the actual number of videocassettes examined by the BBFC would have been considerably lower. Nevertheless, the added responsibility saw the BBFC grow from "a small, family-sized operation with a staff of twelve" in 1982, to an organisation comprised of fifty in 1985.[45] As is the case now, every video passing through their doors at Soho Square in London would have been seen by a minimum of two examiners. Most classifications were straightforward and could have been based on this initial observation, in which case the Board aimed to release their decision seventy-two hours after viewing. If a film proved to be 'troublesome' however, classification would likely have been delayed indefinitely, with the original examiners referring the work to a second team or even to senior staff. Should the Board feel the need for changes or cuts, these requirements were put to the film company in writing.

The credo of the Board is that the integrity of a work should be preserved whenever possible, whilst balancing the requirements of the law and the public interest. Imagery — and in some instances 'taste'[46] — can often throw this balance. One area singled out as unacceptable by the BBFC in their *Annual Report 1985*, was that of genuine, unsimulated cruelty to animals, said to be "a particular problem in foreign language works which have been produced in countries where animal welfare is not generally accorded the same importance as in the English-speaking world." The major concern however, remained the matter of rape and sexual violence, regarded in the Report as a worrying trend in cinema since the seventies.[47] "The Board is even stricter with such depictions on video than on film, since the fact that a scene might be searched out and repeated endlessly out of context in the privacy of one's own home could condition some viewers to find the behaviour sexually exciting, not just on film, but in real life." By way of example:

> For the cinema, the sight of a man scarring the breasts of a prostitute with electric curling tongs had been excised; on video the whole idea was cut. Threats and injury to breasts with knives, razors and lighted cigarettes were cut from video works classified '18', as was the sexual taunting of a woman bound and gagged.

Graham Bright had assured the press that the objective of his Bill was to stamp out the video nasties "straight away." But in order to determine what would be suitable for viewing in the home and by whom, all material would need to be evaluated. This meant not only sadistic and violent films, but everything else — from children's cartoons to television sitcoms — would require an examination by the BBFC. In the case of feature films already passed by the Board for viewing in a cinema, further examination was necessary.

These were factors that Bright and his stalwarts evidently hadn't anticipated (and one which, according to the BVA, Bright reputedly thought absurd). The MP had optimistically told *The Guardian* that on top of the "thirty nasties that will not get a classification", there were only some 200 to 300 films which needed to be looked at.

With the introduction of the Video Recordings Act, a register of all films released theatrically in Britain[48] — some 58,000 titles — was made available by the Home Office. What benefits were to be had in owning such a list isn't clear (though at a cost of £20, the list was obviously beneficial to someone): many titles on video had never seen a theatrical release and so wouldn't be featured, while those titles that did feature wouldn't necessarily receive on video the certificate they had carried theatrically.

Far more relevant was *A Trade Guide to the Video Recordings Act*, a booklet which the BVA compiled to assist those within the industry in carrying out the requirements of the Act. Providing explanatory notes and using language that was less formal than that of the Act itself, the booklet struggled to offer some relief in the face of such a sudden and serious legislative slab. Fundamental aspects of the Act, even in translation, must have seemed pretty unfathomable.[49]

As the BBFC undertook the task of examining and classifying thousands of videocassettes, film distributors would supply retailers with an update on those films which had been granted a certificate. It was then the duty of the retailer to check their stock and keep it in line with the classification process, either by attaching the appropriate BBFC certificate label to videotapes, or removing material from the shelves altogether. "Each day we would receive lists from various companies indicating the certification category granted, and would have to put the correct label on the tape and display box," recalls Chris Glazebrook. "Where a cut had been requested, the original tape had to be withdrawn and replaced with the new certified version."

Not all videos required a certificate from the BBFC. Exempt works included those which, if taken as a whole, were designated to inform, educate or instruct, or were concerned with sport, religion or music.[50] However, in a sub-clause which seemed primarily directed at *Faces of Death* — a documentary which was arguably informative, educational and instructive — a work fitting the above criteria could not be deemed exempt if, to any significant extent, it depicted: (a) human sexual activity or acts of force or restraint associated with such activity; (b) mutilation or torture of, or other acts of gross violence towards, humans or animals; (c) human genital organs or human urinary or excretory functions.[51]

Everything else *did* require a BBFC certificate.

In 1985 it cost companies £4.60 a minute to have the BBFC view previously uncertified product, putting the examination of a video of 1hr 30mins duration at £414 (excluding VAT) — payable in advance. If the Board demanded cuts, the film would need to be resubmitted at a further cost. Lower rates were applicable to films which had been examined previously for a cinema release.[52]

Few small companies could afford the cost of submitting their entire back catalogue for classification, much less when there was uncertainty as to whether the films would come out unscathed — or indeed, come out at all. Many distributors opted instead for liquidation, and as a consequence retailers were left with a surfeit of stock that wasn't about to see a certificate. Once the examination schedule allotted the BBFC had been met, any unclassified videocassette on display would result in prosecution. These tapes, recalls Chris Glazebrook, were supposed to have been destroyed by retailers "breaking the case and pulling the tape from the spool." But with some dealers fearing they might end up losing eighty per cent of their stock this way, an alternative was eagerly sought. The guidebook issued by the BVA stated that prosecutions couldn't be brought under the Video Recordings Act for material currently pending classification. This was an invitation for dealers to try and recoup some cash while they still had the chance. Rather than destroying tapes, they opted instead to sell them off to the public.

The Video Recordings Act effectively cleaned all contentious video titles from the high street, and a lot more besides. The transitional period granted by central government didn't stop some local authorities from continuing to carry out raids. Still seizing videocassettes that had yet to be awarded a certificate was Chief Constable James Anderton, whose campaign in Greater Manchester is described by Steve Ellison as "a witch hunt."[53]

> He would raid all the shops and take out all videos that he felt were obscene. This was after the Video Recordings Act had been put into place and there was a changeover period. Anderton and his men just went all over Manchester looking through video stores, and seize everything that didn't have a certificate. They were seizing children's cartoons, they were seizing everything. And they were making a lot of money for whoever gets the money from the fines that people pay — the courts were full of people having to plead guilty to carrying obscene material.
>
> The way the whole thing was handled was very unfair and it really caused a lot of heartache and caused a lot of people to go out of business. You had a situation where a shop in Walkden, or someplace, would be raided and virtually everything taken — yet a shop fifteen yards down the road, carrying the same stuff, wouldn't be touched because it happened to be outside the Manchester jurisdiction. This was happening all over the place in Greater Manchester. It was alright if you were in Wigan; it was alright if you were somewhere else. But anywhere that Anderton had control... He took issue with films that you might consider to be bad taste.

The major film distributors came through the Video Recordings Act with minimal damage. If anything, they were better off. The way was clear for them to affect the monopoly they had envisaged a couple of years earlier, when the majors created their own distribution networks and cut out the independent wholesalers. (See chapter one.) For a government in favour of an open market, the Video Recordings Act proved rather cataclysmic for small business.

There were other side-effects of the new Bill, notably a period of excessive self-censorship conducted by film companies, and the emergence of a video black market. The underground trade that is created in the wake of any censorial policy was conveniently overlooked in the eagerness to establish the Video Recordings Act.[54] Once uncertified videos were outlawed, they quickly became sought after items by an increasing number of collectors. Video had brought to Britain an exciting new entertainment medium which allowed people to access a wide range of films hitherto denied them. In creating a ban, a whole sub-culture developed for whom the DPP video nasties blacklist became a checklist.

Video controversy was far from over. Titles like *Faces of Death*, *I Spit on Your Grave* and *SS Experiment Camp* may have been removed from the visible landscape, but the mark they left was an indelible one. In the next two chapters we examine the video films that made up the DPP 'banned' list, and some of the many other titles which were lost to the chaos of video legislation.

X–BOMBER
BATTLE OF THE GALAXY
★ A new world of excitement and enthusiasm!
★ A grand scale sci-fi action film!
★ New dimension special effects!

A male
sex fantasy
the point
of no return.
VIOLENT AND UNNERVING!
DEATH GAME
...it really happened!
"DEATH GAME," A FILM BY PETER TRAYNOR
STARRING SONDRA LOCKE, SEYMOUR CASSEL AND COLLEEN CAMP.
Written by ANTHONY OVERMAN and MICHAEL RONALD ROSS.
Music by JIMMIE HASKELL.
Produced by LARRY SPIEGEL and PETER TRAYNOR
Directed by PETER TRAYNOR.

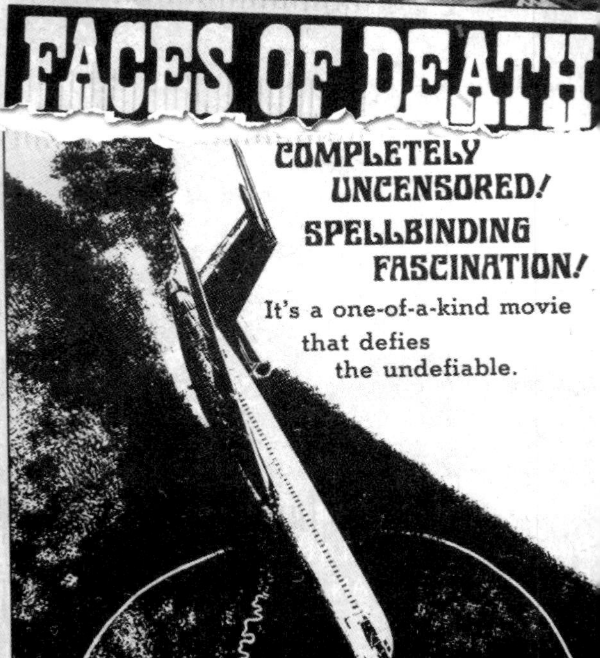
FACES OF DEATH
COMPLETELY
UNCENSORED!
SPELLBINDING
FASCINATION!
It's a one-of-a-kind movie
that defies
the undefiable.

'Draining the blood of the innocent!'[1]

SIEGE

The introduction of video into the domestic market was a blessing to the film aficionado. For the first time a huge variety of full-length feature films could be watched in the home. But the thing that was truly unique about the dawning of the video age in Britain was that it made available films that were not normally accessible to the general public. The nannying system of censorship and the selection criteria of cinema chains were temporarily breached and the avid film viewer had a short-lived moment of freedom. Horror movie fans were those best served, as titles never before seen in the UK became available for rent from a seemingly endless and unlikely range of outlets — from corner shops through to Laundromats. The video distribution system was beneficial to smaller scale productions as shelf space wasn't given over exclusively to Hollywood blockbusters. Indeed, quite the reverse was true. Low-budget films such as William A Levey's *Blackenstein*, Ed Adlum's *Invasion of the Blood Farmers*, Eddie Romero's *Beast of Blood*, Inoshiro Honda's *Matango: Fungus of Terror*; Don Dohler's *Night Beast*, Larry Buchanan's *Mistress of the Apes*, and Michael Findlay's *Shriek of the Mutilated*, began to spring up like uncontrollable weeds. To some people they were an ugly, misunderstood irritant, but to many others they were a much appreciated delight.

> Video was a godsend to the producer of crap films that were never likely to get anywhere near the cinema.
>
> —*Steve Ellison*

The packaging for such videos became increasingly lurid as independent companies struggled to get their product noticed on the shelves. Blood-dripping monsters, flesh-chewing cannibals, Nazi torturers, knife wielding maniacs and gore-choked power-tools were common sights. "The covers of the nasties were terribly important to their image," James Ferman

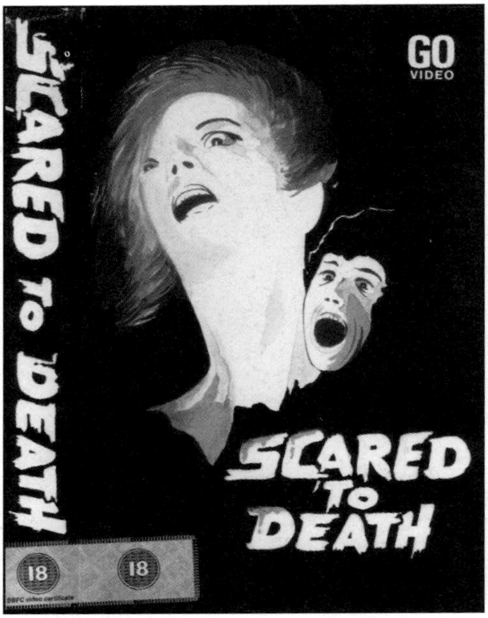

Two examples of child-like, 'coloured-in' video sleeves.

would later deliberate[2]. The covers for Ruggero Deodato's *Cannibal Holocaust*, Abel Ferrara's *The Driller Killer*, and Pete Walker's *Frightmare*, for instance, didn't leave much to the imagination. Yet others would lose the plot entirely and try to sell a genuinely superior horror film in utterly asinine packaging. A fine example of a terribly conceived sleeve which had no discernible connection to the film contained within, was LVC Video's[3] release of *Don't Open the Window*, the American R-rated version of Jorge Grau's excellent *Living Dead at the Manchester Morgue*. Its illustration of a woman closing a window appears to have been painted by a child. Similarly, Christy Cabanne's creaky 1947 shocker *Scared To Death*, starring Bela Lugosi, featured hurried 'coloured-in' artwork that was unlikely to draw the interest of any would-be video-viewer.[4] Medusa's release of Umberto Lenzi's *The Iron Master*, on the other hand, had spectacular Frank Frazetta-like artwork, but this merely disguised a cheap *Quest for Fire* rip-off starring the redoubtable George Eastman.

Many of the earliest videos were packaged in simple boxes made from thin card[5]. Some companies used a standard slipcase for all genre releases, with only a small label stuck to the box and cassette to identify the film. Several titles from Intervision came in this format, including *Onibaba*, *Satan's Slave*, and *Dead of Night*.

Companies were quickly established to take advantage of this new medium, and they capitalised on video's lack of restrictions. Vipco released Lucio Fulci's *Zombie Flesh-Eaters* in the British cinema X certified version and also in a specially-labelled "strong, uncut version" giving potential consumers a choice between the hard or soft. For most people this was the first time a strong horror film had been seen in all its uncensored glory, and the difference in the two versions is quite startling. Throats are torn out and the blood flows in unstoppable torrents, eyeballs are punctured on wooden splinters and intestines are pulled out to be chewed upon.

It wasn't just horror films that were being seen in a new light. TCX was a label specialising in edited hardcore movies. Practically everything but penetration and erections were shown in films such as Alex de Renzy's *Baby Face*, Jim and Artie Mitchell's *Behind the Green Door*, and FX Pope's bizarre *Nightdreams*.

Palace Video could be relied upon for obscure gems. Not only did they release Sam Raimi's *The Evil Dead*, one of the most notorious and popular horrors on video, but they also brought out John Waters' early cult atrocity *Pink Flamingos*. This bad taste shocker showed larger-than-life transvestite Divine consuming dog excrement *for real*, a brief glimpse of fellatio *for real*, and a man showing off his dilating anus — *for real*![6] The sleeve suggested "parental guidance."

Intervision supplied the early Cronenberg movies, *Rabid*, *Shivers* and *The Brood* in addition to strange rarities like Norman Foster's *The Deathhead Virgin*,[7] Jerry Jameson's *The Bat People*, Sean MacGregor's *Devil Times Five*, Ray Danton's *Crypt of the Living Dead*, Al Adamson's *Death Dimension*, and Ray Austin's *House of the Living Dead*. Packaged in flimsy card slipcases these may not have been the connoisseur's choice, but the fact that they were available at all was what mattered.

Once the campaign against the nasties got underway however, any choice the British public had in the matter dissipated. As detailed in UNEASE, scare stories were generated that claimed videos were a threat to the moral stature of the country and a particular menace to children. The Video Recordings Act 1984 was ushered in — a law to control and censor video output, preventing any film from being released on video without a certificate. The cost of certification was prohibitively expensive and caused many of the independent distribution companies to collapse. In addition, few companies that remained solvent were prepared to sink money into the low-budget end of the film market. It was risky to spend close on £1,000 (at today's rates) to release, say, a complete obscurity like the *Death Bed: The Bed That Eats* — regardless of whether it would pass without need for cuts.[8]

Some films would undoubtedly have required cuts, however, and this raised another problem for distributors of low-budget titles. The marketability of Herschell Gordon Lewis' cult classic *Blood Feast*, for example, was dependent entirely on its wild bloodletting. Gore was its *raison d'être*. To obtain a certificate *Blood Feast* would most certainly need to be censored, effectively robbing the film of its purpose as well as its audience.

During the height of the video nasties scare and the phasing in of the certification process, some companies — concerned about the possibility of prosecution — cut scenes from their own releases in a bid to 'play it safe.' (This showed a complete disregard towards customers as, in effect, they were supplying damaged goods.) The original release of Cronenberg's *Videodrome* on the CIC label provides one example of this over-cautiousness. To determine whether their films could be construed as obscene by law, larger distribution companies would employ the services of Geoffrey Robertson, a QC well versed in media law who

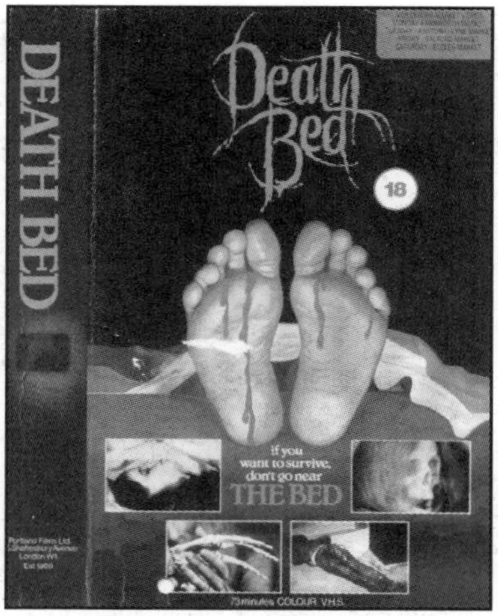

TOP: ***Death Bed: The Bed That Eats*** **– the kind of cinematic oddity that became commercially redundant once distributors had classification fees to consider.**

ABOVE: The generic slipcase of early Intervision horror releases. Only the labels differed. (Norman J Warren, director of *Satan's Slave*, was amazed to learn that Intervision's print contained "revolting" gore footage that he believed he himself had excised prior to the film's release.)

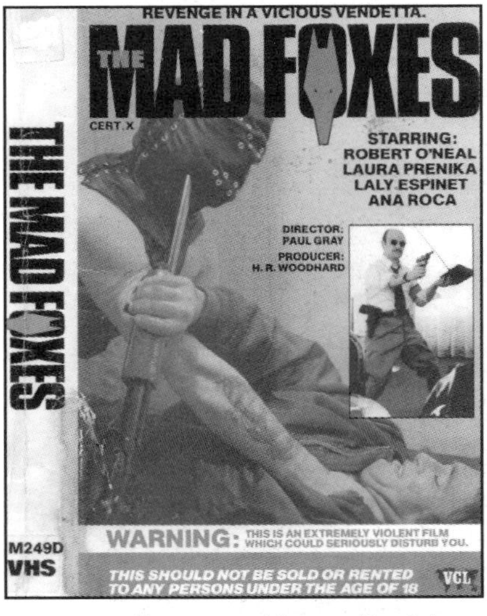

TOP: *Siege* was one of the many films that appeared on video in different versions – all with the same packaging.

ABOVE: Like many video releases, *The Mad Foxes* seemed a prime candidate for the DPP list (more so than some of the movies that did actually make it) but was completely overlooked.

has appeared as counsel in many landmark court cases (see CLAMPDOWN). It was on his advice that CIC removed scenes from *Videodrome*. The film was submitted to the BBFC in 1987 *pre-cut* by several minutes with a running time of 80m 41s. In 1990, once the video nasty hullabaloo had died down, it was re-submitted with a running time of 83m 41s and passed without cuts.[9]

When Polygram Video removed scenes from *Christiane F.* which Robertson had advised could be problematic, James Ferman saw that the film company put them back in again. Robertson also advised Electric Video with regard to cutting *Caligula*. Amongst the scenes removed by the film company were those displaying phallic — or "indecent" — bottles, a particularly asinine decision and one which was erroneously attributed to the BBFC. As Ferman would lament many years later, the Board has "been blamed for that cut ever since!"[10]

Robertson was best trying to serve his employers' interests during a highly volatile and unusual time. He may well have over-reacted in some instances, but the fact remained that film companies and distributors *were* being prosecuted and their offices raided on account of the content of their films.

Apex Video took self-censorship to an extreme. Their release of Andrea Bianchi's eerie zombie epic *Nights of Terror* was cut by one third of its running time — reducing the film from ninety-two minutes to an astonishingly limp and violence free fifty-nine minutes *before* submitting it for classification. The film had obviously been selected for distribution before the Video Recordings Act became law. Evidently having no desire to submit the video more than once to the BBFC, Apex removed all of the film's vaguely contentious moments themselves. This way no further cuts would be required and a certificate guaranteed on first submission. It is also possible that Apex thought submitting a full version of *Nights of Terror* might result in outright rejection, giving them no opportunity to make any cuts. Whatever the reason, it seems that the video sleeve had already been printed as it displayed images Apex had actually cut from the film — much to the chagrin of those who rented the thing.

Another adverse side-effect of the VRA panic was that alternate versions of the same film would appear on the market, with identical packaging. One such release was Paul Donovan and Maura O'Connell's *Siege*, a film involving urban warfare and home-made weapons. A sequence showing rednecks executing men in a gay bar at the start of the film was truncated in some prints, while other tapes in circulation were found to be intact. Fate decreed which version actually ended up in the hands of the consumer. It isn't known who made the decision to cut *Siege*, or whether the release of an unabridged version was an oversight. Likewise VTC's release of *Zombie Holocaust* and Interlight's *City of the Living Dead* were available in minutely different versions. Videocassettes of the former sometimes showed the severing of a hand from a corpse in the pre-credit sequence, while copies of the latter sometimes showed a split-second head-drilling sequence unavailable in other identically packaged prints. Other films in the marketplace were also available in alternate versions. Sometimes for no discernible reason (i.e. *Madhouse*) and sometimes the result of a mistake (i.e. *The Burning*). (See next chapter.)

During the formative days of the video nasties campaign, attention was focused on the more extreme examples of uncertified films. *Snuff*, *The Last House on the Left*, *The Driller Killer*, *SS Experiment Camp*, and *I Spit On Your Grave* were amongst the first casualties. Their explicit viciousness gave them little chance of support or any room for appeal. Cinematic mutilation, multiple rape, and dismemberment were considered indefensible, even if the film contained an anti-violence moral message. The titles were condemned by the media and summarily executed without trial. As discussed in the previous chapter, the Director of Public Prosecutions was forced to compile a list of video releases that had been put forward — mainly by pressure groups — as possibly contravening the Obscene Publications Act 1959. The list was astonishingly inconsistent, containing innocuous BBFC certified and censored films on the one hand (such as Tobe Hooper's *The Funhouse* and Lucio Fulci's *The Beyond*), while on the other it omitted titles that positively revelled in contentious imagery (such as Ferdinando Baldi's *Terror Express!*, which was effectively a remake of *Late Night Trains* — a film that *did* feature on the DPP list).

As specific films were vilified in the press and subsequently removed from the shelves of video retailers, they became instant collectors items. The black market which ensued is discussed later in the book. The number of titles reported as having made the DPP list peaked at seventy-five before, gradually dwindling down to thirty-nine. With the exception of *The Big Red One* — a critically acclaimed war movie by Samuel Fuller, which, despite an appearance on early lists, was never seriously considered a nasty (or particularly collectible) — all films are examined and reviewed in detail in the chapter that follows.

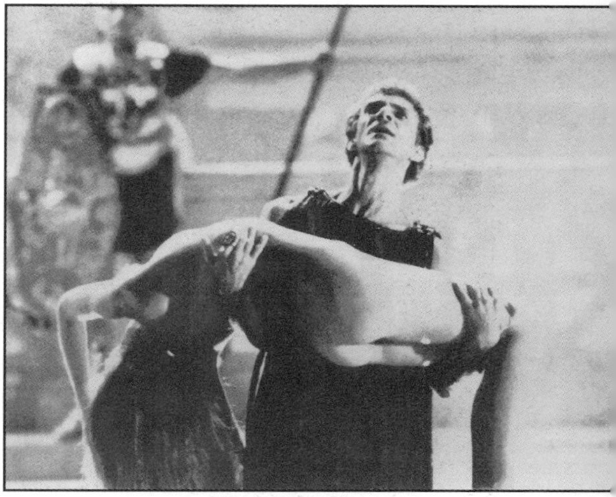

TOP TO BOTTOM: *Caligula* (phallic bottles cut), *Videodrome* (butchered at the behest of CIC) and *Nights of Terror* (censorship in the extreme).

NAME NANCY DANCER
MEASUREMENTS 38/24/36
BORN GARY, IND 12/21/58
DIED N.O., LA. 2/12/78
...and that was only the Beginning
Mardi Gras
MASSACRE
Starring CURT DAWSON & GWEN ARMENT
Also Starring BILL METZO with
LAURA MISCH • CATHRYN LACEY • NANCY DANCER • BUTCH BENIT • WAYNE MACK and RONALD TA
Assistant Producer JOHN STIMAC, Jr • Cinematography by JACK Mc GOWAN • Produced and Directed by J.
IN COLOR
WARNING • DUE TO SHOCKING SCENES OF EXTREME VIOLENCE
• WE RECOMMEND NO ONE UNDER 17 BE ADMITTED.

'Scenes of extreme and explicit violence'

VIDEO NASTIES

ABSURD

SYNOPSIS: Two men are running. In an attempt to escape the other, one of the men accidentally gouges himself while scaling a spiked gate. He gets to make it as far as the door of a nearby house before his intestines spill out through his fingers. "He isn't going to make it," a surgeon woefully confers during emergency treatment on the man. All signs of life drop from the monitors. Then they return.

"It's absurd... completely absurd," puzzles the surgeon. "Recuperative powers like that don't exist."

Sergeant Engleman finds evidence to suggest that the wounded man is from Greece, just like another stranger caught wandering the corridors of the hospital.

The wounded man becomes agitated, attacking a nurse and driving a surgical drill into her skull.

The second man confides to Engleman that he is a priest in pursuit of the wounded one. And not just any priest: "There exists a reality that we do not see," he states. "I serve God with bio-chemistry, more than with rites."

The wounded man's name is Nikos Thanopolous and, as a result of experimental work the priest was conducting at an institute in Greece, Nikos became immortal and escaped. He can regenerate dead cells but, unfortunately, "He does not regenerate cells perfectly... he is insane."

Now he's on the loose again.

One of the doctors, looking at a set of X-rays, notes that Nikos' brain has got bigger.

"It is his brain that is his weak point," says the priest.

Nikos stumbles upon an abattoir. With a machete he attacks a man who is cleaning up. The cleaner tries to stop him with a gun but the bullets have no effect. Nikos grabs the man and sends him head-first into a band saw. The blade penetrates his bald dome.

Later, while setting upon a broken down motorcyclist, Nikos is struck by a hit-and-run driver. Mr Bennett, the driver of the car (and coincidentally owner of the house on whose doorstep Nikos earlier spilled his intestines), has a dinner date with his wife and some friends that evening. The babysitter booked to look after their suitably brattish son Willie and bed-ridden daughter Katya is late. Peggy, the home help, reluctantly agrees to stick around until she arrives.

Peggy tells Willie that if he doesn't go to bed, the "Bogeyman" will get him.

Nikos turns up at the house, deftly sinking a pickaxe into Peggy's head.

When Emily, the babysitter, does show, Peggy is nowhere around.

Emily receives a phone call from a doctor friend at the hospital who fills her in on the recent spate of murders and Nikos. The only way to kill the monster is by destroying his "cerebral mass," he tells her in passing.

Katya, in traction because of a deviation in her spine, draws geometric patterns all day long. Emily tries to comfort the girl by telling her that she is still young and will get better.

Willie says there's a bogeyman in the kitchen. But, as he's cried wolf once too often, no one believes him.

Meanwhile, at the house down the street, Mrs Bennett confronts her husband with regard to his strange, reserved behaviour.

"What's the matter with you, Ian?"

"Nothing," he replies, "other than running over a man today and not stopping to help him."

"Ian!"

Emily discovers Peggy's body and notices the telephone lines have been cut. Barricading herself in the bedroom with Katya, she sends Willie out to alert his parents. Frightened however, he doubles back, forcing Emily to come out of hiding. She is captured, dragged by Nikos into the kitchen and has her head stuffed into a lighted oven. Her face starts to blister and turn purple as she is cooked alive.

Katya makes a concerted effort to struggle free of her sick bed. Hearing the commotion, Nikos breaks his way into the room and she drives her drawing compass into his eyes, blinding him. He searches the room by touch, listening for the girl. Camouflaged by loud church music from her music centre, barely able to stand, Katya makes a shaky retreat from the room.

The priest arrives at the house just in time to free Katya from the monster's clutches, before himself falling victim. Katya takes this opportunity to bring an axe down repeatedly on the monster's neck.

"Look Willie," Katya says, holding Nikos' severed head aloft, "you don't need to be afraid anymore!"

ABSURD

AKA: Rosso sangue (original title); Horrible; The Monster Hunter
ITALY 1981
CAST: George Eastman, Annie Belle, Charles Borromel, Katya Berger, Kasimir Berger
STORY: John Cart [Aristide Massaccesi]
PRODUCER: [not credited]
DIRECTOR: PETER NEWTON [Aristide Massaccesi]

CRITIQUE: Peter Newton is another pseudonym for Italian director Aristide Massaccesi, better known as Joe D'Amato.[1] Not only is this one of his more entertaining films, in many ways it epitomises the romance of the 'nasties' with its excessive blood-letting, dodgy prosthetics, arcane dialogue, clumsy dubbing, competent direction, and simplistic, free-rolling plot.

Together with George Eastman (real name: Luigi Montefiore, the actor who plays the monster), Massaccesi conceived *Absurd* as a sequel to their own successful ***Anthropophagous the Beast***. However, all that really links the two films together is that Eastman stars in each as a homicidal brute who manages to lose his intestines at the end of one film, and lose them again at the start of the other.[2] A more subtle connection is that Nikos is said to originate from Greece, and a Greek island was the setting for ***Anthropophagous***.

Effectively, *Absurd* stands as a 'non-sequel.' In the book *Spaghetti Nightmares*, Eastman relates how he got a part in *Absurd* because of certain scripting problems. Unable to offer a completed script due to other work, Eastman originally gave Massaccesi an outline for the film. He later returned to the project when the script — completed in his absence — proved to be poor. "Since I needed the money," claims Eastman, "I offered to revise the script in return for a part in the film."

Original press announcements for the film state it was to have starred *Black Emanuelle* actress Laura Gemser. This fact, coupled with Eastman 'buying his way into the title role,' suggest that *Absurd* may have been planned as an altogether different film — possibly one in keeping with a straight thematic follow-up to *Anthropophagous*.

One thing's for sure however — there was never any doubt that the film should be completely outrageous and over-the-top.

"We really wanted people to be shocked," Eastman said of both *Absurd* and ***Anthropophagous*** in an interview with *The DarkSide*.[3] "When we wrote them we kept making them more and more shocking."

There is little point trying to rationalise the story. Tim Ferrante, in his review for *Filmfax*,[4] calls *Absurd* "HALLOWEEN ALL'ITALIANA!" and accuses it of being little more than a rip-off of John Carpenter's *Halloween*. However, one curious aspect of *Absurd* is that a priest (played by Edmund Purdom, the narrator of many a mondo film) should be responsible for the maniac that is Nikos. Why make him a priest? With Massaccesi's track record, and Eastman's insinuation that they were only out to shock with the film, there is probably no intended agenda behind it. But nevertheless it does throw an interesting slant on the picture, one that could be interpreted as being critical of the church. Despite the scientific anomaly which he himself has created, the priest still regards Nikos as "evil" and claims him to be possessed by the devil. It's an oxymoron, just like the insistence of the gutter press that so-called video nasties — feature films; spools of magnetic tape encased in plastic — are "evil."

Absurd does occasionally touch on the brilliant, notably in the sequence where Nikos gets his eyes gouged out. (An equally memorable inversion of this scene occurs earlier when Nikos' eyes pop open whilst he is undergoing major

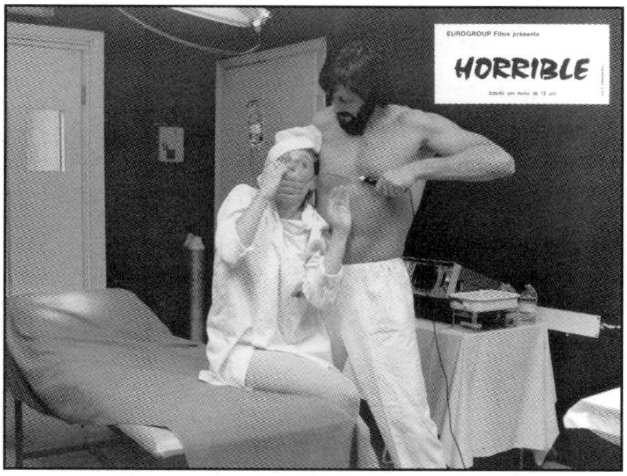

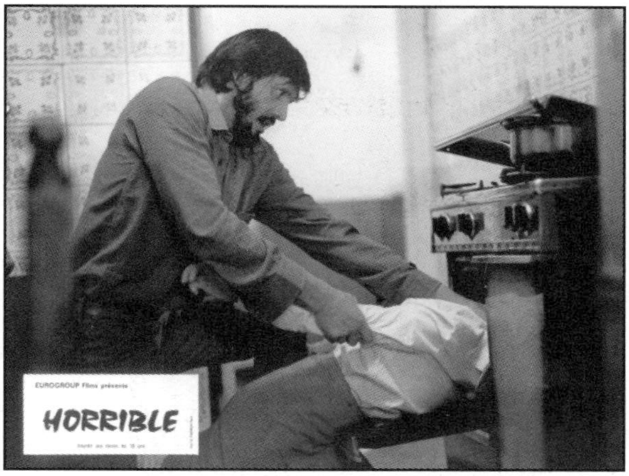

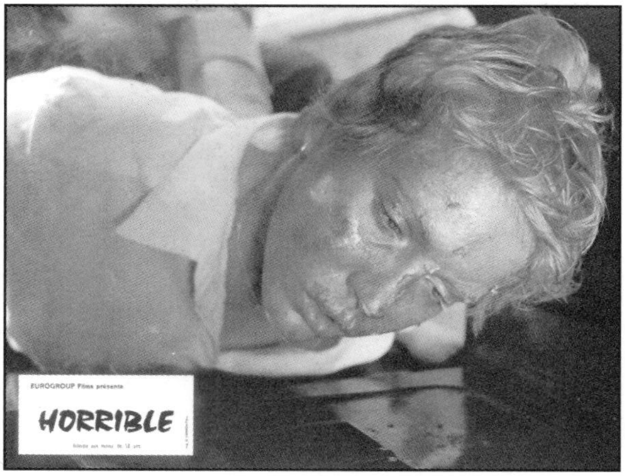

THIS PAGE: *Absurd*, known in France as *Horrible*.

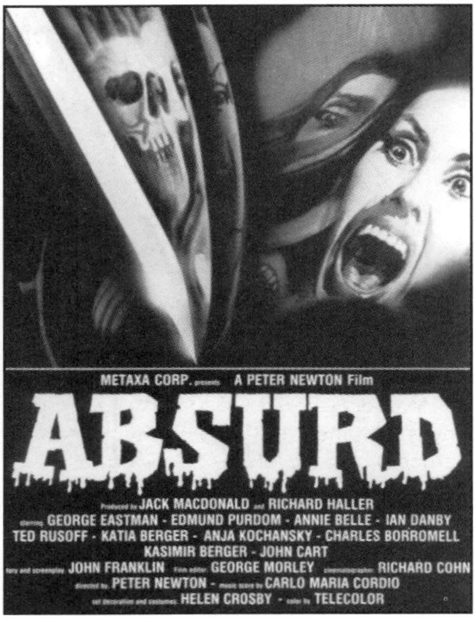

surgery.) Here the film loses its humble exploitation trappings and seems to be playing less *Halloween* and more a twisted homage to Polanski by way of Pasolini — more specifically, Polanski's *Repulsion* and the doomed hero of Pasolini's Sophoclean drama, *Oedipus Rex*. It also owes a tip of the hat to Walter Grauman's *Lady in a Cage*, which in its closing moments has homicidal young thug James Caan (in his first starring role) searching blindly for crippled Olivia de Havilland after she has stuck metal strips into his eyes.

In *Absurd*, having escaped the flailing clutches of the sightless monster in her bedroom, Katya hobbles as best she can down the corridors of the house, supporting herself on its walls. At one point she falls to her knees in the darkened foreground as the monster suddenly appears in the brightly-lit background, silhouetted in the centre of the frame. He too supports himself on the walls of the corridor as he searches blindly for the girl. It's a tense, magnificently crafted scene that compromises the director's reputation for being "one of the top most boring Italian directors,"[5] and deflates somewhat his own assertion that "I'm a businessman and not an artist."[6]

Although it could never top the abortion and auto-cannibalism scenes of ***Anthropophagous*** for sheer tastelessness, *Absurd* is eminently better paced, with nary one horrific set-piece going by before the next starts to unfold. None of the prosthetic effects are particularly convincing (flesh and bone offer no resistance to the assortment of objects that sink into them), but they're all executed with bloodthirsty relish and a liberal spattering of gore.

Given the sadistic bent with which many of the gore scenes are executed, it's unlikely that the film would ever be submitted to the BBFC for classification in an uncut state. Indeed, the murder of Emily the babysitter would probably be justification enough for the Board to reject this film outright. Even though Nikos kills whoever he can lay his hands on, whatever sex they might be, there is an indisputable misogynistic relish to his cooking of Emily's head in the oven. Filmed from within the oven itself, as Emily squirms and bakes in agonising close-up, this particular torment lasts for over a minute[7] but doesn't even end there — she gets stabbed in the neck with a pair of scissors when she pulls herself from death's door to try and stop Nikos capturing Willie.

(Talking of death's door: A lot of emphasis is placed on the door of the Bennetts' house. It seems that whenever it opens, something horrible is revealed behind it. First it opens to show Nikos spilling his guts, then Peggy being murdered, and finally Katya displaying a severed head.)

There is a concerted effort to displace the setting of *Absurd* from Italy to the USA, presumably because the film would be met with greater favour in its home territory if it looked like an American product. As a result, almost every street shot has a fake fire hydrant in view, and the Bennetts get together with their friends to watch (lengthy time-filling bouts of) American football on television. But they snack on pasta, which is a bit of a give-away.

Medusa released two versions of *Absurd*: one cut, the other uncut, both in identical sleeves. The only way to tell the two apart was via the spine of the video itself. If it had a sticker with the film's title, it was uncut; if it had a holographic Medusa seal, then it was the cut version. Some unscrupulous dealers in nasties are known to have duplicated uncut copies of the film over cut versions in order to tout them as more desirable full-uncut originals. Second or even third generation quality playback ought to have alerted dubious viewers to these pirated tapes — by which time, of course, it was invariably too late.

Massaccesi freely admits that he will turn his hand to any kind of movie, and his filmography is testament to that fact, touching on all genres from thrillers through action adventure to hardcore pornography. With hardcore, there is no risk of not making money. Profit is guaranteed, claims the director. But softcore is Massaccesi's forte (he directed the dire *Ladies' Doctor* in 1977, a sex-comedy about a gynaecologist). *Absurd* marked the end of his brief foray into horror cinema, and Massaccesi subsequently joined the post-apocalypse sci-fi bandwagon before going back to porn and his most successful movie to date, *11 Days, 11 Nights*.

He took pride in the fact that some of his films are banned in Britain. "Somebody saw my movies and it had this effect," he told *Flesh & Blood*.[8]

ANTHROPOPHAGOUS THE BEAST

SYNOPSIS: A couple and their dog go down to the deserted beach of a small Greek island. The man sunbathes with his out-sized radio headphones while the girl swims toward a small abandoned boat. Something is watching her from below the surface. As she reaches the boat she is grabbed and dragged beneath the water where she disappears in a cloud of blood and fleshy lumps. The dog senses danger and runs away but the man is unaware of anything other than the music. Whatever attacked the girl is now on the beach advancing on the man. It raises a meat-cleaver and brings it down, splitting his head open.

On the Greek mainland, tourists Carol, Maggie, Danny, Alec and Ernie befriend a lone traveller named Julie. Julie asks if she may join them on their boat for a ride to an island she is planning to visit. The group agree and they all set sail for the island. During the voyage Carol reads tarot cards for the heavily pregnant Maggie and is disturbed by the results. "If you ask the cards about the future and don't get any answer," she explains, "that means there is no future for the person who's asking them." Once on the island they set out to explore the small town and walk Julie to the house where she is to stay. Maggie however, sprains her ankle and decides to stay on board with Starfish, the deck hand.

The whole town seems deserted. Julie and Alec go to the store

ANTHROPOPHAGOUS THE BEAST
AKA: Anthropophagous; Antropofago; The Grim Reaper; Gomia, Terror en el Mar Egeo; Man Beast; Man-Eater; The Savage Island
ITALY 1980
CAST: Tisa Farrow, Saverio Vallone, George Eastman, Margaret Donnelly, Vanessa Steiger, Mark Bodin, Bob Larsen, Simone Baker, Serena Grandi, Rubina Rey
STORY: Luigi Montefiori & Aristide Massaccesi
PRODUCER: Oscar Santaniello
DIRECTOR: JOE D'AMATO [Aristide Massaccesi]

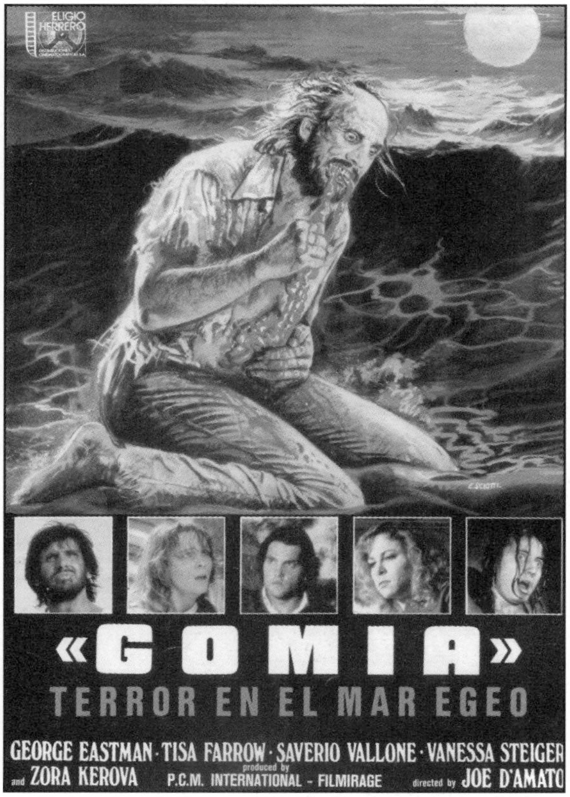

ELIGIO HERRERO
«GOMIA»
TERROR EN EL MAR EGEO
GEORGE EASTMAN · TISA FARROW · SAVERIO VALLONE · VANESSA STEIGER
and ZORA KEROVA produced by P.C.M. INTERNATIONAL - FILMIRAGE directed by JOE D'AMATO

THIS PAGE: A cinematic first: George Eastman attempts to eat his own entrails in *Anthropophagous the Beast*.

NEXT PAGE: Spot the rabbit. The Beast feeds as Ernie looks on.

and find the telegraph machine destroyed. It is the only means of communication with the mainland and records show it hasn't been used for a month. Carol and Ernie see a woman at a window and enter the house. Inside they cannot find her but see a message written in the grime on the window. "Go Away," it warns. Ernie sees the woman making off in the street and goes after her. Carol, intending to follow, stumbles into a corpse sitting in a chair in one of the rooms.

Back at the boat, Maggie asks Starfish to fetch a fresh bucket of water in which to soak her ankle. As he lowers the bucket over the side he is pulled into the water. Maggie goes to see where he is and hoists the tethered bucket back onto the deck only to discover Starfish's severed head in it.

The others have regrouped to examine the corpse in the house and conclude it has been partially eaten. Suddenly concerned about Maggie's safety they rush back to the harbour but see the boat has been set adrift. Unable to do anything else, they go to the house where Julie is to stay, but that also proves deserted. As a storm rages outside, Julie suggests they should look for Maggie in case she got off the boat before it went adrift. Carol says it's useless, "There's an evil on this island, an evil that won't let us get away, an evil that sends out an inhuman diabolic power."

In the night, Julie and Danny are awoken and go to investigate the sound of a piano playing. In the cellar they find the source of the noise: a piano with a kitten walking on the keys. They both relax and laugh, when suddenly a girl lunges from a wine barrel and slashes wildly at Danny. It is Greta, the blind girl Julie has come to attend. They calm her and take her upstairs.

Later they question Greta but she cannot explain the missing inhabitants. Instead she tells them of a strange man on the island, one who smells of blood.

In the night, Greta is woken from her sleep and cries, "He's here." Danny goes downstairs to investigate but finds nothing. He returns to Greta's room, assures her everything is okay and locks the door, unaware that the hideous blood-smelling man is behind it. He advances on Greta who screams, and Danny races back into the room but proves no match for the large man. He is sent sprawling on the floor and the man bites a mouthful of flesh from his shoulder.

The following day, with Danny now dead, Julie, Greta, Ernie and Alec go in search of Carol who has run off and failed to return. They come to a large house, but as they enter it the mystery woman who has been prowling around hangs herself from the stairwell. Upstairs they find Carol and from the upper window Ernie and Alec see that the boat has come nearer to the shore. They leave the three women in the house and head off to the boat. Along the way, Ernie finds Maggie's shoe and makes a detour to search for his wife. He descends into archaic burial catacombs filled with rats and human remains, at the end of which he finds Maggie stuffed in a burial niche, but alive.

In the house Julie discovers a secret room filled with mum-

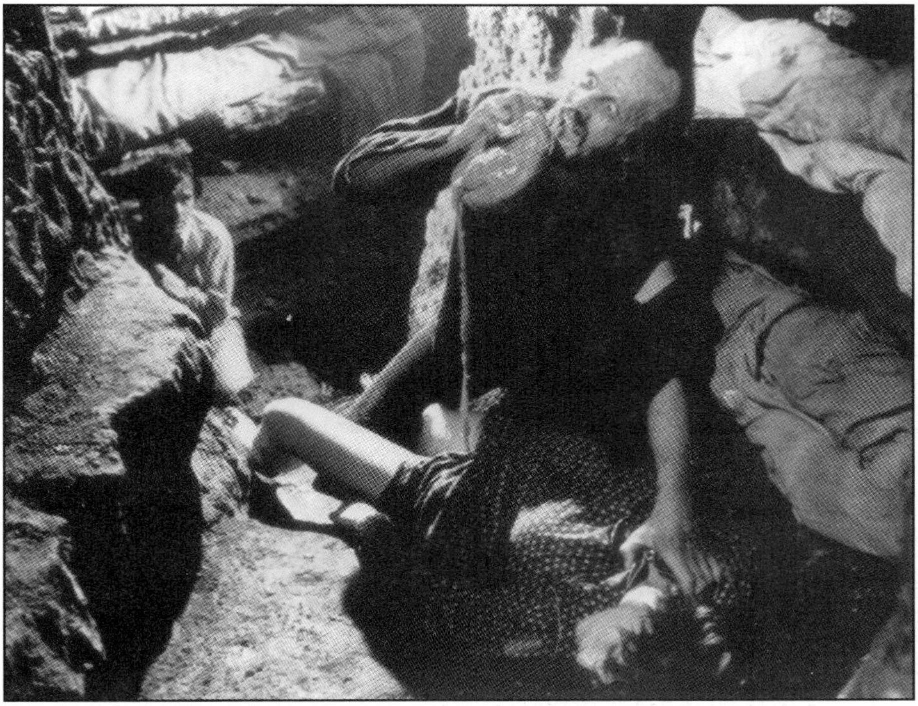

mified corpses. She also finds a diary that tells of the horrible events that have overtaken the island, and learns of a man who was shipwrecked with his wife and child and had to eat the dead body of his son to survive. His wife, so appalled by her husband's actions, killed herself.

In the catacombs the cannibal is advancing on Ernie and Maggie. Ernie begs for their lives, and the killer recalls the fate of his own wife and child — but he is now completely insane and, oblivious to the pleas, drives a knife into Ernie's chest. As Ernie lies dying, he sees the man strangle Maggie before pulling the foetus from her womb and devouring it.

Julie is reading the diary she has found in the secret room, when Carol enters with her throat slit. The cannibal makes a lunge at Julie but she escapes up the stairs. Together with Greta they climb into the loft and lock the trapdoor. Moments later the cannibal smashes his hand through the roof, drags Greta out by her hair and bites open her throat. Julie swings at him with a pickaxe and drives it into his leg. He falls from the roof.

Armed with the pickaxe Julie goes in search of the body, but looking down the well she is grabbed and pulled in. With her hand tangled in the rope she hangs above the water as the cannibal climbs up the rung ladder towards her. She manages to get onto the ladder and out of the well, but is still caught in the rope — the trailing end of which the cannibal now has hold of. As he moves towards her, Alec suddenly appears and drives the pickaxe into the cannibal's stomach. Stumbling to his knees, the cannibal clutches his own intestines as they spill from his wound, then makes an attempt to eat them before he dies.

CRITIQUE: Although he had ventured into the realms of horror with previous titles – the sexually motivated though visceral *Emanuelle in America*, *Emanuelle and the Last Cannibals* and *Erotic Nights of the Living Dead* – *Anthropophagous the Beast*[9] was D'Amato's first specific horror movie and one which he was quite rightly proud of.[10] Without resorting to any sexual content D'Amato needed to generate antipathy as opposed to titillation, something he had failed to achieve in his earlier genre composites. He had provided scenes of abject violence in the two Emanuelle instalments but never induced any sense of atmospheric horror or dread. However, with *Anthropophagous*, he succeeded in producing a viable EC-esque tale of

Greta is dragged through the roof in *Anthropophagous the Beast.*

terror. Location filming and the washed-out colours of the film stock create a unique atmosphere — even the soundtrack is unnerving at times. The fact that George Eastman doesn't have a speaking role helps and he is rigorously disturbing as the lumbering, skin-diseased cannibal. Another major bonus point is the absence of the children and wise-cracking teenagers which are so commonplace in today's formulaic horror movies.

The film contains several grisly moments but it is the realistic scene depicting the aborting and devouring of a near full-term foetus that causes much anxiety. It is a moment of genuinely shocking screen horror. Indeed, the build-up to the scene, with Ernie walking amongst the subterranean shelves of skeletons, only to be followed by the ponderous, heavy-breathing killer, is the most atmospheric moment in the film — pure gothic horror punctuated with an extreme *grand guignol* finale. In a way it is comparable to the eye-slitting scene in Buñuel's *Un Chien Andalou*. In each instance, the viewer is made fully aware of what is about to happen but so appalling is the anticipated climax, he or she doesn't really expect it to be followed through on screen. In *Un Chien Andalou* we see the razor being stropped and the eye being forced open. For a moment we feel 'let off' with a symbolic image of a sliver of cloud cutting across the moon but then the camera abruptly cuts back to the full-screen view of the eye being sliced open. In *Anthropophagous* we see the man throttling the pregnant woman, as his other hand goes beneath her dress and forces its way between her legs. The shot cuts back to the woman's face as she dies from strangulation. For a second the sequence seems over, but then it cuts back to the killer pulling the foetus from between her spread legs and raising it to his jaws.[11]

Another tremendously effective scene occurs when Tisa Farrow is suspended above the well and the scabrous Eastman rises from the murky water. Unfortunately the final climax where the cannibal devours his own intestines, in spite of its poetic symmetry, is a bit too hokey and doesn't have the impact of the foetus-eating scene — possibly because the guts are too thin and stringy to pass off as a human digestive tract. Effective atmosphere is something D'Amato rarely achieves in any of his films yet in this one he succeeds admirably. He is better known for generating tedious longueurs of which, admittedly, there are several in *Anthropophagous* (Ernie and Alec's endless walk to the store to collect antibiotics, amongst them). But these are only minor quibbles and take little away from the film as a whole.

Contrary to popular belief, D'Amato knows exactly what he's doing (even if he can't always afford the time to do it). Courtesy of an article by Thomas M Sipos that appeared in *Midnight Marquee* (No 60), here's how he achieved some of the cost-cutting atmosphere on *Anthropophagous*:

> *Anthrophagous*... cleverly uses day for night photography to simulate lightning: Tisa Farrow (Mia's sister) is chasing Zora Kerova through a forest during a storm. As Farrow's costume and the trees are nearly white, the film stock records an image even though underexposed. We see only the bright trees and Farrow, the underexposed surroundings appearing lost in nighttime darkness. But every so often director [Joe D'Amato] opens the lens aperture — briefly! — to admit more light. When such instances are cued with thunder on the soundtrack, the impression is of lighting illuminating the landscape. But freeze the frame on your VCR and you'll see the 'lightning' is daylight, the entire landscape evenly lit.

Anthropophagous the Beast was released uncut by Videofilm Promotions, and also in a truncated, hard-to-find R-rated form on the Radio Shack video label. At one period it achieved notoriety as a 'snuff' film, identified as such by the ill-informed press, and was even excerpted on national news. A sequel of sorts was ***Absurd***, again directed by D'Amato and featuring George Eastman in another mute role.

AXE

SYNOPSIS: Three men in suits — Steele, Lomax and Billy — break into an apartment and await the arrival of Aubrey. Lomax passes the time by burning holes into female clothing he has found in the wardrobe. Billy keeps watch from the window. Steele, the gang's leader, casually picks his nails.

When Aubrey arrives, Lomax and Steele accuse him of having a "whining mouth," then stub a cigar out in it before accidentally beating him to death. Aubrey's friend, a man who has been cowering in the corner, suddenly leaps from the ninth storey window when attentions are turned towards him.

The gang decide to head out of town to lay low for a while. Billy, the youngest member of the outfit, voices his dissatisfaction and stares distractedly out the back window of the car. Pulling over at a store, Billy waits as his companions go inside and start to kick up a fuss. Steele takes a bite from an apple and throws what's left of it at the cashier.

"Do you call this fresh fruit?" he complains.

"We're very sorry," the cashier replies, in a manner that suggests she might be versed in the apology. "Please take another one if you like."

Steele goes berserk, snatching fruit from the display rack and throwing it at the woman. Afterwards, he makes her take off her blouse at gunpoint. She starts to cry into her hands. The men place an apple on the distraught woman's head and fire at it. Pouring a fizzy drink onto her brassiered breasts, the men leave.

On a farm further on down the road, Lisa looks after her sick grandfather, who is paralysed and unable to communicate. Lisa has a constantly distracted expression on her face, and hums a tuneless tune while chopping the head off a chicken.

The gang turn up. "What do you want?" Lisa asks, completely nonplussed about their presence. When the outlaws discover that she is alone, save for an incapacitated grandfather, they decide to make themselves at home.

Two policemen show. With Steele training a gun on her grandfather, Lisa sends the officers on their way.

During meal time, Billy snaps when his partners make a funny remark about the girl.

Steele and Lomax give chase to a prowler.

In the bathroom, Lisa contemplates slitting her wrists.

At night, feverish with desire, Lomax sneaks into Lisa's bedroom and rapes her. She pulls a cut-throat razor and slices through the back of his neck, killing him.[12] Amazingly, nobody in the house hears Lomax scream, nor do they hear Lisa dragging his corpse into the bathroom, hacking it to pieces with an axe and sticking what's left into a trunk. As Lisa tries to manoeuvre the trunk out of the bathroom the following morning, Billy offers his help. "What have you got in here?" he asks. "Old bowling balls?" He carries the trunk into the attic whereupon he discovers that it actually contains Lomax' body.

Lisa blames the murder on "the other one." Away from the house, Billy asks the girl for help, and mistakenly interprets the cut-throat in her hand as a weapon for him to use against Steele.

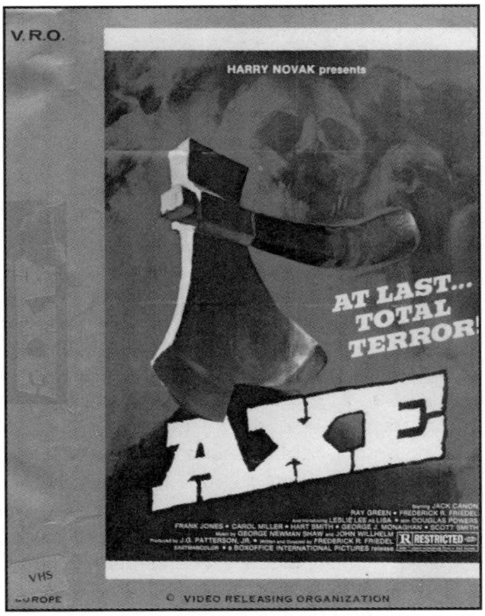

AXE
AKA: Lisa, Lisa; California Axe Massacre; The Axe Murders
USA 1974
CAST: Jack Canon, Ray Green, Frederick R Friedel, and introducing Leslie Lee
STORY: Frederick R Friedel
PRODUCER: J G Petterson Jr
DIRECTOR: FREDERICK R FRIEDEL

"You're way ahead of me," he says. "I'll need that."

Back indoors, Lisa tells Steele that Billy and Lomax have gone for a walk. Steele takes the opportunity to rape the girl, dragging her before her grandfather so that he might have a "real good TV show to watch." Horse racing commentary from the TV set accompanies the struggle. Eventually Lisa manages to reach the axe that sits in the corner of the room and kills Steele with it.

Billy returns and sits down to a bowl of odd-tasting "tomato" soup that Lisa has prepared, in which he discovers a ring belonging to Steele. Steele's bloody body suddenly falls out of the chimney flue.

"No... no... no... no... no..." he mutters.

Running out of the house, the two cops from earlier shoot the reluctant outlaw dead and determine, "That's one of them alright — she sure was right about it."[13]

Lisa hums a tuneless tune as she feeds gramps some more of the soup.

CRITIQUE: One of the most striking things about *Axe* is its peculiar use of sound. The main theme — which also serves to accentuate Lisa's psychosis — is one of the singularly most annoying pieces of music set to film,[14] consisting of a toy keyboard playing a shrill noise that starts high and gets higher. The dubbing is pretty strange, too, no less during the opening sequence where Aubrey is murdered. Here, Steele and Lomax' succession of punches make contact with the same dull, lifeless thud; Aubrey gives a strange non-human gurgling sound when the cigar is extinguished in his mouth; and a fey looped "Ooh" emits from the corner of the room, where Aubrey's effeminate friend lies cringing. "Ooh... Ooh... Ooh... Ooh..."

Things are deliberately ambiguous in *Axe*. There is no clue as to what misdeeds lie behind the gang having to teach Aubrey a lesson. He has squealed on something, that much is clear. But not once do they discuss anything of the events prior to his murder, and no mention is made of loot, or a heist, for which the gang appear appropriately dressed. (One might assume that the intended crime never took place, seeing how the only reason they decide to head off and lie low for a while is because they killed Aubrey.)

Lisa on the other hand is definitely hiding something. We first see her pottering around the farmyard, doing chores, during which she drops an egg. It smashes and she rubs it into the dirt with her bare foot. Later, she opens the refrigerator and we see only broken eggs on a shelf. There is something dark and troubling weighing down on the girl, but we know not what it might be.

The videobox states that Lisa is thirteen-years-old — which would make Lomax and Steele's assault on her even more despicable — but as there is no mention of the girl's age in the film, it's a fact presumably lifted from a pressbook or distribution notes.[15] However, it is evident that Lisa is supposed to be much younger than the actress playing her, given her demeanour and the outlaws not suspecting for a minute she might be capable of anything untoward.

Where are her parents? (She tells the outlaws she has none.)

Why isn't she afraid?

Why is she alone in running the farm and looking after her grandfather?

What is causing her mind to collapse like the eggshells in her fridge?

Bill Landis, in *Sleazoid Express*,[16] describes Lisa as "one of the most haunting female characters ever in an exploitation film."

While Lisa is a cinematic mystery, not much is known about the film's real-life director Frederick R Friedel. Besides *Axe*, Friedel is known to have directed at least one other movie, *Date with a Kidnapper*,[17] which also starred Jack Canon (in the same business suit no less) and shared some of the same production credits. *Date with a Kidnapper* even takes several of the ideas from *Axe* and uses them to a much more confident — if no more logical — end. It's about a guy who kidnaps the daughter of a millionaire and holds her to ransom. Both films have teenaged girls at their centres, suited gangsters whose past crimes are never elaborated on, psychotic rural folk, lonely farm houses, and rapists who are murdered whilst on top of their victims.

The comparatively more polished and satisfying *Date with a Kidnapper* makes *Axe* look like a dry run, and leads one to believe that Friedel kept himself busy in other film work between the two productions.

Interesting to note is that *Date with a Kidnapper* failed to make the nasties list, despite several scenes that are no less harrowing or confrontational than some of those found in *Axe* — an example of how poor distribution[18] and a relatively innocuous title saved many a film from the clutches of the DPP.

Everything in *Axe* is protracted to the point that otherwise mundane actions take on a Zen-like quality. The beating up of Aubrey and the succession of punches, for instance, or Billy taking the trunk containing Lomax' body into the attic — it isn't enough to establish the act, we have to watch it every step of the way. There seems to have been a reluctance to edit down and tighten the movie, which may or may not be connected to the fact that it is already less than seventy minutes long.

Lisa in *Axe*.

But then it goes overboard with 'interesting' camera angles, and Friedel lets slip his aspiration to create 'art' out of the menagerie. (The minimalist cast and one-house setting belies a certain Bergmanesque influence.[19]) In one sequence, a noise heard by Steele and Lomax alerts them to a prowler outside, who then runs off. We haven't seen enough of the unidentified man to establish just what it is he is supposed to be doing, and nobody makes any further reference to the incident — not even the two outlaws after they return from their pursuit of him. In another sequence, Lisa ponders her reflection in the bathroom mirror. The reflection is suddenly bloody. She spots a small black snake curled up in the bottom of the bath. Later, when disposing of Lomax' body — hacking him to pieces and putting what's left in a trunk — at the bottom of the bath, curled up like a snake, is his black necktie.

Axe is relatively free of viscera. The bloodiest moments come from the headless chicken that lies by the sink, and Lomax' dismemberment is implied rather than shown — cutting from Lisa's raised axe to shots of her grandfather's blank face, or courtesy of a silhouette of the scene through the window blind. Even when Billy opens the trunk, we are treated only to his horrified reaction and a momentary replay of Lomax' death throes.

One possible point of contention comes with the sequence in the country store, given that it serves only to humiliate and terrorise an innocent victim without furtherance to the plot.[20] Indeed, it was here that the film lost three minutes when released theatrically as *California Axe Massacre* in 1982. (This footage was replaced when the film was passed for video release in 1999, see APPENDIX II.)

Other elements which might have helped make *Axe* an 'undesirable' include: the videobox claim that Lisa is only thirteen (Lomax calls her a "Nice lookin' woman"), the insinuation of cannibalism, the headless chicken (not in itself, but the tone it conveys through the rest of the film), Aubrey's murder, a child as killer, and the rape sequences (particularly the one accompanied by the sporting commentary on the TV, the dialogue of which was toned down in the recent re-release)...

Executive producer J G 'Pat' Patterson, prior to *Axe*, directed and starred in the terrible *Dr Gore*, which got more attention than it deserved when re-released in the eighties with a tagged-on introduction by Herschell Gordon Lewis. It is Patterson's involvement on *Axe* that makes it unlikely the production should be dated as late as 1977 as some sources suggest. Patterson died in 1974.

THE BEAST IN HEAT

SYNOPSIS: A hypodermic needle injects a solution into the back of a hairy hand. The beautiful female doctor administering the dose turns to an older male colleague and says "You seem perplexed."

"That is quite true," replies the colleague, "because I think what we're doing isn't quite correct. No one can play God, cynically change a human being like we're doing here."

Dr Ellen Kratsch, a lieutenant of Hitler's Third Reich, threatens to remove her estranged colleague's name from the experiments and take all credit for the "remarkable discovery."

The primordial male voice that has been grunting from off-screen up to this point suddenly gurgles loudly, prompting Dr Kratsch to commence "a demonstration that would make the god Eros go green with envy."

As guards bring into the room a naked curvaceous woman, the source of the grunting and gurgling is revealed: a short, flabby, hairy naked man jumping up and down in a cage strewn with straw. He is excited at the sight of the "chosen virgin ... sacrificing herself to science."

The woman is thrown screaming into the cage and the beast-man ravages and rapes her. After some time the woman falls silent and the inexplicable appearance of blood around her mouth impresses that she has been — quite literally — fucked to death.

THE BEAST IN HEAT
TITLE ON PRINT: HORRIFING [sic] EXPERIMENTS OF S.S.LAST DAYS
AKA: La Bestia en Calor; SS Hell Camp; SS Experiment Part 2; Holocauste Nazi–Armes Secrets III Reich
ITALY 1977
CAST: Macha Magall, John Braun, Kim Gatti, Sal Boris
PRODUCER: Eterna Film
DIRECTOR: IVAN KATANSKY [Luigi Batzella]

Kratsch asks one of the observing soldiers whether he finds the spectacle exciting, and slaps him across the face when he replies in the affirmative. "Spineless fool!" she cries. "A soldier of the Third Reich isn't supposed to get excited at *any* spectacle!"

The scene cuts to a mountain railway where members of the Italian resistance are successful in demolishing a bridge of high strategic importance to the Nazis. The news of this latest attack results in Dr Kratsch being assigned to help a captain locate the partisan hideout.

In an attempt to crush the resistance without outside help, the captain orders all the locals to be dragged out of the village. An old woman who raises an objection is gunned down, and a baby snatched from its mother's arms by a group of soldiers is tossed into the air and shot. The exercise doesn't bring the Nazis any closer to locating the partisan hideout.

A philosophical conversation takes place between Don Lorenzo, the village priest, and Drago, one of the members of the resistance. Lorenzo gives Drago his rosary and, with a wink of the eye, concludes their dialogue. "The Lord won't betray you," he says. "He's the best."

Stefan, another member of the resistance, happens to be visiting his family when the Germans make a house-to-house search. He volunteers to give himself up to save the village any further anguish, but his mother will hear none of it, knocks him unconscious and hides him in a cupboard. Stefan comes round only after his sister has been raped and shot point blank in the genitals. He is among those men and women taken to Nazi headquarters for interrogation.

Chained up and nude in a bunker, Stefan is warned by Kratsch that she will make him "talk" and she peels off her tunic to rub her breasts against his chest. This display arouses an adjacent prisoner to the point that he screams half-mad with desire, "Don't waste time with that boy! I want you before I die!"

He is castrated for his trouble.

Elsewhere, a partisan is shot by his compatriots for a being traitor, an action which is quickly followed by German troops mounting an attack on their hideout. (While this battle suggests Kratsch has succeeded in her objective of locating the partisan hideout, in

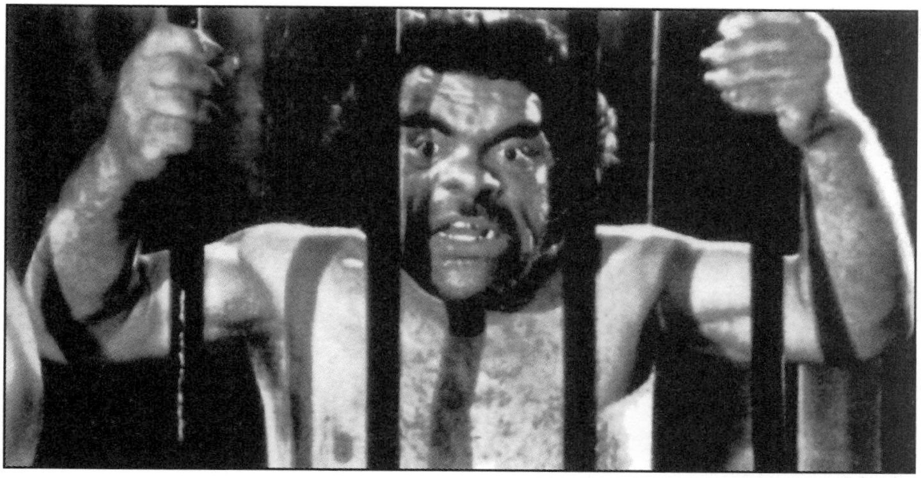

The Beast in *Beast in Heat*.

the next scene she is torturing her prisoners in order to find where the resistance is hiding.)

In her laboratory, Kratsch oversees a multitude of horrors: the hairy man-beast is raping another girl in his cage; a woman has electric shocks administered via electrodes connected to her genitals; a man is suspended head-first over a bath of water as a soldier flogs him; and a woman has a heated bucket containing rats pressed against her stomach. Amidst the growing cacophony of screams and wails, another woman has her fingernails pulled out with pliers. "It hurts," she detachedly tells her tormentors. She lets slip that the village priest knows about the partisan hiding place.

With this information, Kratsch and her two female sidekicks stand and admire the caged beast as he begins to tear pubic hair from between the legs of his latest victim and stuff it in his mouth.

The captain and several soldiers arrive at the church in the village. Irene, the village whore, attempts to throw the troops off the trail and convince them that Don Lorenzo isn't in, that he's perhaps with one of his flock, "someone who's dying."

"At this time of the day?" the Captain retorts, incredulous.

Don Lorenzo refuses to collaborate with the Germans and is taken away, just as allied bombers start an indiscriminate air raid which destroys the church.

As the bombing intensifies, the partisans move on the Nazi headquarters, wherein the beast is busy molesting another victim. "Rape her!" encourages Kratsch, who is dressed inexplicably in a night-gown. "Show her no mercy!"

The girl escapes the cage just as Drago and his men break into the room. The beast grabs Kratsch and tears off her night-gown (to reveal sexy stockings and suspenders). Her screams for mercy at the hands of the blubbery one fall on deaf ears, and the partisan fighters stare with disdain as the Nazi doctor is raped by her own creation. Ultimately both of them are shot dead.

Outside, Drago discovers the corpse of a child lying in some rubble and takes it into his arms. He wanders vacantly into the crossfire, waxing lyrical about there being "a better place" and that soon the child will be "flying high in the sky on a winged horse."

CRITIQUE: *Beast in Heat* opens with a swastika coming into focus, accompanied by a woman's piercing scream and an odd electronic score.[21] The swastika remains centre-screen for the duration of the credits — which only comprise the production company and all of five names. Following the credit for 'Sal Boris' (the actor who plays the Beast), there is an uncomfortable wait of almost a minute-and-a-half before the next name appears, during which time nothing is on screen but that stationary swastika![22]

Part of the reason why elements of *Beast in Heat* seem detached from one another lies in the fact that the director has constructed much of it out of *When the Bell Rings*, an earlier war film of his (described as "tedious" by the *Delirium* guide to Italian exploitation). This material

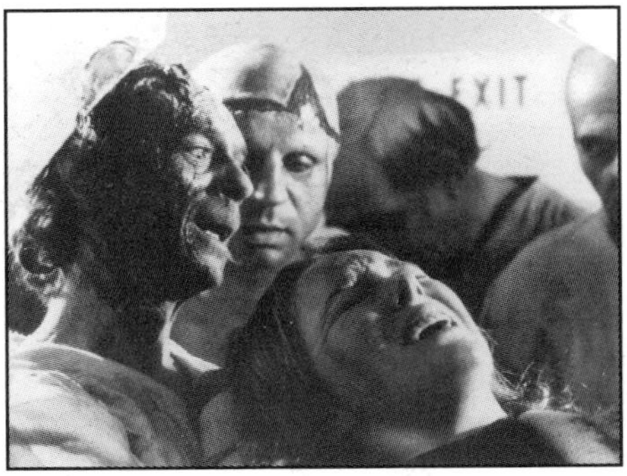

TOP: US poster for *The Beyond*.
ABOVE: Liza is attacked by zombies in *The Beyond*.

is easily identifiable due to the different matching stock and the fact it comprises all the scenes with heavy artillery, aircraft and impressive explosions. In contrast, the rest of the film is noticeably more down-market and generally consists of interior shots, lame 'action' and footage of people arguing.

This would explain why the destination of the villagers in their forced exodus is never revealed (but simply concludes when a baby is thrown up in the air and shot, and several minutes later the villagers find themselves back in their homes as if nothing has happened), nor why Dr Kratsch can drive to the captain's headquarters, help him in locating the resistance, but not actually be seen in the same shot or even the same room or village as him.

(Alas, it's unclear whether this fusing of different films is responsible for the curious sequence where Irene, the village whore, is chased by angry locals for fraternising with the enemy. The chase comes to a dead halt with a Mack Sennett-like gag – a bucket of water is thrown at her but misses and hits someone else.)

The grisly excesses of *Beast in Heat* are unevenly paced, and director Katansky appears torn between making a straight war film and a clone of the Ilsa series, which had starred Dyanne Thorne as a busty, sadistic, sex-crazed Nazi officer.[23] Indeed, the previous year Katansky had covered similar ground with *Desert Tigers*,[24] a film featuring a Nazi camp with a sadomasochistic lesbian doctor called Erika.[25]

Dull action scenes and unnecessary dialogue marks the time between each ridiculous appearance of the beast – played not very seriously by Sal Boris (real name: Salvatore Baccaro), a comedy actor who was called upon more than once to appear in exploitation movies.[26] He gurns at great length into the camera (which gets so close that at one point the lens steams up), mugging wildly while furiously pummelling his flabby buttocks. His surreal performance reaches an absolute nadir with his munching of pubic hair. *Why does this happen?! What train of thought must have been running through the screenwriter's mind to arrive at a point where a rape victim has her pubes ripped out and eaten?!* This absurdity, coupled with the general ineptitude of the film throughout, makes it difficult to qualify *Beast in Heat* as being the most revolting entry in the Italian Nazi cycle as some critics have suggested. It's simply too dumb, and other more competent exercises — like ***Gestapo's Last Orgy*** — are far more alarming and unpleasant.

That said, it's not difficult to see why *Beast in Heat* should have ended up on the 'banned' list: Nazis, rape and titillation are not an acceptable combination.

Other than on the video sleeve, the title *Beast in Heat* is actually nowhere to be found (on what probably remains the most sought after tape on the DPP list — see BLACK MARKET & PIRATES). A Spanish language certificate pops up before the film starts, carrying the original title *La Bestia en Calor*, but it is the rather ham-fisted *Horrifing* [sic] *Experiments of S.S.Last Days* that appears on the actual print itself. Such has been its scarcity that in November 1984 the *Monthly Film Bulletin* suspected the film was merely a re-title for Walerian Borowczyk's female masturbation fantasy *The Beast* — an error that has been compounded elsewhere many times since.

Katansky — who also uses the pseudonyms Ivan Kathansy (with an 'h') and Luigi Batzella — directed many giallos and horror films under his real name Paolo Solvay, including *The Devil's Wedding Night*.

THE BEYOND

SYNOPSIS: In 1927 Louisiana, a torch-bearing lynch mob advance on an isolated hotel. Shvyke, a resident artist, is found in his room finishing a strange painting depicting a Hellish landscape. The mob accuse him of being a warlock and take him to the cellars where he is beaten with chains, nailed to the wall and doused with quick lime which dissolves his flesh.

In the present, Liza Merril has inherited the run-down hotel and is overseeing the process of its renovation. A painter working on scaffolding sees an apparition in one of the rooms and falls from the platform. Liza discovers Shvyke's cobweb-covered painting as the bell rings in room 36, the ill-fated artist's old room now standing empty. Joe the plumber arrives to attend to a leak in the basement and hacks at the water-sodden wall to reveal a hidden area — the place where Shvyke was murdered — only to be clawed in the face by a lunging hand.

While out in her car, Liza encounters a blind woman who introduces herself as Emily. She already knows Liza's name and warns her to leave the hotel.

Martha the housemaid discovers the mutilated body of Joe in the basement. Floating in the floodwater is another decomposed corpse, and both are taken to the hospital for examination by Dr John McCabe. A colleague wires up a brainwave machine to the older corpse by way of an experiment, which begins to activate when the doctor leaves the autopsy room. Joe's wife and daughter Jill arrive with a suit of clothes. Waiting in the corridor Jill hears her mother scream from within the autopsy room, and enters to find her lying on the floor with an acid container spilling its contents onto her face. The foamy pool of dissolving flesh spreads towards the young girl, who seeks safety within a storage cupboard — only to find it contains a living corpse. Later, at the funeral of Joe and his wife, the daughter reveals herself to be in a zombified state.

The blind girl Emily visits Liza at the hotel and explains the building's dark past. She tells her of the painter and how he found a key to one of the gateways to Hell. Emily becomes uneasy and runs out

THE BEYOND
AKA: L'aldilà (original title); Seven Doors of Death
ITALY 1981
CAST: David Warbeck, Catriona MacColl, Sarah Keller, Antoine St John, Veronica Lazar, Giovanni de Nava, Al Cliver, Anthony Flees, Michele Mirabella, Gianpaolo Saccarola, Laura de Marchi, Maria Pia Marsala
STORY: Lucio Fulci
PRODUCER: Fabrizio de Angelis
DIRECTOR: LUCIO FULCI

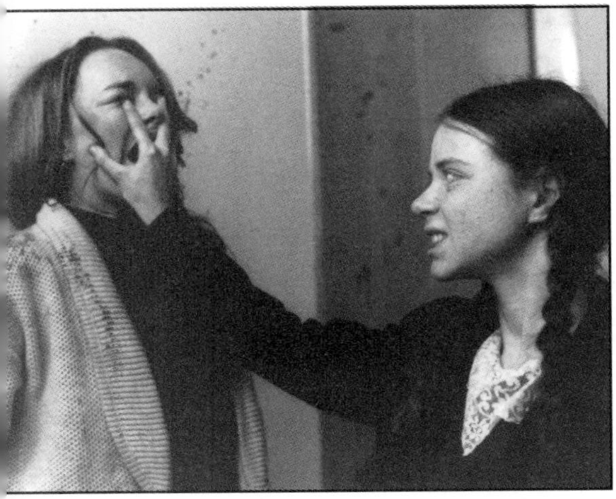

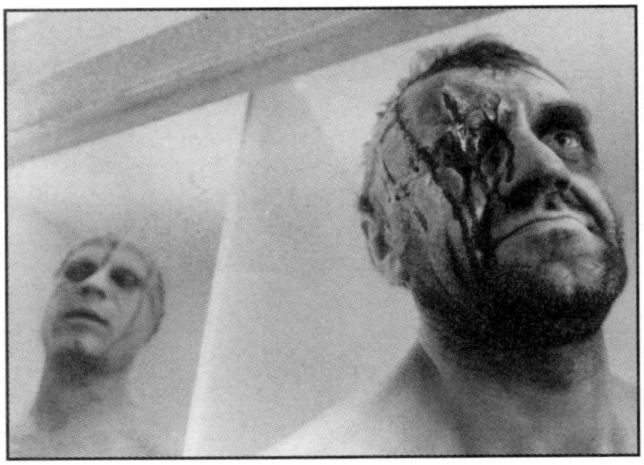

THIS PAGE, FROM TOP: A possessed Jill attacks Liza; Zombies!; Dr McCabe shoots one of the living dead. Scenes from *The Beyond*.

of the room, believing it contains a spiritual presence. Liza thinks it's strange that she made no sound when she ran across the floorboards. The following day Liza opens room 36, where she finds an old book called *Eibon* and sees an image of a crucified corpse nailed to the wall. She runs from the room in terror and finds Dr McCabe who comforts her. Checking out the room, there is no book or body, only two rusty nails sticking from the wall. Liza tells McCabe about Emily but he says he knows of no such blind girl.

Discussing the renovation with the architect, Liza glances in a bookshop window and sees the book of *Eibon* on display. On closer inspection it's another book entirely. The architect goes to the town hall to look at the plans of the hotel, which he locates in a book on a high shelf. The plans don't actually match the layout of the building. A sudden flash of lightning sends him falling from his ladder and he lies paralysed on the floor as, from beneath the shelves, an army of tarantulas approach. They crawl over the motionless architect and devour him. The plan of the hotel slowly fades from the book.

McCabe enters the house where Liza claimed the blind girl lives. It is derelict, but amongst the debris he finds the book of *Eibon*. "The seven dreaded gateways to hell are concealed in seven cursed places," he reads.

Martha is going about her cleaning chores in the hotel when she finds that the bath in room 36 is full of stagnant water. The drain seems to be clogged with hair and as the water runs away it reveals the animated body of Joe, who clambers from the bath and drives Martha's head onto one of the protruding nails in the wall.

Emily is plagued by zombies — they have come to take her back to Hell. She sets her dog on them but the animal turns against her and tears out her throat.

McCabe links the book of *Eibon* to the decomposed corpse that was found in the cellar, a symbol in the book being branded on the corpse's arm. He goes to the hotel to confront Liza, believing she is inventing all the stories and had planted the book in the house so he would find it. Liza denies this and tells him she was just attacked by a zombie in the basement. Together they investigate the cellar and find no zombie. Alarmed by lightning and a rain of blood, they flee the hotel for the hospital — only to discover that it's populated by an army of reanimated corpses. Managing to fight their way through the zombies, Liza and McCabe escape down a spiral staircase that leads them back into the hotel basement. Walking through some collapsed brickwork they find themselves trapped in the Hellish landscape painted by Shvyke.

CRITIQUE: *The Beyond* is one of three films directed by Lucio Fulci to have been included on the DPP list. Judging by the equivocal selection criteria involved however, there could well have been more — notably *City of the Living Dead* and *The Naples Connection*, an extremely violent *French Connection* imitation whose different genre class probably helped it to escape the clutches of the DPP.

The Beyond is a contemporary horror story depicting the resurrected dead plaguing mankind and, despite being cobbled together with ideas from other film sources — such as *The Sentinel*, *Suspiria*, and ***Inferno***[27] — carries all the Fulci hallmarks: sudden lingering close-ups of eyes; exaggerated sound effects; punctuating moments of graphic horror; and a seriously bleak — though confusing — ending. Some of the scenes Fulci fails to pull off and the film would have been better without them. The spider attack sequence, for instance, is all-too unrealistic, the arachnids looking every bit like the mechanical puppets they obviously are. Intercutting the sequence with real tarantulas only emphasises the clumsiness of the automatons and consequently the scene is more amusing than horrifying. When Liza sees the image of the crucified warlock it is in one of the upper rooms, yet the prologue shows the man being dragged from his room and nailed to the cellar wall — effectively composed as they are, there is a lack of continuity and the scenes don't make much sense. Likewise it seems rather ridiculous that a hospital technician would place an EEG-type device on the head of an obviously long-dead corpse.

Unlike Fulci's earlier ***Zombie Flesh-Eaters***, which has a straightforward, even *simplistic* narrative and startling set-pieces, *The Beyond* trips over its own confusion. It almost tries to be too clever with its esoteric mystery and unexplained characters and as a result the film's pace is adversely affected. Moreover, the film lacks any genuinely memorable sequences — like the superbly rendered underwater fight in ***Zombie Flesh-Eaters*** or Christopher George's desperate attempt to save Catriona MacColl from a partially buried coffin with a pick axe in *City of the Living Dead*. The only noteworthy and genuinely creepy image in *The Beyond* comes in its closing moments, where Liza and McCabe discover themselves locked in the nightmare landscape of Shvyke's painting. But Fulci is unable to muster the enthusiasm to do anything with it and the film simply ends here. The director, it seems, had run out of verve and daring ideas, content instead to play around with the rather obvious horror a paralysed man being overrun with (toy) spiders would invoke. Indeed, Fulci's career went into the gutter after *The Beyond* and — with the possible exceptions of ***The House By the Cemetery*** and *The New York Ripper* — he failed to make another film of worth. He even resorted to self-parody in the truly dreadful *A Cat in the Brain*, in which he played the lead role — a demented film director.

The Beyond was released on video with an official BBFC X-certificate — the same version that had been released theatrically in Britain in 1981. Several cuts of a total two minutes duration were made to the original film to achieve this classification, including the removal of the gorier aspects of the spider attack. With the original violence considerably toned down, the only scenes which may have brought the Vampix video release to the attention of the DPP are those depicting the torture and crucifixion of the warlock in the sepia-toned prologue. But even these scenes had been trimmed to remove some of the impact-blows which occurred while the victim was being chain-whipped.

The film was later re-released on the Elephant Video label in an utterly worthless version with all the scenes of violence completely removed.

BLOOD BATH

SYNOPSIS: Frederica, a wheelchair-bound woman living in a sprawling house on the edge of a bay, is murdered by her husband Phillipo. He attempts to make the death look like suicide but as he places the suicide note he too is murdered and his body disposed of. Frank Ventura, an architect, sets off for the bay intending to purchase the property left by the dead woman for development. On the banks of the bay Paul, an eccentric entomologist, and Simon, a fisherman, are arguing.

"You've changed, you know, ever since the countess was murdered," remarks Paul.

"It was *suicide*," reminds Simon.

The pair are being watched from a distance by Rennie, Phillipo's daughter, and her husband Albert who are travelling with their children in their mobile home.

A group of teenagers head for the abandoned resort on the bay while Paul's wife Anna reads tarot cards.

"The sickle of death is about to strike," she tells her husband. "Can't you sense the rattled breathing of death?"

"The only thing I sense is that lecherous Ventura holding the usual orgy in his cottage," he replies.

"You hate Ventura for the exact same reason you hated Frederica's husband — because he knows how to enjoy life and you don't."

Paul explains he only hates the architect because he wants to develop the bay and destroy its natural beauty.

Unaware they are being watched from the woods, the four teenagers are exploring the abandoned buildings when one of the girls decides to go for a swim in the bay. Her companions decide to break into a house that happens to belong to Ventura. In the sea the girl gets herself tangled in a rope, and pulls herself free to find a corpse attached to the other end. It is the body of Phillipo. She runs back to her colleagues but is pursued by an unseen assailant and hacked to death with a machete. The killer goes on to the house and murders the other teenagers.

Rennie and Albert call on Paul to get information on her missing father. Although they are unaware that her father is dead, Rennie learns of the existence of a step-brother: Simon the fisherman, an illegitimate son of Frederica. They go to question Simon about Phillipo's whereabouts but he claims not to have seen him. Rennie pulls back a tarpaulin in Simon's boat to reveal her father's body. Simon explains he has just pulled him from the water, and suggests they go up to Frank Ventura's cottage.

Albert takes Rennie to the house, which seems to be empty. In actual fact, Frank is inside but is ignoring their calls. Albert decides to go back to Paul's to collect the car and tells Paul they have just found the body of Phillipo. In Frank's house Rennie uses the bathroom and discovers the bodies of the murdered teenagers. Before she can get out of the house Frank comes at her with an axe but she manages to stab him with a pair of scissors in self-defence.

Anna hears the commotion and goes over to investigate. Paul heads for Ventura's place in pursuit of his wife and discovers Frank lying bloody on the floor. He runs from the house as Albert arrives with the car. Albert thinks Paul has murdered Frank but Rennie confesses to the killing and tells Albert he must stop Paul from reporting it to the police. Albert catches Paul at his house and strangles him with the telephone wire. Anna finds Frank on the floor and as she leans over the body she is attacked from behind and decapitated. Rennie tells her husband that all the witnesses are now dead and they only need to deal with Simon. Frank's secretary Laura approaches in a car. Rennie says that Laura must also die as she may have seen them at the house.

Laura enters Frank's house and finds him still alive. He asks her to get Simon, which she does only to have Simon confront her about the death of his mother. She explains to him that his mother has been murdered and it was all Frank's idea — she was to seduce Phillipo and get him to kill his wife and make it look like a suicide. Furious Simon strangles Laura and goes in pursuit of Frank. Making his way to the house he encounters Albert and Rennie who murder him. The couple go in search of Frank's will and in the resultant affray Frank is killed.

The following day back at their motor home, Albert and Rennie burn the documents. Their children pop up brandishing a shotgun and shoot them dead thinking they are participating in a game.

They came seeking pleasure, they found death
Blood Bath
Blood Bath
VM 75
VIDEO MOVIES from Hokushin

BLOOD BATH
AKA: A Bay of Blood (original title); Antefatto (working title); Carnage; The Ecology of a Crime; Twitch of the Death Nerve; New House on the Left; The Last House on the Left Part II
ITALY 1971
CAST: Luigi Pistilli, Claudine Auger, Claudio Volonté, Chris Avram, Anna Maria Rosati, Leopold Trieste, Laura Betti, Brigitte Skay, Isa Miranda, Paulo Rubens, Guido Boccaccini, Roberto Bonanni, Giovanni Nuvoletti
STORY: Mario Bava, Joseph McLee, Filippo Ottoni, Dardano Sacchetti, Franco Barberi
PRODUCER: Giuseppe Zaccariello
DIRECTOR: MARIO BAVA

CRITIQUE: There weren't many classy films in the DPP listings but Mario Bava's *Blood Bath* was certainly one of them. This is a stylish, plot-twisting whodunit marred only by the severely frivolous finale. The element of mystery is sustained throughout and even though the violent incidents are graphic they aren't its *raison d'être*. The same can't be said of most of the plot-redundant gore films that were spawned in its wake.

Mario Bava has made many influential films, or to be more precise, influential *sequences*. For example, Bava's 1960 film *Black Sunday* contains a startling eye-piercing scene that was honoured in Fulci's ***Zombie Flesh-Eaters***; his *Blood and Black Lace* features a drowned girl's face peering lifelessly from the bottom of a bath tub filled with water, a scene recreated in Roger Corman's *Bloody Mama*; while *Planet of the Vampires* has a sequence depicting the discovery of a fossilised alien life-form, mimicked almost fifteen years later in Ridley Scott's *Alien*.

Blood Bath is often cited as being the inspiration for the abundant stalk-and-slash movies of the eighties. However, films like *Friday the 13th* and its many sequels (perhaps most notably part 2), mimicked only the grisly murders and abandoned — or simply lacked the skills to realise — the style and panache of Bava's original.

The first graphic murder in *Blood Bath* shows a half-naked girl having her throat chopped deeply with a machete. In another particularly brutal scene a young man is struck full in the face with a machete. Although the impact isn't shown in detail the blade is seen buried deep in the face, then being prised from the massive wound. Effective editing makes the scene horribly realistic. A couple having sex are speared through and pinned to the bed, the spearhead seen penetrating naked flesh. There are other scenes of violence, generally involving stabbing through clothing.

Blood Bath was released on the Hokushin label with an unofficial 18 certificate. Later it was re-released by Redemption Films with a proper 18 certificate. Forty-three seconds of cuts were required in order to achieve this rating.

Martin Scorsese has a great fondness for Bava, calling his films "a kind of Italian Gothic." There's "hardly any story," he says in *Scorsese on Scorsese*,

> just atmosphere, with all that fog and ladies walking down corridors... I could just put them on loops and have one going in one room in my house, one going on in another, as I have many televisions around. I do that sometimes, put different tapes on and just walk around creating a whole mood...

BLOOD FEAST

SYNOPSIS: A woman returns to her apartment and prepares a bath. A local radio news broadcast informs listeners that a maniac is on the prowl and that single young women particularly should take safety precautions. But this woman is too concerned with lathering herself in soapsuds to heed the alarmed newscaster's advice. Indeed, it's too late for safety precautions anyway, as the maniac is already in her home and approaching the bathroom brandishing a kitchen knife. The girl manages but one lingering scream before the madman plunges the knife into her eye. He stares for a moment at the bloody tissue on the blade before proceeding to hack off her leg. The severed limb is placed in a bag and taken from the scene.

At the Homicide Bureau, Detective Pete Thornton and Chief Detective Frank Mason are baffled by the case — the seventh unsolved murder in the last two weeks. They deliberate on the killer's ability to leave not a single clue or print at the murder scenes.

Fuad Ramses is an Egyptian caterer, one who specialises in rare and exotic dishes. Ramses is also the crazed killer terrorising the neighbourhood. Dorothy Fremont, a well-to-do local woman, enters his store and asks him to prepare a dinner party spread for her daughter, something "unusual... totally different." Ramses proposes an ancient banquet, an Egyptian feast that hasn't been served in 5,000 years, and hits his customer with a hypnotic glare. "Yes... yes... we must do it," agrees Fremont in a dislocated voice. A date is set and Mrs Fremont leaves.

Ramses enters a secret room at the back of the shop, replete with red curtains, burning candles, large cooking pots and kettles resting on a table. A statue of the Egyptian goddess Ishtar stands ready for worship. Ramses means to bring Ishtar back to life through an occult ritual, but the process of resurrection requires human blood and flesh to be cooked and served in a ceremonial blood feast. It is for this reason that Ramses has been killing neighbourhood females and collecting their body parts.

Newspaper readers are shocked and startled by the latest murder revelations. "Legs Cut Off," blares *The Daily Chronicle*.

Detectives Thornton and Mason are also distraught by the story and remain thwarted by lack of any substantial lead. The only detail they seem to have uncovered about the latest victim is that she belonged to a book club.

A couple are making out on the beach. The girl is somewhat nervous because of the recent incidents, but her boyfriend assures her everything will be fine as he is there to protect her. "Now prove you love me," he demands seconds before he is struck unconscious by Ramses who has crept up on the pair. With a single machete blow, Ramses chops away the top of the girl's head to reveal her brains, which he collects and bags.

Thornton and Mason are soon on the scene, trying to question the young man who's been rendered a babbling idiot through shock. Thornton contemplates on the fact that the killer has taken the brains of the dead girl. Later the Detectives question the dead girl's parents and discover that she too was a member of a book club.

Ramses is feeding lengths of intestine into a simmering pot. He adds a dash of blood then sets out for another special ingredient.

An inebriated man takes his date home and leaves her at her apartment. As the drunk makes his way back to his car Ramses creeps from hiding and knocks on the woman's door. As she opens the door he attacks her, throwing her onto her bed and using his fingers to rip the tongue from her mouth.

Detective Pete Thornton attends a night-school class with his girlfriend, Suzette Fremont. The study course is Ancient Egyptian Cults and the current lesson is about Ishtar and her notorious blood feast ceremony. After the lesson, Pete and Suzette discuss the current murders. He tells her the only real clue is that the killer is old with grey hair and glowing eyes. He also mentions the book club link that has yet to make any sense to him.

As Thornton drives Suzette home, the radio news informs listeners of a new victim of the maniac, but this girl is still alive. Thornton and Mason make for the hospital to question the victim — whose face has been hacked from the bone — and she describes her attacker as a horrible old man with wild eyes who was cutting her face away for "Itar." Thornton thinks the name sounds familiar but can't quite place it.

Ramses turns out to be the proprietor of the book club. Those members who order copies *of Ancient Weird Religious Rites* are selected as his victims. The latest candidate on Ramses' list is a friend of Suzette Fremont, whom Ramses kidnaps and tortures in his secret room, whipping her to death so that he may collect her blood for use in the imminent blood feast. Meanwhile, Thornton has pieced together 'Itar,' 'Ishtar' and Fuad Ramses (the author of *Ancient Weird Religious Rites*), reasoning that the latter is the killer.

Ramses is busy cooking the body parts for the penultimate liturgy of the blood feast. Thornton and Mason rush down to the caterer's store but the man they seek is no longer there. They discover instead the mutilated remains of his last victim and various choice cuts of human meat. Thornton figures they are the leftovers from the prepared blood feast and suddenly realises that Fuad Ramses is catering for his girlfriend, Suzette. Unable to warn the Fremonts by telephone, the Detectives head for the house.

Ramses is already at the house, intending to sacrifice Suzette as the final offering to Ishtar. He lures the girl away from the party guests so as to decapitate her with his machete, but his murderous deed is thwarted when Suzette's mother interrupts. Ramses makes off and heads to the local dump as Thornton and Mason give chase. The mad caterer attempts to evade arrest by hiding in the back of a garbage truck. Unaware of his presence, the truck driver activates the compression mechanism and Ramses is ground to a pulp.

VHS
VIDEO CASSETTE
You'll Recoil and Shudder as You Witness the Slaughter and Mutilation of Nubile Young Girls – in a Weird and Horrendous Ancient Rite!
NOTHING SO APPALLING IN THE ANNALS OF HORROR!
BLOOD FEAST
Starring Connie Mason
Produced by David F. Friedman
Directed by Herschell G. Lewis
COLOR RUNNING TIME 70 MINUTES
CULTVIDEO DISTRIBUTED EXCLUSIVELY IN THE U.K. BY
ASTRA VIDEO
CULTVIDEO
BLOOD FEAST
ASTRA VIDEO

BLOOD FEAST
USA 1963
CAST: **Connie Mason, Mal Arnold, Thomas Wood, Lyn Bolton, Scott H Hall, Toni Calvert**
STORY: **A Louise Downe**
PRODUCER: **David F Friedman**
DIRECTOR: **HERSCHELL GORDON LEWIS**

CRITIQUE: "I've often compared it with a Walt Whitman poem," H G Lewis once said of *Blood Feast*, "it's no good but it's the first."[28]

Made in 1963, *Blood Feast* is the oldest feature to appear on the DPP list.[29] It seems strange that a clumsy, semi-professional film from the early sixties should be caught up in the controversy surrounding an altogether new era of ultra-violent movies on video. The entire film took just about a week to make — though some sources claim production ran to a full nine days on account of rain — and is populated with a cast of unknown actors. The only person whose name may have been familiar at the time of its release is Connie Mason — not an actor *per se*, but a Playboy model. Even director Lewis himself was under no illusions and in 1981 claimed that the film's producer, David Friedman, had "found her under a rock... Connie Mason was not known for her thespian talent. She had talents but they didn't lie in that direction."

No attempt is made to disguise the film's cheapness or the ineptitude of its actors. Mal Arnold, who plays Fuad Ramses, can at times be seen reading his lines — his eyes scanning an off-screen prompt board. In one flashback sequence he portrays an Egyptian pharaoh carrying out a sacrifice. A woman lies on an altar constructed from concrete blocks as Arnold approaches with a snake. As he backs away he obviously catches his heel on something out of shot — an electric cable perhaps? — and stumbles. The film-makers had no time or inclination to do a re-take. But then, the skill of the actors, the quality of the plot, and the abilities of the production crew were irrelevant to the fundamental purpose of *Blood Feast*. The film was made as a vehicle to test a new concept on a movie-going audience: excessively graphic violence.

Within its first minute, *Blood Feast* has imparted to the audience its first violent incident. A woman is stabbed in the eye. The attack may happen off-screen but the resultant carnage is there for all to see, as the killer gloats over a knife smeared with blood and from which hangs loose slivers of flesh. When the woman loses her leg, the process of amputation is obscured by the killer's head and shoulders, but again there is some revelry in the aftermath — a grisly stump of flesh and bone protruding from the soap suds. Later in the film, a victim has her head split open. Again, budgetary restrictions prevent our witnessing the infliction of the injury. But this is amply compensated by the lingering aftermath, which provides a close-up shot of loose brain matter being fondled by the killer. The final excessive gore effect is an off-screen tongue removal, followed by the ghastly sight of the killer holding a dripping (sheep) tongue, roots and all, above the cranberry sauce-filled mouth of his victim.

In 1973, *The Monster Times*[30] classed *Blood Feast* as a negative ground-breaking film and a cinematic-miracle-in-reverse. In other words, one of a number of films "that have succeeded in establishing totally unprecedented standards of atrocious acting, technical ineptitude and execrable [sic] bad taste." Said editor Joe Kane, "We're sorry to report that *Blood Feast* director Herschell G Lewis did not at once fade into the oblivion he so richly deserved."

Indeed he didn't. Sights as gruesome as those presented in *Blood Feast* had never before been seen in cinemas, and the film launched a very profitable film career for Lewis — as well as cementing cult status for him in years to come.

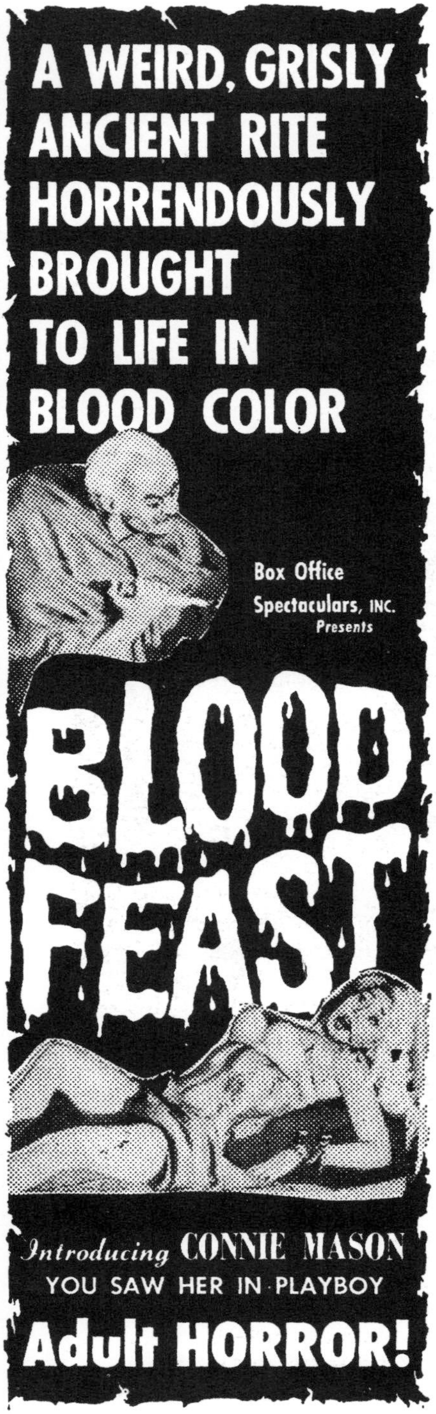
A WEIRD, GRISLY
ANCIENT RITE
HORRENDOUSLY
BROUGHT
TO LIFE IN
BLOOD COLOR
Box Office
Spectaculars, INC.
Presents
BLOOD
FEAST
Introducing CONNIE MASON
YOU SAW HER IN PLAYBOY
Adult HORROR!

Blood Feast was to horror cinema what the Sex Pistols were to rock'n'roll. Lewis and his cohorts had a hit on their hands which was to have an impact on a generation of equally influential film-makers like Tobe Hooper, and wannabes like J G 'Pat' Patterson. They fully intended to exploit their veritable gold mine.

The novelty of gore that *Blood Feast* provided meant that prints of the film would often come back from theatres with key scenes excised by souvenir hunters. At the first anniversary bash of Rick Sullivan's seminal fanzine *Gore Gazette* in November 1981, guest of honour H G Lewis told those in attendance:

> ...one of the problems we always had was getting prints back mangled. Projectionists would cut ten feet out of it, it was a terrible problem because 35mm colour prints were not cheap... some of the prints circulating were cut to shreds and the best effects were gone. What somebody could do with a ten foot 35mm motion picture is beyond me.[31]

(As if this in itself wasn't enough, the film for a time fell into the control of a producer called Stan Kohlberg, who was to cut the front titles off many of the prints and replace them with a card that read "*Blood Feast* made by Stanford Kohlberg.")

Not only did the new popularity and portability of video enable *Blood Feast* to be seen by a completely fresh audience in Britain (thanks to distributors Astra), but it also brought the film renewed interest in its native America. In the seventies *Blood Feast* was regarded by many promoters as kitsch and played as a midnight attraction for a time billed as the "worst film ever made." It took the more discerning video distributors of the eighties to find the right audience for the gore film that started it all.

Lewis followed *Blood Feast* with other gore orientated works, notably *2000 Maniacs* and *Color Me Blood Red* (which, along with *Blood Feast*, constituted Lewis' gore trilogy). Although he made films in other genres, the majority of Lewis' output was horror and he would later direct *Monster A Go-Go*, *A Taste Of Blood*, *The Gruesome Twosome*, *The Wizard Of Gore* and *The Gore Gore Girls*. Although this latter picture extended the atrocities Lewis had begun with *Blood Feast*, offering even more redoubtable carnage (on-screen as well as off), it also showed that after all these films the director had no intention of betraying his cost-cutting acumen:[32] when the finished picture came up short, he didn't bother getting any actors back to shoot additional scenes, but instead stuck two mannequin heads on a table and dubbed dialogue over the top! Many viewers found *The Gore Gore Girls* particularly offensive and misogynistic (one scene shows a woman's nipples being snipped off, with milk pouring from one mutilated teat and chocolate from the other). Lewis evidently determined there was nothing else left for him to show, and with *The Gore Gore Girls* ended his career as a director to concentrate instead on other lines of work, which included writing books on mass communications.

Renewed interest in *Blood Feast* in the eighties led producer Johnny Legend to contact HG Lewis with a view to directing *Blood Feast II* — or *Gore Feast* as it was also announced. Although he had little intention of leaving the "good life" as a writer, word got around that *Blood Feast II* was a viable direct-to-video project in which Lewis had shown serious interest. The film was officially said to be "on ice" in the Winter 1983/84 edition of *The Splatter Times*, no less because Legend had lost the potentially lucrative British market thanks to the video nasties campaign.

Blood Feast was made in the same year as *Carry On Cabby*.

BLOOD RITES

SYNOPSIS: A couple have spent the day on an isolated island and the man decides to take a "look around" alone. He strolls through the woods and comes upon a crazed hunchback who attacks and mutilates him. After ensuring the man is dead the hunchback creeps up on the girl and murders her as well, savagely mutilating her body.

Three sisters, Victoria, Elizabeth and Veronica simultaneously receive a letter from their late father's lawyer, H H Dobbs. They are summoned to his office in New York for an important meeting, whereupon Dobbs informs them that their father has left a will with the specific instruction that the sisters and their husbands must spend three nights in their father's house on the island. Following this a trunk will be brought down from the attic and Dobbs will arrive to read out the terms of the will.

The three women arrive on the island with their husbands Richard, Donald and William. They are met by two maids, Ruth and Martha, and Colin the murderous hunchback. Almost immediately Colin goes into a tantrum as he struggles with the luggage. In his temper he catches a rabbit and eats it alive.

As the guests settle into their rooms they find a huge teddy bear hanging in a closet. One of the maids, Martha, grabs it, quickly insisting they do not touch it as it belongs to Colin. Veronica is suddenly overcome with a strange feeling, one she feels is somehow ominous.

Later, when they retire for the night, Veronica and William find the dead rabbit in their bed, alongside which is a note that reads, "Blessed are the meek for they shall inherit."

Victoria and Robert contemplate the meaning of the note when they are disturbed by a noise in the corridor. Blood is seen seeping under the door. Robert rushes out but finds no one, only a large 'X' daubed in blood on the door. He meets Donald who says he has seen nothing other than a fleeting shadow, and together they go downstairs to investigate. Each taking a drink from a decanter, Robert goes to the cellar and sees someone he recognises, while Donald checks the front door before collapsing, his drink having been drugged.

Victoria is alerted by a noise on the stairs. She goes out to look and finds the body of Robert hanging by its ankles. She collapses in a faint.

The following morning the two maids are discussing the events of the previous night. "Did you tie him up last night?" Ruth asks Martha referring to Colin the hunchback.

Colin takes a bundle of firewood up to Victoria's room and tries to tell her something, but Martha interrupts and sends him away.

Donald is asked to assist Colin with chopping the firewood in the cellar and Martha hands him a leather belt to use on Colin should

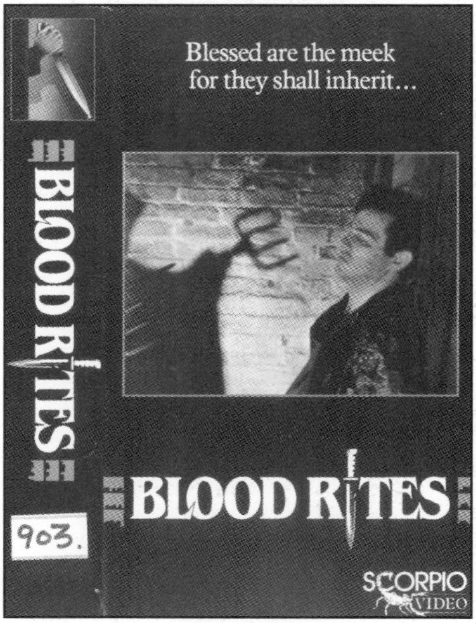
Blessed are the meek
for they shall inherit...
BLOOD RITES
BLOOD RITES
903.
SCORPIO
VIDEO

BLOOD RITES
AKA: The Ghastly Ones (original title)
USA 1967
CAST: Veronica Radburn, Anne Linden, Maggie Rogers, Richards Romanos, Fib La Blaque, Hal Borske, Hal Sherwood, Eileen Haves, Don Williams
STORY: Andy Milligan & Hal Sherwood
PRODUCER: Jerome Fredric
DIRECTOR: ANDY MILLIGAN

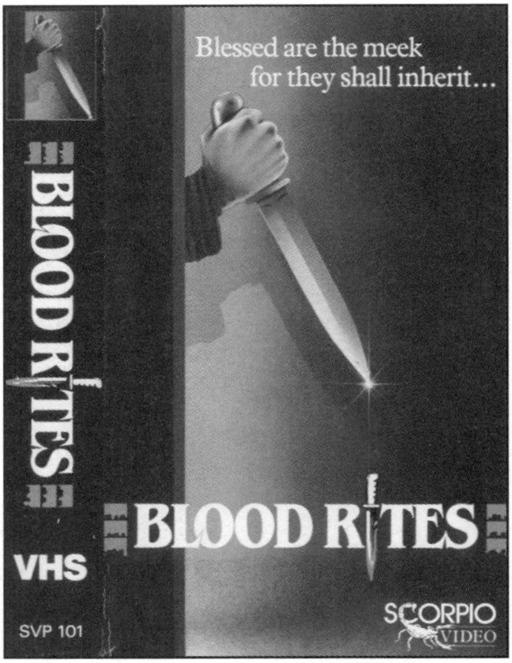

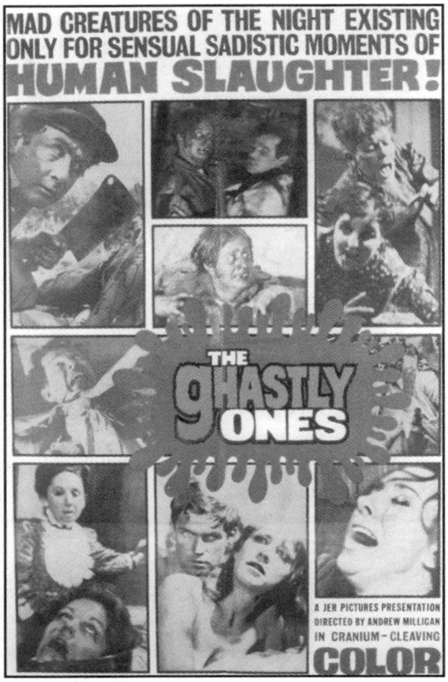

LEFT: ***Blood Rites*** **had a reversible video sleeve (see previous page). This side was for the more discerning video stockist.**
RIGHT: US poster for ***Blood Rites*** **under the film's original title** ***The Ghastly Ones*****.**

he get out of hand. Sorting the wood, Donald finds a plank with a bloody 'X' marked on it when suddenly he is struck from behind. Upon regaining consciousness he finds himself gagged and tied to a workbench. Over him stands a cloaked and hooded figure who proceeds to disembowel him before sawing him in two.

Later, dinner is served and the guests remark on Donald's disappearance. They also enquire after Elizabeth, but the maid assures them she will be down shortly. When the meal is placed on the table it is Elizabeth's severed head that is on the serving dish.

Martha asks William and Colin to bring the trunk down from the attic ready for Lawyer Dobbs, who is scheduled to arrive the following morning. Afterwards, William decides to go in the cellar to look for clues and get to the bottom to the strange things that have been going on. He finds a box, inside which is a photograph. Colin gets himself into a state and snatches the picture away. William is then attacked by the hooded figure and impaled on a pitchfork.

Outside, Martha finds Colin sobbing over the photograph. She takes it from him and realises its significance. Before she can explain she is herself despatched by the hatchet-wielding killer. Colin runs into the house but is caught by the killer on the stairs and set alight. Victoria and Veronica confront the mysterious murderer only to discover that it's actually Ruth the maid, who, it transpires, happens to be their eldest fourth sister. She explains how she intends to kill them, blame all the deaths on Colin and collect the entire inheritance. But Colin is still alive and manages to unbalance Ruth, plunging her down the stairs. The hatchet she carries flies from her hand and implants itself in her head. Victoria and Veronica stare at each other in disbelief.

CRITIQUE: *Blood Rites* is so amateur there are times when the director's agitated instructions to the actors are actually audible on the soundtrack. The colours are washed out and grainy, the film having been shot originally in 16mm on a $700 Auricon camera. But, like the period piece setting, these are characteristic anomalies of an Andy Milligan production and it is Milligan's obvious enthusiasm that makes his films watchable and oddly enjoyable, despite their prevailing inanity.

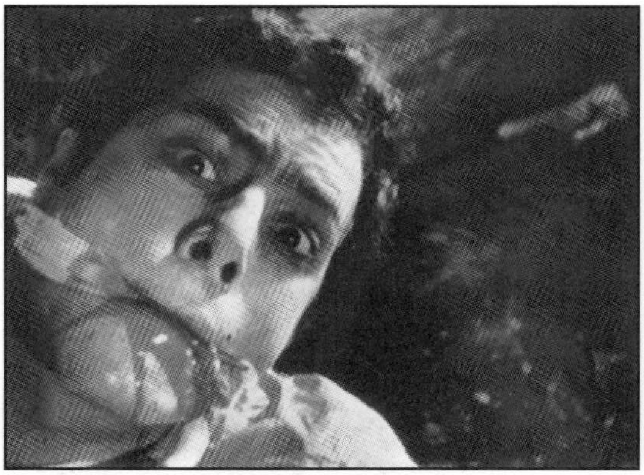

Donald, cut open by the killer in *Blood Rites* – actor Richard Romanus, who later starred in Martin Scorsese's *Mean Streets*.

The soundtrack alternates between static, muffled lines of dialogue and portentous library music. In the pre-credit sequence, when the man leaves his girlfriend to take a look around (the actor interprets "looking around" quite literally, staring into bushes and up at trees as he wanders along), the sound of the undergrowth thumping the microphone is clearly discernible. To pad out the running time, characters will ruminate at great length over the most basic of details — such as the lawyer H H Dobbs' name, and the fact that he's still alive after all these years.

> RICHARD: H H Dobbs? *The* H H Dobbs? Hubert Humphrey Dobbs?... I can't believe it! I thought he'd be dead by now! The first books I read in law school were by H H Dobbs!

The plot of *Blood Rites* has been used countless times over the years since Paul Leni first employed it in his 1927 film, *The Cat and the Canary*. Milligan receives no awards for his own particular red herring ploy (and indeed seems to have completely missed the concept of the diversionary tactic altogether): The viewer perceives Colin as the prime suspect not because he happens to be in the vicinity of each of the killings, but because he is actually seen murdering two people in the opening shot! We *know* Colin is a crazed killer so it's rather condescending to be confronted with the revelation that someone other than him is behind the mystery murders.

However, what Milligan lacks in story line he amply makes up for with his bouts of full frontal gore. The violent moments are few and far between but they stand as being particularly gross, a fact aided immeasurably by the obvious short-comings of the budget — their shoddy execution makes them seem all the more horrible. (Indeed, the effects were created by Milligan himself, who also made the costumes for the cast, drawing on the skills he learned as a dressmaker.)[33] When Colin attacks the lovers in the pre-title sequence, he yanks out the man's eye, only to hold aloft an object that appears to be the size of an apple! His attack on the girl is equally violent and equally unrealistic — he chops off her hand, then lifts her skirt to repeatedly hack at bare mannequin legs.

The murder of Donald (played by Richard Romanus who would go on to secure a central role in Martin Scorsese's *Mean Streets*) is the other main scene of controversy, said by Walter L Gay in *The Sleaze Merchants* to be "realistic enough" to have offended Stephen King. The man is secured to a bench and his shirt is lifted to reveal his bare stomach. The killer then plunges a knife into the abdomen, twisting it, turning it, and pulling out handfuls of bloody matter. Finally a wood saw is used to cut the torso in two. Such scenes are Milligan trademarks.

"The apparent recklessness of the camerawork," noted Tim Lucas of the film in *Video Watchdog*,[34] "lends a tone of accidental, snuff movie authenticity to the slayings."

Another trademark was Milligan's penchant for flailing the camera around in scenes of carnage, which appears a corner-cutting effort to heighten the horror or chaos. During the scene in which William is impaled with a pitchfork, the swirling camera inadvertently reveals a crew member. Other shots are framed peculiarly and are often underlit. Everything is tight and in close-up — indeed there doesn't appear to be a long-shot in the whole movie.

To *Castle of Frankenstein*[35] magazine, Milligan's camera provided some of the "most bleary, indistinct photography ever yet seen." *Demonique*[36] said it was sure to induce eye-straining headaches.

Milligan made several other films with titles bigger and wilder than their content. *Torture Dungeon, Bloodthirsty Butchers, Guru the Mad Monk, The Rats are Coming! The Werewolves*

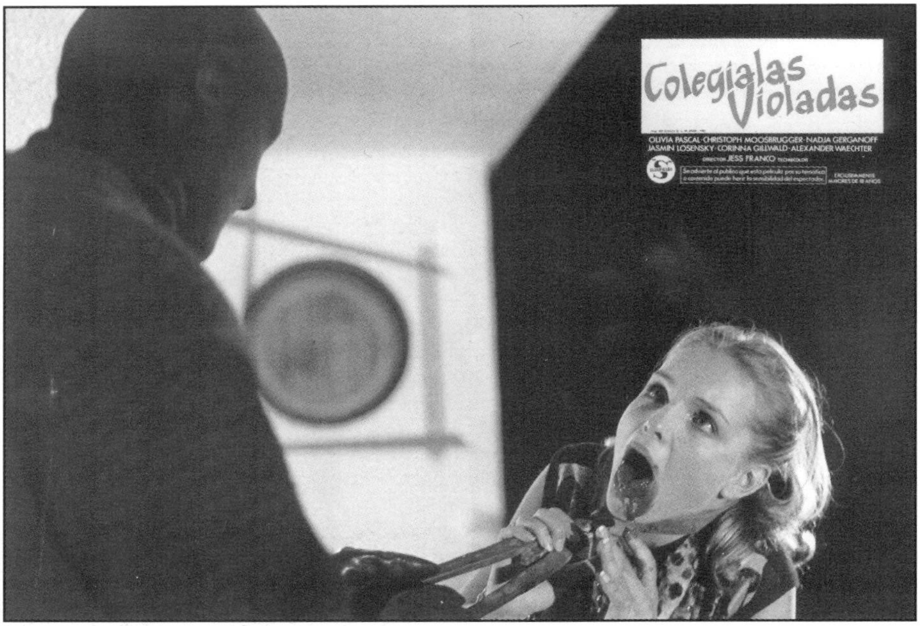

Murder in *Bloody Moon*.

are Here!, *The Man with Two Heads*, *Blood*,[37] and *Carnage* were his most audacious efforts.

Milligan tended to have an effeminate male character at the centre of his films. In *Blood Rites* it is Robert's brother (an incestuous relationship is also heavily implied between the two brothers). In *Torture Dungeon* the Duke of Norfolk describes himself not as bisexual but as "tri-sexual" because he'll "try to have sex with anyone." These characters are obviously intended as an expression of Milligan's own homosexuality, though in real life very few people knew Milligan was gay and the fact only became public with his death from Aids in June 1991.

Blood Rites was released on Scorpio Video without cuts, with a video sleeve that was reversible: one side contained bloody stills from the film, while the other compromised with an inoffensive blood-free artistic representation of a knife.

In 1972, Milligan remade *Blood Rites* as *Legacy of Blood*. Also released on video in the UK this goreless adaptation brought nothing new or different to the story, but served to recoup for Milligan some of the cash he lost on *Blood Rites*. Although the film had turned a tidy profit for its backers J.E.R. Pictures, with whom the director was bound in a three-picture deal,[38] Milligan received only $1,000.

BLOODY MOON

SYNOPSIS: Miguel, a facially disfigured young man, is in the company of his sister Manuela at the Spanish resort owned by their aunt.

"Miguel, don't look at me like that, I'm your sister," she says. "Go back to the dance."

As instructed Miguel makes his way back to the outdoor party. A couple breaks away from the revelry for some privacy. The man removes his Mickey Mouse mask and T-shirt and the loitering Miguel promptly steals them. Now disguised, he meets a girl who mistakes him for somebody else and takes him back to her apartment. On removing his mask she realises her mistake, and is horrified by Miguel's disfigurement. He frantically stabs her to death with a pair of scissors.

Five years later Manuela visits the psychiatric hospital where Miguel has been detained since the murder. She is given custody of her brother but is told, "We can't guarantee your brother is totally cured, therefore you must always keep your eyes open." The doctor also stresses that she must not mention the incident.

Alvaro, the principal at a language school on the resort, is seemingly unconcerned by the financial problems the school is facing. He engages in a discussion with Manuela, which infuriates Maria Gonzales, the ageing and wheelchair-bound Countess who owns the resort. Maria believes her niece, Manuela, is only after her money and tells the girl she has been excluded from her will and that Miguel will now be her sole beneficiary. That night someone invades the Countess' room and attacks her with a burning torch.

As they prepare for a new term at the language school, Angela, one of the students, discusses with her colleagues the rumours about Miguel's murderous past. Unbeknownst to them, Miguel is loitering in the bushes watching. When Angela goes back to her bungalow he follows her, but seeing his reflection in the bathroom mirror she turns and he is gone.

Back at Maria's villa, Miguel approaches his sister in her bedroom.

"For five years I've thought about you, nothing but you," he says as he kisses her legs.

"No Miguel, I'm your sister... We shouldn't start again. Don't you see that people won't let us love each other... If we could just get rid of everyone around us then things could be as they were," she goads.

Following a dance at the resort, Antonio, the general handyman, walks Angela back to her bungalow. They arrange to meet the following day, and Angela is reading in bed when someone breaks in and disconnects the electricity. Before the knife-wielding prowler has a chance to attack however, a fellow student called Eva turns up wanting to borrow a pullover. The intruder stabs her as she tries a garment on for size. Angela runs outside screaming and bumps into Antonio, who calms her and asks to see what has happened, but in the bungalow there is no sign of Eva's body. Antonio finds the book Angela has been reading — a murder mystery story — and concludes it must be her imagination.

The following day during class the girls discuss the missing Eva. Angela hears threats over the headphones the pupils use in their language lessons, and is startled by the sudden appearance of Miguel at the window. She tells Alvaro about the threat on the tuition tape, but when he listens he can find nothing unusual. After class Angela goes in search of Eva and finds the pullover she lent her, stained with blood. She goes down to the harbour and sees Antonio talking to Manuela, and narrowly avoids being crushed by a huge boulder that rolls down the hillside.

Back at the resort she sees Antonio and asks him if he will help her to find Eva. Reluctantly he agrees, but as he takes his garden shears back to the greenhouse notices a snake crawling down the tree under which Angela sits. He rushes back and cuts off the snake's head but Angela, seeing the bloody shears brandished before her, runs away thinking Antonio is the killer.

Angela catches a glimpse of Inga, another student, going by in the Countess' car. The anonymous driver takes the girl out of town to an empty quarry, whereupon Inga is bound to a large stone slab. At first believing it to be part of a kinky sex game, a switch is suddenly thrown and a stone-cutting saw starts up, decapitating Inga. The killer gets in the car and drives back to town, running over a child who had witnessed the incident.

Packing her bags in preparation to leave the resort, Angela attacks a shadowy figure in her bungalow and runs outside to tell Laura she has killed the prowler. Laura investigates and sees it is nothing more than a mannequin, but as Laura goes back to her own bungalow she is attacked and murdered. Angela finds Inga's severed head in her bed and Eva's body behind a curtain. The masked intruder attacks her too but Miguel comes to her assist-

BLOODY MOON
AKA: Die Säge des Todes (original title); Colegialas Violadas; Profonde tenebre
SPAIN/WEST GERMANY 1981
CAST: Olivia Pascal, Christopher Moosbrugger, Nadja Gerganoff, Alexander Waechter, Jasmin Losensky, Corinna Gillwald
STORY: Rayo Casablance
PRODUCER: Wolf C Hartwig
DIRECTOR: JESÚS FRANCO

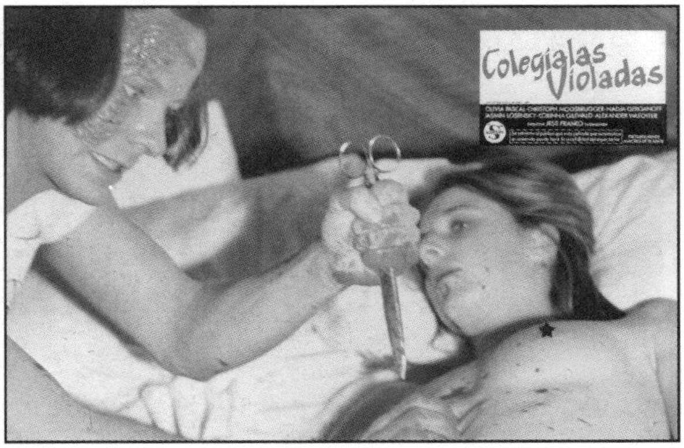

More scenes of mayhem from *Bloody Moon*.
ABOVE: Miguel stabs his blind date.

ance. Angela escapes to the villa and tells Manuela what has been happening. Manuela offers her a drink laced with a drug.

Alvaro comes to the villa and is informed by Manuela that Angela is upstairs and he must kill her like all the others. Manuela's plan is to blame all the murders on Miguel so she can claim the inheritance, and admits that she doesn't love Alvaro.

Having overheard this conversation, Miguel later enters his sister's bedroom only to discover that it is Angela not Manuela in the bed. She wakes up screaming and stabs him in the throat. Running from the room she sees the Countess in her wheelchair and asks for help, only to discover she is dead and horribly burned. Alvaro grabs Angela but before he can kill her Manuela attacks and murders him with a hedge-trimmer, warning Angela to keep silent as the police arrive otherwise she too will be killed. Before he dies, Miguel is able to muster the strength to kill his sister.

CRITIQUE: More of a 'proper' movie than Jesús Franco's usual efforts, *Bloody Moon* still remains an ordeal to sit through. ("You hope the camera remains focused," was the best one critic could wish for of a Franco movie.)[39] Using a tired murder-to-gain-a-family-inheritance plot, like ***Blood Rites*** it opens with a scene identifying a murderous character — in this case Miguel — who happens to be in the vicinity of each subsequent murder but ultimately turns out to be a red herring.

A certain porno quality pervades the film, largely thanks to the fact that every female character looks like a glamour model for whom the boarding school setting is nothing much more than a perfect opportunity to lounge around the pool and hold dance-mad disco parties. (They dance to a weird hybrid of Europop and rock'n'roll tunes, jiving to one particularly asinine record whose lyric comprises only of the words "Shake your baby" and "Rock your baby.")

The largely insinuated incestuous relationship between Manuela and Miguel, which is afforded plenty of angst-ridden screen time is, not surprisingly, just another lame red herring. "If we could just get rid of everyone around us," a frustrated Manuela says at one point, "then things could be as they were." Miguel stares into the distance with menacing intent.

There is one sequence in *Bloody Moon* which does threaten to conjure some genuine atmosphere — that in which Angela hears the killer's voice on her tuition tape — but Franco is more content to take easier routes, and bestow the story with half-hearted, curiously inappropriate diversions in a bid to build and sustain suspense. For instance, every time a student is alone in a darkened room and we are led to believe that the killer is about to strike, Franco will interject some unlikely alternative to the prowler — such a cat or a mannequin throwing a shadow on the wall. In one especially hapless ploy, a little boy is outside the house selling "souvenirs" in the middle of the night.

All the murders take place at night under a full moon. Why this should be the case isn't clear, although it does provide the film with plenty of foreboding full-moon cutaways.

Without a doubt, the most convincing and engaging aspect of *Bloody Moon* are the gruesome special effects (although this doesn't extend to Miguel's disfigured face makeup, which looks nothing so much as a pancake mix gone wrong). The prologue depicting the murder of the girl by Miguel shows him stabbing his victim in the abdomen. The scissors are seen repeatedly penetrating the girl's bare midriff in close-up. When Eva is murdered the knife is shown entering her back and exiting in similarly fine detail through her right breast. Blood on breasts and knives coming into contact with breasts have always been a taboo subject with the BBFC, and it is no surprise that this scene was removed from the certified version of the film some years later.

The decapitation of Inga on the stone saw is probably the most gruelling sequence of all. Not simply because it is depicted in graphic detail, but because the whole process is so slow and protracted — thanks to Franco's unwillingness to waste a single frame of the heavyweight machine as it encroaches on its victim in real time. (The actress is actually secured to real cutting equipment and the machinery propels her alarmingly close to the spinning blade.) To lend some sort of credibility to the whole unlikely scenario, the victim is under the supposed misconception that being tied to rock by a masked stranger is a prelude to some kinky sex. Her unintentionally ridiculous dialogue comprises lines like "I said I was game for anything!"

The sequence is a parody of the clichéd scene from early westerns where the female lead is captured by the masked villain and tied to a railway line. Like the train being stopped at the last moment by the hero, in this instance the blade is stopped inches from the victim's neck by an intervening child who happens to be playing nearby. However, the girl is not rescued from her fate and the man in black restarts the equipment. This time there is a decapitation from which the camera doesn't flinch. The blood that spurts from the resultant stump could be construed as a cheap porn-gore pop shot, if one suspected the wayfaring Franco to be so inclined...

Bloody Moon was released by Interlight Video in a cut as well as an uncut version. Following its ban it was later re-released heavily cut with an 18 certificate on the resurrected Vipco label.

THE BOGEY MAN
TITLE ON PRINT: THE BOGEY MAN
USA 1980
CAST: Suzanna Love, Ron James, John Carradine, Introducing Nicholas Love, Llewelyn Thomas
STORY: Ulli Lommel
PRODUCER: Ulli Lommel
DIRECTOR: ULLI LOMMEL

THE BOGEY MAN

SYNOPSIS: Two children, Willy and Lacey, spy on their drunken mother entertaining a man friend. The woman places one of her stockings over the man's head for a bit of fun when she spots the children at the window. Lacey is sent to her room, but Willy is gagged by the man and tied to a bed. While the adults pick up where they left off,

Lacey cuts her brother free. The man is still wearing the stocking over his head when Willy stabs him repeatedly in the back.

Cut to the present. Lacey and Willy are now adults living with their aunt and uncle on a farm. Lacey is married to Jake and has a son called Kevin, but Willy remains traumatised and hasn't spoken a word since that fateful night.

Lacey tells a priest that she's "afraid something's going to happen." But he claims that no calamity will befall her because she's a Christian. Soon after, a letter arrives from the mother neither she nor Willy have seen for twenty years. The old crone believes she's dying and wishes to see her children one last time. The thought of seeing her mother again however, fills Lacey with dread and Willy takes the letter to his room and burns it.

That night Lacey wakes screaming from a nightmare in which she is being dragged in her underwear across a floor and tied to a bed. Her unseen captor sharpens a set of knives.

Lacey goes to see Dr Warren and under hypnosis says in a gruff voice: "I'll be back and I'm gonna get you!"

The doctor advises Lacey to confront her fears, and agrees with her husband Jake that she should be taken to visit her mother, stopping off along the way at the old house where she grew up. Fortuitously, Lacey's childhood home is up for sale and the couple raise no suspicion posing as prospective buyers. Two teenage sisters show them around as Timmy, a younger brother, plays the fool. Lacey wanders into her mother's old bedroom and is shocked to see a reflection of the stockinged-headed man — murdered all those years ago by Willy. The room behind her is empty, but in the mirror the figure rises from the bed and moves slowly towards her. Lacey screams and smashes the mirror. Apologising to the two girls, Jake escorts his wife and the pieces of the mirror away.

Willy meanwhile is receiving the unwanted attentions of a local girl who has come to collect eggs from the farm. She tells the mute that she likes him because he's different from other boys, but Willy has a psychotic episode and tries to throttle her, letting her go when he sees his reflection in a mirror. He then paints all the mirrors in the house black — excluding the one Jake has just brought home. Jake obsessively fits the tiny shards of his mirror back together as the rest of the household look on.

"Would you mind telling us what this is all about?" Uncle Ernest snaps angrily.

"Wouldn't it be simpler just to get another mirror?" says Aunt Helen.

Peering at her own fragmented image, Lacey tells her husband she sees "Nothing. Nothing but ordinary reflections."

Pieces of a mirror, which mysteriously arrive at Willy's feet in a brown paper bag, later cause a pitchfork in the barn to levitate and narrowly miss impaling him.

Back in the property for sale, a lone glass shard glows red on the floor. The sound of a heartbeat and heavy breathing signifies a malevolent spirit moving around the old house. It forces one of the sisters to cut her T-shirt and then drive a pair of scissors into her throat. The second sister is killed when the door of the bathroom cabinet suddenly swings open and bashes her on the head. Timmy, playing another prank, gets his neck broken.

Lacey takes her son Kevin down to the pier for a spot of fishing. Another stray shard — which has ejected itself from Jake's mirror mosaic — becomes fastened to the sole of the boy's shoe and its reflection in the sunlight wreaks deadly havoc on a group of nearby teenagers. One of the youths becomes distracted by the sound of a heartbeat and heavy breathing, and in an effort to locate its origins sits in his car. A knife on the backseat propels itself through his neck and out his mouth. The boy's girlfriend is also skewered on the knife when she leans into the car and the door slams into the back of her.

After he catches a fish Lacey takes Kevin home, oblivious to the carnage they leave behind. At the farm her blouse starts to rip by itself and Jake struggles against an unseen force to return a sliver back to the mirror. Lacey is adamant that her mother's lover has come back. "When I broke the mirror," she announces, "I released him. Now he's gonna get us."

Uncle Ernest phones for Father Reilly, while Jake goes to see Dr Warren. He quickly returns when the doctor begins to relate the case history of a similar incident, asking Father Reilly whether he believes "in evil as a tangible force." The priest touches the piecemeal mirror and the room starts to glow red. Unbeknownst to them a shard ejects itself and becomes lodged over Lacey's right eye.

Both Ernest and Helen are discovered dead in the barn. When Jake tries to call the sheriff the phone explodes. When they gaze upon Lacey's 'mirror-eye' blood begins to pour down the faces of both Jake and Father Reilly. However, armed with a crucifix, the priest manages to remove the shard and dispose of it down the sink where it bursts into flames.

Jake's mirror is thrown into the well, sending a fireball and an agonised scream into the night sky.

The nightmare seems over and Willy has regained the power of speech, but a last mirror shard is still fastened to the sole of Kevin's shoe. It becomes dislodged and starts to glow as the remaining members of the family prepare to start life anew.

CRITIQUE: *The Bogey Man* is a modestly effective horror movie which tries to invigorate the teens-in-peril sub-genre with a supernatural twist and some extraordinary deaths. Indeed, it accomplishes what it sets out to do without the chest-beating of its follow-up, ***Revenge of the Bogeyman*** (which also found itself on the DPP list), and seems a positive masterpiece by comparison.

With a protagonist whose face remains obscured and who doesn't say a word it's safe to say that Lommel was inspired by John Carpenter's *Halloween* – a film that would be lambasted as being "old hat" in Lommel's follow-up – even down to his use of a main theme that is reminiscent of Carpenter's synthesiser score.

There's a lot of wandering around in almost complete darkness (table lamps provide no discernible illumination), some lame shock tactics (hands reach out menacingly but belong to friends and family not to monsters), and one protracted sequence which fails to go anywhere at all (the carving of a chicken at a dinner table which is accompanied by wrought looks from Lacey and portentous music). Lommel, however, does come up with a few solidly paced scare scenes, notably Lacey being menaced by a reflection in a mirror that doesn't correlate with the room behind her.

The emphasis placed on mirrors gives *The Bogey Man* not only an unusual twist, but also strains of folklore and superstition. For instance, the aforementioned sequence has origins in the belief that peering into a mirror in a death-chamber will reflect a corpse looking over your shoulder. It's a sequence that works well in itself, but the reluctance of the film-makers to exploit the lore to which they're subscribing leaves other scenes quirky and abstract. On the surface there is no rhyme or reason why Willy should get spooked by his own reflection in the barn, or why he should paint all the mirrors in the house black. But looking deeper, these actions do carry a mythical significance that the film is reluctant to divulge.[40] Similarly the mysterious appearance of a paperbag containing mirror shards may seem weird on the surface, but it represents an undisclosed symbolic link: i.e. placing the pieces of a broken mirror into a bag and burying it was thought to counteract any bad luck generated by breaking it in the first place.

Apart from a few oblique references – such as the smashing of a mirror freeing from it everything it's seen – the film-makers don't share with the audience the mythology drawn upon in their story, which is a shame as given this context one feels *The Bogey Man* would be a much stronger work.

German critics of *The Bogey Man* were inclined to read it as not so much a horror film but a social commentary on teenagers in America.[41] A curious stance, no doubt influenced by Lommel having had tutelage under Rainer Werner Fassbinder, the leading voice in Germany's "new cinema."[42] After *Bogey Man*, Lommel's work remained steadfastly in an American vein but with some idiosyncratic ideas and occasional art-house diversions.[43] Certainly in this, his American debut, there is a peculiarity to the way he orchestrates the demise of several (superfluous) players. The deaths of the two sisters and their annoying younger brother, for instance, happen in close succession but the hierarchy seems all wrong: first a sister suffers a gory scissors-impaling after cutting through her T-shirt,[44] then her brother gets his neck broken and finally the remaining sister receives a fatal knock on the head from the door of a bathroom cabinet! No blood, no nipples – nothing.

The scene in which the young man gets a knife through his neck whilst seated in his car is laughably contrived, but this at least has a satisfyingly bloody, genuinely eerie climax.

Both of the above incorporate close-ups of sharp objects penetrating flesh, and rank high in reasons why *The Bogey Man* should have ended up on the DPP list. Other contributing factors may have included images of a distraught child being tied to a bed and gagged, and a bound Lacey being dragged across a floor, tied to a bed and threatened with knives.

Rumour has it that *The Bogey Man* encountered several production problems, notably the disappearance of the soundtrack and a freak snowstorm. These may or may not have contributed to the boom microphone straying into shot and staying there for the duration of Dr Warren's first dialogue. (The 'arty' composition of this sequence – via a mirror no less – ensures that the rogue microphone takes prime position).

And the icing on the cake: Lacey never does get to meet her mother.

THE BURNING

SYNOPSIS: At Camp Blackfoot a group of male campers play a prank on the camp caretaker Cropsy. They creep into his cabin and place a worm-riddled skull with candles burning in the eye sockets at the foot of his bed. Outside, they bang on the window until Cropsy wakes. He sees the glowing head and kicks out at it sending it tumbling onto his bedclothes. Within moments the room is ablaze and Cropsy is caught up in the fire. He eventually escapes engulfed in flame and falls into the lake. The caretaker survives the fire but is horribly disfigured and spends the next five years in hospital undergoing unsuccessful skin grafts. He leaves the hospital wearing a heavy coat and hat to hide his dreadful features. The first thing he does is visit a prostitute but she is repulsed by his appearance. Enraged, he attacks and kills her.

At Camp Stonewater the campers are playing baseball. Retrieving the ball when it is sent into the woods, a girl remains blissfully unaware that Cropsy is creeping up on her brandishing a pair of shears. Before he can attack she finds the ball and runs back to the playing field.

Taking a shower the following morning, Sally hears someone creeping through the cubicle door. She screams and Michelle and Todd run to the showers to find Alfred, the camp misfit, lurking there. He says he was only trying to scare Sally. Glazer — Sally's boyfriend — warns Alfred to keep away. That night Alfred sees Cropsy's face appear at the window but it is gone before anyone else sees anything.

The next day the older campers set off on a canoe trip to Devil's Creek where they will spend the next three days. At night, with the campers gathered round a fire, Todd relates the story of Cropsy. Suddenly, Eddie jumps amongst them wearing a mask and swinging a machete. Everyone laughs at the jape. Eddie takes Karen down to the lake for some skinny dipping. But Eddie comes on too strong for Karen and she leaves only to find that someone has scattered her clothes about the woods. As she collects them Cropsy grabs her and cuts her throat.

THE BURNING
USA 1980
CAST: Brian Matthews, Leah Ayres, Brian Backer, Larry Joshua, Jason Alexander, Ned Eisenberg, Carrick Glenn
STORY: Peter Lawrence, Brad Grey, Bob Weinstein, Harvey Weinstein, Tony Maylam
PRODUCER: Harvey Weinstein
DIRECTOR: TONY MAYLAM

With Karen still missing the following day, Michelle and Todd question Eddie as to her whereabouts. He tells them they had a slight falling out but nothing serious. Someone notices that all the canoes have gone. Glazer blames Alfred for no apparent reason. Todd suspects that Karen took one to go back to Stonewater and accidentally let the others loose. Constructing a raft, several campers volunteer to go back to Stonewater and get assistance. As they paddle down the river they come across one of the canoes and move in closer in order to salvage it. Cropsy is lying in wait however, and all the campers are summarily murdered.

Awaiting the return of their companions, Sally and Glazer break off into the woods to have sex. Having left Sally to get some matches for a fire, Glazer returns to find his girlfriend murdered in the sleeping bag and is also set upon by Cropsy who pins him to a tree with a pair of shears. Alfred witnesses the killing and runs back to camp to alert Todd, who at first suspects Alfred of playing a prank. When finally he agrees to follow him to the woods he finds Glazer's body. Alfred shouts a warning to Todd who, too late, is struck unconscious by Cropsy. Cropsy chases Alfred.

When the raft floats into view, Michelle swims out and finds the butchered remains of her colleagues. Recovering consciousness, Todd makes his way back to the camp and tells Michelle and the remaining campers to take the raft back to Stonewater while he goes in search of Alfred. Alfred meanwhile, has found Cropsy's hideout — a derelict building in the heart of the woods. As he wanders around the ruins Cropsy grabs him and pins him to the wall with his shears. Todd hears Alfred's cries and rushes to his aid. Todd and Cropsy confront each other — Todd carrying an axe, Cropsy a flamethrower. It transpires that Todd was one of the group responsible for the ill-fated prank on Cropsy all those years ago. Todd is knocked to the ground and Cropsy advances with the torch. Alfred manages to pull the shears from the wall and drive them into Cropsy's back. As a police helicopter arrives, Todd and Alfred make their way out of the building but Cropsy springs up again. Todd swings the axe and pins him to a supporting beam while Alfred gets the flame-thrower and sets Cropsy alight.

Cut to an indeterminate future where a group of campers, seated around a campfire, listen to the updated story of Cropsy and how his body was never found....

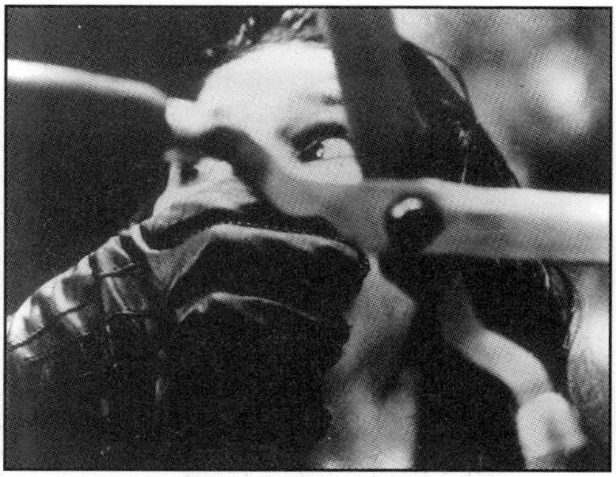

Promiscuity – and shears – brings death in *The Burning*.

CRITIQUE: *The Burning* is an uninspired retread of *Friday the 13th* even down to the similar Summer Camp setting in which a group of teenagers are selectively murdered one-by-one in grisly fashion. Such a basic idea when attached to a simplistic plot yields very little in the way of absorbing entertainment. Indeed, for things to happen and the story to 'progress,' people have to behave in a stupid and irrational manner: having sex in unlikely places, for instance, or wandering alone in dark woods.

There is an attempt to inject the proceedings with some *Porky's*-style slapstick humour (a film made the same year and also aimed at a predominately teen audience). At times it succeeds, notably in the scene in which the obnoxious Glazer is shot in the pants with an air pistol. When *The Burning* endeavours to shock however, it fails miserably, simply because it declines to stray from hackneyed formulae and chooses instead to offer clichés. A bird suddenly flying out from behind an opened door accompanied by a jolt on the soundtrack, for example, irritates rather than startles. The teen sex sequences and imperilled shower scene are simply *de rigueur* – as is the sudden lunging into shot of the apparently dead killer at the end.

Matters aren't helped at all by Rick Wakeman's vitriolic soundtrack (comprising "electronic janglings"[45] wherever Cropsy goes), or by the generally apathetic performances of the cast. However, two young actors who marked their debut in *The Burning* did go on to greater things – Jason Alexander and Holly Hunter.[46]

The clever special effects were created by Tom Savini who was considered something of a maestro in horror prosthetics at the time, having worked on *Friday the 13th* and many subsequent successful genre productions. (Savini turned down *Friday the 13th Part 2* in order to work on *The Burning*.) As tended to be the case on many of the films in which he was involved, Savini's gruesome decapitations and imaginatively staged mayhem provided the core around which everything else revolved. It's probably fair to say that the American stalk-and-slash genre owes as much to Savini's ingenious prosthetic skills as it does the influence of Mario Bava's ***Blood Bath***.

Thanks to Savini, for a time during the eighties the special effects man was held in almost as high a regard as the director. Many fans flocked to see horror films because they featured the talents of Rob Bottin (*The Thing*), Rick Baker (*Videodrome*), and other rising stars all creating unique, larger-than-life, mind-blowing fantasies on the screen. The popularity of these artists ensured that the appearance of their names in a film's credits was interpreted as an endorsement, and would often draw audiences in to an otherwise unremarkable picture – as was the case with Savini and the likes of *Rosemary's Killer*, ***Nightmares in a Damaged Brain*** and, of course, *The Burning*.

When Thorn EMI submitted *The Burning* to the BBFC, fifteen seconds of cuts were requested for a pre-VRA X-certificate. These cuts were agreed upon, but the company inadvertently mass-produced and released duplicates of the uncut master. The result was that in September 1983, police raided Thorn EMI offices and seized the master-tape and videocassette copies of the film. On June 21, 1984, Uxbridge Magistrates Court cleared the company of obscenity charges. (Defending, Richard Du Cann said that *The Burning* was "simply a bogeyman story... The horrific scenes take up only a minuscule amount of a film predominantly made up of some of the most boring teenage dialogue you are ever likely to witness.")

Although Thorn EMI recalled the uncut tape and offered to replace it free-of-charge with the slightly shorter certified version, not everyone did so. The company repeated its offer when the film was cleared of obscenity, and warned dealers that continued distribution of the uncensored print would be liable to prosecution.

The cut version of *The Burning* was identifiable by a date stamp on a two-colour label, as opposed to the uncut version which was date-free with a single-colour label. Another giveaway was that the two versions could also be identified by the thickness of the videobox lid: the cut version was released in a standard video case, while the uncut film was enclosed in a more substantial heavy-duty box.

The censored film was ultimately re-released by Vipco.

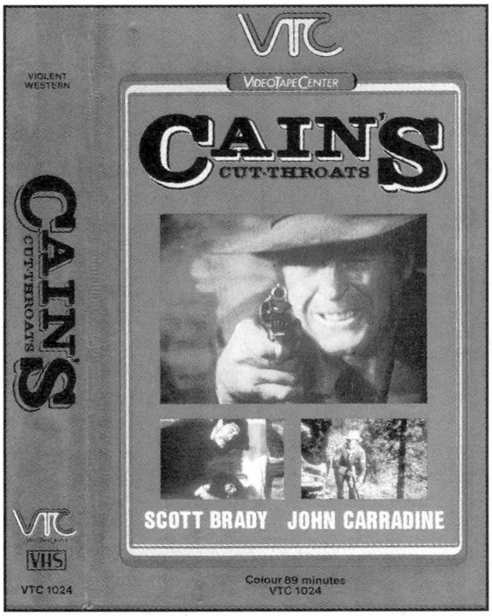

CAIN'S CUTTHROATS
AKA: Cain's Way; Caine's Way; The Blood Seekers; Justice Cain
USA 1969
CAST: John Carradine, Scott Brady, Bruce Kimball, Russ McCubbin, Tereza Thaw, Valda Hansen
STORY: Will Denmark
PRODUCERS: Kent Osborne & Budd Dell
DIRECTOR: KENT OSBORNE

CAIN'S CUTTHROATS

SYNOPSIS: The year is 1870. A gang of outlaws, led by one-eyed Amison, ambush a Yankee payroll wagon and a brief shootout ensues before the Yankee soldiers are overpowered. Billy Joe, one of the gang members, jumps into the back of the wagon to collect the money chest and finding it chained to the wrist of an old soldier, hacks off the man's hand. Once they have the money the gang shoot dead the soldiers as well as a wounded colleague, whose injuries would only slow them down.

Amison says they will visit their wartime leader, Captain Justice Cain, so they can form an army to take on the Yankees again. Cain, now living on a farmstead with his wife and child, is not pleased to see the men from his past but tells them they can water their horses and use his tools to break open the chest. When Amison makes known his proposition, Cain points out that the war is over and that he personally wants nothing more to do with violence. Trying to change his mind, Billy Joe grabs Cain and reminds him that in the past he would have obeyed any order for the captain.

"Take your hands off me you simple little bastard," shouts Cain.

"You should not have said that" retorts Billy Joe. "I think the world of you, but you shouldn't call me no bastard."

Cain's wife comes out to see what the commotion is about.

"A nigger!" shouts one of the men. "The captain's married to a high and mighty nigger!"

A scuffle ensues and the gang jump Cain, beating him up. Cain's wife tries to help but is thrown down whereupon Amison decides that she should be raped. With Cain tied to a post and his young boy brought out to watch, Amison is first to take the woman. When he's done, Billy Joe takes his place but the woman flinches and sends the young outlaw into a rage. He beats her to death. Cain yells at him, again calling him a "bastard" and Billy Joe responds by shooting both him and his son. The gang set fire to the house and leave.

A travelling preacher by the name of Simms notices the fire and finds Cain alive, vowing to kill the men who murdered his wife and child. They team-up when Cain learns that Simms is not only a preacher, but also a bounty hunter already on the trail of the Amison gang. Simms asks that Cain doesn't mutilate the heads of the outlaws, as the heads are all he requires to collect the reward.

They are able to catch up and kill two gang members by nightfall, before the others are alerted and escape. The following day they find a third having sex and Cain shoots him in the head.

"I distinctly asked you not to mutilate the heads," Simms complains. Unconcerned about the death of her partner, Rita asks if she can join the two men, promising to lead them to Amison in return.

Elsewhere, there is the threat of revolt as gang member Barrett wants to take off with all the money. Amison remonstrates that Cain is close on their trail and suggests they should turn the tables and hunt him down instead. They find Cain with his two companions camped by a river, and open fire from a ridge but find themselves quickly being outgunned and pinned down. Amison talks Barrett into surrendering so that he can get a shot at Cain, but double-crosses his colleague and shoots him in the back before making off.

Barrett is still alive and Rita says they should get him to a doctor. She awakens the following morning to discover the outlaw has died and suspects the unsympathetic Cain of having killed him in the night.

In a nearby town, Billy Joe prepares to spend some of his money on a prostitute. She is disgusted however, when he refers to her as his mother. Billy Joe strangles her and in his drunken state runs to a water trough where he is shot in the chest and groin by Cain. As he lies dying Billy Joe tells Cain that Amison has been captured and is going to be executed. Rita and Simms are appalled with Cain for prolonging the man's death.

Now alone, Cain finds Amison as he faces a Yankee firing squad. Moments before he is executed, Amison taunts Cain for failing to kill him personally as promised.

CRITIQUE: *Cain's Cutthroats* is an obscure western using a regularly utilised plot in which a decent man seeks revenge on those who murdered his kinfolk. (It was virtually remade as *The Deadly Trackers* starring Richard Harris in 1973.) Although the film slows down considerably after the first twenty minutes it is unusually brutal for its time — the gang rape of the mother in front of her young son being particularly truculent. After this, the film changes pace completely. Indeed, Cain loses the sympathy of his hardened travelling companions when he shoots the deranged Billy Joe in the groin and chest, then slaps the dying man around in order to extract information. "It ain't natural," retorts Simms before he and Rita ride off, leaving Cain behind.

The cast are typical B-movie types and the ubiquitous John Carradine obviously revels in his role of the ambiguous preacher-cum-bounty hunter, delivering Biblical platitudes the one moment and hacking the head from a corpse the next. He also delivers some of the best lines, saying of the outlaw who is killed whilst having sex: "He wenteth before he cameth." (For no discernible reason, Simms dresses up as a woman during the shootout with Amison and Barrett on the ridge.)

At times, the camaraderie between Simms and Cain is reminiscent of the light-hearted episodes that would off-set the violence in westerns from Clint Eastwood's Malpaso film company (such as *The Outlaw Josey Wales*, which also bears a thematic resemblance to *Cain's Cutthroats*).

Cain's Cutthroats appeared briefly on a listing of banned and suspect titles in the video trade press, a fact which has largely been forgotten by collectors and genre historians, possibly due to the film being a western as opposed to a horror picture. The violence generally consists of brief though fairly bloody shootouts in the style of *The Wild Bunch* — made the same year — with the gang revelling in the brutality. They bicker like schoolchildren when not committing some misdeed on other people; acts of murder and rape cause them to laugh uncontrollably. One of the first victims to fall to the gang, a Yankee soldier on the payroll wagon, is shot in the belly bringing a fleeting glimpse of a gaping, offal-wound. (Notably, *Soldier Blue* was made the following year.) But it is probably the rape sequence that caused most concern, even if it isn't unduly explicit. The continuous racial insults and the fact that a minor is forced to watch certainly intensifies the unpleasant event.

The film was released uncertified on the VTC label under the category of "violent western." Prior to this, in 1978, it had a theatrical run as *Cain's Way*, shorn of four minutes. Under this title however, the film appears to have run on slightly longer, making more of the futility of Cain's plight. (Cain is abandoned because, as the preacher puts it, he is no longer motivated by revenge but by "a lust for killing.") According to the *Monthly Film Bulletin*, the execution of Amison at the film's end causes Cain, cheated of his prey, to fall to his knees in front of the body. The VTC print on the other hand ends suddenly with a freeze frame of Amison's slumped body, over which the credits play.[47]

Cain's Cutthroats marked Kent Osborne's only foray into directing. As an actor, Osborne appeared in a number of movies by low-budget film-maker Al Adamson, one of which was a western entitled *Five Bloody Graves* made in 1969 (featuring a narrator in the form of Death!). The two productions share several of the same cast members — no less Scott Brady (who plays Cain in *Cain's Cutthroats*) and John Carradine, who plays a preacher in both — and there is every likelihood that they were made back-to-back. The two film-makers certainly appear to have spurred one another on with a desire to make a raw and gritty western, far removed from the other westerns of this era: Walter L Gay in *The Sleaze Merchants* describes Adamson's *Five Bloody Graves* as a "savage storm of ferocious Indian assaults, shooting, rape, torture, and assorted other mayhem."

CANNIBAL APOCALYPSE
AKA: Apocalypse Domani (original title); Cannibals in the Streets; Invasion of the Flesh Hunters; Savage Apocalypse
ITALY/SPAIN 1980
CAST: John Saxon, John Morghen, Elizabeth Turner, Tony King, Cindy Hamilton, Ray Williams
STORY: Anthony M Dawson, José Luis Martinez Molla, Dardano Sacchetti, Maurizio & Sandro Amati
PRODUCERS: Maurizio & Sandro Amati
DIRECTOR: ANTHONY M DAWSON [Antonio Margheriti]

CANNIBAL APOCALYPSE

SYNOPSIS: During the conflict in Vietnam a rescue team is sent out to retrieve American prisoners of war. Norman Hopper commands one such team and leads a raid on a Vietcong lair where two GIs are held. The captive soldiers, Bukowski and Thompson, are confined in a dug out cell. A gun battle results in the destruction of the Vietcong and a burning soldier falls into the pit. The two soldiers grab the burning body and attempt to devour it. Hopper finds the men and offers a hand to them, but Thompson lunges and bites his outstretched arm.

Hopper wakes from his flashback nightmare. He goes downstairs to get a drink from the refrigerator and is drawn to the raw, dripping meat on the shelf. Jane, his wife, is concerned about his psychological state. She speaks to Bill, a doctor from the Hospital of Nervous Disorders who had initially treated her husband. He tells her not to worry as Bukowski and Thompson were more serious cases than Hopper but are now practically cured.

While Jane is at work, Mary the young niece of Hopper's neighbour, calls round to borrow a hairdryer. He invites her in and she makes a pass at him. The telephone rings and it's Bukowski informing Hopper of his release from hospital, reminding him of their time together in Vietnam and asking him to come out for a drink. Hopper refuses and turns his attention back to Mary. He raises her pullover to kiss her stomach but her reaction is one of pain — as if she has just been bitten.

Bukowski visits a cinema to watch a war movie. In front of him sit a couple who show more interest in each other than the film playing. Unable to resist, Bukowski bites a chunk of flesh from the woman's shoulder and is pursued from the cinema into a shopping mall by a gang of bikers. Having found a rack of shotguns and ammunition in a store, Bukowski blasts a biker and a security guard to death.

The police lay siege to the building trapping Bukowski inside and he opens fire when officers ask him to come out. Jane hears the news of a Vietnam vet being involved in a shootout and, worried that it might be her husband, phones home. She is relieved when Hopper answers. Hearing of the situation at the mall, Hopper concludes it must be Bukowski and goes to investigate. Hopper is able to convince Bukowski to give himself up.

Bukowski is taken to the hospital where his army buddy Thompson is a patient and together they attack the head nurse, managing to inflict a severe bite on her leg before being dragged off her. Dr Morris cannot understand the relapse in the men's behaviour and has them both restrained and drugged.

Bill phones Jane to tell her that Hopper may be suffering the same symptoms as the other two men, and asks her to bring him down to the hospital for an examination. Hopper has overheard the conversation, and for a moment Jane fears that he is about to attack her. Instead, he tells her that he loves her and volunteers to go to the hospital.

At the police station, an officer who was bitten by Bukowski following the stand-off at the shopping mall, has torn off and started to devour a colleague's breast. The chief shoots him dead and the injured officer is rushed to hospital. Before she dies the officer grabs at Bill and claws into his neck.

Hopper is undergoing tests at the hospital where Helen, the head nurse, is showing signs of infection. She approaches Dr Morris and kisses him before biting off his tongue. As the doctor falls to the floor she beats him to death with a paperweight and releases Bukowski and Thompson. Hopper murders an orderly who was about to report the escape and the four of them leave the hospital in a stolen ambulance.

Their first stop is a garage where they kill a mechanic and gleefully saw off his leg. From the parking lot they steal a car but are confronted by the biker gang, who demand that Bukowski is handed over so they can deal with him for killing their buddy earlier. A fight ensues resulting in the violent deaths of the bikers. A squad car arrives and the escapees retreat down into the sewer system.

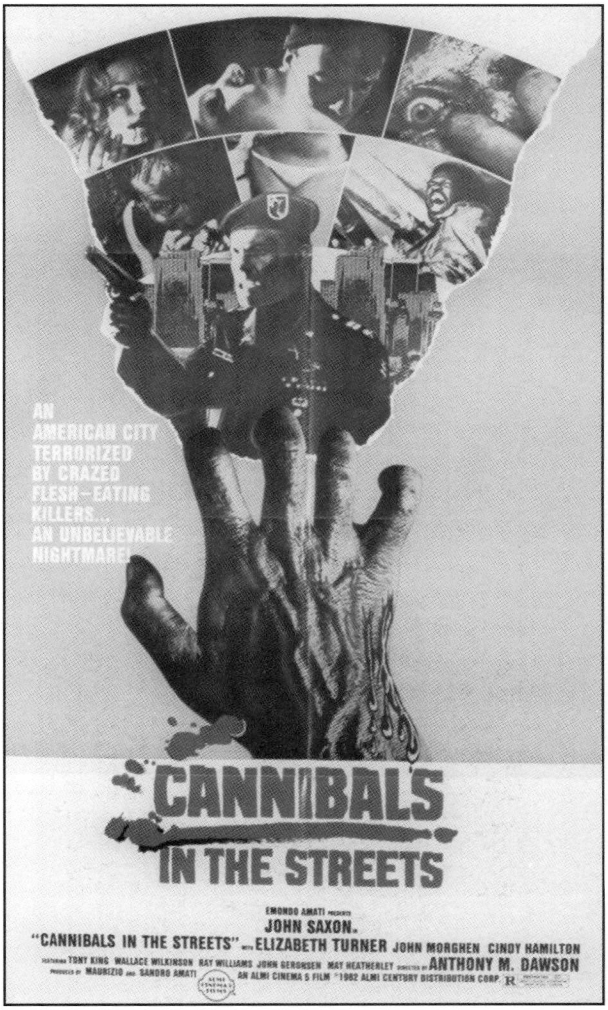

US poster for *Cannibal Apocalypse*, under the title *Cannibals in the Streets*.

With the exits sealed off, the police send armed men down after the killers. Helen refuses to enter a tunnel infested with rats and is gunned down by the police. Bukowski is trapped against a metal grille and also shot. Thompson runs into the path of a flame-thrower and is burned to death. Hopper, though injured, manages to find an unguarded exit and make his way back home where Jane ultimately finds him there dressed in his army uniform and carrying a gun. She backs away thinking he is about to kill her and when Bill enters she runs to him for protection. But Bill, himself now carrying the virus, bites into Jane's breast before Hopper can shoot him.

The police arrive and, hearing gunshots, break into the house to find Hopper and his wife dead. Next door Mary and her brother — chewing on something — watch from the window. Behind the children in the refrigerator are the chopped-up remains of their aunt.

CRITIQUE: *Cannibal Apocalypse* was a spin-off from the deteriorating Italian cannibal genre and the Vietnam resurgence initiated by Francis Ford Coppola's *Apocalypse Now*.[48] The Vietnam sequence is over almost before the opening credits have finished however, and the film

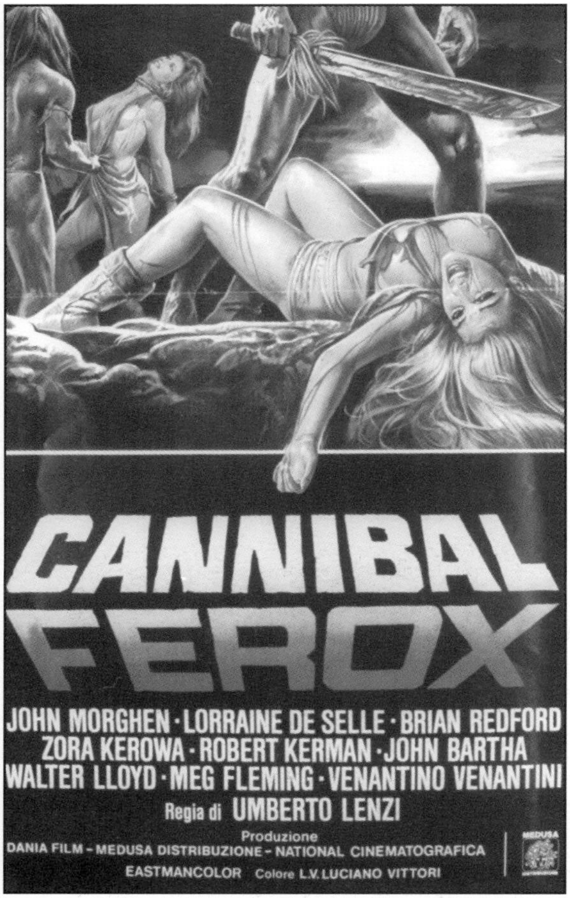

comes across as a confused hybrid of both genres achieving little merit in either field. John Saxon's deteriorating character (Norman) is the only one that holds any interest as he fails to align himself back in society after his wartime experience. But it is a mystery virus that ails him, not the usual 'psychological trauma' of the war veteran. In this respect director Antonio Margheriti (using the name Anthony M Dawson) tries to break from tradition, though in reality he has only produced a contemporary modification of the Dracula and vampire myth: Saxon travels to a distant and uncivilised country (Vietnam substituting Transylvania) where he is bitten and contaminated with a behaviour-modifying virus. Though he tries to fight off his desire for human blood he eventually succumbs and sides with those who infected him. Others who survive attacks by the pack also become flesh-eating psychotics. The final shot is an out-of-place fairytale-like ending where the girl peers through the window and the camera zooms past and focuses on the remains of her once-nagging aunt stored in the fridge.

Viewed today, the scenes where the precocious youngster makes a pass at Saxon seem far more alarming any of the film's flesh-rending. She seems hardly older than twelve, but at one point Saxon lifts her dress to reveal a tiny G-string and barely visible fringe of immature pubic hair.[49]

Saxon told *Is it... Uncut?*[50] that he found the English version of the *Cannibal Apocalypse* script interesting,[51] but that it gave no clue as to the film-makers' real intent — which was to cash in on Japan and Germany's penchant for "bloody cannibalism at its most vulgar." Saxon claims to have only discovered this

> later when we were ready to do a scene, and I asked "Where did this meat we are all supposed to be devouring like this come from?"... did I find out this was supposed to be human flesh. And more specifically when I came to understand (not clear in the English translation to me) that this meat included the testicles of one of our brother soldiers, I asked Margheriti to exclude me from the scene which he did. However, I was now in almost suicidal despair...

The film was a big hit in Korea apparently. Margheriti denies it was his intention to include so much gore, and puts the fact that there is an abundance of it in *Cannibal Apocalypse* down to the producers, who he says wanted to cash-in on the trend launched by George Romero's *Dawn of the Dead*.

"I've always tried to capture an effect of gracefulness and gentleness," the director said in *Spaghetti Nightmares*.

The British video release of *Cannibal Apocalypse* was an unexpurgated version. Although the gore effects are extreme they are not particularly well done. The penchant for splatter results in some strangely protracted scenes. A shot of the garage mechanic having his leg severed with a grinding disk, for instance (replete with arteries and bone visible in the wound), seems to go on forever. Other mutilations include eyeballs enucleated with fingers, chunks of flesh being bitten and torn, and John Morghen (playing Bukowski) having his entire body contents blasted out of his abdomen in the final sewer scenes. (The resultant gaping hole which is used as a framing device for the background action is an idea lifted wholesale from John Huston's *The Life and Times of Judge Roy Bean*.)[52] Replay's video sleeve displayed a self-imposed, though unofficial XX-certificate.

CANNIBAL FEROX

SYNOPSIS: Mike Logan has ripped off a drug gang to the tune of $100,000 and disappeared from his New York apartment.

On a boat on the Amazon, Patricia, Gloria and her brother Rudy are headed deeper into the jungles of South America. Patricia thinks they're are on vacation until being told their destination is actually a tiny village rumoured to be inhabited by cannibals. For the dissertation she is writing, Gloria intends to prove that the practice of cannibalism does not exist, and that "the mythical lie of cannibal ferox[53] in this isolated village was only an alibi to justify the cruelty of the conquistadors."

A fellow passenger on the boat hands to Patricia a small animal, its purpose being to draw snakes that may otherwise attack the three travellers. "The life of the weak for that of the strong," says Rudy. "It's the law of the jungle."

On dry land, the group get their jeep stuck in mud after swerving to avoid an iguana. Rudy stomps on what appears to be a giant mosquito that threatens Pat (it obviously isn't a Black Widow as Gloria implies). Unable to retrieve their vehicle, the team's plan of action — dictated by the flip of a coin — is to continue on foot. They encounter a native man sitting alone, munching slowly and methodically on giant grubs.[54] He seems oblivious to the strangers who are stood only feet away.

The group make camp. The little animal that is intended to draw snakes away from the group is attacked and crushed slowly to death by an anaconda.

"Oh, poor little thing!" comments Gloria.

The group follow a scream to find a clearing which contains the bodies of two dead natives. Into the clearing stagger two white men — Joe and Mike Logan from New York.

"Help us! Cannibals! They attacked us!" Mike cries.

Joe lies wounded as Mike extols the virtues of cocaine and relates the story of how they came to the jungle to look for emeralds, before they were taken prisoner by cannibals. He relates how a Portuguese companion of theirs was tied to a stake, castrated and had his genitals eaten before his very eyes. That's when Mike and Joe managed to escape.

The part about genitals being devoured plays over in Gloria's mind, sitting uneasily with her theory that cannibalism is a myth. The following morning she has to be rescued from a pit by Mike, but reprimands him when he enthusiastically kills a small pig.

"You get off on ecology, twat?" Mike snaps back.

A leopard devours a monkey.

The group happen across the cannibal village, but the place is deserted except for some old men who appear to be frightened of the strangers. Upon seeing a badly mutilated corpse tied to a stake and several dead bodies scattered about the floor, crawling with maggots, Gloria realises she is desperately wrong about her theory and agrees to head back home. But when Joe takes a turn for the worse they decide to stay in the village until he is able to travel again.

Sharing the coke he keeps in a container around his neck, Mike and Pat have sex. "Hey, how would you like to make an Indio girl?" he suggests, leading Pat to the riverbank where some Indio chil-

CANNIBAL FEROX
AKA: Make Them Die Slowly; Let Them Die Slowly; Die Rache der Kannibalen; Woman from Deep River
ITALY 1981
CAST: John Morghen, Lorraine de Selle, Brian Redford, Zora Kerowa, Walter Lloyd, Meg Fleming
STORY: Umberto Lenzi
EXEC PRODUCER: Antonio Crescenzi
DIRECTOR: UMBERTO LENZI

dren are playing. Mike encourages Pat to run a knife over a child's pubescent breast, but when he tries to get Pat to cut the girl, she refuses.

"She's only a filthy little cannibal," Mike snaps, shooting the child when she attempts to run away.

Joe has a relapse, but before he dies he warns the group that Mike is psychotic and that his story about the emeralds isn't true. The two of them had to flee New York because of their involvement in a drug sting, and arrived in the village suspecting there were emeralds hidden there. It was Mike in a drug-frenzy who tortured the figure tied to the stake, plucking out his eye with a knife and castrating him. On fleeing the village with a young guide (whom Mike later killed for fun), they were followed and that's when Joe was wounded by a spear.

Mike does a runner with Pat, taking all the equipment and $5,000 in cash belonging to Gloria. Rudy remains philosophical. "Spilled milk is spilled milk," he says.

When the young men of the village return, Joe's body makes for an impromptu feast. The natives split his chest in two and drag his organs out.

Rudy and Gloria fail to escape, and are reunited with Pat when thrown into a bamboo cage. The Indios wreak a terrible revenge on Mike, however, tying him to a stake, castrating him and cauterising the wound so he doesn't bleed to death. His genitals are eaten before his eyes.

"Will we be tortured like that, or killed?" asks one of the girls.

The following day, the Indios take the prisoners upstream to another camp. Rudy makes a run for it, but is forced out of his aquatic hiding place by piranha fish and killed by a poisoned dart.

Holed up and awaiting their fate, Gloria prevents Pat from feeding on the lump of meat left for them by the tribesmen. "No," she says. "It could be Rudy's!" Mike escapes from his cage, but doesn't get far before he is caught and has a hand hacked off. He watches as overhead a plane carrying his girlfriend gives up its search and flies away. The cannibals slice off the top of his head with a machete and feast on his still warm brains.

Later, Pat is suspended by two large hooks that have been forced through her breasts.

Gloria, the only one left, is freed from her bonds by a sympathetic native boy. Despite her young guide being killed in a booby trap, she makes it back to civilisation.

Three months pass. In an award ceremony at New York University, a phased Gloria accepts a Doctor's Degree in Anthropology. She seems not to have given the true facts about her Amazonian ordeal, and instead told everyone her travelling companions died when their canoe capsized. The title of her dissertation is "Cannibalism: End of a Myth."

CRITIQUE: Considering that Lenzi actually went to the Amazon to film *Cannibal Ferox*, he doesn't make an awful lot out of the fact and the locations could be pretty much anywhere. Even the opening shots — looking down on the jungle from a plane with the superimposed legend "RIO DELLE AMAZZONI" — are ill-matched and appear to be taken from some other source.

Perhaps more exasperating is the New York subplot that serves only to provide this Italian movie with its quota of Americana cutaways (each accompanied by a brash 'Big Apple' score). Though there is a suggestion that the two disparate threads may cross when Mike's girlfriend Myrna makes a deal with the NYPD, the nearest we actually get to it is Myrna travelling to the Amazon and flying unwittingly over Mike's head in a search plane before giving up and heading off out of the picture.

Although he had made ***Deep River Savages*** back in 1972, it was only the success of Ruggero Deadoto's ***Cannibal Holocaust*** almost a decade later that prompted Lenzi to return to the genre, a purely financial decision the director claims.[55] Indeed *Cannibal Ferox* is essentially a rehash of Deodato's yarn but without the technical embroidery that makes Deodato's movie so special. It even incorporates similar-sounding musical passages for its similarly composed shots. Most blatant of these is probably Rudy photographing the mutilated body he finds tied to a stake on first entering the village, a direct lift of the scene in ***Cannibal Holocaust*** where the film-making team happen upon a dead native woman impaled on a stake. But it isn't enough to merely mimic scenes, Lenzi has to be seen to go one up. His *coup de grâce*: a live and screaming female victim, impaled through each breast.

Lenzi also employs the inverted racism of Deodato's film by teaming primitive flesh-eating savages with belligerent white protagonists, who are amoral and completely unsympathetic, but whose presence ultimately serves only to demean the primitive peoples yet further.

And in the end, Gloria's anthropological bent serves to point out the obvious (in a dialogue that virtually paraphrases the closing line in ***Cannibal Holocaust***):

> What a fool I was, thinking I had to leave New York to find the reasons behind cannibalism... It's us and our superior society!

Elsewhere in the movie, the cannibals toy with twentieth-century artefacts such as a credit card,[56] a wristwatch and a camera. But the out-of-place objects have no significance in this film — they are just images that Lenzi has borrowed from Deodato.

Lenzi has jettisoned the film-within-a-film framework of Deodato's movie and cranked up the viciousness. Not content with the usual consortium of real animal mutilation[57] and prosthetic limb hacking, we are treated to graphic depictions of eye gouging, genitals being hacked off and breasts being punctured with meat hooks (for a tribe still reliant on stone cutting tools, where these iron hooks might have come from is a mystery). *Fangoria* described the result as "a stupefyingly vicious piece of garbage with absolutely no redeeming values whatsoever."[58] The film was evidently too much for horror hostess Elvira as well, as its release on the US Thrillervideo label came without the endorsement that she bestowed on other movies from the same company.

In Britain, Replay Video released two versions of the film: the first was a complete version carrying a self-imposed XX-certificate, in a package that had on its cover nothing but the title, some cast credits, and the warning:

> Due to the specific and horrific nature of this film this area is not graphically illustrated to avoid offence.

The re-release carried a BBFC 18 certificate, and was cut. The sleeve in this instance featured the same warning as above, but also included a drawing of blood-red bones and the (nonsensical) axiom:

> WOULD YOU BELIEVE IRON-AGE MAN STILL LIVES
> THEY FOUND OUT!

The video sleeve for the latter was without two strong scenes that had appeared on the reverse of the sleeve before it. Both sleeves however, carried the same running time and reference number.

The DPP list makes no differentiation between the two versions and both are effectively banned. Whether *Cannibal Ferox* is "Banned in 31 Countries" as several of its American distributors have claimed is impossible to verify, however. (It's not an unreasonable figure, but who would be collating such information?) For *Eaten Alive*, Lenzi's next digression into cannibal territory (his third and final entry in the sub-genre), opposition seems to have increased proportionally and the distributors boasted of a ban in *thirty-eight* countries.[59]

CANNIBAL HOLOCAUST

SYNOPSIS: A team of young documentary film-makers has gone missing in the jungles of South America. After two months a search party is mobilised, partly funded by the TV company for whom the film-makers were working. Quick to find their trail, the search party locate the decomposed body of Felipe, a guide from the missing expedition. Eventually, after winning an uneasy alliance with the primitive Yamamono tribe, they find the skeletal remains of the rest of the expedition. It is clear that the film-makers caused considerable unrest in the jungle, and the Yamamonos have created an inimical tableau from what's left of them, strewn together with camera parts and unopened cans of film. The search over, the crew returns to New York with the film reels.

Even before all the film has been developed, the TV studio wants to broadcast the found footage. They request that Professor Monroe, the man who brought the footage back — being "an eyewitness as well as a scientist" — should lend his name to the project and help formulate a coherent documentary. While the negative is slowly and carefully being processed, demanding "special treatment... because of the humidity," Monroe acquaints himself with the documentary film-makers through an earlier film of theirs called *The Last Road to Hell*. He is reliably informed that the brutalities and deaths depicted in the film were perpetrated at the behest of the film-makers themselves, for the sake of camera: in an African township, a firing squad guns down a line of men, a boy is shot point-blank through the chest by soldiers, and corpses are stockpiled.

CANNIBAL HOLOCAUST
ITALY 1979
CAST: Robert Kerman, Francesca Ciardi, Perry Pirkanen, Luca Giorgio Barbareschi, Salvatore Basile
STORY: Gianfranco Clerici
PRODUCER: Giovani Masini
DIRECTOR: RUGGERO DEODATO

Knowing something of their illicit methods, Monroe analyses the jungle expedition footage, to be broadcast by the station as *The Green Inferno*.

From here on, film-makers Alan Yates, Faye Daniels, Jack Anders and Mark Tommaso are the real focus of *Cannibal Holocaust*, living through the newly discovered footage — shaky, scratched, unfocused, *cinéma-vérité* style that it is. The first reel shows the team about to board the plane that will take them to South America, joking and fooling around, and introducing their guide, Felipe. The next roll of film — without sound for a few minutes — follows the team as they enter the jungle itself. Two of the men pull from the river a huge turtle, dismember it, and cook and eat it.

Deeper in the jungle, Faye screams as a poisonous spider crawls up her arm. The team insist on filming the potentially deadly encounter before knocking the spider to the ground. Felipe is bitten on the foot by a snake. Although the venom is extracted immediately, the team demands — not without relish — that the leg must be amputated anyway and Felipe dies as a result.

Spying a group of natives out hunting, and wounding one with a gunshot to the leg so that they can tail him, the crew find the village of the Yacumo tribe. They shoot a tethered piglet for the hell of it. After terrorising the villagers, they corral them into a hut and set it alight so that their documentary may include atrocities meted out by "warring tribes." Impromptu narration made by the film-makers claims the incident to be the "daily survival of the strong overcoming the weak." Many natives are burned alive. Later, Alan and Faye make wild passionate love.

Back at the TV studios, Professor Monroe voices his growing concern over the validity of the documentary, but is rebuked. "Today people want sensationalism," he is told. "The more you rape their senses, the happier they are." He manages to convince the studio executives that before transmission of *The Green Inferno* commences they should at least "see the stuff even your editors didn't have the stomach to put together."

In a darkened auditorium, the lights lower and the intrepid explorers flicker once again into life.

The men capture a young girl of the Yamamono tribe and rape her. The team then find a clearing where the body of a woman is impaled on a stake through her lower torso. The wooden shaft exits the body through the woman's mouth. Alan, feigning sobriety, comments on the "unimaginable horror" that stands before them. The film jumps forward: the team are surrounded by the Yamamonos. They open fire on the darting figures, but Jack is hit by a spear in his belly. Without hesitation, Alan shoots his colleague dead, and Mark films the swift dismemberment of Jack's body by swarming Yamamono. The natives castrate the corpse and hack it in two, feeding on intestines. "Keep rolling," one of the team cries. "We're gonna get an Oscar for this!" The camera turns on the remaining members of the team. Faye is captured and Alan falls injured, calling to Mark. But Mark cannot afford to stop filming to help, instead he turns his camera on Faye, who is raped and bludgeoned until dead. Her severed head is held aloft. Obsessively, Mark keeps hold of the camera even as he himself is captured. He turns it on himself, recording the last moments of life as his own head is bashed repeatedly on the ground.

With the sight of Mark's bloodied, staring face, the film ends. The auditorium is silent. A station executive calls for the material to be destroyed. Monroe walks out onto a busy New York street, pauses for a moment, and asks himself "I wonder who the real cannibals are?"

CRITIQUE: Despite its clichés and portentous dialogue, *Cannibal Holocaust* is a very clever and powerful film. What is basically a threadbare adventure yarn — and a return to the themes of an earlier jungle adventure of Deodato's called *Cannibal* — has been given a complete refurbishment thanks to some shaky handheld camerawork! Together with gratuitous animal slaughter and Third World actors who aren't afraid to munch on ugly looking food, the handheld camera infuses the film with a *newsreel veneer* — one that has succeeded in fooling people for two decades into believing all that is shown on-screen is real, including the murders.[60] (And those who aren't fooled tend to read the film as a piece of social commentary and then denigrate it because it's *only* exploitation.)[61]

Controversy has hounded the film from the start. Shortly after opening in Italy, it was confiscated and declared obscene by the high court, while an old law pertaining to cruelty against guinea pigs no less helped to get

TOP: Cannibals hold aloft a head in *Cannibal Holocaust*.
ABOVE: An adultress being put to death – one of the rites Monroe and his team witness while searching for the missing film-makers. *Cannibal Holocaust*.

the film banned outright.[62] The ruling was overturned in 1983. In France, following an article in the magazine *Photo*,[63] news began to spread that *Cannibal Holocaust* "was the [film] in which men were really dismembered, beheaded, castrated and *mangiati vivi*!"[64] This completely erroneous fact continues to be trotted out by the ill-informed and by lazy journalists. In Britain in April 1993, a raid on a comic mart in Birmingham (emotively referred to as a 'children's fair' by the press) was reported as having resulted in "the first known seizure in the city of a snuff video"[65] — in reality, a copy of *Cannibal Holocaust*.

Far from being a snuff film, *Cannibal Holocaust* does however contain scenes in which people are shot dead for real. This footage comprises *The Last Road to Hell* segment, the film the documentary crew are said to have made prior to their ill-fated trip into the jungle — in actual fact, atrocity footage of (what appears to be) blacks being executed under a Third World dictatorship which director Deodato "bought from an English company."[66] (The same footage is also utilised in several mondo documentaries.) The undeniable authenticity of this segment, despite it looking nothing like the rest of the movie, helps to enforce the misconception that everything about *Cannibal Holocaust* is *real*. Writes Mikita Brottman in her book *Offensive Films*: "*The Last Road to Hell* is a fleeting and crucial glimpse of the unimaginable reality that *Cannibal Holocaust* (falsely) disguises itself as."

Cannibal Holocaust exists world-wide in a multitude of slightly differing prints of various running times. (Although the fabled 'piranha baiting' sequence — a still for which has appeared in several fan publications over the years — has yet to materialise in any of them.) The British video print of *Cannibal Holocaust* is an example of the migraine-inducing myriad forms the film is wont to take: not content with censoring whole passages, someone down the line has taken to removing *bits* of other scenes. These part-expurgated sections include a sequence in which Professor Monroe and his team observe a heavily pregnant native being clubbed about the belly, an act described by the professor as "social surgery." The clubbing part is still in the British version but, outside of a single long-shot, all shots which show the woman to be pregnant have been cut. And with the cuts the reason for Monroe's diagnosis will be lost on all but the most eager-eyed viewers. (The complete sequence, which can be found in European prints of the film, not only shows the woman's bloated belly being clubbed, but also the foetus which is induced by the primitive abortionists.) Another trimmed sequence concerns the native found impaled on a stake by the documentary film crew. Here, all shots below the woman's waist have been removed, revealing to the viewer the stake leaving the woman's mouth, but not the part entering between her legs.

It is difficult to ascertain the quantifying element that determines why one scene should be cut and another left intact. In another sequence, Monroe's team encounter another woman who is being violated with a grotesque makeshift dildo for being an adulteress. Unlike the abortion meted out on the native woman earlier, this sequence remains intact in the British print. (Curiously, the British print runs twice back-to-back the sequence in which the men from the documentary team chase a girl of the Yamamono tribe, prior to them raping her.)

Unlike some directors who have worked in the exploitation field, Deodato isn't embarrassed about the excesses of his filmic past. Indeed, he stands by *Cannibal Holocaust* and to this day claims it to be his best film. "*Cannibal Holocaust* is a splendid film," he says in *Spaghetti Nightmares*. "Even when I see it today, I can't understand how I managed to direct it with such finesse and expertise! It certainly couldn't have been done any better."[67]

As to his own hand-held camerawork, Deodato has claimed the result to be "realistic beyond belief."

> To be a good director you have to be at least fifty years old, before that age you are really nothing. When you are young you shoot movies from your heart like I did with *Cannibal Holocaust*, not really from your head. At the time I directed that film I was very depressed due to [a] terrorist group called Brigado Rosso (Red Brigade). I saw all that violence in the newspapers and many journalists exploited that violence in a very bad way I think.
>
> —*Ruggero Deodato, European Trash Cinema Vol 2 No 7*

Deodato's film seems to have been the prime inspiration for *The Blair Witch Project*, an independent American feature and box office smash that can fairly be described as *Cannibal Holocaust*-Lite. Here a team of young film-makers who have set out to document the legends surrounding a wood (in which a group of teenagers have already supposedly gone missing), come up against much more than they bargained for. The consequence being that they are neither seen nor heard from again but, courtesy of the cameras they so resolutely refused to switch off, their story lives in the form of found-footage.

THE CANNIBAL MAN

SYNOPSIS: Marcos has a poorly paid job at the Flory soup factory, and lives in a dilapidated shack surrounded by arid wasteland on which wild dogs roam. His nearest neighbours are the faceless well-to-do occupants of a newly opened tower block. From the top floor of this complex a young man with binoculars observes local boys playing football and, through his skylight, Marcos himself.

Marcos wakes in the morning and looks at the pictures of glamorous women tacked to his wall. At the local café, Rosa playfully chides him that her soup is made with real meat, unlike the produce to come out of the place where he works.

That evening, Marcos meets his fiancé Paola. She is keeping their relationship a secret from her family until Marcos can get a better paid job at the factory. When the couple are kicked out of a taxi for being overly amorous, a ruckus results in Marcos striking dead the driver with a rock.

As Marcos is returning home he bumps into Nestor, the man from the expensive tower block who has been surreptitiously observing him. Nestor tells Marcos that his family are away and he hopes the two of them can get better acquainted. It seems that Marcos is unable to step out of his front door without running into Nestor.

After work the following day, Paola goes to see Marcos to discuss the incident of the night before. Incidental sounds become accentuated as the two of them make love. When she suggests they go to the authorities with regard to the taxi driver's death, Marcos categorically refuses.

"The police will never listen to someone as poor as I am," he tells Paola. "The police will listen to the rich only."

Locked in a kiss, Marcos throttles Paola with his bare hands and dumps the body in his bedroom. He is contemplative and withdrawn when his brother Steve returns from a lorry driving job a day early.

"You sure are a strange one," says Steve. "I can hardly believe you're my brother."

On confiding to Steve the fact that he has murdered two people, Marcos is dismayed to hear that his brother is also threatening to go to the police. With a wrench Marcos bashes in Steve's head and dumps the body alongside Paola's in the bedroom.

In a fleeting conversation he has with Nestor the following day, the troubled Marcos is told he sounds "like a demagogue."

Carmen is waiting on the doorstep when Marcos arrives home. She wants to know why Steve, her fiancé, hasn't shown for their date. Despite his gentle protestations, Carmen refuses to leave and suspects he might be hiding something in the bedroom. Her inquisitiveness leads to her demise as Marcos slowly and without

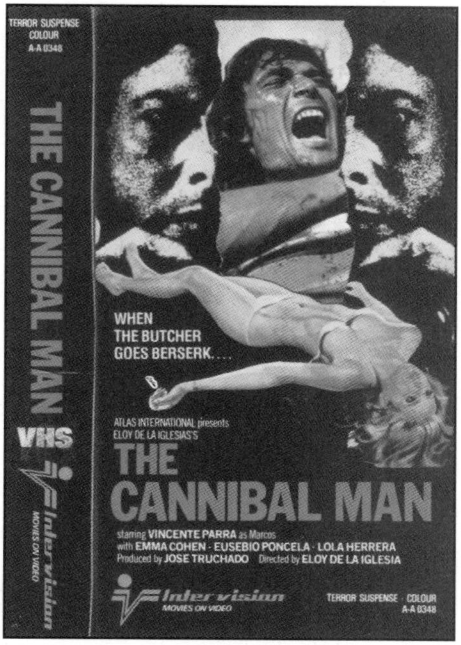

THE CANNIBAL MAN
AKA: The Apartment on the 13th Floor; La semana del asesino (original title)
SPAIN 1972
CAST: Vincent Parra, Emma Cohen, Eusebio Poncela, Vicky Lagos, Lola Herrera
STORY: Eloy de la Iglesia & Anthony Fos (dialogues by Robert H Oliver)
PRODUCER: Joe Truchado
DIRECTOR: ELOY DE LA IGLESIA

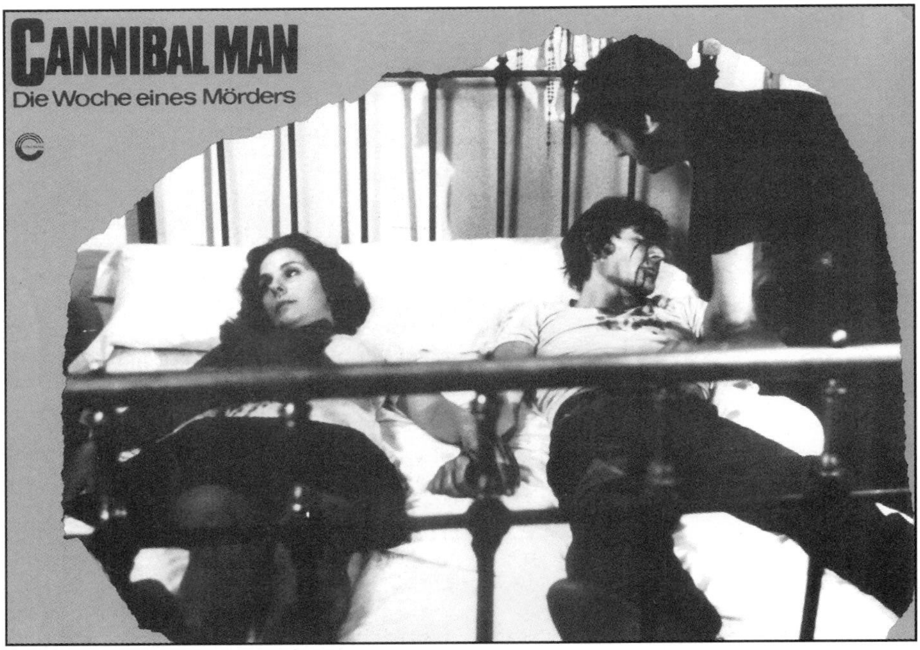

Marcos tends to the corpses of his girlfriend Paola, and his brother Steve. *The Cannibal Man.*

emotion cuts her throat with a knife.

Nestor invites Marcos to go for a drink and says he believes them both to be "pariahs or outcasts." Later he ambiguously tells Marcos he should try and bury his memories.

Looking for his daughter, Carmen's father arrives at the house and is swiftly despatched with a meat cleaver in the face. Marcos then decides to do something about the bodies and starts hacking them into pieces, taking the bits to work in a sports bag and dumping them into the machine that makes the soup. In order to try and conceal the growing stench, he also sprays the house with air freshener and perfume.

After a late night snack at Rose's café, Marcos is invited by Nestor to join him for a swim at his club. Frolicking in the water and taking a shower, it is the first time we see Marcos relaxed and enjoying himself.

"If I was curious I would ask what's bothering you," says Nestor. "But I'm not curious."

The next day Marcos goes to work looking fresh and invigorated, only to be derided by his work mates. It seems Marcos has been promoted and he's not welcome as part of the gang anymore.

Ironically his new job entails feeding the soup machine. Marcos empties another load from his sports bag.

At Rose's café, Marcos is unable to eat his meal when told the soup is not the usual kind they serve but comes from the factory. He leaves, heaving. The following day Rose pays him a visit to see how he's feeling. She notices the smell but he blames it on the garbage. With sounds of children playing outside, they make love on the sofa.

She offers to come in and clean for him everyday, but his strange reserved attitude and dialogue gives the game away. As Rose backs away, Marcos tells her to put her trust and faith in him but then he accuses her of having to come and spoil everything. He bashes he head against the wall.

Deathly pale he decides to take a walk. Dogs are sniffing at his door as he leaves. When he returns later that evening, the stench is so bad he cannot stand to be in the house. Nestor arrives.

"You seem to be lonely," he says.

"I am lonely," replies Marcos, and accepts Nestor's invitation to go back to his place for a chat and a drink.

The apartment is spacious and elegantly furnished. In the younger man's company, Marcos is once again relaxed and at ease. A boxing match can be heard playing on the TV as Nestor confides he is aware of the murders committed by

Marcos, having viewed them through his binoculars.

Marcos attacks him, holding a broken glass to Nestor's throat, but backs down when his host shows no fear. Nestor explains it's because he doesn't care whether he lives or dies.

In a moment of lucidity, Marcos says he knows what he must do and bids farewell. He phones the police and confesses to the six murders.

Nestor observes from his luxury apartment.

CRITIQUE: It is unfortunate that Eloy de la Iglesia's *La semana del asesino*[68] was titled *The Cannibal Man* for British distribution. Not only is it something of a misnomer, with the lead character never actually devouring human flesh (nor do we see anyone else doing so for that matter), but also because without such an inflammatory title there is always the possibility that this obscure little movie would have been overlooked in the trawl for video nasties.

Made in Spain while the country was still under the rule of General Franco, *The Cannibal Man* is one of several horror films that emerged in the slightly liberalised years prior to the dictator's death in 1975.[69] There is the theme of observing and being observed running through the movie, beginning and ending as it does with scenes of Nestor spying on Marcos through his binoculars, and passers-by giving wayward glances. Along the same lines there is the desire of the victims to see what lies behind closed doors, close-ups of eyes, mirrors, Marcos positioning the bodies of his victims face-down (prompting Carmen's father to accuse his dead daughter of being unable to look him in the face, before himself getting a meat cleaver between the eyes), and so on. Concurrent to this theme — and no doubt another aspect of it — is repressed sexuality. Marcos doesn't consider himself to be homosexual, despite the fact that his only happiness in the movie arises from the short time he spends relaxing with Nestor.[70] His sexual relations with women all end in murder ('little death,' indeed!),[71] and even masturbating to the tacky bikini-clad beauties on his wall at the beginning of the film proves an arduous, uncomfortable task.

Confined to a future in which there can be no transgression for the working class, homosexuality is a life as far removed as the expensive apartments that Marcos must face everyday. When he and Paola are caught petting in the back of a taxi cab and told to get out, it is without aforethought that Marcos remarks to the driver, "What are you? Some kind of homosexual?" It's a derogatory comment alright, but also an absurd and to Marcos a completely alien one.

This is also the first and only time the term "homosexual" is used in the film, and it can be perceived as a veiled reference to Marcos' own self-doubt.[72]

In his native Spain de la Iglesia made something of a name for himself for provocative subject matter, usually with a homo-erotic element. His first film was *Fantasía... 3* (1966), a trilogy based on the fairy tales of Hans Christian Andersen. By 1987, de la Iglesia had directed something like twenty-one films (including an adaptation of Henry James' ghost story *The Turn of the Screw*), after which drugs got the better of him and he was more or less living on the streets as a heroin addict — as one source claims. He appears to have overcome this problem and returned to film-making in recent years.

Given the dictatorial climate in which it was made and de la Iglesia's track record, it's inevitable that we should find political and sexual subtexts within *The Cannibal Man*. However there are some ideas that are so subjugated they are open to most any kind of interpretation, not least of which is the great emphasis placed on dogs: Nestor is always out walking his dog; packs of wild dogs constantly roam the area; dogs sniff at doors and are locked into other rooms; and, most pointed of all, a sick dog draws a crowd of onlookers. The latter appears a scene of symbolic overload, as a deathly pale Marcos — having just killed Rosa, his last victim — comes across a group congregating around a prone bitch fastened to a leash. Someone in the crowd suggests they call a veterinarian for the sick animal. After what seems an eternity someone else replies, "Is there one nearby?" Raising half a smile Marcos continues on his way.

The cheap dubbing sits uneasily with the film's art-house aspirations, while the gratuitous shots of Marcos in the abattoir environment of his factory seem to have been inserted only to draw a parallel with *Blood of the Beasts*, George Franju's art-house documentary on the slaughterhouses of Paris. The first of these sequences plays before the opening credits roll and show Marcos nonchalantly munching on a sandwich, while around him workers hack at cows suspended on hooks. The beasts have their throats cut and the torrents of blood are caught in buckets or mopped into rivers along the tiled floor. Returning to this environment later on in the film, a sequence in which Marcos wheels meat-parts from one end of the building to the other cleverly segues the obviously real carnage of the slaughterhouse with the fictionalised tale that is unfolding.

It's unlikely that the director intended these scenes to be somehow indicative of Marcos' unbalanced state of mind. If anything — given the ghastly TV ads which promote Flory soups as being like "mama used to make" — the slaughterhouse seems more a wry social comment on consumerism and commercialism.[73] ('Wry' like the pinball game called 'Top Secret' that Marcos plays in Rose's café.)

Outside of these scenes, the gore in *The Cannibal Man* is fleeting but effective. Steve being struck on the head with a wrench results in a plume of blood, while the meat cleaver that lands in the face of Carmen's father is an image that recurs in *Friday the 13th Part 2*. The dismemberment of the bodies is always represented by a shadow on a wall, or is carried out behind the closed door of the bedroom (onto which a crash zoom accompanies each sound made by the striking meat cleaver).

The Cannibal Man was certificated and released by Redemption in the nineties, with one second cut.

CANNIBAL TERROR
SPAIN 1981
CAST: Tony Fontaine, Sylvia Solar, Burt Altman, Pamela Stanford, Gerard LeMaine, Michael Lavry,
STORY: H L Rostaine & Ilona Kunesova
PRODUCER: Marius Lasoeur
DIRECTOR: ALLAN W STEEVE [Julio Perez Tabernero]

CANNIBAL TERROR

SYNOPSIS: Two petty crooks, Mario and Roberto, are tired of small-time burglary. Nina, their girlfriend, talks them into kidnapping Florence, the child of a wealthy couple who she had spoken to earlier that day. After snatching the child, an accomplice is involved in a traffic accident and is taken away by the police. The kidnappers fear their colleague may say something incriminating and so telephone Pepe, a fixer, who arranges a secure hideout for them. He instructs them to meet Mickey, who will drive them to Antonio's house located across the border in "Indian territory."

They fly out to an arranged pick-up point where Mickey awaits them in a jeep. To their surprise Mickey is a woman. She instructs them to make their way through the forest on foot while she distracts the guards at the border crossing. She also warns them of the danger of local cannibals. They meet up across the border and set off for the hideout, but the jeep overheats and stalls. Mickey walks down to the river to collect some water and is soon surrounded by cannibals. She tries to escape but is overpowered. Hearing gunshots the kidnappers get back in the jeep and drive off. Mickey is taken back to the natives' village where she is placed in a skull-adorned hut, ritually dissected by the chief and devoured.

The kidnappers eventually arrive at Antonio's house and tell him Pepe has sent them. He allows them into his home and introduces them to his wife Manuela. Antonio tells his wife he has some business to take care of. "I'll be gone for two or three days," he says. "Be a good girl." Once he has gone Manuela puts down her broom and bathes in a tub in the garden. Mario watches her from behind a screen and when she sees him spying, quickly dresses and runs into the forest. Mario follows, catches her, ties her to a tree and rapes her.

Antonio arrives back at the house "sooner than I thought" and asks Roberto the whereabouts of Manuela. He shrugs his shoulders and Antonio searches the forest. He eventually finds his wife still tied to the tree and she tells him of her ordeal at the hands of Mario.

There is a party atmosphere at the house and Mario believes Manuela mustn't have spoken to her husband about the incident earlier. The following morning Antonio asks Mario if he would like to go hunting — he agrees and together they set off for the forest. Meanwhile, Manuela reports the fact that her visitors have a kidnapped child with them.

Antonio and Mario arrive at the location of the rape and Mario realises something is going on. He turns on Antonio but his rifle has no ammunition. Antonio orders him to tie himself to the tree. Making sure he is secure, Antonio leaves — but not before signalling the cannibals, who come creeping out of the trees towards the bound man.

Florence's parents are tipped off about the location of their kidnapped daughter. They organise a rescue team and head off for the jungle hideout. Roberto and Nina evade capture and escape with the child into the jungle, where they discover the half-eaten remains of Mario. Before long they are captured by the cannibals and taken to their village. Not far behind is the rescue team which engages in a gun battle with the natives.

Roberto and Nina are bound to tree trunks and tortured. Nina is devoured where she stands, while Roberto is taken to the chief's hut and first dismembered.

Antonio arrives with Florence's parents and the cannibal chief is talked into giving back their unharmed child.

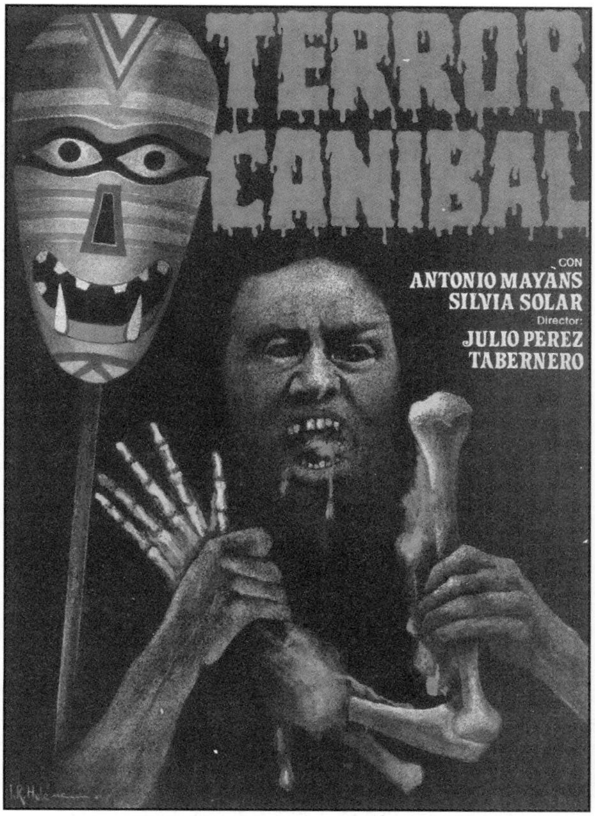

CRITIQUE: Many people originally suspected that Allan W Steeve, director of *Cannibal Terror*, was actually Jesús Franco under another one of his pseudonyms. However, the film is now widely regarded to be the work of Julio Perez Tabernero, a former actor who took up directing in the early seventies with *Sexy Cat*, a horror movie centred around the mysterious murders that befall a film crew.

Nevertheless, there is the unmistakable imprint of Jesús Franco about *Cannibal Terror*. While it is difficult to believe that anyone could or should want to mimic Franco's torpid directing style, there is the strongest likelihood that Franco did have considerable input into the project.

For a start, the film was made at the same time as Franco's two ultra-cheap cannibal movies, ***The Devil Hunter*** and *Cannibals*, both of which shared stock footage and many of the same actors. Some of the same footage, actors and locations also appear in *Cannibal Terror* (the start of which could "easily be mistaken for a holiday ad," according to a review in *Hi-Tech Terror*).[74] The plots for *Cannibal Terror* and *Cannibals* are virtually interchangeable, with each story revolving around parents in search of their jungle-captive offspring.

John Boorman would utilise this same basic idea several years later for his considerably more upmarket *The Emerald Forest*.

Other Franco characteristics apparent in *Cannibal Terror* include his complete lack of film-making tolerance and scant regard to matters of detail and realism. Disjointed musical accompaniment,[75] actors statically pondering non-events (usually through bushes) and flesh-munching in extreme close-up also belies a certain Franco input.

Cannibal Terror is a chore. It is cheap and inept, with a fatuous story line that is at once

The fabulously coiffured 'savages' of *Cannibal Terror* await directions.

stupefyingly simple and yet convoluting to the point of distraction. Dialogue is dubbed — seemingly without the benefit of a script.[76] The party at the hideout is a cacophony of arrhythmical musical sounds with someone's voice "la la la"-ing tunelessly over the top. The jungle soundtrack comprises an unending loop of a single birdcall. The supposed heart of the jungle is a cluster of palm trees some one hundred yards from a busy road with vehicles visible in the distance. Most of the jungle natives are actually Caucasian, wearing body paint and carrying sticks mounted with cheap plastic skulls. Some tribesman sport Elvis Presley sideburns, or moustaches, and several look every inch like out-of-condition businessmen without their clothes on. Few of them can refrain from laughing when they are supposed to be engaged in a tribal dance (of which there are many) or cannibalising their victims and tugging on raw offal.

One inexplicable scene which would appear to have some great importance (due to it being shown more than once), features a native crawling into shot and trying to snatch a bone from the big chief's bone collection. He is turned away in the manner of a bad comedy sketch, only to return later whereupon the routine is played out again.

Much of the film's running time is devoted to characters wandering from one location to another, simply looking at the surrounding flora. But then, no matter how many miles they travel, that same bird is still audible in the background!

The blurb on the videobox calls the film "fast-paced," but it takes almost a dialogue-free half-hour for the cast to wade across a shallow stream.

Cannibal Terror was marketed on the strength of its gore content alone ("Don't view on a full stomach!" warned the posters). The video sleeve depicted a group of cannibals gorging on raw flesh — an effect comprised largely of genuine offal and coloured food stuffs. Some of the scenes of carnage were achieved by concealing a slaughtered pig carcass in clothing worn by the actor, which was then systematically hacked open by the natives who then dragged out its entrails.

"Nyam, nyam, nyam," go the actors as they chow down on the meat.

The depiction of anthropophagy wasn't tolerated by the DPP. As it was with almost any film with 'cannibal' in its title that came to the DPP's attention, *Cannibal Terror* quickly found itself on the video nasties list. Curiously, *Cannibals*, the film that was almost identical, escaped the DPP unnoticed.

Originally released on Modern Films Video, uncertified and uncut, *Cannibal Terror* is unlikely ever to ever see a re-release in the UK.

CONTAMINATION

SYNOPSIS: Authorities in Manhattan are bewildered when the *Caribbean Lady* sails into port completely bereft of its crew. A radio report from the captain the previous night made no suggestion of anything untoward, but there's a weird smell and an investigative team in protective clothing soon discover horribly mutilated bodies secreted about the ship. A trail of "green gunk" leads the team to the hold where they find boxes filled with big green eggs. One of the eggs, making a strange noise and glowing, suddenly bursts and the slime that is expelled causes violent reactions on contact with the men: their flesh pustulates and their innards erupt, leaving gaping holes where their stomachs once were. Only Lieutenant Arris escapes, a clowning police officer who's drafted in by Colonel Stella Holmes to help get to the bottom of the mystery. The Colonel — of Special Division Five — calls for "Emergency Plan Number Seven" to be put into effect.

Scientists deduce that the eggs are comprised of an "intensive culture of unknown bacteria" and demonstrate the effect the slime has on living tissue by causing a white rat to explode. Based upon nothing more solid than "women's intuition," the Colonel announces that the eggs on the *Caribbean Lady* were bound for the sewers of New York.

A warehouse in the Bronx is raided and discovered to already contain hundreds of the eggs. Following a shootout, the warehouse custodians give themselves up but are killed when several eggs erupt and shower them with slime.

As with the cargo on the ship, the deadly payload in the warehouse is destroyed. "National Security is at stake," reflects the Colonel. "Possibly more than that."

The scientists conclude that the eggs are of extraterrestrial origin, and the Colonel decides to visit Commander Hubbard — an astronaut on the last manned mission to Mars. Kicked out of service and ridiculed because of his supposed sightings on the red planet, Hubbard is now alcoholic and a recluse who bears a grudge toward the government. The sight of the Colonel rekindles his anger and results in a mystifyingly frank exchange:

"Come on, Colonel," snaps Hubbard, "what is it you want to know? *How many times I screw?*"

To which the Colonel replies: "If you're always in this condition it's quite obvious you couldn't get it up — even if you used a crane."[77]

With the discovery of the eggs, the Colonel tells Hubbard that she now knows he was telling the truth about his sighting on Mars and shows him photographic evidence. Hubbard runs through the story of how he and fellow astronaut Hamilton, on landing on Mars' "polar icecap," discovered a cave full of eggs. From deep within the cave a bright light emanated and completely gripped Hamilton's mind. But on returning to earth the astronaut denied this and refused to corroborate Hubbard's story.

Having convinced Hubbard to join her and Arris, the team head off to South America to investigate the origin of the cargo on the *Caribbean Lady*. In a pep talk at their hotel, the Colonel advises her companions not to take anything for granted. "Remember, we're dealing with something from beyond our planet."

While the Colonel is taking a shower, a mysterious figure locks a glowing egg in the bathroom. Arris and Hubbard debate in the hallway whether to go to lunch when they hear her muffled cries: "Let me out of here! There's an egg!"

Hamilton wasn't killed in a car accident as everyone believes, but is overseeing the cultivation of alien eggs from his coffee com-

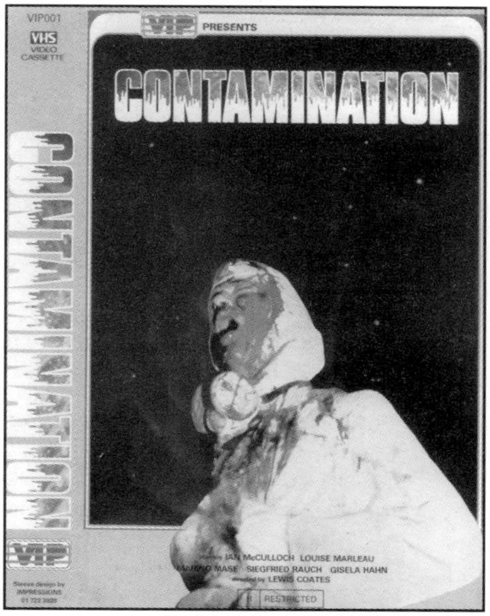

CONTAMINATION
AKA: Alien Contamination; Toxic Spawn
ITALY/GERMANY 1980
CAST: Ian McCulloch, Louise Marleay, Marino Masé, Siegfried Rauch, Gisela Hahn, Carlo de Mejo
STORY: Lewis Coates & Erich Tomek
PRODUCER: Claudio Mancini
DIRECTOR: LEWIS COATES [Luigi Cozzi]

CONTAMINATION
18
Reaches beyond 'ALIEN' to new extremes of terror.
Starring
IAN McCULLOCH
LOUISE MARLEAU
GISELA HAHN
Directed by
LEWIS COATES
AT LAST IT'S LEGAL
BBFC Certified
RELEASE DATE 19th JUNE
EUROPEAN CREATIVE FILMS
GUARANTEED T.V. AND CABLE HOLDBACK

"At last it's legal!" Advertisement for the the re-released, BBFC certified, cut, *Contamination*.

pany front in Brazil. He has some kind of 'egg-link' and reacts in horror when sensing that the Colonel isn't dead and one of his eggs has been sacrificed in vain. He brings down a plane in which Hubbard circles aimlessly overhead, and takes Arris and the Colonel hostage when they arrive at his plant posing as potential buyers.

Arris is mesmerised by the mountainous "Cyclops" — a monstrosity that has grown from a seed Hamilton brought back from Mars. Drawn toward it against his will, the thing devours him. Hamilton next forces the Colonel to gaze into the creature's pulsating orb…

Having recovered from his crash landing and infiltrated the underground complex, Hubbard destroys the incubation quarters for the alien eggs and arrives in time to save the Colonel from the slavering protrusions of the Cyclops. Levelling his revolver at the glowing orb, Hubbard has a flashback to the cave on Mars.

"Damn you!" he cries in defiance and pulls the trigger. The monster bursts into flames.

Hamilton's empathy with the dying creature causes his chest to erupt in a slow motion shower of gore.

Special Division Five arrive to mop up the mess.

Hubbard looks up at the night sky. "Mars," he says, "the Cyclops star."

A lone alien egg glows unnoticed amongst some garbage on a New York street…

CRITIQUE: Luigi Cozzi had a modest hit in 1978 with *Starcrash*, a film the director describes as "science fiction for kids." Cozzi intended to follow this surreal *Star Wars* cash-in with two sequels, but problems between the potential investors and producers ensured that neither film got off the ground.[78] Fortuitously, another box-office smash arrived enabling Cozzi to stay with a sci-fi theme for his next film, the inspiration for which was altogether more adult than *Star Wars*.

More than anything else, the big talking point of Ridley Scott's *Alien* was the chest-burster scene. And for Italian scriptwriters and financiers intent on jumping the next money-spinning trend, it was inevitable the idea of chest-bursting should find its way into their own adult-orientated sci-fi movie — even if the intended title of *Alien 2* had to be scuppered for fear of legal repercussions from Twentieth Century-Fox.[79] But why stop there? *Alien* had proven a success with just one chest-burster scene, how about they made a movie with *lots* of chest-bursting scenes?

And so it is with *Contamination* — a film that is content to play virtually the same special effect over and over. Neither is there anything to distinguish one chest-bursting from the next, as most all the victims are attired head-to-toe in protective white overalls and are wearing face masks. But at least the displays of bloody entrails are consistently spectacular[80] and — together with Goblin's musical soundtrack — provide much needed remuneration for the ludicrous dialogue and sorry story line.

It was for these displays of erupting viscera that *Contamination* was quarantined on the DPP list. With these scenes cut, European Creative Films were able to secure an 18 certificate and release the film with an advertising campaign that boasted "At last it's legal — BBFC Certificated." The promotion also promised that *Contamination* "reaches beyond *Alien* to new extremes of terror," whilst cheekily incorporating the same gory image that VIP had used for their original (uncut) video packaging.

With a love for science fiction, particularly "trash movies from the fifties,"[81] Cozzi considers *Contamination* to be his most effective film. When pressed about the similarities the opening sequence shares with Lucio Fulci's earlier ***Zombie Flesh-Eaters***, in which a deserted ship also sails into New York, Cozzi claims not to have seen it because "I don't like that style of movie."[82]

This is difficult to accept as Cozzi even borrows the leading man from ***Zombie Flesh-Eaters***: the classically trained British actor, Ian McCulloch. *Contamination* was the last of three horror pictures McCulloch made in Italy and effectively marked the end of his career, with the actor not having had an interview for a film since. "I thought I was absolutely terrible in *Contamination*," McCulloch told *The DarkSide*.[83] In spite of this, it's his solid performance that helps to hold movie together.

While not being hostile toward his Italian film work[84] — indeed he embraces these films as "the best working vacations an actor could have... and they made money"[85] — McCulloch doesn't pretend ***Zombie Flesh-Eaters***, *Zombie Holocaust*[86] and *Contamination* are anything other than "silly."

With regard to the latter, he recalls in his *DarkSide* interview the reservations he had while working on the film:

> I went out one night with the actress Louise Marleau [who plays Colonel Holmes in the movie] and I mentioned to her that it was a pretty bad script. The next night we met Cozzi, and I was aghast when she said "Ian thinks this is crap!" I may have thought it, but I would never have had the bad manners to say that to someone who was employing me.

The original theatrical trailer for *Contamination* can be found on VIP's video ***The Living Dead***. In between brief teasers of the gore-explosions on offer, the trailer flashes up the title *Contamination* repeatedly. This pounds dramatically closer and closer with each appearance. Alas, no concession has been made for the transfer of the trailer to the small screen, and the viewer is left watching a trailer for a movie that appears latterly to be called 'TAMINAT.'

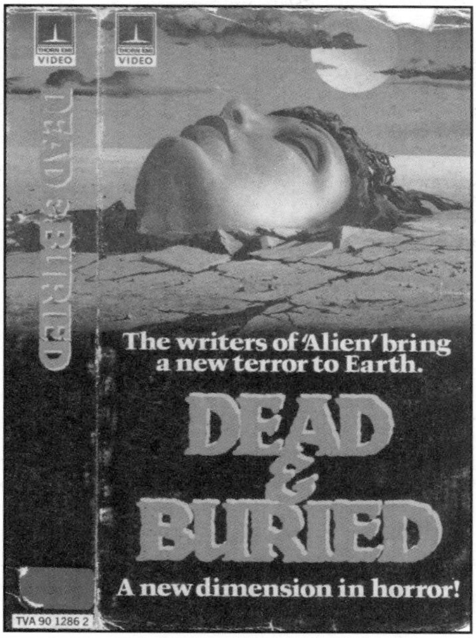

DEAD AND BURIED
USA 1981
CAST: James Farentino, Melody Anderson, Dennis Redfield, Jack Albertson, Robert Englund, Lisa Blount, Nancy Locke Hauser
STORY: Ronald Shusset, Dan O'Bannon, Jeff Millar, Alex Stern
PRODUCERS: Ronald Shussett & Robert Fentress
DIRECTOR: GARY A SHERMAN

DEAD AND BURIED

SYNOPSIS: In the small isolated coastal town of Potter's Bluff, George, a freelance photographer, takes pictures on the beach. He meets a beautiful local girl who chats to him and poses for some pictures. She removes her top and asks George if he wants her, but then grabs his camera as a group of locals spring up, attack him, and tie him to a post before dousing him in petrol and setting him alight. The gathered crowd photograph and film him. Later George's overturned car is found burning with him inside. Sheriff Gillis awaits Dobbs the coroner to pronounce him dead, but Dobbs discovers that the man is still alive despite his appalling injuries.

The following day Gillis is questioned by locals in the café about the night's events. The waitress who serves his coffee is the woman who threw the match on the petrol-soaked photographer. That night a vagrant is set upon at the boat yard. As he is beaten and stabbed to death several of the townsfolk film his ordeal.

At the mortuary, Gillis asks Dobbs whether it may have been possible that the photographer was placed in the vehicle after being burned elsewhere. Before Dobbs can answer, a call comes through informing Gillis about the discovery of the vagrant's corpse. After seeing the body, Gillis decides it's a murder case and also suspects that someone tried to murder the photographer as well. He asks Ben, the local hotelier, if any of his guests are missing. Ben tells him that one man hasn't been back to the hotel for some time. Checking the missing man's room, they find it full of photography books but no clues as to the identity of its former occupant. Ben tells Gillis that Julie — Gillis' wife — knows the identity of the mystery guest. Somewhat suspicious, Gillis asks his wife about the man. She tells him his name is George and she bought some photographic equipment from him for the school. Later Gillis tries to get more information on George from the school principal, but is informed that the school hasn't bought any such equipment nor heard of George.

Gillis tries to question the charred victim in the hospital, but the doctor refuses him permission. In the meantime, the girl from the beach enters George's room and stabs him in the eye with a hypodermic needle, killing him.

Sometime later a family arrive in Potter's Bluff trying to find the Seaview Hotel. They ask for directions at the café and also enquire as to where they might get their car refuelled. The waitress introduces them to Freddy, the garage attendant — in actual fact, George the photographer, alive and healthy. Driving to the hotel the family are forced off the road after a figure runs in front of them. They seek help in a nearby house and are set upon by the residents, but manage to get back to their car and escape at speed. Gillis on patrol is distracted by the passing car and accidentally runs into someone crossing the road. He gets out to assist the fallen man, only to find that the man's arm has been severed and is caught in the radiator grille. The man gets up from the road, strikes Gillis, and retrieves his arm before making off. Gillis gives chase but loses the man. Back at home he happens across a book on witchcraft. He questions Julie about it and she assures him she is doing a school project on the subject.

The following day, Gillis takes a roll of film that his wife has given him to be developed — it is supposedly another class project. Still suspicious of his wife, Gillis tells the shop assistant to let no one but him have the film. Later he receives a call concerning an empty car that has been pulled out of the sea — it is the vehicle belonging to the family who were forced off the road. Gillis takes samples of skin from the grille of his car and takes them to the lab for analysis. Ben, the hotel owner, contacts Gillis and tells him he has seen the missing photographer working at the filling station. Gillis assures him it is impossible, as the man is dead. But Ben suggests that he asks Julie to identify him. Gillis later drives to the gas station with his wife but she doesn't seem to recognise the attendant.

A young hitchhiker is picked up by the vagrant who was recently murdered. He drives the girl into Potter's Bluff where a group surround her and beat her to death with a boulder. Dobbs reconstructs the girl at the mortuary. Later, she is brought back to life.

At the lab, a forensic scientist tells Gillis that the flesh samples are more than three months dead. Gillis cannot believe it and the scientist promises to study the samples further. The scientist later uncovers something, but before he can divulge the information is set upon by the residents and murdered.

The next day Dobbs reports the missing body of the hitchhiker to Gillis. He also tells the sheriff that his wife has been to see him regularly asking about the black arts. A call comes through from the St Louis Police Department who request the return of the body of the photographer as they have identified him. Gillis exhumes the body only to find the coffin contains nothing but a human heart.

Gillis goes in search of Dobbs but cannot find him. He discovers however, that Dobbs was censured by the medical board for inappropriate use of dead bodies.

Collecting the roll of film he had earlier taken to be developed, Gillis discovers that the footage shows his wife stabbing a man to death. He goes back to the mortuary where he finds Dobbs running all the films shot by the locals, each depicting the current murders. Dobbs has been rebuilding the disfigured corpses and reanimating them. Julie, it transpires, is also a living zombie. She turns up at the mortuary and only realises she is dead after Gillis has fired several bullets into her. Gillis shoots Dobbs while Julie sets off for the cemetery, where she climbs into the photographer's empty grave. Gillis helps her bury herself. The townsfolk arrive to pay their last respects — all are Dobbs' zombies.

Gillis returns back to the mortuary where Dobbs has reanimated himself. Film is running that shows the man who Julie murdered is Gillis himself — he too is one the living dead. As the flesh begins to crumble from Gillis' hands, Dobbs offers to repair them.

CRITIQUE: At a production cost of $6 million, *Dead and Buried* is one of the unusual high-budget — 'respectful' — movies that offended the DPP, despite the fact that the violence content is nothing remarkable. The film comes across as a modified version of *Invasion of the Body Snatchers*, but falls far short of attaining the quality or calibre of that film. Indeed, *Dead and Buried* at times resembles an amalgam of classic horror movie moments. When Gillis finds the book on demonology and has suspicions about his wife, it is a situation we recognise as having been done before, but better, in *Night of the Eagle*.

Another film that appears to have proven a big influence on the *Dead and Buried* scriptwriters is *Scream and Scream Again*. This too has a plot that involves a mad doctor creating superhuman zombies. In it Michael Gothard, playing one of the zombies, is apprehended and handcuffed to the bumper of a police car. To the surprise of the police however, Gothard manages to escape and his torn-off arm is discovered hanging from the front of the vehicle. In *Dead and Buried*, the scene is recreated when sheriff Gillis finds on his car radiator a detached arm, the mutilated owner of which simply gets up and runs away.

Both films have other noteworthy similarities, such as a zombified murderous nurse, a scene in which a killer and victim meet for the first time and try to guess each other's names, and a climax where an apparently normal person is revealed to be a 'zombie.'

The overwhelming impression is that *Dead and Buried* is bereft of any real weight of its own. The film struggles to make a feature-length production out of what is essentially a basic, one-note story line that would perhaps be better suited to a half-hour episode of *The Twilight Zone* or five pages of an EC comic. It takes an awfully long time to arrive at what is a rather thin punchline — one that is patently evident from an early stage of the film.

The film relies too much on contrivance to generate any kind of *frisson* or interest. One of the few ominous moments comes when Gillis exhumes the body of George, but finds only a bundle of clothing in a coffin containing the man's heart.

Dead and Buried was released by Thorn EMI. The scenes that probably caused offence are those depicting the hypodermic needle in the eye and the acid infusion into the face of the lab assistant. It was eventually dropped from the list and re-released.

Dead and Buried derived more publicity than it deserved because of its association with the box office smash *Alien*. Dan O'Bannon worked on the screenplays for both films, a fact prominently displayed on the unimaginative *Dead and Buried* poster and video sleeve.

The most memorable aspect of seeing *Dead and Buried* on its original theatrical run — for one of the authors of this book at least — was the fact that it was supported by a short British obscurity entitled *The Orchard End Murder*. Set within an apple orchard in which a murdered woman is buried by a hunchbacked station-keeper and his simple-minded assistant, it had an atmosphere and contained images that were to have far more a lasting impact than anything in *Dead and Buried*.[87]

One correspondent told the authors of this book that, during the early eighties, "the first video shop in Burnley town centre was informing its customers that *Dead and Buried* was a genuine snuff film."

DEATH TRAP

SYNOPSIS: Miss Hattie, the Madam of the local whorehouse, tells a girl to leave when she refuses to co-operate with a rough client called Buck. The sympathetic cook offers the girl a few dollars and points her in the direction of the Starlight

Hotel, a run-down place on the edge of the swamp which has a fenced-off pool containing a large pet crocodile. Judd the proprietor of the Starlight books the girl in. Suspecting she may have come from Hattie's place however, he then attacks her. Hitting her repeatedly with a rake, Judd throws the girl to the crocodile.

Faye and Roy roll up with their daughter Angie, and ask Judd how far it is to town. The family dog manages to scramble into the crocodile pen and is eaten in full view of the young girl, prompting the family to take a room and stay for the night.

Next to arrive is Harvey Wood with his daughter Libby, in search of his other daughter who has gone missing. Judd recognises from a photograph that she is the girl he murdered earlier, but tells Harvey he'll probably find her at the whorehouse.

After arguing with his wife, Roy decides to shoot the crocodile that ate their dog. As he takes a pot shot into the pool Judd attacks him with a scythe, following which the crocodile crashes through the railings of the porch and drags Roy into the pool. Judd examines the gunshot blast he took in his leg, revealing it to be an artificial limb from the knee down. He takes the suitcases from the family's car upstairs and hears Faye in the bathroom. He enters and attacks her, drags her into a room and ties her to the bed. Angie witnesses the attack on her mother and runs from the house with Judd in pursuit. She seeks refuge in the crawlspace under the building.

Sheriff Martin takes Harvey and Libby to see Hattie at the whorehouse, but the Madam claims not to recognise the missing girl in the photograph they present to her. Having been dropped off back at the hotel by the sheriff, Harvey hears Angie crying underneath the building and is about to investigate when Judd drives the scythe through his neck and drags him into the crocodile pool. The Sheriff takes Libby to the local bar to get some food, but first has to evict Buck who is with his girlfriend Lynette causing trouble around the pool table.

Buck takes his girl to the Starlight for some privacy and they rent a room. They are disturbed by the loud music which Judd plays in order to drown out the noise made by Faye tied to his bed. Buck goes to complain but while looking for Judd he hears Angie in the crawlspace. On the porch trying to determine where the sound is coming from, Buck is attacked by Judd and pushed into the pool. The crocodile devours him. Lynette tries to find Buck and is chased through the woods by the scythe-wielding Judd. She makes it to the road and is picked up by a passing car.

Libby arrives back at the hotel and discovers Faye tied to the bed. Judd, meanwhile, has located Angie's hiding place and is trying to drive his crocodile under the hotel to get the little girl. But Libby and Faye rush to her assistance and a fight with Judd spills out onto the porch. Having rescued Angie, Faye pushes Judd into the pool where he is eaten by his own pet. All that remains is his unpalatable wooden leg floating on the surface.

DEATH TRAP

AKA: Horror Hotel; Eaten Alive; Starlight Slaughter; Legend of the Bayou; Swamp Beast (working title)

USA 1976

CAST: Neville Brand, Robert Englund, Mel Ferrer, Carolyn Jones, Marilyn Burns, Stuart Whitman, William Finley, Kyle Richards, Roberta Collins

STORY: Tobe Hooper, Mardi Rustam, Alvin L. Fast, Kim Henkel

PRODUCERS: Mardi Rustam, Mohammed Rustam, Samir Rustam, Larry Huly, Robert Kantor, Alvin L Fast

DIRECTOR: TOBE HOOPER

CRITIQUE: *Death Trap* is Tobe Hooper's flawed follow-up to *The Texas Chain Saw Massacre* and comparisons between the two films are unavoidable. Hooper tries in vain to recreate the atmosphere of his vastly superior debut, even down to a thrifty reprise of *Texas Chain Saw*'s 'final girl' sequence: where originally it was Marilyn Burns narrowly escaping a weapon-wielding psychopath in the guise of the pig-squealing Leatherface, now it is Janus Blyth (as Lynette) chased by the babbling Judd.

"Where? Where? *Whe-e-e-e-re*?" Judd bewails when his intended victim is whisked away by an anonymous passer-by (just like in *Texas Chain Saw*), falling to his knees and hacking at nothing in particular with his scythe. It's a poor substitute for chainsaw-reeling dementia.

Hooper also tries to recreate the 'prolonged climax' that so defined *Texas Chain Saw*, wherein the whole film seemed to be one long adrenaline rush. In *Death Trap*, however, the result is more a caustic irritant, with the incessant screaming of the victims — sometimes several at once — blurring into Brand's inane mutterings, and a musical soundtrack that comprises country and western songs with industrial-strength electronic blips and bleeps.

Although the assembled performers attack their roles with gusto, the fact that *Death Trap* utilises 'name' actors robs it of the power and verisimilitude that the cast of unknowns lent to *Texas Chain Saw*. The all-too-obvious studio sets illuminated with primary coloured lighting also give the suggestion of a theatrical play ("menacingly unreal," said a delighted reviewer in *The Splatter Times*).[88] Whereas *Texas Chain Saw* was shot for the most part in blazing sunlight, *Death Trap* is dark and shadowy to the point of total screen blackout. This achieves nothing other than eyestrain and apathy. And whereas the earlier film seemed all too credible (and, as the poster campaign posited, the audience really did agonise over "Who will survive and what will be left for them?"), it is difficult to take anything in *Death Trap* seriously at all. Indeed, why do all these people want to stay in such a decrepit hotel as the Starlight, which is "an hour from town" no less? More to the point, what are they all doing in the middle of nowhere to even find the place?

What *Death Trap* lacks in atmosphere, it tries to make up for with bloody deaths. Although not overtly gory there is a good deal more blood spilled than in *Texas Chain Saw*. The opening murder by rake is particularly brutal — even though the weapon blows occur off screen — and Mel Ferrer's demise with the scythe through his neck is probably explicit enough to have landed the film on the DPP list.

Commentators have noted that *Death Trap* bears a resemblance to some comic stories published by EC in the fifties, such as 'Horror We? How's Bayou?' and in particular 'Country Clubbing' (both in *The Haunt of Fear*). With their swamp settings, crumbling isolated shacks, mad men and crocodiles, similarities between these strips and Hooper's film are easy to draw. However, it's only fair to note that EC themselves weren't adverse to lifting ideas...

TOP: Neville Brand swings his scythe in *Death Trap*.
ABOVE: US ad for *Death Trap* under the title *Legend of the Bayou*.

Like *The Texas Chain Saw Massacre* (and no doubt some of the EC stories), *Death Trap* was based loosely on a true crime incident. Judd of the Starlight is a rendition of Joseph Ball who, in the late 1920s owned The Sociable Inn, a gin mill which had a concrete-lined pool containing five alligators. To entertain his buddies he would throw live stray cats and dogs to the reptiles. Ball also murdered around twenty-five women and fed their chopped-up remains to the alligators. After the police started to make inquiries about a missing person, Judd committed suicide with a gunshot to the head on September 24, 1938.

Hooper claimed that studio interference together with a disagreement with the producer of *Death Trap* resulted in a film that he wasn't entirely happy with. Similar circumstances were said by Hooper to have plagued and also spoiled his later productions.

Death Trap was released uncertified by Vipco in video cases that sometimes carried the same "strong uncut version" sticker which appeared on the uncensored version of ***Zombie Flesh-Eaters***. This may have been a packaging error because, unlike that other film, there was no discernible difference between the *Death Trap* that carried the warning and those that didn't. Vipco re-released the film in a cut and certified version almost a decade after it was banned.

Hooper would next direct a made-for-TV adaptation of Stephen King's *Salem's Lot*, before returning to the big screen with ***The Funhouse***. This too found itself on the DPP list.

DEEP RIVER SAVAGES

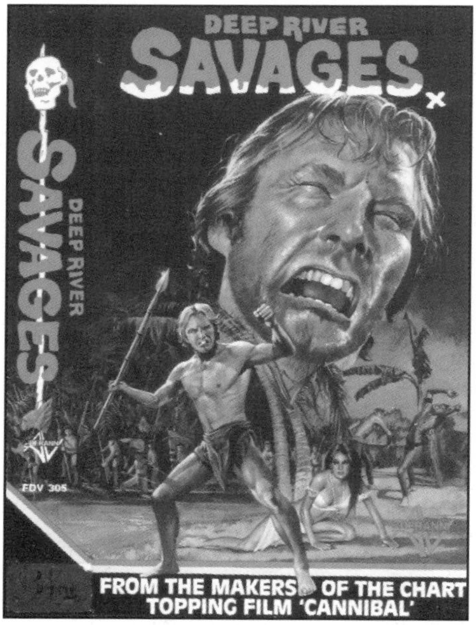

DEEP RIVER SAVAGES
AKA: Il paese del sesso selvaggio (original title); The Man from Deep River; Sacrifice
ITALY 1972
CAST: Ivan Rassimov, Me Me Lay, Pratitsak Singhara, Sulallewan Suwantat, Ong Ard, Prapas Chindang, Tuan Tevan
STORY: Francesco Barilli & Massimo d'Avack
PRODUCER: M G Rossi
DIRECTOR: UMBERTO LENZI

SYNOPSIS: Bradley, an English photographer in Thailand, collides with a man in a bar who pulls a knife. Turning the knife on his attacker, Bradley stabs the man in the stomach and runs from the scene. The next day he travels to a village on the outskirts of the jungle with the intention of exploring the river with a guide. He hires a boat and asks the villager not to divulge his whereabouts should anyone ask. Bradley and Tuan set off up-river. Not having been so deep into the jungle before, Tuan becomes uneasy.

The next day Bradley awakes to find Tuan is missing. He sees something in the water and swims over to investigate, only to find that it's Tuan's body. Bradley is suddenly caught up in a net and hauled ashore by a group of primitive tribesmen. Because of his diving suit and flippers they think of him as some kind of man-fish, and carry him back to their village. Immobilised and suspended off the ground, Bradley is horrified to see two prisoners from a rival tribe brought before him only to get their tongues cut out.

Bradley is used as a slave to assist the villagers and Mariya, one of the tribeswomen takes an interest in him. An elderly woman who can speak English offers to help Bradley. When a helicopter flies overhead, Bradley tries to attract its attention but fails and the men in the village attack him. Only Mariya prevents them from killing him. Because of his attempt to escape he is tied up again.

One day a man is killed when a wooden effigy falls from a rooftop and crushes him. The funerary rite involves the deceased being cremated, with the man's wife then copulating with each male member of the village in his ashes. The elderly lady tells Bradley this may be a good time to escape and so he takes the opportunity to run from the village. The men soon notice he is missing and hunt him down. Bradley is challenged to a fight by one of the natives and wins. The defeated tribesman respects the wounded Bradley's bravery and instructs the others not to harm him.

The helicopter appears overhead again but Bradley is too weak to attempt to draw its attention. He is taken back to the village where he undergoes an initiation ceremony, secured to a vertical rotating shaft in a specially adapted hut. As Bradley is rotated on the shaft, darts are fired from blowpipes into his flesh. The next day he is placed out in the blazing sun without water. The final part of the ritual involves eating raw monkey brains.

When a child has a breathing problem Bradley recognises the symptoms and saves him with a tracheotomy, much to the chagrin of the witchdoctor. Eventually he takes Mariya as his wife and soon she becomes pregnant. Unknown to Bradley however, the witchdoctor is providing her with potions that cause her to become sick.

A woman and boy stray from the village and are captured by a rival tribe. The boy, though injured, manages to escape but the woman is raped, killed and devoured. Bradley witnesses the act and with a group of tribesmen attacks and kills the cannibals. Bradley slices out the tongue of a captive without any hesitation or remorse.

Mariya has fallen seriously ill and ultimately goes blind, so Bradley decides to take her to civilisation to seek proper medical attention. Knowing the elders will not allow it, he takes a canoe in the night, but before long the two of them are caught and brought back to the village. The elderly woman who assisted them has her hand amputated. During the night the cannibal tribe attacks and burns the village.

The survivors relocate their village. Mariya finally gives birth to a boy, but dies shortly afterwards. For a moment it seems that Bradley has rejected the primitive lifestyle, hacking in despair the skulls suspended from a nearby tree. When the helicopter flies overhead again however, he makes no attempt to signal to it. Bradley has finally chosen to stay with the tribe — moreover, it seems he is now leader.

CRITIQUE: This was the first in a long line of popular Italian cannibal movies. *Deep River Savages* uses a plot and several scenes that are characteristic of the 1970 western, *A Man Called Horse*: a civilised Englishman encounters a primitive culture, undergoes intolerable initiation, accepts the antediluvian ways as an improvement on his own advanced culture and finally attains a high-ranking status in the adoptive society. Indeed, Ivan Rassimov in the role of Bradley at times looks like the young Richard Harris who starred in that earlier film, and some effort is made to have him sound like him too. ("I can't take any more, do you understand? You bloody savages!")

Like most cannibal films there seems to exist an evolutionary timeline within the jungle. The further along this line one progresses the more feral the inhabitants become. As such it is the unclean, ugly men from deeper in the forest who are the cannibals, not the tribe by the river Bradley is assimilated into. The more distant from civilisation they are, the more brutal they behave.

Though anthropophagy plays only a small role in this particular story,[89] throughout the film there are scenes of genuine animal slaughter and mutilation. The scenes of animal butchery are thoroughly unpleasant. For instance, an alligator has a knife pushed through the base of its head whereupon blood bubbles and foams from the wound. The creature is then skinned alive. A mongoose and cobra are forced to fight to the death. A live monkey has the top of its skull cut off to reveal its brains. As Mariya gives birth a sacrificial goat has its throat sliced clean open.

As is generally the case in cannibal movies, a disclaimer of sorts appears after the opening credits which in this instance states that

> even though some of the rites and ceremonies shown are perhaps gruesome and repugnant they are portrayed as they are actually carried out. Only the story is imaginary.

Umberto Lenzi would go on to make two further Third World cannibal films — *Eaten Alive* in 1980 and ***Cannibal Ferox*** in 1981 — each sleazier and more violent than its predecessor. Lenzi claims not to be proud of these forays into the cannibal sub-genre and considers himself primarily a director of action and horror pictures. His expansive filmography incorporates all manner of diverse movies — historical melodrama, spy adventure, war, westerns, comedy, crime — and Lenzi is recognised as a director who can readily adapt to whatever genre is in vogue (albeit not always with satisfying results).

Unfortunately for Lenzi, it is the cannibal genre for which he is best known. "I really hate those movies!" he said in one interview.[90] "It is very sad that I am always mentioned because of those cannibal movies."

For all his protestations however, Lenzi wasn't about to let someone else steal his thunder. "I'd like to make something clear," the director said of the cannibal genre he so despised...

> Ruggero Deodato said in an interview that he invented this type of film, that Umberto Lenzi copied his ideas and his successful films. This is not true! The first cannibal film was mine, *Deep River Savages;* it went very well so the producers wanted to make a second part. I was already busy with other projects and so I refused. The film was given to Deodato and called [*Cannibal*]. If you check the actors, you'll find Me Me Lay and Ivan Rassimov in both films.[91]

Deep River Savages looks every bit the forbearer of a genre that would, in a few short years, transmute into a riot of animal mutilation and innard-chomping. Also of note is the fact that much of the dialogue is presented in the natives' original tongue, without the benefit of subtitles, and whenever Me Me Lay gets her smiling flowery face into a shot the soundtrack goes all gushy.

DELIRIUM

SYNOPSIS: Susan Norcross returns home one night to find her flatmate Jennifer murdered, her body pinned to the back of a door with a spear. Chief suspect is a man named Charlie, who had been offered a job interview by Susan's boss earlier in the day.

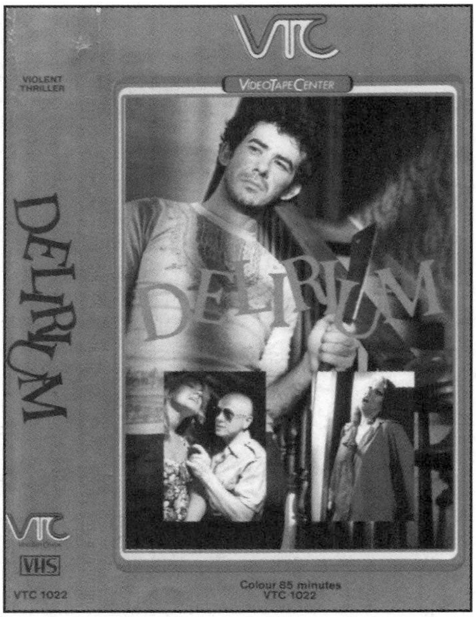

DELIRIUM
AKA: Psycho Puppet
USA 1979 [?]
CAST: Turk Cekovsky, Debi Chaney, Terry Ten Broek, Barron Winchester, Bob Winters, Garrett Bergfeld, Nick Panouzis
STORY: James Lowe, Eddie Krell & Richard Yalem
PRODUCERS: Sunny Vest & Peter Maris
DIRECTOR: PETER MARIS

Charlie running through a field has a flashback to Jennifer's murder. A war veteran, Charlie also suffers flashbacks of The Nam in which he witnesses limbs being blown off and heads exploding. He steals a car and picks up a hitchhiker in hotpants, but says nothing to the girl who becomes frightened at his erratic, high speed driving. Eventually he comes to a stop at a beach. "Are you OK?" the girl asks before casually announcing she's going for a swim, stripping off her clothes and jumping into the sea.

Her taunts when he won't join her and the resonance of Jennifer saying "I'm gonna tell everyone you can't get it up" cause Charlie to go berserk and strangle the hitchhiker.

Detectives Dollinger and Mead pay Susan's boss a visit, but the evasive Donald Andrews claims not to have given the mysterious Charlie an interview. As soon as the officers leave, Andrews makes a phone call and that evening attends a meeting chaired by Stern — a bald-headed man in sunglasses. Stern, another Nam vet, is in charge of an underground organisation which sets to amend what it perceives as major miscarriages of justice. Unfortunately, one of their operatives — Charlie — has gone off the rails, even showing up at Andrews' office for money. The group all have "a position to maintain in the community" and this makes them nervous.

Stern brings in a man who has recently been cleared of rape and murder in a court of law — a verdict which is revoked by the assembled group who charge him guilty and sentence him to death. Like the others before him, the man's death is made to look like suicide and his body is dumped.

One member of the group who had been particularly outspoken about Stern and his slip-up with Charlie is later killed in a car bomb explosion.

Charlie finds a secluded farmhouse and attacks a woman, stabbing a pitchfork into her neck.

Following her flatmate's funeral, Susan goes for a coffee with Detective Mead. She tells him that she can't understand how her boss can know nothing about the mysterious Charlie. "Let's change the subject," says the Detective, and makes some small talk.

Back at work, Susan catches a snippet of a suspicious conversation Andrews has on the phone. Later, the Detectives discover that Andrews had a daughter who was murdered, and that the suspect who walked free on a technicality was found dead shortly afterwards. Verdict: suicide.

Charlie finds another secluded house. He grabs a meat cleaver from the kitchen and makes his way slowly upstairs to where a woman is taking a bath. But Charlie's attentions are diverted when a grocery boy arrives, and he chops off the surrogate victim's hand before sinking the meat cleaver repeatedly into his back. Meantime, the bathing woman appears at the top of the stairs with a shotgun and blasts Charlie dead.

When an attempt is made on Susan's life by one of Stern's men, Andrews reminds Stern that "This organisation was formed to *protect*the innocent," not to kill them. Andrews calls for an immediate meeting, but is followed by his secretary to the group's clandestine headquarters — an abandoned warehouse. Getting a message to the police, Susan investigates further but is caught.

A scuffle ensues in which Andrews is shot dead by Stern and the rest of the group are killed when a crate of ammunition is struck by a stray bullet. An heavily armed Stern escapes with Susan as hostage, but is wounded in a gun battle with police once outside the building. In his delirium, Stern runs for cover. He's back in The Nam and believes the police chopper overhead is coming to rescue him and his platoon. (Cut back and forth with actual Nam footage.) When the chopper makes no attempt to land, Stern leaves his cover and yells, "Don't leave us — you son of a bitch!"

A mystified police officer guns Stern down.

VTC issued *Delirium* in two different video sleeves (see also previous page). The above proved more obscure.

CRITIQUE: It does come as something of a shock when *Delirium* loses its central character only forty minutes into the picture, but it's no surprise that what little drive and focus it had gained from the psychotic Charlie is lost once he's gone. And with him go the few objectionable scenes of blood-letting: a spear bursting messily out of a chest (replete with a squirt of blood); a close-up of a pitchfork penetrating a neck; repeated body blows with a meat cleaver (including one close-up of an impact wound); and Charlie's struggle with the nude hitchhiker, which goes on for some time. By way of replacement we get close-ups of several exploding squibs in the film's climactic shootout.

The major let-down is that without Charlie, the film puts its emphasis on a love interest and the rather dull, tail-chasing Detectives. These two clowns do little more than collate at some length information which is redundant to the viewer, having already been disclosed in previous scenes. When the Broadwater County Sheriff informs the Detectives that their suspect Charlie has turned up dead, for instance, it comes after we have just witnessed him being killed with a shotgun.

Delirium over-stretches its limited budget to the point that scenes supposedly tense or horrific come over instead as plain silly. The Nam flashbacks are a case in point, with a building site doubling as a cut-rate jungle and a dilapidated prefab representing a Vietnamese village. The inept gunfights between a handful of motley US troops and an unseen enemy comes courtesy of "The World War II Re-enactment Society," who get a special credit at the end of the film. An abundance of library music (some of which is recognisable from TV)[92] doesn't help matters much, either. Nor, for that matter, does the array of incidental characters who look for all intent and purposes to have been written into the script in exchange for a small non-refundable cash-in-hand payment. (These include an elderly police chief who is constantly poised on the steps of the Police Department for no reason other than to ask how the case is going, and a motorist who knocks over one of Stern's henchmen by mistake.)

There are some dumb scenes, though these are not without a certain charm — notably when Andrews, suspecting his secretary might be listening in on his phone calls, goes down to the public phone in the lobby to hold his irate conversations with Stern. The sight of the pint-sized Stern 'dragging' the considerably taller Susan through the abandoned warehouse is also pretty funny (so too the bizarre little exclamatory noises Susan makes as he does so: "Ow... Yow... Oh!"). In the house where Charlie advances on the woman in the bath, he makes plenty of noise banging into things, but the intended victim remains oblivious to his approach, happy to shrug off each new noise as nothing untoward.

One scene even has a certain art-house quality about it: A group of young children playing on the beach spot the dead body of the naked hitchhiker floating past. Calling to their (unseen) parents, they one-by-one run out of the frame.

At the heart of this illogical and rather dull movie lies an interesting conspiratorial-vigilante idea. This was borrowed by Peter Hyams for his own 1983 film *The Star Chamber* — with equally disappointing results.

With sixteen seconds of cuts, *Delirium* (a movie whose producer is a man called Sunny Vest) was given a certificate and released by Viz Movies and Vidage as *Psycho Puppet*.

THE DEVIL HUNTER
TITLE ON PRINT: DEVIL HUNTER
AKA: The Man Hunter; Mandingo Manhunter; Il Cacciatore di Uomini
SPAIN/FRANCE/GERMANY 1980
CAST: Ursula Fellner, Robert Foster, Antonio de Cabo, Gisella Hahn
STORY: Julius Valery
PRODUCTION: JE Films
DIRECTOR: CLIFFORD BROWN [Jesús Franco]

THE DEVIL HUNTER

SYNOPSIS: A native woman is being chased through the jungle. The film cuts between shots of the chase and beautiful film star Laura Crawford arriving at a hotel amidst a small flurry of reporters. Laura has come to check out locations for her new film.

Reporter: "Can you give me your opinion of men in this country?"

Miss Crawford: "I have no opinion of men — I just love them."

Reporter (deadpan): "Oh, I see."

Back in the jungle, the native woman is captured, hog-tied and transported by four men to a sacrificial spot. Before they get there, the men stop and stare apprehensively at a cliff face. A nearby tribe honours a bug-eyed effigy carved into a totem pole.

With the sacrificial victim in position, a man-monster with bulging, bloodshot eyes lumbers out of the jungle. The four men watch from a safe distance as the beast feels the woman's breasts, bites her neck, and ultimately rips open her stomach to feed on her entrails.

In her hotel room, whilst having a bath, Miss Crawford is kidnapped and taken to a hideout in the jungle. The kidnappers — who are unaware of the sacrifice or of the existence of the cannibalistic man-monster — want $6 million from Laura's film company for the actress' safe return. The studio is willing to pay it, and employ Peter Weston to make the drop-off. Weston is getting a substantial sum for his trouble, but if he brings back the girl *and* the ransom money, he gets an even bigger cut.

Miss Crawford is chained up in the jungle hideout. Chris, one of the kidnappers,[93] teases her breasts with a knife. Chris is a nervous type. He hates the jungle and swears a lot. A colleague, Maquillaje, twirls a flower in his fingers and tells him that "Back in my country, we have these flowers and we used to offer them to the virgins."

"Flowers — Shit!" yells Chris. "Damn it! Damn it! Damn it! Damn it!"

The wild vegetation gives him the creeps.

Thomas, the leader of the kidnap gang, molests then rapes Laura.

Weston receives instructions to go to the rocky beach of a nearby island, and is flown there by a pilot friend of his called Jack.

"There's the beach," exclaims Weston from the helicopter, looking down on nothing but vegetation.

After landing, Peter queries Jack's need for a gun and tells the pilot, "We're not in Vietnam."

Two minutes into the jungle, in search of the kidnappers, Jack has a Nam flashback (consisting of the sound of gunfire and shots of tree tops).

"Oh… Oh my poor head!" Jack cries. "Wait a minute — let me take a pill."

The switch doesn't go according to plan. The kidnappers discover that Weston is planning a double-cross and open fire on the two men. Although they make it to back their chopper, it is immobilised by a bullet and they have to bail out. The kidnappers disperse back into the jungle, where they inadvertently lose Laura.

Chris and Maquillaje spot a set of strange footprints and ponder their origins. Maquillaje momentarily loses sight of his companion, until blood dripping onto his head alerts him to Chris' mutilated body hanging from a tree. Chris' head falls off. Maquillaje runs away.

On the other side of the island, Jack and Peter discover the kidnappers' motorboat. A topless woman is on board, who Weston punches unconscious.

Jack: "What was that?"

Weston: "A girl."

Jack: "What happened?"

Weston: "She started screaming. I had to knock her out — what else could I do?" (She wasn't screaming, but did pull a gun.)

The Devil Hunter **announced under the title** ***The Man Hunter*****.**

Jack: "I hope the others didn't hear her scream." (Jack was directly behind Peter and he didn't hear a scream.)

At the hideout, Maquillaje sobs uncontrollably at Thomas' feet while telling him about Chris.

The local tribespeople capture Laura.

On the motorboat, Weston tells Jack that because the kidnappers believe they are dead following the helicopter explosion, they now have the upper hand. Then he calls the kidnappers on his walkie-talkie.

"I know it's you on the other end of this walkie-talkie, Weston," says Thomas. "What the hell d'you want from me?"

"I'm pretty sure it's a surprise to you," says Weston, "but it's me, Peter Weston."

Weston sets out to find the kidnappers. While he's gone, Jack makes love to the girl on the boat. The man-monster climbs on board, kills Jack by grabbing his face (!) and pulls intestines from the girl.

Thomas and Maquillaje go in search of Laura. They spot her being bathed by the natives in a waterfall. It's up to Peter to save the day however, when a series of sudden, fatalistic encounters befall the kidnappers: Maquillaje drops into a pit of deadly spears; a female kidnapper is clobbered to death by the man-monster back at the hideout; and Thomas gets his head bashed against a rock in combat with Weston.

Laura is tied to the sacrificial spot, but instead of being killed by the monster, it throws her over its shoulder and makes off with her. Weston gives chase and fights the beast on the precipice of a cliff top. Following a couple of shrewd kung fu-type moves, the monster lifts Weston above its head and throws him over the edge. But, clinging on by his very fingertips, Weston forces a branch into the monster's mouth and scrambles back up again.

In the nearby village, the natives sense that something is amiss and leave their bug-eyed effigy to see what it might be.

Following a few ill-placed punches, Weston manages to catch the monster off-balance and send it hurtling to its death on the rocks below. With their god now dead, the tribesmen run back to the village and demolish the totem pole, leaving our hero and a topless Laura Crawford to head home, better off to the tune of $6 million.

CRITIQUE: *Devil Hunter* started out under the directorship of Amando de Ossorio — who was responsible for the Blind Dead series of films[94] — but Jesús Franco stepped in and completed the film under the pseudonym Clifford Brown.[95] It doesn't look like de Ossorio made much headway as *Devil Hunter* feels every inch a Franco film, utilising some of the same actors as his jungle adventure of the previous year, *Cannibals* — as well as being laced with such familiar Franco traits as crash zooms to nowhere, dreamy music, and a propensity to get the whole damn thing over with as quickly and painlessly as possible.

The result is perhaps an even more alienating Franco movie than most, with no concession whatsoever made towards the viewer: the film supinely unfolds, failing to generate any tension, suspense, or emotion. (This may explain why the few reviews of the movie that do exist contain glaring plot inaccuracies. *The Aurum Film Encyclopedia*, for instance, states erroneously that a "priestess tears out young mens' hearts and eats them," while Michael Weldon's *The Psychotronic Video Guide* suggests that the film contains "Nam-vet cannibals.")

Part of the ethereal quality lies in the fact that many characters speak with their backs to the camera, or with their faces hidden beneath some object such as a hat. No doubt this is to better facilitate a little post-production embroidery,[96] but a whole conversation might take place with no direct evidence as to who is having it. The dubbing itself is some of the worst ever committed to celluloid, with completely lacklustre deliveries from everyone concerned. The dialogue is in the tradition of a porno loop, and dire enough to suggest that it's being made up on the spot. Characters will blabber inanely and often contradict themselves. Many of the male voices seem to dubbed by the same person, who tries to adopt as many diverse accents as he can muster. These are pretty terrible in themselves, but are made worse in that they come and go on a whim. Jack occasionally has what could loosely be termed a Texan twang to his voice, while stiff upper lip Thomas talks as though he literally has marbles in his mouth.

Sound effects are no better, with the characters seeming at times to be treading down a gravel path as opposed to walking through a jungle. The punches thrown in fight scenes land with a sound reminiscent of a hand slapping water. Everything has a horrible resonance to it, as though events have been dubbed from within a small cardboard box.

All of which helps to distance *Devil Hunter* from the viewer. And while the poor sound and dubbing can be dismissed as a technical shortcoming, the musical soundtrack cannot. The music — composed by Franco himself — comprises of two main themes. The first is a strangely alluring lounge number, replete with haunting vocals. The second is a percussive piece, pounding out a tribal rhythm. Both are competent in themselves, but the manner in which they are used is jarring. As the film cuts between the beautiful Laura Crawford touring the city at the beginning of the film, and the native girl running through the jungle, the music abruptly jumps between the easy-flowing lounge number and the pounding tribal drums. Back and forth, back and forth.

The monster is a tall, well-built black gent in a loin cloth (according to Franco, a six-foot Polish basketball player), with large white eyes. As if to compensate for this rather lacklustre makeup effect, each appearance of the creature is accompanied by a cacophonous roar on the soundtrack.

Several of the tribespeople in the one-hut village are undoubtedly crew members. As was the case in Allan W Steeve's ***Cannibal Terror***, no attempt has been made to hide the fact they're white (and they all dance apprehensively to a white guy playing the bongos). Other unintentionally humorous shortcomings include the scene where the monster bludgeons a kidnapper with a rock, resulting in a spray of blood being squirted into shot. The actor makes no attempt to hide his amusement when it strikes him in the face. Later, when the monster is killed, the tribespeople are quick to destroy the mighty totem pole effigy in their village. So insecure and lightweight is the totem pole however, that the very first touch sends it bouncing to the ground almost taking the guy behind it down, too. Under a barrage of gunfire from the kidnappers after his failed double-cross, Weston, despite being in plain view, manages to dodge the bullets by rolling up and down the beach, flipping this way and that.

And while it can be night time on one side of the island, it can be sunny on the other — as per the scene where Weston speaks to Thomas on the walkie-talkie.

Devil Hunter has very little gore. With the exception of the woman on the motorboat — whose intestines are left exposed after being attacked by the monster — viscera is either implied or off-screen. Franco appears not to have the time nor patience to offer much in the way of special makeup effects. When the monster rips open the stomach of the sacrificial victim early in the film, it's courtesy of sleight of hand, except that a rather lame camera angle and a late cutaway from the scene completely destroys the illusion.

Looking towards reasons why the film might not have been submitted for certification following the Video Recordings Act 1984, scenes such as Weston beating a kidnapper's head repeatedly against a rock probably wouldn't win it any favours. On top of that, there's perhaps a little too much emphasis on women being held captive, molested and raped — indeed we see more of Laura being terrorised in chains than we do of the monster or anything else for that matter. The camera also lingers for a long time on the pubis of the woman being transported through the jungle at the beginning of the film, and on the bottom of a pretty village girl who does a frenetic dance. (US distributors Trans World Entertainment labelled the film "Adult" as opposed to "Horror" for their release.) Cannibalism is an obvious point of contention, outlined by the DPP as one of the factors that may render a film obscene (even if, as with *Devil Hunter*, it is far from being a convincing depiction of violence).

Franco has claimed that *Devil Hunter* was the unaccredited inspiration for the Arnold Schwarzenegger blockbuster *Predator*. "It's exactly the same," the director said in an interview,[97] "except instead of a creature from another planet we had a sort of Yeti."[98]

That said, Weston's battle with the monster on the cliff tops at the film's end appears to be a kind of Franco re-enactment of the Empire State sequence in *King Kong*.

DON'T GO IN THE HOUSE

SYNOPSIS: As a child Donny Kohler was tortured by his mother. She held his arms over the gas stove and burned him whenever he misbehaved. He now works in a waste incineration plant and when one colleague is engulfed in flames following an explosion, Donny stands by and watches. He is reprimanded for failing to assist the man and his buddy Bob offers to take him for a beer after work to console him. Donny refuses, saying he needs to get home to attend to his sick mother.

When Donny arrives home he discovers his mother has died and voices in his head tell him he can now do whatever he wants. He plays his music at full volume, bounces on the furniture and lights a cigarette which he then stubs out on mother's favourite statuette. Later he takes a box of matches to his mother's corpse and begins to burn her flesh.

He skips work and lines a room in the house with steel sheeting. He buys an asbestos fireproof suit and decides to get some flowers

DON'T GO IN THE HOUSE
AKA: The Burning (working title)
USA 1979
CAST: Dan Grimaldi, Robert Osth, Ruth Dardick
STORY: Joseph Ellison, Ellen Hammill, Joseph R Masefield
PRODUCER: Ellen Hammill
DIRECTOR: JOSEPH ELLISON

for his mother. The florist shop has just closed but Kathy, the shopkeeper, opens up to allow Donny to purchase his bouquet. As a result, Kathy misses her bus but accepts a lift from Donny who first wants to take his flowers home. At the house Donny suggests that she comes in to meet his mother, and reluctantly Kathy agrees. Once in the house Donny claims his mother is much sicker than he thought and he will have to wait for the doctor to arrive before he can take Kathy home. Kathy asks if she can phone a cab as she doesn't wish to wait any longer, but Donny beats her unconscious before she can complete the call. When she comes round she is naked and suspended from the ceiling of the steel-lined room. Donny suddenly enters dressed in his asbestos suit, pours petrol over the woman and sets her ablaze with a flame-thrower.

The following day in his truck, Donny happens across a woman whose car has broken down. He offers her a lift to the next service station and she accepts. "You don't mind if I drop these things off at my house, do you?" he asks. "It's on the way." Like Kathy, the woman is duly burned to death.

Donny dresses the charred bodies of his victims in his mother's clothes, and seats them all in armchairs in a small upstairs room. He thinks they're laughing at him.

"You're all bitches — selfish and vain," he tells the corpses.

Bobby gives Donny a call telling him that he must report for work otherwise he will lose his job. Donny is now seeing things in the house — fleeting shadows and images of the burned victims in the mirror. His dreams are also plagued with fire and the calcined reanimated women. Donny flees to the church when he sees an apparition of his dead mother on the stairs, and shows his scarred arms to Father Garritty explaining that his mother burned him as a child. The priest tells Donny that he must forgive her. Donny goes home and does just that.

He phones Bobby and asks him out to the cinema. Pleased that Donny is coming out of his shell, Bobby instead suggests they go to the disco where he has two girls lined up. They pair off with the girls at the club but Donny refuses to dance. His date tries to pull Donny onto the dance floor, inadvertently tugging his arms over the candle on the table. Donny reacts by throwing the burning candle at her, igniting the girl's hair, and makes a hasty retreat. Driving home he picks up two girls on their way to a club, and talks them into going back to his place for a party.

Worried by the incident at the club, Bobby goes to Father Garritty and the two of them head over to Donny's house. They find his truck parked up but Donny refuses to come to the door. They break in, find the two girls locked in the steel-lined room and rescue them. Donny confronts Father Garritty and sets him alight with the flame-thrower. The priest manages to stumble out of the house in flames. Donny is shocked to see the bodies of his victims in the upstairs room suddenly become animated and start to close in on him. He turns his flame-thrower on them and succeeds in setting the house and himself ablaze.

Elsewhere a mother is reprimanding her child. She slaps and beats him and the child listens to the voices in his head telling him that everything is going to be all right.

CRITIQUE: *Don't Go in the House* is the progeny of Tobe Hooper's *Texas Chain Saw Massacre* (with the flame-thrower substituting the chainsaw), Alan Ormsby's *Deranged* and Alfred Hitchcock's *Psycho* — all of which were rudimentarily based on the real-life crimes of Edward Gein. It lacks the impact and visceral panache of these other films but does provide some incisive and genuinely creepy moments of its own.

Stephen Thrower in his review of the film for *Eyeball*,[99] rightly claimed the first fiery murder to be "one of the most outrageous scenes ever to feature in a 'video nasty.'" While *Don't Go in the House* was shocking on its release back in the eighties, today it is so wide of social perceptions of acceptability it looks like it comes from a different planet entirely. It is impossible to imagine any contemporary theatrical production would dare subject an audience to such morally formidable imagery...

Kathy is suspended naked from the ceiling of a home-made crematorium. Clinical panelled walls offer no clue as to what fate awaits her. Donny, dressed in a flame-retardant suit, enters the room and without uttering a word pours gasoline over her. As the helpless woman screams, he ignites her with a flame-thrower and watches her burn. She continues to scream as the flames engulf her.

This is the only murder that is played out in any detail, but it's more than enough to set the tone for the entire picture. Beyond any amount of dodgy cannibal gut-munching or eye-gorging zombie effects work, the sight of a woman being incinerated in a bare steel room epitomises the excesses of the films on the DPP list, and — forgive us a moment — quantifies the 'nasty' in video nasty. (Those who consider it misogynistic may wish also to consider that the film's producer and co-writer is a woman.)

The film was shot initially for European distribution only (which might explain the full-frontal nudity, uncommon for an American R-rated production). When Film Ventures, a small independent studio, saw the end result they decided it had potential for a wider market and paid for the film — which was shot without sound — to be dubbed into English. Special makeup expert Tom Brumberger told *Fangoria* how he achieved such convincing work on a budget as tight as the one afforded him on *Don't Go in the House*:

> I suggested to [Film Ventures] that we try not to attach prosthetics to the actresses, because the prosthetics could only make them look larger — and when you're burned, you *shrink*, as you lose fluid. The director wanted the victims absolutely charred black, and skeletal, so I suggested that he use dancers who would be much slimmer than the actresses, but the same height. So that's what we did...[100]

Outside of his burn-chamber, Donny is just a simple-minded boyish misfit suffering oedipal withdrawal. In one scene, his pal Bobby prominently reads a copy of *Mad* magazine as if that little detail somehow paints a picture we don't already know. Elsewhere, Donny goes to buy a "dynamite outfit" for his disco date and an effeminate salesman threatens to undermine the dense atmosphere with some cheap laughs, but it doesn't happen. Director Joseph Ellison wants nothing to undermine the tone established in the opening murder scene.

In a recent interview, Alan Ormsby claimed that he interjected his similarly themed film *Deranged* with black humour because he felt he couldn't make it any other way; the story was simply too gruesome — and in a sense, ridiculous — to translate in a po-faced fashion. We have the opposite situation with *Don't Go in the House*. While it is void of humour — and a markedly less rounded film than *Deranged* — it's also difficult to imagine how any attempt at levity would settle following the first murder scene.

Naturally, the film's overt unpleasantness also negates any sincerity that may have been intended in the depiction of child abuse — *Don't Go in the House* identifying with the popular theory that the abused themselves become abusers in later life.

When the film was released theatrically in Britain in January 1982, the reviewer for *Screen International* gave credit to director Joseph Ellison for "stressing the Gothic horror elements instead of exploiting the gruesome potential of the murders." However, the two minutes of cuts excised by the BBFC might very well have made it seem that way. There was no such concession when *Don't go In the House* appeared on video courtesy of distributors Arcade, who released the film uncut.

Although there is no blood loss in the film, it is quite obvious where the contention lies. However, given the selection criteria that brought many of the films to the attention of the DPP, the video sleeve alone would probably have been enough to land *Don't Go in the House* on the nasties list. (Over a blackened corpse, suspended by its hands, the blurb on the videobox reads: "In a steel room built for revenge they die burning... in chains.")

The film was later reprieved from the prosecution list and re-released with over three minutes of cuts on the Apex label.

Don't Go in the House was filmed under the title *The Burning* — not to be confused with Tony Maylam's film of the same name which also featured on the list.

DON'T GO IN THE WOODS... ALONE!

SYNOPSIS: A young woman runs in fear through the woods, her camera discarded by a stream.

While looking through his binoculars, an ornithologist notices a small commotion in a nearby bush and is attacked. The unseen assailant first strikes him in the face and then hacks off an arm. The arm falls to the floor and a death blow is delivered.

There are other groups of people travelling through other areas of the woods independent to one another. These include two teams of backpackers, two couples in trailers, a fisherman, a lone individual in a wheelchair, and a landscape painter.

"Another missing persons report?" says the fat sheriff to his deputy in the nearby town, on the disappearance of the ornithologist.

One team of backpackers sit around a campfire at night listening to a spooky tale. Elsewhere, amorous couple Dick and Cherry are trying to make out in their camper van. They hear a noise and Dick goes to ward off the "Peeping Tom." He's gone a long time and Cherry begins to get worried when suddenly Dick's bloody face slaps against the window. The camper van, perched precariously on a ledge, is sent tumbling down the mountainside in darkness.

The sheriff and his men arrive in the woods.

A woman is murdered whilst painting at an easel. Blood is spattered over her canvas. The infant who had been playing close by is taken from her carriage by the assailant.

Elsewhere, another attack takes place, this time on the backpackers, who are locked into their sleeping bags and stabbed repeatedly.

We get our first glimpse of the killer — a wild man wearing furs and carrying a spear and machete — when a fisherman is murdered with a bear trap.

Craig, Peter, Ingrid and Joanne, who make up a second team of young backpackers, talk of Bigfoot stalking the woods, oblivious to the threat that lies in wait. Peter goes off on his own after being chided by the others. Whilst he is gone, Craig locks one of the girls into her sleeping bag, ties it to a tree and hoists her into the air for a prank. The girl cuts a hole into the bag in time to see the figure of the wildman approaching below, and the subsequent death of Craig.[101] The girl in the sleeping bag is spared.

Peter meets up with Ingrid and they accidentally discover the wild man's hideout. In it is the body of Craig. The wild man returns and the two of them run for their lives. Peter accidentally spears a backpacker thinking it's the killer. "I'm sorry… I'm sorry… I'm sorry," he calmly tells the dying man.

Peter and Ingrid fall asleep. When they awake the following morning, they discover they've made it to the edge of the woods and the safety of the town.

At the local hospital, Peter fulfils a doctor's fears and becomes "irrational," running off to find Joanne who is left in the woods.

Joanne, meanwhile, has found the wildman's hideout and is hacked to death when he suddenly returns.

The man in a wheelchair treks alone through the woods, sometimes rolling backwards out of control, panting and struggling to manoeuvre his chair across the rough terrain. With a sigh of contentment and relief, he finally reaches the summit of the mountain he has been climbing… just as a machete swings out of nowhere and chops off his head.

Peter stabs the wildman with a spear. Both he and Ingrid are locked in a stabbing frenzy, continuing to bring their knives down on the wildman long after he is dead. The sheriff and his men emerge from the undergrowth and watch in horror.

A little later, seemingly without charges or having taken any statements, the Sheriff allows Peter and Ingrid to go free. An officer waves to the couple and ruminates, "Sometimes it makes you wonder."

The child whose mother was murdered at her easel, hacks at the ground with an axe, forgotten and all alone in the woods.

DON'T GO IN THE WOODS... ALONE!
TITLE ON PRINT: **DON'T GO IN THE WOODS**
USA 1980
CAST: **Jack McClelland, Mary Gail Artz, James P Hayden, Ken Carter, Larry Roupe, Angie Brown**
STORY: **Garth Eliassen**
PRODUCERS: **Roberto & Suzette Gomez**
DIRECTOR: **JAMES BRYAN**

CRITIQUE: In terms of budget[102] and technical competence, this film sits at the bottom of the nasties list. Director James Bryan appears not to have grasped even the most rudimentary aspects of film-making, and *Don't Go in the Woods* (which surely must be his one and only feature)[103] suffers every cinematic pitfall imaginable — from being underlit through to utilising characters who look, dress, talk and behave exactly the same (in the same woodland settings). It also has the most ham-fisted editing ever to grace a theatrically released production (it had a cinema release in the US, but not in Britain).[104] Indeed, frayed to begin with, continuity comes to a complete standstill in the 'action' sequences, courtesy of editing that doesn't adhere to any rational sense of rhythm or timing.

As a consequence, *Don't Go in the Woods* completely detaches the viewer's interest. Nothing about this film draws you in (outside of the fact that it has been 'banned'). The musical soundtrack consists of synthesised 'themes' played back-to-back without a break, underpinned by a succession of digital beeps and squeaks. This drone starts with the opening titles and doesn't halt until the final credits, where a terrible song based upon 'The Teddy Bears Picnic' takes over. A series of electronic 'wows' is offered in lieu of any actual tension.

(The man trekking through the woods alone in his wheelchair is presumably a tasteless stab at humour, given that each appearance of his has a 'comedy' musical accompaniment.)

Like the music, the film plays out without any sense of depth or dynamic. Although the events in the film seem to take place over a period of only a day or two, the timeframe could easily be spanning weeks, months or even years. Everything is unclear and confusing.

Donald Farmer, in *The Splatter Times*,[105] determined, "Another reason to stay away is the constantly shaky camerawork – anyone sitting too close to the screen could probably get motion sickness."

The majority of blood-letting is buried in the film's ineptitude. Several of the early attacks in the woods – when the identity of the attacker is still being guarded – are so spectacularly incompetent and surreal, that they could effectively be depicting *anything*. (And perhaps detractors *did* read much more into these scenes than is actually taking place?) The only gore sequences that allow the viewer enough of a handle for any real criticism, include the attack on Joanne in the wildman's lair (he slashes her repeatedly with a knife as she tries to clamber through a skylight) and the scene in which Peter and Ingrid maniacally stab the wildman even after his death. The special effects don't extend to anything more gratuitous than close-ups of slashed and bloodied clothing, but both these sequences are needlessly protracted, with the death of Joanne – caught in the skylight[106] – being particularly unpleasant.

The non-actors don't bring nearly enough unintentional humour to the proceedings, although the sequence with the lovers in the camper van is guaranteed to raise a smile. "Dick... Dick..." the woman hollers in a completely dispassionate manner when her man is taking an inordinately long time to check out the prowler. When the camper van is subsequently sent tumbling down the mountainside – undoubtedly the single greatest expense in the movie – the viewer gets a sense of relative extravagance, even though the incident is related in almost complete darkness and very nearly wasted.

One of the earliest entries in the generic stalk-and-slash cycle of films, *Don't Go in the Woods* is a shining example of how inclusion on the DPP list has bestowed a piece of complete crap with notoriety and near-legendary status. Why else are we still discussing James Bryan?

For reasons unknown, US distributors Manson International, extended the original title for their poster artwork of *Don't Go in the Woods* to reflect the advice of one of the characters in the film: 'Don't Go In the Woods... Alone!'[107] It is this artwork which also adorns the British videobox.

Though the sub-genre that comprises yeti and bigfoot cinema is minuscule, several films on the DPP list are a part of it: *Don't Go in the Woods*, ***Night of the Demon*** and ***The Werewolf and the Yeti***. On top of these, ***Anthropophagous the Beast*** and ***The Devil Hunter*** arguably fit the category of stalking-hairy-man-thing.

DON'T GO NEAR THE PARK

SYNOPSIS: Some 12,000 years ago, an old medicine woman curses her two grown-up children, Gar and Tra. Her curse condemns both to a life of perpetual dying — they will never reach death but instead will age ten years for each one they are alive. They face a 12,000 year wait before such planetary alignments occur as will allow them to sacrifice a descendant to rid themselves of their curse and attain eternal life. The old lady disappears in a cloud of smoke and Gar says, "We will do what we must to survive — and we *will* survive."

In the present, a boy is fishing on a riverbank. Gar, using the name Mark and dressed in a business suit, approaches him and engages him in conversation. He slips a garrotte over the boy's head and strangles him. The boy is dragged to a clearing and Mark tears open his abdomen. Reaching in, he pulls out handfuls of innards to devour, and as he eats, the dead boy ages and mummifies while Mark's complexion rejuvenates. An aged and decrepit Tra, now called Patty, hobbles up to Mark. She insists that he must stop wasting time, and should find himself a woman to bear his child for sacrifice. Later, at a carnival, Mark sees a likely looking girl and follows her home. Fortunately for him, her house has a room to rent, which Mark takes.

A girl is running through the woods chasing her dog. She follows it into a barn and steps into a bear trap. Patty offers to help but instead disembowels the girl to eat her entrails. Patty then also regenerates.

While Mark is out of the house his landlady explores his room. She finds an attaché case that contains an ancient smoking pipe and a newspaper report concerning the recent missing child. Mark enters the room and catches her snooping. He hypnotises her and she undresses for him. Later they marry and have a daughter who Mark names Bondi. He shows much affection towards the girl and little towards his wife, buying Bondi a gold medallion for her sixteenth birthday. His wife is furious at his favouritism and decides to leave. Bondi is so upset by the break-up that she leaves home, too, getting a lift from a group of men who drive her out of the city and attempt to rape her in the back of their van. As she is being molested she grabs the medallion and screams for her father to help her. The medallion glows and the driver loses control of the van, whereupon it plunges off a bridge and explodes.

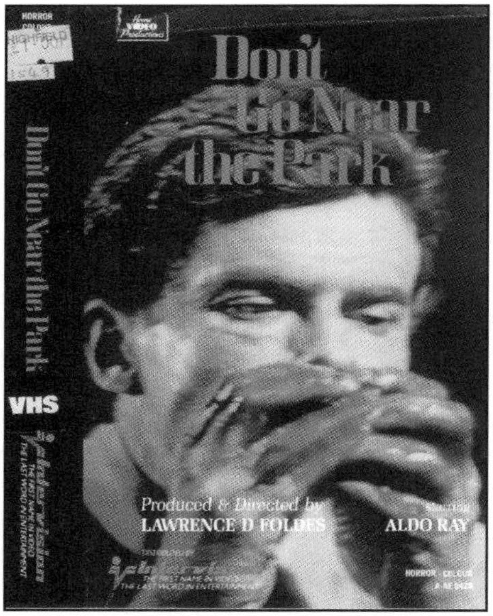

DON'T GO NEAR THE PARK
AKA: Night Stalker
USA 1979
CAST: Aldo Ray, Meeno Peluce, Tamara Taylor, Barbara Monker, Linnea Quigley, Crackers Phinn
STORY: Linwood Chase & Lawrence D Foldes
PRODUCER: Lawrence D Foldes
DIRECTOR: LAWRENCE D FOLDES

Bondi, unharmed, finds her way to the derelict shack where Patty lives. Patty recognises the medallion and invites her to stay and there she meets two runaway boys, Nick and Cowboy.

Nick is selling flowers on a street corner when a knife-wielding thug harasses him. A man named Taft comes to his aid and they develop a friendship. Taft has been researching the legends associated with the park and he warns Nick of the dangers. He tells him of an evil woman named Patranella who used to live there in the last century.

Nick and Bondi become suspicious about Patty thinking she may actually be the legendary Patranella. Later that night Nick follows Patty and observes her murdering and cannibalising a lone camper.

Bondi, running from the shack after a terrifying nightmare, stumbles into a cave. There, surrounded by corpses, she finds her father who tells Bondi the time is right for her sacrifice and tries to rape her. Patty intervenes, striking him with a rock, pointing out that for the ritual to work Bondi must remain a virgin. Cowboy finds his way into the cave and tries to save Bondi, but Mark zaps him with beams from his eyes. Mark and Patty get into a fight and Patty tells Bondi to swallow the medallion. This she does, causing her to transform into Mark and Patty's mother. Using her powers she reanimates the strewn corpses which rise to kill both Mark and Patty.

Bondi returns to her normal self and she and Cowboy find Nick. Taft arrives and digs them out of the collapsed cave.

Later, the three go back to the shack only to find it is about to be demolished. They venture deeper into the park and come across a children's playground. Nick climbs on the slide and asks Bondi to push him, but instead she wraps her arms around him and tears open his stomach. Bondi has appropriated the cannibal legacy of her ancestors.

CRITIQUE: *Don't Go Near the Park* would undoubtedly have faded into oblivion unnoticed and unmissed had the DPP not immortalised it with 'nasty' status.

At times it has the air of a made-for-TV feature, but then suddenly it swings into graphic mutilation and cannibalism. In these occasional and very short gore scenes, abdomens are torn open and their contents scooped out and devoured.

But rubbery gore alone does not a good horror movie make. And while campaigners were stirring up a fuss with regard to video nasties, incompetent films like *Don't Go Near the Park* attained a popularity they most assuredly didn't deserve. Nobody who reviewed the film prior to or during the media backlash had a single good word to say about it (nobody has had a good word to say about it since, but with the film now being so highly desired by collectors, that hardly seems important). Reviewing the latest horror releases, Liam T Sanford in the July 1983 edition of *Video Viewer* called *Don't Go Near the Park* "brainless junk." So brainless in fact, he felt compelled to advise readers that

> Many moronic movies now being made available on videotape were originally perpetrated by used-car salesmen, opticians, lawyers, dentists and greengrocers. Whether intended as a tax fiddle or a money-spinner, they don't give a gnat's earlobe about quality.
> Enlisting the dubious aid of family friends, in-laws, outlaws and casual acquaintances to fill in on both sides of the camera, they then proceed to toss together the sort of trash that gives 'splatter' a bad name...

Knowing now how bad the few gore scenes are, let us peruse the sleazy underbelly that has passed most commentators by. First up is the use of the barely-of-age Linnea Quigley in an adult role (Mark's wife, complete with shower scene). Although she would go on to become something of a B-movie queen featuring in the likes of *Return of the Living Dead* and *Graduation Day* (in which she was hired to replace an actress who refused to remove her top), this was one of the first movie parts for Quigley. The film may have had nudity, she later confided to Jewel Shepard, but it "also gave me a few lines."[108]

Don't Go Near the Park has an odd mix of dubious themes: cannibalism, incest, and subliminal paedophilia. At one point eight-year-old Nick (played by Meeno Peluce), tries to grope the breasts of the sleeping Bondi (Tamara Taylor), but she wakes and stops him, telling him he'll have to wait until he's at least twelve before he does anything like that. In another scene, Bondi remarks that she is sick of being molested. Indeed, the molester who rips open her blouse, bares her immature breasts and gropes at her thighs in the back of the van is none other than the director himself, Lawrence D Foldes.

Many times during the film, the camera will be specifically positioned in order to get an unobstructed view up Bondi's skirt. When she and Nick escape from Patranella's room by climbing out the window and down a tree, we don't see Nick descend, but — courtesy of the camera below — we do see the short-skirted Bondi as she stretches her legs from branch to branch.

Perhaps most alarming is Aldo Ray, who plays Taft... This once respected actor, veteran of movies like *The Naked and the Dead*, *We're No Angels* and *The Green Berets*, was driven out of the Hollywood mainstream due to his heavy drinking. Until his death in 1991, the only parts then offered to him were courtesy of low-budget film-makers, who liked the idea of a former name star in their humble productions. Volume one of *The X-Rated Videotape Guide* also recognises Ray as "the first regular Hollywood actor to appear in a porno film" (in reference to his pants-on appearance in Anne Perry's *Sweet Savage*, an explicit western). In *Don't Go Near the Park*, Taft, an old man, picks up Nick from the street. He takes the young boy home, where he lives alone, and invites him to stay with him as his special friend. Towards the end of the film, the three youngsters — Cowboy, Bondi and Nick — are all sleeping half-naked in Taft's apartment while he looks on, smiling.

If nothing else such sleazy moments throw a whole new light on the otherwise ridiculous on-screen proclamation that *Don't Go Near the Park* "is based on actual occurrences which happened over the centuries"!

Foldes went on to direct the altogether more competent *Young Warriors* and *Nightforce*, the latter starring Linda Blair.

DON'T LOOK IN THE BASEMENT

SYNOPSIS: A sanatorium is the setting for this film. In the pre-credit sequence, we are introduced to the sanatorium's founder, a Dr Stephens, who has some radical ideas about psychiatry. He is convinced that the treatment of mental illness lies with encouraging patients to live out their fantasies. He gives the Judge, an axe murderer, the chore of chopping wood. "Reach for it, Judge!" coaches Stephens. Unfortunately, the Judge goes berserk and sinks the axe into the doctor.

Dr Masters steps up as Stephen's replacement, referring to the patients as her "family."

Following the unrelated death of another member of staff — murdered with her own suitcase when she threatens to leave — Charlotte Beale arrives at the hospital to start work as a nurse. She is a little shocked to discover that the patients are free to wander the corridors at will, and is unable to go anywhere in the building without a succession of warnings. Mrs Callingham, a loopy old lady who is later attacked in the night, tells her to get out while she can.

The other residents include Sergeant Jaffee, who stands at a window in his army fatigues, barking commands and watching diligently for an unseen enemy. Sam, a giant Black man and the subject of an unsuccessful lobotomy by Dr Stephens, craves nothing but popsicles. Harriett believes a child's doll to be her flesh and blood baby. Danny is a crazed young man who calls everyone else "crazy."

After the telephone lines are mysteriously cut, a repairman arrives and suffers untoward advances from the house nymphomaniac, Allyson. "You love me," she demands, forcing him backwards into a cupboard. "You love me. Say it!"

Dr Masters' temperament is becoming increasingly unstable. She tells Sgt Jaffe that her power is "absolute" and that she will punish anyone who challenges it.

Nurse Charlotte takes time out with Danny in the grounds. They talk. He pecks her on the cheek and picks for her a flower. She walks out of shot. He laughs maniacally for a long time.

Later that night, as Charlotte lies sleeping in her bed, the Judge appears over her brandishing an axe. Suddenly, Danny walks in with a mad glint in his eye and tries to climb on top of Charlotte. The Judge sends him on his way, and explains to the nurse:

"He needs watching. I'm sure you know. You can be sure there'll be other times… times for other things. Unlike your friend Danny, I choose only perfect moments. Perfect moments to work out perfect destinies for so many lives."

Sam is in the kitchen helping himself to a popsicle. He finds the body of the telephone repairman. When he shows his discovery to Allyson, the nymphomaniac sobs, "She'll kill anyone who threatens to expose her."

The mayhem begins to escalate. A patient who attempts to steal some pills from a cabinet is forced, head-first, onto a paper spike by a killer who is hidden in shadow. It is revealed that Dr Masters is perpetrating the crimes and that it's a case of the lunatics having taken over the asylum. More of a twist is the fact that the real head of the sanatorium, Dr Stephens, isn't dead. Nobody knows he's alive but Sam, who has been helping him to convalesce in the basement — until Nurse Charlotte goes prowling around, gets a shock and clobbers the good doctor with one of Sam's toy boats.

The Judge leads a murderous revolt against Dr Masters. "The trial has been held," he announces. "The verdict is guilty."

Suffering from a lobotomy flashback and saving Nurse Charlotte from certain death, Sam slaughters his fellow residents with an axe after he finds she has been murdered by the residents. As Charlotte escapes in the rain, Sam is left alone, sobbing.

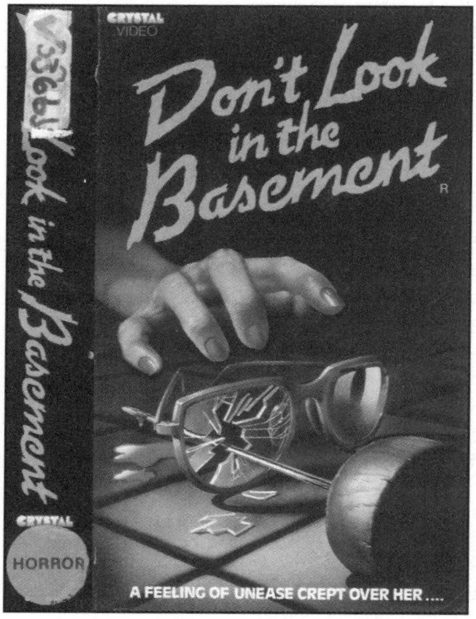

DON'T LOOK IN THE BASEMENT
TITLE ON PRINT: "DON'T LOOK IN THE BASEMENT"
AKA: The Forgotten (original title); Death Ward #13
USA 1973
CAST: William Bill McGhee, Jessie Lee Fulton, Robert Dracup, Harryette Warren, Michael Harvey, Jessie Kirby
STORY: Tim Pope
PRODUCER: S F Brownrigg
DIRECTOR: S F BROWNRIGG

CRITIQUE: It's certainly not much of a surprise to hear that Dr Masters is insane, having already given the game away right at the beginning when she declared that the patients were her "family." What does come as a jolt however, is the ambiguity as to whether Charlotte herself might also be delusional in her role as nurse.[109] From the moment she arrives, Charlotte is viewed as an outsider and never once is there anything to suggest she might be anything other than a nurse.[110] In the film's climax, when Masters' real place in the sanatorium is divulged and Charlotte confronts the other patients for confirmation, the Judge informs her, "You too are a patient my dear." Indeed, when Charlotte arrives at the sanatorium to take up her new post, and at the film's end when she leaves, we don't actually see her go anywhere but the grounds. From the onset, she is a part of the unstable, insular little world of Dr Stephens.

"Yet another slice of raw garbage," David Bartholomew wrote of this film in *The Monster Times*. But out of his budgetary short-comings, director S F Brownrigg successfully creates an oppressive atmosphere and several supremely weird moments. The curiously framed low-angle shots, for instance, which reach a subjective nadir during Danny and Charlotte's conversation in the grounds: half of the frame is focussed on grass blowing in the wind, in spite of the human activity which is taking place in the top half of the picture. Most noteworthy though is the sequence near the end, where Charlotte decides she must escape the place but... cannot find the door! (Presumably now's the time to cue in the limp promotional blurb from the videobox: "A feeling of unease crept over her...") "I can't find a way out!" Charlotte cries in desperation, leading her to the basement and the unnecessary discovery that Dr Stephens is still alive.

We never do get a clear glimpse of the exit, not once throughout the entire duration of the film. Like some psychological black star, the little world of *Don't Look in the Basement* is in a state of collapse, drawing its inhabitants inexorably towards its bloody cataclysmic breakdown and taking all means of escape with it.

Charlotte getting lost in the tiny building in which she lives is a masterstroke of paranoiac cinema, but one arising as much out of low-budget necessity as it is design. In what might be the director's only published interview, Brownrigg explained in *Draculina*[111] that *Don't Look in the Basement*

> was put together rather hurriedly... and we did put it together along the lines that I try to do the low-budget pictures, and that is we try to keep the script, until after we get the thing financed, kind of loose so that we can go to the actual location and write the script around the location where we're going to shoot.

Sherold F Brownrigg worked in commercial and industrial films for a company in Dallas, Texas, before turning his hand to feature films. His first stint was as a soundman on several of Larry Buchanan's early movies. As a director, he made just five movies, the first of which was *Don't Look in the Basement*.[112] Shot in just twelve days, it introduced the actors that would become repertory players in Brownrigg's other movies[113] and enjoyed a brief theatrical run in the South under its original title *The Forgotten*. When Hallmark picked it up, the title was changed to *Don't Look in the Basement* and distributed in a succession of horror double-bills and triple-bills across America.[114]

In its unexpurgated form, the film has a reputation of being something of a gore opus. The version released in Britain is considerably cut however, with almost every gore scene showing evidence of tampering. It seems that this truncated version is the responsibility of an American video company, who, according to *Demonique*, excised twelve minutes from the film to create "what seems their own nearly PG rated version." [115] Even the final axe massacre is a reserved affair, constituting in the main 'reaction shots' and some blood being spattered onto walls.[116]

"We were trying to out do everybody in blood and everything," Brownrigg told *Draculina*. Not a big horror film fan, Brownrigg's ambition was first to create a suspense movie in the manner of Hitchcock but, lacking any commercial clout, he went the route that offered "less chance for an investor to lose their money." Sure enough, *Don't Look in the Basement* was a success. Brownrigg stuck with horror through the seventies, directing *Poor White Trash Part 2*,[117] *Don't Open the Door*, and *Keep My Grave Open*.[118]

Despite turning a tidy profit for his distributors, Brownrigg claims not to have made the type of money he should and got disillusioned to the point that after this quartet of horror made only one more movie — a teen sex comedy called *Thinkin' Big*, which he subsequently disowned. After this he returned full-time to commercials, sales films, and "producing an outdoor hunting and fishing show for Star Sportsmen."

In John McCarty's book *The Sleaze Merchants*, exploitation director Bret McCormick[119] says that he and Brownrigg — "a close pal" — had penned a sequel to *Don't Look in the Basement* which they hoped to get onto the video shelves someday. Alas, Brownrigg died in 1997 at the age of fifty-nine.

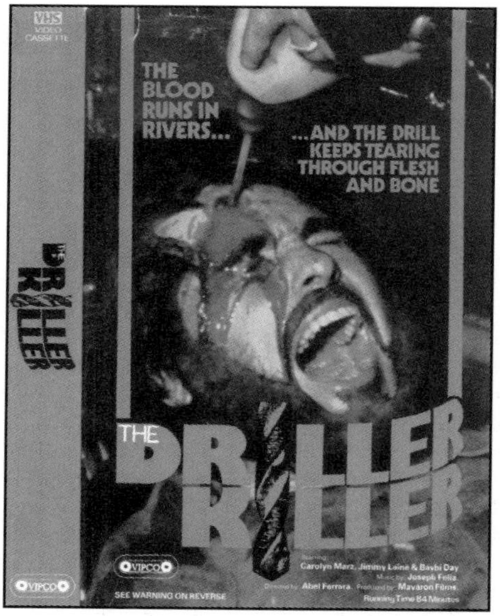

THE DRILLER KILLER
USA 1979
CAST: Jimmy Laine, Carol Marz, Baybi Day, Harry Schultz, Alan Wynroth
STORY: N G St John
PRODUCER: Rochelle Weisberg
DIRECTOR: ABEL FERRARA

THE DRILLER KILLER

SYNOPSIS: Reno, a struggling artist, is disgusted when a vagrant reaches out and touches his hand in a church. He runs from the building and jumps into a taxi with his girlfriend.

"What happened in there?" Carol asks.

"Some degenerate bum... wino... got a grip of my hand," says Reno, rubbing his hand as though contaminated.

The following day he is woken by his flat-mate Pamela who is trying, for no discernible reason, to drill a hole in the door with a power drill. Reno spends some time working on a huge canvas, a painting of a buffalo which he can't seem to finish. His concentration is thrown completely when unpaid bills arrive. So annoyed is he with the size of the phone bill that he rips the telephone from the wall and throws it through the window. Pamela and Carol simply look at him in bewilderment.

With a serious cash flow problem he goes to see his art agent and asks for a $500 advance, but the agent wants the painting finished before he will hand over any more money. When Carol tells Reno that as far as she can tell the painting is finished, Reno points out that she is no art aficionado and only *he* will know when it is completed. An advertisement on TV promotes a new device called the Porta Pak, a belt of batteries that provides portable power to any domestic electrical appliance.

Tony Coca-Cola and his band The Roosters move into the apartment below. Their all-night practice sessions make Reno's work much more difficult, and so he goes out for a walk, harassing the bums who hang around the area. Reno goes to the supervisor and complains about the noise the band is making.

"If you don't get rid of those cats, I ain't payin' the rent," Reno threatens.

"Waddaya mean, 'won't pay the rent'?" responds the supervisor. "You don't pay the rent anyway!"

Nevertheless, to appease Reno, the supervisor hands him a freshly skinned rabbit ready for cooking. Reno toys and mutilates the carcass, before going to the local hardware store where he buys a Porta Pak. That night, equipped with the Pak and power drill, he takes to the streets and murders a bum.

The Roosters are having a gig and hoping to secure a contract. Reno watches the band for a while but finds them too noisy. He leaves the show and goes on a killing spree with his power drill, running around the streets like a crazed gunman.

Having scored a contract, Tony from the band asks Reno to paint his portrait. As he poses he plays his guitar and sings, much to the annoyance of a vagrant trying to sleep in the alley down below, whom Reno later tortures and kills.

Reno decides the Buffalo painting is finished and calls in the dealer, who is far from impressed by what he sees. "No, no, no, no, this is *shit*!" he shouts before walking out. Carol has had enough of this impoverished lifestyle and decides to go back to her ex-husband, Stephen, despite Reno's attempts to stop her.

Alone, Reno calls the art dealer and invites him to come round again, promising him something worthwhile. Reno uses Carol's makeup to feminise his face. When the dealer arrives he is summarily drilled through the chest and pinned to the door. Pamela returns to the apartment and discovers the body but she is unable to escape from Reno.

Carol is taking a shower at Stephen's apartment when Reno enters and kills him. With the place in darkness, Carol fails to see her ex-husband's body, nor does she realise that the shape under the bedsheet is Reno... waiting.

CRITIQUE: *The Driller Killer* is more an art-house film than a horror film, yet too much of a horror film to sit comfortably with the former's convention and as a result tends to alienate both audiences.[120] Had Reno gone out and murdered in a more conventional manner, say with a gun, things would have been much simpler. The focus would have been taken away from the means of murder, but — as the title of the film corroborates — the emphasis is on *how* he kills rather than *why*.

What confounds matters further is the fact that director Abel Ferrara doesn't suggest there is anything deeply significant in Reno's *modus operandi*. "To me it's a comedy," he said in an interview for *Shock Xpress*.

> Like drilling people, that's a joke, that was our sense of fun! The idea is a documentary about a dear friend of mine. I played the role of my friend. He lived in that attic with those two girls, they were his real girlfriends. I played the role because it was shot over a long period of time, and we couldn't interest an actor in staying with a film shot in bits and pieces.[121]

When we see Reno go on his kill spree, running unnoticed around the streets and brandishing his power drill like a revolver, we can well believe Ferrara that the film is a comedy at heart.

Reno sees his world collapsing and his greatest fear is that he will soon be joining the 'degenerate bums' he so despises. Killing them, wiping them out, will forestall the inevitable — or so he believes. When the awful Roosters get themselves a lucrative contract and Reno loses his own painting deal, he can't comprehend the injustice and he feels he's on a road to nowhere. Carol leaving him only compounds his downfall. From this point on, Reno ceases to focus his anger on vagrants and instead begins to destroy his peers.

When James Ferman reflected upon gory video sleeves in the early eighties and the part they played in generating the nasties backlash (see previous chapter), he singled out as a particular pertinent example the artwork for *The Driller Killer*. Given the film's art-house aspirations however, the director of the BBFC had no qualms that *The Driller Killer* could be passed with only a few cuts. Ironic then that the killings and their lingering grisliness should actually detract from the film as a whole. When Reno murders his first victim, barely has the drill bit touched the clothing of the vagrant than a fountain of blood is gushing in the air. Though the effects themselves are cleverly realised — in particular the drilling of the head as shown on the garish sleeve — they seem almost superfluous.

The Driller Killer was released on the Vipco label uncertified and with the few gore scenes intact. After fifteen years in uncertified limbo, the film was finally submitted to the BBFC in 1999 by Visual Films and passed 18 with cuts. This version also reinstated some non-violent scenes that had been missing from Vipco's original print and utilised considerably tamer video sleeve artwork.

Part of *The Driller Killer*'s regeneration as something of an 'acceptable' nasty is down to Ferrara's partial assimilation into the mainstream, with a remake of Don Siegel's *Invasion of the Body Snatchers* and episodes of *Miami Vice* under his belt (we say 'partial assimilation' because other features like *Dangerous Game* and *The Funeral* are far from typical mainstream fare). On top of this is the recognition that *The Driller Killer* — Ferrara's first major feature — offers some kind of social comment. Ferrara said of its New York City setting:

> That's where I live, the awfulness is there... A lot of the film is real, but if we staged something, we were sure there was something twice as bad going on two blocks away![122]

With the importance — nay, reverence — now attributed to the punk rock era, where once *The Driller Killer* was largely perceived to be a horrible scruffy lout, now it's also seen to be 'art' (as if the two couldn't co-exist before historians got a handle on them). Punk credibility is provided in an early title card which advises that the film be played loud, its use of the bargain-basement punksters The Roosters, and the rumour that Ferrara tried to get David Johansen of the New York Dolls to play the role of Reno.

THE EVIL DEAD

THE EVIL DEAD
AKA: Book of the Dead (original title)
USA 1982
CAST: Bruce Campbell, Ellen Sandweiss, Betsy Baker, Hal Delrich, Sarah York
STORY: Sam Raimi
PRODUCER: Robert G Tapert
DIRECTOR: SAM RAIMI

SYNOPSIS: Five young people are heading for a vacation in an isolated forest. An unstable bridge is all that links their shack with the outside world, and as they approach the run-down building a swaying porch seat suspended on chain beats a rhythm against the wall. Scotty is first out of the car. When he reaches the keys hidden on top of the doorframe, the swaying chair comes to a standstill. Scotty looks on, puzzled, as the others unload the car.

Later, Cheryl is sketching the clock on the wall when the pendulum suddenly stops swinging, fixed at an angle that defies gravity. She hears something calling from the woods: "Join us." Losing control of her hand, she scrawls a disturbing face-like form on her drawing pad.

While the group are eating, a trapdoor to the cellar suddenly bursts open and Scotty volunteers to go down to investigate. The others wait in the room and call to him. When they hear no reply, Ashley goes down to find him. The cellars are expansive and divided into smaller rooms. Ashley finds Scotty who has discovered a pile of interesting junk, amongst which is a strange-looking book, some kind of ceremonial dagger, and a tape machine. They carry the stuff upstairs and play the tape, only to hear the owner of the shack relate occult practices and his experiments with the strange book. It is revealed that the book is bound in human skin and contains incantations to summon ancient Sumerian demons. Scotty winds the tape on and plays some mysterious chanting. Outside, in the woods, something is erupting from the ground. Cheryl is disturbed by the tape and demands it to be turned off, just as a tree branch crashes through the window.

Ashley gives Linda a pendant, unaware that outside the window they are being watched. Moving from window to window, the unseen entity then focuses on Cheryl who is alone in her room. She becomes aware that she is being watched and goes outside to investigate. Wandering into the woods, the foliage suddenly comes alive and attacks her but she manages to break free and run back to the shack. She tells her friends what has happened but they think she is just being hysterical. Cheryl refuses to stay any longer and demands to be taken back to town. Ashley volunteers to drive her but the car won't start.

"I know it's not going to start. It's not going to let us leave," Cheryl says when suddenly the engine bursts into life. They drive off but get no further than the ravine because the bridge has collapsed.

Back at the shack Linda and Shelly are playing with a pack of cards. Linda asks Shelly to guess what card she is looking at, but Cheryl — who is facing the other way — interrupts and begins to correctly name the cards even before they are turned over. When she turns around her features have altered. Levitating and speaking in a demonic voice, she lunges at the others and manages to stab Linda in the ankle with a pencil. She turns on Ashley but Scotty manages to overpower her and throw her into the cellar, whereupon he locks the trapdoor. Ashley carries the injured Linda to her room and they all decide to leave first thing in the morning.

Shelly becomes possessed herself and transforms after the unseen thing from the woods bursts through the window of her room. When Scotty is alerted by the noise, she lunges at him. They fight, crashing into the main room and Shelly ends up being thrown into the fire. Scotty rescues her from the flames, but she continues fighting. Even being stabbed with the ornate dagger doesn't stop her, and Scotty is ultimately forced to beat her to the floor with an axe and dismember her.

Having buried Shelly's remains in the woods, Scotty says he can't wait until morning and decides to leave on foot. When Ashley points out that Linda can't walk, he says that she's his problem and leaves anyway. Ashley checks on Linda and examines the wound on her ankle, which suddenly spreads rapidly from her ankle up her leg. She rises from the bed transformed like the others.

Scotty bursts back into the shack severely wounded and, before he dies, tells Ashley that Cheryl was right about the trees being alive.

Linda is taunting Ashley, and Cheryl is trying to break out of the cellar. Ashley arms himself with a shotgun and is about to shoot Linda when she reverts to her normal self. Cheryl also claims to be okay but, as Ashley is about to open up the cellar door, Cheryl and Linda switch back to their demonic selves. He drags Linda outside and attempts to leave her in the woods, but she follows him back into the shack and attacks him with the knife. Ashley manages to immobilise her and prepares to dismember her body with a chainsaw in the workshed. He is unable to bring himself to do it however and buries her, whereupon she scrambles from her grave and attacks him. Ashley finally decapitates Linda with a shovel but back in the shack discovers that Cheryl has escaped from the cellar. He sees her outside and shoots her. He goes into the cellar to retrieve more shells and the cellar walls leak blood. Back upstairs he is attacked by Cheryl and the reanimated Scotty. As they fight around the room the book falls close to the fire which causes Scotty to emit smoke. Ashley manages to hurl the book fully into the flames and both Cheryl and Scotty decompose before his eyes.

TOP: *The Evil Dead* at Cannes.
ABOVE: Panels from 'House of Evil,' *Eerie* No 4 (1966).

Dawn breaks and Ashley prepares for his trek back to the road. As he leaves the hut an invisible demon rises from the ground and seizes him.

CRITIQUE: *The Evil Dead* was Sam Raimi's debut feature and, as so often seems the case, it remains his best and most striking work. It was Raimi's maverick style as much as the outlandish special effects and camera work that propelled the movie into instant cult classic status. From the opening moment when the camera glides over a sinister-looking pond the film rarely lets up. Whether rushing through the woods knocking down trees in its path, or providing forced perspective shots of characters, the camera technique generates an excitement all of its own.

Raimi — an ardent horror movie and Three Stooges fan — borrows ideas from many sources, yet manages to convert them into something almost wholly unique. The scenes in the forest, for instance, evoke the chilling woodland chase sequence in Jacques Tourneur's *Night of the Demon*. The 'above the rafters' point-of-view shot of Ashley in *The Evil Dead*'s latter half appear remarkably similar to the Steadycam shots in Kubrick's *The Shining*, where Danny rides his pedal car through hotel corridors (even down to replicating the strange on-off sound effects of that film as the car crosses rugs and wooden floor surfaces).[123]

There are also some cryptic references in the film, such as a poster for Wes Craven's *The Hills Have Eyes* which is on a wall of the cellar torn in half. This isn't so much a homage to Craven as an amicable dig at a movie that frightened Raimi. In *The Hills Have Eyes* a torn poster for *Jaws* can be seen on a wall, as if to signify that however scary that particular film was things here are scarier... Raimi considered his own film to be even scarier, hence the poster on his wall.[124]

There are times when the film's pace slips and its amateurish origins are revealed. While this generally serves to enhance the picture's charm,[125] there are moments when it can be merely exasperating, such as the scenes in which Ashley gets entangled in the collapsed bookshelves. There is no discernible reason why Ashley can't get back on his feet, yet he struggles under the flimsy woodwork as though he were trapped beneath a truck. Minor complaints aside, *The Evil Dead* achieves exactly what it set out to accomplish and provides a relentless assault on the senses.

Even the limited acting capacity of Bruce Campbell as Ashley does nothing to diminish the impact of the film. If anything, the sight of Campbell desperately trying to express fear and panic serve to amplify the madness of the piece. He shakes and babbles in a hyper-nervous state as the objects in the building around him take on hallucinatory qualities. Blood starts to poor from the walls, a wall mirror loses its natural solid state and — most inspired of all, when Ashley finds he needs only stave off the demons a little longer before dawn breaks — time itself reverses! If Raimi never picked up a camera again this scene alone ought to secure for him auteur status.

Having already made many Super-8 shorts together, Sam Raimi, Bruce Campbell and Robert Tapert raised money for *The Evil Dead* by showing to potential backers *Within the Woods* — a half-hour condensed treatment of their *Evil Dead* screenplay. With a budget ranging anywhere from $90,000 to $420,000 (depending on the source), *The Evil Dead* took three years to make. Raimi claims he never had particularly high hopes and was happy to simply have the film play the drive-in circuit. "We wanted a film that would stop people kissing in their cars and turn their attention to the screen," he told *Starburst* magazine.[126]

The picture soon grew to be an international success carrying an endorsement from Stephen King no less, who considered it a work of genius not to mention "the most ferociously original" horror movie of the year.[127]

A possible influential source for the basic story can be found in issue No 4 of the comic *Eerie*, published by Warren in 1966. A Joe Orlando and Archie Goodwin strip titled 'House of Evil' concerns a man, Lee Hargraves, who goes to an isolated house in search of his brother. The house seems deserted and Hargraves finds a tape recorder which he plays. A narrator on the tape — Hargraves' brother — tells of the house's history and the original owners who used the place to summon demons. As the tape plays it lures a hideous zombie-like creature into the room. Hargraves attacks it with a chair and the thing crumbles and decomposes into a slimy mess. It turns out the thing was Hargraves' brother infected by the house's evil. Hargraves himself is now infected and transforming.

As if that strip in itself wasn't enough to draw a comparison, in the same issue there is a strip in which a man decapitates his lover and she returns from the dead, her severed head talking to him while the headless body wanders around — strikingly reminiscent to the killing and subsequent resurrection of Ashley's girlfriend.

The film was followed by two sequels which, despite considerably higher production values, were played for juvenile laughs and were downright inferior to the original.[128] (The best thing that can be said for the third instalment, *Army of Darkness*, is that it had a great tentative title in *The Medieval Dead*.)

The Evil Dead was released on the Palace video label in the same slightly censored state it was released theatrically in the UK. The film is overtly gory but in such a cartoonish and over-the-top manner that it is impossible to be offended by it... although it evidently did offend some people...

For perhaps no other reason than it had 'evil' in the title, *The Evil Dead* was singled out by anti-video nasties protestors (led by Mary Whitehouse) as being particularly objectionable. This in spite of it being essentially a good old-fashioned scare story, a criteria which most campaigners claimed differentiated the horrors of the video nasties from traditional, more acceptable horrors. The film was the subject of many courtroom battles around the country (film director David Puttnam was amongst the defence witnesses ready to give evidence). After it and Palace had been cleared of obscenity at Snaresbrook Crown Court, in what was regarded as something of a test case, Judge Owen Stable QC criticised the DPP and in summing-up said

> I regard it as quite lamentable that in relation to a single film that there should have been over forty separate pieces of litigation up and down the country. I am concerned with what this chaotic state of affairs does to the reputation of the administration of justice.

The Evil Dead was re-released with a few additional cuts, though again the reasoning behind some of these decisions — i.e. trimming a shot where Linda has a pencil twisted into her ankle — was baffling. In an interview with *Killing Moon*,[129] principal examiner Guy Phelps was asked why *The Evil Dead* should be cut while other over-the-top films, such as *Society* and *Bad Taste*, were passed intact. He replied:

> *Society* and *Bad Taste* didn't seem to have any handle on reality; they were clearly placed in the completely fantasy world. You can obviously say the same about *The Evil Dead*, but within that there were moments where the violence to the people took you into a much more realistic handling of violence. The wriggling of a pencil deep into someone's ankle gives you a very real jolt of pain in a way the taking of the top of the man's head off in *Bad Taste* clearly didn't — it was obviously ludicrous and fairly painless as well!
>
> I think the particular problem with horror is that there are two ways of looking at these things. The public at large see them as quite real, whereas the horror buff sees them as totally unreal. So for them the horror film is not at all dangerous for the public at large, as we all saw in 1982-3, it clearly is.

EVILSPEAK

SYNOPSIS: On a rocky beach in sixteenth-century Spain, devil worshipper Lorenzo Esteban is banished from the country by the Inquisition. He conducts one final ritual before his exile and decapitates a willing sacrifice.

In modern-day America a football game is underway at West Andover Military Academy. Coopersmith, an accident prone, orphaned, welfare case, lets the side down and the team loses the match. Bubba, the leader of the class, bullies Coopersmith and insists he shouldn't play in the next game. The team coach tells Bubba that anyone can play but, in a whispered aside, hints that if Coopersmith where to have an accident...

On open day, Coopersmith is assigned "punishment duty" and has to clean out the cluttered cellar. The rest of the academy enjoys themselves and the Reverend explains to one visitor how the land on which the academy is built was given to Lorenzo Esteban as his place of exile prior to his execution. "Mmmm... how interesting," replies the visitor, "and *strange*."

A portrait of the Satanist hangs on the chapel wall.

In the cellars, Coopersmith uncovers a secret chamber that contains occult paraphernalia and Esteban's book on devil worship. That night Coopersmith has a nightmare about Esteban and he wakes late for class, his electric alarm clock having been unplugged and his clothes tied in knots by Bubba's gang. In one lesson Coopersmith utilises the computer to translate pages from Esteban's book. It explains how to conduct rituals that will enable the return of the Satanist himself.

When the lessons are over Coopersmith has to report to the colonel because of his persistent lateness. He is punished verbally and physically, and when he leaves doesn't realise that Esteban's book has fallen unnoticed into the wastebin.

Assigned further punishment duties Coopersmith is made to slop out the pigs on the farm. Meanwhile, the colonel's secretary finds the book and tries to prise off the decorative motif on its cover. As she does so, the pigs become frenzied and almost attack Coopersmith.

Back in his dorm, Coopersmith discovers that his model catapult — part of an important class project — has been wrecked by Bubba and his gang. He also realises that his book has gone and confronts Bubba, but believes the bully when he claims to know nothing about it.

Coopersmith takes a computer down into the cellars so he can work on the translation without being disturbed. He thinks he has all the instructions and ingredients to perform the resurrection ritual, but when h inputs the data is informed that two ingredients are missing — consecrated host and blood. Coopersmith misses dinner so the chef takes pity on him and cooks him up a steak. He also shows the boy a litter of puppies, allowing Coopersmith to take the runt.

In the cellar the computer still demands the two missing ingredients. Coopersmith goes to the chapel but doesn't have the nerve to steal any wafers. He tries to finish the ritual without the necessary parts and is surprised to hear strange noises. He goes to investigate and is set upon by strange looking creatures. He passes out unaware that the attackers are Bubba and his gang in fancy dress. When Coopersmith comes round he thinks the ritual was successful.

The next day Coopersmith and his puppy are discovered by Sarge, the alcoholic caretaker who lives in the cellar. He looks like he's about to kill the dog when Coopersmith kicks him between the legs. "I'm going to show you how to turn a little boy into a little girl," Sarge threatens Coopersmith, but some supernatural force intervenes and kills him.

Coopersmith rushes to tell the colonel but is reprimanded for his untidy appearance and sent away. Meanwhile, in her dormitory, the secretary is still trying to remove the motif from the book. The pigs become frenzied, break from their pen, herd into her room and eat the secretary alive. The book fades and disappears.

Teenage models competing for the title of Miss Heavy Artillery put on a show for the academy. The colonel tells Coopersmith that he won't be playing in the big match the following day, and soon after Coopersmith is bullied once again by Bubba's gang. Finding the secret chamber in the cellar, the gang read the rituals on the computer and sacrifice the puppy, but the computer still demands human blood.

The next day Coopersmith finds the dead dog. Incensed and no longer inhibited, he goes to the chapel and takes the wafers. He then murders a member of the academy staff who follows him to

EVILSPEAK
USA 1981
CAST: Clint Howard, R G Armstrong, Joseph Cortes, Claude Earl Jones, Hatywood Nelson, Don Stark, Charles Tyner, Hamilton Camp, Louie Gravance, Jim Greenleaf, Lynn Hancock, Loren Lester, Kathy McCullen, Lenny Montana
STORY: Joseph Garofalo
PRODUCERS: Sylvio Tabet & Eric Weston
DIRECTOR: ERIC WESTON

Spot the difference. *Evilspeak* promotional artwork, during and after production (LEFT AND RIGHT). The latter image depicts Clint Howard – although this was altered again for the videobox art (PREVIOUS PAGE).

the cellar and uses his blood to finalise the ritual. Bubba's gang are in the chapel when Coopersmith crashes through the floor, levitating and wielding a sword. Behind him follows the herd of pigs. Coopersmith despatches all his tormentors and is duly interned in a psychiatric hospital. The computer continues to flash a message and indicates that if the ritual is performed Coopersmith will return.

CRITIQUE: Child star of the sixties TV show *Gentle Ben*, with some ninety film appearances in thirty years, *Evilspeak* marked the first star part for the young adult Clint Howard. He attacks the role of Coopersmith with gusto, seemingly perfectly attuned to the downtrodden, ham-fisted student. Indeed, as a result of *Evilspeak*, the diminutive pudgy-faced actor would be called to appear in more and more films in the horror genre (though it would be over a decade before his next leading role, a homicidal mental patient in *Ice Cream Man*). Thanks to his brother Ron Howard, director of hits like *EdTV*, *Splash* and *Backdraft*, Clint's career is not relegated to low-budget dreck but occasionally crosses over to big-budget Hollywood productions. For his role in *Apollo 13* – brother Ron's most successful movie to date in which Clint played a mission control technician – he received a shared cast award.

Howard doesn't denigrate the more modest productions he's called to work in, and rarely turns any part down. The fact that, in his own words, he's "a funny looking guy," hasn't hindered his career in the least. "God has seen fit that I'm a character actor," he told *Psychotronic*.[130] "In my own head, I'm not a leading man. I'm not a hero in my own head."

Of all the movies he's appeared in, it is *Evilspeak* for which Howard has a particular fondness. Because the story incorporated a computer, the actor considers it ahead of its time (the computer isn't actually called to do very much beyond flash digital text on the screen and project some rather improbable swirling pentangles. At one point it looks like Esteban has his own 'logo').

Eric Weston never managed to breakthrough with *Evilspeak*, despite the relative compe-

Fiona Richmond and Linda Hayden (blonde) get it on in *Exposé*.

tence he showed as a director. Howard has suggested that the movie was the first in a prospective trilogy, hence the tagged-on digital message warning that the wrath of Coopersmith can be evoked in a ritual. For all of Weston's directorial promise and Howard's capacity as an actor, the premise of *Evilspeak* is not so good you'd want to see it pan into a second or third instalment. Indeed the story is formulaic to the point of tedium. With everything being stacked so unfavourably towards Coopersmith it ought to be a pleasure to see him avenge himself. (He doesn't belong... He's chubby... Everybody hates and deceives him — even the Reverend... He's hopeless at sports ... He's an orphan... Sarge wants to sodomise him... They call him names... They kill his cute l'il puppy...) But Coopersmith's revenge is an inevitability — a particularly lame one at that — about which the only good thing is the fact that it draws the film closer to its end.

The gore effects are relatively few, but fairly visceral. They include the decapitation of a topless woman, a brief shot of a pig pulling innards from the naked secretary, and the possessed Sarge sinking his hand into Bubba's chest and removing a heart. With a few cuts, the Board had no problem passing *Evilspeak* as 18 some years after it featured on the DPP list.

EXPOSÉ

SYNOPSIS: Over gently swaying wheat fields, the voice of a young woman discusses the typing post she has seen advertised. Elsewhere, a storm is brewing. Best-selling novelist Paul Martin leads his girlfriend Suzanne to his bedroom. She strips off, he dons surgical gloves, and they have sex. Unflattering wide-angle shots of Suzanne's face cause Paul to have a panic attack. He begins to shake and sweat profusely, imagining that a man in a dinner suit is standing outside the house with a knife. In his delirium, Paul sees bloodied wrists, the pages of a book flipping by, and a manuscript titled *Straw Summer* bearing his name.

Paul has just two weeks in which to come up with a new bestseller. Not even the quiet country cottage in which he has secluded himself is helping, and he blames his slow progress on the lack of a typist to whom he can dictate his book.

His girlfriend leaves.

After calling his agent — during which the table lamp flickers on and off — Paul sits alone on the stairs, muttering a soliloquy: "To harass; to worry; to importune; to pursue; to persecute; decay; crumble; rot; die!"

A man with troubles, Paul retires to his bedroom and imagines himself with a knife in his bloodied hands.

The agency calls back with the news that they have found a typist. Paul drives to meet her at the train station, and thinks that

Linda, his new secretary, looks familiar. He tells her that he doesn't trust people and that they have a lot of work to get through.

A short stop on the way back to the house results in Linda being accosted by two young men on bicycles.[131] Fighting dirty, Paul leaves them squirming on the floor and quickly drives away.

The following day, after a spot of dictation, Linda goes to make coffee and starts to snoop around the house. She is particularly inquisitive about Paul's bedroom. Back in her own room, she slips a hand into her knickers and masturbates in front of a photograph of her late husband. A storm breaks out (as it did the last time there was any sex on-screen).

"Everything alright?" Paul asks on Linda's return to the study.

"Fine," she replies.

"You've been a long time."

"In coming?" she says, suggestively biting into a biscuit.

Later, while Linda is out of the house, still insistent that he has met the girl before, Paul starts to rummage through her belongings. He pulls from her suitcase a pair of knickers, a dildo, and *The Oxford Book of Latin Verse*.

Linda is lying in a wheat field, masturbating again. She looks up to see the two thugs from earlier. They rape her at gunpoint, but Linda manages to win their shotgun and shoots them both. She says nothing of the incident to anybody.

Without Paul's knowledge, Linda dismisses Mrs Aston, the housekeeper.

Paul is a boor. He talks about himself all the time. He even believes that this new book of his "may be in line for the Pulitzer Prize." Over an evening drink, Paul tells Linda that he feels happy and content, and that they're getting to know each other well. Suddenly, he has a fit of paranoia and insists that "they" are out to get him. In a drunken stupor he collapses onto the floor and dreams again about the man in the dinner suit, rubber gloves, and a knife penetrating flesh in close-up.

When he regains consciousness, he suspects that Linda is masturbating in her room. She is.

(Time becomes meaningless, as day slips into night, and night drifts back to day. Paul is flat-out drunk one moment, and stone-cold sober the next.)

For reasons unknown, Mrs Aston slips back into the house — only to get her throat cut by an unseen assailant.

More table lamps flicker on and off inexplicably.[132]

During dictation, Paul makes a pass at Linda. When she rejects his advances, he throws a tantrum and invites Suzanne, his girlfriend, back over. But Linda makes a pass at Suzanne, and Paul throws an even bigger tantrum. Later, inadvertently interrupting Paul and Suzanne while they are making violent love, Linda runs out of the house and drives off in one of the cars. Paul attempts to follow her, but is soon given the slip. Linda returns to the house to continue what she started with Suzanne.

As the two girls reach their climax, Paul — discovering the brakes on the car have been tampered with — crashes into a pond.

Suzanne discovers the body of Mrs Aston in Linda's wardrobe, and hides in the bathroom (where for no reason she flushes the toilet and turns on the shower). Linda comes in and slashes Suzanne's naked torso with a knife, before stabbing her and leaving her dead in the bathtub.

Paul returns to the house on foot. "There's no one I can trust," he moans. When he inquires about Suzanne, Linda says she's taking a nap.

Linda insists that they finish the book. Indeed, she effectively writes the ending by herself, refusing to heed anything that Paul dictates or suggests. When it's finished, she tells the author that she is going to kill him. Donning the rubber gloves, Linda slashes Paul

EXPOSÉ
TITLE ON PRINT: THE HOUSE ON STRAW HILL
AKA: Trauma
GREAT BRITAIN 1975
CAST: Linda Hayden, Fiona Richmond, Patsy Smart, Karl Howman, Vic Armstrong
STORY: James Kenelm Clarke
PRODUCER: Brian Smedley-Aston
DIRECTOR: JAMES KENELM CLARKE

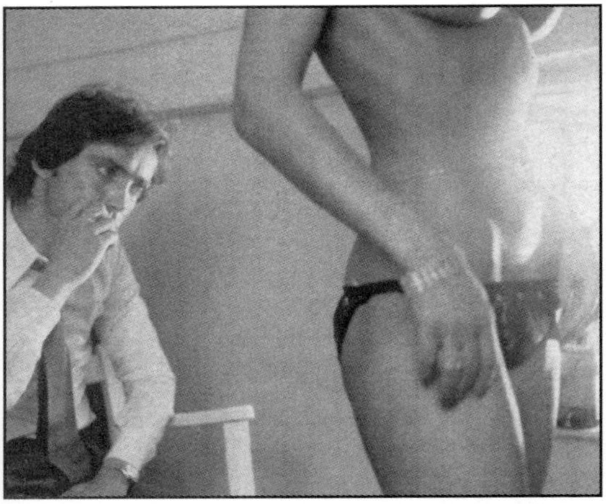

Paul (Udo Kier) gets nervous in *Exposé*.

across the face with a knife and gives chase to him through the house. He manages to grab the shotgun that has been hanging on the wall (as the table lamp flashes again) and the hunter momentarily becomes the hunted. A fight in the garden shed results in Linda getting the shotgun and Paul the knife. He runs into a field and throws the knife away as Linda, with the shotgun, catches up. She explains to Paul why he must die. Her husband was the late-Simon Hindstatt, the *real* author of Paul's previous best-selling novel. Paul stole the book, a fact which drove Simon to commit suicide.

Linda squeezes the trigger. The shotgun isn't loaded. Just then, one of the rapists from earlier lunges into shot, stabs Linda with the knife that Paul disposed of moments earlier, and dies. The paranoid Paul is surrounded by dead bodies.

CRITIQUE: James Kenelm Clarke's sex and horror hybrid was released theatrically in Britain in 1976 as *Exposé*. Under this title it was packaged for video release by Intervision, despite the title on the video print itself being *The House on Straw Hill*.[133]

These differing titles give some clue to the problem that faced Clarke's film.

Although Udo Kier (who plays Paul Martin) and Linda Hayden (Linda) were both familiar names in exploitation cinema,[134] the film's big selling point was that it featured Fiona Richmond (Suzanne) — "Britain's Number One Sex Symbol." A celebrity in most part due to the monthly column she wrote for Paul Raymond's *Men Only* magazine, much of the film's promotion was geared around Richmond and the fact that *Exposé* marked her feature length movie debut. Indeed, Fiona's piece in the January 1976 edition of *Men Only* was a set-report for the soon-to-be released movie. It might not have offered much by way of insight — the guys in the crew were said to be "dishy" and Fiona "could cheerfully have given them all one" — but it does prove what a last-minute decision it was to change the title. In the article, the film is refereed throughout as *The House on Straw Hill*, and Fiona pegs its release down as "very soon." In actually fact, not two months later, the *Monthly Film Bulletin* had reviewed the film as *Exposé*. British distributors Target International were responsible for the title change,[135] *Exposé* being an obvious attempt to make the whole thing seem more 'naughty' than it actually was — as evidenced in the advertising blurb that promised of Fiona, "Nothing is left to the imagination."

The initial, better-suited title of *The House on Straw Hill* is obviously derivative of Sam Peckinpah's disturbing *Straw Dogs*, a film from which Kenelm Clarke draws some inspiration.[136] The sexual connotations in the title and marketing of *Exposé*, however, suggests something akin to a skin-flick.

> Proves that if adult-film makers would add explicit sex to a good story they might produce more interesting films. This one has the story, but implied sex, including rape, is not detailed.
>
> —*The X-Rated Videotape Guide I*

> Slow, pointless softcore porn number… horror fans should fast forward their VCR's to the last twenty minutes.
>
> —*Hi-Tech Terror No 20*

The film's uneasy combination of eroticism and horror could have won little favour with the powers that be. Scenes of soft-porn lovemaking are either interrupted by Paul's violent hallucinations, or, in the case of the lesbian romp between Linda and Suzanne, followed by vicious, sadistic murder. Linda's bout of masturbation and subsequent rape in the field makes for a particularly uneasy alliance, given that she shows no signs of fear or emotion throughout the ordeal. The BBFC would undoubtedly construe the victim's failure to respond to the sex attack in the same negative way as they would the sight of a victim who suddenly enjoys her ordeal — as evidenced in their cuts for *Exposé*'s re-release in 1997.

Director Clarke worked on BBC2's documentary programme *Man Alive*, and it was a report on the British sexploitation business that prompted him to take up film-making. No sooner had the report aired in 1975 than Clarke had acquired funding from Paul Raymond[137] and was directing Fiona Richmond in a trio of films: *Exposé*, *Let's Get Laid!* and *Hardcore*. For the latter two, Clarke resorted to the British tradition of lame sex-comedy.

Exposé was one of the more elusive films to make it to the DPP list. While it definitely suffered from poor distribution, one suspects that the film also fell foul of its own marketing in that the drawing power of Fiona Richmond had diminished considerably by the time it made it to video. She may well have been "Britain's Number One Sex Symbol" back in 1975, when the film was made, but by the eighties that crown had been relinquished. Porn's hierarchy had shifted in favour of a more explicit stable of models, courtesy of Mary Millington, and David Sullivan's publishing empire. Those people who wanted pornographic videos could readily get hold of cut-down versions of notorious American titles (like *Deep Throat* and *Debbie Does Dallas*), or fully uncut hardcore courtesy of mail order companies like Videx and Taboo,[138] who advertised regularly in film and video magazines.

Ironically, given the current retro chic and the modest success of the Saucy Seventies series of movies released by Medusa recently,[139] Fiona Richmond has once again come to the fore as "Britain's Biggest Sex Star of the Seventies." Siren Video have re-mastered and reissued *Exposé* — together with *Let's Get Laid!* and *Hardcore* — with Fiona as the key selling point. Passed with fifty-one seconds of cuts, Siren's video is missing much of Suzanne's murder as well as the aforementioned rape of Linda.

It was noted in the *Aurum Film Encyclopedia* that on the film's original theatrical release the censor cut thirty minutes — a fact compounded by *Psychotronic*[140] in their review some years later. However, this is unlikely. Producer Smedley-Aston recalls that only a little self-imposed cutting was ever made, specifically a shot of blood running own Suzanne's legs following her murder.[141]

Clarke is reported as saying he intends to remake *Exposé*.

FACES OF DEATH
AKA: Junk
USA/JAPAN 1979
CONSULTANT NARRATOR: Dr Frances B Gröss [Michael Carr]
PRODUCER: Rosilyn T Scott
WRITER: Alan Black
DIRECTOR: CONAN LE CILAIRE

FACES OF DEATH

SYNOPSIS: "Prepare yourself for a journey — a journey into a world where each new step may give you a better understanding of your own reality."

With that caveat *Faces of Death* offloads a succession of film clips that look at man's mortality, and the mysteries and rites surrounding death. An early warning as to the exact nature of this supposed 'factual' and 'serious' investigation comes with the appearance of the aptly named host, the self-proclaimed "doctor of the pathological sciences" Dr Frances B Gröss (an actor whose real identity is revealed in the end credits).[142]

Faces of Death opens with footage of open heart surgery, accompanied by the beating of a heart on the soundtrack. Both film and soundtrack are slowed down to a dead halt for the credits. With numerous shots of cadavers in a mortuary and a close-up of an autopsy, Gröss walks in — his hair unkempt and glasses askew — removing a pair of surgical gloves and disposing of them in a pedal bin (in a room that looks more like a kitchen than a doctor's surgery). An assistant passes him a jar which he studies momentarily, before continuing with a story of how a recurring funeral-dream made him want to travel the world and study death. Gröss supplies a banal voice-over and often bizarre philosophical musing to each of the film clips that follow.

The first stop in his guileless compilation is Guanajuato, Mexico, where exhumed corpses are found to be mummified because of rich minerals in the earth. The eerie synthesiser score compliments Gröss' observation that the bodies have "faces frozen with the final vision."

This is followed by brief shots of a bull fight, and a lengthy episode involving fighting dogs. Two bloodied pit bull terriers bite and tear at one another courtesy of footage that plays in slow motion. "If this appears inhuman," says Gröss, "remember, these animals know only one way of life; they have been conditioned by man to declare war on their own kind."

The Amazon jungle brings film of animals feeding in their natural habitat. A swimming snake is supposedly attacked by a school of piranha fish and stripped of its flesh — an encounter which has obviously been fabricated in the editing room. Similarly, footage of natives hunting a monkey with a blowgun, and a tribe of head-hunters displaying shrunken heads, comprise of mismatched stock which gives the appearance of having its origins elsewhere.

In Africa, Masai tribesmen bleed a cow before slaughtering and cooking it.

Back in the Western world, a sombre rendition of 'Old McDonald Had A Farm' accompanies film of a farmhand pulling a chicken from a pen and hacking off its head. Threatening low-angle shots give the proceedings a sinister edge. Lambs are stunned with an electric gun and cows are bled to death in a slaughterhouse, a place described by Gröss as the "ultimate killing machine."

One of the film's most notorious segments follows. Said to take place in the Al-Ahram, a restaurant in the Middle East, two Western couples eagerly await the culinary delight of fresh monkey brains. A small screaming monkey is secured in a contraption that allows only its head to protrude through the centre of the table, and the two male diners proceed to pound he skull with tiny clubs until the animal is dead. The women look on, nauseous. The waiter opens the cranium and dishes up the bloody matter, which some of the tourists chew upon apprehensively. Everything about the scene smacks of fabrication, from the opening stock footage of an anonymous Middle Eastern city, to the obviously Caucasian staff of the restaurant (which, incidentally, has only one table, around which our four diners are seated) and the rubber monkey head which is substituted during the bludgeoning scenes.[143]

Hunting is the next topic with scenes of shark fishing, men clubbing seals for their fur, and poachers — "the murderers of nature" — skinning alligators. The latter reptile "gets his own chance at revenge" in the subsequent scenario: a news cameraman is on hand when a game warden is called to investigate reports of a fifteen-foot alligator in a lake close to a residential area. The warden spots something by a bank, throws a lasso into the reeds and is yanked out of his boat by something unseen. Camera jostle, snatches of images and frantic screams from onlookers imply that the warden is being savaged. A bloodied torso is eventually pulled ashore.

A news conference in France, 1968, results in a speaker being assassinated. Gröss claims to have tracked down the gunman, one Francois Gordon, who demonstrates his prowess by shooting watermelon targets in a clearing. (Another makeshift target, the top-half of a mannequin, explodes into a fiery ball when hit.)

In rural America, 1973, family man Mike Lawrence has gone psychotic, killed his family and is locked in a gun battle with police. The shootout ends in his death. Inside the house, a film camera manages to glimpse the bodies of Lawrence's wife and children before being turned away by a hand over the lens. "Perhaps there's a Mike Lawrence in each of us waiting to explode," says Gröss.

A brief interview with Thomas Noguchi, celebrated coroner of Los Angeles, follows. Cadavers are wheeled through the city morgue. An X-ray reveals a bullet embedded in the torso of a gang war victim. As the camera glides through the autopsy room, faces of corpses are seen being peeled back like masks, empty chest cavities glare skyward, dead babies are opened up and massive sutures produce quilts of human flesh.

Combat footage taken during WWII merges into film of a Nazi rally and bodies from concentration camps being exhumed following the Allied victory. "This face of death," intones Gröss of the Holocaust, "is by far the most devastating… I personally don't know if this kind of situation can repeat itself, but if it does, we all deserve a life in Hell."[144]

The bubonic plague, a cholera epidemic in India, and the malnourished in Biafra constitute the section on diseases (how malnutrition fits this isn't clear). Surgeons operate on a cancerous dog for purposes of research.

The marvel of modern transportation offers film of a luckless parachutist falling to his death at an air show. "I wonder what thoughts ran through this man's mind as he plummeted through the skies at eighty miles per hour?" asks Gröss, before rebuking the medical opinion that suggested the man had a fatal coronary in mid-air and was saved any undue suffering. He plays the film again in slow motion to indicate that the figure is struggling frantically right up until the very moment of impact.

A stunt on a movie set goes wrong and a car jumps a low bluff only to miss its safe target. The driver is pronounced dead.[145]

There follows news footage of a derailed train — although genuine itself, the cutaways to close-up bloodied limbs look suspect. Non-bogus footage of a woman cyclist killed by a truck culminates with a paramedic scooping detritus from the tarmac into a small plastic bag. The terrible aftermath of a mid-air collision between aircraft over San Diego (illustrated with still photographs of a Boeing 727 plummeting earthward in flames) features bodies being strewn over streets and houses. News cameras pick out the corpses and detached limbs that are spread across roof tops, gardens, and asphalt. "This disaster could be the most *gruesome* face of death," reports Gröss. As with the dubbed sobbing of a bystander in the footage of the dead cyclist, here a loop of a police siren plays incessantly.

The final investigation concerns the spirit world, and in particular the case of one Joseph Binder, architect, who claims his house is haunted by the spirits of his recently deceased wife and son. After a two-week vigil, paranormal investigators successfully capture psychic sounds and images on their "sensitive instruments" — along with a set of footprints in the flour they spread across the bedroom floor. A medium channels the spirits of "Diane" and "Mark," but the film stops suddenly with a scream… only to return with Gröss back in his office, holding up one of the ludicrous spirit photos as proof-positive that life after death exists.

A song called 'Life' brings *Faces of Death* to an end.

CRITIQUE: Given the 'shocking' nature of some of the footage that is left intact, it is puzzling why Atlantis Video Productions chose to remove a whole chunk of *Faces of Death* for the British market. The excised footage – which can still be found in the American print of the film – comprises all the material that originally fell between the Los Angeles autopsy room film and the stock footage of WWII.[146] It is probable that the reason for this wholesale removal lies in the video company wanting to save cash on magnetic tape, a fate which befell at least one other film on the nasties list (***The Driller Killer***).

According to the press book, *Faces of Death* took three years to make, comprised a team that "could have been hired by the United Nations," and answers "the unasked questions we've always had about death." But the production is shrouded in some mystery, and all the credits are obviously pseudonyms.[147] Dr Frances B Gröss, we are informed, works as a county coroner, while director Conan Le Cilaire

> has directed adventure stories from diving to scalling [sic] mountains. He is a man with a great love of celluloid. The intensity of *Faces of Death* will no doubt place him in a league all his own amongst his associates in the film world.

Into a league of his own unquestionably, but there is no

'FACES OF DEATH' DUE AT CANNES 'MARKET'

Tokyo.

Having recently had its preem in Los Angeles, "Faces of Death" by Rosilyn T. Scott and directed by Conan Le Cilaire, will be given its international launch in the market of the Cannes Festival. World-wide distribution rights have been picked up by Telecas of Japan, whose president Kenzo Kuroda will be on the Riviera, supported by two principal aides.

Among the "Faces of Death" described in the film are sequences dealing with a flesh-eating cult in San Francisco; self-immolation by a Buddhist monk; a game warden in Florida being mutilated and devoured by an alligator; and an execution by decapitation in the Middle East.

In other sequences two pit bull terriers fight to the death, while in a restaurant in India a waiter serves a live monkey with its head secured in the middle of a table. The diners are then presented with mallets and bang the monkey's head until it dies. The waiter then serves the brains.

TOP: Scene excised from the British print of *Faces of Death*.
ABOVE: Announcement in *Variety*, May 7, 1980.

hint at what these other works of Le Cilaire's might be. The same ambiguity surrounds producer Rosilyn T Scott (said to have "worked on several documentaries and docu-dramas"), writer Alan Black (described as being "a 'film doctor' for numerous movies throughout the world"), composer Gene Kauer (responsible for composing and conducting "the music for many major pictures out of Hollywood"), and director of photography Michael Golden (who is nothing less than "a leading cinematographer in the United States").

The inspiration for *Faces of Death* undoubtedly lies in an earlier film: Robert Emenegger and Allan Sandler's *Death: The Ultimate Mystery*. Although altogether more reserved in its use of grisly imagery, this earlier production looks almost like a dry-run for *Faces of Death* and the two films share many striking similarities. Most obvious being the use of a lone figure on a journey of self-discovery — who in each film starts his trip with a visit to the mummies of Guanajuato, Mexico.

Faces of Death is part of a cycle known as the mondo film — or 'shockumentaries' — feature-length documentaries that seek more to entertain and shock than to inform. The mondo film had its Golden Age in the sixties and seventies, exciting audiences with exotic and ghoulish images from around the globe. Thanks to recent camcorder technology and the home-video market, the mondo film has seen a recent rejuvenation in the form of cheaply produced, direct-to-video compilations, consisting of true gore footage captured by newshounds or culled from police files and the like.

It was Gualtiero Jacopetti who created the blueprint for the mondo genre in 1962, with his film *Mondo Cane*. Subsequent productions adhered closely to Jacopetti's successful formula — the bare bones of which would have a haughty narrator guiding the viewer through a succession of perilously linked film clips, accompanied by an overblown musical score and a sappy closing song. Some films devoted themselves to a specific topic, such as witchcraft, the mysterious continent of Asia, or sex. As the decades wore on, the world which mondo films had helped to span was getting smaller, and material that had once appeared exotic and alluring in these films seemed now dated and quaint.

Faces of Death changed that, stripping all extraneous matter away from the genus to leave the only subject still regarded as taboo. After hardcore pornography had crossed into the mainstream with movies like *Deep Throat* and *The Devil in Miss Jones* in the early-seventies, sex as a draw for mondo audiences was effectively redundant. Conan Le Cilaire helped to reshape mondo, shifting into a territory that sought only to pummel the viewer with a non-stop barrage of gruesome deaths and disasters.

Made in 1979 by an American team for the Japanese market, *Faces of Death* proved enormously popular in the Orient and even secured a place in Hong Kong's All-time Top Twenty Grossers list for 1980. It fared less well when released theatrically in the US in 1981, but later on video was a surprising success and established itself as one of the top rental hits in the country.

So popular in fact that several sequels were spawned, with *Faces of Death* parts II, III, and IV being directed again by the "man with a great love for celluloid," Le Cilaire. All these films follow the same pattern, with Dr Gröss[148] — substituted by a Dr Louis Flellis in part IV[149] — guiding the viewer through footage relating to his thoughts and theories on death.

The series appears to have come to its true end with the fourth instalment, but the title continued for a spell thanks to a German entrepreneur by the name of Uwe Schier who bought the rights to the title at the beginning of 1990. His instalments in the series — aimed solely at the German market — bear little relation to the earlier films and consist mainly of true life gore footage culled from already available sources and set to classical music.[150]

It is hard to imagine that any audience could be fooled by the patently fabricated sequences of *Faces of Death*.[151] But they were and evidently continue to be (as will be seen in BLACK MARKET & PIRATES). The camera most certainly can lie and a deceptive narrative can often go unquestioned. Back in the eighties, the film bludgeoned an audience yet to experience a daily influx of Reality TV shows and true crime reconstructions. In the nineties and beyond, the fact that the film is unobtainable in Britain and attitudes are governed by hearsay and jaundiced news reports, it is little wonder that *Faces of Death* has acquired a somewhat legendary status. It was certainly one of the films that figured prominently in the Government spearhead to outlaw the nasties.

In 1998, Gorgon Video, the current US video distributors of *Faces of Death*, made a short feature entitled *Faces of Death Fact or Fiction?*[152] Despite the questionable sincerity, the short does provide a little interesting background to the series and addresses the contentious issue of passing fabricated material off as genuine. A man hidden in shadow with a voice distortion box is introduced as director Conan Le Cilaire, described by the narrator as a "dark genius... born in the slums of Marseille." Le Cilaire admits that many scenes in the films are indeed simulated, because last minute legal responsibilities prevented him from using the source material. Other insights have more of a ring of truth about them. For instance, *Faces of Death*'s monkey brain sequence was a simulation originally based on a South East Asian culinary custom. The Japanese clients for the film, Le Cilaire explains, didn't want to show Asians in a bad light and demanded the setting be changed to the Middle East. As for the plane accident over San Diego towards the end of the film, in which human carnage litters the streets, the director claims the footage was in a can marked "Body Parts" and cost him $50 from a news agency.

Faces of Death Fact or Fiction? also boasts a special guest appearance by Dr Louis Flellis. Having supposedly deteriorated mentally and physically since his last *Faces of Death* appearance, the demented host is wheeled before the camera clutching an oxygen mask in the one hand and holding a cigar in the other. When challenged about the authenticity of some scenes, in a rare moment of lucidity Flellis responds, "What isn't simulated when you think about it?"

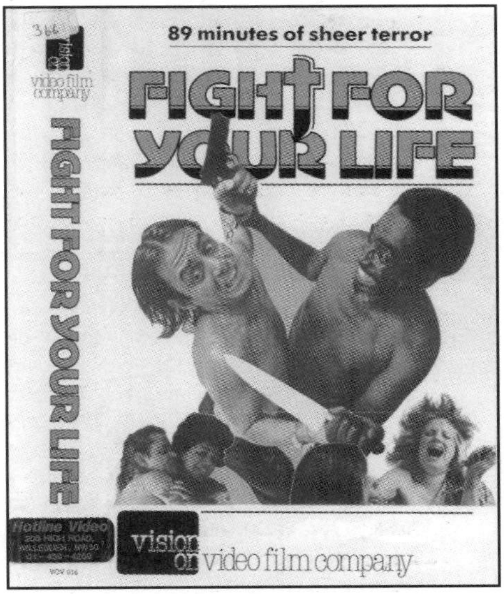

FIGHT FOR YOUR LIFE

SYNOPSIS: Following a road accident and a shootout, three dangerous felons escape from a police truck, cold-bloodedly shooting point-blank an unconscious police officer. They make a getaway in a Mercedes belonging to a pimp who happens to have pulled over to slap one of his bitches. An all-points bulletin identifies the escapees as Chino Rodriguez, Chow Ling and Jesse Lee Kane, wanted for the collective crimes of manslaughter, assault, arson, child-beating and first degree murder. "Consider all three extremely dangerous," the report concludes. "Especially Kane."

According to an old cellmate, Kane kills for the fun of it and fights dirty, too.

The gang's first obstacle is a toll booth. They have no money. Chino panics that they'll get caught, while Chow laughs, and Kane at the last minute finds some cash in the pimp's stolen car.

The Turners are a black family sitting down to a meal together — Ted Turner is a minister who believes that one day the "meek

FIGHT FOR YOUR LIFE
AKA: I Hate Your Guts; Blood Bath at 1313 Fury Road; Getting Even; Stayin' Alive; The Hostage's Bloody Revenge; The Killing Machine; Held Hostage
USA 1977
CAST: William J Sanderson, Robert Judd, Reginald Blythewood, Lela Small, Daniel Faraldo, Catherine Peppers, Yvonne Ross, Peter Yoshida
STORY: Straw Weisman
PRODUCERS: William Mishkin & Robert A Endelson
DIRECTOR: ROBERT A ENDELSON

STAND UP AND CHEER THE BROTHER WHO TAUGHT AMERICA THE MEANING OF THE WORD 'COURAGE'
FIGHT FOR YOUR LIFE
AND EXPERIENCE THE JOY OF TOTAL REVENGE

shall inherit the Earth." This philosophy is not shared by the rest of his family however, particularly crippled Grandma and young Floyd. Even Mrs Turner is less than happy to hear that Karen — a white girl — has been invited around for Thanksgiving dinner.[153]

The fugitives stop for gas and kill the pump attendant. Further down the road they hold up a liquor store in which Turner's daughter Corrie happens to be a customer. Kane shoots the cashier and points his gun at a toddler's head, laughing when he pulls the trigger and the gun is out of ammo. They take Corrie prisoner, getting her to direct them to her parents' house so that they might switch cars.

Turner has used the vehicle to drive to church. Awaiting his return, the fugitives hold the family hostage. Virtually every line of dialogue is peppered with racial slurs but, as Kane has the gun, they're nearly all directed at the Turners.[154]

Kane proceeds to get drunk. When Turner does return home, Kane has decided the gang ought to take full advantage of their situation before getting on their way. This includes dining with the Turners, a meal which sees Chino taking masticated food from his mouth and trying to offer it to Floyd. The fugitive angrily tells the family that in his country he has to eat garbage from the floor — and that they ought to do likewise. (They don't, because Kane intervenes.)

In his drunken state, Kane divulges something of his upbringing, of how he was abandoned by his mother as a child and "thrown to the animals" in prison whereupon he was raped by a black man.

Despite his son's protestations to "stand up to him," Turner refuses to lift a fist against Kane. When Kane wants his shoes shined, Turner instead explains that "The measure of a man is dignity."

"The measure of a man is power," Kane snaps back, waving the gun.

Karen — the white girl who mom so adamantly didn't want in the house — turns up after being unable to get through on the phone. Chow chases after her through the surrounding woods, catches her, rapes her and ultimately throws her off a cliff to her death. Chow also spies Joey, a friend of Floyd's, lurking nearby. He grabs the boy, pins him to the floor and smashes in his head with a rock (in slow motion). When Chow returns to the house, he brandishes Karen's underwear and gloats over the rape.

Grandma finds Kane's Achilles' heel when she riles the outlaw with comments pertaining to his manhood and his time in prison as a boy. Shortly after, Turner is beaten unconscious with his own Bible,[155] during which time the gang take it in turns to systematically rape his virgin daughter, Corrie.

The police finally locate the killers' whereabouts and surround the house. In the woods they discover the bludgeoned body of Joey — who happens to be the deputy's son. The shock causes the deputy to make a suicide run for the house and in the commotion that ensues the family win possession of the gun. Instead of giving the gang over to the police, however, Turner — who has finally had as much as he can take — tells his family "Now it's our turn." He manages to convince the police that they are still being held hostage by the gang. Retribution comes with Chino being shot in the genitals and dying a horrible, lingering death, and Chow fatally wounding himself on broken glass after trying to escape through a window. Kane is shot dead by Turner who first makes the fugitive accept some home truths.

CRITIQUE: *Fight For Your Life* is an extremely uncomfortable piece of cinema and one of the most powerful films on the DPP list. The theme of intruders breaking into a secluded house and submitting their victims to a series of degradations is not an uncommon one in exploitation cinema — several other titles on the nasties list share it, as does William Fruet's *Death Weekend*, which was released the same year as Endelson's film, and *Hostage Girls*,[156] a hardcore variant. It's a cinematic tradition that appears to have its genus in William Wyler's *The Desperate Hours* (1955).[157] However, *Fight For Your Life* substitutes the class divide usually evidenced in these types of film with one of race[158] — a turnabout owing much to the success of blaxploitation movies, which had hit their stride in the mid-seventies with the *Shaft* series and the likes of *The Candy Tangerine Man*.

Black does win through over white in the end, and the promotional campaign for *Fight For Your Life* sometimes used this fact as its selling point. "Stand up and cheer the Brother who taught America the meaning of the word 'courage'... and experience the joy of total revenge," ran one by-line, making the film look even more like a blaxploitation piece.[159] In reality, it's nothing of the sort, but a cleverly ambiguous blast of high-octane exploitation.

Despite appearing on first glance to side with the Turner family, *Fight For Your Life* doesn't do them any favours. For virtually the entire time they're on-screen, the Turners are subjected to ridicule and abuse. Beyond that, the first racial slur in the film comes not from the convicts but from Mrs Turner herself, and her opinions with regard to the white girl Karen. Certainly, Turner 'wins' out in the end and kills Kane,[160] but his 'joy of total revenge' is an act which takes all of two minutes to accomplish. Not exactly a brilliant *denouement*, given the humiliation he's had to endure to get to it. (Indeed, so swift is Turner's retribution, the film-makers try and give it some extra clout by running Kane's demise in slow motion.) However, these couple of minutes of retribution are a commercial necessity. Without them, Kane's racism would remain unchecked, and the film would be quite possibly unmarketable. With them, the film eventually opens itself to a part of the audience it has so completely alienated for most of its running time.

As Steve Puchalski notes in his review for *Shock Cinema*:[161]

> You couldn't have paid me to be the only white face in a Harlem theatre when [*Fight For Your Life*] was first shown! But the most frightening aspect of the flick is the fact it was probably enjoyed on both sides of the Mason-Dixie, for totally different reasons.

While *Fight For Your Life* on the one hand was marketed as a piece of black power propaganda, for white liberal audiences it was promoted as an out-and-out action film with no hint of racial intolerance — as per the blurb on the British videobox which simply states that *Fight For Your Life* is "eighty-nine minutes of sheer terror."

As unrelenting and inflammatory as the racial slurs appear to be, it is unlikely that they were the primary reason for the film being banned in Britain. Only a few years prior to *Fight For Your Life*, the BBFC had deliberated over another film which they feared might stir up racial feelings. This was *Uncle Tom*, a pseudo-historical reconstruction filmed in a documentary-like manner. Made by the Italian team of Gualtiero Jacopetti and Franco Prosperi — co-directors on *Mondo Cane*, and the 'fathers' of mondo cinema — it was supposedly an inquiry into conditions of slavery in the Deep South during the early nineteenth-century. But, as Guy Phelps notes in his book *Film Censorship*, the film was "in fact totally voyeuristic and exploitative. The blacks are shown to be little more than animals and the camera gloats at the treatment they receive from whites."

Uncle Tom received a theatrical release in Britain in 1973, after cuts of forty minutes had been made,[162] which included the removal of the last reel in its entirety. According to Phelps, the BBFC in general would have liked to have banned the film outright. Director Stephen Murphy however, "was not eager to expand the issues upon which 'social undesirability' becomes cause enough for rejection." As a result, *Uncle Tom* was screened for the Race Relations Board, who ultimately agreed with Murphy and felt it shouldn't be banned because the social issue was not entirely relevant — the film degraded both blacks and whites.

Still puzzling over *Uncle Tom*, the Board consulted the Race Relations Act which stipulated that in order to secure a conviction, it had to be proven that the handlers[163] of a work fully intended to stir up racial hatred. This was unlikely as *Uncle Tom* was dealing with a very real, emotive era in man's history, and that the despicable treatment of black slaves served to degrade the white characters.[164]

The Board didn't suffer the same consternation over *Fight For Your Life*, rejecting it seemingly without aforethought when it was submitted in 1981 with a view to a theatrical release.[165] It was never submitted for video classification following the introduction of the Video Recordings Act.

Something else draws the two films together: The Ted Turner character in *Fight For Your Life* is obviously a 'nod' to Nat Turner, the slave leader (and religious fanatic) who, in 1831, mounted the only sustained slave revolt. The final reel in *Uncle Tom* — the one the BBFC excised completely — focused upon the writings of Nat Turner and brought them 'up-to-date' in a hypothetical scenario that sees white families being slaughtered by blacks.[166] Given these parallels it's highly likely that *Uncle Tom* was the inspiration for Endelson's film.

Fight For Your Life is part of a very isolated tradition of commercial cinema, with the film-makers presenting racial stereotypes and slurs in an almost amoral fashion with no underlying racist agenda of their own. It doesn't fit in with the blaxploitation films of the seventies nor the more recent anti-KKK 'message' films, like *Mississippi Burning* and *A Time To Kill*.

While cuts may be made in *Cliffhanger* on the basis that some audiences in East End cinemas supposedly cheered the racist remarks made by a cockney villain about his black accomplice,[167] what cuts can be made when the central character in, say, *Dawn of the Dead* gets jeered by some audience members for *being* black?[168]

Neither the DPP outline with regard to horror videos nor the Video Recordings Act 1984 (and its numerous amendments) make any reference to racism.[169] After voicing his concern that the heroin use in Tarantino's *Pulp Fiction* was a potentially harmful influence, speaking at the ICA[170] James Ferman then responded to a question from the audience on the abundance of the word "nigger" in that same film by saying "At 18, we don't ban language."

So would *Fight For Your Life* be granted a video certificate if submitted to the BBFC? Not likely, with or without cuts.

FOREST OF FEAR
AKA: Bloodeaters
USA 1979
CAST: Charles Austin, Beverly Shapiro, Dennis Helfend, Kevin Hanlon, Judy Brown, Pat Kellis, Roger Miles, Philip Garfinkel, Bob Larson, Hariet Miller, Paul Haskin, John Amplas
STORY: Charles McCrann
PRODUCER: Charles McCrann
DIRECTOR: CHARLES McCRANN

FOREST OF FEAR

SYNOPSIS: A small group of hippies are cultivating a marijuana crop in a remote part of an unidentified forest. Two Federal agents, scouring an area of sixty square miles, finally get lucky and find a clue that leads them to the hippies' base camp. They close in on a clearing where a hippie girl dressed only in a pair of yellow knickers is washing herself.

"Federal officers," the men call, "stand where you are!" But the girl panics, runs and is shot dead.

Standing over the body the two agents are surprised by the gender of their victim. "Holy shit!" they exclaim "It's a woman!" Two hippies then jump out of the undergrowth and kill both men, stabbing one repeatedly in the back and garrotting the other.

There is dissent amongst the hippies as to whether they should leave or stay. The general consensus is that they take what they can of the $2 million dope harvest and pull out as soon as possible.

Cut to a small office in Washington where Briggs and Phillips, two more government agents, discuss "Operation Torpedo." Briggs is worried that the hippies will slip through the net and suggests they drop Dromax, a powerful new herbicide, on the whole area. Phillips alerts Briggs to the fact that testing on Dromax isn't yet complete, that it might well have dangerous side effects, and is off-limits to their particular operation anyway. But he warms to the idea when Briggs confides that he can access a large consignment of

Dromax without anyone knowing, and that success in Operation Torpedo will undoubtedly go down well at headquarters.

Briggs and Phillips employ a down-at-heel crop duster pilot for the job and fabricate a flood warning to keep fellow officers away from the sector. Forestry agent Tom Cole isn't about to let reports of a little flooding come in the way of his fishing trip, however, and — oblivious to the threat of the hippie drug growers — heads off for the restricted area with his brother Jay and wife Polly.

Meanwhile the drop has been completed and all but two of the hippies are covered in Dromax, coughing up blood and fighting for water. Even the pilot of the dusting plane is looking decidedly the worse for wear. That evening, with dark circles around his eyes, a zombie-like gait and emitting a low moan, he staggers menacingly towards his wife. Not even broken glass under his bare feet impedes his progress…

The hippies who were caught by the Dromax are feeling "as sick as hell" (but not too sick to play a practical joke). The only two members of the group to have avoided the herbicide are attacked and chased by their suddenly homicidal companions. Having run no more than a few yards, the hunted stop to drink from a stream, inadvertently spill a little blood on a rock, and hide in the undergrowth. The pursuing hippies pick up the trail almost immediately when one of them stops to take a drink (at the same spot) and spies the blood. They find their prey and kill them.

Skipping through the forest to a happy refrain come another two characters: Jimmy and Amy, children who have strayed from their parents' barbecue. Stumbling upon the hippies' now deserted camp, Jimmy discovers a mutilated body.

Elsewhere, the parents of the children are attacked by the killer hippies. The father has a hand hacked off and is swiftly murdered; sinking a knife into one assailant's eye allows the mother to escape. She is spotted by the driver of a pickup truck who warns the hysterical, incoherent woman, "I ain't runnin' no taxi cab."

Having travelled no more than a few yards, the reluctant Samaritan pulls over to investigate another figure in the road ahead. Alas, this one turns out to be an infected hippie who guts him with a knife. A second hippie attacks the woman in the vehicle, ripping out her throat with his teeth.

Agents Briggs and Phillips discover that, despite the flood warning, Tom Cole has gone into the forest after all. It's imperative they reach him before he learns about their covert crop spraying operation.

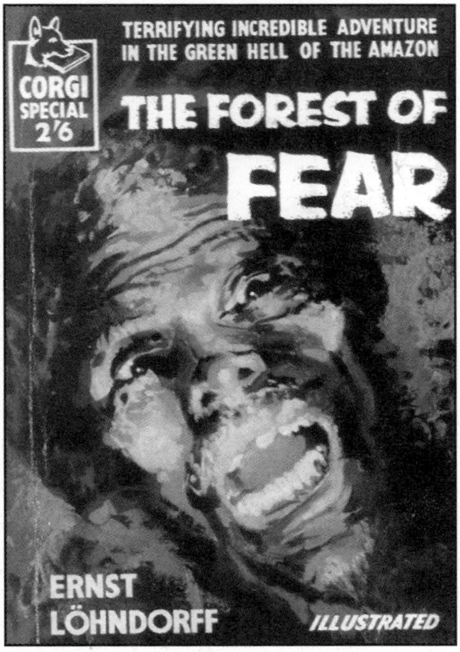

TOP: Trade ad.

ABOVE: *The Forest of Fear*, Ernst Löhndorff's recollections of an Amazonian adventure. It would seem that Charles McCrann borrowed this book's title – and the cover of Corgi's 1957 printing – for his film and its promotional artwork (see previous page).

Tom, meanwhile, is investigating strange sounds in the undergrowth. The buzz of flies promises another corpse but offers instead the children Amy and Jimmy, still searching for their parents. With adult help — and a string of racist jokes from Jay, Tom's brother — it isn't long before a camper van is found. But no sign of any parents. A quick search of the area uncovers a detached limb and offal. Jay is bludgeoned with a rock and mutilated by hippies, but Tom, Polly and the children manage to escape to a secluded shack, whose owner begrudgingly lets them in for $20.

Tom tries to impress upon the hermit that cannibals are roaming the forest, but the hermit will hear none of it. He tells Tom of his pals the hippies and their marijuana patch, and how the dust that the government spayed missed their drug crop but caught his dog and vegetable patch killing them both.

Otto and the Baron flanked by "zambies."
Frankenstein (Andy Warhol's).

That night the shack is besieged by the hippies. Despite only a fleeting contact with the crazed attackers Tom irrationally deduces that "nothing seems to stop them." Everyone flees the shack except the hermit, who mistakenly believes that in their deranged state the hippies will still consider him their friend. They don't.

The following morning the group is discovered by Briggs and Phillips, who are about to dispose of the eyewitnesses when the killer hippies arrive on the scene. In the ensuing bloodbath all the hippies are killed, as are Polly, Phillips and Briggs — the latter courtesy of an axe in the back, a knife in the neck and orange-coloured blood pouring from the mouth.

CRITIQUE: Sad it may be, but the most exciting thing about *Forest of Fear* is spotting a baby-faced John Amplas — an actor who had previously played the lead in George Romero's *Martin* — in the role of Agent Henry Phillips. Acquiring Amplas was presumably something of a coup for the *Forest of Fear* film-makers: not only is he the only 'name' actor in their movie, but his presence accentuates a connection — albeit tenuous — between their work and that of Romero's (whose *Night of the Living Dead* and *The Crazies* obviously influenced *Forest of Fear*).[171]

McCrann doesn't appear to have made any other film besides this 16mm effort, and nothing outside of *Forest of Fear* is known about him. He is one of the great unknowns of low-budget cinema, obscure to the point that even the most persevering of film zines has yet to come up with a feature or factoid on him.

McCrann's characters completely lack colour and depth. Everyone is a cipher, operating under ambiguous adjuncts like "agent" out of tiny offices in "Washington," or — as in the case of the child Jimmy — are suffering a mental disability. (Moreover, the children are played by two young adults, who appear to be in their mid-twenties.) Jimmy really doesn't have much to do. He rubs a curiously phallic teddy bear and delivers a half dozen mumbled words which have no bearing on anyone or anything.

McCrann takes a couple of stabs at generating tension, but these instances fall flat or come across as being just plain weird. None weirder though than the mother who momentarily escapes death by driving a knife into a hippie's eye and finds herself on a dirt track. Crawling along hysterical with fear, she spots a pickup truck in the mid-distance. (Considering the film is set in a remote area of forest, an awful lot of people are converging on it.) The truck driver, who has been fiddling under the hood, drives away blissfully unaware of the woman desperately trying to attract his attention. Not too far down the road the truck pulls over again and the guy checks under the hood a second time. About to drive off he spots the woman in his rear view mirror... This all constitutes a rather laborious set-piece, whose whole attitude is skew-whiff thanks to the radio upon which everything hangs: the guy can't hear the woman because he has the radio in his pickup switched on — but it's not enough that the radio should be *on*, it has to on *very loud* because it's not playing music but conversation. But it's not even real conversation, it's playing what sounds like a made-up language. The driver of the pickup is driving around listening to a very loud made-up language on his radio.

For no logical reason the British release of *Forest of Fear* is missing a whole chunk of footage. This missing sequence adds little to the film itself, but does highlight another miserable misfire on McCrann's part to incorporate elements of tension, suspense and shock.

Where the British print concludes with Tom and the children gathering around the body of Polly — a scene that jumps abruptly to the end credits — the original version continues to run for several more minutes, showing Tom clearing his desk having quit his job and heading off to see how the children, Jimmy and Amy, are coping. He pulls in for gas and — snapped out of a daydream by a fat pump attendant — continues on his journey until the end credits roll.

Presumably this coda is meant to impart a feeling of the horror being far from over, that the hulking pump attendant — who pops out of nowhere with a sneeze into the camera — is yet another Dromax-infected crazy. But nothing about the sequence works and the supposed jolt simply comes over as absurd — lost to McCrann's shortcomings as a director.

The gore effects in *Forest of Fear* fair marginally better and mercifully aren't locked on screen for too long (a major failing with low-budget film work is the reluctance to cut away). There is a passable hand-being-lopped-off scene and a couple of instances of actual spilled offal, but there is an aversion to depicting the actual killings, which tend to take place out of shot.[172]

There is little reason why *Forest of Fear* shouldn't be granted a certificate if submitted to the BBFC. Perhaps the opening scene with the Federal agents being garrotted and stabbed repeatedly would be truncated (it follows lengthy shots of a hippie girl soaping her breasts), but nothing beyond this ought to hinder the film in getting a release... excepting of course the idea of putting such drivel before a paying public.

Forest of Fear also happens to have the most succinct opening credits of any film on the DPP list which read, in their entirety, "CM Productions presents *Forest of Fear*."

FRANKENSTEIN (ANDY WARHOL'S)

SYNOPSIS: For his experiments, the Baron is looking for a head with the perfect nose — or "nasum." In a thick accent that is at times close to being impenetrable, he explains to his assistant Otto: "Ve have to find the right head for zis torso. It has to be a man who strongly quavers [sic] vimmen."

In his laboratory, he and Otto stitch together body parts in the quest to build perfect male and female mates, whom the Baron intends to be the start of a new race, "responding only to my bidding."

Trunks are considered useless and are discarded in a heap once their organs have been removed.

Though she knows nothing of her husband's work, Katrin shares the Baron's ideas on physical perfection, removing their two children from school because she believes it is full of "urchins." Of her son she says, "I've always looked for beauty. In fact, I insist on it."

Taking the children on a picnic in the castle grounds, Katrin happens across Nicholas, the shepherd boy, who is frolicking with a local girl. She reprimands him and orders to see him back at the castle the following day.

The children — who never speak a word — spy on their father as he tells Otto they must go to the bordello, where they will find the head for their male "zambie" in the guise of "a man who likes to make love to anything."

Nicholas, the shepherd boy, is a regular at the bordello. He tries to initiate his quiet friend to the pleasures of the flesh, but his friend — who wants to become a monk — seems more interested

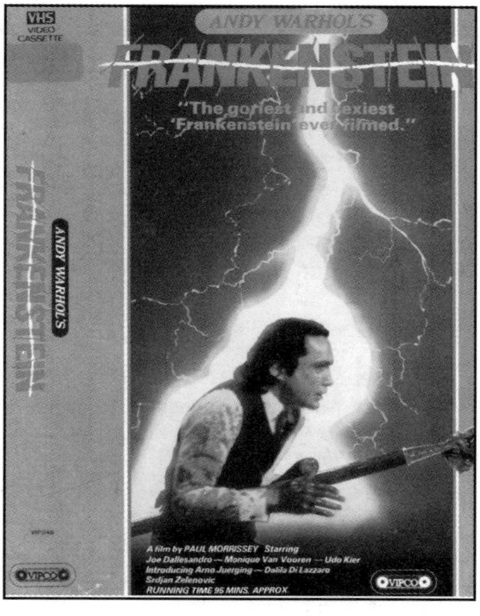

FRANKENSTEIN (ANDY WARHOL'S)
TITLE ON PRINT: FLESH FOR FRANKENSTEIN
AKA: Il mostro e in tavola... barone Frankenstein! (trans: The Monster is on the table... Baron Frankenstein!); Andy Warhol's Frankenstein
ITALY/FRANCE 1973
CAST: Joe Dallesandro, Monique van Vooren, Udo Kier, Arno Juerging, Dalila Lazzaro, Srojan Zelenovic
STORY: Paul Morrissey
PRODUCER: Andrew Braunsberg
DIRECTOR: PAUL MORRISSEY

One of Frankenstein's creations, and the doctor's entrails on the end of a lance.
Frankenstein (Andy Warhol's).

in looking at Nicholas than he does the girls. As the two of them are returning home through the woods, Otto and the Baron pounce. Otto renders the drunk Nicholas unconscious while his friend — who certainly has the right "nasum" — is decapitated by the Baron with a pair of shears.

Back at the lab, Baron sews the head onto his male zombie. "My work is the continuation of the unfinished business of man on earth," he proclaims.

Nicholas arrives at the castle for his meeting with Katrin, which she conducts from her bedroom. Though she chastises him for his disgusting actions, her real intentions are openly apparent. Katrin confides that the Baron doesn't love her and that theirs is a marriage in name only. Despite suffering the loss of his friend the night before, Nicholas makes love to Katrin and she asks him to come to work in the castle. The children are spying on the couple.

In the lab, the Baron snips through the ugly sutures on his female zombie and announces, "I go into her digestive parts."

"Kidney! Gall bladder! Liver! mmm…" he says with much pleasure, dipping his hands into the wound and pulling out some offal.

"Why are you looking at me?" he yells at Otto. "You filthy thing — turn around!"

After applying electricity, the Baron's creations are able to move at his command. He takes them to dinner and introduces them to his wife and children as guests who are assisting him in his laboratory work. He dismisses their strange wooden demeanour as a medical condition.

Nicholas, who has been promoted to waiter, recognises his friend's head.

As the Baron spies on his wife's infidelities with Nicholas, Otto catches the housemaid nosing around the lab. Lusting after her, he eventually corners the woman and drives his hand into her stomach. She collapses onto a steel grating, through which her innards spill.

With an eye on its genitalia, the Baron wonders why the female zombie's kisses are failing to arouse the male zombie. He deduces that someone has been tampering with his work and goes off to investigate. While the Baron is away, Nicholas sneaks into the lab via a hidden passage shown to him by the children. He offers his zombified buddy the chance to escape and be reunited with his real body, but his buddy doesn't want to go; he wants to be dead.

The Baron is alerted to Nicholas' suspicions by his wife, and returns to the lab where he succeeds in chaining Nicholas up. As a reward, the sex-crazed Katrin is allowed to spend time alone with his male creation, but its embraces crush her to death. Fretting in that all his years of faithful service to the Baron he never once has been rewarded, Otto decides to take his own pleasure with the female zombie. Unfortunately, his idea of sexual satisfaction has been perverted by the Baron and he sinks his hands into her midriff. The creature screams and drops to the floor in a pool of blood.

"She... She's ruined!" cries an incredulous Baron at the sight of the lifeless creature and throttles his dim-witted assistant, while remonstrating of his own technique, "I studied how to do it!"

The male zombie wanders into the lab carrying the broken body of Katrin who, it transpires, is not only the Baron's wife but his sister.[173] In his apoplectic rage, the Baron blames Nicholas for everything and orders the zombie to kill him. But the creature turns on his master and runs him through with a lance. As it penetrates the Baron, one of his organs is skewered on the tip of the lance where it wobbles precariously. The zombie kills himself by ripping open his sutures and allowing his own organs to tumble out.

As Nicholas dangles impotently from his chains in the middle of the lab, the two children wander in and grab a scalpel. They throw one another a knowing look and begin to winch Nicholas even higher.

CRITIQUE: *Flesh for Frankenstein*[174] is inexorably linked with *Blood for Dracula*. Shot back-to-back in Italy over a two-month period, both films star Udo Kier in the title role and utilise virtually the same cast and crew.

Despite lending his name to the posters and credits, Andy Warhol didn't contribute anything to either movie.[175] However, the association with Warhol and actor Joe Dallesandro was a prerequisite in Morrissey securing the deal with the Italian backers.

Paul Morrissey joined Andy Warhol's Factory in the sixties where he worked as a production assistant and cameraman. He gradually moved into directing and brought to the Factory's rash cinematic work a formality and accessibility lacking in its earlier output. Indeed his trilogy of *Flesh*,[176] *Trash* and *Heat* — each of which starred Dallesandro — are perhaps the most popular films the Factory ever produced.

Having no interest in the horror genre as such, the idea that he could make a film in 3-D and in Europe with European actors appealed greatly to Morrissey leading him to accept the offer to make a Frankenstein picture. Estimating he could bring the film in for $350,000 within three weeks, the response from the backers was one of surprise and Morrissey was offered a budget of almost a million dollars if he would make not one but two films.

The backers wanted Dallesandro and understood the kudos Warhol's name would have, but were concerned that the result would somehow be systematic of the Factory and not be commercial enough — at least, this is the reason Antonio Margheriti gives for having been asked to "supervise" *Flesh for Frankenstein* and direct some sequences himself.

In an interview with *The DarkSide*,[177] Margheriti claims that Morrissey had no script,

> just fourteen pages of what is to happen, and they made decisions with the actors about what the dialogue would be, writing the script all night for the next day. Because Carlo [Ponti, executive producer] was worried about all of this, he worked a kind of blackmail on me, he said: "Tony, you want to make that picture in Australia we talked about? If so, you have to be with the Morrissey shoot first."

Although Margheriti unquestionably did film parts of *Flesh for Frankenstein*, quite what and how much has been open to question. The general consensus is that he filmed only pick-up shots with the two children wandering around the lab and castle, although Margheriti claims also to have shot some of the gore effects.[178] Margheriti's name doesn't appear on prints of the film outside of Italy (because the American distributors believed it would detract from Warhol and the film's art-house alliance), while in Italy — under the pseudonym 'Anthony Dawson' — Margheriti is credited with being its director. This rather curious turnaround is founded on the fact that in Italy, with an Italian director, the film became eligible for a state subsidy.

Initially, Warhol's name on both *Flesh for Frankenstein* and *Blood for Dracula* took precedence over that of Morrissey's directorship.[179] (Morrissey has said that "Andy's idea of making a movie is going to the premiere.") Now of late, Morrissey is being usurped once again as some sourcebooks and critics erroneously credit his work to Antonio Margheriti.

Both films however, have an attitude that is completely removed from Italian horror. For instance, they have humour and irony, attributes alien to Italian genre pictures (certainly they're absent from the films of Margheriti). And it's debatable whether Udo Kier would have landed the title roles in the two films without a chance meeting with Morrissey on a plane. Morrissey, always keen to cast players who sound right as well as look right made the perfect choice with Kier, and it's impossible to perceive these films being anywhere near as entertaining without the presence of the German actor. Although he had already appeared in the highly controversial and altogether more sombre *Mark of the Devil* (also as a Baron), it was his role in Morrissey's films and the association with Warhol that established Kier as a cult figure. Suddenly he was in *Vogue* magazine.

As the bombastic Baron in *Flesh for Frankenstein*,[180] Kier espouses his demented ideals of sex, death and power, and admonishes his assistant Otto for being "filthy," in an accent and manner that is at once hilarious and a little sad.

In one of the film's most notorious sequences, the Baron fist-fucks his female zombie's stomach cavity and decries, "To know death, Otto, you have to fuck life in the gall bladder!" This oft quoted line of dialogue,[181] states Michael Ferguson in his book *Little Joe Superstar*, was inspired by the director's disdain at the critical idolatry heaped upon Bertolucci's *Last Tango in Paris* the previous year. In Bertolucci's film, after having sodomised Maria Schneider and prior to his requesting she stick her fingers into his rectum, Marlon Brando explains that the man she is looking for will remain elusive until she goes "right up into the ass of death; right up in his ass until you find a womb of fear, and then maybe, maybe then you'll be able to find him."

Morrissey thought this to be a ridiculous line of dialogue.

Ferguson also makes the valid observation that Kier may have mixed up "life" and "death" in his delivery. Understandable given that the actors only ever saw what passed as their scripts hours before shooting commenced. (One particularly lengthy diatribe is clearly being read by Kier from pages placed on the workbench before him.)

The most priceless moment comes at the end of the film, when the male zombie revolts and the Baron loses a hand trying to flee it. With blood gushing from the stump, the Baron staggers around the lab, trying hopelessly to join his hand back to his wrist before throwing it at Nicholas in frustration. *"It's all your fault!"* he yells at the shepherd boy who remains suspended helplessly in mid-air.

Flesh for Frankenstein was heavily cut when released theatrically in Britain in 1975, losing about seven minutes. The critic in *World of Horror* deduced that the film's 3-D process — so proudly boasted in the advertising — had only really been successful in one scene of the film. In truth, almost all the scenes that did exploit the gimmick had been removed — ironic given that a supporting feature on this first run was *Violence in the Cinema Part 1*,[182] a "convincing and grisly" short which included an eye gouging and a woman having a breast hacked off.[183]

Flesh for Frankenstein was later re-released 'flat' on a double-bill with *Blood for Dracula* — a film which reverses the political accent from that of fascism to socialism. Enjoyable it is, but *Blood for Dracula* stands as a rather sanitised and unevenly paced work by comparison. Despite initial arrangements that it too would be made in 3-D, the idea was scrapped when the confines of the location in which much of the *Dracula* takes place proved impractical for the Space-Vision camera.

Vipco's video release of *Flesh for Frankenstein* — residing on the DPP list — is uncut. Viewed today, the wild abandon with which real sheep guts are brandished remains a little shocking, particularly given the sexualised context in which the Baron conducts his business, holding the raw (spoiled and stinking) offal to his cheek and plucking oversized seminal vesicles from containers. Guts are gleefully thrust into the camera, or come tumbling toward it, as in the scenes where the maid is killed by Otto and the male zombie tears open his own sutures. When the Baron decapitates Nicholas' buddy with a pair of shears during the ambush in the forest, Otto clubs the headless torso as it stands bolt upright spraying blood into the air.

One of the last shots of the film has the Baron delivering a final soliloquy with half his stomach swaying from the point of a lance, several feet in front of his face. It's an arresting image that seems several light-years removed from any other horror film made before or since.

As Katrin says to Nicholas when he broaches the subject of her husband's work: "Things that are strange to you are very well planned by the Baron." And that's the benchmark with which we ought to measure this movie.

It should be noted that *Flesh for Frankenstein* was made the same year as Hammer's *Frankenstein and the Monster from Hell*, the last of the British studio's lengthy run in with Mary Shelley's monster. The two films are as removed as Hammer's original Monster was to the Universal Frankensteins of the 1930s. Except for one rather convoluting link...

Following their work together on *Four Flies on Grey Velvet*, Dario Argento and Luigi Cozzi began looking to their next venture, which was intended to be a new interpretation of the Frankenstein legend. They planned to transpose the original story to 1920s pre-Nazi Germany, with the Monster allegorising the birth of Nazism. According to Cozzi, interviewed in *Psychotronic Video*,[184] no backers were interested. "They said Frankenstein was dead, and anyway, no one who wanted to see a horror movie cared about politics."

It's odd that Argento and Cozzi should be given the thumbs down only to have Morrissey's Italian-backed Frankenstein project appearing shortly after. Even more ironic given the political, fascistic charge of Morrissey's film.

And the convoluting link? Hammer was one of the potential investors approached by Argento and Cozzi to fund their Frankenstein.

FROZEN SCREAM

SYNOPSIS: A couple in a swimming pool are attacked and murdered by a caped and hooded man wielding a hammer. Another similar hooded figure carries an unconscious woman to a house that has a laboratory in the basement. Lil Stanhope, a doctor experimenting in immortality, implants a device in the woman's neck.

Ann Gerhard telephones her husband Tom and informs him she will be home shortly. Outside Tom's house a hooded figure loiters in the bushes. Tom tries to reach Father O'Brian and leaves a message requesting that the priest calls him back urgently. When the phone rings moments later, Tom thinks it's O'Brian but hears instead a sinister laugh and a voice saying, "The angel will be there in a few minutes." Tom hangs up and grabs his gun when he hears someone breaking into his house. A hooded man at the top of the stairs attacks him and Tom opens fire. At the front door is another similarly dressed man whom Tom shoots. Both men get up apparently unharmed, grab Tom and inject him with a solution. The men flee when Ann arrives, leaving Tom lying dead.

The following day, Ann awakens in a hospital bed where she is looked after by Dr Lil Stanhope. Detective Kevin McGuire wishes to speak to Lil about some missing students who had attended her lectures, but she assures him she knows nothing of their whereabouts.

Lil and her colleague-lover Dr Sven Johnson are concerned about the Detective and the fact that he is acquainted with Ann. Meanwhile, Ann dreams about Tom and a mysterious attractive blonde named Catherine. Tom transforms into a living skeleton and Ann wakes up. Lil tells her she is well enough to leave the hospital and offers to drive her home, but the patient is disappointed that Lil hasn't helped her to analyse her dreams as promised. "You haven't said anything about the one I had last night," Ann complains. Lil

FROZEN SCREAM
USA 1981 [84?]
CAST: Lynne Kocol, Renee Harmon, Thomas Gowen, Wolf Muser, Bob Rochelle, Lee James
STORY: Renee Harmon, Doug Ferrin, Michael Soney, Celeste Hammond
PRODUCER: Renee Harmon
DIRECTOR: FRANK ROACH

says the dream must be related to the group-meeting on the beach some time ago, attended by Tom, Ann and Father O'Brian.

Lil asks Ann if she will come back to the university and help her with her work, but Ann is not keen on the idea and declines. At home she is startled by an image of Tom in the mirror but this turns out to be a reflection of Catherine, who Lil has assigned to look after Ann.

Lil tells Sven she is afraid of the work they are doing because it goes against nature. Sven assures her they are close to making a breakthrough.

Detective Kevin McGuire meets Ann at the university and wishes to speak to her about Tom. Ann first has to telephone Catherine and tell her she will be late home. Knowing that the pair are together, Catherine then makes a phone call and says to whoever's on the line, "She's with *him*."

Kevin tells Ann about Lil and Sven's illicit practices, and says that Tom was also involved. She doesn't believe him but later Father O'Brian explains he is aware of the experiments the group had conducted with rats. They would inject the rodents with poison and then revive them at much lower temperatures. Tom had been concerned as to whether rats had souls or not. Father O'Brian is later strangled in his confessional.

At home Ann receives a phone call from Tom, who tells her he is cold and numb. Having heard someone breaking into the house, Ann sees an apparition of Tom and runs to Catherine's room. She isn't there, but a hooded man holds a knife to Ann's throat and warns her not to speak to anyone. When Catherine returns Ann remarks on how cold she feels.

Sven and Lil are worried about Ann becoming a threat to their work. Ann manages to get Sven's files from the hospital and finds they relate to Tom and two other men, Bob and Kirk. Ann recognises one of these men as her hooded attacker, and now believes Tom is still alive.

Ann is invited to a Halloween celebration at Sven's home and she takes the opportunity to look into his private laboratory. She has to go and hide when Sven suddenly walks in with Bob, instructing him that she must be got rid of after the party. Ann manages to get away but is followed by Bob, who promptly loses her after being distracted by a dog which he then strangles. Having spotted Tom standing at an upstairs window in Sven's house, Ann discovers a refrigerated room wherein Tom and two other men lie in suspended animation. She later returns to the freezer room with Kevin but is set upon by Bob and Kirk. In the ensuing battle, Kevin manages to kill Bob, but stumbles into the path of an approaching car and is run over. Pursued by Kirk, Ann hides in a building but is discovered. Kirk kills a watchman and advances on Ann when Lil turns up and stops him from harming her.

Regaining consciousness Ann finds herself strapped to a table in the lab. Sven and Lil are about to operate and transform her into an immortal when Lil has second thoughts and shoots Sven. She tells Ann that she will be released if she will join her in her work. Ann agrees but when released tries to escape. Father O'Brian enters the lab and Ann runs to him for help, only to find that he has been transformed. He restrains the girl while Lil administers an injection.

Dropped off at the hospital by the driver who collided with him, Kevin comes round to see Lil, Ann and Father O'Brian standing over his bed. Lil injects him with the immortality serum.

CRITIQUE: When it first gets underway this film looks like it might turn out to be an obscure, hitherto unknown little gem. Unfortunately, it quickly becomes evident this isn't going to be the case. *Frozen Scream* is strange and dream-like alright, no thanks to any deliberate surrealism engendered by a talented auteur, but rather because the film is so completely unkempt and disorderly. Everyone appears to be in a somnambulistic state, regardless of whether they are the resurrected dead of Lil and Sven's experiments.[185] Characters talk to one another as if nailed to the spot, fearing to move in case they slip out of focus. None of the cast appear to have grasped the basic principles of acting, and emotions are conveyed through a succession of stares. For example, the hooded intruders[186] give a crazed, excitable stare, while Ann in order to project a feeling of perplexion or fright stares back that much harder.

Lil just stares for no reason at all, often in tight close-ups.

Only once in the whole movie do the film-makers even attempt a panning shot. (Panning onto Catherine as she stares past the telephone.)

The plot is confusing in itself, yet is made all the more arduous by the curious accent Renee Harmon (as Lil) at times adopts. "Why Cassarin?" she asks after Sven has recommended that Catherine keeps an eye on Ann. "I could stay vivver avile."

Some of the confusion can probably be attributed to the fact that four writers are credited with scripting the story, and it's probably safe to surmise that they did so without much collaboration between themselves. Clumsy editing, in which characters suddenly appear out of context adds to the chaos, as do the dream sequences and flashbacks which occur with startling regularity in the film's first half and then cease altogether.

The continuity is also flawed. When a hooded killer is seen carrying a female victim to the lab in the opening reel, her face appears horribly mutilated, yet once inside the lab she is completely unblemished.

The music, an irritating synthesised score of a type unduly popular amongst the nasties, is the same as that used in ***Don't Go in the Woods*** and credited to H Kingsley Thurber III (although none of the other credits match, the two movies do share a similar transcendental quality).

There are many unintentionally humorous incidents, notably the footsteps that are wildly out of synch when Ann is being chased as the film's end (when she stops they carry on going) and the big hand that slips into the confessional to strangle Father O'Brian (he conveniently doesn't notice it's there, despite the fact that it lingers in front of his face for long enough). When Lil saves Ann from certain death at the hands of Kirk, Lil reprimands the reanimated killer with the line: "Feel your forehead, Kirk... It's hot in here."

Frozen Scream is another example of a film that was unnecessarily targeted by the DPP. Maybe its junior-grade appearance and the lowly videosleeve — images seemingly lifted straight off a TV screen — were enough to land it on the list. The only actual scenes that may have designated *Frozen Scream* a nasty are those depicting the aftermath of an axe attack, with the tool implanted in a woman's head, and the attack on the night watchman which results in a sliver of glass protruding from his eye. There is also a trauma-to-the-eye scene implied at the film's end, when Lil administers the serum to Kevin. As the needle descends on his screaming face, the screen goes blood-red and the credits roll.

Frozen Scream is tame enough, if not good enough, for late-night television.

THE FUNHOUSE

SYNOPSIS: Amy is given a scare in the shower when her younger brother Joey does a *Psycho* re-enactment with a rubber knife. Incensed, she warns the boy that she'll get her own back on him when he's least expecting it.

Amy has a date with Buzz, a guy who works in a gas station. Her parents, who disapprove of Buzz and the lateness of the hour, tell Amy not to go to the carnival because two girls were found murdered in the last town at which it stopped. But that's just where the couple are headed — on a double date with Liz and Richie.

The kids have a fun time on the rides and games.

Whilst in the toilets, Liz chides Amy for still being a virgin. Suddenly an old hag appears and proclaims "God is watching you."

The kids go into a freakshow tent and the sight of two cows with deformed heads makes the girls want to leave. However, Richie convinces them to take a look at the special exhibit, a baby in a jar of formaldehyde with a hideously shaped head.

The barkers at the carnival seem drawn to Amy and she's equally fascinated with them.

Amy gets her palm read by Madame Zena, a fortune-teller with a thick European accent. But the accent disappears when Amy's friends make one too many wise cracks and she throws them out.

THE FUNHOUSE
USA 1981
CAST: Elizabeth Berridge, Shawn Carson, Jeanne Austin, Jack McDermott, Cooper Huckabee, Largo Woodruff, Miles Chapin, David Carson, Sonia Zomina, Kevin Conway
STORY: Larry Block
PRODUCERS: Derek Power & Steven Bernhardt
DIRECTOR: TOBE HOOPER

"Don't come back," Madame Zena hollers, "or I'll break every bone in yer fuckin' body!"

Richie has the bright idea that the four of them should spend the night in the Funhouse. Consequently, the cars that take the two couples into the attraction, leave it empty — to the bemusement of the strange carnival helper in a monster mask.

Joey, who has sneaked out of the house and followed his sister at a distance, is equally puzzled. As the carnival begins to wind down for the night and people leave, he gets scared by the old hag and runs straight into a carny hand.

In the Funhouse, the two couples stop their petting when a light comes on in a room beneath them. Through the floorboards they witness the Funhouse helper in the monster mask and Madame Zena. Able to communicate only in grunts, the masked man tries to procure the impatient crone's sexual services and hands her some money from a cash box. When he ejaculates prematurely he wants the money back. When he doesn't get it, he kills her and panics.

The group decide to get the hell out of the Funhouse. Thinking they've found an exit that doesn't take them through the room below, Richie slips the money from the cash box into his pocket. But it's not an exit and the group end up back where they started — only to witness the masked one return with the Funhouse barker.

"You really did it this time, didn't ya?" says the barker on seeing Madame Zena's body. "You killed one of the family. I should have wrung your ugly neck the day you were born and have done with it!"

The barker discovers that the money in the cash box is missing and his accusations send the masked one into a rage. He punishes himself with self-inflicted punches to the head before ripping off his mask to reveal a hideously deformed cleft head and huge teeth.

Richie inadvertently alerts the barker to their presence when he drops his lighter through the floorboards. Unable to coax the group down, under his breath the barker tells the monster "We've got work to do," convincing him to do one last "bad thing."

The Funhouse bursts into life and Richie is dragged away by a noose from above. When the cars start rolling again, Buzz sinks an axe into the head of the shadowy figure riding in front — only to discover it's Richie.

Liz falls through a trapdoor that promptly snaps shut again. She comes face to face with the drooling monster and offers to make him "feel good" before sinking a knife into his back. The creature goes berserk and tears at the girl with his huge clawing hands.

Amy's parents meanwhile have arrived at the carnival following a call made by the carny hand who found their frightened son (and seem completely oblivious to the overly affectionate manner in which the stranger handles the boy). Amy sees her parents leaving, unable to attract their attention over the noise of the Funhouse and the huge extractor fan that stands between them.

The remaining two teenagers are confronted by the barker who tells them that "blood is thicker than water," and that the monster is only looking out for his family. In a scuffle, the barker is run-through with a prop sword.[187] Buzz is killed when the monster appears, and Amy is driven to hide in the heart of the Funhouse — a room containing the cogs, motors and pulleys that drive the cars and attractions. With no way out, she awaits the arrival of the monster but manages to ultimately crush him between two giant cogs.

It's daylight when Amy steps from the Funhouse. The carnival attractions are being dismantled as she makes her dazed way through the park.

CRITIQUE: *The Funhouse* met with much disappointment from fans expecting another *Texas Chain Saw Massacre* of director Tobe Hooper, and simply confirmed the slide into mediocrity that was already beginning to show with ***Death Trap***, his second feature.

The Funhouse is Hooper's first movie with major studio backing and it completely lacks the gritty, claustrophobic edge of either *Texas Chain Saw* or *Death Trap* — which, unfortunately, is an argument that can also be levelled at every subsequent Hooper production to date.

Hooper clearly intends *The Funhouse* to be a homage — or a return — to the traditional scares of early horror films.[188] Not content with the trite *Psycho*-inspired bathroom scene that opens the movie, he feels compelled to signpost his intention through the entire first half. There are posters featuring classic Universal monsters adorning Joey's bedroom walls; the carnival monster wears a Boris Karloff Frankenstein mask; and, should any viewer still be missing the point, a clip from *Bride of Frankenstein* plays on TV as Amy leaves for her date with Buzz.[189]

Even the violence and bloodshed is always just out of frame.

But Hooper fails to add any depth to his characters (the two protagonists, the carnival barker and the monster, don't even have names).[190] Amy is a virgin,[191] and seemingly content to display that fact in a little-girl outfit that belongs to a completely different time zone. Her friend Liz — big-girl outfit — chides her several times for "saving it," but her own promiscuity ultimately proves her downfall. These are attributes drawn without aforethought from other movies in an attempt to lend a contemporaneous air to the proceedings — which, it has to be said, is infinitely more preferable to the film's own trite efforts, courtesy of such embarrassingly 'hip' dialogue as "When you're stoned, Charles Manson is a terrific guy."

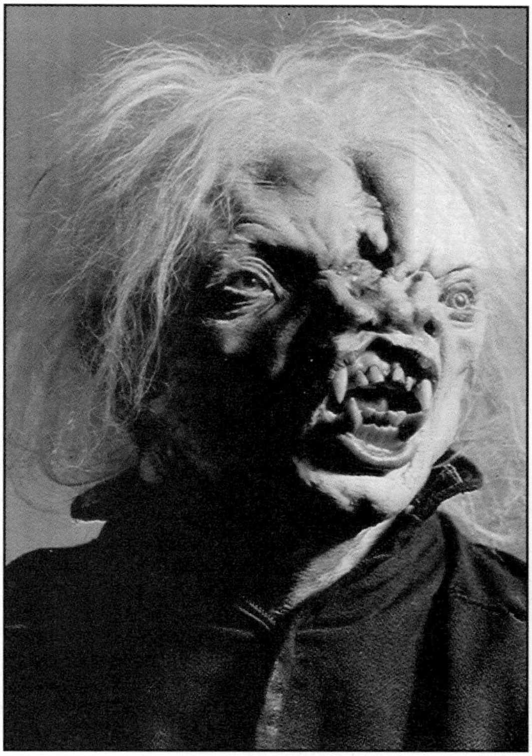

The monster in *The Funhouse*.

Distancing oneself from Hooper's earlier, better pictures, *The Funhouse* might provide the less-discerning viewer with some pleasing moments. Most notable are the garish carnival attractions with their bright neon lights and art brut murals; the barkers — all of whom are played by a suitably weary Kevin Conway — drawing crowds with cries of "Alive! Alive! Alive!" and "Terrifying! Terrifying! Terrifying!"; and the inside of the freakshow tent, a guaranteed attention-grabber that is afforded only a fleeting glimpse here.

There is also a burlesque attraction in which a motley bunch of women flash their leather-hides at a packed male audience. While this curiously displaced segment doesn't serve to develop the plot any, it does add to the atmosphere — a facet attributable to Hooper's insistence on using an actual working carnival for the film. Brought to the Ivan Tors studio in Florida from Akron, Ohio, the carnival however, didn't come without a price, and soon production was beset with problems.

The limited shooting schedule was a major handicap, particularly given union rules with regard to shooting at night.[192] Ultimately many sequences had to be compromised in order to try and bring the film in on time — a pressure which weighed on the film-makers in the guise of a completion guarantor who wandered around the set, looking to protect the investors' money.

Some scripted shots were left out entirely, which may or may not explain why *The Funhouse* has a particularly unsatisfying ending (Amy wandering off into the distance) and why some nagging subtexts which go unexplored. For instance, the supernatural flourishes; Amy being drawn to the barkers and they to her; and why do two different grown men come onto Joey during the course of the movie?

Hooper was only able to deliver one rough cut before leaving the film for another commitment, which turned out to be an aborted involvement in *Venom*, shot in England.[193] He returned to *The Funhouse* for the final stages of post-production.

There is no logical reason why this innocuous little film found itself for a brief spell on the DPP list. The bloodletting is very discriminate, and there is no twisted sexual activity (unless, of course, someone decided Amy in the opening shower scene looked a little too young to be flashing her breasts).

Perhaps the reference to Hooper having directed *The Texas Chain Saw Massacre* on the videobox was reason enough?[194]

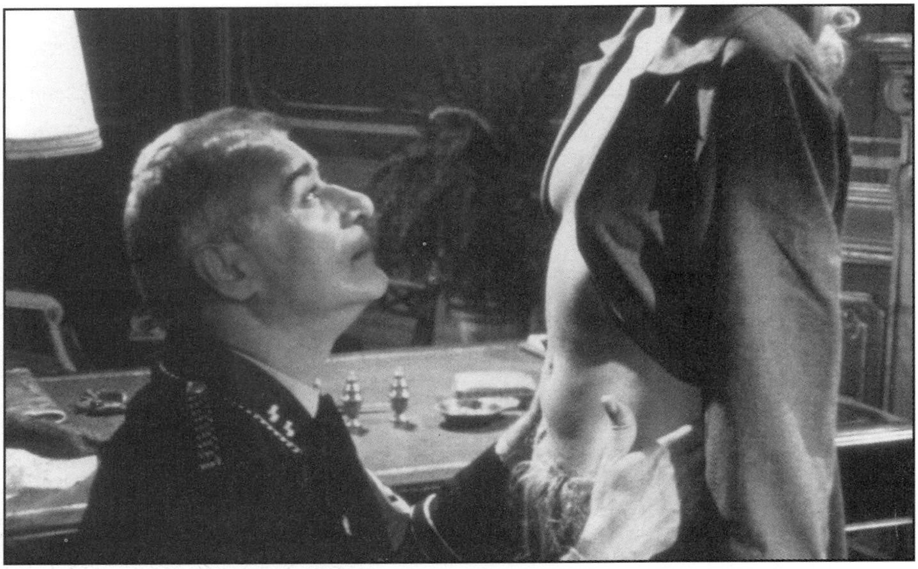

Lise delights von Schtarke by wearing a girdle made from human scalps.
Gestapo's Last Orgy.

GESTAPO'S LAST ORGY

SYNOPSIS: After being released from prison, former Nazi death camp commandant Conrad von Schtarke returns to the ruins of his camp to meet Lise, one of the surviving prisoners. As he drives to the place he recalls his trial at Nuremberg… The judge asks a survivor what happened to her sister in the camp.

"Rebecca was very beautiful. She was twenty-years-old. They cut all the tendons and ligaments in her legs so that she was unable to walk."

"Why did they do that?"

"She was trying to avoid the attention of two of the camp's officers. She ran away so the two officers got the idea without the use of her legs Rebecca could only crawl at their feet. So from then on all the men had to do was pick her up from the floor, throw her on the bed and use her. Then they would throw her back on the floor and leave her there until one of them wanted her again."

"How did she die?"

"One day she managed to drag herself to an oil truck. She hid by the rear wheels and waited for the truck to go down the hill. She was crushed like a worm."

Von Schtarke arrives at the location of the ruined camp where Lise is waiting for him. He lets her into his car and embraces her.

"How did you find me?" he asks.

"I looked for you," replies the vacant-looking Lise.

Von Schtarke explains how he has been rehabilitated after several years in prison.

"Lise, thanks," he says. "When you were on the witness stand we were able to stop those bastards on the bench. They'd have killed me."

"Your lawyer was good. You must have paid him well," responds Lise as though she had nothing to do with von Schtarke escaping execution.

"Germany should have paid him. I was just a soldier doing my duty… One thing, why did you want me to be here today?" he asks as his hands grope at the girl.

"I met you here, then," Lise reminds him.

Together they drive through the rusting gates and into the camp itself, reduced now to derelict brick structures overgrown with weeds. They wander separately around the grounds. Lise finds a rusted harmonica and flashes back to her time in the camp: a young officer is playing the harmonica and observing his comrades raping the inmates.

New inmates are being brought in and separated off into different areas of the camp. When a mother refuses to hand over her son, the Nazi warden beats her to death.

In a gymnasium the purpose of the camp is revealed. Standing before von Schtarke is a group of naked young men — some of them battle scarred — fresh from the front. They are shown a series of slides. In one of these a naked woman is seen eating from a dog's bowl and being taken from behind by an officer. The next slide shows two naked women tied together so each has their face in the other's genitals. "Those two are mother and daughter," continues von Schtarke, "but that does not prevent them from having incestuous and unnatural relations. They are incapable of feeling the sacred ties of the family. No human being could behave in that way. They asked never to be separated so we tied them in that position and they will stay that way until death do them part."

The next slide shows an officer excreting into a bucket, followed by a naked woman smearing herself with the faeces.

"Just like dogs who find agreeable certain sensations which for the human race are repellent," the commandant points out, "this girl loves to smell the excrement of a man. And of course, more — she eats it — she smears her body with it — she is happy like with a drug — she masturbates — she comes. Lights."

A selection of women prisoners has been herded into the gym and the soldiers are ordered to rape them. Later, when the prisoners return to their quarters, older women and any who are pregnant are marched away and burned alive in a brick-lined oven. Knowing that only the healthy and attractive women will be required, a group of prisoners turn on a fellow inmate and mutilate her face to ensure themselves a better chance of survival. Lise watches the attack in horror.

The following day Alma, a female commandant, arrives at the camp. She enters the prison block and thrusts her hand between the legs of each woman. One girl is selected and dragged outside, where she is thrown into the dog pen and devoured. Lise learns that the girl was picked because she was menstruating and the smell drives the dogs into a frenzy. She is also told that Alma and von Schtarke run the camp together.

Having enjoyed a luxurious meal, von Schtarke, in a drunken state, notices Lise for the first time. He orders her over, removes her top and runs his pistol over her breasts. He tells her that he could kill her quite easily and Lise says she would rather die than live in the camp. He forces her to fellate him but she bites his penis in the hope that von Schtarke will shoot her. From this point on, he is determined to break her and have her crawling at his feet in fear of him.

He tells her she will not be killed until she utterly fears death.

Alma takes Lise to her room and displays her collection of human hair wigs, skin lamp shades and baby skin gloves. Lise still refuses to be intimidated and lies without emotion as Alma runs a knife over her body while threatening to skin her. From a corner von Schtarke watches excitedly. When Lise is sent away Alma turns to von Schtarke. Noticing he has ejaculated in his trousers she administers punishment by forcing the handle of her whip into his rectum.

The next day von Schtarke binds the naked Lise and whips her. She still refuses to cry or beg for mercy so von Schtarke orders a guard to rape her. Later she is suspended upside down over a tank of rats. Von Schtarke lowers her gradually, explaining how the rodents will eat out her eyes and devour the flesh from her face before burrowing into her brain. Lise shows no fear. Von Schtarke feels he cannot allow the rats to get to her unless she breaks, so he punches her in the stomach and leaves her suspended.

In the prison block, Anna gives herself to Lieutenant Weismann, the warden. In return she asks that Lise be saved from von Schtarke. But Weismann has his way then betrays her and turns her over to

GESTAPO'S LAST ORGY

TITLE ON PRINT: **THE GESTAPO'S LAST ORGY**

AKA: **L'ultima orgia del III Reich (original title); Caligula Reincarnated as Hitler; Orgies du III Reich; Des Filles Pour Le Bourreau; Bourreaux SS**

ITALY 1977

CAST: **Daniela Levy, Marc Loud, Maristella Greco, Fulvio Riccardi, Atineska Nemour, Caterina Barbero**

STORY: **Antonio Lucarella**

PRODUCER: **Ruggero Gorgoglione**

DIRECTOR: **CESARE CANEVARI**

von Schtarke. She and Lise are suspended over a vat of quicklime and Anna is plunged into the caustic liquid. Her dissolving corpse is hoisted out so Lise can see what fate will soon befall her. Even this cannot break Lise however, and she is turned over to the camp doctor who diagnoses Lise as being mentally ill. During treatment he discovers that Lise's wish to die stems from the fact that she believes she betrayed her family by turning them over to the Nazis. The doctor investigates and discovers that it was a priest, not Lise, who turned them in. On hearing the news Lise suddenly transforms.

"Life, now I want life. Life!" she declares after making love with the doctor. Soon after she succumbs to von Schtarke and rushes to his room to fellate his pistol. Later she delights him by wearing a girdle made from the hair of murdered prisoners. They declare their love for one another — she refuses to save a friend from death and he strangles Alma. Lise soon becomes pregnant but when the baby boy is born von Schtarke has it put to death because it has Jewish blood.

In the ruins of the camp von Schtarke and Lise have sex. Lise is void of any emotion as she retrieves a pistol from her handbag. A few shots ring out and together they fall to the ground.

CRITIQUE: Like their short-lived series of cannibal movies, the Italian-lensed Nazi camp genre was more intent on depicting brutality and sadism than it was a means of making any moral statement. Derived in part from Liliana Cavani's *The Night Porter* and in whole from the works of de Sade, *The Gestapo's Last Orgy* depicts a lot of extreme cruelty yet has very little to say. Other entries in this unpleasant cycle also found their way onto the DPP list (see ***Beast in Heat*** and ***SS Experiment Camp***), while some managed to slip by seemingly unnoticed (*SS Girls* and *The Red Nights of the Gestapo*, albeit cut). Compared to the greasy sexual and sadistic excesses of *The Gestapo's Last Orgy* they all seem positively slight and frivolous.

The use of a familiar quotation from Nietsche[195] which follows the opening credits in no way raises the film from the level of the toilet pan. Everything about it stretches credibility. Von Schtarke is said to have received a lenient prison sentence for being in charge of a camp that tortured, raped and murdered nearly 4,000 prisoners. When the story flashes back from the present-day to WWII, von Schtarke and Lise don't look a day younger. Lise's moment of passion with the Nazi doctor, where they roll back and forth across a bed, goes on for so long it becomes a laughing matter. The sequence is made even more embarrassingly humorous by the song 'Lise' which plays in tandem with their naked frolicking.

There are other moments of cinematographic incompetence. When Alma, the female commandant, first comes to the camp she is seen arriving on an open boat. As the camera circles the craft a man can be seen hiding in the bottom of the vessel crouched on his knees with his backside thrust up in the air. He is not a character in the film, but perhaps the real-life boat owner keeping an eye on his craft. Supposedly some months later, when Lise is using the boat, the man is seen again in exactly the same position. At one point he even peeps over the side and looks directly at the camera before quickly ducking back down 'out of sight.'

When von Schtarke threatens Lise with rats, he demonstrates their voracity by placing his hand into the glass tank in which they're contained. When the creatures become visible they are seen not to be rats at all but tiny gerbils that sniff curiously at his hand. "They're voracious little beasts aren't they?" he intones. "My blood excites them." But the gerbils don't look threatening at all, they're hardly bigger than von Schtarke's thumb.[196]

Lise's character is incomprehensible. Her desire to die stems from the mistaken belief that she betrayed her family to the Nazis. Once this error has been rectified and Lise learns she wasn't to blame at all, she is ecstatic with an absolute desire to live. Yet, incongruously, she becomes a thoroughly unpleasant person and begins to betray her friends and conform to Nazi ideals. At one point she willingly wears a human hair girdle made from the scalps of her one-time companions to please von Schtarke.

Of course, it isn't technical incompetence and an asinine screenplay that landed *Gestapo's Last Orgy* on the banned list. Yet these characteristics serve to make an unpleasant film even sleazier. The content of the lecture and slideshow (should that be *side-show*?) which von Schtarke gives to the troops is straight out of Krafft-Ebing's *Psychopathia Sexualis*. Forcible incest and half-starved women made to eat from dog bowls are regarded as "the object of a certain sexual stimulation." The whole thing comes over like loose-leaf case studies lifted from the good doctor's book. In one of the film's typically objectionable diatribes, von Schtarke advises his troops that

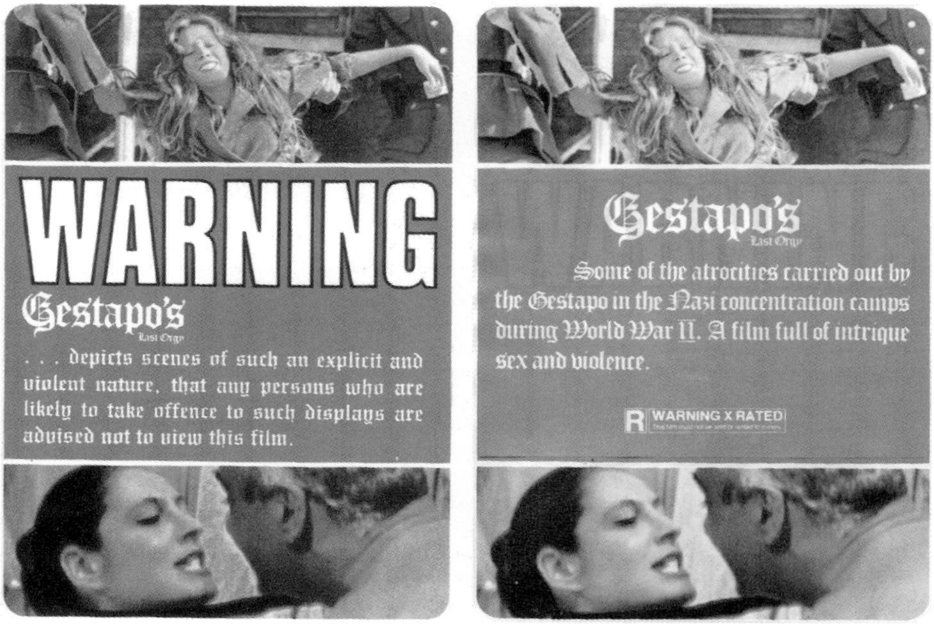

The reverse of the video sleeve for *Gestapo's Last Orgy*. Originally printed with a warning (LEFT), some editions had a sticker highlighting the fact that the content concerned Nazi concentration camps, "full of intrigue sex and violence" (RIGHT).

> a soldier of the Third Reich never makes love to a girl of the Hebrew race. He limits himself to taking pleasure, dominating her, demonstrating to her that she is nothing but filth and he is perfection. He should cause her great suffering. Pain of body and of mind. Never must a Jew be allowed the honour of orgasm with an Aryan.

The only time the film rises above cheap sexploitation and manages to instil a sense of real drama is when the elderly and infirm women are sent to the cremation oven. As they walk sheepishly down the brick tunnel, the film loses its colour temporarily. It may be a technical fault rather than a deliberate effect, but it does afford the sequence a truly sinister and disturbing significance — perhaps only because the momentary colour loss transforms the movie into what looks like newsreel footage and gives the feeling that suddenly it's 'all too real.'[197] There is also something uniquely disagreeable in seeing a heavily pregnant naked woman running back and forth between huge plumes of burning gas — which is as much a medical concern as an ethical one.

There are no singular scenes in *The Gestapo's Last Orgy* that could be attributed to its banning, and there is less actual bloodletting here than in *Schindler's List*. Like the other films of its ilk, it is the entire context that lies at the root of the problem; the subject matter and the manner in which the film-makers have handled it. As reprehensible as these films are, racism is not the film-makers intention. The sexual tortures and horrors are not here to remind the audience of a historic atrocity, but to titillate and excite. Nowhere is this so blatant as in the scene where soldiers begin to masturbate while viewing von Schtarke's slides (despite the commandant's insistence that it is a non-Aryan animal-like behaviour).

Nevertheless a film such as this doesn't need to be banned. It is so unappealing, uninteresting and unexciting that it fails as a piece of film entertainment on virtually every level. Had it not been drawn to the public's attention by the process of classifying it as a nasty, like the Nazi camp genre as a whole, it would have long since died a natural and unmourned death.

THE HOUSE BY THE CEMETERY

SYNOPSIS: In an old house, a young woman finds her lover dead, his brains hanging out. Upon this discovery an unseen assailant drives a knife into the back of her skull, the blade of which exits from her mouth. Her body is dragged through a door which creaks slowly closed.

In New York, Lucy Boyle is preparing to accompany her husband Norman on a business trip. Their son Bobby is transfixed by a photograph hanging on the wall, and tells mom that the girl in the picture is warning him he shouldn't go.

When the family Boyle arrive in New Whitby, Boston, the girl in the picture (who no one else can see) introduces herself to Bobby as May.

At the old Freudstein place, which is to be home for the Boyles for the next six months, Lucy recognises the isolated building as being the one in the photograph that so mesmerised Bobby back in New York. The fact that it's situated right alongside a cemetery doesn't help matters and Lucy wants to leave. But Norman convinces her to take some of her pills and to treat the stay as a vacation. After all, once he completes the research started by his dead predecessor Dr Peterson — said to have killed his mistress before taking his own life — he'll qualify for a better teaching job and they'll all be better off.

THE HOUSE BY THE CEMETERY
AKA: Freudstein (announced under this title); Quella villa accanto al cimitero (original title)
ITALY 1981
CAST: Katherine MacColl, Paolo Malco, Ania Pieroni, Giovanni Frezza, Silvia Collatine, Dagmar Lassander
STORY: Elisa Livia Briganti
PRODUCER: Fabrizio de Angelis
DIRECTOR: LUCIO FULCI

A babysitter by the name of Ann arrives. She throws glances that suggest all is not what it seems with the girl. Sure enough, in the middle of the night, Norman finds Ann trying to remove the boards that block off the cellar door.

The next day Norman goes to the library where Peterson's notes are held, and discovers that much of the material is seemingly unrelated to his designated research field — suicide. The work conducted prior to the man's death focuses instead upon Dr Freudstein, a turn of the century surgeon banned from the medical profession on account of his bizarre experiments.

Norman returns home to find his wife crying. She has discovered a tombstone (bearing the inscription "Jacob Tess Freudstein") sunk into the floor beneath a rug in the hall. The following morning, having taken some of her pills, Lucy is feeling much better and Norman manages to open the cellar door with a key he has found. But once inside he is attacked by a bat that sinks its teeth into his hand and proves reticent to relinquish its grip even when a knife is twisted into it. The episode convinces Norman they ought to give up the house for another one.

When the estate agent arrives for her appointment, she finds the place empty. Her foot falls through a crack in the tombstone in the hall and, unable to free herself, she is attacked and murdered by an unseen assailant who drives the tip of a poker into her chest a couple of times. Her body is dragged behind a door which slams shut.

Ann is mopping up the blood when Lucy walks in. Throwing another one of her strange glances, the girl seems unperturbed by the mess and, as if by way of explanation, tells Lucy she has made coffee.

Lucy tells her husband that the babysitter "is a real weirdo."

Back at the library, Norman discovers an audio cassette on which Dr Peterson feverishly explains that he has lost all critical perspective — and that he is frightened. "How many have wandered innocently into the spider's web," the recording continues, "how many more to come?"

Peterson gets more excitable: "Blood! Blood! Not only blood — *his voice*! I hear it! I hear it everywhere!... He's here! Do you believe me now!!... No! No, not the children! No!!"

(Cut to Bobby playing with his toys.)

Norman destroys the cassette.

Ann mistakenly thinks that Bobby has gone down into the cellar and, worried, goes after him. She is decapitated with a knife. After being alerted by the screams, the boy ventures into the cellar and mom struggles frantically to free him when he fears someone is coming to get him.

Wise to the fact that Freudstein is still beneath the house and is regenerating his cells with human victims, Norman dashes home and takes an axe to the cellar door. He warns Bobby to stand back, unaware that the boy's head is being pressed against the timber on the other side. Each splintering blow from the axe narrowly avoids contact with the child.

We get our first look at Freudstein: a towering man with a heavy overcoat and mutant face. His domain is littered with his recent victims. Norman struggles with the monster, but a knife driven into its stomach has no effect other than to release slop and maggots from the resultant wound. Freudstein reciprocates by ripping Norman's throat out.

Lucy and Bob attempt to escape up a ladder which terminates directly underneath the tombstone in the hall. The crack in the tombstone proves too tight a squeeze for mom and she is dragged back down, her head hammering on each step. It looks as though Bobby might go the same way, but kicking wildly and with May's helping hand from above, he pulls free.

But free in what sense? The setting is clearly of a bygone age, and May's mother — Mrs Freudstein — tells the girl that she shouldn't forget her manners now that Bobby is staying.

Gothic imagery from *The House by the Cemetery*.
TOP: The house...
ABOVE: Trapped in the tombstone in the hallway.

CRITIQUE: The fourth and final instalment in Fulci's 'living dead' series... While *The House by the Cemetery* doesn't adhere to the narrative trajectory of either ***Zombie Flesh-Eaters***, ***The Beyond***, or *City of the Living Dead*, there is continuity in its use of common motifs, familiar actors and gory pay-offs. It's a lot more insular in its makeup than those films, focusing its story — and all of its action — on an autumnal New England house.[198] However, there are still plenty of inconsistencies. For instance, just where exactly is Dr Peterson supposed to have died? In the Freudstein house where he killed his mistress before committing suicide, or in the library where he hung himself from a rail? Both are trotted out as statements of fact.

Other facets of the story can be interpreted as a means to disorientate the audience. Various townspeople are adamant they remember Norman from some previous visit, for example (although he denies ever being to the town before). Norman also destroys Peterson's cassette recording and is completely unphased at the discovery of a tombstone in the house. Also noteworthy is the sinister manner in which Ann, the babysitter, goes about her business.[199] Whatever secrets Norman and Ann may have, in the end they both die trying to save Bob — who, it needs to be said, suffers from particularly appalling dubbing, his voice coming courtesy of an adult mimicking a child. (The obtrusive dubbing extends to the sound of footfalls around the house: everyone clomps about the place as if they're wearing hobnailed boots.)

Perhaps the most tantalising element of the story — enforced in the early stages but allowed to peter away completely later on — is that Lucy is taking prescription pills which are said to induce hallucinations. It's interesting to speculate how the final nightmare in the cellar might have been handled had the 'acid' idea been carried through!

There are many well-crafted scenes in *Cemetery*, but if we have to single out just one it would be Bob's discovery of Ann's decapitated head: entering the cellar alone, the boy gets to the foot of the iron steps when he hears the pounding of something bouncing down behind him — it may be one of his toys, but somehow he knows it won't be — and out of the shadows the babysitter's head comes to a dead stop.

After the dynamic head-stabbing that occurs in the opening minutes, *The House By The Cemetery* settles down to some restrained mood-building and a blood-free sobriety not often seen in Italian exploitation of this era. It isn't until the encroachment of the halfway mark that the film embarks on its series of remarkably gory set-pieces. The first of these takes the form of a corny bat-attack that breathlessly intensifies until a mini-bloodbath ensues and the winged mammal succumbs to its multiple stab wounds. Subsequent killings are of the human kind, but are all meted out with the same unnerving intensity.

There aren't many telltale signs that Vampix' release is victim to cuts, indeed the only real evidence of censorial tampering comes with the death of Mrs Gittelson, the estate agent (which has an 'irregular' feel about it). But while everything else might appear intact — i.e. without discernible jumps in sound or picture — it's an impression that owes as much to the *longevity* of the gore scenes as it does the dexterity of the censor's film-snipping hand. In other words, the gore as it exists is interminable and horribly brutal — what could be missing?

A lot.

The estate agent in the Vampix release gets a poker rammed into her chest. After some twisting and turning and the pooling of blood, the tool is removed and sunk through the victim's blouse into her left breast. In its original uncut form, these shots are complemented with plenty of bloody close-ups and the penetration of the left breast is considerably more protracted. But it doesn't end there: in a sequence excised in its entirety from the Vampix release, the killer then drives the poker into Gittelson's neck. Its withdrawal results in a spectacular explosion of blood from the perfectly formed wound, which is shot from differing camera angles and played in both real-time and slow motion.[200]

Other excised scenes include some *cinéma-vérité* camerawork in the Freudstein cellar (over which Peterson's tape recording is being played), revealing a close-up of a mutilated, innards-on-display torso.

When Ann is decapitated, the Vampix print shows a single neck slash before cutting away. In its entirety, the sequence continues with the knife being brought down a second time, on the opposite side of the girl's neck, ultimately creating two horrendous wounds.

As Bob's head is pressed by Freudstein against the cellar door that Norman tries to break down with an axe, Vampix omit one final blow that actually has the axe striking the boy's head and drawing blood. Both Freudstein and the boy reel away from the impact, the preposterous consequence of which has Bob being merely grazed and Freudstein losing a hand.

Apart from the truncation of more gory debris in Freudstein's subterranean laboratory, Norman's throat ripping is the last scene to suffer cuts.

Vampix' *House by the Cemetery* is the same print that was released theatrically in Britain (even opening with the original X-certificate). In spite of the cuts, and the fact the print is discernibly much darker than it ought to be, the film positively shines when compared to its subsequent British releases on the Elephant and Vipco video labels — where less discerning, more brutal censoring serves to completely eradicate the 'point' of the film (the latter print missing seven-and-a-half minutes).

"Damn tombstones!" cries Mrs Gittelson, the estate agent, as she struggles to negotiate her vehicle off the Freudstein property.

Fulci's next film would be *The New York Ripper*, a psychotic and misogynistic visual feast that was rejected outright by the BBFC. Stories of the print receiving a police escort out of the country are true.

HOUSE ON THE EDGE OF THE PARK

SYNOPSIS: Driving home at night a girl is forced off the road by another car and raped by its driver, Alex. He strangles her to death as he reaches orgasm and steals the girl's (cheap-looking) locket before leaving.

In an indeterminate future-time, Alex and his dim-witted friend Ricky are preparing to go for a night on the town, when a car pulls into the garage that Alex runs. Although the obnoxious Alex tells the well-to-do young couple the garage is closed for the evening, Ricky fixes the vehicle's minor problem and as a result the two of them are invited to a private party.

Arriving at a secluded house where a handful of formally dressed, stuffy guests are socialising, Ricky immediately starts to dance to the terrible disco music playing. "Just remember," whispers Alex to his friend, "we're among rich people."

Ricky is happy to be the centre of attention, but is unable to see that the joke is on him.

When one of the female guests decides to go upstairs Alex follows and, at her request, joins her in the shower. But when the woman declines to have sex, Alex rejoins the party a frustrated man and becomes incensed when he sees Ricky being humiliated yet further in a crooked game of poker.

"You're great, Alex!" the doe-eyed Ricky elatedly cries when his buddy uncovers the scam.

Things take a turn for the worse when Alex hurls abuse at the women (he calls them "twot") and pulls a cut-throat razor on the men — Tom and Howard — when they rush him.

Instead of wanting to leave, Alex volunteers that it's now his and Ricky's turn to have some fun, and encourages his pal to rape the woman of his choice. Howard tries to intervene when Alex tears the knickers off Gloria, but is soon overpowered by the bigger man, who throws him into the swimming pool and pisses on him before tying him up.

"Now, let's have a party!" Alex announces, locking all the doors.

Ricky has had a change of heart and tells his buddy that Gloria is afraid and he doesn't want to do it this way. Exasperated, Alex takes over but tosses the woman to one side when it seems she's beginning to enjoy his attentions.

Tom causes a distraction in order that Gloria can try and phone for help, but gets his head bashed repeatedly against a table for his troubles. Alex rapes the woman with whom he took a shower earlier. She fights him at first but then enjoys it. Later, he demands that she has a lesbian petting session with another guest, but this is interrupted by the doorbell ringing.

The caller is a young girl by the name of Cindy. As the other party guests look on disgustedly, Alex turns to the new arrival and slowly cuts off her clothes with his razor. The waif stands topless and sobbing, attempting to cover herself with her hands. "Hellooo

HOUSE ON THE EDGE OF THE PARK

AKA: La casa sperduta nel parco (original title); Der Schlitzer; Trampa para un violador; The House at the Edge of the Park

ITALY 1980

CAST: David A Hess, Annie Belle, Cristian Borromeo, Giovanni Lombardo Radice, Marie Claude Joseph, Gabrielle di Giulio, and with a special appearance by Lorraine de Selle

STORY: Gianfranco Clerici & Vincenzo Mannino

PRODUCER: Giovanni Masini

DIRECTOR: RUGGERO DEODATO

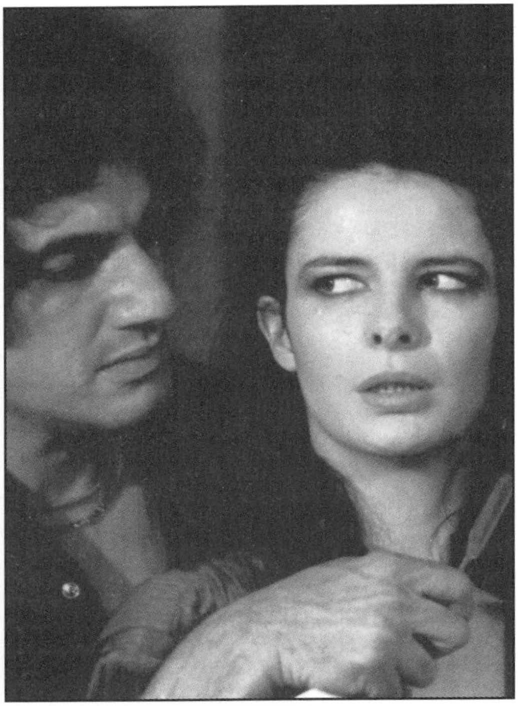

lady," Alex drools, making the final transition into psychosis with a love song that invokes the film's sickly main theme.[201] Forcing the girl to remove her jeans, he then gropes her crotch through her knickers and is somehow able to deduce that "She's a virgin!"

Ricky gives chase to Gloria who has made a run for freedom. He captures her in the bushes outside and comforts her with the fact that he doesn't want to hurt her — he feels bad. She reciprocates with tenderness and soon the two are kissing and making love. Gloria's orgasmic cries are intercut with the scenes of the petrified Cindy being menaced inside the house with the cut-throat razor.

Ricky talks Gloria into returning inside because he is certain he can convince Alex to leave now that he's had his fun. He is proven wrong however; Alex has no intention of leaving. Instead, he turns his attentions back to Cindy and tells her that "they say you always remember the first time," before throwing the naked girl onto a couch and slashing her arm with the razor. He gets 'off' on this and proceeds to slice her breasts (four times), abdomen and upper thighs.

"Alex... you'll come to a point where you won't be able to stop," Ricky pleads. Alex responds to this insubordination by stabbing his pal in the belly whereupon he is instantly struck by remorse. "Why did you make me do it?" he pleads of the dying man in his arms.

With Alex distracted, Tom takes a pistol from a nearby drawer and shoots Alex in the leg, driving him outside with a second and third shot from the gun.

"Filthy animal," Tom mutters, explaining to the dying man that the loose alternator wire on his car was all part of a plan to get him to the house. It transpires that it was Tom's sister who Alex raped at the beginning of the picture.

Alex is shot in the groin, which throws the man wailing into the swimming pool. From here on each of the guests takes a pot-shot until Alex' body floats lifelessly in the water.

Howard then takes aim at the dying Ricky, but is prevented from firing by Gloria.

Tom telephones the police, ready to tell them that he has shot an intruder in self-defence.

CRITIQUE: Director Ruggero Deodato attempts to elevate this odious film with some rather ineffectual stabs at issues of class and society, and seems to be implying that compared to

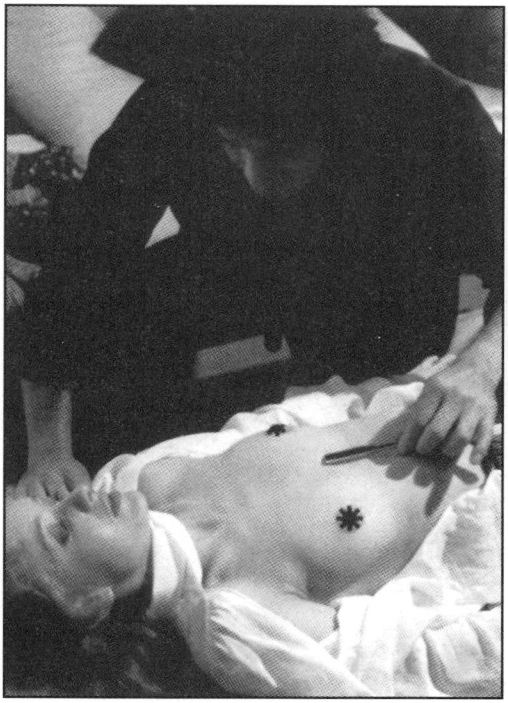

House on the Edge of the Park.
PREVIOUS PAGE, FROM LEFT: Alex and Ricky take over the party; Alex threatens Gloria.
THIS PAGE: Alex violates Cindy.

the 'toffs' of the world a reprobate like Alex isn't so bad after all. The film suggests that for all his shortcomings, if misguided and insane, at least Alex is honest and loyal. Take his devotion to the dim-witted Ricky, for instance, his best buddy whom he stabs in the belly – this act of destruction draws from Alex the following heartfelt plea:

> They did this to you!... They're all fuckin' bastards — all of them! They did this to you! They're trying to turn us against each other! Just look at them — what do they know about friendship anyway!

Not a lot – as suggested in the closing moments of the film when Gloria, the girl with whom Ricky had sex, turns to Howard and decides to break off an indeterminate relationship. (They might be married or might only be dating, the audience is given no clue.) Rich people don't really love one another in the way that Alex and Ricky do.

The sophisticates are painted as a lot bored with their lives. Money has given them much, but robbed them of even more. Into this flam of finery and etiquette come our two protagonists, who are the brunt of some humiliation but at the same time hold a rugged appeal over the other guests – particularly Alex who the women regard as a "stud." At the party, Alex and Ricky are first portrayed as a couple of 'regular' guys simply out of their depth, while their hosts are a scheming lot who not only make fun of a retard like Ricky, but are prepared to take advantage of him also. But Alex quickly gets wise. He isn't fooled by the charade and in his own callous way even manages to make a valid observation or two, inadvertently recognising Glenda – the black girl with a bald head – as not so much a guest but a symbol of 'polite society' decadence like himself. They tell him he should be in a cage; he calls Glenda "Roots."

House on the Edge of the Park is a virtual reprise of Wes Craven's ***The Last House on the Left***, lifting David Hess from that movie and typecasting him forever as one of cinema's most degenerate villains. Like that earlier production, here a family avenge the rape and murder of a loved one, albeit in a more cold and calculated way. By the end of *House on the Edge of the Park*, revenge has become something else entirely — a turn-on for some of the guests; another twisted kick for those who can afford it.

House on the Edge of the Park has lost none of its shock value. If anything, it's more shocking viewed in these post-politically correct times than when it first appeared back in the early eighties. Certainly it traverses an uncomfortable line with using rape for titillation and having victims getting turned on by their ordeal — a major point of contention for the BBFC. But Deodato goes much further than that. With the arrival of Cindy, the teenager who initially flirts with Alex before realising what is actually going on, the film charts a territory so dark it seems out of place even in a film as morally disjointed as this. The girl is displayed for the audience (literally, she faces the camera in the centre of the shot) and humiliated; she is a virgin, for which she is humiliated even further. When finally Alex takes his cut-throat razor to her, the evident sexual satisfaction he derives in slicing her flesh is intercut with the orgasmic thrusts of Ricky and Gloria elsewhere. There aren't too many ways this lengthy passage of sexual sadism can be interpreted. At the time *House on the Edge of the Park* was being made, even hardcore pornographic features had given up trying to tackle this kind of fantasy extreme, not that many had ever bothered to do so with such conviction anyway.[202]

It is around this sequence that a possible myth has evolved. Numerous people claim to have seen a rather questionable scene in *House* that certainly doesn't exist in the British print (which was released uncut) and has yet to appear in any video version elsewhere. These rumours appear to have their origin in the US, where more than one viewer has stated they remember the scene from a theatrical screening around the mid-eighties. Rick Sullivan wrote in *Gore Gazette*[203] around this time:

> *House* offers what has to be one of the sickest scenes ever committed to celluloid: [David] Hess rips the panties off one of the party guests and is about to rape her when he notices that a white string is dangling from between her legs. He crudely shouts "Hey, look what I found" and pulls out a bloody tampon for all to see while the humiliated girl sobs with embarrassment.

It's almost inconceivable that a bloody tampon would be dangled in front of cinema audiences, even those savouring the rare exploitational pedigree of a movie such as this one. On top of that, it's hard to imagine how such a scene would fit in what is essentially a tightly edited sequence — in a close-up shot, the film has already shown Alex feeling through the girl's panties and declaring her to be a virgin. Hess himself in an interview has supposedly denied that such a scene was ever filmed.

So how has the idea of such a scene come about? It could simply be the ramblings of an overworked Rick Sullivan,[204] whose critique has since passed into legend (people who have never seen the film frequently speak of the 'tampon scene'), or it may be that the print playing theatrically back in 1985 was doctored. After all, such a thing happened with ***I Spit On Your Grave***. Then again, in 'Interesting,' an episode of the British comedy series *The Young Ones* (broadcast by the BBC in December 1982), a character called Rik unwittingly pulls a tampon from a girl's handbag during a party and starts playing around with it...

HUMAN EXPERIMENTS

SYNOPSIS: Rachel Foster is a country and western singer touring the clubs with a series of solo performances. Her first venue is in an out-of-town bar run by the obnoxious Mr Tibbs. After her performance Tibbs comes onto her, pointing out that "These one night stands must get pretty lonely for a sweet young lady like yourself." Rachel turns down Tibbs' offer, telling him she has to be up early in the morning. "Cunt," mutters Tibbs under his breath. From her room Rachel telephones her next venue to confirm the booking but is told that the bar is closing down. While she sleeps Tibbs slides an envelope containing her fee under her door.

The following morning as she prepares to leave, Rachel realises she has been underpaid and confronts Tibbs in his office. He tells her he has deducted money for her drinks, room and taxes. Rachel argues that such deductions were not part of the agreement, and so takes cash from Tibbs' desk counting out what she is due. "I wouldn't do that if I were you," threatens Tibbs, who introduces Rachel to his brother the sheriff sitting in the corner. The sheriff orders her to put the money back and leave.

Rachel drives from the place in a temper. Later, on the highway, a woman stumbles into the road and Rachel swerves to miss her. The car ends up stuck in a field and she goes to a nearby farmhouse for assistance. Knocking on the door and getting no reply she goes inside to use the telephone, but discovers the occupants of the house are lying dead from gunshot wounds. A little boy sits in a chair holding a rifle that he slowly levels at Rachel. She grabs a gun from a wall mounting and fires at the boy striking him in the chest. The sheriff happens upon the scene and Rachel is arrested, charged with murder and the attempted murder of the boy, who is taken to hospital in a coma. Following her trial she is found guilty, sentenced to life imprisonment and taken to the local Gates Correctional Facility.

Dr Kline, the facility's resident psychiatrist, is particularly interested in the fact that Rachel has no family or close friends. He tells her that he is going to be her friend. Unknown to the inmates, the prison has a series of subterranean cells in which Kline's patients are treated. Kline has developed a method of rehabilitation in which the patient is regressed to childhood and brought back to adulthood as a different and much-improved person. One woman undergoing the treatment is sitting in a cell filled with child's toys. She is fed with a baby's bottle and a sign on the wall reads, "My Name is Rita." Rita is taken to Kline's residence and treated like an adult, given a proper meal and instructed on how to eat by the doctor. Rita, like a baby, throws the food in the doctor's face and he advances on her. Rita is never seen again.

One night Rachel hears someone groaning in another cell. She finds her cell door open and goes to investigate, only to discover an inmate has hung herself. She calls for the guard but no one comes to help. The following morning Rachel is informed that the prisoner has been paroled and that she must have imagined the hanging. Kline puts her on tranquillisers.

Months go by and Rachel and another inmate decide to try and escape. During a concert they feign illness and visit the nurse, attack her and retreat to the basement where Rachel's accomplice claims to know of an escape route. In the basement they get separated and Rachel discovers the body of the inmate she saw hanging, then begins to hallucinate and sees the family she is convicted of murdering. She crawls through a ventilation shaft and is engulfed in cockroaches and centipedes, before reaching the other side and finding herself in a spacious cell. Kline is present along with two hooded executioners, who take Rachel to an awaiting noose and simulate hanging her. Kline promises she will be reborn.

Rachel is in a cell filled with toys. A sign reads "My Name is Sarah."

Following months of treatment the warden learns that the boy who Rachel is accused of shooting has come out of his coma and confessed to the murders. She tells Kline that Rachel is innocent and the experiment has to be stopped. Realising that he will be investigated if she is released, Kline brainwashes Rachel/Sarah into believing that the warden is a threat to her. He slips a gun into her bag as they both go to the warden's office to sign the release documents. Once in the office, Kline reminds Rachel that the warden doesn't love her, only he does. Rachel takes the gun from her bag but only fires upon the specimen jars that line the shelves. She is released and continues with her singing career.

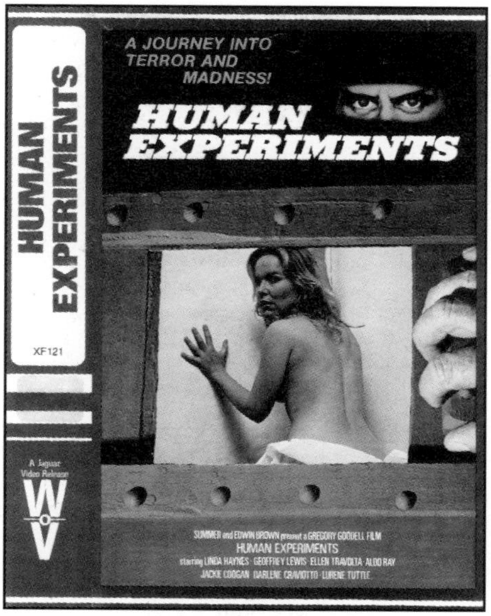

HUMAN EXPERIMENTS
USA 1979
CAST: Linda Haynes, Geoffrey Lewis, Ellen Travolta, Aldo Ray, Jackie Coogan, Darlene Craviotti, Lurene Tuttle
STORY: Richard Rothstein
PRODUCERS: Gregory Goodell & Summer Brown
DIRECTOR: GREGORY GOODELL

CRITIQUE: Despite a promising opening *Human Experiments* soon slips into a tiresome women-in-prison saga featuring the prerequisite hard-boiled guard and big butch prison dyke. The few male characters are redneck misogynists who come straight from the gene pool of *Macon County Line* and *Jackson County Jail*, films that had similar plots concerning outsiders who were wrongly accused of a serious crime. However, *Human Experiments* dwells more on the psychological torment of the heroine rather than the physical abuse administered to the female characters of those two earlier films.

The concept of Kline's bizarre experiment is unique and interesting but isn't explored in any depth. We only witness the outcome of the experiments, even when it is Rachel — the central character — who is subjected to the regressive treatment.

We are never too sure about what is exactly going on in the prison and who amongst the other prisoners are in on the plot (if indeed any of them are). Following Rachel's transformation into Sarah she is reintroduced to her inmate acquaintances as Sarah and none of them remark on the fact that it is really Rachel. It is also unclear whether Rachel is at times hallucinating — the noises she hears at night, the bodies she discovers, the masses of insects — or if she is actually embroiled in some hideous reality. Such a lack of clarity is detrimental to the film.

There is no particular scene that could remotely identify *Human Experiments* as a video nasty (though when it played theatrically in 1980, the *Monthly Film Bulletin* records that the film was cut by a staggering eight minutes). It can only be concluded that it was placed on the DPP list because of its title alone — in that the word 'experiment' may have somehow erratically linked the film to ***SS Experiment Camp***. Indeed, *Human Experiments* would not be out of place on television — though perhaps with Aldo Ray's single utterance of the word "cunt" being replaced with something less severe.

Human Experiments was released on World of Video 2000. Vipco re-released Michael Laughlin's unrelated *Dead Kids* under the title of *Human Experiments* in the nineties, no doubt in an attempt to fool people into believing that — along with truncated versions of ***The Slayer***, ***Shogun Assassin*** and ***Zombie Flesh-Eaters*** — it was another entry in their own line of BBFC certified video nasty re-issues.

Husband and wife team of executive producer Edwin Brown and co-producer Summer Brown were, prior to *Human Experiments*, better known for sex films. Under the name Sandra Winters, Summer co-produced the 1974 *China Girl* (a film apparently made before its star, Annette Haven, had her teeth capped) which also featured a doctor experimenting on the human brain and memory faculties.

I MISS YOU HUGS & KISSES
TITLE ON PRINT: I MISS YOU, HUGS AND KISSES
AKA: Left for Dead
CANADA 1978
CAST: Elke Sommer, Donald Pilon, Chuck Shamata, Cindy Girling, George Touliatos, Cec Linder, and introducing George Chuvalo
STORY: Murray Markowitz
PRODUCERS: Charles Zakery Markowitz & Murray Markowitz
DIRECTOR: MURRAY MARKOWITZ

I MISS YOU HUGS & KISSES

SYNOPSIS: Magdalene Kruschen is bludgeoned to death in her garage by someone wielding an iron bar. The attacker strikes her twice and a plume of blood erupts from a spot removed from the actual point of impact. Blood pumps from the prone figure on the floor.

Wealthy Charles Kruschen is charged with the murder of his wife. At the trial, Charles reminisces on events dating back twenty years. B&W footage of the 1956 Hungarian uprising plays, and the convicted man is back in his childhood, escaping from the advancing Russian troops for Canada.

Having slipped across the border, the story then jumps forward to show Charles as quite the successful businessman in his new country. He gives a speech at a party and (in a flashback within the flashback) explains how his first job on arriving in Canada was working at a slaughterhouse.

There is a brief sojourn to the courtroom of the present before Charles recounts how he met his wife, Magdalene. Magdalene was a model he met at Gershen Isen's photographic studio — Gershen being a good buddy with whom Charles had escaped Hungary. He tells Gershen they plan to marry.

"Let me tell you," Gershen responds to the news, "all she is is a money-grabbing little nothing from a little village near Hamburg, who's going to wind up as a fat hausfrau. That's right, not even a good whore. All she's got is that face, those tits, and an ever-open door of a cunt!"

This outburst doesn't deter Charles and the wedding goes ahead. But the marriage turns sour, and before long Charles begins to imagine his wife being murdered. First she is being bludgeoned in a shady part of town, then electrocuted in a swimming pool and finally run over by his car.

Gershen testifies that he and the accused discussed ways of killing Magdalene. It also transpires Gershen was blackmailing Magdalene with some compromising photos he had of her. In a flashback he tells Magdalene that he hates Charles because "he got the money… and he got you."

Pauline Corte takes the witness stand. She is a student from France with whom Charles has fallen in love and had an affair. The two of them are seen frolicking beneath autumnal skies, riding bicycles, watching boats and drinking wine. Pauline tells the court that Charles is a kind man, a lonely man, and that "he wanted love."

When Magdalene finds out about the affair, she arranges a meeting with Tibor Zanopek — a figure from way back who was shot while trying to escape Hungary and left for dead by Charles. He is now a boxing coach and bears a grudge. Magdalene offers Zanopek $10,000 to have his prize fighter beat her husband until he's dead. "Dead?" replies the boxer, "Naw, I only break arms and legs."

But Zanopek proceeds to take advance payments for the job, without any intention of seeing it through.

Meanwhile, an escapee from an institution for the criminally insane enters the fray. He picks up a lone female hitchhiker, drives to a secluded spot, kills her, and rapes her.

Once again, Magdalene is seen being bludgeoned by an anonymous attacker.

Charles finds his wife's bloodied body after returning from a shopping trip with his daughter. And although he couldn't possibly have committed the murder, an unscrupulous Detective successfully pins the crime on him.

Charles is locked in a prison cell, his hair fallen out and face erupting in boils. He pens a letter to his love, Pauline, and signs off, "I miss you, hugs and kisses."

CRITIQUE: Several minutes into *I Miss You, Hugs and Kisses*, a notice rolls by:

> The film you are about to see is fiction although the basic idea for the film was inspired by an actual event, the circumstances and characters have been deliberately and extensively altered so that any resemblance to the actual events or actual persons living or dead is purely coincidental.

The same disclaimer appears again during the end credits (on the tail of a notice that proclaims "This film is dedicated to Ms. Elaine Green on the occasion of her marriage").

Despite the sentence passed on Charles Kruschen by the court, the film-makers obviously don't believe he committed the murder — in spite of his lurid daydreams and negotiations on how best to kill his wife. Instead, they suggest that any one of a number of people could have committed the crime, with an emphasis on the boxing coach Tibor Zanopek and the madman John MacGregor as being most likely the real perpetrators. Zanopek is said to have gone round to collect another "advance payment" from Magdalene on the night of her murder, and was himself later killed in a high-speed police chase (but how this links to the murder is never explained); MacGregor, on the other hand, already having killed several strangers, was simply in the area at the time. Such unresolved hypothesising would have been better suited to a more widely known criminal case, but the 'actual events' on which this film is supposedly based are long forgotten[205] and, presented as a work of fiction, its open-endedness comes over simply as sloppy, confusing and ultimately frustrating.

Not that the film is helped in having a structure that would give Peter Greenaway a headache. There are flashbacks within flashbacks, slotted together seemingly at random, and 'major' characters who don't get so much as an introduction but instead are dropped cold into the story (except for MacGregor, who literally drives down a road and into shot).

There are several contentious scenes in *I Miss You, Hugs and Kisses*. One of them is the sex-murder perpetrated by MacGregor, who drags his victim to the ground, stabs her and proceeds to rape her while the knife remains jutting from her belly.[206] A flashback to the incident shows the girl being stabbed twice again in close-up, blood slowly pooling around the blade as MacGregor has necrophilic sex. The other notable contentious scene features the brutal bludgeoning of Magdalene Kruschen (played by Elke Sommer), which is the hinge pin from which everything in the film hangs. Should there be any doubt about the importance of this event, the film-makers trot it out with shocking regularity, first playing it over the opening credits and later several times in close succession. Here, as George Kruschen contemplates the guilty verdict just handed to him by the courts, the film attempts to undermine the sentence by placing each of the other suspects at the crime scene, weapon in hand, delivering the fatal blow. Gershen — Charles's buddy — jumps out of the shadows and strikes Magdalene across the head, as does Zanopek in a mirror scene, then MacGregor, and finally the boxing champ who had refused the $10,000 offer to kill Kruschen. Although clumsily executed from a technical viewpoint, the reign of slow-motion blows and bright syrupy blood gushing through platinum blonde hair makes for an unsettling visceral onslaught nonetheless.

Other scenes that might have raised a few eyebrows include the chicken slaughterhouse footage which serves to illustrate Kruschen's first job, and the police removal of clothes from Magdalene's bloodied corpse, which lingers unhealthily on scissors cutting through underwear.

Director Murray Markowitz has made at least one other film, *Recommendation for Mercy*. Howard Shore who composed the music for *I Miss You, Hugs and Kisses* went on to score David Cronenberg's *Videodrome*. The picture of Elke Sommer that adorns the sleeve for Intercity Video's pre-certificated video release is not a still taken from Markowitz' film.

With 1m 6s of cuts, *I Miss You, Hugs and Kisses* was granted an 18 certificate when re-released by Heron Home Entertainment in 1986 under the title of *Drop Dead Dearest*.

I Miss You, Hugs and Kisses was ideally suited to a residency on the videos nasties list. In itself it belongs to no specific genre: it isn't a murder-mystery, nor a thriller, and it isn't a horror film. The DPP managed to give it an identity — not to mention a collector's price.

I SPIT ON YOUR GRAVE

SYNOPSIS: A budding novelist, Jennifer Hill sets out on vacation from her home in New York City to a secluded summerhouse in the countryside. After driving for three straight hours, and not far from her destination, she pulls up for gas. "Feels good to stretch my legs," she tells Johnny, the creepy pump attendant. His layabout friends — Andy and Stanley — fool amongst themselves in the background.

Arriving at the summerhouse, Jennifer goes skinny-dipping in the river that runs by the property. Refreshed, she takes delivery of some groceries, courtesy of a retarded local boy named Matthew. They engage in some small talk, and Matthew later brags to his three buddies at the gas station that he has seen the stranger's "tits." When the group chide him for still being a virgin and offer to fix him up with a broad, Matthew innocently tells the gang he has already found someone special in Miss Hill — who has given him a dollar tip.

The conversation has terrible repercussions for Jennifer.

Following several nuisance episodes — such as distracting Jennifer from her novel writing and prowling around outside the summerhouse in the middle of the night — the gang embarks on a day of physical abuse and rape. It starts when Jennifer is dragged upstream, and pushed around by a couple of the gang members. She attempts to run away, but her path is blocked by Johnny (still in his garage overalls and cap) who steps out of the undergrowth. Johnny rips off her swimsuit and, holding her down with his two buddies, calls to Matthew, "We got her for you!"

"I can't!" Matthew whimpers from a distance.

Johnny rapes Jennifer. The sequence is full of shots of Johnny's hideously contorted face. When he's through, the men back off in silence. Some of them look almost guilty.

Jennifer, dishevelled and sobbing, crawls slowly away. The gang cajole Matthew that if he doesn't go after her and make a man of himself, he's going to die a virgin. Instead he runs away.

Jennifer continues on a solitary, dazed trek through the woods, as a mournful musical refrain gently filters into hearshot. She steps into a clearing to see one of the men perched on a boulder, playing a harmonica. The rest of the gang close in, and hold her face-down over the rock while she is sodomised. The rape is played out in real time. When it's over, the men say nothing but get in their motorboat and head back upstream. Jennifer rolls off the rock, shaking. She makes it back to the summerhouse, and stands before it, uncertain.

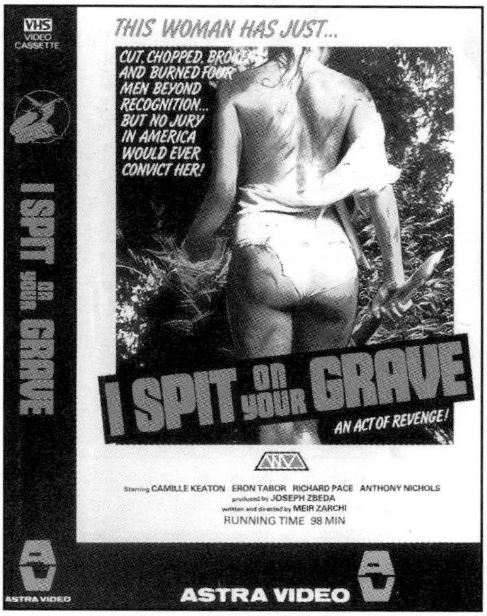

Now clothed and in a state of shock, Jennifer is subjected to yet further abuse when the gang returns that evening with Matthew. After two swigs of alcohol, the retarded delivery boy becomes an instant extravert, stripping off to his socks and finally managing to rape the girl. One of the men finds Jennifer's manuscript and reads aloud from it, mocking it, before tearing it to pieces. "Total submission, that's what I like in a woman," says another, as he unsuccessfully tries to get the now unconscious Jennifer to fellate him.

This proves the most brutal attack of all, leaving Jennifer kicked, beaten, abused with a bottle, and half-dead. The gang retreat, but ultimately decide it would be better if she was dead and send Matthew back to do the deed. Contrary to what he later tells his buddies however, the delivery boy lets Jennifer be. Two weeks pass before they start to wonder why nobody has reported the murder.

Jennifer Hill pieces together her life (alluded to in the taping up of the torn manuscript). Dressed in mourning, she drives to a deserted church, and asks forgiveness for the retribution she has in mind.[207] Back at the summerhouse she phones the grocery store and requests a delivery. Matthew nervously shows up, telling Jennifer that he hates her. "You brought nothing but bad luck with you!" Because of her — or rather, because his fellow rapists found out he'd lied about killing her — Matthew no longer has any friends in town.

Tempting him with sex, Jennifer leads Matthew into a trap. She throws a noose around his neck and hangs him until dead (with his trousers wrapped around his ankles).

The next in line for Jennifer's cold, deliberate plan of vengeance, is Johnny. With the promise of sex, she coaxes him into the woods, where she pulls out a revolver and forces him to strip naked. He pleads that the rape wasn't his fault, but was all down to her having exposed her "damn sexy legs" when she first arrived in town — and for having "tits with no bra."

Jennifer gives up the gun and invites Johnny to share a hot bath, where she masturbates him ("God bless your hands") before

I SPIT ON YOUR GRAVE
AKA: The Rape and Revenge of Jennifer Hill (original title); Day of the Woman
USA 1978
CAST: Camille Keaton, Eron Tabor, Richard Pace, Anthony Nichols, Gunter Kleeman
STORY: Meir Zarchi
PRODUCERS: Joseph Zbeda & Leir Zarchi
DIRECTOR: MEIR ZARCHI

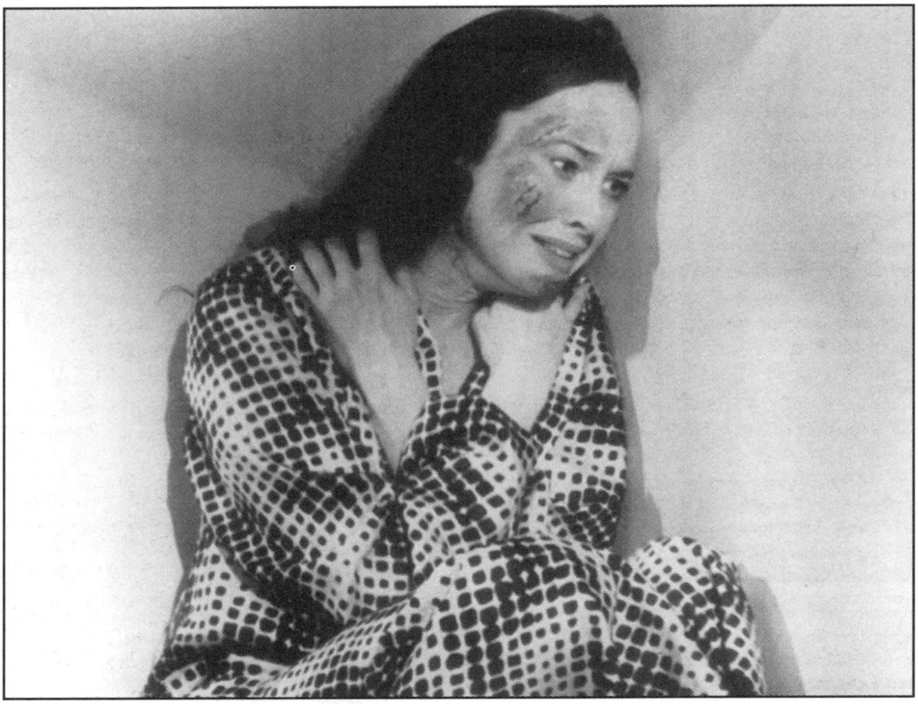

using a secreted knife to castrate him.

"That's so sweet it's painful!" says Johnny before realising quite what has happened.

With Johnny locked in the bathroom bleeding to death and screaming his lungs out, Jennifer retires to the front room, gazing vacantly from her rocking chair as a classical record plays.

The remaining two members of the gang arrive in their motorboat looking for their missing buddy. They are killed when Jennifer tricks them out of their boat, sinking an axe into the back of one, and driving the boat's propeller into the chest of the other.

The film ends with Jennifer speeding along the river, a half-smile crossing her lips.

CRITIQUE: *I Spit On Your Grave* is probably the most notorious of all the titles on the DPP list, and its title was prominently featured whenever the media undertook their condemnation of the video nasties. As a result, gang rape became another despicable factor of what the nasties were supposedly all about.

> *I Spit on Your Grave* has the distinction of being among the most loathsome films of all time.
>
> —*Kim Newman, Nightmare Movies*

> Unpleasant as this film is, it at least shows a woman fighting back.
>
> —*David J Hogan, Dark Romance*

The controversy that surrounded the film in Britain was preceded by a storm of protest on the other side of the Atlantic, when film critics Roger Ebert[208] and Gene Siskel — in their PBS TV show *Sneak Previews* — urged people to boycott the theatres that screened it. But of course, not many people heeded the advice. The film had been fairing rather badly in New

York, managing only a handful of dates at 42nd Street's Anco Theatre and other decrepit joints. With its video release however, sales went ballistic, and *I Spit On Your Grave* out-sold then recent Academy Award winner *Ordinary People* by about twenty-to-one in some places, getting as high as number twenty-four in *Billboard*'s best-sellers list for 1981.

The star of the film, Camille Keaton herself, was moved to pen a reply to the critic for the *Los Angeles Times* who described *I Spit On Your Grave* as "a sleazy film about interracial sex."

> There is no interracial sex... Further, I personally resent the implication of [critic Lewis] Beale's sweeping generalisation... "films noted for their hilariously inept actors." Having made more than a half-dozen films in Europe and having won the Best Actress Award at the Sitges Film Festival for *I Spit On Your Grave*, my professional credentials are well-established.[209]

There was controversy of a different kind when it was discovered that theatrical and video prints displaying an R-rating — supposedly trimmed by seventeen minutes[210] — were in actual fact full uncut X-rated prints of the film. Bill Landis was one critic who figured something was amiss. "I agree with Ebert on this being the most extreme R-rated film," he wrote in *Sleazoid Express*.[211] The MPAA filed a federal lawsuit against Wizard Video and the Jerry Gross Organization — the respective video and theatrical distributors — for misuse of their trademarked R symbol in advertising the film. But it took them a year to catch onto the ratings masquerade, according to Camille Keaton.[212] "You know the scene where I'm raped on the rock?" she told *Draculina*.[213] "If that's in the film, you know it's the [uncut] version."

I Spit On Your Grave has only ever had a video release in Britain, distributed under the Astra Video and Wizard Video labels. The latter was always much more difficult to obtain, but — outside of having a smaller label stuck on the cassette itself — is believed to have been identical to the Astra release in every way.[214] The British prints also carried the misappropriated US R-rat-

I Spit on your Grave.

PREVIOUS PAGE: Jennifer Hill tries to come to terms with her ordeal.
THIS PAGE, TOP: UK trade advertisement.
ABOVE: The men are dead and Jennifer rides out of the picture.

ing, which pops up at the end of the film, cutting the closing credits short.

According to director Zarchi, the film has its genesis in a true life incident that occurred one Sunday afternoon in October 1974. Driving to a park with his eight-year-old daughter and a friend, Zarchi spotted a girl wandering naked in a state of shock.[215] She had been raped. After dropping his daughter off at home, Zarchi and his companion took the girl to the police.

"Now of course I realise we should've taken her to a hospital," Zarchi reflected in *Fangoria*.[216] "We found out when we took her to the police just what the word bureaucracy means — how old are you? what's your name? why were you in the park? what time was it? should we notify your mother?"

The police insisted on filling out papers, despite the fact the girl was hysterical. It transpired that two men had raped, sodomised and beaten the girl, even breaking her jaw. They were about to kill her, but she convinced them that she couldn't see anything on account of them having taken her glasses.

Zarchi was later to visit a friend in Kent, Connecticut, and saw the riverside house and petrol station that became the key locales in *I Spit On Your Grave*. They became his springboard for the rape-revenge story, which drew on his experience with the girl from the park and the further indignity she suffered when taken to the police.

"So Jennifer Hills did not report it," Zarchi said of his fictional rape victim, "and took the law into her own hands."

Further inspiration, which Zarchi fails to mention in his interview with *Fangoria*, undoubtedly comes from *Straw Dogs* and *Deliverance*, two hit movies dealing with themes of displaced city folk, rape and revenge. (Indeed, one early poster for Zarchi's film — under the title *The Rape and Revenge of Jennifer Hill*[217] — carried on it the blurb "More Devastating than *Deliverance*!") Other films to which *I Spit On Your Grave* bears some relation include Michael Winner's *Death Wish*; Timothy Gulfas' *Revenge For a Rape*, a TV movie in which a pregnant woman on a deer hunting trip is raped by three local rednecks; and Lamont Johnson's *Lipstick*, about a beautiful model who kills the man who rapes her and her daughter.

Particularly worthy of note is *They Call Her One Eye*, a 1972 Swedish movie. As well as utilising a rape-revenge scenario it has a gun-toting leading lady (Christina Lindberg), blinded in one eye by a pimp, who bears more than a passing resemblance to Camille Keaton. Supposedly banned in its country of origin, the original uncut print of *They Call Her One Eye* contained hardcore inserts. Its release in the US as *Hookers Revenge* came with the ad line "It began with a rape. It ended in a massacre."

Indeed, Zarchi's recollection of true life events that took place in 1974 bear a similarity to a TV movie of that same year called *A Case of Rape*. Directed by Boris Sagal, it told the story of a young woman who goes to the police after being raped, which only leads to red tape, further humiliation, scepticism, and the ordeal of a court case.

According to the BBFC, no topic is taboo if dealt with in the right way. Zarchi's film would seem to fall outside that criteria because it doesn't rise to the question of what is right or what is wrong. The film-makers simply present the events without imposing on them any kind of morality — morality is left to the viewer. *I Spit On Your Grave* doesn't condemn rape, ergo it must be condoning it.

It doesn't criticise Jennifer's subsequent murder of the four men either, but that is never an issue with the film's detractors.[218] And while the men pay for their crime, Jennifer rides off unchallenged following hers. No one who sees *I Spit On Your Grave* can be left with any doubt that the men in it deserve their fate. Jennifer's ordeal is perceived as inherently more terrible than the murder of her rapists, due to the way the film is structured. "How can you say anything bad about the way Jennifer Hills takes revenge?" queried Zarchi in his *Fangoria* interview. He offers the rapists no excuse for their crime, no shield to hide behind, no dysfunctional background... in fact, no background at all. The only instance in which any of the three men is presented as three-dimensional — a brief scene where Johnny is shown to be a family man (tellingly only via long-shot) — serves only to provide Zarchi with the opportunity of dropping him from an even greater height, i.e. not only is he a rapist, but a cheat and a liar, too.

Sympathy throughout lies with Jennifer. She is the only 'real' person here. We start the film with Jennifer and journey with her to the summerhouse; we are privy to the work she does on her manuscript, listening as she mentally recites a part of it; we share in the solitude and beauty of her riverside retreat, and also in her anger as the jerks disrupt the peace in their motorboat. When Jennifer changes out of her swimming costume, the camera modestly pulls right back to the far bank of the river. Even the rape scenes when they come are largely played from her point-of-view — and we suffer the ugly, distorted, grunting faces of the men pressing down.

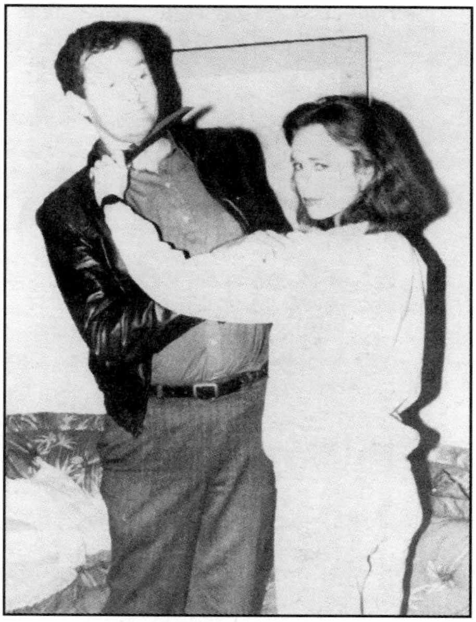

Camille Keaton fools around with Donald Farmer, director of the ill-fated, unofficial sequel to *I Spit On Your Grave*.

I Spit On Your Grave is very *anti*-cinema. The camera often comes to a complete standstill, locking onto shots for an uncomfortably long time without cutaways. The acts of rape appear to be played out in real time. In other words, the film utilises the convention of pornographic loops to further alienate its audience. ("The scope of the screenplay would've fit nicely into a twenty-minute Mitchell Bros peep-show reel," proffered Ralph Darren in his review for *Demonique*.)[219] The absence of music also imbues the film with a cold, callous edge. Not only does the film reject a main title theme, it also refuses to diffuse the shocking nature of the story with incidental music.

The common notion that the film has no music at all however, or that the harmonica piece is the only music in the film, is wrong. There is also music in the church where Jennifer goes to ask forgiveness, and Jennifer later plays a classical record[220] while Johnny bleeds to death in the bathroom upstairs. Of the three short pieces, it is only the harmonica that is used in a traditional filmic sense — changing tempo, heightening tension and working as a prelude to the events unfolding on-screen.[221] But it comes about in such a subtle, clever way, that it alone could testify to the skill at work behind the camera. Further examples of strikingly poignant and lyrical moments come with the scenes where Jennifer's swimsuit is casually tossed aside by the rapists as they leave the second rape scene, and with the terrible, haunting post-trauma shots of Jennifer sitting silently, unmoving on the staircase of the summerhouse. Without a doubt, the primitive, distancing quality of the film is a premeditated effort on the part of the film-maker (Zarchi wrote, directed, edited and cast the film[222] — his only other known directorial effort[223] is *Don't Mess With My Sister!*, which *The Psychotronic Video Guide* likens to Scorsese's *After Hours*).

After *I Spit* was re-mastered for a laserdisc release by Elite Entertainment, Michael Gingold in *Fangoria*[224] remarked that Zarchi's "simplistic approach comes to look less like low-budget craftlessness and more intentionally disaffected."

Following Zarchi's success, some films tried to tackle the rape-revenge story in a decidedly more mainstream manner. Most notable — rather, most similar — of these were Abel Ferrara's *Angel of Vengeance*, Tony Garnett's *Handgun* and Richard Gardener's *Deadly Daphne's Revenge*. Al Adamson's *Girls For Rent*, a film made before *I Spit On Your Grave*, found itself acquiring the title *I Spit On Your Corpse* when released onto videotape in the eighties. A shot lifted from a scene where mob hitwoman Georgina Spelvin rapes a retarded guy featured on its sleeve. More recently there has been Todd Morris's *A Gun For Jennifer*, whose by-line is "Dead men don't rape."

I Spit On Your Grave is believed to have initially been released on the drive-in circuit in the late-seventies as *Day of the Woman*.[225] According to some sources, under this title the film ran a few minutes longer. When Jerry Gross acquired it for distribution in the eighties, the title was changed to *I Spit On Your Grave* and some dialogue and several linking shots were excised.[226]

The film has a history of being chopped up for no good reason. On a double-bill with Lucio Fulci's *City of the Living Dead*, a rare early screening of *I Spit On Your Grave* was thwarted after the projectionist at the Fabian Theatre in Paterson discovered someone had stolen the print — not only had they stolen it, but they had gone to the trouble of splicing its title and opening credits onto another film in it its place, in the hope that no one in the audience would notice! (The other film turned out to be John Newland's *The Legend of Hillbilly John*, about a man with a silver-string guitar who fights evil.)

An unofficial sequel tentatively titled *Return to the Grave* went into production but was never completed. Shot on video by Donald Farmer, one-time editor of *The Splatter Times*, the *raison d'être* for the sequel was Camille Keaton's willingness to reprise her most famous role, and when she pulled out partway through, the follow-up was shelved.[227]

INFERNO

SYNOPSIS: Rose has discovered a secret related to the New York hotel in which she lives. According to an old book titled *The Three Mothers*, the hotel was one of three structures built specifically for the evil entities noted in its text. The location of these dwellings could be identified by a sickly sweet smell as the immediate surrounding area would become infected with evil and the air poisoned. Underneath each was the name and a portrait of the Mother for whom the house was constructed.

Rose relates her discovery in a letter to her brother Mark, a music student in Rome. She asks Kazanian, the crippled owner of the antique shop from whom she bought the book, whether the story is true. He replies cryptically, "The only true mystery is that our very lives are governed by dead people." To test the story's authenticity Rose goes to the basement of the building in search of a name and portrait, and locates a room below ground level that is completely filled with water. Swimming to the bottom, having dropped her keys, she sees a portrait of Mother Tenebrarum and is terrified when a decomposing corpse floats towards her. She escapes from the room and makes her way back to her apartment.

Mark receives Rose's letter and opens it during a music class, but is distracted from reading it by a beguiling and beautiful young woman. She mouths something to him but Mark doesn't understand. Suddenly the doors burst open, a wind rushes into the lecture room and the mystery woman leaves. When the class is over, the dazed Mark inadvertently leaves behind the letter and Sarah, a friend, picks it up. From the letter, Sarah is able to identify a building in Rome which was constructed for another of the Mothers, and upon investigation finds there is a smell surrounding the building as described in Rose's letter. Inside is a library in which Sarah is able to locate a copy of *The Three Mothers*, but as she comes to leave she loses her way and ends up in the basement in some kind of alchemist's laboratory. A cloaked figure advances threateningly when it notices the book Sarah is carrying, causing her to drop the volume and run away. Finding the exit, the frightened girl asks a man, Carlo, to keep her company at her apartment until a friend arrives. Phoning Mark to say she has his letter, the power in the apartment suddenly surges on and off. Carlo goes to check the fuses but gets a knife driven through his neck by an intruder who then kills Sarah.

INFERNO
ITALY 1980
CAST: Irene Miracle, Leigh McCloskey, Daria Nicolodi, Eleonora Giorgi, Alida Valli, Sacha Pitoeff, Veronica Lazar
STORY: Dario Argento
PRODUCER: Claudio Argento
DIRECTOR: DARIO ARGENTO

When Mark arrives he finds the letter torn to pieces, but manages to glean from it some information. He phones his sister Rose in New York who asks him to come over right away.

Mark arrives in New York unaware that Rose has since been murdered. Sharing an elevator with a wheelchair-bound man cared for by a nurse, he makes his way to Rose's apartment where he meets a friend of his late sister called Elise. She tells him about the strange system of pipes that run throughout the building which amplify and carry sounds, and how she and Rose used them to speak to one another. Elise's butler reminds her that it's time for her medication. Later she returns to Mark and — about to impart information Rose had given to her concerning the Three Mothers — is disturbed by a sinister laugh echoing through the pipe system. Mark follows a feint trail of blood to a door that leads to the service area of the building. Frightened, Elise stays behind only to then follow when she discovers a bloody handprint in Rose's room. Confronting an unconscious Mark being dragged by a cloaked figure, she runs back upstairs where she finds the only unlocked exit leads to the attic. Here she is attacked by a pack of cats and, as she struggles with the animals, is stabbed to death by the mysterious figure.

Mark recovers and tries to find Elise. Kazanian complains to Carol, the proprietress, about the roaming cats and threatens to inform the health authority. Mark asks Kazanian if he knew his sister, to which the antique dealer replies only in that he sold books to her. As an aside he informs Mark there will be a lunar eclipse that night and urges him to watch.

Having caught many of the stray cats and tied them in a sack, Kazanian struggles to the park and drowns them in the lake. The deed accomplished, he falls from his crutches and is set upon by rats spilling from a sewer pipe. His cries for help are heard by a food stall worker who rushes over, but instead of assisting the fallen man, he hacks into Kazanian's neck with a butcher's knife and rolls the body toward the sewer pipe as food for the rats.

Following the disappearance of Elise, her butler locates Elise's valuables and agrees to split them with Carol, but he is murdered when the lights suddenly go out. Drawn to the commotion and illuminating the darkened room with a candle, Carol discovers the butler's mutilated corpse and accidentally sets light to the room and to herself.

While pacing his room, Mark realises there is an unusually deep crawlspace between the floors of the building. He breaks a hole to find an old scroll pertaining to the Three Mothers. Upon further investigation, he discovers a hatchway that leads to a secret part of the building where he meets the old wheelchair-bound man with whom he shared an elevator earlier. Lacking any vocal chords the old man is only able to speak through an electronic device. He identifies himself as Varelli, the architect of all the Three Mothers' buildings, and urges Mark to come closer so that others won't hear. But as Mark nears, Varelli attempts to inject him with a poison whereupon the old man is knocked from his wheelchair and strangled with the cable that connects his neck to the voice unit.

As the fire caused by Carol continues to rage, Mark locates Varelli's 'nurse' in another secret room, and she reveals herself to be the Mother of Shadows. She becomes Death — but before destroying Mark he escapes and the blazing structure collapses around her.

CRITIQUE: Being a continuation of the Three Mothers story that began with *Suspiria*, Dario Argento's *Inferno* comes across as much a remake as a sequel. Like *Suspiria* the plot revolves around a protagonist being trapped within a stylised house of evil, culminating in a climactic confrontation and the fiery destruction of the house. Although it has its moments, *Inferno* lacks the terror invoked by its predecessor. Indeed, the film is more a series of glamorous, cleverly shot incidents than it is a coherent narrative. (Lucio Fulci was impressed enough to adopt a similarly free approach for his own ***The Beyond*** and ***The House By the Cemetery*** the following year, the latter even borrowing Argento's 'house of evil' environment.) The opening sequence in the submerged room may *look* good but it doesn't make much sense. How is the room lit, for instance? What is its purpose? Why does the floating corpse gravitate to Rose?[228] Later, what is the relevance of the mystery girl in Mark's music class? She is credited as 'music student' but appears more a phantasm, whose unintelligible words could either be a warning or a curse. It seems all these elements are included for no reason other than visual appeal.

"This is an alchemist's picture," was Argento's justification, "if you don't understand it, well, me too, I don't understand! This is what the story is. Alchemy is a mystery, you know."[229]

Nevertheless, this disparate quality is a little too confusing and contrived in *Inferno*, ultimately detracting from the picture. It doesn't help that the visual composite is accompanied by a powerful (i.e. loud) but infuriating and equally disjointed soundtrack by Keith Emerson — which evidently tries to emulate the grandeur of Goblin's *Suspiria* soundtrack, but only once comes anywhere close. Thrown into this potpourri are some tantalising minutiae which serve no purpose. For instance, a title card informs viewers at one point that the setting is "New York — The Same Night in April," but it's not information of any relevance. The voiceless, wheelchair-bound Valleri makes a confusing earlier appearance as a vocal, able-bodied librarian in Rome, leading the fated Sarah to a copy of *The Three Mothers*. The doors that Elise finds locked as she runs from the cloaked figure, are represented by fantastic close-ups of lock mechanisms being systematically engaged — the implication being that some revelatory significance is about to be divulged (or 'unlocked'). There isn't.

The concept of infectious evil emanating into the area surrounding the house however, is cleverly and subtly achieved. When Sarah gets out of a taxi, a tiny needle extends from the door handle to puncture her thumb, and Kazanian's cries for assistance lead to his apparent helper unexpectedly hacking him to death (one of the best sequences in the film). Anyone, it seems could be part of the conspiracy and such a prospect makes for good psychological horror.

The violence is tame in comparison to that found in *Suspiria* which, incidentally, wasn't banned.

The projected Three Mothers trilogy remains incomplete, although Argento still insists that he will film the concluding instalment soon. ("Maybe in the next two or three years," he said back in 1994.) *Suspiria* revolved around the house belonging to the Mother of Sighs in Freiburg, *Inferno* around that of the Mother of Shadows, and no doubt the third was scheduled to take place within the Roman dwelling of the Mother of Tears. The concept is original and creepy, but it seems that poor response to *Inferno* may have ruined forever the possibility to see the series drawn to a proper close. However, the director would use ideas from *Inferno* as a springboard for his next feature, ***Tenebrae***, where a book would prove to be the key to an altogether more down-to-earth thriller.[230]

ISLAND OF DEATH

SYNOPSIS: Christopher and Celia arrive on the Greek island of Mykonos. Looking for accommodation they visit a shop run by an American named Paul. He suggests they should rent a house rather than go to a hotel and gives them an address — a place owned by Hanna, whose husband is away. Hannah asks the couple if they are married and they confirm that they are.

While walking around the town, Celia asks Christopher to make love to her. "What, right here?" he asks. They enter a public phone box and Christopher telephones his mother in London.

"Guess what I'm doing," he asks her.

"Christopher, where are you?" queries his mother.

"You won't believe it, mother. I'm in a telephone booth on a small Greek island and I'm making love to Celia!"

Christopher's mother is thoroughly disgusted and she insists that he stops at once. Outside her house in a car is a Detective named Foster who has a line tap on the phone. He calls into headquarters and tells them he's located the man.

Later Christopher and Celia go to a restaurant, where Christopher notices a man dining alone. "I don't like that man," he says. "He's a dirty bastard. You don't know what he's thinking about you." Celia isn't interested but Christopher invites the stranger to dine with them and introduces Celia as his cousin. The man's name is Jean-Claude and he is on the island to renovate a chapel.

When they get back to their apartment Christopher sees Hannah making love to a man. "The bitch," he intones. "If I were her husband I'd kill her."

The next morning he wakes wanting sex but Celia is too tired. He wanders outside and finds Hannah's pet goat. He unties the animal and takes it to the back of the garden where he copulates with it then stabs it repeatedly.

Celia goes to the chapel where Jean-Claude is working and soon the two of them are playfully daubing each other with whitewash. From a field, Christopher watches and takes photographs as the couple begin to have sex. When they're finished, he throws a noose around Jean-Claude's neck and beats him. Celia takes photographs as Christopher nails the man to the ground through the palms of his hands. "Poor thing," observes Celia, "he's fainted." Christopher suggests a drink and pours whitewash down the man's throat until he chokes to death.

The couple bump into Paul, the American shop-owner, who invites them to an engagement party that night. "Who's the lucky girl?" asks Celia. "Girl?" laughs Paul. At the party Paul introduces the couple to Jonathan, his catamite and bride-to-be.

Once the party is over Christopher and Celia return to Paul's home with the camera and a gun. They break in and watch Paul and Jonathan fondling each other. Christopher hands Celia the gun and camera then takes an ornamental sword from the wall. "God punishes perversion and I am the angel with the flaming sword sent to kill dirty worms," he announces as he advances on the two men. He knocks Jonathan unconscious and Paul runs screaming from the house. Christopher chases after him, eventually catching up and hacking him to death. Celia stays with Jonathan, running the gun over his body before inserting it in his mouth and blowing out his brains.

Back at the apartment Christopher and Celia masturbate while looking at photographs of their victims.

Patricia, an old Epicurean they met at the engagement party, tells the couple about the apparent crime of passion in which Jonathan murdered Paul then killed himself. Patricia introduces them to Lesley, a lesbian barmaid.

That night, while Celia dreams about a man who rapes her and kills her partner, Christopher lies awake with Lesley on his mind. He leaves the apartment and follows the barmaid as she makes her way home, then observes as she injects herself with drugs and has sex with another woman.

The lucky ones got their brains blown out!!
VHS
ISLAND OF DEATH
ISLAND OF DEATH
AVI 003
100 MINS APPROX
NICO MASTORAKIS

ISLAND OF DEATH
AKA: A Craving for Lust; Island of Perversion; Psychic Killer II; Devils in Mykonos
UK/GREECE 1972 [75?]
CAST: Bob Belling, Jane Ryall, Jessica Dublin, Gerarlo Gonalons, Janice McConnel, Clay Huff
STORY: Nico Mastorakis
PRODUCER: Nico Mastorakis
DIRECTOR: NICO MASTORAKIS

Detective Foster arrives on the island in a private plane he has hired, and soon discovers where Christopher is staying. Returning home having spent the day out, Christopher and Celia meet Hannah who tells them that someone is waiting for them at the apartment. Christopher suspects it may be Foster. Having given up waiting, the Detective returns to his plane only to find Christopher waiting for him — he throws a noose around the Detective's neck and starts the engine. Foster manages to grab a wing support as the plane takes off, but as the aircraft circles the island he soon loses his strength and hangs himself in mid-air.

Christopher decides he would like to visit Patricia and have sex with her. He tells Celia she can watch, and she agrees so long as there is no more killing. Christopher arrives at Patricia's apartment on the pretext that Celia is ill and he wants some cold milk. Patricia offers to pay Christopher for sex and he climbs onto the bed, but instead of indulging in foreplay he urinates over her. At first she is disgusted but then she enjoys it. During oral sex Patricia bites Christopher and he beats her unconscious. Celia rushes in and Christopher tells her they must now kill the woman. Carrying her to a building site, Christopher decapitates Patricia with a bulldozer.

Some days later Christopher decides to go fishing. Celia stays at home but is attacked by two intruders who attempt to rape her. Christopher arrives home, shoots one of the men with a spear-gun and drowns the other in the toilet. They report the incident to the police and suggest that the two men may have been responsible for all the recent killings. A novelist called Dimitri calls at the apartment wanting details of the recent attack for a book he is writing.

Later Christopher decides they must get rid of Lesley as she knows he was with Patricia on the night she died. Celia goes to see the barmaid at home, telling her that she has had a fight with Christopher. He watches through the window and takes photographs as Lesley seduces Celia, entering after Lesley has injected herself with drugs. Sitting astride the prone woman he pours a bottle of gin down her throat, then injects her with a massive dose of the drug. Lesley dies almost instantly and Christopher uses an aerosol deodorant as a flame-thrower to burn away her face.

The next morning Christopher tries to rape Hannah in the shower but she manages to fight him off. Meanwhile Dimitri has called at Lesley's apartment and discovered her body. Finding the carton for a roll of film on the balcony, he suspects Christopher of the murder and informs the police. As Christopher is killing Hannah with a sickle, he notices the police activity and wakes Celia. Together they run off to the hills where they encounter a shepherd. Celia points out that he was the man in her dream. "Nonsense," remarks Christopher, "he may be primitive but he's innocent." The shepherd offers the couple food and drink in his hut, but later rapes Celia. Christopher doesn't help and instead takes photographs — until the shepherd knocks him unconscious and sodomises him. Celia watches.

Christopher is bound and thrown into a pit of lime. Christopher and Celia are revealed now not to be husband and wife or cousins, but brother and sister. He begs her for help but she refuses, returning instead to the shepherd for more sex. It begins to rain and the dry lime covering Christopher suddenly becomes corrosive. Celia smiles as she hears her brother's dying screams.

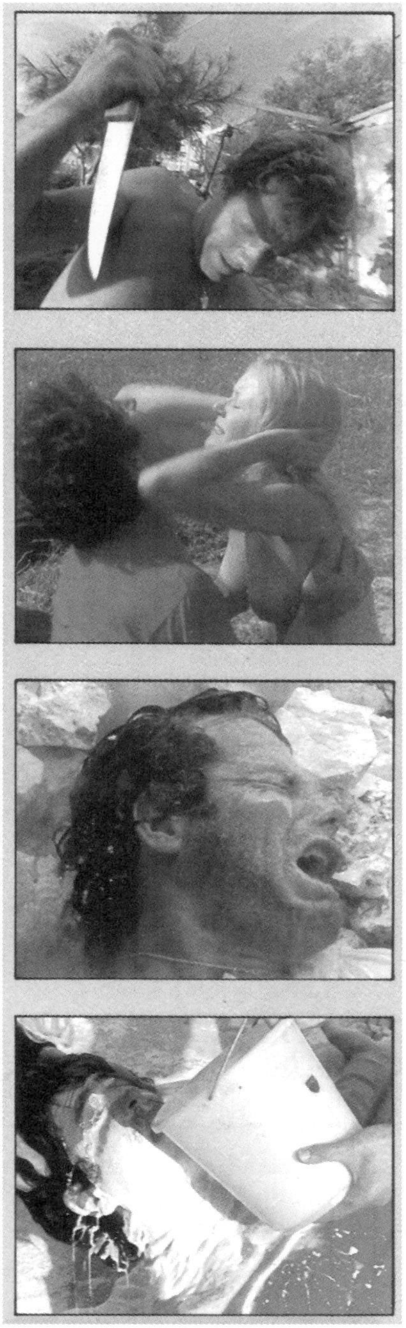

Rape, murder and whitewash on the *Island of Death*.

CRITIQUE: Regarded as something of a Jack-of-all-trades in his native Greece, Nico Mastorakis is not only a film-maker but in his early days also applied himself to songwriting, radio producing and quiz show hosting. His first directing work was in documentaries and a TV sci-fi series by the name of *Conspiracy of Silence*. His first full-length feature film was a rather slipshod ill-received erotic thriller with fantasy elements (inexplicably cut from the British theatrical print, reducing the running time by some thirty minutes) entitled *Death Has Blue Eyes*. His second picture was *Island of Death*, a film to which Mastorakis brings to bear much of his multi-faceted experience, not only directing, writing and producing it, but also penning the oddly inappropriate closing theme song ("Mother, I see the wonders of the day...").

While being interviewed for *Video — The Magazine* Mastorakis was surprised to hear that *Island of Death* featured on the DPP's nasties list because, he claimed, it had already been distributed theatrically in Britain by GTO, "a reputable company."

In actual fact, it was distributed in 1978 by Winstone Films (under the title *A Craving for Lust*) and suffered some eighteen minutes of cuts. On video it had no cuts.

Said Mastorakis of the production:

> I had no money. All the people in it were amateurs. We were going up to people who looked American in the street and asking them if they could act! We shot it quickly and I did everything on it, wrote, produced, directed, photographed and edited.

In the interview, Mastorakis reflected that the "movie was ahead of its time," and claimed he deliberately intended the violence "to be very realistic" in order to show "how horrible it was."

With scenes showing death by aircraft and death by whitewash, it's debatable whether the violence in the film is realistic. However, there can be no doubting that *Island of Death* is horrible.

The lucky ones got their brains blown out!!
ISLAND OF DEATH
Available for video

Whether it's intentional or not, the film would seem to be for Mastorakis some kind of comment on his homeland Greece, where ninety-seven per cent of the population is Greek Orthodox. Christopher's attempts to clean up the streets of Mykonos parallels the country's intolerance of anything that transgresses Christian values. Indeed, *Island of Death* can be read as a metaphor of the Crusades, with the aptly named Christopher remarking to Celia at one point that he is on a "crusade against perversion."

Yet Christopher is repulsed by the perversions of other people and blind to his own absolute wickedness. He is actually far more corrupt than any of the characters he castigates, and the one person he believes to be pure — the farmer — is the one who is as twisted as himself. Christopher is finally destroyed in a manner apt for the middle ages, with rain and lime reacting to generate intense heat, burning him alive.

The Detective Foster character is a somewhat unnecessary addition. There is no explanation as to who he is or why he is hunting Christopher (then again, there is no valid reason why Mykonos should be singled out by Christopher for cleansing). No sooner does Foster arrive on the island than he is despatched again in one of the most ludicrously implausible ways imaginable. To get into the position where Christopher can hang Foster from his own plane requires utmost suspension of disbelief, and would be arduous even in a teen stalk-and-slash picture.

Within moments of arriving on the island, it becomes clear that Christopher and Celia are not the ordinary vacationing couple they at first appear. (Mastorakis shot the film at out-of-season Mykonos locations, which does give an air of something being askew right from the off-set.) When the couple jump into a phonebooth for sex, during the course of which Christopher antagonises his mother on the phone, any initial feeling that *Island of Death* might be embarking on a familiar trajectory is quickly and irrevocably dashed.

The film is jaw-droppingly unusual, and its excesses are completely absent from the director's later film ventures (though *Zero Boys*, like *Island of Death*, does contain a scene in which a man is forced to suck on the barrel of a revolver).

After its catalogue of sexual horrors, Mastorakis attempts a final twist, waiting until the last moment to reveal that Christopher and Celia are in fact brother and sister.

"You've got to help me," cries Christopher from the lime pit. "I'm your brother!"

"Shhh! You promised not to tell anyone," responds Celia.

By this point however, nothing can heighten the sleaziness and after all that has gone before, this particular revelation seems somehow *inevitable*.

For a film to include such a varying degree of sexual perversions is unusual: homosexuality, incest, sodomy, bestiality and urolagnia. Then to ice such a cake with drug-taking, rape, mutilation and murder makes for one unrelenting movie. But such an array of depravities does not make the film interesting or outrageous in same way as, say, Tinto Brass' *Caligula*. Indeed, the film as a whole is generally dreary and boring (travelling an awfully long way to level a simple accusation: that perversion is but a narrow thread made taut by those who seek to define it). It is this assortment of depraved themes rather than any particular invidious scene that secured *Island of Death*'s banned status. (See also SEX & WRECKS.)

KILLER NUN

SYNOPSIS: A nun during confession refuses to forgive a man who she claims has ruined her life. The confessor insists that forgiveness is the only option, but because of what the man did to her she wants to "take revenge on all men, to snuff them out like he snuffed out my happiness."

Sister Gertrude oversees the elderly and infirm residents of a hospice. She is addicted to morphine and believes she still suffers from cancer, despite having had an operation some time ago to remove a brain tumour. Assisting the resident doctor who asks her to pass a scalpel, Sister Gertrude suddenly freezes at the sight of the instruments.

"What's wrong with you this morning?" asks the doctor.

"You know what is wrong."

"You can't still be suffering from post-operative shock."

"It's cancer, doctor. Cancer," she responds.

One of the patients remarks that "Sister Gertrude could freak out any second."

In the recovery ward Gertrude removes the intravenous supply from a particularly frail woman. The doctor notices just in time and reconnects the tube.

While everyone is in the dining area eating their meals, Gertrude relates from a book the story of a martyr, speaking in detail of the terrible pain the woman suffered under torture. The elderly diners are annoying her and the Sister's attention is particularly diverted by a glass containing dentures. She reprimands Josephine for having the false teeth on view, throws them to the floor and crushes them under her foot. The shock traumatises the old lady.

KILLER NUN
TITLE ON PRINT: THE KILLER NUN
AKA: Suor Omicidi (original title); Deadly Habit; La Petite Soeur du Diable; La Nonne Qui Tue
ITALY 1978
CAST: Anita Ekberg, Alida Valli, Massimo Serato, Daniele Dublino, Lou Castel, Joe Dallesandro, Laura Nucci, Paola Morra
STORY: Giulio Berruti & Albert Tarallo
PRODUCER: Enzo Gallo
DIRECTOR: GIULIO BERRUTI

Sister Mathieu is searching through medical records when she finds and destroys a set of X-rays. Later, she comforts the depressed Gertrude and tells her there is no proof now that she is not sick.

"Have you gone mad?" asks Gertrude.

"No, I love you," replies Mathieu.

The following day Josephine is in a serious condition and the doctor asks Gertrude to quickly bring her medication. The Sister deliberately takes her time however, and the delay results in the death of Josephine. Gertrude goes through the old woman's belongings and steals a diamond ring.

Dressed in regular clothing the Sister leaves the hospice and sells the ring to a jeweller in town. She then goes to a bar and picks up a man with whom she copulates in the hallway of a boarding house.

Back at the hospice Gertrude injects herself with morphine and collapses. She is carried to her bed by an elderly man, who is suddenly attacked with a bedside lamp and beaten to death. Mathieu thinks Gertrude is responsible for the death, but tells her friend she will protect her. Gertrude insists she has done nothing wrong.

The doctor is dismissed following rumours spread by Gertrude, and a younger man, Dr Patrick, comes to take his place. He arrives on the day Sister Gertrude and a group of patients are playing 'The Truth Game.' Peter asks the Sister why she killed the old man, whereupon the game is drawn to an abrupt halt and the residents are ushered back inside. Gertrude is later appalled to see an elderly wheelchair-bound man copulating with a younger patient. The following day, the man is found murdered on the lawn.

Gertrude puts the patients through a vigorous exercise routine, which is halted by Dr Patrick who reports his doubts about the Sister to the hospice principal. The patients grow increasingly suspicious of Gertrude, and one night an unseen assailant attacks her. An elderly lady who thinks she may have seen something is abducted by an unseen assailant who ties her up, tortures her with pins and a scalpel before finally leaving her dead in the laundry chute. In a state of shock, Gertrude is also found at the bottom of the chute with track marks on her arm.

Gertrude carries the crippled Peter to the basement that night and demands to know why he thinks she is a murderer. He refuses to speak so she takes away his crutches, leaves him and goes back to her room for another dose of morphine. Peter manages to crawl out of the basement but is kicked to death at the top of the steps.

"There is confusion in my head," Sister Gertrude tells the Mother Superior prior to being taken away for "special treatment." To avoid a scandal, the Sister is placed in a cell and poisoned. Too late she recalls the moment when the old man was battered to death with the bedside lamp and realises that the killer was Mathieu.

CRITIQUE: According to the opening credits *Killer Nun* is based on a true incident (occurring recently in Belgium, states the videobox). This may well be the case, as history is rife with accounts of sadistic Sisters, lesbian Sisters and Sisters who threaten to be an embarrassment to the Church. (It would be nice to think there existed documentation of a Sister smashing dentures underfoot while screaming "Disgusting! Disgusting! Disgusting!")

Like Nazis and cannibals, nuns offered film-makers a seemingly inexhaustible potential for exploitation, and the cloistered life was the focus of many productions through the seventies and eighties. Sometimes it didn't even have to stretch to a cloistered life. As with Hammer's *To the Devil—A Daughter*, a pretty face in a habit would often suffice.

The nun as an exploitable commodity stretches back beyond these other sub-genres however, and indeed beyond cinema itself. It enabled authors like Matthew Lewis to scandalise eighteenth-century English folk with *The Monk*, and Denis Diderot the French with *The Nun*, where the idea of chaste women living apart from men wasn't only titillating but also ammunition against the church.

Killer Nun isn't typical of its oeuvre, introducing drug addiction, the infirm, and murder into the usual stocking-top sexploitative fare. The script is actually quite witty, too, which is another anomaly.

Anita Ekberg is perfectly cast as Sister Gertrude, and it's refreshing that a central role in a film such as this has gone to someone who neither looks like a glamour model and is actually over the age of twenty-five. (There are some concessions however, like blue eye shadow — not normally a requisite of nun-life.) There is a credibility to Gertrude's plea of "I need m-morphine!" And when she surreptitiously takes a ride into the city, there is a sense of genuine desperation in the old girl's attempts to entice a stranger with a flash of her stocking tops. Only a flash, mind you — lest he notices the bruises.

There isn't an awful lot of blood-letting or perversion, although the torture of the old woman near the end of the film — she has pins forced into her face and eyes — meant several seconds of cuts when *Killer Nun* was re-released through Redemption in the nineties.

It is the sequence leading up to the bludgeoning of the man with a lampshade that proves the film's standout piece. Indeed, with its pounding score and rapid editing of multifarious scenarios, it offers a somewhat frustrating glimpse at what director Giulio Berruti could *really* have achieved with *Killer Nun*...

After injecting herself with morphine and asking God for absolution, Sister Gertrude collapses on the floor. Discovered by one of the patients, she starts to suffer flashbacks and at the same time begins to hallucinate. She sees herself on the operating table, her cancerous tumour exposed ready for removal. This is intercut with shots of the Sister about to interfere with the unidentified corpse of a naked young man in a morgue, as well as shots of her own eye in extreme close-up, her own drugged-up self being dragged to her bed by the old man, and a veiled woman dressed in black who — we presume — is the Angel of Death. On top of all this is a pounding score by Alessandro Alessandroni that sounds like Morricone crossed with Goblin.

Nothing else in the film quite matches the flair and energy of this sequence, although some viewers will get a rise out of Gertrude tormenting the infatuated Sister Mathieu, demanding that the novice dons the silk stockings she has bought her or suffer a beating. "I'm the worst kind of prostitute," Mathieu is made to say — a sentiment which is evidently true, as later she laps at Dr Patrick's flies, promising him "anything" so long as he doesn't report that it was her who supplied Gertrude with morphine.

The young Sister obviously has got a lot more than this to hide, but the film is content to beat a hasty retreat once the church administers its "special treatment" to Sister Gertrude.

THE LAST HOUSE ON THE LEFT

SYNOPSIS: It is Mari Collingwood's seventeenth birthday and she is getting ready to spend the day with her friend Phyllis. "I want you to be careful tonight," remarks John, her father. "Your mother tells me the place you're going is in a bad neighbourhood." ("Hey, no bra," he also comments, pointing out that he can see his daughter's nipples as plain as day.) The girls are going to see a notorious band named Bloodlust, a fact that Estelle, Mari's mother, thinks is counterpoint to the "love generation" her daughter is supposedly a part of.

Father gives Mari a CND peace-symbol pendant as a birthday gift.

Mari tells Phyllis that she feels like a woman for the first time in her life and the two of them drive to the concert. The radio broadcasts a report about two recently escaped convicts: Krug Stillo serving life for murder and Fred 'Weasel' Pudowski, a child molester. The pair got away in a car driven by Krug's heroin addicted son Junior, and in the company of a female passenger called Sadie.

In a cheap down-town apartment, Weasel and Sadie are listening to the same radio broadcast. When Krug and Junior enter, an argument ensues over Sadie and the matter of sex.

THE LAST HOUSE ON THE LEFT
AKA: Sex Crime of the Century; Krug and Company; The Men's Room; Night of Vengeance (shooting title)
USA 1972
CAST: David Hess, Lucy Grantheim, Sandra Cassel, Marc Scheffier, Jeraime Rain, Fred Lincoln
STORY: Wes Craven
PRODUCER: Sean S Cunningham
DIRECTOR: WES CRAVEN

"I ain't puttin' out any more until I get a couple more chicks around here," Sadie snaps.

Trying to score a little dope, Mari and Phyllis encounter Junior on the street. He says he can help and takes them up to the apartment. The door is locked behind them and Krug springs up from his hiding place, telling the girls not to worry, "We just want some company, that's all."

Phyllis threatens to scream but Weasel pulls a flick knife on her. While Krug unbuttons her blouse, Weasel tries to kiss the girl's bared breasts but she spits in his face.

"Do that again and you're dead," he tells her.

"It would be a shame to get this floor all messed up with blood," remarks Krug. "You see, there are other ways of doing things." Krug thumps Phyllis in the gut and she collapses on the floor. Mari looks on horrified as the two men then rape her friend.

Mari's parents are preparing a birthday party, but become anxious when their daughter fails to return. Her father tries to shrug it off, suggesting that Mari is simply stating she is now an adult. The next day Mari's mother phones the concert manager who tells her the band had finished playing at 2 AM. They decide to wait for another hour before phoning the police.

The two girls are bundled into the boot of Krug's car and driven from the city. "What do you think the sex crime of the century was?" Weasel idly asks as they head for the Canadian border. Some time later the car breaks down and Krug opens the trunk to get the toolkit, but is bitten on the hand by Phyllis. The girls are dragged from the car, gagged, and marched into the woods to a small clearing.

John and Estelle report their missing daughter to the police and two officers call round to take details. When they leave they notice the abandoned car by the driveway but think it of no importance.

In the woods, Krug tells Weasel to cut Mari if her friend doesn't do exactly as he tells her. He orders Phyllis to "Piss your pants."

"You sick mother," she retorts and Weasel cuts Mari's flesh.

Krug repeats the command and this time the girl urinates. The gang roll about in laughter as Phyllis soaks her jeans. Next they tell her to hit Mari as hard as she can but Junior, not getting off on the violence, suggests instead the girls should be made to have sex together. Mari and Phyllis are ordered to strip naked and play around with each other. Krug soon becomes bored however, and tells Weasel to look after things while he goes to the car to fetch "something to cut some firewood with."

Phyllis asks Weasel if she can get dressed as she is getting cold, and whispers to Mari that they ought to make a break for it. Phyllis runs into the woods and is chased by Weasel and Sadie. Mari meanwhile tries to talk Junior into letting her go. He is afraid of what Krug might do to him if he does, but Mari says she will be his friend and offers Junior her birthday pendant.

Sadie catches Phyllis but is struck on the head with a rock. Phyllis finds her way into a graveyard and sees a busy road by the tree line, when her escape is cut off by Krug wielding a machete. As she backs away from him, Weasel and Sadie catch up. Weasel drives his knife into the girl's back and Phyllis falls to the ground, crawling away into the trees. After standing around for a moment the gang follow her trail and find the girl propped against a tree.

"How's your back, baby?" Weasel asks, and Phyllis spits in his face again. Krug holds the girl up while Weasel stabs her several times in the stomach. Sadie takes a turn and carries out a frenzied attack that culminates in her tugging loops of intestine from Phyllis' ruptured belly.

Mari has almost convinced Junior into letting her go when the gang returns. They show Mari her friend's severed hand and hold her down while Krug carves his name in her chest. Krug then rapes her, after which Mari grabs her clothes and walks into the lake in a state of shock. The bemused gang watches for a moment, then Weasel hands Krug a revolver with which he shoots her dead.

Washing themselves in the lake, and with the car still out of action, the gang go to the nearest house for assistance — which just so happens to belong to the Collingwood family, whose daughter Mari they have just murdered. Looking respectable in their clean clothes and combed hair the outlaws are fed and made guests for the night.

Mari's parents become somewhat suspicious when their guests don't seem to be able to get each other's names right.

Later that night Estelle finds Junior being sick in the bathroom and notices he is wearing a peace pendant identical to the one given to Mari. As she helps him back to the bedroom she overhears the

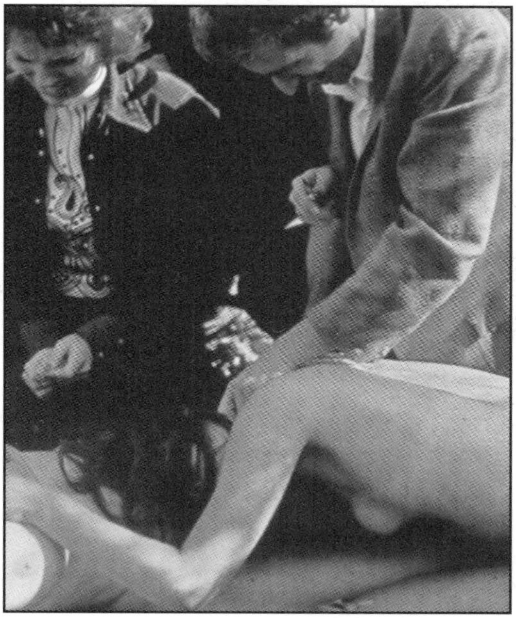

The Last House on the Left.

TOP: Krug's name carved into Mari's chest.
ABOVE: Sadie gleefully watches as Weasel forces the two girls upon each other.

gang discussing the killings and sees that their suitcase contains bloodied clothing. Estelle tells John and together they go to the lake where they find the body of their daughter.

Weasel wakes following a disturbing nightmare. He goes downstairs to get a drink and finds Estelle in the lounge. She tells him she's fallen out with her husband. "I could make love to a looker like you with my hands tied behind my back," Weasel boasts, and Estelle invites him outside to do just that. With his hands securely tied Estelle unzips Weasel's fly and begins to fellate him, biting off his penis at the moment of his orgasm.

Weasel's screams wake the rest of the gang. John fires at Krug with a shotgun but only manages to wound him and a fight ensues. Despite the booby-traps that John has placed around the house, Krug takes the upper hand but soon has to deal with Junior, who appears with the revolver and insists that he stops fighting. As Krug talks his son into taking his own life, John grabs a chainsaw from the cellar and runs Krug through with it. Sadie, having fallen into the swimming pool while trying to escape, gets her throat cut by Estelle.

CRITIQUE: A contemporary remake of Ingmar Bergman's *The Virgin Spring*, Wes Craven's *The Last House on the Left* contains a murder sequence that, for sheer brutal intensity, has never been surpassed in any film since. Even a quarter of a century after it was made.

It was Craven's intention to portray what a real murder — as opposed to a cinematic murder — would be like, and he succeeded unequivocally. The uncompromising portrayal of the killers, their subjugation, torture and murder of the two young girls, and the *cinéma-vérité* style combine to bring a stamp of authenticity to the proceedings.[231] The viewer is left with the impression that by watching, they themselves are partaking in something truly dreadful.

Prior to *The Last House on the Left*, the director-producer team of Wes Craven and Sean Cunningham had only previously worked on a pseudo-documentary by the name of *Together* (and, it is rumoured, some porn). With little idea of film-making techniques, and no idea that it would ever be shown outside of Boston, they set out to make *Last House*. "Nobody was ever going to see it," reasoned Craven, "and nobody was ever going to know that we did it."[232]

With that proviso the team determined they could go all the way and make something which more established, and possibly competent, film-makers would not dare to do.[233] Amazingly, given these sense-pummelling criteria and the film-makers' inexperience, there are many lyrical moments in the film — simple, almost overlooked aspects of comparative tranquillity that serve to heighten the horror. For instance, the scene in which the killers idly pull pieces of grass from their blood-covered hands (contrary to most movie gore, the blood actually looks *real* in this film); or Weasel being momentarily sympathetic towards Phyllis and allowing her to dress before killing her; or the two petrified girls clutching one another naked, their sobs obscured by a sympathetic music score. After Weasel has stabbed Phyllis in the back, the gang does nothing to stop the girl crawling off into the woods. (We get tight close-ups of faces and then a low-angle shot, a familiar pattern during the course of this whole torture and murder sequence.) If it's concern, guilt or sympathy that keeps the gang at bay, it quickly dissipates and there follows the horrifyingly frenzied attack in which Sadie 'loses it' and disembowels the girl.

Having gone on to make many subsequent successful horror films, such as *A Nightmare on Elm Street* and *Scream*, Craven told *Shock Xpress*[234] he could never return to the intensity of *Last House* because now

> people can find out where I live. Back then, nobody knew where I was. I wasn't in nice hotels like this, I was sleeping on the producer's floor and shooting in people's backyards. As a matter of fact, we lost the first day's shooting because the people whose house we were using came back unexpectedly.

One of Craven's failings in *Last House* is the overstated nastiness of the outlaws. He introduces them by way of a radio news report which is so wildly descriptive — and so obviously the absolute antithesis of the neat and tidy Collingwoods — that it becomes Pythonesque. We learn that Krug (who is seen popping a kid's balloon in the street) was convicted of killing a priest and two nuns, Fred was a child-molester, Junior a heroin addict and Sadie an "animal-like woman" who kicked to death a police dog.

FROM THE MAKERS OF
"LAST HOUSE ON THE LEFT" AND
"FRIDAY THE 13TH"...
THE "HOUSE" THAT SET
THE STANDARD FOR TERROR
IS BACK!
LAST
HOUSE
ON THE
LEFT
PART II
Directed by DANNY STEINMAN
("Friday the 13th Part V")
NOW IN PRE-PRODUCTION

Trade advertisement for the official and – fortunately – never realised sequel to *Last House on the Left*.

The latter half of the film is where Craven drifts from his goal of realism and returns to a more traditional cinematic model, a downslide which begins when the killers arrive at the Collingwood house. It isn't enough that they should unwittingly happen to turn to the family of their last murder victim for assistance, but it defies logic that the Collingwoods should invite such a motley crew to spend the night as their guests — no less when they are so overwhelmingly concerned about the safety of their missing daughter. Another stretch of credibility comes in the way Mari's mother chooses to kill the loathsome Weasel. Once she has the man's hands tied behind his back it is ludicrous to think she would fellate him to orgasm and bite off his penis.[235]

The bumbling sheriff and the dim-witted deputy who arrive to take details of the Collingwoods' missing daughter are an unnecessary and inexplicable appendage to the film. They are evidently supposed to break the tension by offering light comic relief — coming across like Abbot and Costello or something out of *Cannonball Run* — but there is no need, nor any room for their broadside buffoonery.

Such a nasty piece of work are Fred 'Weasel' Pudowski and Krug Stillo that Craven resurrected and reinvented them as a composite monster called Freddy Krueger several years later in *A Nightmare on Elm Street*.

It would be comforting (and easy) to derive from *Last House* a parallel with social unrest and the Vietnam war, and indeed to an extent this is possible. But there is something telling in the fact that as Phyllis and Mari drive to the city and the rock concert, the refrain of a horrible song promises "The road leads to nowhere..."[236]

The two girls are an inversion of the Driver who sits in his Chevy at the end of Monte Hellman's *Two-Lane Blacktop*. Whereas he gazes disillusioned from his car at the start of yet another race, the two girls in *Last House* are embarking on a journey in which their joy for life only makes them look stupid. *Two-Lane Blacktop* finishes with the celluloid itself setting on fire, analogous of the end of the sixties, the era in which the film was made. *Last House* on the other hand begins with the declaration that the events depicted are "true." They might well be, but flower-power is over and the audience, burned by the sixties, doesn't really care. It's going to take something more than love and peace to elicit change or motivate them now.

"Few images," writes David A Szulkin in his book *Wes Craven's Last House on the Left*, "capture the burnt-out desperation of the early seventies as well as the shot of Junior Stillo sliding down a wall with his brains blown out and a peace-symbol ornament dangling around his neck."

The Collingwood home isn't last or on the left, and indeed Wes Craven regards the title of the film as a "nothing title" dreamed up by someone in advertising but liked by the producer.

The formidable David Hess went on to virtually reprise the role of Krug in Ruggero Deodato's ***House on the Edge of the Park*** and Pasquale Festa Campanile's *Hitch Hike*. Other film-makers and distributors attempted to cash-in on the success of *Last House on the Left*, and a plethora of similar sounding, similar themed movies followed in its wake, amongst them ***Late Night Trains***.

Craven himself did pen a script for an official sequel to his most infamous movie, but Krug and Weasel coming back from Hell wasn't a concept that particularly thrilled the producers. If for that we ought to be thankful, let us consider the idea of teens on a rafting trip ending up on Krug's island, which by all accounts was a story they preferred.

Last House on the Left was released uncertified in the UK on Replay video, and was missing some incidental footage of the two comedy cops having to hitch a ride on the roof of a truck after their squad car runs out of gas.[237] With regard to gore it was essentially an uncut print. It should be noted however, that *Last House* is one of those movies that exists in a multitude of slightly different forms around the world. Otherwise unreleased out-take footage of Phyllis' disembowelling appeared in Britain as part of a tagged on ending to the pseudo-documentary film *Confessions of a Blue Movie Star*, where it was presented as a genuine snuff film clip.[238] This material also disappeared with the introduction of the Video Recordings Act.

Last House on the Left was submitted to the BBFC for classification in February 2000 but was rejected. It had been rejected once before in July 1974.

LATE NIGHT TRAINS

SYNOPSIS: Two teenage cousins Margaret and Lisa are travelling to Lisa's parents' for Christmas via the overnight train from Munich to Italy. On board they encounter two young men — thugs who earlier robbed a man and slashed a woman's fur coat for amusement — and help them to evade the ticket collector.

One of the young men eyes an attractive woman travelling alone. When she goes to the toilet he follows and forces his way in, but instantly she succumbs to his advances and they have sex. Meanwhile the other thug gets into a fight with a passenger and pulls a knife. Shocked, Lisa and Margaret run to another carriage.

Following a bomb scare, the train is stopped at a station and searched. The girls are able to secure passage on another, altogether less crowded train where they settle into a compartment of their own and prepare to eat their sandwiches. When the train sets off they are disturbed to hear a harmonica playing and decide to find a carriage with other people in it. The harmonica actually belongs to Curly, one of the thugs who, together with the woman who has now latched onto them, have also jumped trains. They force their way into the compartment and prevent the girls from leaving.

Curly goes to the toilet to inject himself with heroin. Blackie meanwhile, the thug with the leather-jacket, shares the girls' food with the woman, and the girls are made to watch as she and Blackie then have sex. Following his fix, Curly amuses himself by tormenting Lisa with a knife, cutting off a portion of her hair and then forcing her to masturbate him. Margaret is struck in the mouth and knocked unconscious when she tries to escape the compartment. The lights in the already darkened train go out.

In the corridor an elderly man accidentally breaks the handle from the door connecting the carriages, effectively isolating the end carriage from the rest of the train. Hearing a scream he goes to investigate, and witnesses Lisa having her panties removed and crotch inspected by the woman. When the thugs realise they have an audience they drag him in into the carriage and instruct him to rape Margaret. Lisa lurches to the window to vomit, and the man, who has finished having sex, slips from the compartment unnoticed and leaves the train at the next stop. The woman guesses that Lisa is a virgin and Curly unsuccessfully tries to rape her. Angry at his failure he decides to deflower the girl with his switchblade. He slowly raises the blade between Lisa's legs but the woman, impatient, grabs Curly's hand and thrusts it upwards. Lisa dies from the wound, and Margaret manages to escape half-naked from the compartment. She runs down the corridor (only to find the door to the next carriage won't open) and jumps from the speeding train to her death.

Lisa's body is thrown from the train by the gang, as are the girls' belongings — with the exception of the tie Lisa bought for her father which Curly decides to keep. Blackie angrily tells the woman — mopping up the blood from the floor — that the deaths are all her fault, but she assures him no one will find out. In the ruckus with Blackie she injures her knee. They all get off at the next stop.

Waiting at the station are Lisa's parents, Julio and Laura. When the girls fail to alight, the station attendant tells the couple they must have caught the next train which is delayed. The attendant asks if Julio — a doctor — can see to the injured woman who has just disembarked. He does, recommending that the wound be treated in a hospital. As it's Christmas however, he agrees to treat it himself at home and the gang are invited back for lunch..

Laura notices the distinctive tie worn by Curly is similar to the one Lisa intended to give her father as a present — a fact described to her earlier over the telephone. She mentions this to Julio but he says it is just a coincidence. The radio reports the discovery of an unidentified teenage girl's body on the railway line and the two thugs eye each other nervously.

Having also heard the report, the elderly man who raped Margaret anonymously calls the police and describes to them the three people he saw with the girls.

As Julio prepares to head back to the station and meet the train he thinks the girls will be on, a radio bulletin reports the discovery of a second dead teenager on the railway line. Personal artefacts have enabled the police to identify this victim and Julio's suspicions are confirmed. He also realises the killers are his houseguests. In a frenzy he grabs the woman, but she convinces him the murders had nothing to do with her — it was the other two. Inside his treatment room, Julio finds Curly injecting drugs and stabs him several times before grabbing a shotgun and pursuing Blackie. After a chase through the woods the thug is wounded and ends up back in the grounds of the house, unable to run any further. Julio catches up, stands over him and reloads the gun. Ignoring his wife's plea to stop, Julio discharges the weapon.

The woman prepares to slip away as police sirens are heard.

CRITIQUE: *Late Night Trains* is a direct imitation of Wes Craven's ***Last House on the Left*** but falls far short of the power and verisimilitude of the film it tries to emulate. The similarities to ***Last House*** are intrusively prominent and include: (i) two upper-middle class teenage girls being held against their will, raped and murdered by deranged drug-infused yobs; (ii) parents who await the arrival of their daughter and prepare a celebratory party (in this instance for Christmas rather than a birthday as in ***Last House***); (iii) a father who is a doctor; (iv) the killers ending up as guests in the parents' home of one of their victims; (v) a mother who becomes suspicious upon

LATE NIGHT TRAINS

TITLE ON PRINT: **NIGHT TRAIN MURDERS**

AKA: **L'ultimo treno della notte (original title); Don't Ride on Late Night Trains; Torture Train; Second House from the Left; Last House on the Left II; The New House on the Left**

ITALY 1974

CAST: **Flavio Bucci, Macha Meril, Irene Miracle, Gianfranco de Grassi, Enrico Maria Salerno, Marino Berti, Franco Fabrizi, Laura d'Angelo**

STORY: **[not credited]**

PRODUCERS: **Pino Bucci & Paolo Infascelli**

DIRECTOR: **ALDO LADO**

seeing an item belonging to her daughter worn around the neck of a killer; (vi) a female gang member who is in many way more ruthless than her male associates; (vii) one gang member who really doesn't want the girls to come to any harm, and so on.

Indeed, one of the thugs (Flavio Bucci) even resembles David Hess and it was probably this reason alone that he was cast for the part. The intensity of his performance, however — along with everyone else in the film — is best described as prosaic and comes nowhere close to Hess' frightening portrayal of spiritual desolation.

So derivative are the thugs in *Late Night Trains* that they don't even have names of their own. The credits do identify Bucci as 'Blackie' and Gianfranco de Gassi as 'Curly,' but nowhere in the film are these (ridiculous) names actually utilised. Macha Meril is credited simply as 'The Lady on the Train.'

The villains are too unconvincing and stereotyped to generate any real antipathy (Blackie and Curly even mug a man dressed as Santa Claus in the opening reel). We are to believe that the woman who boards the train smartly dressed, well-spoken and knowledgeable (she strikes up a conversation on philosophy with a fellow passenger) requires just a good fuck with a stranger in the toilets to revert to her uninhibited, conscience-free, primordial 'other' (should the audience misinterpret all the wriggling and commotion going on in the toilet as something other than sex, director Lado throws in a train-going-into-tunnel shot).

"We just want to have fun, nothing more," she tells the girls prior to their humiliation, torture and rape. Cold and callous, she shows not the slightest remorse after she has forced a switchblade knife into Lisa's groin, an act which brings about her death.

"You're a mad woman, lady!" Blackie subsequently accuses the woman.

To which she retorts, "What did I do wrong? It was just one of those things."

The victims, too, are unrealistic and essentially nothing more than objects around which the villains of the piece can play out their misdeeds. At the start of the film the girls are portrayed as naïve and silly, taking naughty pleasure in smoking a cigarette (inadvertently crushing the cigarette of a fellow passenger from whom they take a light) and rubbing themselves up against the vibrating walls of the train. Not much by way of characterisation, but it's all the girls are afforded. After they switch trains they do little more than simper and await their fate.

The confines of a train provide an ideal situation in which to create a claustrophobic atmosphere, but Lado spoils all efforts to capitalise on the opportunity. The means by which the carriage is isolated from the rest of the train — with the connecting door handle coming away in a passenger's hand — is a bit too convenient and unintentionally comical. Similarly farcical is that the same passenger then manages to watch the girls being abused, standing unnoticed at the compartment door for several minutes, despite the fact he's in plain view and constantly moving around to find a better vantage point.

It's convenient that the lights are out for much of the ordeal. Shaken by events on the previous train however, it's a mystery that the girls should locate a carriage that is dimly lit and empty in the first place.

A musical score by Ennio Morricone does little to complement the film, though there is a nod in the direction of Sergio Leone's *Once Upon a Time in America* — also scored by Morricone. In Leone's movie Charles Bronson is always heard before he is seen, playing a sinister dirge on his harmonica. Likewise, similar downbeat phrases on the mouth organ introduce the junkie's appearance in Lado's film. (Strangely, 'A Flower's All You Need' by Demis Roussos provides *Late Night Trains* with its opening and closing song.)

Although the film is a catalogue of unpleasantness, *Late Night Trains* does more by implication than by actually showing anything outright. The only gore is a brief stock footage scene at the film's beginning which shows a scalpel cutting flesh — a procedure supposedly being carried out by Lisa's father. The only nudity comes via brief scenes of the half-naked Margaret running from the gang down the corridor of the train, prior to hurling herself out of the window.[239]

These factors aside, it is unlikely that the BBFC would grant the film a certificate if ever submitted — isolated incidents of sexual violence are often justification enough to warrant cuts or a rejection, let alone a film based almost entirely around such acts. However, *Late Night Trains* also contains that most reviled of concepts: 'porno-rape,' the rape victim who begins to enjoy her ordeal.

Released on the Video Warehouse International label, the sleeve for *Late Night Trains* claimed it had been voted "Best Late Night Horror Film" in 1978, though by whom or what organisation is not divulged. (The videobox for ***Nightmares in a Damaged Brain*** carried a similarly obtuse accolade, hailing Scavolini's film as "the American Cult Terror film of 1982.") Lacking any kind of certification — other than a self-imposed but unexplained "AX" — *Late Night Trains* carried a warning that its content "may contain scenes liable to cause distress to viewers with a nervous disposition."

In its favour, the circumstances that lead the killers to the family home of one of their victims — courtesy of stolen train tickets — is marginally more credible than that which led Krug and his gang to the Collingwood residence in ***Last House on the Left***.

THE LIVING DEAD

SYNOPSIS: Bleak, post-industrial Manchester — a city dead on its rush-hour feet. Commuters stare vacantly from crowded bus shelters and gridlocked motor vehicles. Even the abstraction of a female streaker dodging the traffic does little to stir any reaction.

After packing his saddlebag, George, the proprietor of a city centre art and antiques shop,[240] closes up for the weekend and heads off on his motorcycle for the rolling hills of the Lake District. The unhealthy, exhaust-fumed claustrophobia of the city soon slip into the beauty and tranquillity of the Lakes, as George burns up the miles on his Norton. Before he can reach his destination in Windermere however, his cycle is knocked out of action on a petrol station forecourt when a woman reverses into it. George is quick to check on the condition of the items in his saddlebag — most notably a statuette. Discovering that it hasn't been damaged in the accident, he announces "It could've been worse." But it's an uncharacteristically sympathetic lull for George, who carries a chip on his shoulder through the duration of the movie. He demands that the driver of the offending car — Edna Simmons, on her way to see her sister — takes a detour so that he might be dropped off in Windermere.[241] To be on the safe side, he also demands that he drive the car.

At one point in their journey, the couple find themselves on a narrow stretch of road, stuck behind a truck which carries the markings "City of Manchester Mortuary," and whose driver refuses to let them pass. It's an omen.

Edna becomes increasingly anxious at the thought of arriving late at her sister Katie's house, and so, begrudgingly, George agrees to drive to Katie's first. They get lost. Leaving Edna and the car outside a cemetery, George goes to ask for directions at a farm, where it so happens the Department of Agriculture are testing a new form of pest control — an "ultrasonic radiation" device that attacks primitive nervous systems. George voices his disapproval, suggesting that the scientists ought to leave mother nature well alone. The farmer makes a backhanded remark about "city folk."[242] The scientists manage to get the machine to work and it emanates a high-pitch pulsating hum.

Awaiting George's return, Edna is attacked by a bearded, scruffy-looking man who appears to have lumbered out of a stream.

THE LIVING DEAD
TITLE ON PRINT: THE LIVING DEAD AT MANCHESTER MORGUE
AKA: The Living Dead at the Manchester Morgue; No Profanar el Sueño de los Muertos (original title); Don't Open the Window; Let Sleeping Corpses Lie; Breakfast at Manchester Morgue; Invasion der Zombies; Les Massacre des Morts-Vivants
SPAIN/ITALY 1974
CAST: Ray Lovelock, Christine Galbo, Arthur Kennedy
STORY: Sandro Continenza & Marcello Coscia
PRODUCER: Edmondo Amati
DIRECTOR: JORGE GRAU

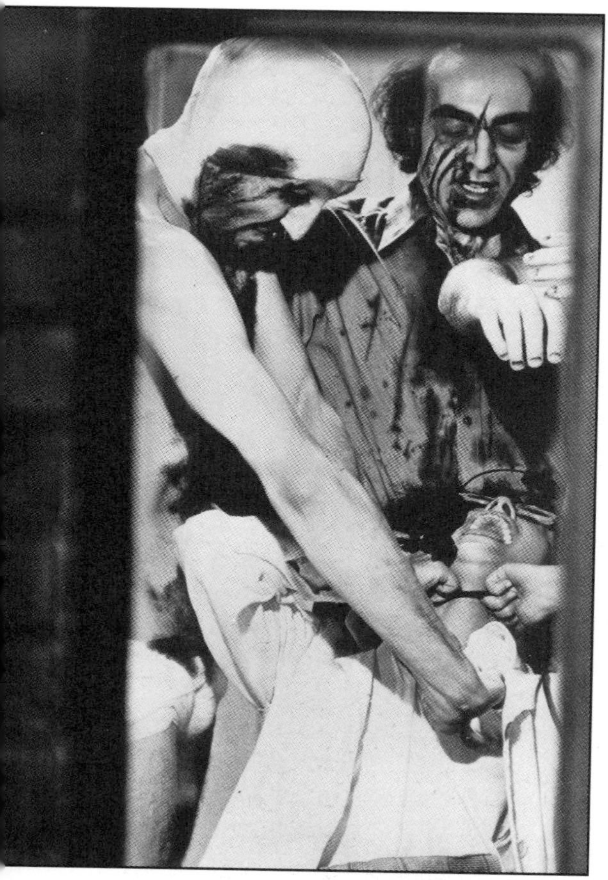

The dead attack the telephone receptionist at the hospital. *The Living Dead.*

She manages to escape and find George, who simply humours her when the assailant is nowhere to be seen. The farmer claims the description of the man fits that of "Guthrie, the loony," a local tramp — except Guthrie was found drowned in the stream the previous week.

Later that evening, awaiting George and Edna's arrival, Katie and her husband Martin are having another of their frequent arguments. It transpires that Katie is a drug fiend and, despite her protestations to the contrary, even in this secluded country retreat still hasn't managed to stay clean. It is while preparing a fix of heroin from a secret stash that she is menaced by Guthrie, who emerges from the shadows. She runs for Martin, who is working on a series of nature photographs by a waterfall. With his automatic camera and flash clicking away, Martin grapples with the homicidal stranger. Despite two solid blows to head with a rock, Guthrie still overpowers and kills Martin. He is frightened away by George and Edna's car headlights.

The police are called in, led by a no-nonsense Irish Sergeant called McCormick, who believes not a word of what Katie says.[243] With a magnifying glass McCormick leers at a contact sheet of snaps showing Katie in the bath, and pointedly asks of the woman (whose husband has just been murdered), "Can you tell us what these pictures are all about?" When he hears that Katie has a drug problem and that Martin had been contemplating putting her into care — hence his calling Edna to the cottage — McCormick comes to the hasty conclusion that Katie must be the murderer, having crushed her husband's chest in a drug frenzy.

"Don't get hysterical," McCormick snaps at the distraught woman.

When George tells the Sergeant that he had nothing to do with any of this and wants to leave, the Sergeant grabs him by his lapels and shakes him, yelling, "You're all the same the lot of you — with your long hair and faggot clothes, drugs, sex, every sort of filth." The Sergeant accuses George of being an accessory to murder, and tells both him and Edna to get a room at the Old Owl Hotel and not to leave town.

Before they leave the scene, George snatches the roll of film that was left clicking away when Martin was killed and decides they ought to get it developed for themselves. But the photos reveal nothing and the theft only serves to further incriminate the couple in the eyes of McCormick.

Shortly after arriving at the Old Owl Hotel, Edna hears that Katie has been admitted to hospital having suffered a breakdown. It is at the hospital that George learns of several babies born with apparent "homicidal tendencies" in the last couple of days. What's more, they all come from the same area in which the new pest-control machine is operating.

Could this device — which drives insects mad, causing them to attack one another — be affecting new-born babies, whose nervous systems are still yet at an elementary stage? The doctor seems to think it's a probability, but refuses to act on a mere hunch.

Edna sees a photograph of "Guthrie, the loony" in the obituary column of a local newspaper and is positive that it's the man who attacked her. George takes Edna to the cemetery to prove that the dead aren't in the habit of walking around.

McCormick puts a man on their tail.

The cemetery is deserted. In a crypt, George and Edna find Guthrie's coffin, but it's empty. They also find that the caretaker has been murdered. Suddenly, the crypt door slams shut and Guthrie lumbers out of nowhere. George spears the somnambulist through the belly, but the attack fails to stop him. As George and Edna scramble for another way out, Guthrie turns his attention to two corpses, reanimating them by applying freshly spilled blood to their eyelids.

Escaping from the crypt, George and Edna bump into the police officer tailing them, and all three find themselves cornered in the caretaker's quarters. The three corpses are outside bashing on the door. A rifle-shot to the head has no detrimental effect and the police officer decides he has to reach his walkie-talkie outside and call for assistance. "Maybe you'll think better of the police if I can pull this off," the officer tells George as he makes a run for it. He's quickly incapacitated by the three zombies, managing only to blurt one message out to McCormick: "There are dead people trying to kill me!"

The zombies pull out the man's guts, and munch slowly and expressionlessly on the offal. One of the dead lifts a plucked eyeball to her mouth.

George finds that the zombies can be stopped with fire. By the time the police arrive on the scene (seemingly hours later — sometime at night), both he and Edna are gone. Viewing the carnage, McCormick accuses the couple of being "A couple of drug crazy maniacs."

"Or worse than that, Sergeant," interjects Perkins, a coroner. "Have you ever come across any of these 'Satanists' in your investigations?"

"No, but I've heard about them."

The suspects know nothing of these new incriminations. George goes to knock the ultrasonic radiation machine out of action, while Edna travels back to her sister's cottage in search of the police — only to be attacked and wounded by her reanimated brother-in-law, Martin. George finds her in a state of shock and takes her to a garage to await an ambulance.[244] He himself sets out to torch Martin, but is ambushed by the police and taken in for questioning (at the Old Owl Hotel, no less, where the police too appear to have taken residence).[245]

McCormick won't hear of any nonsense about the dead coming back to life. For him, further evidence of ritual murder comes with the discovery of the antique statuette that George has been carrying in his saddlebag. On hearing that Martin's body has been taken to the hospital and fearing for Edna's safety, George escapes (incapacitating an officer by throwing a towel in his face and jumping out a window).

But it's already too late. By the time George arrives, Martin has already devoured a medic and resurrected two other corpses who together have swept through the hospital. Not only have they torn a breast from a chatty telephone receptionist and disembowelled her, the zombies have succeeded in killing Katie, Edna and a doctor.

George torches the ghouls before McCormick can unload several shots from his revolver, killing his suspect with malice.

On his way back to the hotel, a smug McCormick explains to one officer: "Justice has been a bit slow in these parts with all this permissive rot going on. Maybe people have learned a thing or two from my example here."

Waiting for the Sergeant in the shadows of his room is the reanimated George...

CRITIQUE: It's probably wisest to clarify the title of this film straight away. The original theatrical print from the seventies carried the title *The Living Dead at the Manchester Morgue*. The subsequent video print carried a truncated variant of this – the grammatically dubious *The Living Dead at Manchester Morgue*[246] – while the videobox simply stated *The Living Dead*.

> This is probably the most depressing film we've seen since *The Mutations*...
> —*Lee Kennedy, World of Horror*

> A step beyond in gore?
> —*John Fleming, The House of Hammer*

The early part of the 1970s were a time when cinematic horror shifted into a higher, more viscerally demanding gear – directly proportional to the nudity flooding British art-house cinemas courtesy of continental soft-porn.[247] Warhol had put his name to Frankenstein and Dracula; a multitude of Italian *Exorcist* clones were intent on 'out-possessing' Friedkin's blockbusting original;[248] English-speaking audiences also managed to catch up on some of the burgeoning bloody obsessions of Hispanic horror (given a general release courtesy of small but enterprising distributors like Variety, Miracle and Grand National); and with *Frankenstein and the Monster from Hell*, the institutionalised Hammer Films went into gore-frenzy, breathing life into its hideous creation one last time before tearing it apart again, literally. Exciting new glossy publications like *Kung Fu Monthly* made pin-ups of Bruce Lee, while *Monster Mag* did the same with such unlikely stars as vampires, skeletons and assorted grisly film moments — blowing them up to gory wall-dwarfing detail.[249]

The changing tide of horror cinema polarised itself in 1974 with the release of *The Texas Chain Saw Massacre*. Strains of the realism and unrelenting, almost ethereal excess of this film could be found in other horror pictures of the same year, such as *Deranged*, *Vampyres*, and *The Living Dead at the Manchester Morgue*.

Common to all is the palpable, underlying threat of explicit horror that refuses to be swept politely out of shot come the pay-off. They have a grittiness, a *frisson*, largely absent from the even gorier heights scaled by the stalk-and-slash movies that proliferated in the decade to follow.

The Living Dead at the Manchester Morgue has often been described as a rehash of George Romero's *Night of the Living Dead*. (Alan Frank, writing in *Horror Films*, claims Jorge Grau's film to be superior to Romero's "in almost every way," but Frank is most certainly in the minority.) Seeing as Romero pretty much defined the lore of the zombie, parallels with *Night of the Living Dead* can be drawn from most every zombie film to have emerged since.[250] Like *Night of the Living Dead*, Grau introduces a lone zombie in the shadow of a cemetery at the film's beginning. And, like Romero, he has his anti-hero needlessly killed at the film's close. Contrary to Romero's unchallenged method of killing the living dead, however, bullets to the head fail to stop Grau's zombies (only fire can do that). But then, Grau seems uncertain of his own criteria — or at least his four screenwriters do — and his zombies at times appear to possess supernatural traits. For instance, despite there being the inference that it could be a type of "plague" that enables Guthrie to raise the dead in the crypt, the action of placing blood on eyelids actually smacks more of *ritualism* than it does a method of contamination. Other curious disclosures about Guthrie include his image failing to appear on the photographs George and Edna take to be developed, and his habit of seeming to materialise out of nowhere prior to each attack.[251]

The Living Dead came to be on the DPP list because of four key scenes depicting lingering, unflinching shots of cannibalism and flesh-rending. These comprise of George's attack on the undead in the crypt with a spike (which features a close-up impalement of a neck); the cannibalism of the policeman in the cemetery (which shows ghouls removing innards and feeding on them); the attack on the telephone receptionist at the hospital (which has ghouls tearing a breast away and feeding on it); [252] and a zombie sinking an axe into the face of a doctor at the hospital.

In this respect, *The Living Dead* is a relatively 'easy' film for the BBFC — remove these scenes and the contention is gone (as indeed proved the case with the re-release noted below).[253] Unlike say, ***I Spit On Your Grave***, where the problem is more indigenous, the potency of *The Living Dead* can be diffused with the cut of the censor's scissors, without any need to disassemble the whole feature.

It would do *The Living Dead* a disservice to analyse it only in terms of Giannetto de Rossi's gore effects. Competent though these are, coming from the effects technician who was later to lend his skills to ***Contamination*** and ***Zombie Flesh-Eaters*** amongst others,[254] there is something else to the film that sets it apart from such simple-minded gore-driven exercises. Several small details — such as the corpse in the crypt having nose plugs and the serenity of the zombies when feeding — help to make an unnerving whole. But it is Grau, a director working on foreign soil, seeing the English countryside as an outsider, who really sets the whole thing on edge.

Grau engages the beauty of *this blessèd plot*[255] — the bleakness, the isolation, the greens of the rolling hills — to haunting effect. So infatuated is he with preserving this vista, Grau goes to the trouble of removing *all extraneous players from it*.[256] With the exception of the opening shots in city centre Manchester and the end 'crowd scene' outside the hospital, there is not a single person in *The Living Dead* who shouldn't be there. That is to say that everyone in the film has a design, a part to play; there are no 'extras.' As George heads for the hills at the film's beginning, the city and everyone in it is seen to methodically peel away. George is leaving behind a landscape that has emasculated its inhabitants only to enter one which looks to have *devoured* its inhabitants. By the time George reaches the garage for refuelling, there is no turning back: no one is left who doesn't belong; no one is left who George doesn't have to meet. Here, on the garage forecourt, it is Edna and the attendant who agrees to fix his bike. Later, in the hills, it is the farmer and the two men from the Department of Environment — no farmhands, no wife or family, no one out taking a stroll, no other travellers on the roads.

When viewed from this angle, the landscape in *The Living Dead* comes alive, and a rather oblique reference to "ecological problems" announced on the car radio after George and Edna first meet, takes on a whole deeper meaning. The landscape is alive and it has these dead things to do its bidding.

The same isolation is to be found in the village, where George, Edna and Sgt McCormick can wander the streets and bump into no one but one another. There are no other guests in the Old Owl Hotel... there is no one in the chemist shop but the man who develops the roll of photographs for George and Edna... George's friends in Windermere are faceless and voiceless entities on the other end of a phone line. The only people who inhabit *The Living Dead* are those with whom the principal characters — or the film/landscape — must have some direct interaction. Take for instance the hospital, whose corridors are always empty, and where three shadowy figures in beds — seen only once in medium-shot — represent the entire sick population of Southgate. When one of the babies attacks a nurse, there is nobody the doctor can call for assistance but George, who happens to be passing.

ABOVE: George being interrogated by Sgt McCormick at 'THE OLD OLW' hotel. *The Living Dead.*

The film's soundtrack — boasting several variations on the excellent main theme, including the catchy-titled 'Manchester M2 6LD'[257] — incorporates strange guttural noises which director Grau himself describes as being the "voice of the dead." In an article that appeared in the Belgian magazine *Fandom's Film Gallery*, Grau relates how he was inspired by and sought to recreate sounds "that are sometimes uttered by corpses when they are moved and caused by exhaling the air from their dead lungs."[258] The effect is a chilling one. Interestingly however, despite the sound accompanying each appearance of the zombies in the film, it never once looks like the zombies are actually making the noise (returning us to the theory of the carnivorous landscape).

On the subject of sound, *The Living Dead* is often regarded as being the first horror film to utilise a stereophonic soundtrack. However, André de Toth's 1953 *House of Wax* — as well as being presented with the attraction of 3-D — was originally screened with a stereo soundtrack.

The Living Dead was granted an 18 certificate when submitted to the BBFC by European Creative Films (ECF) at the end of 1985. Ron Gale, chief executive for ECF, told the press that he was "very pleased" and added, "I know there are a lot of people out there who want horror." As well as being nearly two minutes shorter than Grau had intended, the ECF print of the film that the authors of this book viewed also suffered from an execrable soundtrack, obliterating much of the film's mood.

Grau has numerous film credits to his name, but his only other genre entry remains *The Legend of Blood Castle*. As to why specifically a morgue in Manchester, the idea belonged to producer Edmondo Amati, who was obsessed with both Manchester and *Night of the Living Dead*. Speaking on Channel 4's *Eurotika!*, Grau said, "For him the magic word was Manchester. For him a horror movie had to be set in Manchester."

LOVE CAMP 7

SYNOPSIS: A voiceover informs viewers: "The story you are about to see is true. It is based on actual fact as told by one who lived it."

In a small office in the city of London, a business meeting is drawing to a close. A map on the wall steers the conversation to WWII. Prompted by an associate, the grey-haired Mr Latham recalls how — as a Major in the army — he effectively won the war for the Allies.

"If it hadn't been for him," says the associate, "we might all be speaking German here today."

Latham's tale concerns a prototype jet aircraft the Nazis were working on. A spy, one Martha Grossman, was found by the Nazis to be Jewish and confined to a special women's camp where prisoners were used as sex slaves for front line officers of the Third Reich. Having lost all track of the jet aircraft experiment and fearing they may be defeated in the air, the Allies came up with a plan to reach Grossman and find out all she knows...

A Place of Total Despair
All the youthful beauty of Europe Enslaved for the pleasure of the 3rd Reich
LOVE CAMP 7
LOVE CAMP 7
ABBEY VIDEO
This is the film that goes beyond X
ADULTS ONLY

LOVE CAMP 7
USA 1968
CAST: R W Cresse, Maria Lease; Kathy Williams; Bruce Kemp; John Aiderman; Rodger Steel; Rod Willmouth; Dave Friedman
STORY: R W Cresse
PRODUCER: R W Cresse
DIRECTOR: R L FROST

In a meeting with military bigwigs, Major Latham[259] explains that two WAC officers — Linda Harman and Grace Freeman — have undergone rigorous training and will be used to infiltrate the camp, where they will become "less than whores."

Once behind enemy lines, Captain Calais of the French underground helps the two women with their new identities. Soon after, as planned, they are amongst those women arrested by the Gestapo and sent to the Nazi camp.

In the courtyard,[260] the camp commandant greets the new arrivals. "Velcome ladies, to Love Camp Number 7... I cannot guarantee that you will *love* Love Camp 7. But I can guarantee you will love *in* Love Camp 7."

The Commandant refers to a pregnant girl as "distorted" and has her removed, while the rest of the group are hosed down. A happy dog belonging to one of the guards snaps and barks at the stream of water.

Moving to an office, in a speech that mirrors the one delivered previously, the Commandment thumps his desk and tells the new girls what is required of them. If they refuse to co-operate, the alternatives are "Auschwitz, Belsen, Dauchau."

A medical examination follows. In order that "none of you Jewish ladies will have any of your high sensitivities offended," a female doctor has been secured (who makes a self-conscious "Heil Hitler" salute on entering the room). Stripped naked, the first girl is flung onto the Commandant's desk and, held roughly down by several lecherous guards, is 'examined' by the doctor. When another girl resists, the Commandant thrashes her with his crop and tells her things are going to get much worse.

Miss Kaufman is taken to the barracks beaten and bruised.

Her continued punishment is to spend a day on the 'Seat of Honour,' a cheap wooden sawhorse over which the victim is painfully suspended. The other prisoners are forbidden to help her in any way, so when one of them offers Kaufman a sip of water the Commandant — peeking through the door of the barracks — throws a fit.

"Schnell! Schnell!" he bellows, ordering the prisoners to strip and forcing each of them to hold aloft a bucket at arm's length. When one girl tires and lowers her bucket she is beaten.

The following day, Kaufman is removed from the blood-stained Seat of Honour and ordered by the Commandant to lick his boots to see if she's learned her lesson. She certainly has and enthusiastically engages in the task.

One of the motley, unlikely bunch of soldiers guarding the compound is a private by the name of Godhardt. He tells one of the prisoners — unbeknownst to him one of the spies — that he doesn't agree with what he sees and feels guilty. As he is making his apology and having sex with the prisoner (because it's expected of him), the sound of a hulking obnoxious soldier can be heard manhandling another girl in the background.

Godhardt requests that the Commandment gives him a transfer. He wants to get back to fighting the war, but more importantly doesn't agree with the doctor's experiments in sterilisation that are taking place in the camp. The Commandant refuses the request and reminds Godhardt that "these people aren't human beings."

Love Camp 7 **was available on the Leeds based Abbey Video (PREVIOUS PAGE) and London based Mountain Video (ABOVE) labels. Quite how the same film came to be distributed by two separate companies at the same time is a mystery. The same thing happened with some of the other nasties.**

In order to reach Martha Grossman, who is in the detention room (a punishment for having claimed to feel ill), one of the spies causes a ruckus whilst entertaining an officer and is carted off to join her. After suffering a severe flogging by the Commandant for her insurrection, the spy wins Martha's confidence and is told all the former scientist knows about the Nazis' jet aircraft.

On the third day, General Erich von Hamer arrives in the camp. Having spent a year fighting alongside Rommel, the General has been given the post of "new area commander" and warns the Commandant that he's not here for pleasure. However, after ordering cleaner quarters for his visiting officers and lingerie for the women, von Hamer requests a private lesbian show. The prisoners strip and perform as the General looks on, a film of sweat on his face and his mouth twitching uncontrollably.

Attired in their fine new underwear, the prisoners are prepared for a party in the Commandant's office. Private Godhardt makes one last impassioned attempt to stop his fellow soldiers from ill-treating the women, but it gets him nowhere.[261]

The orgy takes place to the accompaniment of some odd German music playing on a gramophone. With the arrival of the French Resistance outside the camp, the two female agents spring into action, hitting German officers over the head with ornaments and driving a corkscrew into the throat of one soldier. The Commandant is blinded with a wine bottle and proceeds to fire his pistol arbitrarily, hitting one of the spies before himself falling into the corpses entangled on the floor.

Cut to present day London and the conclusion of Latham's story... Martha Grossman is married and living in the States, while the WAC officer who survived Love Camp 7 is now Latham's own wife.

CRITIQUE: *Love Camp 7* falls into a category of motion picture known colloquially as 'Kinkies' which, along with 'Roughies' and 'Ghoulies,' emerged in the politically volatile era of late-sixties America and constituted a harder-edged form of sexploitation cinema. Key features of the story line in these films tended to be acts of sadism, rape, drugs and murder, peppered liberally with plenty of female flesh.

Hardcore was still several years away but Kinkies *et al* went as far as possible with their sexual content short of actually breaking the law. Many scenes in *Love Camp 7* are awash with writhing naked bodies engaged in sex, but are orchestrated so as to avoid depicting actual pubic hair.[262]

A PLACE OF TOTAL
DESPAIR!
LOVE CAMP 7
ADULTS
ALL THE YOUTHFUL
BEAUTY OF EUROPE ENSLAVED
FOR THE PLEASURE OF
THE 3RD REICH
IN EASTMAN COLOR
FROM OLYMPIC INTERNATIONAL

Somehow this tends only to heighten the inherent nastiness of the film. The sex acts constitutes naked women being pawed and mauled by overweight men who keep their trousers on. The camera wobbles and twists with each gasp and grunt.[263]

With the exception of Godhardt and the actor who plays Major Latham — who one suspects had little inkling of the film into which his scenes would be inserted — all the men in *Love Camp 7* are horrid. Even the Italian Allied commander (who looks like a young Ron Jeremy and claims in a funny accent to be aged "forty sevron") has a leer on his face when he meets the two WAC officers who must become "less than whores" in order to save the free world.

Worst of all is the camp Commandant, a sadist with a yellow streak who thinks nothing of flogging the women for the slightest transgression, but who turns into a snivelling wretch at the prospect of having to give up the luxury of his post for actual frontline combat. Indeed, the power-crazed manner in which he lords over the camp, making unreasonable, effete demands from behind his desk, has more than a passing suggestion of Peter Ustinov's Emperor Nero in *Quo Vadis?*.

Bob Cresse, the film's producer, cast himself in the role of Commandment and there is no doubting that he throws himself heart and soul into the part. Having built a career in the transient world of exploitation film-making and distribution, Cresse made it clear he wasn't someone to be messed around with. He had in his employment two full-time bodyguards, and wasn't adverse to flashing the revolver he carried, even sticking the barrel into the mouth of one reneging exhibitor and threatening to blow his head off unless he paid his fees.[264] Cresse also had a liking for Nazi regalia, so much so that it spurred him to come up with the idea of *Love Camp 7*. Speaking of Cresse in an interview he gave *RE/Search #10: Incredibly Strange Films*, Dave Friedman — who has a walk-on part in the film — noted that

> Cresse was a weird kid... very domineering... Cresse really wants to be a Nazi more than anything else in the world, that's his whole thing. He *really* believed he was a Nazi.

But *Love Camp 7* gave Cresse more than just the opportunity to don a uniform and strut about with a swastika armband. It allowed him to engage in another predilection: flagellation — of which there is plenty in *Love Camp 7*. Cresse, "who apparently never cast an actress he didn't want to whip,"[265] flogs a woman with his crop in an early scene. For a film whose special effects work is sparse and unconvincing, the resultant welts on the woman's chest and back are remarkably realistic. However there is no debating the authenticity of the thrashing Cresse administers later in the film. Naked and trussed with her hands behind her back, in a way that forces her to bend double in evident discomfort, one of the spies is flogged by Cresse without the sanctity of any cutaways as leather strikes flesh. As with all the scenes of debasement in the film, the flagellation here goes on for quite some time, red welts materialising before the viewer's eyes.

Contrasting with this are the very funny scenes in which Cresse throws a fit of rage and starts to bark the only word in German in appears to know: "Schnell!" As if by way of compensation, he invariably adds to this several impassioned pleas for the aid of a soldier with the *über total* Teutonic name of "Klaus Müller!"[266]

The director of *Love Camp 7* is the prolific R L Frost, who had a long-running association with Cresse working on a spate of mondo documentaries[267] — their *Mondo Bizarro* featured Nazi-garbed actors in what is supposed to be a clandestine theatre performance filmed in Germany — and before that the nudie-monster crossover, *The House on Bare Mountain*.

As well as Frost's ability to make good, tight exploitation movies on next to no budget, his skill as a cameraman was called for in providing imported pictures with special sex inserts for the US market. Frost was hired by Twentieth Century-Fox to direct *Race With the Devil*, an action-horror film which Frost had co-written and whose name cast included Peter Fonda and Warren Oates. However, years spent working with meagre budgets betrayed Frost and he was swiftly fired[268] for unnerving "producers by not shooting an excessive amount of film, only what he needed."[269]

Love Camp 7 was a big success on the grindhouse circuit. But because of a growing rivalry, neither Frost not Cresse followed it up and it was left to the enterprising Dave Friedman[270] to make a deal with Canadian investors and produce a Nazi camp cash-in. However, so effectual was the resultant *Ilsa, She-Wolf of the SS* that it wasn't released until 1974 (the same year as Liliana Cavani's controversial *The Night Porter*) and even then Friedman had his name removed from the credits.[271]

The Italians, quick to tap a commercial vein, embarked on a cycle of sleazy Nazi themed movies that ran in fits and starts through the latter part of the seventies. The cycle burned itself out before the decade was over.

Love Camp 7 was released in Britain by Market Video and Abbey Video. Although the artwork differed greatly for each release, both sleeves carried the same synopsis and a warning that "This is the film that goes beyond X. ADULTS ONLY."

MADHOUSE
AKA: There was a Little Girl (original title; this title also appears on the British video, but is preceded by a tacked on card reading: Madhouse)
USA/ITALY 1981
CAST: Trish Everly, Michael Maere, Morgan Hart, Jerry Fujikara
STORY: Ovidio G Assonitis, Stephen Blakely, Peter Sheperd, Robert Gandus
PRODUCER: Ovidio G Assonitis
DIRECTOR: OVIDIO G ASSONITIS

MADHOUSE

SYNOPSIS: Julia Sullivan is a teacher at a school for deaf children. Her uncle has told her she ought to visit her sister Mary in hospital, a fact which concerns her although she isn't quite sure why. "There's always been a strange kind of bond between us," Julia tells a colleague. At the hospital Julia is warned by her uncle, Father James, that she might not recognise her sister. Julia reminds him that they are identical twins. "Not any more," he responds, telling her that Mary is suffering from a potentially fatal skin disorder which has deformed her features. Julia goes into the ward alone to see her sister and immediately Mary grabs her wrist. She is incensed with Julia because she isn't suffering from the same disease and reminds her of the terrible things she used to do to Julia on her birthday, threatening to "make it hurt again." Julia pulls away and runs from the ward.

Later Julia tells her boyfriend Sam, a psychiatrist, that she has a twin sister. Sam is amazed she hasn't told him before. "She was the mistress and I was the slave," Julia explains. "She had this dog, a really vicious animal. She would just lift her hand and it would obey."

Julia relates how Mary would torture her with matches and needles. When Sam asks why she didn't tell anyone, Julia replies that Mary had so much power over her that, "it was almost as if I was doing it to myself."

Julia's apartment is situated in a large house currently undergoing renovation. The only other occupant is Amantha who lives in the attic. Suddenly the lights fail and Julia goes to the basement,

where she finds Mr Kimura the handyman changing fuses. She reprimands him for coming into her flat when she's not in. Later that night she receives a series of mysterious phone calls in which the caller refuses to speak. At the hospital a security guard patrolling the grounds is attacked and killed by a large dog, which is then taken away in a car.

The following day at the school, Father James arrives to tell Julia that her sister has escaped from the hospital. Later, Mr Kimura is loading supplies in the basement when he encounters the savage dog. He backs away and runs into Mary, who raises a knife and stabs him in the heart.

The next day Julia takes Sacha, her favourite pupil, to church to listen to her uncle give a sermon. After the service she introduces Sacha to her uncle, telling him that she won't be in town on her birthday as she's going to San Francisco with Sam.

Julia thinks she hears a dog prowling around the house that night.

While playing with a Frisbee in the local park, Sacha is attacked and killed by the dog. Julia is convinced that Mary is somehow responsible. When she tells Father James her suspicions he responds, "It's irrational, completely irrational." The death of the child results in Julia cancelling her trip to San Francisco with Sam.

Sam finds claw marks on the door to Julia's flat and tells her to keep it locked. Having to work the night shift, he asks Helen, a work colleague of Julia's, to stay over and keep her company. On hearing noises in the night, Helen investigates the empty floors of the building only to be attacked and killed by the dog. Julia goes to work the following morning thinking that Helen must have already left.

Amantha, the neighbour, sees Father John struggling with a large bag in the street. Believing he is preparing a birthday surprise for Julia, she helps carry the bag into the basement where she quips, "That feels just like a body in there." "Oh, it is," responds the priest, opening the bag to reveal the security guard savaged by the dog at the hospital. Father James stabs Amantha to death after which he goes to meet Julia at the school, telling her "I've got a wonderful surprise ready for you."

Back at the house Father James blindfolds Julia and walks her into the basement. Around a decorated table he has seated the bodies of the recent murder victims. "I invited all of your friends," he tells the girl as he removes the blindfold. Julia runs away only to be confronted by Mary.

On his way to the airport the taxi in which Sam is travelling gets a flat tyre. As the cabby changes the wheel, Sam takes the opportunity to read through his speech but the pages of the document are blown away in the wind and he has to return to the flat to get another copy.

At the birthday party, Mary is contemplating disfiguring Julia so they will once again look alike. Father James complains about people being afraid of dying but to show how easy it is he stabs Mary in the back.

Sam hears the ravings of Father James coming up from the basement. He goes down to investigate and is set upon by the dog, but manages to kill it with a power drill. Picking up a small axe he searches the other rooms, finding Julia tied to a chair and her uncle raving and singing nursery rhymes. Father James is surprised to see Sam and decides to take the body of Mary out of the room "for a nap." Trying to untie Julia, Sam is threatened by Father James who returns wielding a knife. Julia slips free, grabs the axe and kills her uncle with a ferocity that shocks Sam. She wanders from the room covered in blood and in a state of shock. Suddenly, Mary lunges up at her and in her dying breath mutters, "You'll never be free. Never!"

CRITIQUE: There's no scientific explanation, we are informed, for the virus that is attacking and disfiguring Mary. Similarly, we might argue, there's no real reason why any of these murders should be taking place. When Julia takes one of her pupils to church, Father James gives a sermon that attacks sisters who are selfish and deny kinfolk love and comfort, while great is the reward that awaits "those who honour familial love."

There are lots of clues given to indicate that Julia's clergyman uncle might be a homicidal psychopath, but his sermon is the nearest we get to an explanation why he should be helping Mary with a bunch of birthday-treat murders.

Madhouse is a rather predictable and clichéd whodunit that offers nothing original or particularly surprising. Neither should it prove particularly taxing trying to figure that Father James is somehow involved in the murders, given that he's featured on the videobox holding a knife with a mad look on his face. *Madhouse* comes across like a bland TV movie save for the odd moment of violence. Indeed, Trish Everly (as Julia) looks like she might have stepped straight out of *Dallas* or any one of a number of glamorous soaps, emoting breathlessly whole chunks of expositional dialogue. On the other hand, Dennis Robertson (as Father James) is a positive cauldron of seething, barely contained malevolence, happily singing nursery rhymes one minute and sinking a knife into someone's back the next.

In Britain the film was available in two versions, one showing the drilling of the dog's head while the other was without (there was no way to differentiate from the packaging which print of the film was which). In its uncut form, the sequence is particularly unpleasant, and an over-the-top piece of nastiness in an otherwise compromising movie. The actual dog is substituted with a rather tacky fake dog for the drilling – although it's debatable whether the film-makers' intended the sight of a pooch getting its head drilled to look *too* real!

It's unlikely that *Madhouse* would pose much of a problem with the BBFC if submitted with this one sequence excised.

The only other graphic scenes of violence occur in the opening credits (a dummy having its faced smashed repeatedly and bloodily with a rock) and the axing to death of Father James in the closing moments, replete with streaks of flesh dangling from the wound.

The juxtaposition of maddening nursery rhymes and menacing strings in Riz Ortolani's score conjures up the composer's earlier work on mondo films (such as *Brutes and Savages*) and on other banned titles, ***Cannibal Holocaust*** and ***House on the Edge of the Park***. These soundtracks were similarly overbearing and cheery at times, counterpoint to the havoc being unleashed on the screen.

The polished look and traditional scares of *Madhouse* are a million miles from the DPP films of some of Assonitis' countrymen, notably such Italian films as ***Absurd***, ***Late Night Trains*** and ***Gestapo's Last Orgy***. Indeed, it seems a million miles from some of Assonitis' other work, which includes the rather more raw-edged and visceral *Beyond the Door* and *The Curse*.

It might be interesting to note that *Madhouse* was made the same year as the similar celebratory motivated slasher *Happy Birthday To Me*.

MARDI GRAS MASSACRE

SYNOPSIS: Two prostitutes walk into a public bar and ask Sam the bartender how the action is. A wealthy-looking suited man enters and introduces himself to the girls. He tells them he is new to the city and looking for something "different" to which they reply that anything is available at a price. Upon his asking who the most evil woman in the place might be, the girls point out Shirley, a young hooker sitting alone at a table. The man approaches Shirley.

"Hello," he says. "I understand you are the most evil woman here."

"Listen, honey. I could probably take first prize in any evil contest," responds the hooker. He pays her $200 in advance and they both leave for his apartment.

At the apartment the man tells Shirley he wants her on a special bed — a curious altar-like structure. She undresses in a red-curtained room while the man goes off to prepare himself. Drawing aside the curtains he reappears robed and masked, stood in front of a looming Toltec statue. After a brief massage with oils the woman is bound to the altar and the man informs her that she is to be sacrificed to Evil. With a blade he slices open her hand ("that accepted the money for your evil"), gouges the sole of one foot ("that brought you misdeeds") and cuts open her torso to remove her heart ("the part of you you use for your evil"). The organ is offered to the Toltec statue.

The following day the police find the hooker's body dumped on a railway line, and two Detectives discuss with the coroner the possibility of sacrificial murders. Later they go to Sam's bar to question him and the regular prostitutes. One of the girls, Sherri, describes the man who took Shirley away and distinctly remembers that he wore a large ornamental ring. One of the Detectives takes Sherri to lunch and then to bed.

The killer visits a bar and a hooker introduces herself. He tells her he's looking for someone very evil, and is soon fixed up with a girl who he takes back to his apartment.

"Are you sure you're really evil?" he asks.

"Honey, I'm as evil as you can get," she retorts.

"Then let's not waste any more time."

He leads her to the sacrificial chamber where she strips and lies down allowing herself to be tied. He oils her body and tells her, "I'll go to the next room now and prepare for you." The man returns wearing his extravagant costume and brandishing the sacrificial knife. As with the previous victim he stabs her hand and foot before removing her heart. The organ is fed to the idol.

The police receive a call concerning the latest killing. The captain insists that the case be wrapped up before the Mardi Gras begins. "Stop the bad publicity about the killings," demands the mayor, "or you'll ruin Mardi Gras and cost us a lot of business."

MARDI GRAS MASSACRE
USA 1978
CAST: Curt Dawson, Gwen Arment, Laura Misch, Cathryn Lacey, Nancy Dancer, Butch Benit, William Metzo, Ronald Tanet, Wayne Mack
STORY: Jack Weis
PRODUCER: Jack Weis
DIRECTOR: JACK WEIS

The two Detectives visit Dr Lewis, an expert on ancient sacrifices. Meanwhile, in a strip joint, the killer is attracted to a dancer wearing novelty horns and a devil's fork, but is unaware that she has been told to work on him by a pimp. The stripper takes him to Exchange Alley where the pimp lies in wait, ready to pounce and steal his money. A scuffle takes place during which the pimp is stabbed with his own knife.

Still in need of a victim the killer visits another strip joint and does a deal with Catfish, a rhyme-speaking pimp. Having acquired a whore, the killer returns to his apartment and orders a Chinese takeaway over the phone. While the girl is in the shower the food arrives and the deliveryman can't help but notice the customer's ornate ring.

After the meal the hooker is taken to the killing room where she dances for the man. He asks her age and when she replies "nineteen," he demands that she leaves. She refuses to go however, and is sacrificed in the same manner as the previous victims.

Back at the station the captain reminds the two Detectives that Tuesday is Mardi Gras and the killer must be found. Consequently they tour the streets questioning people but come up with no new leads. They figure the killer may have moved on, satisfied with three murders. In reality, he is preparing for a triple sacrifice and has already paid in advance for the whores — Sherri being one of them.

During the festivities the two cops mix among the revellers. The masked killer slips by them and meets with the three girls, whom he then takes back to his apartment and drugs.

At the Chinese takeaway the cops brandish a sketch of the killer's ring which the deliveryman duly recognises, and he provides the address of the man to which he made the recent delivery. The cops however go for a drink at Sam's bar to give back-up time to arrive, and Sam tells them he's seen Sherri with the wanted man. They raid the apartment and rescue the three women, but the killer absconds down the fire escape.

A car chase ensues and the killer leads the cops to the docks. Seeing no way out he drives his station wagon towards the edge of

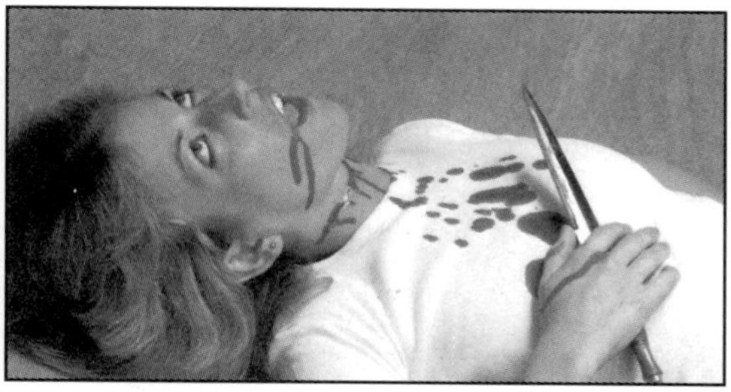

PREVIOUS PAGE: *Mardi Gras Massacre* on the Market Video label.
THIS PAGE, LEFT: *Mardi Gras Massacre* on the Gold Star label. TOP RIGHT: The reverse of the Market Video sleeve featured an image not actually in the film. ABOVE RIGHT: The reverse of the Gold Star label showed one of the generic gore scenes from *Mardi Gras Massacre* (ironically, from an angle different to the one featured doggedly throughout the film).

the quay and plunges into the water. When the vehicle is eventually retrieved there is no sign of the man — only the mask he wore for the Mardi Gras.

CRITIQUE: One wonders how on earth the killer in *Mardi Gras Massacre* transports the enormous stone idol around from town to town or indeed, if we consider information the Detectives receive from Interpol, country to county. His common-or-garden apartment doesn't look big enough to have an all-purpose sacrificial chamber — a sound-proof one at that.

Mardi Gras Massacre mixes film genres in the hope of hitting at least one target, combining elements of *Jaws* (town officials refuse to halt festivities and risk losing business!) and the disco craze sparked by *Saturday Night Fever* (dancing and music!), yet fails to achieve anything of significance as a whole. The plot closely resembles that of ***Blood Feast***, with the sacrifice of women to an ancient deity culminating in the ultimate sacrifice being thwarted at the last moment. The two cops fumble around doing very little other than appearing confused, although this does serve to generate unintentional laughter. For instance, they literally scour the night streets looking for clues, coming down heavy on miscreants like the bum they beat up in a doorway and the crazed tap dancer they question in the middle of a crowd of people. All this is depicted in medium shot, which gives an heightened sense of the absurd to an already absurd situation. The actors who play the cops behave as though they are *Starsky and Hutch*.

Given the incompetence of the cops and the weird surplus of individuals in the film, it's not inconceivable that the blatantly unstable killer (asking for "evil" women with his Boris Karloff demeanour) should be able to pass from bar to club without attracting the slightest attention.

Catfish, the scat-singing rhyme-talking pimp is almost as big a nut as he is: "I may not be honest, but you've got my promise," Catfish tells the killer with complete nonextant street credibility.

Dr Lewis,[272] the expert on ancient sacrificial rites whom the two Detectives visit, blurts

out with utmost conviction "Human sacrifice — not uncommon today," and then wrongly credits the Manson family with being devil worshippers.

The generally uneventful story line is punctuated with infrequent acts of sacrifice, which are graphic but rather ridiculous. The scenes which caused the film to be placed on the DPP list are easy to isolate, comprising shots of the victims having their torso cut open and their heart extracted. This occurs on three occasions, but as each is filmed in the same way and at the same static angle viewers may be excused for thinking the same effect is being repeated over again.

It is not clear why the film-makers should go to the trouble and expense of creating several life-like torso models — it's probably safe to assume that they are the single most expensive items in the entire production — only to film their destruction in a manner that renders them virtually interchangeable. The more astute will notice differences in the way the sacrificial dagger slices through the (accommodatingly pliable) flesh, the way in which the killer places his hand so not to reveal too much of the emptiness that lies beneath the growing wound, and the way that each torso has differently shaped breasts and nipples to correspond with the live actress. All in all they're a prosthetic worthy of any major movie production.

Contrary to the title, all the killings occur *before* the Mardi Gras and none take place on the actual day of the festival.

Mardi Gras Massacre tries to generate tension with a weird howling synthesised wind sound. Used indiscriminately, this will switch — usually mid-sacrifice — back to the pounding disco-funk score that otherwise dominates the soundtrack. Indeed, the film has a lengthy sequence set in a discotheque for no discernible reason other than to feature some gratuitous sign-of-the-times dancing (***Don't Go in the House*** has a similar sequence). The use of self-contained pop compositions on the soundtrack is reminiscent of the feel-good movie sounds of *Car Wash*, *Saturday Night Fever* and the like.

In February 1998, a professor at Lafayette University included clips from *Mardi Gras Massacre* in a lecture exploring stereotypes and inaccuracies in films that portray the Pre-Columbian people of Latin America — notably Hollywood's penchant for crazy, bloodthirsty Aztec priests.[273]

Crypt of Dark Secrets is often cited as being an alternative title for *Mardi Gras Massacre*, but it's actually an earlier — even more obscure — movie made by Weis in 1976, which has found a recent video release in America under the title of *Dark Secrets*. It concerns a Vietnam veteran who is brought back to life in a voodoo ceremony, sharing the Louisiana setting and some of the same cast members as *Mardi Gras Massacre*. According to *Psychotronic Video*,[274] its "FX are surprisingly excellent" although *Video Watchdog*[275] claimed the film to be "a truly excruciating sixty-nine minutes that will tax the patience of even the most devoted horror completist."

NIGHT OF THE BLOODY APES

SYNOPSIS: A police lieutenant called Arthur is watching his girlfriend Lucy during one of her professional wrestling matches. During the bout Lucy's opponent Elena is thrown from the ring and suffers a fractured skull, whereupon she is rushed to the local hospital. Dr Krauman is the head surgeon at the hospital, but he happens to be breaking into the local zoo with Goyo, his crippled assistant. They tranquillise and steal a gorilla, taking the animal to Krauman's home where it is caged in a basement laboratory. Krauman's son, Julio, is suffering from leukaemia. Summoned back to the hospital to operate on the comatose Elena, Krauman hears word from the specialists that nothing can be done to save his son. His days are numbered, they say.

Krauman has his own plans however and proposes an operation in his basement lab. "The transfusions of human blood have been ineffective against his terrible leukaemia," the doctor enlightens his assistant. "I feel the blood from an animal as powerful as that of a gorilla might annihilate what is causing the cancer in his blood."

Goyo is unsure about the feasibility of such an operation but Krauman tells him he will also transplant the heart. "Move the table over to the cage and prepare the gorilla," he orders. Krauman then transplants the gorilla's heart into the body of his son. With the operation appearing to be a success the body of the ape is incinerated.

The gorilla is reported missing and zoo officials inform the authorities that they must be prepared to shoot the animal on sight. Meanwhile, still concerned about Elena, Lucy loses her latest wrestling bout. After the match she decides to retire from the ring once her contract has expired. Arthur suggests they go out for a meal that evening but his plans are scuppered when he is summoned to see the police chief.

Julio is recovering from his operation when he unexpectedly transforms into an ape-like creature and escapes from the lab with Krauman and his assistant in pursuit. He climbs into an apartment and attacks a woman who is taking a shower, killing her during a struggle. Other residents are alerted by the girl's screams and Julio leaves, only to be spotted by Krauman, shot with a tranquilliser dart and taken back to the lab.

"I was prepared for everything, but not for this," remarks Krauman, concluding that his son's condition may be corrected if he removes the gorilla heart and replaces it with a human one. He decides to use the comatose Elena as the donor, but while they are kidnapping the woman the drug wears off Julio and he breaks free again. He attacks a courting couple in the park, killing the man while the woman manages to escape and seek help. A bystander goes to see if he can assist but he too is killed by the ape-man, as is a passer-by on the street. Krauman returns from the hospital and with his assistant goes in search of the missing Julio, who they are quickly able to locate in the park thanks to the police activity. They get to him first, tranquillise him and get him back to the lab.

Arthur questions the woman who survived the assault and from her description deduces the attacker must be the gorilla that escaped from the zoo. With all the evidence of the attacks at his disposal, he later reasons that they are looking for a half-human half-beast creature. While searching for the monster he calls Lucy and asks her to meet him later by the park.

Krauman successfully transplants Elena's heart and Julio transforms from the ape back to his normal self. Once he regains consciousness however, he transforms back into the creature and decapitates Krauman's assistant. The sight of his son carrying Goyo's torn-off head causes Krauman to stumble and strike his head on some furniture. Still able to recognise his father, Julio carefully lifts Krauman onto the bed and then goes out onto the street where he kills a passing patrolman. Lucy witnesses the attack and runs into the park with Julio in pursuit, closely followed by Arthur who has heard her screams. Having revived, Krauman is able to prevent Arthur from shooting Julio, whose ape features have again subsided. Convalescing in the hospital, Julio changes back to his brute form and kills two orderlies, before grabbing a little girl and carrying her to the roof. Watched by a crowd of alarmed citizens and policemen, Arthur and Krauman manage to talk him into relinquishing the child, whereupon Julio is shot by the police. As he dies he

NIGHT OF THE BLOODY APES

AKA: La Horriplante bestia humana (original title); Feast of Flesh; Horror y Sexo; Gomar, The Human Gorilla; Korang, La Terrificante Bestia Umana [?]

MEXICO 1968

CAST: Armando Silvestre, Norma Lazareno, José Elias Moreno, Carlo Lopez Moctezuma, Juan Fava

STORY: René Cardona & René Cardona Jr

PRODUCER: Alfredo Salazar

DIRECTOR: RENÉ CARDONA

The Bloody Ape in *Night of the Bloody Apes* claims his first victim (TOP), and later carries a child to the hospital roof (ABOVE).

transforms back to human form.

CRITIQUE: René Cardona spent five decades in the Mexican film business, as an actor, writer and producer, as well as a director in exploitation films whose subject matter ranged from westerns to wrestling superheroes. He co-wrote *Night of the Bloody Apes* with his son, who was himself to enjoy a film-making career. In many ways *Bloody Apes* comes over as a kind of homage to the classic movie monsters, with its strain of mad scientist, Frankenstein monster and lycanthrope. The film opens with 'blood' pouring behind the credits, and closes with a chase across the rooftops with frightened townspeople gathered below. Even the dramatic score echoes the Universal monsters era.

Night of the Bloody Apes bears a particular resemblance to William Beaudine's 1943 *The Ape Man*, wherein Bela Lugosi injects himself with ape serum and takes on ape-like attributes, resorting to killing others for the human spinal fluid he needs to regain his human features. (Cardona appears to have been impressed enough by Beaudine's film to explore its ideas on at least one other occasion outside of *Bloody Apes* — and his 1962 film *Wrestling Women Vs. the Aztec Ape* also features mad scientists and gorillas.)

Cardona tries to modernise the archaic B-movie plot by throwing in scenes of wrestling, partial nudity and graphic gore, all of which raise laughs rather than their supposed intended response. The wrestling sequences (three in the first half-hour) are overlong and irrelevant to the plot, thrown in to appease the fans of Mexican wrestling, around which an entire film genre had grown (but one that has little appeal to filmgoers outside its country of origin). Scenes that incorporated nudity were filmed in a cautious manner — not unlike early naturist documentaries — with conveniently placed objects obscuring the vital areas of the body. The woman who is attacked in the shower by the monster even manages to turn her leg discretely while unconscious to obscure any wisp of pubis.

The gore effects are plentiful, but remarkably cheesy and their rubber origins all too evident. When a victim has his scalp torn off, for instance, a plastic tube taped to the top of his head is clearly visible, supplying blood to the wound. When an eye gouging occurs it seems that the effect is achieved courtesy of a rubber mask having mashed potato squeezed from the eyehole. The lengthy scenes depicting Julio's operations are stock footage inserts showing transplantation surgery and a still beating heart being cut from its donor (with plenty of cutaways to

Dr Krauman[276] mopping his sweating brow). The fact that the footage doesn't correspond with the actors, their actions or the colour of the stock it is sandwiched between is evidently of little importance to the film-makers. What's more, it incorporates more hands around the operating table than there are people in Krauman's lab.

The special effects depicting the transformation of Julio into the ape adopt the same methods – but are technically inferior – to those used on Lon Chaney Jr in *The Wolf Man* (1941). However, as tends to be the case, the cheap makeup job somehow renders the sight of the creature all the more disgusting and horrific.

On top of the gloriously wild and cut-price blood-letting, there are plenty of other factors that go to make *Night of the Bloody Apes* such an enjoyable experience. These include the Hispanic beat cop who speaks in a strange Irish accent; the diminutive Lucy who seems to gain extra pounds once she has donned her mask and got into the wrestling ring; the small studio set that passes as an area of the park to which all the characters seem drawn (and in which a struggling victim inadvertently kicks up the grass to reveal a concrete floor); the flimsy wooden boards that are nailed haphazardly across the lab window following Krauman's concern that no precaution can be great enough; the elderly woman who discovers a dead body in the street and screams "Oh! A dead man! A dead man! A dead man!" (pre-dating Edith Massey's Egg Lady in *Pink Flamingos* by several years).[277]

We almost hope that the phone never rings in the Krauman household because it invariably means that Goyo, the assistant, will traipse through several rooms and a staircase (in real time and with a gammy leg) in order to tell the doctor that he has a call waiting.

As to why his son turns into a bloody ape, Krauman explains to his assistant:

> KRAUMAN: I was prepared for a case of refusal, for auto-immunisation which might affect the normal tissues — such as the pleura and the red blood cells — but I never thought it would affect the cerebrum.
> GOYO: The cerebrum?
> KRAUMAN: Yes. And what is more probable is that the heart of a gorilla is much too potent for any human, and the volume of blood to the cerebrum — which couldn't control this great pressure — damaged the superior parts. And when this happens man becomes... an animal completely without control, giving origin to the transmutation. The malignancy of the case is that the process might occur each forty-five seconds, the time it takes for the blood to circulate through the normal body.

The film was described by *Monster Mag*[278] as being "based on an absolutely true and plausible occurrence." The unaccredited reviewer was aghast at the incredible advancements in medical science which made *Night of the Bloody Apes* so credible. "What horror can an eminent physician create in a state of terrible mental stress?" he wrote.

After all the murder and mayhem that has gone before, Lucy closes the film with the deadpan understatement: "It's unfortunate – really sad."

Originally released theatrically in Britain in 1974 with one minute of cuts, *Night of the Bloody Apes* was made available on video by Iver Film Services (IFS) with a warning that "this film contains scenes of extreme violence."[279] The distinctive IFS packaging for horror films tended to feature specially commissioned photographic work (the cover for *Bloody Apes* was a surgeon's bloodied hands; ***Night of the Demon*** was a darkened moonlight sky; *Pigs* was a pig's head with a bloody mouth) and often carried the film's American rating.

The film has been made available again with cuts.

NIGHT OF THE DEMON

SYNOPSIS: Recovering in a hospital bed with the lower half of his face bandaged, Professor Nugent explains to the doctors and a Detective how he encountered a creature — "a demon" — in the forest.

A man is on a camping holiday when he is disturbed by something in the woods. Attacked, he falls to the ground with one of his arms torn from its socket. The blood that flows from the stump fills a huge footprint in the soft earth. The man's daughter, Carla Thomas, is invited as a special guest to one of Professor Nugent's lectures at the university. Nugent addresses the anthropology students on the possible existence of the Sasquatch, and Carla relates another incident that took place near to where her father was killed: a couple of lovers were in their van when some creature pulled the man from the vehicle and killed him. The woman died from shock.

Nugent organises a team of students to go to the areas where sightings of the creature have been reported. They first visit a man named Carlson who has written about the creature, but Carlson proves evasive and goes off hunting, so the team decide to make camp by his cabin. Elsewhere in the forest a lone camper is attacked and killed by the Bigfoot. Later when Carlson has returned, Warren, one of the students, calls at his cabin with a bottle of whiskey. Carlson gets uneasy when Warren mentions Bigfoot and he tells him of a woman they call "Crazy Wanda" who has seen the animal.

The following day the group goes to town to question people about Wanda. They learn that she lives alone, that her father committed suicide some years ago, and that she had a baby who was "awful to look at."

The team travel further up river and make camp. Nugent warns them they are now in Bigfoot territory and relates a story about a motorcyclist who was killed in the area. Later that night Nugent and Warren investigate strange sounds in the woods. They observe a ceremony in which townsfolk are worshipping an anthropoid effigy and a woman is about to be ritually raped. After Nugent fires shots in the air the people disperse.

The following morning the group wake to find their boat has gone.

"The pole's been completely pulled out of the ground," remarks one of the students.

"What could have done that?" asks Carla.

"Something huge, like an elephant," suggests Warren.

Nugent finds a footprint in the mud and asks Gary to make a cast of it before setting off in search of Wanda's home. In the night Gary is attacked and injured by the creature.

When finally they locate her cabin, the team discover that the mute Wanda is the same woman who was to be raped during the ritual. Nugent asks her about Bigfoot and Gary shows her the plaster cast of the footprint, the sight of which causes Wanda to become hysterical and she smashes the cast. The team leave her to calm down, and at the camp Nugent informs the party that a woodsman was axed to death not far from where they are currently situated. He also relates an incident in which two girl scouts were killed by the creature, and suggests someone must keep watch throughout the night.

During Pete's watch he investigates a sound in the woods, only to be attacked by the creature causing him to discharge a shotgun into his own face. The others can find no sign of their colleague, only the gun and a bloodstain on a tree.

The next morning they hypnotise Wanda so she is able to speak, and she tells them how she was rejected by her pious father and attacked and raped by the Bigfoot. Despite her father's attempts to bring about a miscarriage after she became pregnant, Wanda gave birth to a mutated infant which her father promptly destroyed. Wanda later burned her father alive in revenge. To confirm the story Nugent and Warren dig up the baby's grave and the skeletal remains they uncover suggest some kind of deformed creature. From within the forest Bigfoot sees them disturbing the grave of its offspring and attacks. They manage to get back to the cabin and barricade themselves in, but in no time at all the creature is able to break in and kill all the students. Nugent himself survives the attack but is horribly scarred.

At the hospital, after hearing his story, the doctor concludes that the creature doesn't exist and Nugent is criminally insane.

NIGHT OF THE DEMON
USA 1980
CAST: Michael J Cutt, Joy Allen, Bob Collins, Jodi Lazarus, Richard Fields, Michael Lang, Melaine Graham
STORY: Jim L Ball Mike Williams
PRODUCER: Jim L Ball
DIRECTOR: JAMES C WASSON

CRITIQUE: James Wasson's *Night of the Demon* is an oddly engaging film. Despite its cheapness, lousy acting and trite script the film is immensely watchable, with a dynamism that kicks off right from the opening pre-title killing: a man preparing to go fishing is attacked and has his arm ripped off. Although this is only shown in shadow, the victim manages to stagger into shot displaying his ragged wounds before falling to the ground and bleeding into the outsize footprint left by the thing that attacked him. Shoddily done to say the least, but it's an attention-grabbing opening scene and non-too-succinctly plots what mayhem lies ahead.

Barely have the titles finished than we are witnessing another Bigfoot attack. In what may be Wasson's tip of the hat to the famous Roger Patterson footage — on which the image of a supposedly genuine Sasquatch was captured in 1967[280] — this sequence is related to the anthropology students via footage accidentally caught on a home movie camera. Again the sequence is ludicrously awkward, but has an essence which transcends the humble budget and is greater than the sum of its parts.

Another attack features a couple making out in the back of a van in the woods (a bout of lovemaking that seems to go on for an eternity — not helped at all by the particularly unattractive couple doing the loving). Something outside the window catches the woman's eye. She suspects at first that it's a peeping tom and continues with a wry smile on her face, but it turns out to be the creature. Having stared through the back window of the van and got a clear view of the man's naked pummelling backside, the creature pulls open the door and yanks the man outside. Frozen to the spot, the woman listens to the path the creature takes across the top of the vehicle, her lover screaming in agony. First with a handprint on the windscreen he finally comes into view again. For an awfully long time his bloodied face is perfectly still, emitting a strange guttural death rattle. The camera eventually focuses on the woman and stays with her as she slowly succumbs to shock and dies.

And fundamentally that is all the film is: a succession of events, generally in flashback (or flashback-within-flashbacks if one considers that the whole tale is related by a convalescing Nugent), that occur every ten minutes-or-so and are tied together by the investigations of the research group. It seems that wherever the team camps, Nugent has a story concerning people being "horribly mutilated" nearby.

The film-makers belie a certain film-making experience, in spite of the fact their names are unknown. Cutaways and dissolves are plentiful, and feature in all the right places (unlike that other woodlands nasty ***Don't Go in the Woods***). The camera is far from static and the cheesy dialogue rarely descends to out-and-out stupidity. (Although there is a good laugh to be had when two of the team disrupt the ritual about to take place and inadvertently cause a container of flammable liquid to catch fire. Of the growing blaze, Nugent tells his concerned student: "We're not equipped to handle it. Let them take care of it — they live in the woods.")

The team that goes in search of the creature is composed of the most disagreeable and incompetent people imaginable. An absolute lack of any anthropological expertise is highlighted when one of them deduces, in all seriousness, that their boat has been pulled from its mooring post by something "like an elephant."

The flashback depicting Wanda's bestial impregnation and the conflict with her pious father are possibly the most competent and adept parts of the film. His attempts to induce a miscarriage in his daughter fail. When finally she gives birth to a revolting monstrosity that screams like a chimpanzee, complemented by an expression on her father's face that is at once joy and terror, the result is quite chilling. Like ***Cannibal Holocaust***, *Night of the Demon* appears to have been another inspiration for the makers of *The Blair Witch Project*. The sequence in which the team wanders around the small township asking people their opinion of the mysterious "Crazy Wanda" is notably similar to passages in that later film.

The film's frequent Bigfoot attack segments, narrated by Nugent, are its *raison d'être* (as if to spell that fact out, there is only one tight close-up shot in the whole movie that doesn't feature a grisly gore effect). Each one of these is progressively more violent, culminating in the all-out assault on the anthropologists themselves — a sequence which is credited on the video sleeve as "the most gruesome blood bath ever filmed" (but is essentially another retread of Romero's *Night of the Living Dead*, in which those holed up in a barricaded shack are forced to fight off the ultimately overwhelming force of the aggressor).

The team constantly stray too close to the windows of the shack, in spite of the imminent wounding that befalls anyone within reach of the creature's powerful claws. The dream-like state this sequence invokes is compounded once the creature manages to break through the window-bars and get into the building. As the Bigfoot contemplates its new environment, the team slowly manoeuvre their way around the room. Unable to get out the front door, they make a run for a back room. The film switches to slow-motion, and the creature embarks on an orgy of sadistic mutilation. One student is shaken to death; another is throttled; one student is forced onto a saw blade and from the resultant wound the creature rips intestines which it then uses to flail the boy's colleagues (the most memorable and the silliest sequence); another student is impaled on a pitchfork and yet another has his throat cut open on broken glass. Nugent has his faced pushed onto burning coals — hence his hospitalisation.

As if that isn't gloriously gory or tasteless enough, earlier in the film the creature captures two girl scouts and bashes them together repeatedly until dead (neither girl relinquishes the knife they are holding, adding to the flesh-rending mayhem). A woodcutter is chopped in the shoulder and the camera seems unable to pull free of the blood-pumping wound. Blood... pumping... endlessly...

In a sequence that has passed into (video nasty) legend, Nugent embarks on the tale of a motorcyclist who had his penis torn off by the monster. Cut to the motorcyclist travelling from a long way away, down a mountainside road. He (eventually) pulls over for a rest and decides to urinate. Suddenly, from the bushes springs the Bigfoot who grabs the man's penis and lifts him off the floor, ultimately leaving him to stumble with a blood-oozing groin stump back to his cycle, where he squirts a few drops of crimson urine on the chrome before dropping dead.

Night of the Demon was released uncut on the IFS label. The gore was unconvincing but rather graphic, and a warning identical to that of ***Night of the Bloody Apes*** appeared on the video sleeve. As the gory madness is all part of the film's strange appeal there would be little point in releasing a bowdlerised version.

Night of the Demon typifies the kind of complete obscurity that would never have seen the light of day in Britain if not for the momentary leeway afforded it by pre-certified videocassettes.

NIGHTMARE MAKER
TITLE ON PRINT: BUTCHER, BAKER, NIGHTMARE MAKER
AKA: Night Warning; Thrilled To Death
USA 1981
CAST: Jimmy McNichol, Susan Tyrrell, Bo Svenson, Marcia Lewis, Julia Duffy, Steve Eastin, Caskey Swaim, Britt Leach
STORY: Alan Jay Glueckman & Boon Collins
PRODUCER: Stephen Breimer
DIRECTOR: WILLIAM ASHER

NIGHTMARE MAKER

SYNOPSIS: A young couple on a mountain road discover that the brakes of their car don't work. After dodging some traffic at high-speed, they run into the back of a truck, sending one of the logs it is carrying straight through their windscreen and into the head of the driver. The car goes tumbling down the mountainside. Then it flips over a second, even greater precipice, before smashing flat at the bottom. Then it explodes.

Fourteen years later and the seventeen-year-old Billy — who everyone believes is the orphaned son of the couple killed so spectacularly — has grown up living with his Aunt Cheryl. Cheryl is protective to say the least. When Coach Landers suggests that Billy — his most promising pupil — ought to try for a scholarship when he leaves school, Cheryl is dead against the idea. "College is for rich kids and people with brains," she tells the lad, "you wouldn't fit in."

Cheryl wants Billy to stay with her… always. She sits contemplating out loud to herself ways to keep him at home.

Whilst Billy is at school, a TV repairman comes to the house and Cheryl makes a pass at him. When he rejects her advances, she stabs him to death with a kitchen knife. Billy returns home, finds the bloody scene and calls the police.

Cheryl claims that she stabbed the guy in self-defence after he tried to rape her. Lieutenant Joe Carlson isn't convinced. He notices that the "poor guy didn't even get his pecker out."

Carlson sees some inkling of the strange relationship between the woman and her nephew. But, upon discovering that Coach Landers is homosexual and years ago had a brief affair with the TV repairman, deduces that Billy too must be homosexual. He thinks that it was Billy who murdered the TV repairman following a lovers' quarrel.

"Are you a fag?" Carlson pressures Billy. The Lieutenant becomes completely obsessed with this notion, even badgering Julie — Billy's long-term girlfriend — as to whether they are "making it." She refuses to answer such a personal question. Carlson takes that to mean Billy's a fag.

One of the other men on the case — Sergeant Cook — starts to question Carlson's theory (primarily because he has caught a glimpse of Billy and Julie in the sack through a window), but the hot-headed Lieutenant will hear none of it. Cook turns up more clues, and believes that Billy's parents were murdered, the brakes on their car having shown signs of tampering. When Cook tells Carlson that he thinks Cheryl is guilty of the murder, and that an old boyfriend of hers from years ago is still officially missing, the Lieutenant tells the Sergeant to shut up and take a vacation.

Aunt Cheryl is nuts. She screams, mugs and wails almost incessantly. She also has a shrine to her "missing" boyfriend in the cellar. In reality, this missing boyfriend is Billy's father, and Cheryl his mother. Fearing that her sister and brother-in-law were about to take the illegitimate Billy away to allay a public scandal, Cheryl tampered with the brakes on their car and 'adopted' the child.[281]

The day of Billy's all-important basketball trial arrives. If he can impress the scouts who will be watching, he will undoubtedly get his scholarship. But Cheryl spikes his milk, causing him to collapse part-way through the game. He awakens in the new bedroom his aunt has fixed up for him in the attic, full of toys and teddy bears. She tells him that she doesn't want him to go back to school, on account of it being full of "perverts."

Billy finally appreciates that something is seriously amiss when he finds a box of news clippings and personal belongings that Cheryl has been hiding in her room. Julie tries to distract Cheryl as Billy snoops around his aunt's room, but Cheryl knocks the girl unconscious with a meat tenderiser and sticks her body in the cellar. When she recovers, she finds the head of Cheryl's old boyfriend pickled in a jar.

A storm brews outside.

Cheryl murders a suspicious neighbour with a machete, and hacks to death Sergeant Cook, who has arrived at the house looking for Julie.

Cradling Billy in her arms, Cheryl tells him "I'm your girlfriend, now!"

But the boy stabs her and telephones Coach Landers for help, just as Cheryl recovers enough to slash him with a knife. Billy runs her through with a poker.

The homophobic Carlson turns up as Landers is bent over Billy, administering First Aid. Despite Julie's pleas that Cheryl is responsible, Carlson is en-

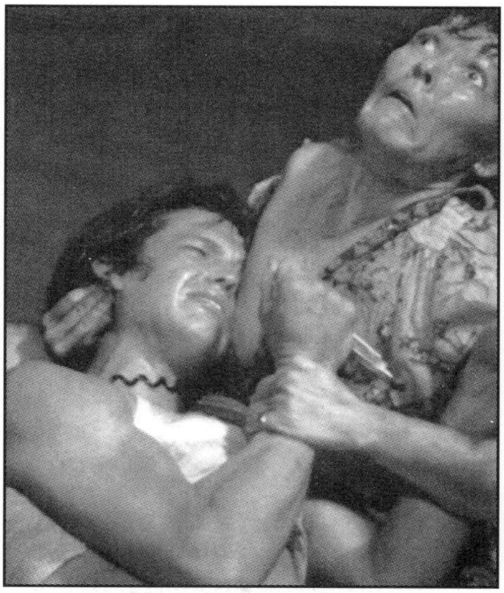

TOP: Susan Tyrrell emotes!

raged that a "fag" has murdered his Sergeant and slowly aims his gun. Billy fires first, however. A closing title relates that Billy stood trial for the slaying of Lieutenant Carlson, but was acquitted on the grounds of temporary insanity. He and Julie are said to be attending the University of Denver.

CRITIQUE: The outspoken Susan Tyrrell (who plays Aunt Cheryl) said of this film in an interview for *Psychotronic Video*: "I liked it because it gave me a chance to go berserk. I always like that, but I don't need a piece of shit movie to make me go berserk... It looks like it was written on the spot, it was a mess... I was trying to make it funny." [282]

Indeed, Tyrrell's performance as Aunt Cheryl is one of the more endearing aspects of *Nightmare Maker*. Her demeanour and facial expressions following the murder of the TV repairman and the final bloody assault are show-stopping. They *could* be called "funny" but not in the context that springs immediately to mind. Tyrrell takes her performance into a realm of *ultra-acting*, as if she is attempting to express multi-personalities in the same body, at the same time. In these scenes of transmutation, Tyrrell is recreating characters from another movie — hip to the fact that director Asher is attempting to emulate Brian de Palma's *Carrie*. Tyrrell stands motionless, drenched in blood, arms in a mannequin-lock, her face in ecstatic delirium — or a state of catatonia. Is she Sissy Spacek or Piper Laurie? No, she is both. Both at once.

Like *Carrie*, a mother's puritanical protectiveness toward her offspring lies at the heart of *Nightmare Maker*. Also like *Carrie*, Cheryl's house is adorned with religious iconography and holy pictures,[283] but Asher seems at a loss to make anything of it, outside of allowing mom to share in Lieutenant Carlson's vehement homophobia and come out with Biblical proclamations like "Do you know that homosexuals are very, very sick?"

(Lieutenant Carlson is a completely bewildering character. How did he manage to ever solve a case if his only detection constitutes whether or not a "fag" might be involved, ignoring any real evidence that might come to light? At one point he is shown interrogating a suspect with a gun pointing at their head, forcing them to sit on the floor of his office.)

William Asher is a competent enough director, having worked for many years on TV's *I Love Lucy* and created the hugely successful Beach Party cycle of movies for AIP in the sixties.[284] But *Nightmare Maker* was a unique departure into horror for him. Not surprising, then, that while it has some unorthodox and unpleasant elements, it carries all the hallmarks of a TV Movie of the Week — looking like a TV movie and starring faces familiar from TV.[285]

Nightmare Maker is a concerted effort to break out of type for Asher — an attempt to draw a cloud over "the longest summer on record," as he once referred to his Beach Party movies. Interestingly, an essential ingredient in the winning Beach Party formula was that they presented to the youth market an idealised, carefree vision of youth, one without the authoritarian shadow of parents looming over it; in effect, a direct reversal of *Nightmare Maker*.

It was announced in 1985 that *Nightmare Maker* was among a further four titles to be dropped by the DPP from the nasties list. It came too late for Atlantis, however, the label who had distributed the film — they had gone bust.

Nightmare Maker remains a banned title. Despite the DPP having dropped it, when Film View Video submitted it to the BBFC in 1987 under the title *The Evil Protégé* (a title that makes no sense at all in the context of the movie), it was refused a certificate and rejected outright.[286]

So where does the contention lie? Outside of the opening car accident, and its spectacular shot of a log knocking a head off its shoulders (repeated again in flashback), the film gets no more viscerally graphic than a hand being hacked off with an axe and several stabbings (through clothing). Also, Tyrrell does get drenched in blood while dressed in a low-cut top, possibly treading too finely the BBFC's concern about blood-on-breasts. But it's unlikely that any of these scenes in themselves posed a problem (they could, after all, be cut). Perhaps these factors together with *Nightmare Maker*'s theme of incest and anti-gay crusading proved problematic?

A quick word on Atlantis: They had one of the great, cheesy logos of the video boom. The word 'Atlantis' ripples up from the bottom of the screen, comes to rest in the middle and dematerialises by spinning slowly in fabulous, state-of-the-art, eighties pop promo fashion. And, in case you should miss it, the copyright warning on *Nightmare Maker* pops up twice before the main feature starts,[287] and once after it has ended.

NIGHTMARES IN A DAMAGED BRAIN

SYNOPSIS: George Tatum is having a listless night's sleep. He pulls back the blood-soaked sheets and finds a woman's decapitated head in his bed. Its eyes suddenly spring open. George awakes screaming — but for real this time — trussed up in a straightjacket, a patient in a hospital for the criminally insane.

THE FIRST NIGHT

FLORIDA

Kathy the babysitter is having trouble with the Temper children in her care. The two girls won't sleep because they believe someone is looking through the window. Kathy comforts them but later has a feeling herself of being watched. She goes outside to investigate and a shadowy figure on the roof of the house causes her to scream. The police can find no sign of an intruder, but the smirk on the face of C J Temper — a blond-haired rapscallion also in her care — suggests it was him playing a prank.

THE FIRST NIGHT

NEW YORK

George is under sedation but still having bad dreams. This time he's a smartly dressed child witnessing his mother and father engaged in a kinky sex game. The image breaks down with glimpses of blood spattering onto the walls.

A group of doctors observe that George's recurring nightmares are probably triggered by some childhood trauma that he refuses or is unable to divulge. Elsewhere, seated in front of a bank of TV monitors, a man with a cigar relates to somebody on the end of a phone line that George — a schizophrenic, suffering amnesia and seizures, responsible for the sexual mutilation and murder of a Brooklyn family — is now cured. The prognosis, which runs contrary to what the doctors have been witnessing in their patient, concludes with the officious-looking man stating that they've successfully "taken a dangerous psychotic and completely rebuilt him. Programming him for future government or private sector use will be our next step."

A free man again, George heads straight for a Times Square peepshow. In a private booth watching a woman masturbate, he suffers a violent and crippling flashback, collapsing to the floor with thick white foam pouring out his mouth.

NIGHTMARE'S IN A DAMAGED BRAIN
TITLE ON PRINT: SCAVOLINI'S NIGHTMARES IN A DAMAGED BRAIN
AKA: Nightmare; Dark Games (working title)
USA 1981
CAST: Baird Stafford, Sharon Smith, and introducing: C J Cooke, Mik Cribben, Danny Ronan, John Watkins
PRODUCER: John L Watkins
DIRECTOR: ROMANO SCAVOLINI

THE SECOND DAY

The doctor assigned to treat George is worried because his patient hasn't kept his appointment. Unbeknown to the doctor, George is miles away bound for Florida. When the car he's driving breaks down, George goes in search of another vehicle. This he acquires from a woman whose throat he cuts and belly he stabs. George apologises meekly to his victim, witnessing again the head-in-the-bed flashback.

THE THIRD DAY

Following another series of flashbacks, George presses on with his journey and ultimately arrives at his intended destination — the home of Temper family. He watches from across the street as the young C J empties the garbage. C J terrifies the rest of the family by covering himself in ketchup and pretending that the stranger he saw in the street has stabbed him.

Despite the anguish this prank causes, the boy is back to his old tricks with Kathy the babysitter that evening. As she's taking a shower, he sneaks up on her wearing a mask.

THE FOURTH DAY

"C J is not normal! He's evil!" an exasperated Kathy tells the boy's mother as she quits her babysitter job.

Looking at some Polaroids they have just taken, mom and her boyfriend Bob are alarmed by one print which shows a strange figure in an upstairs window of their house. They rush into the house to investigate but can find no one. Bob suggests it might be their imagination (even though he has the evidence of the photo in his hand). Unbeknownst to either of them, George is hiding in the house.

During a family picnic on the beach, C J spies George — the mysterious figure he saw loitering outside the house the previous day — but no one will believe him. Bob asks if C J ever heard of the "boy who cried wolf"?

In the middle of the night, mom gets an obscene phone call from a man who claims she's sleeping in his bed.

THE FIFTH DAY

"It's happened again!" George yells down the phone at his doctor. The doctor tries to comfort him but George collapses onto the floor with thick foam coming out of his mouth again. Later in the day he murders a young girl who is inexplicably drawn to investigate a derelict building after jogging at the side of a lake. A pal of C J's called Tony decides to follow the girl and frighten her, but after wandering around the darkened building he too meets an untimely end. That night the police and an ambulance crew turn up at the Temper household with Tony's body on a stretcher. A man wearing a tie who might or might not be a cop, shows C J the corpse and splutters accusingly, "You know him, dontcha?"

There is no mention of the dead girl.

THE FINAL DAY

The man with the cigar from the beginning of the picture believes he has picked up George's trail and heads off for Florida with the doctor.

George has crept back into the Temper household, and this time removes underwear from a drawer in mom's bedroom.

Mom has to go to an important business function with Bob and convinces Kathy to return one last time to baby-sit. With the kids asleep in bed, Kathy sits downstairs watching horror films on TV. Her boyfriend Joey sneaks into the house and the two of them make out. Afterwards, whilst Kathy is taking a shower, the killer dons the mask C J wore earlier and strangles Joey. He sinks an icepick into Kathy's back, fatally wounding her as she tries to call the police. Disturbed by the noise, C J is alerted to the masked intruder and helps his sisters out of the house to safety. The boy then takes a revolver from under the bed and pumps several bullets into the killer, but he won't stay down. The boy swaps the pistol for a rifle and plugs him again in the belly.

"C J, you don't understand," comes a sobbing voice from behind the mask, and George's fragmented dream unfolds in its entirety:

George as a child arrives home one day to hear strange noises from upstairs. He quietly makes his way to his parents' bedroom and spies his father tied to the bed and his mother straddled over him dressed in sexy underwear, slapping him across the face. Bewildered and upset, the young George gets an axe and kills them both. First he swings it at his mother's neck, causing a plume of blood to squirt from a massive wound. A second strike removes the head from her shoulders and it bounces to the floor. George hacks at the body several times before turning his attention to his bound and helpless father, bringing the axe down squarely on his forehead. From the wound blood pumps onto the sheet. George contemplates his bloodied self in the mirror as the time zone switches back to the present, with the adult George slumped at the bottom of the stairs of the Temper household.

When mom sees George's unmasked face she screams, *"It's my husband!"*

CRITIQUE: Some notoriety surrounds this film on both sides of the Atlantic, stemming in each

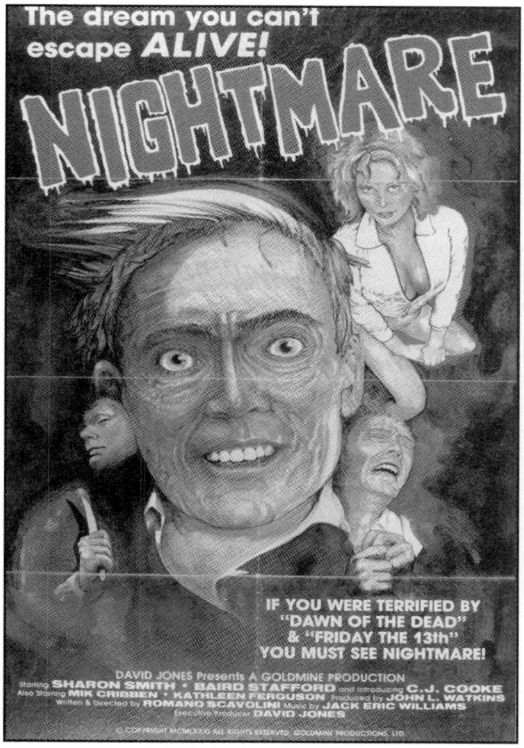

case from the special makeup effects. Though grisly by any definition, in Britain these effects were responsible for getting the film banned, while in the US the protest was of a more discriminating nature. Under its US title of — simply — *Nightmare*, the film accredited the makeup work to Tom Savini, whose imaginatively gory work had made him something of a star and box office draw in his own right. (See ***The Burning*** for further information.) To this day however, he denies having anything but the most superficial association with *Nightmare* and rejects outright the credit for its makeup effects.

When the film was first released, Savini's was the most prominent name in the advertising. He threatened to sue on the grounds that his only involvement was to offer advice in the decapitation sequence and nothing more. With this, his name was masked from posters with black tape and removed from the credits of the film playing across New York. (It reappeared at a later date.)

Romano Scavolini, the film's director, recollects that Savini was called in to supervise the prosthetics of effects man Lester Lorraine but featured in a much greater capacity once shooting got underway. He says Savini was very active in the film, in actual fact crucial to it, but claims he can understand — and even admires — Savini's resentment at the apparent exploitation of his name over that of a fellow technician.[288]

Alas, Scavolini has some exaggerated notions on the quality and influence of his own film, claiming in an interview in *Spaghetti Nightmares* that it remains "one of America's biggest cult movies" and that it's the only work by Savini that has been "a total success."

Naturally, such declarations are not shared by Savini, who thought the film "came and went" (which is a lot nearer to the truth). In an interview elsewhere in *Spaghetti Nightmares*,

Savini himself reflects

> They never hired me to do the film. So when I was in New York, I met Lester Lorraine and chatted with him about some of the effects and stuff, but I never actually worked on the film. Apart from that I'd only had a brief chat on the phone in the early days of the project when it was known as *Dark Games.*

However laudable Savini's reasons are for disassociating himself from *Nightmare*, he clearly did visit the set — as evidenced in a photograph reproduced in the book, in which the makeup maestro demonstratively holds the axe that chops the woman's head off in the recurring flashback scene.

In Britain, the video release of *Nightmares in a Damaged Brain* closely followed a theatrical run of the film, which had played with forty-eight seconds of cuts. Press screenings of the movie were shrouded in secrecy and came with a complementary vomit bag, a tired novelty that failed to win over any critics. Not even the title of the movie was made known until projection was underway.

Scavolini makes no pretence about the film being anything but an exercise to shock the audience with gore,[289] but claims that the theme of secret experiments on the mentally ill was a delicate issue and an embarrassment to the American government. This, he says, ultimately brought about the hostile reaction to the film.

The British video distributor sought to continue the decidedly tacky promotion evidenced in the press screenings with a stunt that was to backfire horribly. At a video trade show held in Manchester in May 1982, British distributors World of Video 2000 launched *Nightmares in a Damaged Brain* with a dealer competition: on their stand was the brain[290] of the film's lead character in a pickling jar — could you guess its weight and win £50? The company perceived this gimmick as so brilliant they chose to incorporate it into the sleeve design for the video — a composite that implies actor Baird Stafford (George) is in a jar with a brain as blood oozes out of his eyes. Whether the police that raided the roadshow and confiscated the exhibit were also a part of the gimmick is not known, but the tasteless prank reached the press and served only to aggravate the increasing dissent that horror videos were facing.

It is understood that World of Video 2000 pulled the same stunt for reporters outside a hospital in Surrey. Again the campaign concluded with police intervention.

Such promotional antics brought *Nightmares* to the attention of the DPP, who successfully prosecuted and helped to secure for it a place as one of the most notorious of the video nasties.

Following police raids in which videocassettes of the film were seized, three men and their parent company April Electronics, were charged with possessing obscene articles for publication and gain. They entered the special defence that *Nightmares* was "in the public good." Alas it took the jury five-and-a-half hours to decide it wasn't. (Having watched the film themselves earlier in the day, presumably the nine men and three women of the jury left the courtroom suitably depraved and corrupted by the experience.)

April Electronics went into liquidation. Company secretary David Hamilton-Grant, received an eighteen-month prison sentence of which twelve months were suspended.[291] Two colleagues — Malcolm Fancey and Roger Morley — got between them a suspended sentence and fines. (See also CLAMPDOWN.)

One issue raised in the trial was that the video print was "left unedited," unlike the theatrical print which had undergone cuts by the BBFC in order to attain an X-certificate. Compulsory video certification was a couple of years away at the time the tapes were confiscated in October 1982, so while the 'X' which also adorned the video sleeve may not have been wholly accurate, it needn't have been displayed at all. The forty-eight seconds difference between theatrical and video prints — which included a close-up shot of an icepick being buried in Kathy's back — obviously helped sway the jury. However, in hindsight, it serves only to illustrate the terrible ambiguity which allowed the law to be wielded almost at a whim, and the minefield that lay before British video companies.

Scavolini made many short films for Italian TV in the sixties before embarking on his first feature *A Mosca Cieca*, a controversial movie focusing on violence and the human condition. Scavolini claims even today the government allows him only to show it "privately to an audience of no more than fifteen people."[292]

After travelling extensively as a journalist and war photographer, Scavolini made several more movies and documentaries in Italy before settling in the US in 1976. Despite the infamy of *Nightmares*, he seems only to have directed one feature since — *Dogtags*, a grisly war film set within the Vietnam conflict, which utilises the framing device of its predecessor and is divided into 'days' ("The First Day," etc).

He denies that *Nightmares* was influenced by John Carpenter's *Halloween*, but it could be that Scavolini did derive some inspiration from Ulli Lommel's ***The Bogey Man*** of the previous year. Both movies feature grisly deaths which are precipitated by flashbacks to a young boy who murders a parent figure engaged in kinky sex.

There have been rumours that early in his career Scavolini had a hand in making hardcore porn movies. We have been unable to verify this information and one Italian source told us, "Nobody knows anything about this. I think if Scavolini did make some porn movies, he made them when he was working in the USA... It's not so easy to hide your name making porn here."

In all likelihood, these rumours probably have their origins in Scavolini's convincing portrayal of the sleazy peepshow sequences at the beginning of *Nightmares*, courtesy of some over-excited critics.

Nightmares in a Damaged Brain has a musical theme that sounds like an outtake from Pink Floyd's *Dark Side of the Moon*. It also features a brief shot before the end credits of C J in the back of a police car. Suddenly, rather disconcertingly, the boy winks at the camera. Scavolini claims that he shot six different endings for the film, each of which offered a different take on the relationship between George and the Temper family. Husband and father proved the most effective.

POSSESSION

SYNOPSIS: After a lengthy absence away on business, Marc returns to his Berlin home to find his wife Anna in a strange mood. When she telephones from "down town" one morning, in need of "time of think," he suspects she's having an affair and riffles through her belongings. Marc's suspicions are confirmed with the discovery of a postcard from a man named Heinrich.

Marc confronts his wife in the Café Einstein, and has to be physically restrained when he goes into a rage and attacks her. He spends the next three weeks alone in a hotel room, suffering some kind of breakdown. He looks terrible, is unable to speak, wanders the rooms aimlessly, shakes uncontrollably on the bed... until suddenly he gets up and returns home.

He uses the fact that Bob, their young son, has been left unsupervised to try and make peace with Anna, threatening to take custody of the child if she refuses to let him back into their lives.

With Anna claiming to have gone to visit her friend Marge, Marc gets a mysterious phone call from a man he suspects is Heinrich. "Anna is with me," says the stranger, "and she'll stay with me."

After dropping Bob off at school — and meeting Helen, a teacher who looks identical to Anna but with longer hair and different-coloured eyes — Marc goes to confront Heinrich.

The philosophical, well-spoken Heinrich is a touchy-feely kind of guy who shows no remorse, and even tells Marc that he has "reached a state of perfect harmony" with the man's wife. Concerning the recent mysterious phone call however, Heinrich is innocent.

Marc returns home and has a fight with Anna, slapping her across the face several times, following which she runs into the street with blood pouring from her mouth and causes a traffic accident.

She moves out of the flat, and on one of her occasional visits acknowledges to Marc that she is very happy. But her demeanour is even stranger these days, and she seems unable to communicate properly, ultimately cutting herself with an electric knife out of a sense of guilt or frustration. Marc reciprocates by cutting his own arm.

The Detective agency Marc has employed puts a man on Anna's tail, and he follows her to a deserted flat near the Berlin wall. The Detective gains access to the apartment by posing as a safety inspector. At first Anna is completely distraught by the intrusion but, unable to turn the man away, resigns herself to the fact he must die or her secret will be out. In the bathroom the Detective catches sight of a giant cocoon as Anna sinks a broken bottle repeatedly into his neck.

Heinrich calls on Marc with the intention of discussing "the redistribution of our paths in this fundamentally vulgar structure called the triangle." Having met Helen — Bob's school teacher — a second time, Marc is more at peace with himself and claims to be wiser.

"There is nothing to fear except God," says Heinrich. "Whatever that means to you."

"To me God is a disease," replies Marc.

The Detective agency is concerned that their man following Anna has failed to return. The boss (and lover) of the missing Detective goes to Anna's apartment to investigate, but is disorientated by the strange tentacled creature that he finds there. Anna shoots him with his own revolver.

Marc watches a home movie of his wife putting a class of young ballerinas through their paces. She is very firm with the children and reduces one girl to tears with an extended exercise that is sadistic and sexual. Anna trashes Marc's apartment. "I feel nothing for no one!" she yells at him. Later she agonises beneath a statue of Jesus in a church, and then suffers a prolonged and agonising 'spiritual miscarriage' in a deserted underpass, throwing herself into the walls and writhing on the floor.

When Marc deduces that he is no longer captivated by his wife, he telephones Heinrich and gives to him the address of her apartment.

Heinrich arrives with a bag of weed and tells Anna not to resist him. Catching sight of the creature — which has developed humanoid form — causes him to temporarily go blind however, and Heinrich stumbles into the kitchen where he discovers parts of Anna's previous victims. After she stabs him in the shoulder he manages to escape and call Marc, requesting that he comes to help him. Marc is elated by Heinrich's predicament and tells Bob "Mummy's calling me."

Leaving the boy in the care of their friend Marge, Marc finds Heinrich bleeding in the toilet of a bar, babbling one moment that he's at peace with himself, demanding the next that Marc sends him on a long trip to restore his harmony. Instead, Marc murders him and leaves him with his head down a toilet bowl.

Marc returns home to find Anna waiting. She fears that her own flat is no longer safe, and has cut Marge's throat because she tried to take "it" away from her. Marc understands and suggests they use the dead woman's home as a safehouse.

Leaving Bob in the care of Helen, Marc goes to the safehouse and is disturbed to find his wife having sex with the creature. He goes to console Heinrich's mother, who tells him she has identified her son's body, but his "soul wasn't there."

Watching a dead dog float down a river, Marc is visited by a former work associate who presses him to return to his post. "Our man won't confide or deal with your successor," the stranger says. "He wants you."

Marc declines and later finds that police cars are surrounding the safehouse. He causes a disturbance, allowing Anna to escape, but is badly wounded himself during the shootout that ensues. Losing blood and collapsing on a strange stairwell, he is surprised to see that Anna has found him. She is accompanied by the creature, whose transformation is "finished" and now looks just like Marc.

In an ironic twist, given that Anna finally has the perfect partner in the replicant, she is happy to die in Marc's arms when the police open fire from the foot of the stairwell.

The creature escapes.

The doorbell to Helen's apartment rings, but Bob doesn't want her to answer it and goes to hide. Through the frosted glass Helen sees the replicant-Marc, but she suffers some kind of panic attack and turns away.

POSSESSION
AKA: Night the Screaming Stops
FRANCE/WEST GERMANY 1981
CAST: Isabelle Adjani, Sam Neill, Margit Carstensen, Heinz Bennent
STORY: Andrzej Zulawski
PRODUCER: Marie-Laure Reyre
DIRECTOR: ANDRZEJ ZULAWSKI

VTC released *Possession* with two different video sleeves. The more common one (ABOVE) seemed to be printed 'back-to-front.'

CRITIQUE: *Possession* was never meant for the DPP list, an opinion shared by jurors who ruled that the scene where Anna makes love to the tentacle creature — "octopus sex" as it came to be known in the press — would be unlikely to deprave and corrupt. Viewed as a video nasty, the film is relatively blood-free and disconcertingly well-acted. Viewed on its own terms, without the ridiculous stigma that arose from its association with the DPP, *Possession* has a subversive quality that is more potent and unsettling than any scene of prosthetic carnage.

It goes without saying that *Possession* doesn't adhere to a strict linear narrative. Approaching it with a linear frame of mind will spoil the pickings to be had. For its British theatrical release in 1982, *Continental Film and Video Review* devoted considerable space to deciphering the film's mystical and symbolic reference points,[293] even noting that the original poster art closely paralleled *The Idol of Perversity*, a painting by Belgian Symbolist Jean Delville. (Arguably another of Delville's paintings, *The Treasures of Satan*, provides inspiration for the film's evolving tentacle-creature.)

But reading it as some kind of manifesto is perhaps as detrimental as not reading anything into the film at all. It isn't necessary to decipher *Possession* — it works best as a fever dream. Though director Zulawski isn't adverse to symbolism and subtexts, his use of them is as likely to be the antithesis of what critics believe the film to be actually saying. Though there appears some catechismal significance to the unfolding events, with Anna visiting a church, later declaring that God is in her and so forth, it comes to naught. (Or, if we prefer, is flipped on its head like a cosmic joke as the spiritually enlightened Heinrich — a sinister character but ultimately a comedic one — is led dick-first to his death in a public toilet "in a flood of shit.")

The more one tries to 'read' the film, the more infuriating it gets because while there are clearly symbolic and psychological properties at work, nothing is really being said; for all its colourful and labyrinthine facets, *Possession* is a love story at heart.

In an interview that appeared in *Eyeball*,[294] Zulawski stated that "cinema is eyes" and

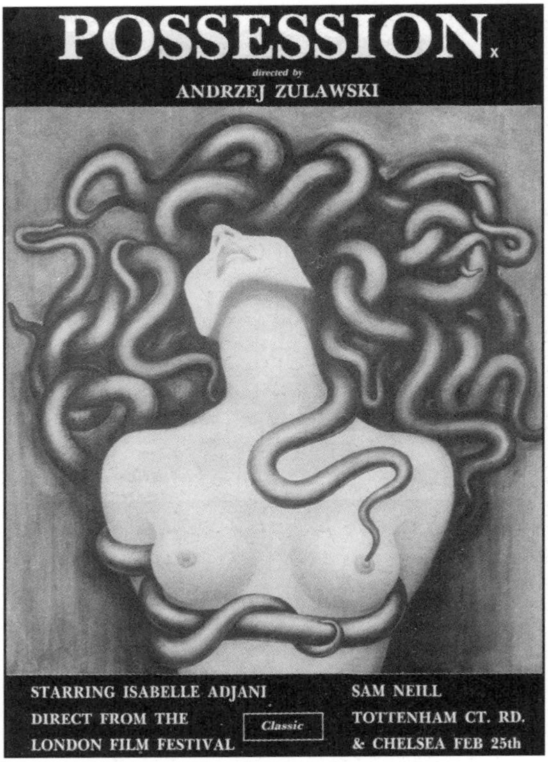

claimed it wasn't important for a director to impart a message. He declared *Possession* to be "essentially a very true-to-life autobiographical story," with much of its dialogue being transcribed from experience.[295] Naturally however, the creature — the aspect of the film that viewers find most problematic — isn't drawn from real events, but provides a fairy tale element to the story.

Said Zulawski in *Eyeball*:

> When I wrote *Possession* as a script I gave it to a dear friend who is a Polish critic... and said "tell me what you think." And he said to me "You should never show the monster, you should always guess," you know, a shadow or something, she goes in, you never see it because it is impossible... All right, but this is the reason I'm making the film! Because otherwise, write or tell it but don't film... Because this is cinema, and I will never hide, a door will never close at the right moment, a light will never go out. If you invent it, think it, then find a way to show it... otherwise do something else.[296]

Viewing the film as a fairy tale spares us from having to assemble the film into a coherent whole; it is better to accept that some pieces simply cannot be made to lock together. What, for instance, is to be made of the air raid sound at the film's end, which commences when Helen is unwittingly about to open the door to Marc's squirming doppelganger? Has war broken out (on account of Marc refusing to return to the job whose precise nature is never revealed, but seems to involve some political subterfuge)? Or is the very fabric of the film coming apart now that anti-Marc is at the door of Helen, the anti-Anna? If we opt for the latter we get a tidy inversion of the film's opening sequence, where the real Marc — "Coming up from the wars," as he puts it — returns home to the real Anna. ('Home' being Berlin, a city which Zulawski chose for the setting of *Possession* because he regarded it as an anonymous city, a nowhere place.)

This cyclic Yin-Yang duality element is at the heart of *Possession*: As Marc becomes progressively more 'balanced' over the course of the film, his wife degenerates. They die together and are reborn.

It is impossible to imagine *Possession* with anyone but Sam Neill in the role of the vexed husband, and the same can be said of Heinz Bennent as the cod-mystic Heinrich. They fall into their parts almost seamlessly. But unquestionably it is Isabelle Adjani who is the star of the film. She has an innocent, pre-Raphaelite look about her, with beautiful dark eyes that seem forever in search of something completely removed from this world. When the Detective arrives at her flat on the heels of his missing colleague, we understand why he should be frightened of this outwardly delicate creature going about her chores. In one scene of high emotional drama, she thinks nothing of deliberately pacing in front of a moving truck and causing it to crash (there is never any question that it might actually knock her over). Anna carries traits of both Marc and Heinrich, the rage of one and the mysticism of the other, producing an amorality all of her own. In a flashback which shows her tutoring a class of

Anna puts a ballerina through her paces. *Possession*.

young ballerina hopefuls, Anna is fixated by the shortcoming of one girl during exercises and demands that the student lift her leg higher. It isn't good enough — higher, higher! But it can never be good enough and it becomes apparent that the girl is merely an excuse for Anna's own failings. "That's why I'm with you," she tells the camera, "because you say 'I' for me."

The interpolation of a woman openly venting her sexual frustrations while systematically reducing a little girl to tears is certainly not a comfortable one, but Adjani goes even further physically and emotionally in a later scene...

It is perhaps *Possession*'s best remembered scene: Anna is travelling back to her flat with groceries when suddenly she breaks into laughter. As she makes her way through an underpass, the laughter switches to anguish and before long Anna is in the throes of a violent fit, hurling herself from one wall to the other. After several minutes in this volatile state she collapses to her knees, dry heaves until she is purple, and 'miscarries.' The ferocity and conviction of her performance in this sequence is gut-wrenching, and it's satisfying to know that *Possession* landed Adjani with the award for Best Actress at the Cannes Film Festival.

Zulawski has stated that he gives his actors trance exercises, little programmes that last several days. And it was because she was in one such trance, claims the director, Adjani was able to give such an intense performance, taking physical knocks without feeling any pain.

After seeing the film for the first time, Zulawski says that the actress locked herself in a bathroom and tried to commit suicide!

> But it's Adjani, it's not real. She committed suicide with a Gillette G2, you know, you can cut zero-zero-one millimetre of your skin with that, these twin blades... It was only to show she was suffering so much having seen herself and she said to me this memorable sentence. "You don't have the right to put the camera in this way because it looks inside one's soul" — and her soul is dark, I think, and she knows it.[297]

Possession exists in a number of different forms. The film was shot in English but there is a French language version (with Adjani dubbing her own character)[298] and numerous other prints of radically varying lengths. The original pre-certificate video version from VTC —

which landed on the DPP list — is complete at 118 minutes. When acquitted and re-released however, it suffered cuts.

Possession was issued again on video more recently by the newly formed Visual Film label, under a masthead proclaiming it to be "The Director's Cut."

In America, audiences got to see only a hideously truncated version when Limelight removed almost forty minutes from the film. Little wonder the reviewer for *Cinefantastique* was so scathing, not to mention presumptuous in writing that some of the cut material consisted of "shockingly explicit sex scenes." This is the kind of misinformed statement that breeds apocryphal tales, and one such legend has grown around the sequence in the underpass where Anna throws a fit. Several sources have erroneously stated that even at five minutes duration this sequence is truncated, that it originally ran for ten minutes.

Limelight did no for favours cutting the film for a Stateside release, but it faired even worse when Rugged Films picked it up in 1985. So that they could utilise a bunch of posters left over from Amando de Ossorio's *When the Screaming Stops*,[299] an earlier film the company had distributed, the company pasted the word 'Night' over 'When' on the posters and promoted *Possession* as *Night the Screaming Stops*. It mattered not a jot that the campaign bore no relation to the film itself. Rugged Films didn't even bother to remove the promise of a free vomit bag, a gimmick which had accompanied de Ossorio's modest chiller.

PRANKS
AKA: The Dorm that Dripped Blood; Death Dorm
USA 1981
CAST: Laurie Lapinski, Stephen Sachs, David Snow, Pamela Holland, Dennis Ely, Woody Roll
STORY: Stephen Carpenter, Jeffrey Obrow & Stacey Giachino
PRODUCER: Jeffrey Obrow
DIRECTORS: JEFF OBROW & STEPHEN CARPENTER

PRANKS

SYNOPSIS: A college dormitory is sold off for conversion into apartments, and five students — Joanne, Diana, Patricia, Brian and Craig — remain behind at the end of term to clear the building. Diana lets Joanne know that she won't be able to stay to help after all and her parents later arrive to take her home. Waiting for their daughter in the car, Diana's mother gets impatient and sends her husband to hurry the girl along. On the stairs he is confronted by someone wielding a spiked baseball bat and is beaten to death. The killer climbs into the back of the car and garrottes Diana's mother. When Diana finds her murdered parents she faints, only to have the killer drive the car over her head and then dispose of the bodies.

The following morning Patricia sees a dubious-looking man lurking by the waste bins. She reports his presence to Joanne who believes it to be John, a misfit resident who should no longer be in the building. The caretaker approaches Joanne and tells her that his power drill has gone missing — Joanne immediately suspects John and goes to his room to have a word, but he is not there. She then encounters a stranger standing by his truck, who introduces himself as Bobby Lee, bringing a cheque for some of the furniture being sold off. He tells her that he was around the buildings the other night and asks Joanne if she's staying alone.

That night, as the four students are playing pool, a figure appears at the window and terrifies Patricia. It is John and they decide to confront him, splitting into two groups to find him. They fail, although Craig admits to almost catching him. In the early hours Bobby Lee gives Joanne a call and arranges to have a drink with her.

Whilst having a wash, the caretaker is grabbed from behind and murdered with his missing power drill. Later Craig and Brian encounter misfit John near the trash dump. Craig goes after him and warns him to stay away.

That evening some food is stolen and Craig suspects John, going after him again. Joanne goes to get Brian, but while they are away someone wielding a spiked baseball bat smashes the dining table. Finding the damage Joanne calls the police and reports John, only to be told that they have just picked up a guy fitting his description.

Later that night Joanne hears someone prowling on the roof, following which both the phone and power are cut. Brian is attacked as he makes his way up the stairs to comfort Joanne and Patricia, and when he doesn't show, Craig suggests that he and Patricia should go and look for him. Attempting to fix the electricity supply, Craig is struck by an unseen assailant and Patricia is placed in an industrial pressure cooker.

Craig is relating to Joanne the story of how he came to be knocked unconscious, when suddenly they hear someone moving around outside — it is John carrying a machete. They make a run for it, but John attacks Craig and knocks him out before going after Joanne. She happens to find the dismembered body of Brian partially hidden in a room, before wounding John and giving him the slip. She bumps into Craig, who has recovered, and the pair once again encounter John. Craig wrestles with the misfit whom Joanne subsequently strikes and kills. Craig then confesses that he's the real murderer, and that John was really only trying to help her.

Craig takes Joanne around the basement showing her the numerous bodies. She escapes but is soon caught again. Bobby Lee, the man with the chequebook from earlier, arrives and hears the commotion. He rushes to the basement to help Joanne, but ends up in combat with Craig. Bobby Lee has the upper hand when the police arrive. Craig forces the innocent man to make a sudden move and the police, who have guns trained on the two men, shoot Bobby Lee dead. Craig tells the cops that there are more victims upstairs. While they go off to investigate Craig picks up the still-unconscious Joanne and pushes her into the incinerator.

A headful of steam. *Pranks*.

CRITIQUE: *Pranks* was initially conceived by a group of college pals who weren't particularly enamoured by the prospect of having to look for real work. They came up with a three-minute show reel with which they hoped to generate financial backing for a full-length feature and thereby launch their career in the movies (for directors Obrow and Carpenter it succeeded). Although the show reel generated interest, there appears to have been little elaboration in converting it to a fully fledged production and — despite the supposed three months it took to write — *Pranks* looks for all intent and purposes a vague idea padded out to eighty-plus minutes, the tedium of which certainly belies its humble origins. The film is utterly overlong, filled with uninteresting characters and is constructed around a dreary, clichéd plot.

"Why don't we split up and look for him?" is the kind of dullard dialogue that would have seemed contrived back in the 1940s, but which finds a place here.

Co-director Jeff Obrow told *Fangoria* that *Pranks* was "the type of film where the audience is constantly putting themselves in the place of the characters, wondering what they will do next." [300]

The men in the film are all presented as red herrings, while right up until the end the real killer is only ever depicted through the prowling menace of point-of-view camera angles — hardly ground-breaking or taxing. And what is the film's big *denouement*? That Craig's unrequited love for Joanne has pushed him over the edge into an indiscriminate killing spree.

The relentless music is an uninspired modification of the *Psycho* theme (as it's also the title theme, a sense of desperation permeates before the film has even got underway).

Although Diana and her father are murdered in a singularly unpleasant fashion — she has her head run over by a car and he is struck by a spiked baseball bat — these are portrayed either off-screen or in a blink-and-it's-over manner. The only scenes that could be considered 'nasty' are those in which a man has his hand split open with a knife (an unexplained pre-credit sequence that takes place during a party but is never referred to again), and the scene in which the caretaker has his head drilled. Although the latter does show the drill bit penetrating the skull, it again is very brief, cutting quickly away without elaboration or detail.[301] *Pranks* was eventually re-released with this scene removed.

By contrast, the film's ending — in which Joanne is stuffed into an incinerator — is unexpectedly downbeat and somewhat out of character of the rest of the film, as indeed it is the stalk-and-slash genre as a whole.

The directorial team of Obrow and Carpenter went on next to direct the markedly better *The Kindred*.

PRISONER OF THE CANNIBAL GOD
AKA: Mountain of the Cannibal God; Slave of the Cannibal God; La Montagna del dio Cannibale (original title); The Mountain in the Jungle; El dios de los Canibales
ITALY 1979
CAST: Ursula Andress, Stacy Keach, Claudio Cassinelli, Antonio Marsina, Franco Fantasia, Lanfranco Spinola, Carlo Longhi, Luigina Rocchi, Akushia Sellajaah, Dudley Wanaguru, T M Munna, M Suki
STORY: Cesare Frugoni & Sergio Martino
PRODUCER: Luciano Martino
DIRECTOR: SERGIO MARTINO

PRISONER OF THE CANNIBAL GOD

SYNOPSIS: Susan Stevenson arrives in New Guinea to discover what has happened to her husband, Henry, who failed to return from an unauthorised expedition to the Maraba region. The New Guinea government has failed to find any trace of Henry and offer no further help because of the underhand way in which the expedition was organised. The British ambassador suggests that she seek the assistance of American anthropologist Edward Foster.

The following day Susan and her brother Arthur visit Foster. He tells them that he knew Henry very well, was aware of his last expedition, but was surprised at how secretive he was about it. Foster suspects his destination was a sacred mountain in the Maraba region. Susan asks him if he will lead a search party into that area. "It's hard enough for a man but for a woman it would be nearly impossible," Foster remarks, but the offer of good money convinces him to undertake the task.

The police don't want anyone to go near the area (because of "the curse"), but an obliging helicopter pilot drops the group off as close to the sacred mountain as he is able. Foster, Susan and Arthur are assisted by a group of native helpers — one of whom, named Asaro, constantly eyes Susan. "Why does he look at me that strange way?" she asks. "Don't worry, he's shy," explains Foster.

Hacking their way through the undergrowth, Susan becomes entangled in the foliage and a tarantula creeps towards her. Foster hears her screams and kills the spider, but the natives believe this is a bad omen and so must perform a ritual which involves sacrificing an iguana and eating its raw innards. When a helicopter hovers overhead Foster instructs everyone to hide. Arthur attacks the natives for having lit a fire which could have attracted the attention of the helicopter. The team reach the coast the next day and use an inflatable boat to cross to the island. On the beach a knife is found which Susan recognises as belonging to her husband. They continue through the jungle and as night falls make camp, unaware they are being watched by masked natives.

The following morning the team discovers that Asaro is missing, but continue their journey to the sacred mountain. Crossing a river one helper is dragged to his death by a crocodile. Back on land another helper is lost in a brutal animal trap and the last helper runs away in panic. Foster and Arthur give chase leaving Susan alone, during which time she is confronted by a masked native but saved when another explorer named Manolo suddenly appears.

When Foster and Arthur return, Manolo takes the group to a nearby mission run by Father Moses, an old friend of Foster's. Foster believes the masked natives are members of the Puka, a tribe of cannibals. He relates the story of how he was captured by the Puka six years ago and was only allowed to survive because he treated a sick son of the tribe's elder.

At night one of the masked natives is seen in the mission grounds.

"Maybe you're still being chased by the ghosts of your cannibals," remarks Manolo.

"That's right," retorts Foster, "you don't forget the taste of human flesh."

Manolo is shocked to learn that Foster was forced to partake in a Puka flesh-eating ritual, and Foster admits to wanting to get back to the mountain in order to wipe out any remaining Puka.

In a hut Arthur is visited by a native girl, the new wife of the chief, unaware that her elderly husband is watching her. As they have sex a masked native creeps into the hut and kills the girl with a spear. Foster gives chase and kills the masked attacker following a confrontation that leaves him with a wounded leg. He discovers that the attacker was Asaro, and recounts to the others that Asaro was the boy from the Puka tribe he cured and with whom he managed to escape the cannibals. The others believe that Asaro was probably the last of the Puka.

When the chief of the tribe is found hanging from a tree Father Moses expels the group from the mission. The four head for the mountain and have to ascend a dangerous waterfall. Halfway up Foster finds himself in trouble, but Arthur refuses to help and Foster falls to his death. Furious with Arthur's behaviour Manolo almost turns back but is convinced to go on by Susan, and eventually they reach the base of the mountain. In a cave, Arthur gets excited about the readings on his Geiger counter. Susan admits that she and Arthur weren't looking for her husband at all, but were seeking the uranium deposits that Henry had set out to find.

Without warning the group is surrounded by Puka and Arthur is killed. The group is taken to a huge cavern in which the tribe lives. Fixed in a crude frame is the putrefying body of Henry Stevenson with a clicking Geiger counter in his chest cavity. The Puka believe him to be a god — the Geiger counter his living heart — and aware that Susan is his wife they prepare her for worship. The natives carve and devour Arthur's body, offering some of the flesh to Susan. She eats it regardless of Manolo's warnings. During the night Manolo is tormented by a dwarf but manages to kick him to the ground, splitting his skull open. Retrieving the dwarf's knife Manolo cuts himself free, rescues Susan and the two of them escape to the river and freedom.

CRITIQUE: Even the presence of Ursula Andress and Stacy Keach can't raise *Prisoner of the Cannibal God* above the status of mediocre adventure film. With the interminable edits of stock footage and borrowed scenes previously used in other cannibal films, the whole thing is a thoroughly dull viewing experience. As with most cannibal films the plot revolves around the greed of the civilised Caucasian invading and conflicting with primitive culture. The journey to the mountain is long and ponderous and the ascent of the waterfall itself seems to take forever.

The slow progress of the film is interrupted with brief moments of violence in which either a wild animal will be killed or a member of the exploration team will die violently. When Foster kills the spider that threatens Susan at the beginning of the journey, it comes as little surprise that the helpers determine a sacrifice is needed to redress the balance. They cut up a small lizard, skin it and eat it. As the helpers chomp on the offal, Foster reminds the disgusted onlookers that "It's part of their religion."

The final scenes in the cave show the Puka slowly disembowelling the corpse of Arthur, protracting the horrible image by removing his intestines slowly and deliberately, in the manner a magician might draw a string of silk scarves from a hat.

Although the excesses of *Prisoner of the Cannibal God* aren't quite as intense or as often as those featured in, say, ***Cannibal Holocaust*** — showing instead "the (relatively) lighter side of Italian cannibal picture," as noted in the *Delirium* guidebook — the film remains fairly typical of the genre. The killings progress through an evolutionary/racial perspective. First an insect is killed, then a reptile. Next a crocodile kills a black man, black men die at the hands of black men, white man kills black man in self-defence, white man dies from white man's negligence, and finally the 'ultimate' taboo: white man is killed and devoured by black men.

Sergio Martino — who, typically for a jobbing Italian director, has worked in genres as diverse as mondo, giallo thrillers and sex comedies — credits *Prisoner of the Cannibal God* with being one of his most successful films in the foreign markets (he followed it with the jungle-themed fantasies of *Island of Mutations* and *The Great Alligator*). The concept of a jungle adventure yarn with two name stars — predating the big-budget adventure heroics of Michael Douglas and Kathleen Turner in *Romancing the Stone* — certainly succeeded in drawing crowds that may not have otherwise cared to see exposed entrails and animal slaughter. *Screen International* were surprised to see an actor of Stacy Keach's stature partaking in such a gruesome venture, but determined that the rest of the cast toiled as hard, including

> Ursula Andress who leaps about on rocks, slogs up the mountain foothills, swims in the river, and strips down to the skin, as if *Dr No* had been filmed no more than a couple of years ago.

Hokushin released *Prisoner of the Cannibal God* on video carrying the BBFC X-certificate granted the film for its theatrical run in 1979 (when it was relatively well received by the *Monthly Film Bulletin*, who regarded it as being "executed with spirited authenticity"). The videoboxes were of the older cardboard slipcase variety, and a sticker — 'Video Movies' — obscured the wording 'Entertainment in Video with Hokushin,' presumably because Entertainment in Video was the name of a company in its own right.

It ought to be noted that the plane which screeches down the runway at the beginning of the picture, bringing Susan into New Guinea, is frozen abruptly so that a written introduction may enlighten viewers:

> New Guinea is perhaps the last region on Earth which still contains immense unexplored areas shrouded in mystery, where life has remained at its primordial level...

As if it was all an afterthought, the text promptly disappears and the plane continues with its noisy landing.

REVENGE OF THE BOGEY MAN

SYNOPSIS: Lacey arrives at the Hollywood Hills home of her old school chum Bonnie. Bonnie is married to Mickey, a European film director who's at loggerheads with his producer over his current movie.

That evening over dinner, Bonnie and Mickey ask Lacey about the murders in her home town and whether the killer has yet been apprehended. Lacey tells them the killer is a supernatural entity and proceeds to relate the whole sorry tale (flashbacks comprising of sequences lifted ad hoc from Ulli Lommel's original ***The Bogey Man***). The grisly tale commences with Lacey as a three-year-old infant witnessing the murder of their mother's abusive lover, and continues to the story of a girl who stabbed herself in the throat with a pair of scissors.

Joseph, a manservant in Bonnie and Mickey's household, takes an interest in the tale, as does the couple's young daughter who has come to listen at the door.

That night in bed, Bonnie and Mickey deduce Lacey has suffered some kind of breakdown.

"Bummer," Bonnie says, before hitting on the idea that Lacey's story would make a great movie. Mickey thinks they'd be exploiting her, but Bonnie reminds him that he needs a hit movie, that he can't keep making critically acclaimed films which no one pays to see.

Bonnie goes to comfort their daughter who has awoken in the night with nightmares about bogeymen. Meanwhile, Mickey walks into Lacey's bedroom in his night-gown and watches her remove a small box from beneath her pillow. Lacey explains that she keeps in the box "an Indian arrowhead that a medicine man from the Chinkatink tribe gave to me." She tells him about the good forces inherent in this and several other objects she pulls from the ornate case. Not so the last item however, which is a fragment of mirror that once possessed her. "Only I must touch it," she says of this. "Only I."

Joseph, the prowling manservant, has been listening at the door.

The following day by the pool, light reflected on the water causes Lacey to have another flashback. She is brought back to the present by the voices of Joseph and Bonnie's daughter. Bernie, Mickey's producer, is sat reading a copy of Kenneth Anger's *Hollywood Babylon*. Flipping to a picture of the Viennese director Erich von Stroheim, he recalls that Joseph worked for one of von Stroheim's stars. "When she died," he says of the manservant, "he had no place to go. Bonnie found him walking down the hill."

Bonnie throws a small party for Lacey. The guest list comprises "low-budget Hollywood types" whom she hopes will be able to make something of Lacey's story.

Joseph sneaks into Lacey's bedroom and takes the mirror shard from the box under her pillow.

Lacey is introduced to the guests and relates to them her story.

Bernie tries to convince Mickey that he should direct a film based on Lacey's story, but Mickey doesn't want to make a horror picture.

"If you don't do this film somebody else will," says the exasperated producer, "because it's *now*!"

Slowly, inevitably, the guests at the party pair off for a little fun, and it isn't long before the first young couple are being menaced by a set of garden implements. A spatter of blood on the ground denotes their rather ambiguous deaths.

Another couple, in the bathroom, are subjected to failing lights and vibrating toiletries, before death comes via toothbrush and shaving foam. In the carport, Bernie is dragged through the sunroof of his car by a length of hose and the girl to whom he was offering a film part looks for him under the vehicle. A stepladder knocks her mouth over the exhaust pipe, asphyxiating her when the engine starts. Another couple are killed in the kitchen by a pair of barbecue tongs and a corkscrew.

Having discovered some of the dead bodies, Lacey and Bonnie spy Joseph by the side of the pool with the mirror shard in his hand. Sensing he is behind the deaths, the two women drown the manservant just as Mickey arrives back at the house from someplace undisclosed.

Lacey claims to have remained immune to the mirror because she knew the secret of the evil force that inhabited it, but adds "it used Joseph and possessed him to seek revenge against those who wanted to exploit it."

Later, as Lacey tends to Joseph's grave, a gloved hand erupts through the earth and the mirror shard in its grasp causes the car Bonnie is waiting in to explode.

CRITIQUE: So much extraneous dialogue is spent on film-makers and film-making, one gets the impression *Revenge of the Bogeyman* has a forgotten subtext within its lame splatter façade. The movie opens with Mickey shooting topless scenes because producer Bernie wants to turn his proposed art-house movie into a film that'll make money. He also wants to change the title from *Natalie and the Age of Diminishing Expectations* to the more personable *Kiss and Tell*. "In America exploitation is a genre," Bernie impresses upon the "artsy fartsy" European director.

The two have much the same argument again later in the picture, when Bernie sees big screen potential in Lacey's story and believes it could open up a new kind of horror film. "*Halloween* and stuff like that is old hat," Bernie tells Mickey.

Even Bonnie wants her husband to turn to movies that'll make money.

This latent anti-Hollywood stance takes on a greater significance given that the part of "arty fartsy" Mickey is actually played by German director Ulli Lommel — who, moping around in a leather jacket is neither likeable nor a rebel, just a bit pathetic. Lommel directed the original ***Bogey Man*** but isn't credited as director on this follow-up — that's a dubious honour most sources bestow on one 'Bruce Starr.' In the British print at least,[302] Starr is actually credited only as Line Producer and no credit is given for a director at all (although a title card does proclaim *Revenge of the Bogeyman* to be "An Ulli Lommel Film").

Lommel is often regarded as a 'serious' filmmaker thanks to an early association with Fassbinder

REVENGE OF THE BOGEY MAN
TITLE ON PRINT: REVENGE OF THE BOOGEYMAN
USA 1982
CAST: Suzanna Love, Shannah Hall, Sholto von Douglas, John Carradine
STORY: [not credited]
EXEC PRODUCERS: David Dubay & Jochem Breitenstein
DIRECTOR: [NOT CREDITED; ULLI LOMMEL]

Trade ad for *The Bogey Man* (which also featured on the DPP list), a film from which much of the sequel was derived.

and a powerful directorial debut in *Tenderness of the Wolves*. Subsequent commercial success with ***The Bogey Man*** obviously weighed heavily on the director's artistic sensitivities however, manifesting itself in the strange Mickey character for the follow-up, through whom Lommel berates the very genre to which he is contributing.

Whoever Bruce Starr might be,[303] Lommel can't shirk all responsibility for *Revenge of the Bogeyman*. Footage from his original film constitutes an inordinately large amount of its running time, while plenty of the new material bears distinctive idiosyncratic traits. Furthermore, Suzanna Love — Lommel's wife until 1987 — once again appears in the starring role.

Trauma to the mouth is common to both films, while the preposterous death by electric toothbrush in *Revenge* — sadly, the film's highlight — is also replicated in Lommel's thriller of the subsequent year, *Double Jeopardy* (prompting one critic to ruminate whether the director has "an oral hygiene fetish").[304]

The most disappointing thing about *Revenge of the Bogeyman* is the pervasive sense of negligence. Despite the resources and evident talent to hand, no effort at all has been made, and it looks every inch like the filmmakers had their sights set firmly on their bank balance throughout its production. The fact that almost half the running time is padded with footage from the first movie is pretty indefensible, but *Revenge of the Bogeyman* constantly denigrates other films and genres to win kudos and propel itself to a position of chimerical superiority.

Midway through the picture, a guest encourages Mickey to take on the Lacey project, reasoning that "Brian de Palma spent $18 million on that bomb of his, *Blow Out*. You could make fifty movies for that."[305] The same guest then confesses to never personally watching horror films. Whatever significance the dialogue concerning de Palma may appear to hold,[306] it is turned on its head in the penultimate scene — the hand that reaches out from the grave is a direct lift from a de Palma movie (*Carrie*).[307]

A close-up on Mickey's face during *Revenge*'s farcical closing moments reveals not an expression of horror, shock or incredulity, but one of barely concealed boredom. It'd be reassuring to interpret these passages and dialogues as somehow indicative of the tired state of exploitation in general, but more likely Lommel really is bored.

Jokes are delivered with hopeless aplomb; battery operated toys jump suddenly to life for no better reason than to emulate similar scenes which proved effective in *Close Encounters of the Third Kind*; eerie lighting lends desperately needed 'mood' to periods of absolute static; and the fanfare that comes with Joseph being identified as the killer overlooks the fact his manservant white gloves have been in evidence every time a murder is committed.

Its association with the original ***Bogey Man*** is the only reason this travesty ended up on the DPP list. Unlike that first film however, *Revenge* is completely bereft of gore, and even the plentiful flashbacks to the gore scenes in ***Bogey Man*** have been removed.[308]

The two films were released by different video companies, at a time when certification was yet to be made compulsory. Presumably therefore, VTC — distributors of *Revenge of the Bogeyman* — were either sensitive to the rising backlash concerning violent videos and cut the film themselves, or acquired a heavily butchered US print.

After a ten year hiatus the series was resurrected with the direct-to-video *Boogey Man 3*. Lommel was producer.

SHOGUN ASSASSIN

SYNOPSIS: Lone Wolf, the Shogun's chief executioner, becomes so formidable that the Shogun decides he must be assassinated. Ninjas are sent to his home and maliciously kill his wife. Vowing revenge and clutching his infant son Daigoro in one hand, Lone Wolf wipes out several of the aged Shogun's men. He agrees to a duel with the Shogun's son for his freedom but, arranging the time and place, the Shogun ensures that his offspring will have the glare of the sun to his advantage. The two men race at each other with their swords, but at the moment of contact Lone Wolf ducks to reveal Daigoro strapped to his back — on his forehead is a mirror that reflects the sunlight back at the Shogun's son. Lone Wolf decapitates his blinded foe.

Later the Shogun sends his men to kill Daigoro, pointing out that the deal only included the sparing of Lone Wolf's life and not that of his son. Lone Wolf cuts down the men and kills another of the Shogun's sons during the battle, leaving the scene pushing Daigoro along in his wooden pram. Lone Wolf's reputation soon spreads and he is asked by a group of peasants to assassinate the evil brother of the Shogun who is about to return to the territory. He accepts the task and goes in pursuit of the Lord but he is forewarned about the three men who escort him — the Masters of Death.

The Shogun's men recruit a band of female ninjas to seek and kill Lone Wolf. Posing as peasants they attack Lone Wolf, but he fights them off killing all except the leader — "the Supreme Ninja" — who manages to escape. Later Lone Wolf is attacked in a forest by an armed gang but he manages to destroy them all. The Supreme Ninja returns to the Shogun's men and together they deduce that Lone Wolf's power must come from the child — if the child were separated from him he would be easy to kill.

Travelling one night, Lone Wolf becomes ill and has to take shelter in a hut. Daigoro takes care of him but is lured out of the hut when he hears singing. It is the female ninja accompanied by several of the Shogun's men. Lone Wolf recovers to find Daigoro suspended above a well, and is told the child will die if he doesn't surrender. "Kill him if you dare," threatens Lone Wolf, "it won't weaken me." Lone Wolf tells his son to prepare to meet his mother and then attacks the men, stepping on the rope to which Daigoro is attached and halting his descent into the well. Killing his attackers he hoists the boy out of the hole unharmed. The Supreme Ninja is left untouched because she resembles Lone Wolf's murdered wife.

Still awaiting an opportunity to assassinate him, the Supreme Ninja follows Lone Wolf onto a ship. Here they encounter the Masters of Death, bodyguards of the Lord that Lone Wolf has been paid

SHOGUN ASSASSIN
USA 1980
CAST: Tomisaburo Wakayama, Kayo Matsuo, Minoru Ohki, Shoji Kohayashi, Shin Kishida
SCREENPLAY: Kazuo Koike, Robert Houston & David Weisman
PRODUCER: David Weisman
DIRECTOR: ROBERT HOUSTON
[*Shogun Assassin* is a composite of two episodes in the Japanese 'Baby Cart' series of films directed by Kenji Misumi in the early seventies.]

"When I was little, my father was famous..."
Lone Wolf and son. *Shogun Assassin*.

to assassinate. A group of rebels attack the all-powerful Masters but are soon slaughtered. When a fire breaks out, Lone Wolf jumps into the sea with his son and swims for shore, along the way disarming the ninja as she tries to kill him. All three spend the night in a hut huddled together to keep from freezing to death.

The next day the Supreme Ninja chooses not to kill Lone Wolf and returns to the Shogun.

Escorting the Shogun's brother across a stretch of desert, the Masters of Death thwart a rebel ambush and kill all the attackers. They resume their march before falling in a battle with Lone Wolf — who then finishes off the guards and kills the Lord, thus completing his task. Father and son wander off into the desert.

CRITIQUE: *Shogun Assassin* opens with the voiceover narration of Lone Wolf's infant child: "When I was little, my father was famous. He was the greatest samurai in the Empire."

With these innocent words there commences one extraordinary bloodbath that for eighty-five minutes rarely lets up.

"He was the Shogun's decapitator," Daigoro continues. "He cut off the heads of a 131 Lords... for the Shogun."

The renegade Lone Wolf speaks very little. Following the murder of his wife and the subsequent double-dealing by the decrepit, evil Shogun, he has become something of a demon spirit wandering the highways of sixteenth-century Japan with his infant. "He became an assassin who walks the road of vengeance," says the boy, "and he took me with him." Lone Wolf easily demolishes those who stand in his way with a few deft strokes of his powerful sword (so deft and powerful in fact that when he chops at a foe, he cuts them virtually clean in two, along with anything else that happens to be in the way). Lone Wolf plunges his sword through necks, breaks the swords of others in battle, and even manages to hurl his sword into opponents.

The bloodletting is stylish to the point of being beautiful. Decapitations and limb-hackings are followed by a momentary stillness, where both victor and victim stand motionless – until a crimson gush from the horrific wound engages the action once again and the victim collapses to the ground. It is as if Lone Wolf's retribution is so swift the victim needs time to contemplate and recognise his own demise – his mind and automatic reflexes momentarily frozen (possibly space and time, too). In his battle with the Masters of Death, when Lone Wolf swings his sword into the head of one opponent, logic and the law of physics are caught unaware. The victim stands bolt upright, and long moments pass before eventually his straw hat falls away in half and his head slowly, unnaturally, splits asunder. A stream of blood flies into the air for several feet to provide the tableau with its finishing touch.

In another memorable sequence, the female ninjas prove their mettle and skill by pitting themselves against the best fighter their male counterparts can offer. In what is a very lopsided exercise (several against one), the male ninja is told to try to leave the room, but is brought down and mercilessly hacked to pieces by the women as he attempts to carry out the task. His facial features are sliced away, then his limbs, leaving the man a raw bloody stump.

Not only does *Shogun Assassin* have episodes of wild exaggerated violence, it also has moments of poignancy – in particular the time when Daigoro tries to carry water to his father who has fallen ill. Each trip to the river yields nothing as the water spills from the infant's tiny cupped hands. Finally he brings the water in his mouth and dribbles it onto his father's lips. Another poignant moment in the film may have caused offence in the more brittle minded. Following the sinking of the ship on which they're travelling, Daigoro sits between his naked father and the ninja woman as they try to keep warm. The boy looks from his father's chest to her breasts, then brushes her nipple with his hand causing it to become erect.

The film's drive is augmented by the voiceover narration of the infant (in actual fact the voice of comedienne/actress Sandra Bernhard – a remarkable performance that has fooled fans and critics alike into thinking a genuine non-actor child was utilised). Stumbling over his words, his childish observations provide a brilliant and touching counterpoint to the mayhem being unleashed. A fairy tale quality is established in the opening moments when Daigoro tells of the senile Shogun, for whom his father had once worked. The Shogun locked himself away because he believed his people were conspiring against him. "People said he had a lot of enemies," relates Daigoro, "but he killed more people than that."

The boy even has a few fighting tricks of his own, and pats various sensitive parts of his wooden cart to unleash a multitude of deadly blades.[309]

The idea of a young child in the company of a professional assassin, and being exposed to violence and death, was further explored in Jean Luc Besson's *Léon* which, in some respects, could be considered a remake of *Shogun Assassin*. John Carpenter took the Masters of Death idea – assassins who, respectively, utilise a spiked club, a studded glove and a claw – and recreated them as the Three Storms in his own *Big Trouble in Little China*.

Shogun Assassin is constructed from two episodes of the cult Japanese 'Baby Cart' series of films (of which there were six) – namely *Sword of Vengeance* and *Baby Cart at the River Styx*.[310] It works very well as a seamless composite, and indeed is better than the source material in some respects. For a start, it removes much expositional dialogue and concentrates almost exclusively on an action-packed narrative (the English language dialogue was written specifically to match the lips of the characters on-screen). Neither do the original films have Daigoro's voiceovers.[311]

Not much of the bloodletting in the two original Japanese films failed to make the transition to *Shogun Assassin* (a title, incidentally, intended to cash-in on the *Shogun* TV mini-series). Conspicuous by its absence however, is a shot of Lone Wolf slicing through the breasts and nipple of an attacking female ninja assassin – a fight sequence which otherwise makes the transition from the original Japanese source to *Shogun Assassin* intact.

Shogun Assassin is so awash with blood that no single scene can be responsible for its banned status. However this welter of spectacularly choreographed violence was soon dropped from the DPP list and the film subsequently re-released. (The two source films from which *Shogun Assassin* was constructed have also recently been made available in Britain.)

THE SLAYER

SYNOPSIS: "I was having that nightmare again," Kay tells David, her husband. "Something was after me."

David convinces Kay they ought to take a vacation, and so they set off to a secluded island with Kay's brother Eric and his wife Brooke. The only route to the wind swept, out-of-season resort is via a private plane. On landing, Kay tells the pilot, Mr Marsh, that she has dreamt of this place before. She isn't the first, he tells her.

On the trek across the island to their accommodation, Kay spots a derelict building that looks identical to one in a painting of hers.

Once settled in their holiday home, Mr Marsh turns up at the door.

"I came back to warn you," he says, apprehensively. "There's a storm moving up from the gulf."

But it's not just the storm he's trying to warn them about.

An old man sits on the beach gutting fishes, lamenting on how he's spending too much time alone on the islands. A shadow looms over him and someone or something smashes in his head with an oar. Could it be another one of Kay's dreams? According to David, Kay is building a "wall of depression" around her and he thinks she's slipping over the edge. She tells him that she's afraid she'll fall asleep and awaken to find her life has been replaced by a dream.

The storm arrives.

In the night, David hears strange noises coming from the cellar and goes to investigate. The sounds seems to emanate from a overhead hatch leading to an elevator shaft. He climbs up, sticks his head through the opening, and gets it caught. The stepladders fall away and he is left hanging by the neck. His legs give a couple of death twitches.

Kay dreams that she is kissing David's decapitated head. When she awakens, she tells Eric and Brooke that her husband is dead. They spend the day searching for him without success. The next morning, Kay goes to a derelict theatre and discovers David's headless body hanging upside down.

THE SLAYER
AKA: Nightmare Island (working title)
USA 1981
CAST: Sarah Kendall, Frederick Flynn, Carol Kottenbrook, Alam McRae, Michael Holmes
STORY: J S Cardone & William R Ewing
PRODUCER: William R Ewing
DIRECTOR: J S CARDONE

Back at the house, Eric fires a distress flare.

That night, Kay drinks masses of coffee in order to try and stay awake. She believes that if she falls asleep they'll all be killed. She tells the others that she has seen the killer in her dreams — the same dream she's had since a child — and that soon the killer won't need her or her dreams to exist.

Eric and Brooke slip her a sedative.

"What if everything Kay's said is true?" ponders Brooke later.

On the assumption that they haven't actually seen him leave the island, Eric goes in search of Mr Marsh, the pilot. With his flashlight, Eric looks around an old boathouse. A shadow moves across the window, followed by the sound of creaking doors. Eric is killed with a fishing rod that hooks him in the throat and reels him out to sea.

Worried, Brooke goes out looking for her husband. She too finds the old boathouse, before being attacked and run through with a pitchfork.

The following morning Kay finds the bodies. "Stay awake... Stay awake..." she says out loud, barricading herself in the house.

Night falls, and the storm comes again.

Kay tries to fight sleep with more coffee and by stubbing cigarettes out in the palm of her hand.

The power fails and the lights go out. Kay stabs a hand that reaches towards her. It turns out to belong to Mr Marsh, who she accidentally kills with a flare and manages to set fire to the house.

Framed in the doorway of the house is a stupid-looking monster. Kay screams — only to awaken as a little girl in her parents' house. The whole story has been a premonition dream...

CRITIQUE: A dream world that infringes on reality, with a killer who is able to transgress the boundaries of sleep. That's the fascinating concept of J S Cardone's *The Slayer*. So fascinating a concept in fact, that Wes Craven adopted it for his own *A Nightmare on Elm Street* two years later. Unlike Cardone's film however, *Elm Street* proved to be a huge success.

The dream sequence that opens *The Slayer* is subtle and effective, with Kay's pallid face peering, wide-eyed from a black backdrop. Cutting between open doorways and a swinging pendulum, the whole sequence is reminiscent of German Expressionist cinema and, unfortunately, offers a calibre of production that the rest of the film struggles vainly to maintain. Cardone fails to fully exploit the potential of *The Slayer* and instead relegates the idea of a deadly dream state to the back burner for most of the running time. The film plays more as a stalk-and-slash movie tinged with an element of the supernatural, and adhering to a tradition of obvious clichés and scare tactics (with an inordinate number of doors creaking and shutters banging throughout the duration). It also features the usual stock of tired characters who insist on the group 'splitting up' so that they may go searching for missing companions on their own (and are gone, it seems, for stretches of several days at a time – in lieu of anything better the plot has to offer). *The Slayer* doesn't really bother to explore the more interesting avenues promised by Kay's predicament until the very end of the picture, by which time it's late enough to qualify as a twist ending. (Kay waking up as a little girl, only to discover that her dream is a reality yet to happen, is a pretty good twist nonetheless.)

The characters in *The Slayer* – like the stalk-and-slash sub-genre in general – serve only to be slaughtered in a variety of graphic and disagreeable ways. The first character to be murdered, the fisherman on the beach who gets an oar smashed across his head, has no bearing whatsoever on the story. No one is aware of his presence. No one finds the body. The guy just sits on the beach – of a supposedly deserted island[312] – gutting fishes. The entirety of his screen time comprises the moment of his effectively rendered death. But it's interesting how his gutting of real fish plies the scene with an expectation of a demise far worse than a mere oar across the head. If nothing else, his brief presence lends the film and subsequent murders an *attitude*.

The simplicity of the fisherman's death is amply made up for in the series of orchestrated deaths which follow. Indeed, David's demise is particularly contrived and convoluting. After an eternity of following a noise around the house, David finds himself in the cellar, standing under a trapdoor that leads to an elevator shaft. A pair of stepladders enables him to access the shaft, whereupon David gets his head caught, loses balance on the stepladders and hangs himself.

But it is Brooke's murder that is the most salacious and explicit,[313] and the one sequence cut on the film's re-release by Vipco in the nineties.[314] Searching the boathouse for her husband (and appearing to find something significant in the name of a boat she sees there), Brooke is frightened by an unseen assailant. She attempts to escape through a boarded window, but is impaled on a pitchfork which is seen penetrating her back and exiting through her chest. The murder – which culminates with the fork prongs jutting out from the woman's bosom – treads an area of sexual violence that the BBFC abhors. With Brooke's nipples clearly visible through her blood-soaked frock the sequence becomes totally unacceptable.

Following *The Slayer*, Cardone went on to direct other films with themes concerning dream states and shifting realities (*Shadowzone* and *Shadow Hunter*). A downside to this of course is that dream realities also provide the perfect opportunity to squander the plot on red herrings, and a story line which never needs to fully be resolved.

The Slayer was released by Continental video in the US on a double-bill with Fred Olen Ray's *Scalps*. Canadian author L A Morse in his book *Video Trash & Treasures* recalls that Cardone's name had been removed from some video versions of *The Slayer*.

SNUFF

SYNOPSIS: In a run-down factory complex appropriated by a band of hippies as their home, a girl is challenged for being a "greedy bitch." Under the command of their leader, Satán, the hippies torture her with a knife.

Satán is a guru figure to his all-girl followers, who hang on every word he says and even kill under his command. When Terri London, a porno actress, flies into Buenos Aires, a convoluting chain of circumstances allows Satán to mix in elite social circles.

Unbeknown to her doting producer, Terri London rekindles a love affair with Horst, a millionaire living with his father. In turn, Horst dumps his long-standing girlfriend Angelica, who goes to seek solace in Satán. He tells the girl, "You do not know yet the way we live."

At a carnival, Terri slips away and has sex with Horst, while her producer friend is kept occupied by Angelica dancing on his table. As Terri reaches a climax, Angelica stabs the producer through the heart.

Terri is called in for questioning about the murder, and is interviewed by a Detective who conducts his investigation from a desk in the open air outside a barn.

Horst collects Terri from the police-barn and takes her to meet his father — a lecherous old man who claims to sell munitions to the Germans. "Surely you don't find that shocking?!" the old man snaps at an altogether indifferent Terri.

Satán and Angelica show up at the mansion, and quickly get thrown out again when they advocate killing rich people to avenge the sufferings of the poor.

Back at the factory hideaway, Satán initiates Angelica into his band of female followers. While the rest of the girls are out robbing a provisions store, he tells the new initiate, "I demand more than anyone else could. How can you call that freedom?"

"It's what I want," Angelica replies, and has a flashback to her troubled childhood.

Shortly afterwards, Satán determines that now "the time has come for slaughter!" and orders his followers to attack the Horst mansion. The girls steal their way into the grounds while a drunken orgy is in progress, and kill everyone in sight. Horst himself is tied to a tree and castrated. The assassins make their way through the mansion, and find a sleeping, heavily pregnant Terri London in bed with Horst's lecherous father. The old man, begging for his life, is shot dead. Terri, pinned to the bed, pleads of the demented Angelica, "What good does it do to torment me like this?"

"No good," Angelica snaps back and plunges the knife into the pregnant belly.

With Terri's scream, a voice off-camera yells "CUT!" and the scene cuts away to reveal a studio set. It's a rather unconvincing representation of the Horst bedroom in long-shot, and there are actors and actresses wandering around, supposedly those of the previous scene but obviously not the same people. Surrounding them are the trappings of a film studio. A boorish director confides to a pretty production assistant, "That was a gory scene and it really turned me on."

She confesses, "It turned me on."

The director convinces the girl that everyone else will soon be gone, and they ought to get on the bed and "turn each other on."

The other people in the room don't leave, however, and slowly turn their attentions toward the couple on the bed, filming them. Startled by this realisation, the girl struggles to free herself from the director's grip.

"Do all of you wanna get a good scene?" the director hollers at his crew, calling for assistance in holding down the girl. His hands now free, the director reaches for 'Angelica's' knife from the last scene, and slices across the girl's shoulder. Blood the colour of raspberry pours from the wound. The director encourages the girl to scream, taking from his back pocket a pair of pliers and cutting off one of her fingers. He then uses an electric saw to remove a hand at the wrist. The girl's soft moans fall silent when the director cuts into her stomach with a knife, drawing effortlessly down to her geni-

THE ORIGINAL LEGENDARY ATROCITY
SHOT AND BANNED IN NEW YORK
SNUFF
THE ACTORS AND ACTRESSES WHO DEDICATED
THEIR LIVES TO MAKING THIS FILM WERE
NEVER SEEN OR HEARD FROM AGAIN.

SNUFF
AKA: Slaughter (original title); American Cannibale
ARGENTINA/USA 1971/76
CAST: [not credited]
STORY: [not credited]
PRODUCERS: [not credited; Michael Findlay & Jack Frost]
DIRECTOR: [NOT CREDITED; MICHAEL FINDLAY & CARTER STEVENS]

talia. The thumping of a heartbeat swells onto the soundtrack. The director sinks his hand into the wound and the posthumous fist-fuck delivers a handful of entrails. Muttering to himself, he slips his hand in for more, reaching deeper and pulling out the girl's heart. Dipping his hand in a third time, he ecstatically throws his bloody catch of entrails into the air. Freeze frame. The film runs into leader-tape and then blackness. A voice whispers, "Shit, shit… we ran out of film."

A second voice asks, "Did you get it? Did you get it all?"

"Yeah, we got it all."

"Let's get outa here."

The sound of breathing. Ends.

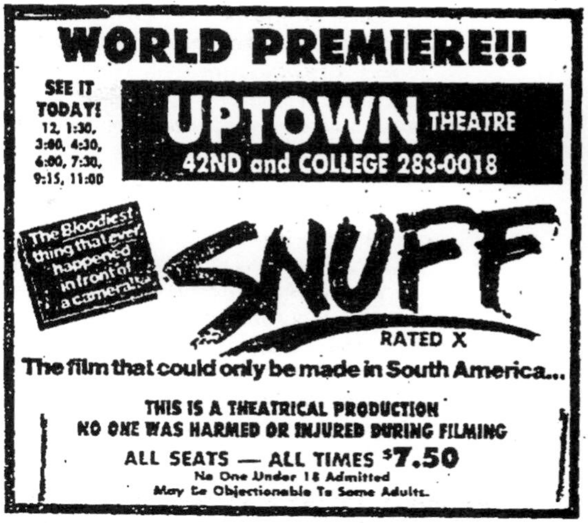

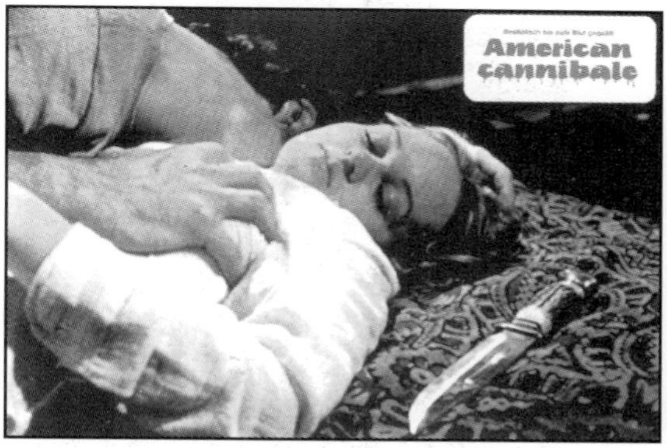

ABOVE: Prelude to 'murder': tacked on footage at the end of *Snuff* (under its German title).

CRITIQUE: "The original nasty" — is how *The Sunday Times* described *Snuff* back in November 1982. The ending of the film tries to motivate the viewer into believing they are privy to some great conspiratorial secret; that these last five minutes offer a fleeting glimpse of something so abhorrent it can only be referred to in breathless, hushed tones.

Jerky, *cinéma-vérité* camerawork is a technique often used to create a sense of urgency and 'heightened reality' from staged scenes. Mondo documentary film-makers,[315] and indeed the makers of *Snuff*, used it to fool viewers into thinking that what they were witnessing was a document of fact.

At the turn of the century, pulp horror writers like H P Lovecraft often presented tales in the form of a forgotten manuscript or diary that had fallen into the hands of the narrator. As the story unfolded, the incredulous narrator would slowly come to terms with the lurking horror that the script invariably spoke of — until, too late, the evil would be at his very door, bashing it down. The stories were presented as a 'warning' to the rest of mankind.

In this instance 'snuff films' are the 'lurking horror' — human sacrifices perpetrated for the benefit of a film camera, supposedly circulated as entertainment to those people becoming increasingly jaded by conventional pornography.[316]

These films were said to be distributed via underground networks and were difficult to locate. *Snuff* purported to be a rare insight into this hitherto hidden cinema and 'clued' audiences in with an ambiguous advertising campaign that promised

The film that could only be made in South America… Where Life is *CHEAP!*

The Bloodiest thing that ever happened in front of a camera!

No one who actually sat through the ridiculous 'snuff' footage however, was liable to be fooled into thinking it was anything but a combination of cheap prosthetic effects and animal innards. Still, after having endured seventy interminable minutes of plodding direction and Satán's pontifications, this impromptu tagged-on ending came as a blessed relief (signalling the end of the film if nothing else).

Snuff started out as a cash-in on the media furore surrounding the Tate/LaBianca slayings for which Charles Manson and members of his hippie followers were being charged. It was filmed in 1971 in Argentina under the title of *Slaughter*, by the husband-and-wife team Michael and Roberta Findlay.[317] In Argentina, the Findlays were able to hire a film crew for just $60 a week, and complete the film in four weeks at a total cost of $30,000.[318] (Maybe not for the reason insinuated in the film's advertising, but the film really was "made in South America... where Life is *CHEAP!*") Sound was dubbed in later, partly because many of the players spoke no English — which is why some conversations and reactions in the film seem stilted.

The Findlays weren't particularly concerned about coming up with an original story of their own and so shot *Slaughter* as a virtual reconstruction of the most sensational aspect of the Manson Family case — that of the attack on the home of Roman Polanski and the murder of Polanski's actress wife, Sharon Tate. Eight-and-a-half months pregnant, Tate was stabbed a total of sixteen times and left to die. Several guests were also murdered.

Though it was one of the first films to exploit hippie cult hysteria,[319] *Slaughter* never got released. It was simply too awful a film for distributors to risk investing in.[320] Eventually, Allan Shackleton of the Monarch Releasing Corporation picked it up, but kept it shelved until 1976.[321] Originally, the film didn't include the behind-the-scenes cutaway which supposedly featured the on-camera murder of a crew member. This was something Shackleton himself formulated.

Roberta Findlay recollected in an interview in *CCVL*,[322] that in the mid-seventies rumours of so-called snuff films began to circulate. "I don't know that they ever existed," Findlay said. "Maybe they did, maybe they didn't. Shackleton was reading the paper and said, 'Hey, that's a great idea, that's what I'll call the film.' And that's what he did."

In actual fact there is every possibility that the newspaper reports featured in the *New York Post* dated October 2, 1975, and the *Daily News* the following day, originated from Shackleton himself. Both articles speak of a film rumoured to have been made in Argentina in which a woman is stabbed. The New York Detective who is quoted in both newspapers as saying that such films were the ultimate obscenity and available through underworld sources, later told the FBI that he had never even heard of snuff films before the reporter from the *New York Post* got in touch.

Starting the whole ball rolling, however, was the *National Decency Reporter*, the Newsletter of Citizens for Decency through Law, Inc. In their edition dated November-December 1974, an article entitled 'Perversion for Profit' claimed that young people were on a slippery slope. "Just as the liquor industry depends on alcoholics," stated the anonymous writer of the piece, "the sexual pervert constitutes pornography's major market." Moreover, as many as twenty-five snuff films were said to have been in current circulation, and they claimed that the only defence was "for an outraged citizenry to *demand* strict enforcement of obscenity laws."[323] (See also APPENDIX III.)

Shackleton changed the title of the film he had sitting around from *Slaughter* to *Snuff*, removed all credits, and got a porn director by the name of Carter Stevens to shoot the now notorious coda.[324] The new footage was brief but provided Shackleton with the angle he needed to spring the film into a crowded and competitive marketplace. With an advertising campaign that made no mention of Manson or killer hippies — but which insinuated that the carnage on-screen was genuine, and that a life was being taken for purposes of entertainment — Shackleton foisted *Snuff* onto a public very much familiar with the recent news reports. Not only that, he organised pickets to stand outside theatres that showed the film, and planted 'high profile' FBI agents in the crowds. He also contacted feminist organisations — so outraged by *Deep Throat* — and 'tipped them off.' They in turn picketed theatres and handed out leaflets which called on "women and other persons of conscience" to demonstrate against the film. Naturally, such acts served only to fuel more publicity, and soon *Snuff* — and demonstrations against it — were making primetime news.

In actual fact, the FBI were indeed investigating Shackleton and his film.

The recent Freedom of Information and Privacy Acts has made available numerous FBI files, no less those pertaining to supposed snuff films — or "snuffers." These files reveal how

Shackleton's own *Snuff* was under observation following announcements of its imminent release in the trade papers. When it premiered at the Uptown Theatre in Indianapolis on January 16, 1976, FBI agents and an MD-Pathologist attended the screening. They determined that no hardcore pornography was involved and the closing murder "was a staged theatrical production" (see APPENDIX III). Special Agents who viewed the film in other parts of the country came back with the same conclusion. (Agents who attended the midnight screening at the National Theater, New York, had to first sit through *The Amish Farm and House* and *Life on Mars or Not*, a couple of short documentary features.)

So great was the furore that had built up around *Snuff* that Robert M Morgenthau, district attorney for Manhattan, was pressed to announce publicly that the murder of a woman in the film was a hoax — the actress having been traced and found to be alive and well.

But the attacks on *Snuff* didn't stop once the fact that it was a tasteless scam became known. Feminist organisations simply changed tack and protested the *idea* of a film like *Snuff*. "Whether or not the death depicted in the current film *Snuff* is real or simulated is not the issue," stated flyers distributed by feminists in New York City.

Although more than twenty years have passed since the film was released and 'debunked,' *Snuff* is still largely perceived today as a genuine snuff film by the ignorant. Even many of those who do acknowledge it to be a 'fake' believe that *Snuff* somehow offers tangible proof that genuine snuff films do exist.

In an episode of the BBC fly-on-the-wall documentary series, *Fraud Squad* (aired towards the end of 1998), Trading Standards officers descended on a car boot sale to confront someone suspected of selling illegal videocassettes. Amongst the tapes in the man's possession was a copy of *Snuff* — prompting one officer to remark to the camera that the film featured a real death. (The stall-holder took this opportunity to run away.)

Reporting from a press conference organised by the British Videogram Association (BVA) in April 1983, Liam T Sanford of the *Video Viewer* noted the hostile, knee-jerk reaction the subject of video nasties elicited. To counter the growing backlash, the BVA wanted to propose plans for a certification scheme for movies on video (this being prior to the VRA). Following a Q&A session, where he claims to have been snubbed by the panel for lack of outright condemnation of the nasties, Sanford interviewed Norman Abbott, Chief Executive of the BVA. One of his

The picture they said could NEVER be shown..
The Bloodiest thing that ever happened in front of a camera!!
SNUFF
The film that could only be made in South America...
where Life is CHEAP!

The picture they said could NEVER be shown...
The Bloodiest thing that ever happened in front of a camera!!
SNUFF
The film that could only be made in South America...
where Life is CHEAP!

questions concerned the media's unchecked allegations that *Snuff* was a genuine 'snuff' film, and why the BVA hadn't stepped forward on the matter. Abbott's curious reply: "It probably is not illegal to make a film of a real murder. It's probably not contrary to the Obscene Publications Act."

"But," countered Sanford, " this *isn't* a bona fide bumping off."

Abbott continued:

> Every bulletin from Northern Ireland and Falklands war newsreel, could be held to be obscene because they're showing real killing. If it depraves and corrupts, it doesn't matter if what is depicted is real or simulated under the strict terms of the Act. It's quite another question if you put someone to death. That is *murder* and therefore a crime that should be punished. As far as the Obscene Publications Act is concerned, I don't think the filming of a murder has much relevance on the subject.[325]

The availability of *Snuff* on video in Britain is one vested in some mystery. It could be found languishing on video shelves across the country in the days before certification, and — like so many other films — promptly disappeared soon after the Video Recordings Act was introduced. But who exactly was distributing it isn't clear. Astra picked the film up and scheduled it for release in May 1982, but following hostile press supposedly retracted this decision. No copies had been released, Astra told a *Sunday Times* reporter on May 29, despite big orders. Copies evidently did make it into circulation however, which either suggests that Astra — despite their claims to the contrary — continued to handle the film, or that companies unknown were issuing copies. A report in the *Sunday Times* dated January 16, 1983, noted that

> Thousands of people in Britain who have bought what is considered to be the granddaddy of all 'video nasties,' a noxious movie called *Snuff*, appear to have been conned by black-market pirates.
>
> The pirates have been doing a brisk trade at £15 a copy with a cassette labelled *Snuff*, advertised as 'the original legendary atrocity'...

How people could be "conned" by buying a pirate of a film supposedly not in general release doesn't make sense. The simple fact of the matter is that *Snuff* (replete with professional packaging) was most definitely available prior to the clampdown of the Video Recording Act, even though it was never to have an *official* release in Britain.

In keeping with Shackleton's original promotional gimmick, British copies lacked cast and credit details — a deception which also extended to keeping the identity of the British distributor a secret (no company name appeared on either the videobox or cassette label).[326] In the trade catalogue published by Land of VideoVictoria in the eighties, *Snuff* was one of the titles for which the supplier was listed as "unknown."

The follow-up to *Snuff* that Shackleton predicted in *Boxoffice* in 1975 — to be titled *The Slasher*, another anachronism for snuff films — never materialised.

SS EXPERIMENT CAMP

SYNOPSIS: In a Nazi camp during WWII, a prisoner who refuses to swear her allegiance to the führer is tortured with electricity. Still defiant, a fatal injection is administered and the woman's naked body is taken to a furnace where it contracts and dances in the flames. The next subject isn't so hardy and swears her allegiance after the first shock, wetting herself in the process.

A group of new prisoners arrives at the camp. The all-female group is stripped and herded into a communal shower. Soon after, they are examined by the female doctor who tells them that past and future no longer exist.

That night, from her sleeping quarters, a restless prisoner by the name of Mirelle spies a handsome soldier across the courtyard. They make eyes at one another and he throws her his packet of cigarettes.

Kind-hearted Helmut is amongst six soldiers called back from the front-line to partake in a high priority experiment at the camp: under laboratory conditions they are to copulate with chosen prisoners for the "proliferation of the German empire." States the blond-haired Colonel to Helmut, "We'll rule the world!"

But the Colonel's interest in Helmut is personal as well as professional. It seems that the Colonel had his testicles bitten off whilst trying to rape a woman in a combat zone and believes that Helmut — a "veritable stud" — will prove the perfect donor for a replacement pair.

The "proliferation of the German empire" gets underway and the first soldiers are paired-off with prisoners. One couple have sex partially submerged in a vat of liquid; another two couples are on beds. Fortuitously, Helmut is paired with Mirelle, the girl to whom he gave his cigarettes. She is sedated, but says to him, "For this there was no need to drug me."

One woman who refuses to co-operate is later tortured in the vat when its temperature is first turned up very high (*"This is just the beginning, you frigid, puritanical bitch!"*) and then very low, freezing her to death.

Another body for the crematorium.

The Colonel is interested in experiments concerning the transplantation of the uterus, but when another prisoner dies during surgery Dr Steiner vents his concern that they've killed too many people already. He is told to continue, there being no shortage of subjects.

'Rejected' prisoners are used as whores in the camp's brothel. Here, a boorish sergeant makes no concession to a terrified new girl. "What are ya?," he demands. "Some kind of virgin?" After she is raped (and with blood covering her thighs), the girl stabs the sergeant repeatedly with a fork. This action results in her being strung upside down naked in the middle of the camp and left to die, bleeding from gunshot wounds.

Helmut is apprehensive about being paired off with another girl for the remainder of the experiment, as indeed he is about being separated from Mirelle altogether when it's over. He requests permission to stay at the camp a little longer. Playing into his hands, the Colonel will facilitate the request only if the soldier agrees to undertake another sort of experiment. He doesn't explain to Helmut what exactly this experiment entails, but that "it might affect us both physically."

The doctors are outraged that the Colonel is risking his own life and that of another German on the transplant he requests, but are coerced into performing the operation. Dr Steiner removes testicles the size of chicken eggs from Helmut.

A month passes. Following another series of experiments on the prisoners (in which they have their eardrums burst with high pressure hoses), Steiner reports to the Colonel that clinically the transplant has been a success. Immediately the Colonel plans a demonstration party. While everyone is preoccupied, a sympathetic warden takes Mirelle to see Helmut in his hospital bed. It is only when the two lovebirds are alone that Helmut realises something is wrong.

"It might be nothing!" Mirelle reasons. "It happens sometimes!"

Like a man possessed Helmut dashes off to seek revenge. He finds Dr Steiner in his quarters, reading apocalyptic passages from the Bible, and demands, "Why have you made me into a freak?!" Angst-ridden, the doctor shoots himself in the head.

Armed with a machine-gun, he next races to confront the Colonel who is entertaining female prisoners in his quarters.

"How have you been doing with my balls?" Helmut remonstrates. The women seize this opportunity to kill the Colonel, and Helmut and Mirelle escape the camp — only to be gunned down once outside the gates.[327]

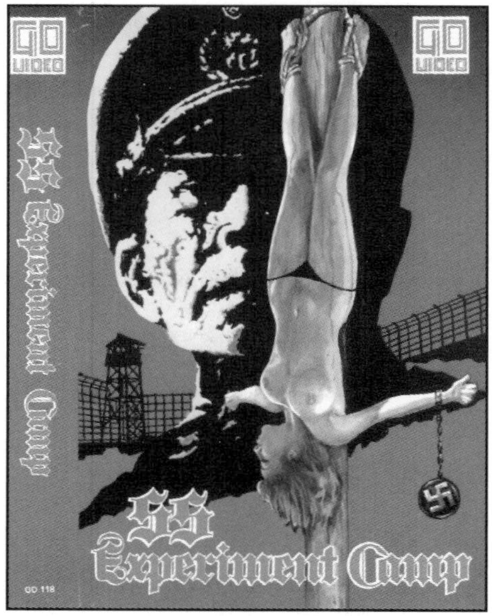

SS EXPERIMENT CAMP

AKA: SS Experiment; SS Experiment Love Camp; Horreur Nazis; Kastrat Commandatur Satirlagher 23; Le Camp des Filles Perdeues; SS Vrouwenkamp

ITALY 1976

CAST: Mircha Carven, Paola Corazzi, Giorgio Cerioni, Giovanna Mainardi, Serafino Profumo, Attilio Dottesio, Patrizia Melega

STORY: Sergio Chiusi

DIR OF PRODUCTION: Mario Caporali

DIRECTOR: SERGIO GARRONE

CRITIQUE: Sergio Garrone has close on two dozen movies to his credit, reflecting the typically eclectic

Trade ad for *SS Experiment Camp* under one of its aliases.

mix of themes and trends found in Italian exploitation. He shot two horror movies starring Klaus Kinski back-to-back in 1974,[328] a cut-rate endeavour which encouraged Garrone to follow suit a couple of years later with *SS Experiment Camp* and the reputedly nastier *SS Camp 5 Women's Hell* (never officially released in Britain). From here Garrone made only a few more films — the last of which had women-in-prison themes — before retiring from the business altogether.[329]

According to an article in *Shock Xpress*,[330] Garrone supposedly made his two Nazi camp films for foreign exploitation markets only, claiming that the Nazi theme was a means of getting the violence of these pictures past the censors intact.

Garrone is obviously riding a bandwagon with these films. But his claim that he "intended neither of them in any way for denunciation" is seemingly supported by *SS Experiment Camp* — which does much to promote the glories of Germany but doesn't once address the prisoners as Jewish.[331] Then again, the whole film seems to be taking place in an alternative dimension, where the trappings appear to be those of WWII but the actual defining points are twisted or erased. Here, prisoners are more concerned with good-looking Nazi soldiers than they are the torment and indignities of life in a concentration camp, passing comments like "There's a beautiful man. He'll be able to cure our insomnia." One prisoner, following a tryst with a lesbian doctor, turns to her friends and tells them "It's incredible — you'll see!" When Helmut and Mirelle manage to steal a little time together, she confides "All this happiness is frightening." ("You're in no position to be in love with someone — especially a Kraut," says a friend, trying to bring the lovesick Mirelle — and indeed the viewer — back down to earth.)

The prisoners all have clearly visible tan-lines and each look a picture of good health. The sole exception is the two women in the pre-credit sequence who are tortured with electricity — they have sunken eyes and sallow complexions, but still the camera steals a wily look at their naked breasts. The clandestine sharing of a cigarette adds to the summer camp atmosphere, as do the beefcake soldiers who lounge around their barracks in shorts pondering the nature of the experiment soon to take place. "With all those beautiful women arriving," says one soldier, "I hope it's a secret mission of a sexual nature."

Another curiously detached moment comes in the form of a nurse with cropped blonde hair, who assists in the transplant of a uterus by rubbing the sedated patient's thigh in a neat little circular motion. Then there are the guards who spot a naked girl making a break for it and exclaim: "Look at that. Where the hell does she think she's going?" Stranger still is the case of Dr Steiner, who is blackmailed into removing Helmut's (unfeasibly large) testicles when the Colonel discovers that he's really a world famous Jewish surgeon by the name of Abraham. It's a wonder the doctor has been able to conceal his identity for so long, given that he spends his evenings in his quarters wearing the garb of a Rabbi.

The scenes inside the crematorium are so surreal that Garrone looks to be interpreting the horror via some kind of experimental dance. As superimposed flames lap, the naked women jerk their limbs in a syncopated fashion.

SS Experiment Camp is one of the most notorious films on the DPP's list — a fact that has little to do with the content of the film (which is mainly softcore sex and some lame gore), and everything to do with its emotive title and notorious ad campaign that accompanied the video release in Britain. (See CLAMPDOWN.)

TENEBRAE

SYNOPSIS: Best-selling American author Peter Neal leaves for Rome and a promotional tour for his latest book *Tenebrae*. At the airport he receives a phone call from his unstable fiancée Jane who, unbeknownst to him, is calling from a phone in the airport lobby. Someone interferes with his luggage as he takes the call.

In a store in Rome a young woman is caught trying to steal a copy of *Tenebrae*, but the shop manager chooses not to report her to the police in exchange for her address and the promise of favours. On her way home she is assaulted by a vagrant but manages to escape and make it home. The vagrant follows her and witnesses her murder by an unseen assailant. She has her throat cut with a razor and her mouth filled with pages torn from Neal's book. The killer also photographs the body and later pushes a note under Neal's hotel apartment door.

Neal attends a press conference arranged by his agent Bulmer, and is introduced to Tilde, a journalist who disagrees with his work. "*Tenebrae* is a sexist novel," she tells him. "Why do you despise women so much?" He later discovers that all the clothes in his bag have been cut up. Arriving at his apartment with Anne his secretary, and Gianni his assistant, Neil is greeted by police who tell him the door was open. The police question Neal on whether he knew the woman who was murdered, and hand him the note that was pushed under the door — it contains a pertinent passage from his book. The killer rings to taunt Neal from a phonebooth in the street, but is gone by the time the police get outside.

Following a quarrel with her lesbian lover, Tilde hears an intruder whisper "filthy, slimy pervert," before she is attacked and murdered with a razor. Tilde's lover is also murdered. Photographs are taken of the bodies and another note is slipped under Neal's door.

The following day Neal does a television interview with Christiano Berti, a curious man who has a particular personal interest in Neal's work. Later Neal thinks he sees fiancée Jane driving past his apartment and when he phones her home in New York he gets no response. Anne suggests that it was probably Jane who cut up his clothing.

The maid from Neal's hotel is walking home when she is chased by a dog and forced to seek sanctuary in a nearby house. There she discovers photographs of the murder victims and other relevant documents. Collecting them together she is disturbed by the murderer and killed with an axe.

Another note is sent to Neal explaining that the latest victim was unintentional. Neal spots similarities between the letter and things Berti has said, so sets off for the TV host's house with Gianni. In the garden they separate, and Gianni witnesses Berti being killed by someone wielding an axe. Running away he finds Neal unconscious on the lawn and helps him back to the car.

Bulmer, Neal's agent, and a Detective Germani advise the author to leave Rome for a few days. Bulmer takes the opportunity to arrange to meet Neal's fiancée Jane, with whom he is having an affair, but is later fatally stabbed by someone he evidently recognises.

Gianni is sure that he is forgetting something important about Berti's death. After taking Neal to the airport he goes back to Berti's house to search for clues, but is garrotted.

Jane is hacked to death after phoning Anne and arranging a meeting. A police officer arrives at the scene and is also axed to death, but this murder is an accident and a babbling Peter Neal

TENEBRAE
AKA: Tenebre (original title); Unsane
ITALY 1982
CAST: Anthony Franciosa, John Saxon, Christian Borromeo, Mirella D'Angelo, Daria Nicolodi
STORY: Dario Argento
PRODUCER: Claudio Argento
DIRECTOR: DARIO ARGENTO

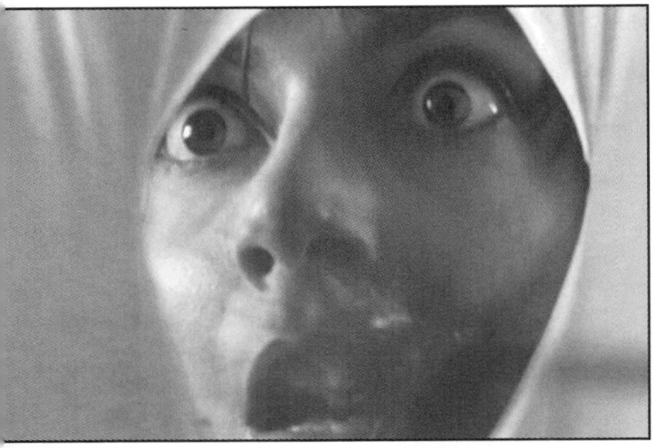

TOP: Tilde is slashed with a razor while dressing.
ABOVE: Approved *Tenebrae* artwork following the Video Recordings Act (compare with previous page).

confesses to the crime when Anne and Detective Germani show up. It transpires that Berti had been committing the murders until Neal, having figured it out, decided to kill him. The traumatised author then took it upon himself to murder his faithless fiancée and his agent.

In what appears a fit of remorse, Neal suddenly pulls a razor from his pocket and cuts his own throat. Detective Germani takes Anne to the car and returns to the house to find Neal gone and a fake razor on the floor. The Detective is killed when the axe-wielding Neal creeps up on him, and he upsets the balance of a huge chrome sculpture as he falls. Anne returns to the house not knowing that Neal lies in wait. As she pushes open the door the sculpture tumbles over and impales Neal. He dies pinned to the wall.

CRITIQUE: Full of energy and confidence — so lacking in Dario Argento's later works — *Tenebrae* bristles with arresting imagery and a cracking musical score from ex-members of Goblin.[332] It also makes a beautiful spectacle out of celluloid murder, with glamorous semi-naked women falling victim to an anonymous black-gloved killer. Death is painted against a backdrop of pure white (underwear) and splashes of impossibly red blood in brightly lit surroundings — the whole thing coming over like *noir* in reverse.

Argento also subverts the sexism argument that dogged horror films of the late-seventies and eighties, by incorporating it into the plot of *Tenebrae*. Tilde, a feminist lesbian journalist no less, accuses Peter Neal of writing sexist books that contain violence against women. For a while it looks like Argento might trounce the argument and reveal it to be another one of the film's many red herrings, but ultimately he seems to support and justify it by having Tilde herself murdered. Like all the victims in *Tenebrae*, Tilde is fundamentally just like the ciphers she accuses Neal of incorporating into his book, and which Argento despatches with suitably unrestrained objectification — even down to having her face hidden as the killer strikes (she is caught drawing a shirt over her head as the killer strikes).

The film's coda, with the falling sculpture impaling Neal, however, does offer a clue to Argento's *real* take on the whole sexism/misogynism debate: he shows murder because it looks good and is engaging — alive the girls look like models; dead they still look like models. "Art as killing, killing as art," stated one critic of *Tenebrae*.[333] Argento doesn't address the issue of sexism earnestly because he doesn't believe in it. To him, "The fact that Peter Neal turns out to be a murderer is just a game, it shows how foolish people can be."[334]

And when *Halls of Horror* asked in 1978 why his movies were so gory, Argento replied succinctly: "Because I make violent movies, and because the blood is an inseparable part of them."[335]

After the supernatural horror of *Suspiria* and ***Inferno***, *Tenebrae* marked Argento's return to the giallo thriller with which he had started his directorial career.[336] (It was supposedly inspired by a true life incident in which a fan obsessed with *Suspiria* threatened to kill the director.) Its original title was *Tenebre*, Italian for 'darkness,' but became *Tenebrae* when released in Britain.[337] Argento had originally conceived that the Peter Neal character should be played by Christopher Walken (Anthony Franciosa got the part), and for reasons unknown has claimed the film to be set five years into the future.

Curiously, the slow panning shot that traverses a whole house in a single take — heralded as a spectacular achievement back in the eighties — now simply appears unnecessary and clumsy.

Tenebrae was passed by the BBFC for theatrical release in 1983, with a few seconds cut from a sequence in which an axe chops off an arm at the film's end. It was this version that Videomedia released on video, and which was determined by the DPP to be a nasty. Further cuts were made to this same sequence when *Tenebrae* was submitted to the BBFC and classified 18 for video release in 1999. (See also SEX AND WRECKS.)

TERROR EYES

SYNOPSIS: When all her pupils have gone home, schoolteacher Miss Anne Barron sits idly on a roundabout in the playground when suddenly she is menaced by a figure whose identity is concealed by a black motorcycle helmet. The figure spins the roundabout faster and faster, silently threatening Anne with a large knife before decapitating her.

The following morning police lieutenant Judd Austin and his sidekick Taj are called to the scene. It's the second killing in a week with the same *modus operandi*: the head of the earlier victim was dumped in a duck pond; here the head is discovered in a bucket of water. No sign of sexual assault in either case, just clean decapitations.

Vincent Millett, professor of anthropology at a night school in the city, has the reputation of being a lady's man. News of his prowess even extends to the nearby Lamplight Café where a waitress volunteers stories of the professor's 'conquests' to Eleanor — who happens to be Millett's personal research assistant and lover. Eleanor leaves in a huff but is followed home by a retarded young man called Gary (whose second name is Downs). Taking a shower, Eleanor hears a noise and fears Gary is trying to break into the house. But it's only Vincent — and the two of them have sex.

An aquarium is the setting for the third murder. As an employee called Kim Morrison is changing out of a wetsuit, she is attacked by the anonymous, knife-wielding killer, who again wears a motorcycle helmet. Slashed several times, her head is then chopped off and thrown into the aquarium where a turtle begins to feed on it.

The police discover that all the victims attended Professor Millett's anthropology class and that he had a sexual fling with each of them.

Overhearing this particular detail causes Eleanor some distress and, pursued by Millett on his motorcycle, she runs to the Lamplight Café. Here she confesses to Millett that she is three months pregnant with his child. But while Millett appears overjoyed by the news, he still flirts with the waitress and dashes off without answering Eleanor's suggestion of marriage.

Doing some last minute chores before locking up, Carol the Lamplight waitress is attacked and murdered by the masked assailant. Her head is discovered the next morning in a sink full of dishwater. The Lieutenant and Taj become suspicious of Gary, the retarded helper, who hasn't been seen for the last couple of days.

TERROR EYES
AKA: Night School
USA 1980
CAST: Leonard Mann, Rachel Ward, Drew Snyder, Joseph R Sicari
STORY: Ruth Avergon
PRODUCERS: Larry Babb & Ruth Avergon
DIRECTOR: KENNETH HUGHES

When it transpires that Gary is a peeping tom with a string of convictions for indecent exposure (and women's underwear stashed in his apartment), Taj is convinced that he's their man. Austin isn't so sure, and makes a return visit to Millett. He isn't at home but Eleanor enlightens the lieutenant on New Guinea head-hunters, whom she and the professor spent some time with over the course of their research (several photographs on Millett's desk show the couple attired in safari garb, surrounded by human skulls). "In taking the heads of the enemies, they are possessing the very life force," Eleanor says of the head-hunters, adding that water is used to cleanse the heads of "evil spirits from the souls of their enemies."

The school registrar, Helene Griffin, consoles an emotional student who claims to have been seduced by Millett. Annoyed that the professor is using the place as a "playground for his sexual exploits," she is adamant that the professor's days at the school are numbered. But it seems Helene is more resentful of the competition, tenderly inviting the distraught girl to spend the night at her place so they can "talk."

That night, both Helene and the student are murdered. Fortuitously, the lieutenant and Taj are in the vicinity—tailing Gary who happens to have been peeping through the governess' window at the time of the crime. The two men give chase and the killer leads them back to Millett's house.

Taking off the motorcycle helmet, Eleanor reveals herself to be the killer. "I did it for us, Vincent," she says. "And our baby!"

In a final selfless act, Vincent Millett dons the killer's garb moments before the police arrive. He is shot down dead.

At the funeral, Austin cryptically asks Eleanor "Is the ceremony over?"

She replies tearfully in the affirmative.

Austin has a shock however when he gets in his car and finds a helmeted figure waiting for him on the back seat... but it's only Taj playing a practical joke. The two of them laugh heartily.

CRITIQUE: This is a lame entry in the stalk-and-slash cycle of films and is far from representative of the director's earlier work, which includes *The Trials of Oscar Wilde*, *Arriverderci, Baby*, *Casino Royale* (co-director), and *Chitty Chitty Bang Bang*.

Given his association with name stars like Peter Sellers, Orson Welles, James Coburn, George Raft, Woody Allen, Tony Curtis, Richard Harris, Alec Guinness, Peter Finch, George Hamilton and even an aged Mae West (in her last "sin-sational" movie, *Sextette*), it is ironic but somehow fitting that the best Hughes could muster for *Terror Eyes* is Rachel Ward — "Burt Reynolds' beautiful leading lady in *Sharkey's Machine*," as the videobox describes her.

Made the same year as *Friday the 13th*, Hughes' film completely lacks the grisly set-pieces and conviction that was to become so essential to the stalk-and-slash genre. Which perhaps goes some way in explaining the film's slim profile and complete absence from many genre related books.

Nothing about the film rings remotely true: Why is the night school exclusive to girls? What manner of Detective is the curiously named Taj, who volunteers nothing but wisecracks when faced with a fresh victim and pulls a lame stunt at the film's end that would have gotten his head blown off in an ideal world?

Not that Hughes passes any opportunity to slip into a cliché: Judd Austin is introduced as a workaholic Detective who, to the chagrin of his girlfriend, gets called to work on his day off. We never do get to see or hear any more of this relationship, so it's completely irrelevant in retrospect. There is also a shower scene that threatens to turn into a bloodbath, but the menacing silhouette belongs not to a killer but to Millett who engages Eleanor in some aquatic foreplay. Nonetheless, the director feels obliged to see the tired *Psycho* reference played out in its entirety: Millett brings into the shower a pot of (blood-red) jam and starts to smear the stuff over Eleanor's body, thereby enabling the scene to close on the sight of crimson-matter going swirling down the drain.[338]

Even the killer being a woman is hardly a twist. Indeed, it's a reversal of Brian de Palma's *Dressed To Kill* of the same year, in which Michael Caine played a killer in drag. Seeing as the only other suspects — Millett and Gary — are so obviously red-herrings anyway most viewers will have Eleanor pegged as the murderer long before her closing 'revelation.'

Despite its relatively gore-free approach, it is likely that the protracted knife threats and relentless hacking at girls who are pleading for their lives steered *Terror Eyes* onto the DPP list..

THE TOOLBOX MURDERS

SYNOPSIS: A man enters an apartment block one night carrying a toolbox. He goes unannounced into an apartment and alarms Mrs Andrews, a middle-aged tenant who, even though inebriated, recognises the man.

"What the hell is going on?" she bemoans. "I call you Monday, you show up Thursday!"

The man simply hums and fits a boring tool into his power drill then sets upon the woman. After killing her he packs away his drill and puts on a ski mask before leaving the room. In another part of the complex, Deborah returns home, prepares for a shower and collects a bag she has left outside her door. She is confronted by the ski-masked killer who knocks her unconscious and carries her into the stairwell where he smashes her skull with a claw hammer. He carries her body back into her room, but before he can mutilate her any further, Deborah's roommate Maria, disturbs him. She tries to escape the killer but is dragged to the floor and stabbed to death with a chisel.

Before leaving the building the killer observes other tenants from the window. Later another resident finds the bloodstains on the stairs and follows them into Deborah's room.

Detective Jamison is assigned to investigate the murders and questions Vance Kingsley, the owner of the apartment block, who is confused as to how anyone could enter the secure building.

Laurie, a student living with her mother and brother Joey, discusses the murders with her friend the following day.

That night the handyman returns to the complex with his toolbox and breaks into an apartment where Dee Ann is taking a bath. He watches the girl in the tub for awhile before chasing her around the rooms and killing her with a nailgun. Elsewhere he attacks and suffocates a student.

Shortly after, Joey and his mother arrive home to find the apartment door open and Laurie missing. When the bodies of the latest victims are found Joey concludes that the killer has kidnapped his sister. Telling the police of his suspicions however, he is treated more like a suspect than someone offering help and decides to find out what happened to his sister without their assistance.

Back at the apartment block he meets Kent, Vance Kingsley's nephew, who is preparing to clean up Mrs Andrew's apartment. Kent seems overly interested in the bloodstains splashed around the place. Joey asks Kent if he will help him break into Dee Ann's apartment to look for any clues that will help locate his sister. Kent agrees, and is disgusted when Joey locates Dee Ann's vibrator and

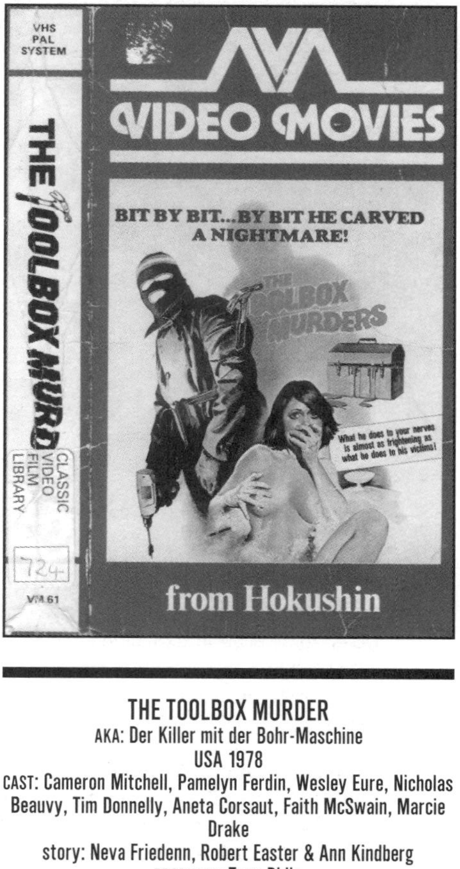

THE TOOLBOX MURDER
AKA: Der Killer mit der Bohr-Maschine
USA 1978
CAST: Cameron Mitchell, Pamelyn Ferdin, Wesley Eure, Nicholas Beauvy, Tim Donnelly, Aneta Corsaut, Faith McSwain, Marcie Drake
story: Neva Friedenn, Robert Easter & Ann Kindberg
PRODUCER: Tony Didio
DIRECTOR: DENNIS DONNELLY

throws it towards him. Kent then spots a nail protruding from the wall and figures she was murdered with a nail gun. He appears unnerved by this discovery.

In the corner of Vance Kingsley's garage is the toolbox used by the killer. Upstairs in the bedroom he has Laurie tied to the bed. Bringing her food, Vance tells Laurie of the death of his own daughter Cathy in a car crash, and how unfair it is that such a beautiful innocent girl should die. He explains that the world is an evil place.

"It's such a bad world. Laurie, it's *bad*. It's *evil*, full of evil. Terrible people... But you see if you get rid of the evil then all that's left is good!"

Vance goes on to explain how he killed the filthy drunk Mrs Andrews, and how he watched Dee Ann masturbate in the bath before he killed her. Confused and mad he momentarily thinks that Laurie is his dead daughter. "Did it hurt when you died?" he asks. Laurie plays along in the hope she will be released, but Vance refits her gag and leaves her tied to the bed.

Later that night Kent climbs up to the window of the room where Laurie is imprisoned. He taps on the glass but is disturbed when Vance enters the room. "I thought I'd sing to you because I haven't done that in a long time," he tells Laurie. "Sometimes I feel like a motherless child..." he croons before falling asleep on Laurie's lap.

The next day as Kent is painting Mrs Andrews apartment, Detective Jamison peers out the window with binoculars. Joey arrives and asks the Detective how Mrs Andrews died. "With a drill," responds Jamison. The information worries Kent.

Joey borrows his mother's car and drives over to Vance's place to examine the contents of his toolbox. But he is followed by Kent who bursts in and asks abruptly, "Need some *tools*, Joey?"

"He did it. Your uncle killed all those women." Joey explains, pointing out the bloodstains on the tools. But Kent doesn't want to know, nor does he want anyone else to know, so he throws flammable liquid over his buddy, sets him alight and burns him to death.

Kent goes upstairs to where Vance is playing with a doll and talking to Laurie. He infuriates his uncle when he tells him he had sex with Cathy, Vance's daughter. They argue, threatening to kill each other, and Vance chases Kent down into the kitchen but is fatally stabbed. Kent returns to the bedroom and before he releases Laurie he rapes her. When Laurie learns that Kent has murdered her brother as well as Vance, she takes the opportunity to stab him with a pair of scissors before escaping and wandering into the night.

CRITIQUE: A caption that appears before the end credits informs viewers that the incidents in *The Toolbox Murders* actually occurred in 1967. But it seems that most of the film's inspiration — including the 'real-life incident' caption — is derived exclusively from Tobe Hooper's *Texas Chain Saw Massacre*: tools are used as murder implements; the killers are family; deceased family members are venerated; and a central female victim is held captive, tortured, humiliated and ultimately escapes to wander the streets dazed and bloodstained...

The deaths that occur in the first part of the film are pretty offensive, even though the version released on video in Britain was heavily cut. As a result of this censorial tampering, the focus of the first murder is a record player on a cabinet, with brief flashes of a bloody drill bit all that remains of the actual killing.[339] It isn't only the violence that is excised — Dee Ann's bath time masturbation sequence is gone completely, despite its 'relevance' to the plot. Only when Vance confesses to having killed Dee Ann do we learn *why* he killed her, muttering something about the "unnatural things" she did to herself.

Even with its hard violence removed, *The Toolbox Murders* remains an unpleasant movie. Cameron Mitchell's portrayal of the crazy killer is unduly nauseating as he not only whistles, hums, grunts and sings during his killing activities but also during his lengthy monologues with the bound Laurie. It is the presence of Mitchell that holds the piece together (his death, incidentally, is as grisly as any of the women he himself kills).

A regular on the popular, long-running TV western *The High Chaparral*, Mitchell was a Hollywood star back in the forties and fifties, appearing in movies like *How To Marry a Millionaire* and *Carousel*. In 1964 he played the lead in Mario Bava's seminal giallo thriller *Blood and Black Lace*, but by the seventies the only parts coming his way were those in low-budget sci-fi and horror, such as *Frankenstein Island* and *Cataclysm*, and later direct-to-video fodder.

Although Mitchell claimed to have no interest in gore pictures — "I *make* 'em, but I don't have to *look* at 'em!" he told Tom Weaver in *Attack of the Monster Movie Makers* — he seemed somewhat proud of his job on *The Toolbox Murders*. Later in the same interview, the actor said

The scene where I sing to the girl I'm holding prisoner was my idea; I thought that actress was quite good, Pamelyn Ferdin. The lollipop I carry around, anything weird like that was my idea! A lot of the odd touches that were any good were mine [laughs]! The human touches — 'cause even a killer is human, you know.

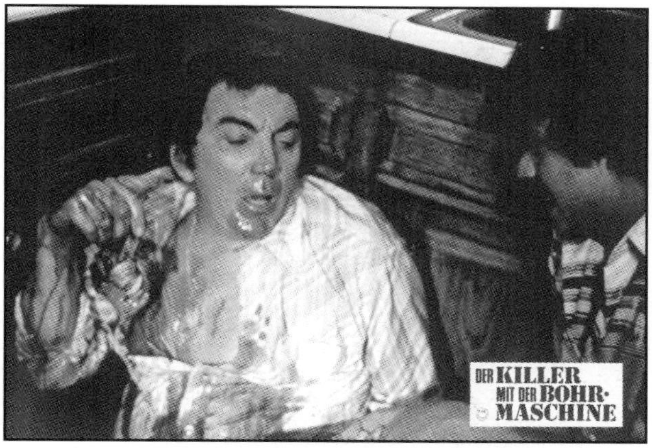

TOP AND ABOVE: Kent confronts and stabs to death his uncle Vance, the Toolbox Murderer. *The Toolbox Murders*.

In the month before he passed away, frail and barely able to raise his voice much above a whisper, Mitchell still managed to delight fans with an impromptu rendition of 'Sometimes I Feel Like A Motherless Child,' the song he sung in *The Toolbox Murders*.[340]

Pamelyn Ferdin, who plays Laurie and to whom Mitchell sings his song, was for many years a popular TV and movie actress, but quit showbusiness after *The Toolbox Murders* to do Barbie doll commercials. More than Vance however, it is Kent who comes over as a truly reprehensible character, pretending to be Laurie's saviour but ultimately raping her. "You can't remain a little girl for the rest of your life," he reasons during the abuse.

To date *The Toolbox Murders* appears to be the only theatrical feature directed by Dennis Donnelly who is usually associated with TV work, having directed episodes of popular shows like *Airwolf*, *The A-Team*, *Falcon Crest*, *Hart to Hart*, *Dallas*, *Hawaii Five-O* and *Charlie's Angels*. Given the opportunity to break out of the otherwise staid TV confines, Donnelley no doubt decided he wanted to go well and truly overboard with *The Toolbox Murders*. "Disgusting and erotic," was the comment made of it by one viewer.[341] Its hackneyed plot does belie a certain TV influence, and the film ultimately comes over as being little more than a particularly twisted episode of any generic TV action show. The actors are given little to play with (although, as we have seen, Mitchell brings a little something of his own to his role) and the whole plot seems unnecessarily long and gory.

The Toolbox Murders did the rounds at the cinemas in the early eighties supporting Fulci's ***Zombie Flesh-Eaters***. The sequence featuring the nailgun murder of Dee Ann (Marianne Walter, said to be porno actress 'Kelly Nichols') was shorn of three minutes and it was this BBFC X-certificate version that Hokushin released on video. Nevertheless, in spite of these cuts and BBFC approval, the film found itself for a time on the DPP list.

Feminists, disturbed by the trend for stalk-and-slash movies, were particularly outraged by the bathtub masturbation and nailgun killing, and it is worth noting that the film's release in Britain came at the tail end of the Yorkshire Ripper 'toolbox' killings. Jane Caputi, in *The*

Age of Sex Crime, described the film as being amongst those offering

> A veritable *Kama Sutra* of possible gynocidal [sic] styles and techniques: different tools, different settings, different victims, and different fetishes to appeal to the imaginations of as many viewers as possible.

Cameron Mitchell said that a *Toolbox Murders* sequel was in the pipeline — indeed in conversation with Tom Weaver he stated ambiguously that he supposed it had been "done." Few people actually admit to liking *The Toolbox Murders* — although Stephen King is supposedly a fan — and there has been no real evidence to suggest a follow-up has ever been imminent.

UNHINGED

SYNOPSIS: Terry, Nancy and Gloria are three girlfriends who are travelling by car to a "music festival." The wail of rock guitars on the radio is interrupted by a local news report on the disappearance of two girls, just as a rainstorm starts and the car careens off the road.

The girls awake to find themselves in an isolated mansion having been rescued by Norman Barnes, a greasy looking fellow who claims he is "a local Jack-of-all-trades."

UNHINGED
AKA: Stark Raving Mad [?]
USA 1982
CAST: Laurel Munson, J E Penner, Sara Ansley, Virginia Settle, John Morrison, Barbara Lusch, Bill Simmonds
STORY: Don Gronquist & Reagan Ramsey
PRODUCER: Don Gronquist
DIRECTOR: DON GRONQUIST

The mansion is owned and inhabited by Marion Penrose and her wheelchair-bound mother Edith, who invite the girls to stay until they have recovered fully. Unfortunately there is no telephone with which the girls can contact their parents, and the village is two miles away through the forest.

Gloria's injuries have confined her to bed but Nancy and Terry accept the Penrose's invitation to dinner. At a lavishly set table, the guests watch as the elderly Penrose acts out a strange ritual in which it looks as if she's about to throttle the pepperpot. As quickly as it starts it's over and the old woman reminisces on better times at Newport, Rhode Island, before accusing Marion of secretly inviting men to the house and defiling the sanctity of their home. "Deny it you slut!" she hollers.

That night, Terry is awoken by noises and through the window spies someone walking around in the dark. She tells Nancy that the heavy breathing she heard sounded like a man "doing himself," and the girls decide that in the morning they'll go and find a telephone.

Through a spy hole someone watches the two girls take a shower. Marion explains to Nancy how to reach the village through the woods, and also prevents Terry from investigating the inside of the garden shed because she claims the timbers are unsafe.

As Nancy is making her way through the woods she gets the feeling she is being watched. A figure is waiting for her and murders her with a scythe. A blood-spattered Nancy tumbles to the floor with a trail of blood drooling from her mouth.

Back at the house Marion explains to Terry the reason for her mother's vitriolic outburst the previous day. It transpires Edith has a hatred of all men springing from the contempt she has for her own husband, whose "infidelity" with a girl of eight or nine she discovered back in Newport, Rhode Island. When Terry says she thinks she heard a man in the night, Marion is steadfast that her mother "will not allow men in this house."

Terry isn't particularly worried that Nancy hasn't yet returned, and that evening dines alone with Edith and Marion as another storm rages. Once again the pompous old woman goes through her strange tabletop ritual and throws disparaging glances at Marion.

That night someone is mooching around the garden shed and Terry is woken again by the sound of heavy breathing. In an attempt to locate its source, she makes her way up to the attic where she finds a revolver, a hunting knife and a photograph of two little boys. (The gasping noises stop.)

Terry is terrified by the appearance of a man's face at her bedroom window but is consoled by Marion, who tells her that it's only her younger brother. In a story which reiterates much of what was said earlier about Edith's hatred of men, Marion explains that as far as Edith is concerned, Carl, her own son, doesn't exist. He has the mind of a five-year-old and is forced to live outside.

A brief exchange takes place between Terry and Norman Barnes, the Jack-of-all-trades who does odd jobs around the place. Norman shows concern that Nancy has gone off by herself in the woods, and claims girls have gone missing in the past.

Someone is spying on Terry as she speaks with the bed-ridden Gloria (the first real encounter with the third girl since arriving at the house). That night, Gloria is murdered with an axe to the head as she sleeps. A storm commences. When Terry pays a return visit to Gloria she is puzzled to find her friend gone, and begins a search which ultimately leads to the shed. Here she finds several dead bodies, various bloody limbs and a jar of eyes (which she knocks to the floor). Frightened by Carl — who she feels is going to kill her — Terry runs from the shed to the attic, grabs the pistol and shoots dead the advancing retard.

AVATAR
Get your slice from the Reaper
RE-ORDER NOW
TV Advertising commences May 19TH
National Press Campaign now running
TV Holdback for 2 years
VIOLENCE BEYOND REASON.
VICTIMS BEYOND HELP...
"Hideous. Just what the market needs." VIDEO BUSINESS
"Gore lovers will wallow in it!" MUSIC AND VIDEO WEEK
Contact your CBS/FOX VIDEO Sales Representative or call Telephone Sales on 01-997 2552

"He was only playing with you!" screams Marion at the sight of her brother's lifeless body. Her voice then suddenly drops an octave as Marion reveals herself to be a man and turns on Terry with the nearby hunting knife. Bringing the knife down repeatedly on the girl — and continuing to do so long after she has stopped screaming — 'Marion' vents her anger with a rant:

> "Do you think it's been easy all these years? *Do you*? Do you think it's been easy trying to take care of my brother, trying to keep my secret from my mother? Trying to keep my own feelings locked up inside? When I told you about Carl I thought you would understand — I thought you'd be different from all the rest. But oh no, you wouldn't believe me. You're just the same as all the *others*! All those years of trying to protect my brother… and that was the only thing that really mattered! But now I am the strong and you are the weak! Now I see you where you really belong — subservient, grovelling, subhuman as I was all those years! Now we're finding out who stands where, *aren't we*? You putrid scum! Fouling the air with your very presence! Now we're finding out, aren't we? Aren't we? Aren't *we-e-e-e-e-e*!"
>
> From downstairs Edith calls, "Do you have another one of your men up there?"
> Adopting a female voice again, Marion replies with some exasperation, "No mother."

CRITIQUE: An early clue to the film's twist ending comes with Norman Barnes the handy man, a name which is clearly analogous to *Psycho*'s Norman Bates.[342] There are plenty of other parallels with Hitchcock's gender-reversal classic, including a reference to the mansion once having bustled with (paying) guests, the domineering mother, women who get spied on

whilst in the shower, and the fact that the *denouement* takes place in an attic (as opposed to a cellar). Even the title — *Unhinged* — doesn't stray too far out of the proverbial ball park.[343] But one gets the impression this is a homage rather than a rip-off, and the result is a relatively mindless, mercifully short, piece of schlock entertainment.

Unhinged opens with Terry taking a shower — a sequence whose purpose is to wallow in as much flesh as possible short of actual pubis (which would probably mean a stronger rating in America). She then chats briefly with her mother on the phone who warns her about the company her daughter keeps and about "gallivanting around the country." It's a seemingly throwaway dialogue that proves to have some resonance when the end of the picture comes.[344]

The same can't be said of the lunatic ritual carried out by old Mrs Penrose every mealtime. These actions serve *no* purpose, other than to pad out the running time and give the other diners the opportunity to stare blankly and throw one another meaningless glances — ergo pad out more running time.

Sequences are separated by empty black film that lingers just a little too long (creating the uncomfortable impression that the film has a fault and has stopped). More time is wasted with extensive aerial shots of the girls' car travelling empty roads in the opening scenes. However, these are the only aerial shots in the film and establish a sense that the budget is considerably larger — and the film itself more 'up-market' — than it actually is.

The Penroses also have a habit of reiterating everything they say.

Thankfully nothing too demanding is asked of the skeletal cast of five, given that the few emotive outbursts from the elderly Penrose come over as ridiculous and contrived. The girls sit around looking pretty — evidently having prepared for their rock concert by bringing along a full wardrobe and plenty of makeup. Terry and Nancy don't seem phased by their car accident at all, but their friend Gloria is conveniently kept in bed and out of sight until the time of her murder.

Though there is the implication of a masturbating voyeur killer, it's hardly enough to get the film banned. *Unhinged*'s most visceral sequence takes place in the shed when Terry stumbles upon the bodies of numerous victims. But even here the bloody carcasses are presented in a pretty abstract way (or incompetently, depending on how you want to interpret the scene) and the camera doesn't hang around the gore for too long. Similarly, the demise of each of the three girls comes spattered with blood a-plenty but precious little is actually shown. The intensity with which Terry is dispatched at the end of the film, however, is fairly brutal. The cross-dressing Marion stabs the pleading girl (who is out of shot) with a hunting knife, enunciating her vitriolic outburst with repeated strikes. Even when Terry's screaming has tapered off to nothing and a cutaway shows her dead eyes, Marion doesn't stall and continues relentlessly to sink the knife down several more times.

The prelude to this sequence also holds one of the few surprises in the film: Marion's dress becomes torn to reveal to Terry a hairy chest beneath.

Unhinged received a theatrical release in Britain in 1983. Don Gronquist has made at least one other film, *The Devil's Keep*. Although sources credit him with also having directed *Stark Raving Mad* in 1982, this seems more likely to be an alternative title for *Unhinged*.

VISITING HOURS

SYNOPSIS: Deborah Ballin is a TV journalist who isn't afraid to speak her mind. When the topic of her show is a housewife who murdered her abusive husband, the nature of Deborah's questions cause the prosecution lawyer in the case to threaten a libel suit. Arriving home that evening, Deborah finds her house in some disarray. Blaming her absent housekeeper for the mess, a man suddenly jumps out of a wardrobe brandishing a knife and tries to kill Deborah. She is forced to exit the room via a dumbwaiter, but the attacker cuts the rope when she is partway down, causing Deborah to crash to the basement.[345] Her injuries land her in hospital.

Unbeknownst to Deborah or the police, the attacker is Colt Hawker, a man troubled by childhood memories of a father who doted on him but by contrast was abusive to his mother. One day his mother retaliated with a pan of boiling fat and left home for good. Hawker has never forgiven her.

The theme of Deborah Ballin's recent TV show, and her defence of the woman in the murder case, has left the journalist a target for Hawker's life-long pent-up rage.

Hawker sets out to finish the journalist off. Posing as a delivery man with flowers, he arrives at the hospital and in a room severs an oxygen line to a woman he thinks is Deborah. He discovers he's made a mistake however, as Deborah has been moved to another room. Hawker sits and watches as the elderly patient struggles for breath, and proceeds to take a few snaps with the camera he has brought along. He stabs a nurse who walks in.

Sheila Munroe, a second nurse, finds the two bodies and raises the alarm. In so doing, she inadvertently becomes drawn into Hawker's plans.[346] He follows her home and watches her from a distance.

At a diner, Hawker picks up a girl and they go back to his place. She comments on the number of framed letters he has hanging on his walls. Most appear to be of a racist nature.

"Do you want the whole goddamn world to yourself?" the girl asks.

"Yeah," Hawker half-smiles. "Yeah, I'd like that."

He rapes the girl.

Dressed as an orderly, Hawker slips back into the hospital. But again he's unable to reach Deborah Ballin. Another botched attempt on her life results in another innocent patient being murdered.

At the Free Clinic, Nurse Munroe happens to tend to the girl who was raped by Hawker. The girl vows to get her own back, and returns to her attacker's apartment in order to trash it. On the wall of a cupboard, she discovers the collage of death photos that Hawker has been accumulating, and recognises that the centrepiece is comprised of pictures of the nurse from the clinic.

Nurse Munroe rushes home after the girl shows her the pictures she has found. When she arrives she finds signs of there having been an intruder in the house, but that her daughter and the babysitter are safely asleep in their beds. As she picks up the phone to call Deborah, a knife seemingly comes out of nowhere and is forced deep into her stomach. Munroe lies bleeding on the floor, while Hawker takes some more snaps.

The nurse is rushed to hospital. Hawker, meanwhile, deliberately injures his own arm so that medics might get him through the heavy security now in place at the hospital entrance. Once inside, he corners Deborah and starts to feel her breasts. She throws alcohol into his face and manages to elude him in the deserted corridors. Finding herself in the X-ray room where Nurse Munroe lies unconscious, Deborah tells a member of staff to get help while she tries to deal with the approaching killer.[347] Leading him away from the prone and defenceless Munroe, Deborah stabs Hawker in the belly.

CRITIQUE: *Visiting Hours* is an overlong, run-of-the-

VISITING HOURS
CANADA 1981
CAST: Lee Grant, William Shatner, Michael Ironside, Lenore Zann, Harvey Atkin, Helen Hughes, Michael J Reynolds, Linda Purl
STORY: Brian Taggert
PRODUCER: Claude Heroux
DIRECTOR: JEAN CLAUDE LORD

mill psycho-on-the-loose tale, which places its action within the confines of a hospital — as do *Halloween II* and *X-Ray*, made around about the same time.[348] With a TV movie quality about it, *Visiting Hours* looks out-of-place next to other films on the DPP list, and it isn't surprising that it should have been dropped before long and given an 18 classification without further cuts (the video print remains the same as the theatrical print, which was cut by a minute).

Visiting Hours, together with ***The Driller Killer***, has the distinction of being one of only two nasties ever to be broadcast on British terrestrial television.

Michael Ironside's performance is one of the film's highlights. As Colt Hawker, obsessively squeezing a rubber ball in his hand, he projects a fragile façade of normality that threatens to collapse at any moment. In the scene where he smashes his own arm in broken glass in order to gain access to the hospital, Ironside lets completely loose with a show of dementia that should have won him an award — popping pills, rolling his eyes back into his head, heaving his chest...

There appear to have been some problems translating Hawker from script to screen, however. Several seemingly important aspects of his character come to light, only to disappear almost immediately without any further ado. For instance, a golden keepsake he wears around his neck — a little bell — is established as being some kind of Achilles' heel. Deborah (Lee Grant) claims to recognise the sound it makes prior to going into surgery, and panics that the killer is in the operating room with her. But that's the only time she hears it. Elsewhere, Hawker's criminal actions appear to be politically as well as psychologically motivated, but the brief tour of the framed hate-letters on his wall and a conversation he has with the girl from the diner is the only inference of this.

Outside of Ironside's eye-rolling performance, the film's only other noteworthy moment comes when Nurse Munroe (Linda Purl) is attacked and stabbed in her home. After searching the house from top to bottom for an intruder and finding none, Munroe — and the audience — relax, feeling that the danger has passed. When the knife stabs her in the belly it comes as a genuine shock, particularly given that the film is in its final stretch and the likeable Munroe has played a pivotal role so far. Alas, the film-makers don't have the nerve to let her die (which would have been an even bigger shock), but instead opt to bring her back for one last pointless appearance — lying unconscious in the X-ray room at the film's end.

Munroe's stabbing might be one reason why *Visiting Hours* found itself on the DPP list. While no more graphic than a blade jutting out of her dress, the attack is still brutally executed. Another reason could be the killer's penchant for observing his victims in their death throes, taking snapshots of the moment.[349]

It ought to be noted that William Shatner is in *Visiting Hours*. Despite second billing to Lee Grant, his character is completely superfluous and his appearance little more than a glorified cameo. Playing TV producer Gary Baylor, Shatner turns up to tell Deborah that he cannot air her show and emotes concern as she lies in her hospital bed. He also has some of the dumbest lines in the movie, delivering them with the weight and conviction of a man who has yet to read the entirety of the script. When the girl tells the police about Hawker's photographs, Baylor arrives on the scene to illuminate everyone. "Look at that, he's created a death mask," he says. When Deborah sits worried in hospital, Baylor tells her that she's "triggered a psychopath."

Jean Claude Lord went on to direct *The Vindicator* and *Mindfield*, which also starred Michael Ironside.

THE WEREWOLF AND THE YETI

SYNOPSIS: A three-man expedition searching for evidence of the yeti in Tibet is attacked and wiped out by the very creature they are attempting to study. The results of their research are discovered and returned to expedition organiser Professor Lacombe in England, who studies the photographs and yeti scalp. "There's no doubt about it," he determines. "It's authentic." With the intention of capturing the creature, Lacombe travels to Tibet with his daughter Sylvia, assistant Melody, and fellow anthropologists Waldemar and Larry.

They travel to Kathmandu and assemble a team of guides and bearers. With Joel, a man familiar with the area, Waldemar sets off to explore a nearby pass. But soon they are lost and Joel, fearing the demons that haunt the area, panics and runs from Waldemar. Following Joel's footprints in the snow, Waldemar finds that they simply come to an end making it appear that the guide has vanished into thin air. Completely lost, Waldemar wanders around the mountainside and eventually comes across a cave in a forest, inside which is a strange shrine guarded by two beautiful sisters. They help the exhausted Waldemar and decide to keep him, as he will make a "passionate lover." He is later horrified to observe his hosts devouring human flesh — one, it transpires, is a vampire, the other a werewolf. Waldemar manages to kill them both but not before being bitten in the chest by the werewolf.

The expedition, concerned about the two missing men, head into the mountains. One of the locals warns them of bandits and suggests that, should they be attacked, it would be better to kill the women rather than have them captured alive.

As the full moon rises, Waldemar transforms into a werewolf, killing and feeding on a group of bandits who were planning an attack on the expedition.

The expedition has set up camp for the night and Sylvia goes for a walk in the woods. She is followed by a drunken team member who tries to molest her, but she slaps him away and runs back to the camp. The man is then set upon by the werewolf. Discovering his body the following morning, the team leaders believe the man was attacked by the yeti. They bury his remains and return to camp, only to find that the guides have all deserted and taken the provisions. As the four make their way back to base camp they are ambushed by bandits from Saka Khan's palace. The professor, Melody and Larry are all captured. Sylvia manages to escape, but is soon captured by three bandits who decide to rape the girl before taking her to the palace. Sylvia is saved from her ordeal when the werewolf kills all three bandits. Sylvia subsequently falls into a faint, during which time Waldemar recovers from his transformation. Together they go in search of Sylvia's father and make their way back to the area of the ambush, only to find Larry skewered on a wooden shaft. Before he dies he tells them that Melody and the professor have been taken to the palace.

Waldemar and Sylvia seek refuge in a monastery where a priest — aware of Waldemar's affliction — tells him of a magic plant that can be used as a cure when it is mixed with the blood of someone who loves him. The priest chains Waldemar to a tree so Sylvia can witness the transformation during the next full moon. Once changed, the werewolf breaks free of its bonds and escapes into the forest, killing a horse rider from the palace.

The priest provides Sylvia with a silver dagger with which to draw her blood when she finds the magic flower. However, she and Waldemar are taken prisoner by the bandits. At the palace they witness an evil priestess torturing Melody. The skin from her back is removed and placed on the diseased back of Kahn.

Sylvia and other prisoners manage to escape from their cell after stabbing a guard with the silver dagger. Some go off to take revenge on the priestess, while Sylvia frees Waldemar and together they fight their way out of the palace (discovering the body of the murdered professor in the process). Outside, Waldemar flees Sylvia as the full moon rises. Alone, she is attacked by the yeti and carried away, but the werewolf comes to her aid once again and is mortally wounded in a battle that leaves the yeti dead. Sylvia finds the magic flower, mixes its petals with her blood and feeds the blend to the werewolf. It transforms back into the healthy Waldemar, now free of his curse.

THE WEREWOLF AND THE YETI

AKA: Night of the Howling Beast; La hombre lobo en la yeti; La Maldición de la Bestia (original title); Hall of the Mountain King; Werewolf Vs. Yeti

SPAIN 1975

CAST: Paul Naschy [Jacinto Molina], Grace Mills, Castillo Escalona, Silvia Solar, Gil Vidal, Luis Induni

STORY: Jacinto Molina

PRODUCER: Modesto Perez Redondo

DIRECTOR: M I BONNS [Miguel Iglesias Bonns]

CRITIQUE: Billed as Spain's greatest horror export, Paul Naschy's early film career was subject to the same censorship problems and restraints as that of Eloy de la Iglesia, director of ***The Cannibal Man*** (and indeed Jesús Franco, who left the country after making his first films). However, where the work of de la Iglesia was more politically subversive and motivated, Naschy just wanted to emulate the Hollywood monster stars. When Naschy made his first horror films in the late-sixties, it wasn't only because he loved the genre but also because he thought they might buck the system and perhaps elevate the Spanish film industry from what Naschy considered its worse period. He was duly considered mad for "making movies about werewolves, vampires and zombies."[350] It is ironic then, that the liberalisation brought about by General Franco's death in 1975 effectively sounded the death knell for the Spanish horror boom which Naschy had helped to create (albeit largely thanks to special export versions of films containing material that couldn't yet be screened in Spain). The genre took a dive once Spanish film-makers found they could show material that had hitherto been considered taboo, and they turned to "cheaper, quicker (and suddenly quite legal and popular) erotic films."[351] Only Naschy steadfastly refused to give up on Spanish horror, continuing to act and direct in a genre whose audience was quickly dwindling away.

> I have always respected the old Universal films from Hollywood and admire the [Lon Chaney Jr] portrayal of the wolfman, because his acting is so profound, so sympathetic, you relate [to] the character and feel for him, so much so you forget the film you are seeing is a made up fantasy, not reality... In my role as the wolfman, I also tried to evoke that same sense of tragedy, that same sense of fate, and that same sympathy...
>
> —*Interview with Paul Naschy, Draculina No 10*

A former competitive weightlifter, Paul Naschy (real name: Jacinto Molina Alvarez) showed a particular fondness for playing werewolves, in each instance portraying the same lycanthropy-afflicted character, Waldemar Daninsky. Several of these films were released on video in the UK, including *Shadow of the Werewolf* and *Curse of the Devil*. However, only *Werewolf and the Yeti* was ascribed to the DPP list despite the fact that they were all equally — though not especially — gory. Indeed other Naschy films seemed more likely candidates for the banned list. *The Blue Eyes of the Broken Doll*, for instance, not only contained several bloody murders, but it even featured highlights from some of them on the video sleeve.

Naschy's movies are generally entertaining with a sufficient Hammeresque grisliness (Hammer being another Naschy favourite) and a suitably sinister atmosphere. *The Werewolf and the Yeti*, however, is unequivocally tedious, mainly due to M I Bonns' flaccid and uninspired direction. This was a far cry from the directors with whom Naschy had previously worked — Carlos Aured and Leon Klimovsky, for instance, had an ability to wring atmosphere from any given situation.

The Naschy werewolf has never been too convincing (less so than Lon Chaney Jr's portrayal of the afflicted Larry Talbot some thirty years previous) and in this instance the clumsy-looking yeti with whom he tangles is even worse. Unlike the classic Universal horror films, in which the monsters lumber around causing mayhem right up to the obligatory climactic confrontation, the yeti appears only at the end of Bonns' film for a brief moment before it is quickly despatched. Neither creature for a single moment looks anything other than a man in a furry suit.

The title of the film, in effect, refers only to the closing moments. The original title, *La Maldición de la Bestia* (The Curse of the Beast), relates to Waldemar's plight and is consequently a lot more accurate.

The only scene that may have caused problems is the flaying sequence, even though it isn't particularly strong (brief scenes of a knife leaving a bloody trail on flesh, a medium-shot of the flesh being peeled off and held aloft, followed by a glimpse of full-frontal nudity).[352] Its association with the torture of women may have given rise to the film's nasty status. Otherwise *The Werewolf and the Yeti* comprises of nothing more horrific than the transformed Waldemar lunging at his foes with his teeth bared, growling and grappling.

"With just TEN SECONDS of cuts," noted *Absurd*, "you could safely show this at a Saturday morning kids' matinee — the kids would lap it up."[353]

Video Programme Distributors Ltd (VPD) only became aware that one of their titles was liable for prosecution under the Obscene Publications Act when they opened the trade papers and saw it included on the DPP list. "Frankly it came as a complete surprise," a spokesperson for the company told the press in the eighties. "As far as any of us know here, *The Werewolf and the Yeti* has never been cited in any prosecution... it does seem a curious situation."

To be on the "safe side" VPD withdrew the title and it has remained unavailable ever since. The DPP should apologise to the nation for this one.

THE WITCH WHO CAME FROM THE SEA

SYNOPSIS: Molly, a spinster, has troubled recollections of her sea-faring father who has been missing for fifteen years. While minding her sister's teenaged boys, Tadd and Tripoli, she recounts how their grandpa was a kind-hearted, generous man who would have put them in irons for the bad language they use. As the children play, Molly's gaze becomes transfixed on two men working out on the beach. She watches them intensely, specifically their bulging trunks. Suddenly, she imagines them both dead.

On their way home, Tadd and Tripoli tell Molly they want a tattoo like grandpa probably had. She replies that he didn't have a tattoo because he was "too nice."

But this isn't a recollection shared by Cathy, her sister, who insists their father was "a drunken bum" and claims she still has a pain where poppa kicked her.

"Poppa was lost at sea," berates Molly.

"Only his brains were lost at sea," retorts her sister.

Watching TV, Molly imagines that the handsome guy in an ad for a shaving razor wants her to sail around the world with him. A football game trips her into what appears to be another dream: in a bedroom with two football players, Molly shares drinks and drugs and starts to get naked. The men think Molly's a little crazy when she starts to refer to them as part of her "crew," tying their arms and legs to the bed. But what they see as kinky fun soon turns into a nightmare as Molly gags them both and, with a razor, reaches out of shot to slice away the first guy's penis. "Aw shit," she says amidst the splashes of blood and muffled screams, "this'll take forever."

Back in front of the TV set and the football game, Molly decides it must be time to head off for her barmaid job at the Boathouse, a place whose owner is called Long John.

The following morning she hears a news report that two football players have been found brutally murdered. Molly is distraught — not because it appears that she committed the deed, but because Tadd and Tripoli have lost a couple of sporting heroes. "Those beautiful men," she sobs down the phone to her sister, "they're dead."

Molly has a flashback to when she was a little girl, helping her father build a model boat. The grizzled man has a look of strange, unnatural emotion about him as he moves closer to his daughter. The sound of seagulls swells up on the soundtrack.

Later, making love to Long John, Molly has another flashback to her childhood. Here she opens a door to see her father naked, a leering grin on his face. "Poppa?" she repeats, bewildered by the hairy sight of him.

A movie star called Billy Batt throws a party and the staff from the Boathouse bar are invited. As Molly later sits admiring Botticelli's *Birth of Venus* on a wall of Batt's house, the movie star explains that

THE WITCH WHO CAME FROM THE SEA
USA 1975 [76?]
CAST: Millie Perkins, Lonny Chapman, Vanessa Brown, Peggy Feury, Jean Pierre Camps, Mark Livingston
STORY: Robert Thom
PRODUCER: Matt Cimber
DIRECTOR: MATT CIMBER [Matteo Ottaviano]

the painting depicts a witch who came from the sea. Without further ado, the two of them retire to a bedroom and kiss. But Molly bites down hard on Batt's lip. After he slaps her away, Molly snaps at his penis and manages to break the man's wrist in the ensuing scuffle. "Could you die for love?" she yells at the actor. "Well, my father did!"

Another guest at the party is Alexander McPeak, the guy who advertises razors on the TV. Molly soon muscles McPeak's girlfriend out of the picture and has a fling with him.

At some indeterminate time, Molly visits a tattoo parlour and gets a picture of a mermaid etched onto her belly. The tattooist, Jack Dracula, has half his face covered in tattoos, a twitchy eye and the misfortune to look like Salvador Dalí. Molly tells him that the "beautiful man" from the TV came to her from the sea. (To which, Jack curiously replies that he doesn't believe in anything obscene.)

Flashback: Molly as a child sits in a bed laughing at a clown on TV. Sitting up next to her is Molly's father who starts yelling.

Cut to the present: McPeak's distraught ex-girlfriend turns up at the actor's door firing a pistol, and the police promptly arrest her, later suspecting that she might be responsible for the sex-murders of the two football players. They think McPeak might be an accomplice, but the incriminating evidence found in his house — an item of clothing — belongs not to his ex-girlfriend but to Molly.

Molly spends the evening with Long John, but some pills given to her at the Boathouse cause her to have a brief, indefinable solarised dream.

She makes love to McPeak, who has been released from police custody. Afterwards, while he is shaving, Molly takes the razor from him and slowly cuts his throat. She then removes his genitals. Covered in blood she panics, and inexplicably awakes in Long John's bed, explaining to him that the blood-covered sheets are due to her having tried to remove her mermaid tattoo with a razor in the night.

The police visit Molly's sister. Although the nervous Cathy tells them nothing, their suspicions concerning the murders are evidently turning toward Molly. This news reaches Long John who deliberates with Molly's pill-popping friend Doris how best to hide the girl.

Molly's mental state is deteriorating, accelerated by drugs given to her by Doris. Molly announces she doesn't want to wear glasses because she doesn't want to look like a hippie. When Long John questions her about McPeak, Molly asks whether the news of his death was on television. "You don't know if it's true or not unless it's on television," she reasons.

Flashback: Molly lies perfectly still as her father has intercourse with her. Suddenly the leering grin on his face drops away and he suffers a fatal heart attack. Molly struggles from beneath his motionless form to spy a mermaid tattoo on his belly.

Tadd and Tripoli arrive at the Boathouse, refusing to believe their mother's claim that Molly is a killer. Seated at her side, completely unperturbed by their aunt's estranged state, the children take it in turns to feed her pills and liquor.

"Doesn't it matter that I didn't hate any of them?" Molly says of her victims, implying in a final babbling rant there may have been more of them.

As the police arrive Molly sees herself on a raft floating on the open sea.

CRITIQUE: Matt Cimber is probably best known for the widely panned *Butterfly*, which starred Stacy Keach and was projected as a starmaking vehicle for the young Pia Zadora, real-life bride of multimillionaire Meshulam Riklis.[354]

Cimber was the last husband of blonde bombshell Jayne Mansfield. He became her publicist and tried to revitalise her flagging career with the title role in his film *Single Room Furnished*, a 'serious' part for Mansfield but a film that would remain without distribution until after her death.

The rest of his filmography includes several obscure trash 'gems,' running the gamut from blaxploitation — *The Black Six* and *The Candy Tangerine Man* — to Indiana Jones-inspired high adventure — *Hundra* and *Yellow Hair and the Fortress of Gold*. At the beginning of the seventies, prior to *Deep Throat* and the hardcore explosion, Cimber was one of the first filmmakers to turn to his hand to 'white coaters,' films which violated the obscenity laws but avoided prosecution by presenting sexually explicit material in an 'educational' context. *Man and Wife* was Cimber's initial foray into this area, and it featured two couples illustrating various sexual positions. At a cost of around $86,000 Cimber claimed it made more than $2.5 million at the box office and quickly followed it up with *He and She*, which covered much the same ground but also demonstrated foreplay and masturbation.

Cimber was involved with at least two other 'sex-ed' films — directing *The Sensually*

Liberated Female (released through the Institute for Adult Education) and producing *Black is Beautiful*, which "despite its pseudo-anthropology" was a success "in the ghetto theatres of cities with substantial black populations."[355]

According to *Psychotronic Video*, Cimber "was last heard making G.L.O.W. wrestling TV shows."

Little of the director's training in explicit motion pictures can be evidenced in *Witch Who Came from the Sea* (although a stray "Ooh, yeah" can be heard in the *ménage à trois* sequence, which utilises heavy reverb throughout). The numerous amorous couplings have a singularly unappealing and unattractive quality about them. But that's probably a blessing, given the truly shocking nature of the final flashback and the repugnant image of infant feet split between pummelling adult thighs. Brief as it is, this surely must stand as the most gratuitous and confrontational depictions of paedophile sex ever to grace a motion picture, and from this point alone it isn't difficult to see why *Witch* was relegated to the DPP list. The scene that follows this one would undoubtedly have caused further problems with its use of minors. It shows Tadd and Tripoli helping their aunt to die, incorporating close-up shots of them dropping pills into her mouth and holding liquor to her lips.

It would be fair to assume that if ever submitted for certification, these scenes — plus the shots of a naked Molly, covered in McPeak's blood — would all require excising before *Witch* stood any chance of seeing a release. But even then, the peculiar atmosphere that pervades the film could ultimately prove a stumbling block. The BBFC are notoriously reticent when it comes to works that refuse to adhere to a linear narrative — it's as if they fear that such films hold some subliminal meaning, awaiting to be untapped.

The Witch Who Came from the Sea is no landmark production and is perhaps too bizarre to be regarded as pure exploitation. It's a horror film with art-house pretensions. It draws obvious inspiration from Lewis John Carlino's *The Sailor Who Fell from Grace with the Sea*,[356] which was described by the *Monthly Film Bulletin* as having "a virtually eventless psychological narrative." Beyond the analogous titles, the two films share some kinky sexcapades, as well as notions concerning the corruption of youth, and the ideology that a sailor's commitment to the sea somehow keeps him pure. Carlino's production even concludes on a sequence where drugs are used to bring about salvation and a 'return' to innocence for a central character.

Millie Perkins is exemplary in her role as the psychotic Molly (it would be six years before she took another part) and — as well as the shocking scenes noted above — the film has some moments of genuine lyricism and tenderness.

Curiously, Tadd and Tripoli feeding their aunt a lethal cocktail of drugs and booze is one of them...

WOMEN BEHIND BARS

SYNOPSIS: In a harbour at a picturesque Mediterranean town near the sea, a robbery takes place and three masked men escape with a suitcase full of diamonds. One of the gang, in a double-cross, shoots his companions and goes to meet his lover Shirley Fields, at the Flamingo Club. She in turn double-crosses him. Shirley hides the diamonds and confesses to the police that she has shot dead her lover in a jealous rage but that she knows nothing of the robbery or missing bounty.

She is taken to an all-woman prison which appears to be centrally located in the town itself. Here, the warden is convinced that Shirley knows more about the "hold-up of the year" than she is letting on, and places a snitch in her cell to try and find out more.

The prisoners — all beautiful — lie naked on their bunks, their heads and breasts framed by the camera.

A gentleman by the name of Milton Warren arrives in the town and books himself into a hotel overlooking the prison. He spies on it through his binoculars. It transpires that Warren is an insurance man investigating the diamond robbery insurance claim. He goes to the prison to interview Shirley, calling to a guard to let him in.

Warren learns nothing from his brief interview with Shirley, and returns to his hotel room where he is met by Bill, the claimant. Bill and Warren are working a scam together — Bill arranged to have his diamonds stolen and Warren secured the insurance money. Now the diamonds are *really* missing. It seems that Shirley has double-crossed everybody.

"If only she has a family," Warren ruminates, "a mother, a father, someone we could threaten to murder if she didn't talk."

The only option open to them, the men deduce, is to spring Shirley from prison.

Back at the prison a woman named Maria is reprimanded for starting a fight in the exercise yard. The warden wants Maria to kneel down and apologise. When she refuses, he tells the guard to flog her "Harder! More! Just a second — I think she's fainted!"

"No, not yet, Colonel," replies the guard.

Following a trip to the infirmary, Maria has to apologise to everyone in the yard individually.

Shirley is the next person to endure the wrath of the warden. This for eating a smuggled note from Warren and not divulging its message. She is strapped naked into a chair and is given electric shocks via electrodes applied to her genitalia (which she could easily pull off despite her bonds). He breasts bounce with each shock and then she faints.

Back in her cell, Shirley finds the gun to which the note referred. She has a quick lesbian fling with Martine, the snitch, and they go to their respective bunks to sleep. In the middle of the night, Shirley awakens and strangles Martine to death.

She is taken to see the warden, who confesses to the prisoner, "I find you as beautiful when you're laughing as when you're suffering."

But Shirley pulls the gun and takes the warden hostage, using him to break out of the prison. Once free she shoots him in the back. Bill is waiting for her, demanding to know where his diamonds are. Shirley tricks him into going into the basement of the Flamingo Club, and there shoots him dead. (Cheesy and wholly inappropriate organ music which featured during the prison torture scenes can now be heard playing through the club's sound system.)[357]

Warren meanwhile books himself out of the hotel, and heads for the train station to meet Shirley, whereupon they intend to travel to Mexico together. In his hand is a briefcase containing the diamonds. He muses to himself: "Neither Shirley or I have any previous criminal record. It is true we've committed murder, but who are the victims? People who deserve to die."

WOMEN BEHIND BARS
FRANCE/BELGIUM 1977
CAST: Lina Romay, Martine Steed, Nathalie Chapell, Roger Darton, Ronald Weiss, Denis Torre
STORY: R Marceignac
DIR OF PRODUCTION: Pierre Querut
DIRECTOR: RICK DECONNINK [Jesús Franco]

CRITIQUE: *Women Behind Bars*[358] fits into a subgenre of exploitation cinema known as women-in-prison movies (WIP for short), a development of the macho Hollywood Prison movies that were made popular in the 1930s, and remain so even today.[359] Initially, much of the drawing power of these movies lay in the fact they offered an insider's view of a world alien to most audiences. While this aspect of their appeal has diminished somewhat over the years, the prison film remains a tantalising draw, thanks to the regimen of motifs which consist of confinement, strict rules, constant surveillance, gruelling day-to-day existence and the underlying threat of violence. This might stand as a potent brew for full-on machismo, but it is easy to see how the same elements can be shifted to an all-female environment for a sexualised, no less potent, result. As well as adopting these same clichés, women-in-prison films have developed a few of their own.[360]

Female penitentiaries have been a focus for movie story lines for almost as long as their male counterparts, but it wasn't until John Cromwell's *Caged* in 1950 that they veered away from social melodrama to portray a grittier, more damning reality. Directors like Jack Hill and Gerry DeLeon, with their respective *The Big Doll House* and *Women in Cages*, took the whole thing a step further by injecting into the mix a liberal dose of torture, rape and nude shower scenes. Before long the genre was stagnant, with directors concentrating less on story and character, and more on the sexploitative elements. Production costs, which had never been much to begin with, were cut even further when the prisons in these films were relocated to isolated settings, like the jungle. The introduction of a slave-trafficking theme also provided a legitimate excuse to downsize the cast and props — and films like Cirio H Santiago's *Hell Hole* would centre upon a mere handful of prisoners incarcerated together in a single barren cell (looking just like every other room in the building). Thanks to the glut of productions lensed in Europe and the Philippines throughout the seventies, the WIP film soon became a blur of interchangeable story lines, with only the increasingly brutal acts of punishment and degradation showing any kind of imagination at all.

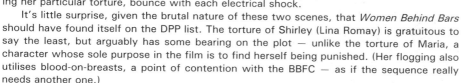

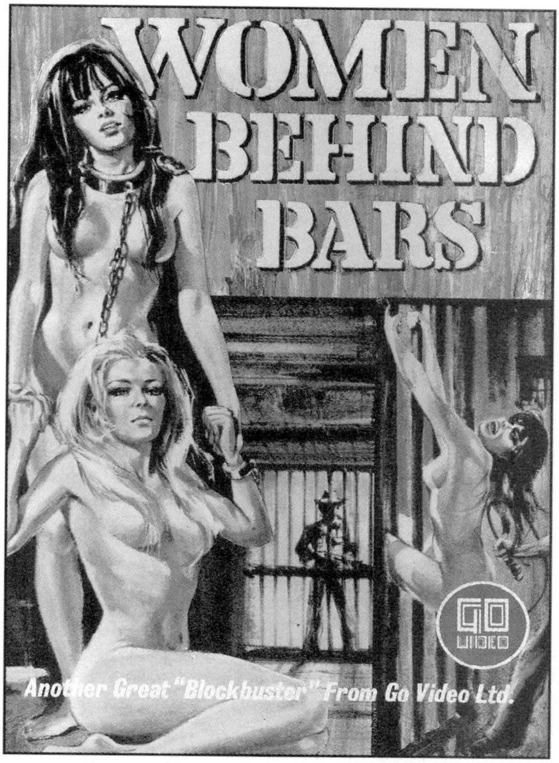

Jesús Franco's *Women Behind Bars* might at first sound like something of an aberration — given that it has a convoluting plot full of double-bluffs — but the fact remains that nothing in the film stands out like the two torture scenes in the prison. In Franco's cinematic mud bath, they provide a few minutes of voyeuristic assiduity.[361]

Maria is subjected to twenty-four lashes in total, filmed in real time, with a crash zoom accompanying each instance of the whip contacting bare flesh. Shirley's bare breasts, during her particular torture, bounce with each electrical shock.

It's little surprise, given the brutal nature of these two scenes, that *Women Behind Bars* should have found itself on the DPP list. The torture of Shirley (Lina Romay) is gratuitous to say the least, but arguably has some bearing on the plot — unlike the torture of Maria, a character whose sole purpose in the film is to find herself being punished. (Her flogging also utilises blood-on-breasts, a point of contention with the BBFC — as if the sequence really needs another one.)

Women Behind Bars came in a year that saw *three* other WIP-themed films from Franco! Indeed, Franco's first foray into the genre in 1968 — *99 Women* — could be described as the template for the decidedly more aggressively-minded WIP features that became so popular in the seventies. It starred Mercedes McCambridge, and, despite the title, rarely featured more than a handful of women on the screen at any given time. Franco followed the success of *99 Women* with *Lovers of Devil's Island, Caged Women, Wanda The Wicked Warden, Women For Cellblock Nine, Love Camp* (1977), and *Sadomania*.[362]

Unrelated to Franco's film was a successful Off Broadway play called *Women Behind Bars*, whose campness and high melodramatics helped to reinvent the WIP genre in the eighties.

Curious details: The opening shot of Franco's *Women Behind Bars* is a panoramic view of the town and railway station which looks like ropy old stock footage. But as characters find themselves at the railway station come the end of the film, presumably it isn't. Dialogue states that the hold-up at the beginning of the film takes place on a Chinese junk, but it doesn't — indeed, there doesn't appear to be a junk in the harbour.

(It is interesting to note that incarcerated women would seem ideally suited to the XXX market. But there are surprisingly few hardcore WIP offshoots. Ted Roter's *Prison Babies* is one, Michel Ricaud's *Women In Prison* is another. Osvaldo de Oliveira's *Bare Behind Bars* gallantly tried to make the best of both worlds by featuring sex of a softcore nature for most of its duration, but it also threw in a couple of brief hardcore encounters for good measure.)

XTRO

SYNOPSIS: Whilst playing with his son Tony, Sam Phillips is abducted by a bright light that suddenly appears in the sky, turning day to night. No one believes the boy's story and three years after the disappearance, Rachel Phillips has given up on her husband and plans to re-marry. But strange things are happening…

An unearthly quadruped is roaming the countryside following the appearance of a second mysterious light. On a lonely stretch of road the creature is struck by a car, killing both its occupants when they stop to investigate. It finds an isolated farmhouse and attacks a woman who is living alone, attaching itself to her mouth and impregnating her with alien seed. The next morning the woman wakes from the ordeal to find the creature reduced to a lifeless skin and her own stomach beginning to bloat up at a phenomenal rate. She discharges onto the kitchen floor and dies giving birth to a fully developed adult male. It's Sam. He bites through the umbilical cord, cleans himself up and dresses in clothes belonging to a victim of his alien 'father.' When he attempts to call Rachel from a public phonebox he is unable to speak and the receiver starts to melt in his hand.

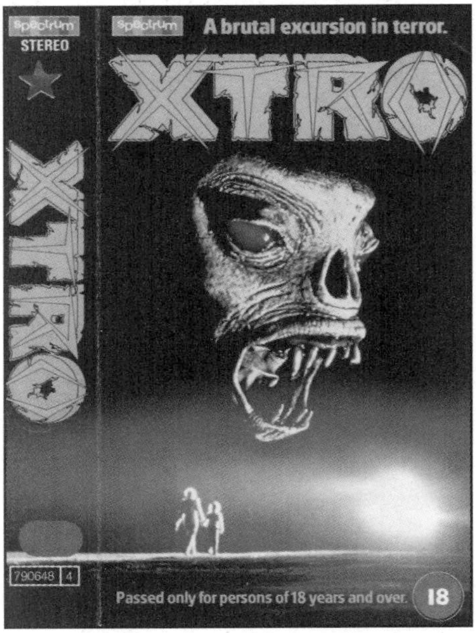

XTRO
AKA: Monstromo; Monstro; The Judas Goat (working titles)
GREAT BRITAIN 1982
CAST: Philip Sayer, Bernice Stegers, Danny Bainin, Maryam d'Abo, Simon Nash
ORIGINAL STORY: Michel Parry & Harry Bromley Davenport
PRODUCER: Mark Forstater
DIRECTOR: HARRY BROMLEY DAVENPORT

In the Phillips household, Tony anticipates his father's return and talks of him incessantly — much to the chagrin of Joe, an American photographer who's planning to become the boy's stepfather. Joe's philosophy is "Look British, think Yiddish."

When Rachel goes to collect Tony from school she is shocked to meet Sam. "I'm back," he says, claiming to have no recollection of the intervening three years.

Rachel lets Sam stay at the apartment, an invitation which doesn't sit easily with Joe.

Shortly after his arrival, Tony finds his father devouring the eggs laid by his pet snake, but is consoled when Sam explains he's not the same any more — that he was changed by "them" so that he could live on their world. Sam then bites into the boy's shoulder, bestowing on him unearthly powers. Analise, the au pair, will be "perfect" he says cryptically.

Tony discovers that he is able to make a spinning top spin by simply willing it. His new-found ability extends to creating life-size replicants of his favourite toys: a dwarf clown, and an Action Man doll that goes and kills an elderly neighbour.

Joe feels he can't stay under the same roof as Sam and so leaves. Rachel doesn't seem particularly perturbed by this development but does later seek Joe's advice after discovering a photo of an anonymous young woman and a fat roll of money in her husband's (stolen) jacket. Needless to say, the photographer isn't interested.

Leaving Tony in the care of Analise, Rachel attempts to jog Sam's memory by taking him to their old cottage retreat — the scene of his abduction and the last thing he claims to be able to remember. Sam has a funny turn and is dismayed to discover that chunks of his scalp and hair are falling out.

Rachel is worried that no one at home is answering the phone. Unbeknownst to her, Tony and his new-found pal the clown are putting into action a grand alien plan in which Analise — having been knocked unconscious and 'impregnated' — is in a cocoon in the bathroom delivering eggs. Any perceived threat is dealt with in a spectacularly adroit manner (Analise's boyfriend is killed by a panther in the kitchen, and a caretaker has his throat cut by a self-propelling spinning top).

Promising Rachel that he'll stop by the apartment and check things out, Joe is side-tracked by a newspaper report concerning the brutal death of a young woman. The accompanying photograph matches that found in Sam's pocket and, concerned for Rachel's safety, Joe heads off for the cottage. Tony, seemingly in anticipation of this move, was waiting by Joe's car and accompanies him. They arrive just as Rachel discovers there is something very wrong with her husband. Fissures are erupting on his face and over his body, progressively worsening until ultimately they reveal Sam's alien form. Tony also takes on an alien appearance. But in spite of this, Joe makes an attempt to stop Sam absconding with the child — only to be killed by an ear-piercing shriek. Hand in hand with his son, Sam boards the alien craft that has landed nearby.

Back in London, Rachel's apartment has taken on a bleached out, curiously dream-like quality. She is happily inspecting the alien eggs in the bathtub until suddenly one of the egg burst open and a disembodied unearthly limb attaches itself to her mouth.

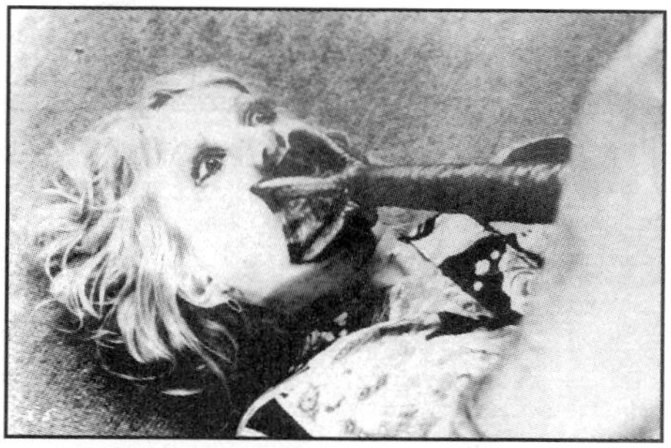

TOP: The host of alien seed in *Xtro*.

CRITIQUE: The alien creature is briefly seen roaming the countryside in the film's early moments and remains a decidedly unnerving aberration — despite being clearly a man in a rubber suit. The unnatural limb shape of the creature is achieved by the strange posture of the man inside the suit, who is upside-down in a crab position. Movement is evidently restricted in this position and thankfully it is only through the use of tight close-ups and point-of-view shots that the film-makers choose to imply the creature's progress through the woods.

Most of the visual effects in *Xtro* rely on similarly inventive flourishes more than they do a sizeable budget, but are no less effective because of it. The alien spacecraft is implied not with intricate model work but with blinding lights, a wind machine, and the occasional animated cut-out. But then what do such concessions matter when the arrival of the thing causes inexplicable, spectacular 'pop art' explosions?

Of course when invention runs dry the audience can fall back on some unpleasant prosthetics, such as the tumescent impregnation scene (replete with bubbling flesh and distended veins) and the adult-birth (in which fleetingly we see a full-grown head exiting a vagina). A distraction of a rather more pleasant kind is Maryam D'Abo as Analise the au pair, who looks like a young Nastassia Kinski. She has two completely gratuitous nude scenes.

According to *Fangoria*,[363] director Harry Bromley Davenport's "strategy" on *Xtro* was to go for fresh talent in the cast as opposed to 'name' stars and that way spend more on the film's 'extensive special effects.' Indeed the résumé of the technicians employed would indicate an extravangza akin to the blockbuster genre movies *Xtro* was so clearly trying to emulate — *Alien*,[364] *An American Werewolf in London* and *Close Encounters of the Third Kind*. But the result has more the look of *Inseminoid*, another low-budget British sci-fi horror picture. Set on a distant planet, this film also incorporates scenes of extraterrestrial rape.

The idea that *Xtro* was destined to be some special effects extravaganza began to dis-

Unnatural limb shapes. *Xtro.*

perse as production progressed. Executive producer and American distributor Robert Shaye actually envisaged *Xtro* should be reliant on special effects to the point that "the plot takes some strange right-angle turns in order to include some of the sequences devised."[365] Realistically, however, they made no pretence that these effects were unlikely to be anything other than modest, rather hit-and-miss affairs.

"On this picture," Shaye said,

> we learned that effects are *more* expensive than we'd thought... And then, not everything that is built, at whatever expense, works. In fact, a good deal of the effects were done and redone after the principal filming was completed, because we really didn't feel we had what we wanted... There are effects in the film that turned out far better than we'd hoped, and some that turned out worse. And there were some that were far worse, where we had to say "no way."

This latter fact may account for several characters being credited in the original cinema release of *Xtro* who don't actually appear in any final print of the film.[366] (Such as 'Consulting Gynaecologist,' 'Van Driver' and 'Petrol Pump Attendant.' If any of these missing characters were assigned an unnatural death, one can but wonder in what form it befell the 'Lavatory Attendant'!) However, *Xtro* is hardly the incoherent mess of a film that so many critics have accused it of being. Certainly at times it appears deliberately obtuse — with its materialisation of clowns, panthers and such like — but Tony's limitless telekinetic abilities cover an awful lot of cracks and can account for just about every indiscretion in the film!

That said, there is no excuse for the dull and protracted live Action Man sequence, which appears to be little more than a showcase for 'human robotics,' so much of a fad in the early eighties. Indeed, the commando here is played by Tok who was a minor celebrity thanks to his convincing robotic performances on British light entertainment programmes. (His robot partner was Tik, who plays the alien creature at the beginning of *Xtro*.)

One sequence that does perhaps fall outside of Tony's telekinetic construct comes at the film's end, when Rachel returns to her London apartment and finds the eggs laid by Analise. The brilliant white, featureless environment gives the sequence a surreal, dream-like look, an unnecessary quality that serves only to befuddle. It ought to be noted that the original cinematic ending differed considerably from the one in the video release. The theatrical print showed Rachel returning to the inexplicably surreal apartment to find "lots of Tony-lookalikes, all murmuring 'Mummy.'"[367] This less graphic alternative is reported to be considerably more disturbing than the blood-spattered, face-hugging finale that adorns the video release. As to why the switch was made, Nigel Burrell in *Flesh & Blood*[368] believes it was because of negative feedback generated by the original ending.

A review in *Starburst* offers the tantalising suggestion that there is even more footage to be mined from *Xtro*, notably some stronger scenes of Sam's adult-birth intended for the Japanese market.[369] In a rare interview with the director himself many years later however, Bromley Davenport told *The DarkSide*[370] that a more explicit model for this scene had been made, but they ultimately couldn't use it "as the Japanese market would never have allowed it in the final cut — it had pubic hair..."

Bromley Davenport has to date made two sequels to *Xtro*. Dealing with a creature from a parallel dimension (*Xtro II: The Second Encounter*) and an alien roaming an island owned by the government (*Xtro III: Watch the Skies*), these films are related to the first in name only.

A 1968 stinker by James A Sullivan originally titled *Night Fright*, was released in Britain as *The Extra Terrestrial Nastie* (the emphasis being on the 'x' in *Extra*) in an attempt to cash-in on the success of *ET* and notoriety of *Xtro*.

Removed from its sci-fi trappings, *Xtro* offers a striking analogy of an incestuous relationship. This can be seen most vividly in the scenes where Sam 'interferes' with his son and later tells him to keep the matter their secret.

ZOMBIE CREEPING FLESH

SYNOPSIS: The Hope Centre is a research facility based in New Guinea, whose purpose it is to produce synthetic food to combat the Third World hunger crisis. When a radioactive leak is detected, maintenance men are sent in to investigate. They find a dead rat which abruptly returns to life and kills one of the workers after squirming under his protective hood. The leak worsens and the entire plant is contaminated with a radioactive cloud. Those affected are transformed into flesh eating zombies and soon enough the whole research station is overrun with the walking dead.

A crack team of commandos is despatched by an unspecified government into New Guinea to close down and secure Hope Centre. Meanwhile, a TV news team that has been sent to cover the recent outbreak of unexplained deaths and cannibalism, arrives at a deserted outpost in the area. One member of the team, Josie, goes to investigate the surrounding buildings, leaving her son in the care of his father. The boy is sick, having been bitten in the stomach by a "crazed native." The other members of the team — Leah and Max the cameraman — go in search of water only to be confronted by a decomposing zombie. They rush back to the outpost pursued by more walking corpses and arrive in time to witness the team of commandos shoot dead the injured boy — it transpires he has died, returned as a zombie, and started to devour his father. Two soldiers go to intercept the zombies advancing from the forest, and discover they can only be stopped with a gunshot to the head. Leah goes in search of Josie only to find her mutilated corpse in one of the buildings. The zombie priest (with a fleshless face) that killed Josie now advances on Leah, but is felled by the soldiers.

Leah and Max join the team of commandos and head to a nearby village. Having gained the trust of the natives they discover the entire village is contaminated and many people have died. By nightfall the village is overwhelmed by zombies. The group escape unharmed but the soldiers are concerned about the journalists interfering with the secrecy of their mission. After their own jeep fails they commandeer the reporters' Land Rover and agree to drop them at the next inhabited location. Stopping to collect water they encounter zombies lurching from the forest. Max films at close hand as the soldiers take pot-shots.

The radio reports on the increasing danger posed by the radioactive cloud over Hope Centre. The United Nations are unable to come up with any solution to the problem.

The group reach an isolated house and split up to explore the rooms. Upstairs, Mike, the commando leader, finds a dead elderly woman in a rocking chair (she has a small animal nesting in her exposed bowels). She suddenly reanimates and Mike is forced to destroy her with a shot to the head. Less fortunate is the soldier who is attacked, overwhelmed and devoured by zombies in the cellar. Soon the whole house is surrounded and the team are forced to flee, eventually reaching the coast where they travel by dinghy to the island-located Hope Centre.

Wandering through the seemingly deserted plant, Max and a soldier are killed by zombies who exit an elevator. Leah and the remaining two soldiers head up to the control room only to be attacked themselves. Mike is bitten in the throat but still manages to fulfil his mission objective to locate and destroy secret documents. Leah is able to deduce that the production of a synthetic food is just a cover, and that the Hope Centre was actually developing a nerve gas. This would turn the people of overcrowded Third World countries into deranged cannibals — eating one another would thereby solve their own population growth and food shortage problems.

Unable to escape, Leah and the remaining soldier are devoured by the zombies.

In an American bar a news bulletin relates a local incident where a limbless corpse has come back to life in a medical school. A couple leaving the bar laugh at the report only to be attacked by the crowds of zombies outside.

CRITIQUE: There was a glut of zombie movies in the late-seventies and early eighties triggered by the success of George Romero's lugubrious *Dawn of the Dead*. The majority of these imitations were poor,[371] with only Lucio Fulci's ***Zombie Flesh-Eaters*** managing to achieve any semblance of a credible identity of its own. Falling into the former camp, of imitating rather than innovating, is Bruno Mattei's *Zombie Creeping Flesh*.

Like Romero, Mattei puts the cause of zombification down to a scientific experiment. Instead of a space probe bringing an unknown virus back to Earth however,[372] the cause of the reanimation in *Zombie Creeping Flesh* is somewhat more cynical, being a manufactured virus spread deliberately throughout the Third World. Both films feature central characters who work in TV, and Mattei closes his movie with a news broadcast reporting on the reanimation of a limbless corpse (inferring that the zombie plague has spread from the Third World to the United States). This would appear an attempt by Mattei to lead audiences into thinking that *Zombie Creeping Flesh* was a prologue to Romero's film (as opposed to simple plagiarism), as *Dawn of the Dead* actually *opens* with such a news broadcast.

ZOMBIE CREEPING FLESH
AKA: Night of the Zombies; Virus (original title); Hell of the Living Dead; Apocalipsis Canibal
ITALY/SPAIN 1981
CAST: Margit Evelyn Newton, Frank Garfeeld, Selan Karay, Robert O'Neal, Gaby Renom, Luis Fonoll
STORY: Claudio Fragasso & J M Cunilles
PRODUCER: Sergio Cortona
DIRECTOR: VINCENT DAWN [Bruno Mattei]

The connection between the two films is more clearly defined in a prologue missing from the UK print of *Zombie Creeping Flesh*, in which a SWAT team storms an embassy under the control of terrorists. This sequence is wholly derivative of the opening moments of Romero's *Dawn*, which also shows a SWAT team storming a building full of terrorists. Both films feature a musical soundtrack by Goblin, indeed Mattei acquired the rights to use passages of music created specifically for Romero's film.

Zombie Creeping Flesh offers nothing new or original, and the masses of stock footage (much of it lifted from Akira Ide's mondo film *Guinea Ama*) only confirms the hastiness and laziness being its production. Each time a character looks up or out in any direction, grainy wildlife documentary footage is inserted to give the illusion of an exotic location.

The film is full of silly overstated dialogue and laughably puerile set-pieces — though perhaps none so puerile as Leah deciding that, in order to be accepted by the natives, she must take off her clothes and wander at length through the jungle daubed in paint. Bruno Mattei — influenced enough by Romero's *Dawn* to choose the pseudonym Vincent 'Dawn'[373] — has claimed that it takes him on average three to four months to complete a movie, "from writing the screenplay to the end product" as he told *European Trash Cinema*.[374] In the same interview Mattei confided he hadn't yet made a film he was happy with, and described the type of cinema he was involved in as "a routine." (He has no qualms about changing direction partway through a production in order to capitalise on fluctuating cinematic trends.)[375]

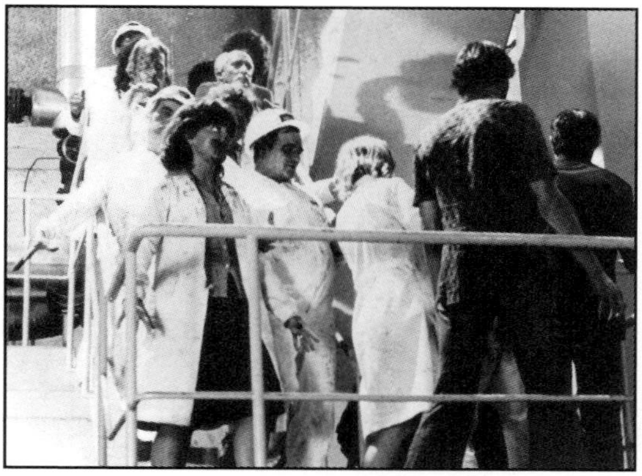

No hope at the Hope Centre. The dead go walkabout in *Zombie Creeping Flesh*.

Like many gore movies, *Zombie Creeping Flesh* attempts to hide its insignificant plot behind gruesome special effects. Unfortunately, most of these were removed for its release in the UK, thus rendering the film even more meaningless. As well as the aforementioned SWAT prologue, several scenes — including documentary footage of real corpses and primitive funerary rites — had been excised from *Zombie Creeping Flesh* for its cinema release in 1982.[376] (In total there were approximately fifteen minutes' worth of cuts.) It was this same version that Merlin released on video, which contained nothing particularly offensive or overtly violent. The film's title and the fact that it had a few fleeting scenes of cannibalism were probably enough to bring it to the attention of the DPP.

While the film itself doesn't have much going for it, it at least should keep conspiracy theorists relatively entertained — the pre-Aids concept of a man-made killer virus being unleashed on the Third World and spreading...?

ZOMBIE FLESH EATERS

SYNOPSIS: An unmanned sailboat enters New York harbour causing problems for other traffic. A patrol boat intercepts the craft and two policemen board to discover the cabin strewn with rubbish. One officer discovers a severed hand when suddenly he is set upon by a lumbering, decomposing man. In the ensuing struggle he pulls lumps of rotten flesh from the assailant before getting his own throat torn out. Advancing on the other cop, the man is shot several times and plunges into the water.

With the boat safely moored in the dock, the police question Ann Bowles, the daughter of the owner of the boat. She confirms the craft belongs to her father but admits she doesn't know where he is.

The body of the murdered cop is being examined at the mortuary. The pathologist is unaware that beneath the sheet the body is beginning to move.

That night Anne sneaks on board the boat to try and find some clue to her father's whereabouts. Also on the boat is investigative newspaper reporter Peter West, sent by his editor to cover the incident and search for leads. They decide to work together and discover a letter addressed to Ann from her father, in which he explains he has contracted a disease and is unable to leave the Caribbean island of Matul. Together they fly out to the Caribbean and meet an American couple by the name of Brian and Susan who own a boat and agree to take them to the island.

"Matul. Not a cool place to hit. Natives claim it's cursed. Avoid it like the plague," Brian says.

Meanwhile on Matul, Dr Menard is trying unsuccessfully to contact the mainland by radio.

"I want to leave this damn island, right now!" shouts his wife.

"Well you can't right now, the radio isn't working," responds Menard, advising his wife he has to leave for the hospital.

"Have they found another one?" she queries. "They have, haven't they? Tell me the truth. Where did they find it this time?"

"They're on the other side of the island," Menard tries to reassure her.

Sailing to the island Susan decides to take some photographs of the reefs, but in the water she is menaced by a shark. Brian manages to get his rifle and fire off a few shots before the shark rams the boat. With this distraction Susan swims to the seabed and hides amongst some rocks, but is grabbed from behind and attacked by a reanimated corpse. As she shakes free of its clutches, the zombie then attacks the shark. Back on board the boat Susan tells her companions that there was a man on the seabed.

On Matul, Menard is tending to the dying people in the hospital. Lucas, his assistant, tells him that everyone is leaving the island.

Back at the house, Menard's wife is taking a shower when she is alerted to a zombie lurking in another room. Just in time she manages to slam a door on it, shearing away its fingers. But the zombie smashes through the louvres of the door, grabs the woman's hair and drags her towards the splintered wood, piercing her eye on a shard.

The boat has been damaged following the shark attack and Brian fires off flares. From the island Lucas sees the distress signal and informs Menard, who goes to investigate. Menard tells the new arrivals that he worked with Ann's father, but that he contracted a disease which reanimates the body after death. The doctor asks the group to take the Land Rover and check on his wife at the house. They do so, only to find her body being devoured by a group of zombies. Fleeing the scene, they run the Land Rover into a tree and succeed in knocking the vehicle — and West's ankle — out of action. They continue their journey on foot, as best they can.

At the hospital, more victims of the strange disease are being brought in. As each victim dies Menard shoots the cadaver in the head.

"Do you know what has caused all this?," the doctor asks his assistant. "Is it voodoo?"

"Lucas not know nothing, man," the assistant replies. "The father of my father always say when the earth spit out the dead they will come back to suck the blood of the living."

"That's nonsense. That's just a stupid superstition," Menard responds.

"Yes, you are right, doctor. You know many more things than Lucas."

"I don't believe that voodoo can bring the dead back to life."

"And Lucas not believe that the dead be dead."

In the forest West is unable to continue on his damaged leg. Brian finds an ancient helmet and realises they are in an ancient Conquistador cemetery. Hands suddenly push up through the earth grabbing at West's ankle and Ann's hair. A worm-riddled corpse rises from the ground and tears out Susan's throat. Bullets fired into its body have no effect, but West finally fells it by splitting its head apart with a wooded cross.

Leaving Susan's body behind them, with the dead rising from their graves, the group finally make it to Menard's hospital where they barricade themselves in. They prepare petrol bombs as the zombies surround the building and start hammering at the doors and windows. Menard goes to retrieve his gun but is bitten in the face by a zombie. Another zombie tears a lump from Lucas' arm and he becomes infected, killing a nurse before attacking Ann. West comes to her aid and finishes Lucas off.

The hospital is soon overrun and Brian, Ann and West escape as the building goes up in flames. Heading back to the boat, Brian runs into the reanimated Susan and in his hesitancy to shoot her is bitten on the arm. At sea, Brian soon collapses from his infected wound and is locked in the bilge. An announcement comes on the radio informing listeners that a national emergency has been declared in New York and the whole of the city is plagued by walking corpses.

The zombified Brian is trying to smash his way out of the bilge as the broadcaster screams — *"Aaaaaaaaaaaargh!"* The living dead have invaded his studio.

ZOMBIE FLESH EATERS
TITLE ON PRINT: ZOMBIE FLESH-EATERS
AKA: Zombi 2; Zombie
ITALY 1979
CAST: Tisa Farrow, Ian McCulloch, Richard Johnson, Al Cliver, Auretta Gay
STORY: Walter Patricarca
PRODUCERS: Ugo Tucci & Fabrizio de Angelis
DIRECTOR: LUCIO FULCI

Zombie Flesh-Eaters.

CRITIQUE: *Zombie Flesh-Eaters* has a satisfying symmetry to it. The concluding sequence on the boat evokes the abandoned vessel of the opening scenes sailing into New York harbour. It was on board this vessel that Ann and West tried to discover the fate of the crew. Now, not only do they have the answer but they themselves face the same terrible fate.

Indeed, quite a number of the memorable scenes in *Zombie Flesh-Eaters* are aquatic. There is the timeless mystery evoked by crewless vessels adrift, the brain-numbing discovery that while out at sea the sanctuary offered by "home" is no more (New York is overrun with the living dead) and, of course, the famous underwater battle between two very different man-eaters...

The astonishing sequence of a corpse walking on the sea bed and fighting with a shark is marred only by some clumsy editing that breaks the continuity. No doubt influenced by the box office draw of *Jaws* and possibly even stuntman Evel Knievel's subsequent (much heralded but cancelled) motorcycle leap across a pool of sharks, the sequence nonetheless remains on first-viewing a jaw-dropping one.[377] In what couldn't have been a comfortable stunt to shoot (regardless of the fact that the shark looks pretty decrepit), the ensuing battle sees the zombie tearing a chunk of flesh from the fish before losing its own arm.

The whole film has a vibrancy to it — whether it is the camera circling a lone member of the living dead wandering through the village, or the rich crimson shock of the horrific wound inflicted upon Susan's throat. Courtesy of a perpetual sandstorm, rolling tumbleweeds, distant pounding of tribal drums, superstitious villagers and Dr Menard's constantly sweating brow, Fulci perfectly attunes cliché and stereotype to capture a stifling sense of decay and timeless death.

Ann: "Drums!"
West: "Getting closer!"
Susan [screaming at the unseen]: "I hate it! You bastards! I can't take it!"
Brian [contemplative]: "Playing a little voodoo on us. It's a sound all of its own."

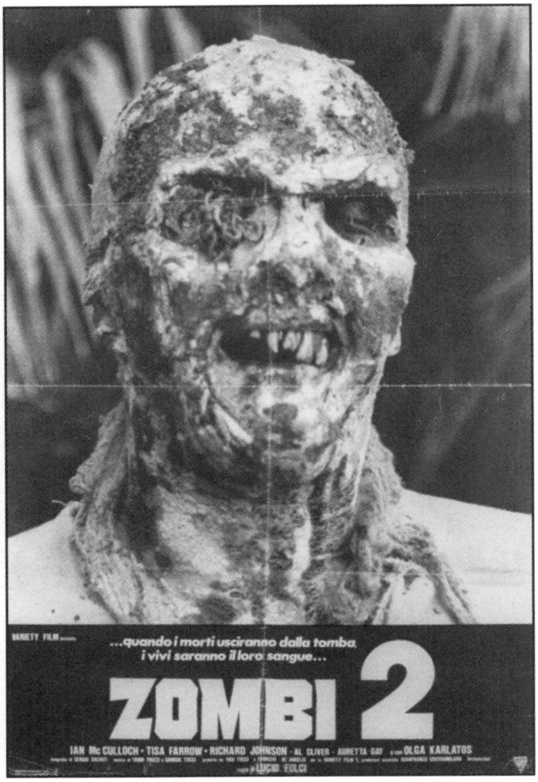

LEFT, TOP AND BOTTOM: Ann, West, Susan and Brian try to make a run for it in *Zombie Flesh-Eaters*.
RIGHT: Fulci's ugly dead.

Menard doesn't believe in voodoo, but the dead coming back to life is a phenomenon that defies logical explanation. "I've tried to apply the disciplines of bacteriology, virology, even of radiology," he says. "We've performed tests for epilepsy and for catalepsy — *nothing fits*!"

Menard constantly ascertains that he *doesn't* believe a curse has been placed upon the island, only to concede that he hasn't got a clue what is really happening. "You ever heard of voodoo?" he responds when West asks him what the Hell is going on. When West replies in the affirmative, Menard dismisses the religious cult as nonsense.

(Curiously, there is much talk of the "evil witchdoctor" said to inhabit the island and whom the natives believe is responsible for the current situation, but he is never actually shown — but then, nor are the natives.)

Trauma to the eye seemed to preoccupy those seeking to censor and ban. The sequence in which Menard's wife has her eye skewered on a wooden splinter was regarded as the most contentious element of the whole movie (certainly it was the most talked about) and the scene was removed by the BBFC when they passed *Zombie Flesh-Eaters* classified 18 for video in later years.[378] (Nine other films that featured on the DPP list also had images of violence upon eyeballs.)[379]

When I was in Atlanta I saw something very funny. I observed three kids playing videogames in the theatre's lobby during a screening of [*Zombie Flesh-Eaters*]. When the aforementioned scene was about to be shown, a fourth kid called his friends so that they wouldn't miss this highlight. This was great to see!

—*Lucio Fulci, European Trash Cinema Vol 2 No 4*

Inspired by Romero's *Dawn of the Dead* (aka *Zombi*), and originally released as *Zombi 2* in an attempt to pass itself off as a bona fide sequel, some critics still consider that Fulci's remodel surpasses the original. (Some don't: Randall Larson said "It's films like this that give the horror genre it's [sic] bad name.")[380] The half-decayed corpses lumbering about the place are certainly uglier, with maggots that issue from every available orifice the moment the camera moves in too close. In comparison to Romero's *Dawn*, the gore is also more outrageous and over-the-top. For instance, when West cuts down a zombie in the cemetery with a blow to the head, it doesn't merely fall to the floor a bloody mess — it falls to the floor a bloody mess that expels the aged contents of its skull into a swelling pool of miasma.

Fulci claimed that the *Zombie Flesh-Eaters* was "based on sensations, hinges on fear, and, of course, horror."[381] This was an approach the director would adopt to varying degrees in several of his later films, most notably ***House By the Cemetery***, ***The Beyond*** and *A Cat in the Brain*. Not only has the latter the unfortunate distinction of being one of the director's last films before he died (a terrible one at that), but it was also recently rejected by the BBFC due in part to "many sequences involving gross violence committed against women, often in a context with clear sexual overtones."[382]

A highly anticipated sequel to *Zombie Flesh-Eaters* arrived in 1988. Titled *Zombi 3* (in keeping with the misappropriated chronology that began with Romero's original film) it had plenty of bloody gore effects but not much else to match the flair, impact or atmosphere of its predecessor. Directorial credit went once again to Fulci, but he was unwell during the troubled production and much of what appeared on screen was actually handled by Bruno Mattei. (*Zombi 3*'s story line has the dead being reanimated by a chemical virus, which was the case with Mattei's own ***Zombie Creeping Flesh***.)

"For the first time in 40 years of film-going I wanted to run from the theatre in pure fright."
–LONDON DAILY TELEGRAPH
MILES FROM ANYWHERE
SO PRIVATE YOU CAN DO
ANYTHING YOU WANT...ANYTHING!
THE HOUSE BY THE LAKE
GRAND PRIZE WINNER "SITGES" INTERNATIONAL TERROR FILM FESTIVAL

'Hard to find rarities'

BLACK MARKET & PIRATES

I remember seeing displays for *I Spit On Your Grave, Cannibal Holocaust* and *SS Experiment Camp* in the video rental shop and thinking that films like that were somehow devaluing horror. I was always interested in horror films but I felt no urgency to see those. There were plenty of other films I wanted to see first. Then one day I walked into the shop and asked for *Tenebrae*, only to be told it was "banned." I couldn't believe it. I got a burning urgency to see all the "banned" stuff. Part of me wanted to know what all the fuss was about, and part of me was desperately missing what I had never been too concerned about in the first place.

—*Adam*

It's great fun being a horror fan in the UK. It's exciting trying to track down uncut horror films.

—*Andrew Allard*[1]

I came across an antiques shop in a country village which doubled as the local video store. A sign in the window said "Video Nasties for Sale." I went in and entered a veritable Aladdin's Cave. Standing in neat rows on a polished wood writing bureau were numerous videos. The first to catch my attention was *Cannibal Ferox* — both versions, the 18 rated and the XX uncut print. Immediately behind it was *Snuff*, the first time I'd seen it since its nationwide disappearance many months ago — a pristine copy, too, by the look of it. Beyond that, *I Spit On*

Your Grave, Cannibal Holocaust, Gestapo's Last Orgy, Last House on the Left. The antiques dealer said they were £8 each and I cursed my lack of ready cash. I picked up *Ferox* and *Snuff* never having seen the former. However, *Ferox* was out on loan so I opted for *I Spit On Your Grave* instead. I asked the chap if he would be interested in trading. I'd give him films he could safely rent out and take the banned titles off his hands. He agreed and over the next few days I picked up a selection of dirt-cheap ex-rental tapes (sold as 'watch'n'wipes' at my local video store). I took the lot to the antique shop and traded them tape for tape. *Ferox* was back in the shop. I exchanged *The Money Pit* for that particular title. I got the best part of my collection from this one shop. Pretty much all the tapes were in excellent condition. The cases were a bit grubby — the shop owner was a heavy smoker and a yellow film coated the protective plastic sleeve. There was a musty smell to the videos, too. Not an unpleasant odour — just what became an associative 'video nasty aroma.' I still have the films after almost fifteen years. The smell lingers vaguely and a quick sniff transports me back to the halcyon days of seeking out banned movies.

—*Kevin*

I started dealing in video nasties when I was fourteen-or-so. You'd buy them from video shops — to the shop owners they were crappy old gore films no one rented anymore — and sell them through ads in the likes of *Fear* and *Samhain.* One time I bought *Anthropohagous, Deep Red* and *Bloody Moon* for £5 each and sold them for £40, £60 and £40 respectively. I made a lot of fucking money, most of which I squandered on McDonald's and Space Invaders. You made a copy before selling the tape and sold copies of that, usually for £10-or-so a go. Likewise imported titles: *Nekromantik, Ilsa, Texas Chain Saw 2*... all very popular.

When I was seventeen, rumours started of police raids. One of my best contacts, A——, rang to tell me to stash my stuff. K—— in Birmingham had had a row with a neighbour, who told police he was a dealer. They raided him and found, amongst videos and so on, a package to be posted to A—— in Hull. On the outside was written "I know someone who's after porn." (A—— dealt in a lot of porn. Most people, me included, had *Deep Throat* and *The Devil In Miss Jones*, but little else.) So they raided him as well. They found 1,250 tapes, six VCRs, and his letter files, including all correspondence I'd sent him, which was a lot! So he rang me to warn me the Old Bill would be round — pretty good of him as he'd been warned not to, with the threat of a harsher sentence if he did.

Suddenly the seventeen-year-old who had hitherto felt pretty cool about having his own video business turned into a rather scared little boy. My dad was very helpful and cool-headed. He was well aware of the situation and had helped me run the business, seeing it as a display of initiative. My mum wasn't — she cried and threatened divorce and various other things unless we burnt all the films. She'd never been any good at handling a crisis. We hid the 250-plus tapes in a suitcase at my grandmother's flat around the corner, telling her it was stuff we'd confiscated from my younger brother. She suspected nothing even when I kept coming round to retrieve films every few days — I was still dealing, albeit on a low-key, much reduced level. I always went to a phone box to call people, though, fearing I'd had my phone tapped!

Shortly after, I came home from school one day to find my bedroom disturbed. The Old Bill had called. They'd taken a few films I'd left lying around to give the impression I hadn't known what was coming — harmless stuff like *Suspiria, The Brood*, and so on — plus they got a load of unrelated stuff, like old diaries, one of which had some gibberish poems that I'd done with a friend way back, containing rhyming couplets about our school teachers. Maybe they thought it was a code, who knows? I could have hidden the videos in the garage, kitchen, living room, anywhere — the police only searched my bedroom. At one point my dad excused himself to go to toilet, and nipped into his own room to stash his Swedish Erotica films under his bed.

A week later, I went with my dad to the local cop shop for an 'interview.' To say I was shitting myself would be something of an understatement. However, the first thing I was told was, "Don't worry, you're in no trouble. We just want to know who you know." Turns out they were basically interested in kiddie porn and 'snuff.' At no point had I ever been offered either

— the network selling uncut copies of *Zombie Flesh-Eaters* and *Cannibal Ferox* is entirely separate and distant to that of paedophile porn and so-called snuff films. The interview was all nice and chummy. I made up some bullshit about giving it all up six months earlier and burning all my stuff. They seemed to swallow it, despite there being one inconsistency: "If you did, how come we have a Xerox of a letter to A—— asking for animal porn dated two months ago?" I said whilst I'd stopped dealing, I was still curious to see this stuff, but always burnt it once I had. The WPC didn't seem entirely convinced I'd buy a tape for £10, watch it once then destroy it, but she let it ride. They asked me for addresses, so I gave those of people I knew had already been busted. Tell a lie — I also gave them the address of a fucker in Essex who'd ripped me off to the tune of £500... I could hardly complain to Trading Standards, could I? The police gave me back everything they'd taken and I left the station a happy boy. I got the search warrant framed, and it still hangs proudly on my wall. Poor old A—— had to give up his Teacher Training course, as his high profile case was perfect for the scumbag local papers to scapegoat him. *"Is this the sort of man you want teaching your children?"* Doubtless they claimed he was a child-pornographer and personal friend of the Horned Beast. He faced a maximum £10,000 fine and six months inside, I think, but ended up with just a £50 fine. I haven't heard from him in years, but wish him well wherever he may be.

I made a *lot* of money from dealing and had a gas. Built up a great video collection, too. Still got them — 400 films and not one of them legal in the UK! I was recently tempted to start dealing again, but I don't think the market's there as it once was. Also, I don't think the police would be as lenient on a twenty-two-year-old as they were a spotty faced adolescent. I'll just have to find a new way to make over £1,000 a month, tax free.

—Eddie

As the Video Recordings Act was making its way through Parliament, interest in the films the law was destined to prohibit began to increase. A good indication of the titles that were unlikely to see their way through the clampdown came courtesy of the DPP index, which remains something of a "shopping list" for collectors. As noted in the chapter previous, rental shops took advantage of the changeover period allotted by Parliament, and sold to the public stock which invariably would need to be destroyed once the legislation came into effect. This became the prime source for the first nasty collectors, who would spend their weekends frequenting out-of-the-way places for possible video goldmines. When the changeover period had ended and the law was in effect, many shops risked a heavy penalty by continuing to sell what remained of their now illegal videocassettes.

Market stalls were another source for collectors. Even into the early part of the nineties, outlawed videocassettes could still be found on the video stalls of some market towns. Although many traders unwittingly threw these tapes in together with legitimate releases, others understood their black market value and potential risks involved, only offering them to select clients (and often running parallel with a brisk under-the-counter trade in porn).

The third and perhaps most important source for banned videos was the classified ad pages in magazines. (Indeed, this is how the authors of the book you are reading became acquainted.) Several publications devoted to video and fantasy film offered their readers a classified ads service, among them *Video—The Magazine*, whose monthly free ads in retrospect give a good indication of how collector interest was influenced by the Video Recordings Act. The service was limited to commercially released tapes only. Introduced in the latter end of 1984, it becomes apparent over the months that more readers are searching for contentious videocassettes, specifically targeting the films that appeared on the DPP list. By 1986, a substantial number of the tapes offered or wanted for exchange were those no longer available on the high street.

Ironically, another source for black market videocassettes seemed to be the police themselves on occasion. The fact that officers were taking videocassettes away didn't necessarily mean they were being removed from circulation. Illegal items such as hardcore pornography and pirate movies often found their way back into public hands after they had been seized. In

SWAPS SWAPS SWAPS SWAPS

OBTAIN

"Island of Death"/"Multiple Maniacs"/"Narrow Edge" (VHS)/"The Beyond" (Beta) — [illegible]

Any C.E.D. Videodiscs. Please state price — Derek [illegible]

"Zombie Flesh Eaters" (full version) — Mr [illegible]

"Tunes Of Glory" (1960 — VHS). Good quality. Top price paid — Duncan [illegible]

"Contamination"/"The Beyond"/"Deep Red" (Beta) — P. Smith, [illegible]

"The Burning"/"Repo Man"/"Mad Max II"/"The Evil Dead"/"The Exorcist"/"Evilspeak"/"Zombie Flesh Eaters"/"Texas Chainsaw Massacre"/"Contamination"/"Living Dead At The Manchester Morgue"/"Friday The 13th"/"The Beyond"/"House By The Cemetery" (VHS) — David Wright [illegible]

"Caged Heat" by Jonathan Demme/"The Story of 'O'" by Just Jaeckin (VHS) — J. [illegible]

"Neil Diamond — Love At The Greek" — Mr H. [illegible]

EXCHANGE

"The Warning"/"The Changeling"/"Samurai Reincarnation"/"Private Eyes" (Beta) for "Cataclysm"/"Mad Max 2" any other good films (Beta) — Steve [illegible]

"Videodrome"/"1984"/"Incubus"/"Spaceship"/"Nightcomers"/"Looking For Mr Goodbar"/"Satan's Slave"/"The Awakening" — [illegible]

"Zombie Flesh Eaters"/"Zombie — City Of the Dead" for "The Deer Hunter"/"Daredevil Drivers" — S. [illegible]

"She-Freak"/"Blood Devils"/"The Devil's Men"/"Mausoleum". Offers — [illegible]

"Give My Regards To Broad Street" (Beta) for "Romancing The Stone"/"War Games"/"Risky Business" (Beta) — Steven [illegible]

"Tenebrae"/"Zombie Flesh Eaters"/"Hills Have Eyes Part 2"/"Dawn Of The Dead"/"Halloween III" for other good horror films (VHS) — G. Jackson [illegible]

"Gremlins"/"Romancing The Stone"/"Trading Places"/"Police Academy" for "Porky's"/"Young Warriors"/"The Key"/"Grizzly"/"Black Sunday" (Barbara Steel) — Marc [illegible]

"Alien Terror" (Beta) for any Elvis Presley film (Beta) — [illegible]

"The Link"/"Screamtime"/"Cujo"/"Blow Out"/"Cat People"/"Schizo"/"Christine"/"The Octagon"/"An Eye For An Eye"/"Forced Vengeance" — [illegible]

"Eating Raoul"/any good comedy (VHS) — C. B. [illegible]

"Straw Dogs" for "The Evil Dead" (VHS) — Scott [illegible]

"S.O.B."/"Jaws III" for "Attack Force Z"/"The Evil Dead" (VHS) — A. [illegible]

"Don't Go In The Woods Alone" (VHS) for "Absurd"/"Suspiria"/"The Beyond"/"Nightmare Maker"/"Madhouse" and others (VHS) — Mr R. Allen, [illegible]

THIS PAGE: Video trades post-Video Recordings Act. *Video–The Magazine.*

NEXT PAGE, TOP: *Samhain*, a magazine whose classified ads section resulted in a smear campaign against its publisher. NEXT PAGE, BELOW: The halcyon days of the long-running and influential horror film magazine *Fangoria*, the first issue of which appeared in 1979 (cover for No 8). Following the Hungerford massacre, a copy of *Fangoria* (No 68 or 69) was brought to the attention of the prime minister Margaret Thatcher by an MP "disgusted" with its content. At least one shopkeeper removed his stock when he heard investigations were afoot to see whether *Fangoria* fell foul of the Obscene Publications Act 1959.

one instance, a school teacher was told by a pupil that their policeman father had brought home a seized pirate copy of Steven Spielberg's *ET*, many months before its official video release. The video was subsequently passed around for others to view. More recently was a case highlighted by the *News of the World*.[2] Following a serious domestic accident, a young couple called for an ambulance. The police also showed up but rather than assisting, spent their time "snooping around the house," particularly the bedroom where they found two VCRs and a collection of video tapes. The police decided to confiscate the tapes in order to examine their content, on the suspicion they might have uncovered some video piracy.[3] The couple denied the tapes were pirates. On examination, officers found the couple were telling the truth. What the tapes did contain however, were home-made movies of the couple in sexual acts — not illegal in itself as the material was made for private viewing only. When the couple asked for their property back, the police told them that a number of the tapes had gone missing and were about to launch an internal investigation.

The interaction that came from swapping films by mail invariably drew collectors together, and provided the beginnings of a network to which the whole underground culture scene in Britain today owes a debt. (See below.) Not everyone who had a videocassette to trade was interested in becoming part of a fan community, but the classifieds provided a gateway for those who did. Once initial contact had been made, the network acquired another link and another possible source for the acquisition of videocassettes.

"I think most collectors would like to own a full set of nasties," one anonymous individual told the authors of this book. "What self-respecting collector *wouldn't* want to own a full set?"

As the number of collectors increased, inevitably the stockpile of pre-certified videocassettes in circulation began to be depleted. Many of the titles on the DPP list had never been widely available in the first place, and distribution of several key films — notably *Faces of Death*, *Anthropophagous the Beast* and *Beast in Heat* — was particularly poor. Once films like this became the target of adverse media attention and police scrutiny in the run up to the Video Recordings Act, they became even more scarce, with stockists diligently removing them from the shelves fearing a raid. In the case of at least one nasty, *I Spit On Your Grave*, the distributor gave retailers a full refund and took away any copies they had in stock.

Although many people had originally been happy to acquire an original tape simply to view before trading it on again for another, this type of friendly dealing was quickly inhibited by dwindling supplies. Fewer collectors were willing to let go of videocassettes that were evidently growing more scarce than others. Another factor which severely curbed such amicability was the increasing likelihood that some unscrupulous trader would try and pass a cheap duplicate off as an original.

Video nasties which were comparatively harder to find naturally fetched higher prices on the black market. According to one dealer,[4] up until several years ago the ten most sought-after nasties remained:

Anthropophagous the Beast
Beast in Heat
Cannibal Ferox (uncut)
Death Trap
Devil Hunter
Flesh for Frankenstein
Island of Death (Nico Mastorakis)
Last House on the Left
Night of the Demon
Zombie Flesh-Eaters (uncut)

Depending on the quality of the tape and packaging, prices would generally range from £15 to £70. Some tapes fetched more, the most notorious example being *Beast in Heat* which has been known to command £250 on the black market. In 1994, the prestigious Lyle Price Guide for *Film & Rock'n'Roll Collectables* also valued *I Spit On Your Grave* on the Wizard label at £250, while the same film on the Astra label was said to be worth only £80.[5]

Says 'Adam', a disgruntled collector:

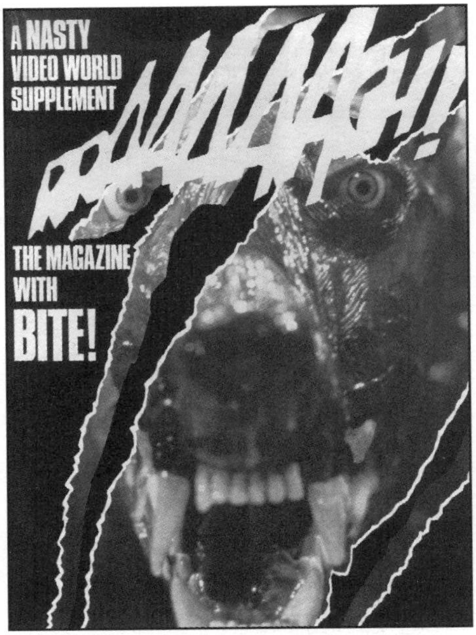

I did actually own an original *Beast in Heat*. I'd bought it for something like £2 off a market stall run by this enterprising young lad — a nice guy, but a little clueless. A couple of times a week he would offload several cratefuls of videos from his van and set up his stall near to the fish market. I tried to get over there at least once a week. This was around about the late-eighties. I remember picking *Beast in Heat* up from his table and thinking it was no big deal, because I never seemed to have much difficulty in finding stuff that had been on the DPP list. I think the tapes he was carrying came from out-of-business video shops, as all the cassettes had labels like 'Please Rewind' or 'Regent Video Centre, Salford'! On one occasion he asked me if I'd like to earn a little cash looking after his stall on Friday as he wouldn't be able to make it. I agreed and he told me that the guy who collects the rent for the stalls would come around, but that I wasn't to give him any money as it would be settled the following morning. Anyway, throughout the day this guy kept coming over for the rent and I kept telling him in good faith it'd be settled the following morning. It never was, of course, as the lad picked up his stock that evening, shared the takings with me and was never seen again! Anyway, getting back to *Beast in Heat*...

To be honest, at that time I didn't have much idea of quite how scarce that particular title was becoming. Like most of the originals I got, I traded it on after I'd made a duplicate for myself. That was the last time I ever traded any tapes, because what I got back in return for *Beast in Heat* was a bootleg copy of the uncut *Absurd*. [See also VIDEO NASTIES.] It breaks my heart now whenever I think that I had an original *Beast in Heat* and let it go!

Interestingly, the copy of the film that I made for myself suffered a defect that I couldn't sort out. Although the original played fine, I couldn't make a decent copy. No matter how I tracked the original, the duplicate kept on breaking up at the precise same moment in the film. Having long since got rid of the duplicate, I was surprised many years later to watch a bootleg that a friend had picked up which had exactly the same fault in exactly the same places! Perhaps my original *Beast in Heat* has been used as the master of countless boots!

Before long there were more people in search of nasties than there were nasties to go around.[6] Of course some ardent collectors were prepared to pay the sometimes exorbitant price for original pre-certificated films, but most people were resigned to seeing banned titles via bootleg cassettes. This became the preferred method of trading and distribution. Anybody who was able to get their hands on a second VCR could, for a nominal cost, pick up a set of suitable co-axial cables from any electrical store, connect their machines together and run off duplicate tapes to their heart's content.

> I bought a double bill of *Zombie Flesh-Eaters* and *I Spit On Your Grave* from this one guy who assured me that his copies were better than most because he was using specialist equipment. His prices were £10 for one film or £15 for two films on a single three-hour tape. When the tape arrived the films looked like any other second or third generation copy might. In fact, the tracking was out on *I Spit On your Grave* and the picture kept rolling.

Originally the means by which collectors could contact one another and trade tapes, classified ads now became the front for a growing cottage industry. People who had traded for nothing got greedy and began selling their bootleg videocassettes. Numerous lists were in circulation, with dealers offering films at a price of anywhere up to £10 a copy. Straight trades would be accepted should the dealer be offered a film he[7] didn't already have, or an original pre-record he could sell on. As the network extended and trading intensified, there was no film on the DPP list that couldn't be located by some dealer somewhere.

Quite often it wasn't enough to trade by mail. The underground network attracted its fair share of curious characters, many of whom desired to make impromptu social calls on their fellow traders.

> After responding to an advert in a video magazine an exchange of tapes was agreed. I had a spare copy of *Absurd*, the uncut version, and this guy was shifting *Cannibal Man*, a title I was having difficulty in finding. After speaking on the phone, B—— said he would be passing by my place and could drop the tape off even though he lived many miles away. I didn't want callers coming round to my house so I asked him to mail the video. He would

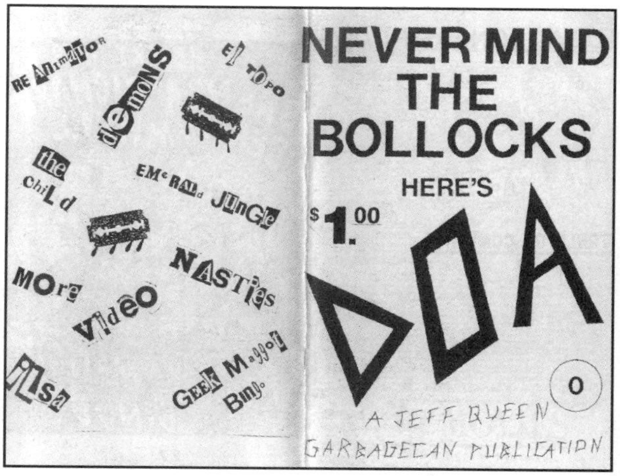

Horror fandom on both sides of the Atlantic owed a debt to the video nasties (and punk rock).

UK (PREVIOUS PAGE, LEFT TO RIGHT): *Roaaaaagh!*, a one-off video nasty supplement given away with *Video World* magazine, 1985; *Video Horror*, part one of a two-part guide primarily reviewing films that featured on the DPP list. Circa 1984.

USA (THIS PAGE, TOP TO BOTTOM): *DOA*, Vol 2 No 0. July-August 1986; *The Splatter Times* No 1, circa 1983. Four of the twelve films reviewed in this American tabloid would later be 'banned' in Britain.

> only do a hand-to-hand swap he insisted and a few hours after the call arrived on my doorstep and handed me a scrappy-looking *Cannibal Man*. I said I'd like to check it out first and slotted it into the video player. He seemed itchy as I perused the quality of the cassette. "I can't hang around too long, my dad's waiting in the car outside," he remarked. "He's just had a heart attack," he added after a pause. I wondered whether he meant his dad had suffered a coronary on the trip over or had had an attack in recent months. But my proper attention was on the film and I wasn't too happy. "I'm not sure about this," I said. The copy of *Absurd* was good quality and at the time I considered it a rarer film, so I was a bit dubious about letting it go. "I do a lot of body building, I'm fit and strong," responded my visitor and he flexed his muscles to further push the point. He went on to tell me how he had a collection of mounted animal heads and other objects of taxidermy. Not sure what his taxidermy hobby had to do with anything, I told him I'd keep *Absurd* and offered him a lesser title instead — I think it was *Forest of Fear*. B—— countered with an additional offer of a copy of *Night of the Bloody Apes* as well as *Cannibal Man* for *Absurd*. I agreed and handed him my tape. "I'll put the film in the post," he promised and disappeared. Weeks passed and no tape arrived. I phoned B—— to ask about the video and he told me that a friend had borrowed it and taken it to America but he'd send it to me on his return. B—— was never to be seen or heard from again. The copy of *Night of the Bloody Apes* was also never seen.

It was enough to put some fans off altogether. "The phone calls started to drive me mad," recalls Adam.

> Many people didn't seem to have a life outside of trading and watching videos. I got lists off a couple of contacts, contacted a couple more and before I knew it I was getting phone calls virtually every night — such-a-body had such-a-film and would I be interested in trading it for this or that? One particular guy, who I remember quite vividly because he always sounded as if he had sinus trouble, would often phone several times in the same evening. Very little small talk or familiarities, just him reeling off fresh titles he had to offer and me doing likewise. It got to be not much fun anymore. He phoned me back twice just to remind me how to pack the cassettes so they didn't get damaged in the mail!
>
> I always considered myself a film fan and only ever swapped videos — a copy-of-yours-gets-a-copy-of-mine, sort of thing. I was well aware that a heavier penalty faced anyone who got caught doing this stuff for profit, but at the end of the day I wasn't in it to get rich. The only time I took money off anyone for a bootleg tape, was when this guy desperately wanted a film I had but had no film to offer in return. He was quite insistent and in the end I told him to send me the cost of a blank tape and I'd run him a copy off. That was the only money I made, the price of a blank videocassette.

The sense of community that came with collecting was aided by a growing number of film-based publications. On the heels of *Fangoria*, a US-based glossy news-stand horror movie magazine launched in 1979, the video boom of the mid eighties had seen something of a revolution in cheaply produced fanzines devoted to obscure and exploitational movies. Interestingly, zines on both sides of the Atlantic started to spring up around the same time and brought to film reviewing the anarchic attitude of the punk rock zine explosion of a few years earlier. Indeed, the irreverent attitude of these small press publications towards the mainstream *Fangoria* was identical to the music zines before them, scornful of the likes of the *NME* and *Rolling Stone* which they perceived as staid and out-of-touch. ("Fuck the Critics," was the philosophy of Jeff Queen's *D.O.A.*, a film/punk crossover zine that regarded exploitation as an art form.) Utilising cut-and-paste layouts and photocopy reproduction, British zines like *Cold Sweat*, *Video Horror* (by the erstwhile 'Horror Consultant'), *Yeeeuuch!*, *Samhain* and *Whiplash Smile* had a natural inclination towards the films that featured on the DPP list, and were predominantly concerned with issues of censorship, often comparing cut prints of domestic video releases with their European and American counterparts. Not suffering the same censorial background, American zine publishers were less inhibitive in their range of subject matter. Nonetheless, the likes of *Sub Human*, *Hi-Tech Terror*, *Video Drive-In!*, *Gore Gazette* and *Slimetime* piqued the interest of British videophiles, reviewing material that — if not already banned in Britain — was unlikely to see a release given the dragnet of the Video Recordings Act.

Fanzines were networked in a similar way to videos, inasmuch as they could be found via the classified ads of news-stand magazines. From here the reader would be patched into other, like-minded small press publications courtesy of the review round-ups that zines invariably carried. Interest in British pre-VRA videocassettes even extended overseas as collectors on the continent sought out the films that were causing so much fuss in the United Kingdom. The Dementia Horror Shop in Sweden was one outlet operating in 1987, which advertised British videos for sale and trade, as well as uncut imports, underground oddities, experimental music, books and zines.

With fanzines, the communal identity of video fandom was established, and with it came a channel of communication that lead to social activities such as late-night video parties and film fairs. These events offered fans the opportunity to meet and make further contacts, as well as buy or trade videocassettes, fanzines and assorted memorabilia. In August 1987, the British exploitation film journal *Shock Xpress* launched Shock Around The Clock, a marathon eighteen-hour horror film festival held at the Scala cinema in London.[8] Featuring ten dodgy movies and a celebrity panel discussion, the Shock festival was an instant sell-out, repeated with equal success on an annual basis over the next few years. It also provided the blueprint for numerous unrelated marathon screenings, such as the northern equivalent Black Sunday.

'Geoff' harkens back to the camaraderie of the collector:

> The film fairs were good fun when they first started on a regular basis. We'd arrive before the doors opened and meet up with some friends in the queue. Swap tapes and stuff. After about an hour-or-so looking around the fair we'd go to a nearby pub, have a couple of drinks and then go back again and maybe pick up some more crap in our semi-inebriated state! I got to know quite a few of the traders, and it was still relatively easy to pick up bargains like, say, originals of *The Toolbox Murders* and *The Witch Who Came From the Sea*, which I got for £15 the pair. Stalls selling pre-certified material and bootlegs weren't that common initially, but they did seem to be a couple more traders dealing in that stuff with each fair. I remember there was a guy who regularly drove over from France just to sell Dutch videos of stuff that was cut or banned over here. And these fairs weren't big events back then, either! It was obviously worth his while bringing a suitcase full of videos all that way, through Customs, for half a day's work. *Crazy Breetish!* His videos were £20 apiece, in the original Dutch sleeve and everything. He had stuff from the banned list, like *House on the Edge of the Park*. I got that off him and that other *Last House* rip-off, *The House by the Lake*... Ultimately, these fairs became busier and busier, and a lot more business orientated. It seemed that some of the people who were getting into videos were doing so purely for gain and no other reason — I mean, picking up films simply so that they could generate a catalogue and sell boots.

The video nasties trade wasn't going unnoticed. Events such as film fairs may have offered anonymity to those collectors in search of elusive, pre-certificated films, but dealers were taking a chance and faced prosecution. But as the activities of the video subculture increased and became more open, so it drew the attentions of moneymakers and the authorities alike. Geoff reiterates:

> There were two guys who started to attend the fairs for a while, who walked around with a list of bootlegs which they kept in the boot of their car. They would flash this list in front of anyone who they thought might be interested. It didn't take a brain surgeon to figure that these guys weren't collectors as such, nor were they really concerned with films apart from the fact that they could make a bit of money from 'banned' tapes. At one fair they clocked me offering someone an original *Blood Rites*, and that's how I got to know what they where up to. They saw me with this tape and came dashing over, offering to trade it for a couple of

> boots on this list of theirs. When I said I wasn't interested, they offered me a bit of cash and I let them have it. They gave me the impression they were trying to get 'heavy.'
> Some months later I ran into these two jokers again at the next fair, where they told me that the tape I'd sold them was faulty. I knew it wasn't. When I offered to take the film back, they told me that they'd already sold it for double what they had given me. *"So? What's the problem?"* Plus they'd made a boot of it and were selling that on their list.
> They disappeared shortly after that and I heard they'd been nicked.

Chris Glazebrook recalls that once the Video Recordings Act came into force, certain unscrupulous video shop dealers would rent out the likes of *SS Experiment Camp* from under-the-counter at £5 or £10 a night. These were the people that the authorities were most concerned with — dealers operating for profit. Although the VRA brought a legitimacy to the industry in outlawing the worse excesses of sex and sadism, piracy and bootlegging were more of a problem than ever as a consequence. Raids continued through the latter part of the eighties and into the nineties, except the onus was not now on the police but on Trading Standards officers and FACT, the Federation Against Copyright Theft (about whom more later). The intensity of the raids was only marginally less than it had been pre-VRA, and commonplace to the point that isolated prosecutions rarely extended beyond the pages of the local press. "Two jailed over sick videos," was a headline that featured in an October 1995 edition of the *Manchester Evening News*. The story was a fairly typical one, concerning market traders who "were caught selling obscene and unclassified movies like *Erotic Clips*, *Cannibal Holocaust* and uncut versions of *The Exorcist* and *Straw Dogs*."

> [W]atchdogs began their investigation after a tip-off. One trading standards officer went undercover and bought illegal tapes on sale with mainstream movies. [One of the stall holders] then showed him boxes marked 'horror' and 'adult' which were stored under the counter and the officer bought some of these.
> When officials identified themselves they seized dozens of pornographic and horror films.

More tapes were recovered from the pair's car and from their homes. Admitting to a total of forty offences under the Obscene Publications and Video Recordings Acts, each of the men received three months imprisonment. The Video Recordings Act made it an offence for anyone to supply a videocassette without a classification certificate, however it has led to few prosecutions. The custodial sentence in this case was influenced by the fact that the "videos were being sold on a public, open market where they could have been purchased by children."

A series of raids that did make it into the pages of the national press occurred in May of 1992. Video collectors across the country feared the worst when their underground network was infiltrated by Trading Standards officers. Reported as the largest operation of its kind, officers in Liverpool were alerted to the "racket" following a raid on a suspected computer software pirate. Other local authorities became involved as officers spent six months undercover and entered into correspondence with dealers. The raids on homes across Britain netted some 3,000 videocassettes and recording equipment, and saw ten people being brought in for questioning. "Some of the films are so sickening," said the chairman of Consumer Protection in Liverpool, "they would be unwatchable for most people." Some journalists noted how many of the films confiscated were video nasties that had appeared on the DPP blacklist, while other reporters keyed into more sensational aspects. The *Daily Star*, for instance, managed to associate the raids with supposed "snuff" films and the murder of schoolboy Jason Swift two years earlier — the sole connection being that the recent sting had uncovered a boy of twelve trading horror videos with his friends. Even the so-called quality press were not immune to such exploitative tactics, and scenes from films that were evidently works of fiction were presented ambiguously, as possibly genuine instances of torture, mutilation and murder.

Following the haul, the foetus-eating scene from *Anthropophagous the Beast* (see VIDEO NASTIES) was used by the press and excerpted on television as some kind of video nasty

MR NASTY SELLS DEATH VIDEOS TO OUR KIDS

NEWS OF THE WORLD INVESTIGATES

BEING DIFFERENT

EVIL Tom Halloran is the Pied Piper of Horror.

He plays the fool to attract a crowd of impressionable children ...then sells them stomach-churning videos of **REAL-LIFE** death, gore and mutilation.

The kids, sucked into believing that anything Halloran does is fun, part with their pocket-money and rush home with films that could warp them forever.

His biggest seller is a video called Faces Of Death. It despicts sequences from real tragedies including a parachutist landing in an alligator park and being eaten alive by the reptiles.

In another scene, a live monkey's head is smashed open with a hammer.

Asian diners are then seen eating the whimpering creature's brains.

There are also close-ups of the mangled victims of fatal car crashes and surgeons carrying out autopsies.

Sinister

Yet another clip shows a woman falling to her death under a lorry.

"Kids are the best customers," said ex-squaddie Halloran with a sinister chuckle. "Adults don't want them.

"A customer is a customer. The kids may be robbing their mums so they can pay them, but that's not my problem.

"As far as I'm concerned, if kids are old enough to be walking around with a tenner, they're old enough to be buying a video off me."

The 35-year-old monster, who touts his grisly wares around the East London borough of Newham, also has a video called Being Different. It shows sad, seriously disfigured people with growths on their heads and stunted limbs.

Wounded

Not content with even that, he hopes to get Army perverts to smuggle him copies of a medical training film, featuring operations on soldiers seriously wounded in the Falklands and Gulf wars.

"A couple of blokes in Germany I'm speaking to soon may bring some back," he leered. "They nick them, you know."

Halloran, who served with the Royal Engineers, boasts that business has doubled since Home Secretary Michael Howard announced tough laws to protect children from video nasties ... and drove his wares underground.

"I'm storing up lots of the Faces Of Death videos," he said.

"They're really popular because it's all blood and guts.

"I'm waiting to see what happens about this new legislation thing, because the price will go up."

The Home Secretary's crackdown on violent videos came after teachers protested at their effect on children.

The British Board of Film Classification will be given powers to ban the worst examples. Jail sentences will also be included in measures to curb under-the-counter supplies of unsuitable videos to children.

The Professional Association of Teachers found in a specially-commissioned study that children secretly deal in horror videos in about 1,000 primary and 600 secondary schools.

Billions

Lavinia Carey, director of the British Video Association, said that the illegal trade in video nasties—worth billions of pounds a year—"needs to be stamped out."

Hopefully Halloran's filthy tricks can be stamped out too.

We have sent our dossier on the Pied Piper straight to the police.

HALLORAN: 'Kids are the best customers'

By GARY JONES

Video nasties seized as ring is smashed

Ian Katz

TRADING standards officers yesterday claimed to have smashed a nationwide underground "horror" video ring after a series of raids across the country.

In the largest operation of its kind, the council investigators, supported by police, seized almost 3,000 videos depicting scenes including torture, mutilation and cannabalism.

Duplicating equipment was also discovered and 10 people were yesterday helping police inquiries after the raids at eight addresses in the North-west, the Midlands, South Wales, Kent and Cornwall. The seizures followed a six-month undercover operation in which Liverpool trading standards officers posed as dealers. Peter Mawdsley, Liverpool's Chief Trading Standards Officer, said children as young as 12 were involved in trading the videos. Titles included Faces of Death, Cannibal Holocaust, and Blood Sucking Freaks.

It is cl[illegible]med th[illegible] some [illegible]os [illegible]

[illegible] movies, in which the victims are killed during filming: "Some are billed as snuff videos but I believe it is more a matter of marketing because most of the people in them are easily identifiable."

His officers were alerted to the racket after a raid on a suspected computer software counterfeiter. Four Liverpool officers spent months infiltrating the ring and 10 other local authorities became involved.

Mr Mawdsley said the network was made up of "enthusiasts" who corresponded. The videos, which sold for between £12 and £90, reportedly include the removal of eyes, tongues, limbs and scalps and people eating human excrement.

The Liverpool investigators have alerted Interpol to the network's connections in Finland, Germany and Ireland. Next week officers start viewing the haul to establish what charges can be brought. They are likely to be charged under the Video Recordings Bill and the Obscene Publications Act. They face fines of up to £20,000 per tape and up to three months' im[illegible]isonment.

LEFT: *News of the World*, May 8, 1994.
RIGHT: *The Guardian*, May 8, 1992.

nadir.

"MR NASTY SELLS DEATH VIDEOS TO OUR KIDS" was the supercharged headline of a report that appeared in the *News of the World* on May 8, 1994. It told of a thirty-five-year-old ex-squaddie by the name of Tom Halloran, who

> plays the fool to attract a crowd of impressionable children... then sells them stomach-churning videos of REAL-LIFE death, gore and mutilation.
> The kids, sucked into believing that anything Halloran does is fun, part with their pocket-money and rush home with films that could warp them forever.

Halloran, operating in East London and described as "evil," a "monster," and "the Pied

Piper of Horror," admitted that *Faces of Death* was his biggest selling video. Several graphic scenes from the film were related by the newspaper, following which Halloran is quoted as saying "Kids are the best customers... kids may be robbing their mums so they can pay them [sic], but that's not my problem."

The report also stated that the stringent laws governing video violence had driven Halloran's "wares underground" — a curious point to make, as Halloran's illegal operation could never exist anywhere but underground in the first place. Wherever it resided, the trade seemed nothing short of endemic amongst youngsters, as per the admonition that "children secretly deal in horror videos in about 1,000 primary and 600 secondary schools."

Children and *Faces of Death* where the subject of another news report when, on April 8, 1995, the *Manchester Evening News* declared "'SNUFF' VIDEO IS FOUND IN SCHOOL." The sensational front page story brought the video into the apocryphal realm of the snuff film, circulating in a school playground no less!

> The sick 'snuff' movie called The Face of Death [sic] ended up in the hands of 15-year-old girl. [sic] She was so horrified that she handed it over to her parents.

Facts pertaining to this particular case did not come from the police or the government, but from an "inter-denominational Christian group called Marantha."[9] Said to "feature more than twenty deaths," the descriptions given of several sequences actually fit those of *Faces of Death IV* and not Conan Le Cilaire's original film. This mistake was repeated in a piece that featured in the Irish paper *Sunday World*, dated September 27, 1998, offering some indication of time scale with regard to pirate videocassettes and their circulation (given that three years had lapsed since the report in the *Manchester Evening News*). It also shows that widespread concern is primarily focussed on the same old films. Beneath a reproduction of the original *Faces of Death* video sleeve, a caption read:

> SICK COVER. The vile video that contains bloody scenes.

The report went on to describe several "slaughterhouse-like scenes" taken from *Faces of Death IV*, concentrating particularly on a sequence depicting guerrilla Michael Stone. At an IRA funeral in Belfast's Milltown cemetery in 1988, loyalist Stone had launched a gun-and-grenade attack which killed three people and wounded sixty others. The footage shows mourners scattering and falling under Stone's hail of bullets, then Stone himself being pursued and attacked by a mob before police were able to pull him to safety. Stone received three life sentences. Under the Good Friday peace agreement between the British and Irish governments however, he was amongst those eligible for an early release (and was actually released in July 2000). There can be no doubting the political intent in associating Stone with the film. A picture of him with his hands up victorious is printed alongside an image of a man 'tied between two horses and ripped asunder on camera' — both may feature in the same film, but beyond that have no connection. Once free, the article proposed that Stone's intention was to live in Ballynahinch and open a business. His evil past however, "will still haunt him — through the pirate video."

It is interesting that outlawed film is not itself the outrage in this instance, but a propaganda tool.

> To some in the loyalist community the video will be a vindication of a man they consider a hero. To others, the video will be the vilest footage they have had to relive and a reminder of how low the human soul can go.

Suspicion of video piracy can be based on nothing more damning than owning two VCRs, as highlighted in the case above, involving a couple's home-made sex films. Indeed, it was the mere suspicion of piracy, together with the stigma attached to horror videos, that lost 'Jimmie', the author of the next tale, his job.

> Last year, shortly after being made redundant, I started an office position through an employment agency on a temp-to-perm basis, with an initial four week trial period. Although a large company, the office consisted of only the department head and three other employees, one being a temp who had been there for sometime. After a while it became obvious I had been brought in to replace this person on a permanent full-time basis.
> During the trial period I was determined to make a good impression, so I kept my head down and got stuck into my work, spending as many hours as possible learning the job. While my training period progressed I tried to get along with everyone (as you do), and we occasionally talked socially about our pastimes and hobbies, my primary one being collecting horror movies.
> Now, let's bear in mind I *did not* gibber fanatically about Giannetto de Rossi's goriest effects, nor did I babble on about the various versions of *Cannibal Holocaust*.
> By the fourth week I was able to do the job without any supervision with all deadlines and quotas met. I was sure I had secured the position I had worked so very hard for — until came 'the final Friday.'
> I returned back from lunch early (yes, I was that conscientious!) when the department secretary came over to the three of us with a dilemma: she said she was taping a film on Channel 4 that night which she wanted to keep, but that she was going out so it would be full of adverts. What could she do?
> Someone suggested she get someone else to tape it for her, leaving out the adverts... but alas she knew no one. I suggested that if she brought the cassette in on Monday, I could re-tape it and edit out all the adverts. Everyone looked at me in astonishment and the secretary said to me with a gasp, "What? You mean you've got more then one video recorder?!"
> I really did not know what to make of her reaction! I just shrugged it off and returned to work.
> Later on in the afternoon my telephone extension rang. It was the woman from my employment agency.
> "How's it coming?" she asked. "Any problems?"
> I told her that I was sure I had got the job as I had progressed very well during my four week trial. There was this short uncomfortable silence at the other end of the line, then she replied, "That's not what I heard. I've been told that you're involved in video piracy. You're finishing at five o'clock and I'm taking you off our records. We can't have someone like you working for us, because you'll give us a bad name."
> And she promptly put the phone down on me, leaving me shocked... What the fuck was going on?!
> Five o'clock came and I still hadn't heard a word from the department head. (In fact, no one had said anything to me at all!) So I grabbed my jacket and went in to see her. She completely ignored me as I entered her office, so I asked whether I had got the job or not. After a short pause she said, "I'm not employing anyone in this department who deals in video piracy and enjoys watching 'snuff films.'"
> I was shocked and told her I didn't know what she was talking about. I demanded to know how she came to these conclusions. She said it had been brought to her attention that I watch horror films and had offered to pirate a film for a member of staff. This was something the company took a very dim view of indeed. She further informed me that I was lucky the police hadn't been alerted to my criminal activities, and then called for me to be removed from the premises. Within moments I was being manhandled from the office by two large security guards. I couldn't believe this was happening, or that such a scenario could be so overblown...
> It has been nearly a year now and I am still out of work. The local employment agencies won't touch me, as these things have a habit of getting around.[10]

Having infiltrated the underground video nasties network, Trading Standards diligently kept up the subterfuge long after their high profile sting of May 1992. Officers continued to bait unsuspecting video dealers with the pretence that they were collectors in search of banned movies. One fresh strategy was the perusal of classified ads in British horror publications like *The DarkSide* and *Samhain*.[11] Although the magazines themselves never advocated that readers deal in video nasties, it was patently obvious what lay at the heart of some of the carefully worded ads. Phraseology used to mask the black market trade typically comprised of "Uncut films for sale," "Copies of rare films available," "VHS and Beta originals," "Good prices/swaps wanted" and "Hard to find rarities." Invitations to make your collection look authentic with colour photocopied video covers were also a bit of a give-away. Often it wasn't even that complicated. The May 1993 edition of *The DarkSide* carried an ad from one K Howell which read:

> UNCUT FILMS. Beyond, Zombie Flesh Eaters, Cannibal, Cannibal Ferox, Faces of Death, Anthropophagous, Xtro, Exorcist. Any two films on one tape £16.

It was hardly surprising that some months later, in February 1994, Trading Standards officers would undertake a second major series of raids. These covered twenty towns nationwide, resulting in a haul of 5,000 videocassettes and twenty people being brought in for police questioning.[12] Meeting with markedly less media fanfare than the first raids, it was noted however that Trading Standards had used the classified ads of the horror press to construct their latest campaign. Jim Potts, chief Standards officer in Preston where the operation was co-ordinated, called for tough action against magazines which allowed dealers to advertise. (Some people suspected that bogus ads were placed by officials themselves in order to lure dealers into the open.[13]) This condemnation lead to a local outcry directed at the publisher of one of the magazines, as well as a call for him to resign from his part time job at a playgroup.

On February 12, two days after the raids had taken place, Exeter's evening newspaper the *Express and Echo* launched a series of leading and defamatory articles against local man John Gullidge, whose magazine *Samhain* was said to specialise "in films and books with titles such as *Zombie Holocaust*, *Driller Killer*, *The Virgin Witch* and *I Spit on your Grave*." Printing a picture of Gullidge beneath a headline that read "Cult horror mag probe," the article implied via a series of contradictory statements that the publisher himself was under investigation and played a pivotal role in the distribution of illegal videos. Furthermore, Gullidge was made to look as if he had declined to comment when contacted by the journalist writing the story. On the contrary. The reporter had chosen to omit the fact that Gullidge had spoken with Trading Standards officers the previous month concerning the matter of classified ads, whereupon the publisher was informed he was within his rights to run such a section so long as he had a "no video nasties" disclaimer.

The Trading Standards link was ignored in subsequent articles on Gullidge, with the *Express and Echo* concentrating instead on the ruckus they had created with their original report. "Resign call to mag boss" was the headline for one story some months later. Gullidge was well liked by staff and children at the playgroup, but several parents had expressed concern that a "cult publisher" — as Gullidge was described by the newspaper — should be employed as a helper with young children. The claim made by the reporter that the Reverend Richard Jeffrey had called for Gullidge to resign however, was refuted on publication of the story, when the vicar denied having said it and apologised to Gullidge for what had appeared in print.

Someone whose mail was placed under surveillance and who consequently fell victim to a raid was William Black. A freelance journalist by profession, Black was a collector of horror films amongst other esoterica, but the circumstance surrounding his case was unique amongst those we heard about in the course of researching this book. In this instance it was the police and not Trading Standards who cast the net.

In Black's own words...

> After answering a personal ad placed by a woman in a national newspaper we began exchanging letters (I used a *nom de plume*). The letters, on both sides, were erotic, openly sexual

and, over time, S&M based.

When photos of the woman began arriving she looked as good as her writing, a young-looking forties. In later photos, leather gear, ropes and a riding crop were in evidence. Other photos showed her in restraint and tied to chairs, sofas, bedheads, a stable door and spread-eagled in an X-position in an open doorway. She made a neat package in an elegant living-room, a bathroom, a stairwell and in what appeared to be a basement or cellar. Not all the pictures were taken in the same house. One could have been described as a manor house, another a step above a council dwelling.

That she had access to money was obvious in one picture where she posed in a full kit of riding gear alongside a handsome black mare.

The woman was married. Her husband agreed to all she was involved in. Occasionally they swapped partners. Sometimes they accepted visitors who stayed at their house. I was obliquely invited. She wrote to a number of other people, men and women. Much later she sent me photos of a number of her correspondents. The women, like herself in her own pictures, were half-naked or sometimes nude or often involved in sex acts. One shot had a girl with the neck of a wine bottle inserted into her vagina, while she herself used a vibrator between her legs.

Her letters were those of an intelligent, even sophisticated woman, feminine and not at all threatening, even when in one photo she posed like a skimpily-dressed Nazi guard wielding a whip.

Though she was the submissive in the photos (there were rarely men in the house) I could tell she was no unthinking sex ragdoll, to be ordered around haphazardly. She appeared fully aware of the reaction she was creating in the dominant one, and the resulting erotic charge she too was experiencing in fulfilling his — and sometimes her — desire.

Her husband never wrote but she said he read all the letters. He was a mysterious figure who was sometimes in the outer regions of my mind when I wrote to her. Someone approving of my sexual ramblings. Someone who would take her to bed to read the sex-charged missives and turn the fantasy writings into heightened sexual reality.

Once she sent me a picture of a semi-nude and slightly buxom girl, who resembled something out of a Russ Meyer movie and resided close to where I lived. I drove past her house, with the knowledge that inside was a young woman with her boyfriend who were into the 'swapping' scene. Though a little too well-fed for my tastes, I wrote but received no reply. Not in your own back garden, perhaps?

Part-way through our correspondences, the woman began to reply with letters written on a word processor. The letters were always signed but gone was the intimacy of hand-written material. I also felt the contents had changed slightly. There appeared to be a new interest in me as a person, a little more probing. Not something I could put my finger on. My letters were answered more quickly, but were shorter in length. Questions I would ask about particular subjects were left unanswered. I began to doubt it was even her writing. That may have been the reason I ended the correspondence — or it could have been that I simply became bored.

Some months later I happened to glance from my bedroom window to see a police van in the street. I assumed they had been to a neighbour's house, though it's not that kind of neighbourhood. After showering and dressing, the phone rang. It was a wrong number the caller explained. In fact it wasn't. It was the police's way of discovering if I was actually in the house. A few minutes later they arrived at the door... five uniformed policemen and two Detectives. Some of them carried hammers, screwdrivers and crowbars and a search warrant was waved before my unbelieving eyes...

I asked three times of nobody in particular what they were looking for. By then I was backed-up into the living-room. It was then that the alarm I felt changed to fear. I tried to remain calm. I felt cold. I couldn't swallow. My mind began to distance itself from what was happening.

The police asked me whether I had any pornographic material in the house. I led them to a

TOP AND ABOVE: Pictures of the correspondent who lead to William Black's appearance in court.

box containing videos. I also showed them my collection of mondos and banned tapes.

When I was informed the warrant had been issued on behalf of the police station's Child Care unit, I sat down and attempted to hide my shaking hands. I watched the events happening as though I wasn't there. It was a medium-shot from a scene in a movie. A climatic act in a stageplay. It was a Roger Cook door-storming incident. But it wasn't. It was my house and me surrounded by police searching for something I knew not what…

The police were searching the house room by room… They expressed no hostility toward me, and went about their business quickly and quietly. No hammers or crowbars were needed. My study — like a set for the film *Twister* — caused a groan or two, but otherwise it was under the bed, over the wardrobe, into the attic, and through every drawer in the house.

My mondo and 'banned' collection caused the older of the Detectives to mutter soberly about the "wild titles." Then the police began to gather all the tapes; those with photocopied covers, tapes in boxes without covers, tapes in dust jackets with details of their contents written on them by myself all piled together.

Originals such as *The Texas Chain Saw Massacre* I to III, *Martin, Nightmares in a Damaged Brain, Blood Sucking Freaks, The Driller Killer,* and many of their ilk were added to the pile.

"I see you have a copy of *Snuff,*" said the younger Detective with a wry smile. He stared at me when I said it was a badly made old thriller.

The tape was added to the growing heap assembled on the living room carpet.

From my mondo collection, the police took *Signal 30, Uncensored News, Mondo Cane* I and II, *Of The Dead, Ecco, The Killing of America, This Violent World, Faces of Death* 1 to 5, *Death Scenes,* and others.

I sat rock still. My body had become part of the chair. If they dragged me away, the furniture would come with me. I felt I was gasping for breath, yet I was calm and barely breathing. I felt almost drunk. The fish bowl I was looking out from appeared to expand, taking me even further away from the events around me.

A constable lifted my copy of *Guinea Pig 2* from a shelf. And *Guinea Pig 3*. And *Guinea Pig 4*. They made a neat stack all on their own.

I love the cinema. I have attended a number of film festivals and I have a large collection of movie documentaries on video, mostly taken from television. They cover the cinema in general, with features on directors, actors, special effects experts, script writers, and interviews with the likes of David Lynch, Clive Barker, David Cronenberg, and others. A few are copies I obtained from advertisers in various cinema and horror magazines, as recommended by Jonathan Ross in the back of his *Incredibly Strange Film Book*.

Other documentaries — again all taken from TV or purchased across the counter at the likes of Virgin — cover True Crime. Some are rare: Ted Bundy's last interview, *Charles Manson Superstar*, Manson: live from Death Row, and many more.

All these were also taken in the search.

My book library was left untouched. No interest was shown in *Porn Gold*, *Araki*, *Memories of an Erotic Bookseller*, *Dada and Surrealism*, or *The Erotic Arts*. Nor even in the book of the film *Death Scenes*. (Why should the representation of an image differ in one medium from that of another?)

Final Truth, *Hunting Humans*, *Alone with the Devil*, works by Masters and Wilson, and none of the other titles among my True Crime books got a look in. And my photographic art books didn't appeal to the police either, books by the likes of Thornton, Knoll, Valleso, Bailey and Klimt.

But the police did find a number of notebooks that I had listed my videos in, and address books going back something like twenty years. A number of ex-girl friends and mates of old were, I presumed, in for a surprise.

Also discovered was a small packet of photos I received from my correspondent. All those involving bondage and any sort of sex act (vibrator use basically) were taken. Other pictures I had of women who had posed for my camera (I fancy myself as a photographer of pretty girls) were given back to me — and some of the poses were explicit.

The search lasted in total two hours. The Detectives questioned me briefly (or in my dazed mind it appeared so) and showed me copies they had of some of the letters I sent to the woman. I noted a number of paragraphs on various pages had been marked in red or green ink. I was asked for the letters I had received from her. But months before I had ended the correspondence and discarded them.

I had not, however, disposed of a number of video tapes she had sent me. They were among those in the box I had handed over earlier. All her tapes had an S&M theme. She had no interest in video nasties or mainstream cinema.

The police informed me that all the tapes would be viewed and assessed, and that it would take some time. I was not arrested or charged with any offence at this stage.

As the officers left the house carrying a number of black bags, a solitary neighbour saw them go. He and a policeman he knew exchanged what seemed like knowing looks. Later they must have got together for a chat because my neighbour began ignoring me after that for a time.

Five months later I was summoned to a police station for an interview. I arrived with a solicitor.

I was questioned about my letters and those of my correspondent — they had all of mine, but none of those she had sent to me. I was also asked about the contents of a small number of the videos taken from my house that had been put to paper.

In the cold light of a police cell interview room, inhabited by two determined Detectives and an elderly solicitor, where your every whispered reply is taped (twice; once for the police and once for my solicitor), talking about sex seemed suddenly akin to being caught naked with a hard-on by your mother.

I was offered a TV and video to review the tapes as their content was read out for the tape recorder. I declined. I wanted, at this stage, to keep my solicitor on my side. The interview lasted two hours.

The police told me my correspondent had received a video tape containing child porn, allegedly sent by me. And that she had sent it back to me. The police search was an attempt to find the tape and anything along similar lines. Nothing relating to child porn was found in my house.

I was shown a photocopy of pages put together by the woman, with the titles of videos on one side and on the other side some comments on their content and their 'hardness' or

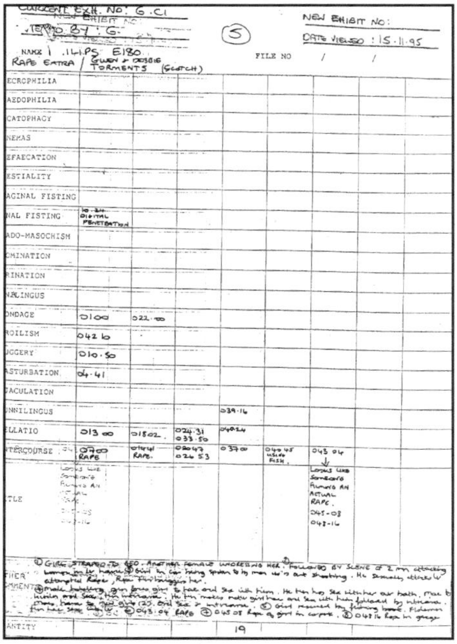

CURRENT EXH. NO: G.C1
VIDEO 84 : G.
NAME | .14.PS E180.
RAPE EXTRA / GWEN & DEBBIE TORMENTS (SCOTCH)

(5)

NEW EXHIBIT NO:
DATE VIEWED : 15.11.95
FILE NO / /

ECROPHILIA								
AEDOPHILIA								
CATOPHAGY								
NEMAS								
EFAECATION								
ESTIALITY								
AGINAL FISTING								
NAL FISTING	10.24 DIGITAL PENETRATION							
ADO-MASOCHISM								
OMINATION								
RINATION								
NALINGUS								
ONDAGE	0100	022.00						
ROILISM	042 6							
UGGERY	010.50							
ASTURBATION	04.41							
JACULATION								
UNNILINGUS				039.16				
ELLATIO	013 00	01802.	024.31 033.50	04024				
NTERCOURSE	0700 RAPE	01441 RAPE.	02047 026 53	03700	04045 USING FISH.	043 04		
TLE	LOOKS LIKE SOMEONE'S FILMING AN ACTUAL RAPE. 045-08 048-16					LOOKS LIKE SOMEONE'S FILMING AN ACTUAL RAPE. 045-08 048-16		
THER COMMENTS	(1) GIRL STRAPPED TO BED. ANOTHER FEMALE UNDRESSING HER. (2) FOLLOWED BY SCENE OF 2 men attacking woman in her home. (3) Girl in car being spoken to by man who's out shooting. He sexually attacks w attempted Rape, Rape [illegible] her. (4) male [illegible] girl forces girl to have oral sex with him. He then has sex with her over bath. [illegible] (5) Girl rescued by fishing boat. Fisherman [illegible] (6) 043.04 RAPE (7) 045 08 Rape of girl in carpark. (8) 048 16 Rape in garage							
ANTITY				19				

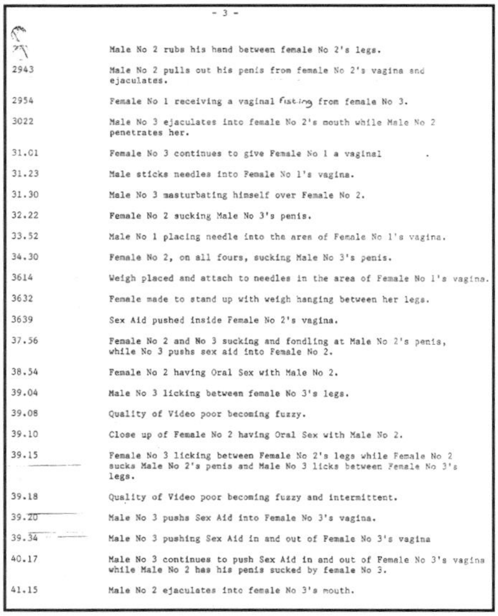

- 3 -

	Male No 2 rubs his hand between female No 2's legs.
2943	Male No 2 pulls out his penis from female No 2's vagina and ejaculates.
2954	Female No 1 receiving a vaginal fisting from female No 3.
3022	Male No 3 ejaculates into female No 2's mouth while Male No 2 penetrates her.
31.01	Female No 3 continues to give Female No 1 a vaginal .
31.23	Male sticks needles into Female No 1's vagina.
31.30	Male No 3 masturbating himself over Female No 2.
32.22	Female No 2 sucking Male No 3's penis.
33.52	Male No 1 placing needle into the area of Female No 1's vagina.
34.30	Female No 2, on all fours, sucking Male No 3's penis.
3614	Weigh placed and attach to needles in the area of Female No 1's vagina.
3632	Female made to stand up with weigh hanging between her legs.
3639	Sex Aid pushed inside Female No 2's vagina.
37.56	Female No 2 and No 3 sucking and fondling at Male No 2's penis, while No 3 pushs sex aid into Female No 2.
38.54	Female No 2 having Oral Sex with Male No 2.
39.04	Male No 3 licking between female No 3's legs.
39.08	Quality of Video poor becoming fuzzy.
39.10	Close up of Female No 2 having Oral Sex with Male No 2.
39.15	Female No 3 licking between Female No 2's legs while Female No 2 sucks Male No 2's penis and Male No 3 licks between Female No 3's legs.
39.18	Quality of Video poor becoming fuzzy and intermittent.
39.20	Male No 3 pushs Sex Aid into Female No 3's vagina.
39.34	Male No 3 pushing Sex Aid in and out of Female No 3's vagina
40.17	Male No 3 continues to push Sex Aid in and out of Female No 3's vagina while Male No 2 has his penis sucked by female No 3.
41.15	Male No 2 ejaculates into female No 3's mouth.

LEFT: Police officers viewed Black's video collection and made comments. This is a typical comment sheet. RIGHT: A minute-by-minute description of one examined video tape.

otherwise, all hand-written: hardcore, softcore, extreme, etc. Each entry was numbered, with the highest number I saw being 150, but there could have been more listings beyond the page I saw. The name of the person she had sent each tape to was also recorded.

There was no record of any of the few tapes I had sent to the woman. The disputed child porn tape was listed on her record sheet as having been sent to me. And then the entry had been scratched through, as though the sender had changed their mind about sending it.

Needless to say, I did not possess, send or receive the tape in question. The tape I was supposed to have sent to her — and she allegedly back to me — was, in fact, found at her house, I was informed during questioning…

Worse was to come. I was told boldly, "You were not writing to a woman, you were writing to a man." Yet, no matter what I was told, I knew the early letters were written by a woman genuinely in search of sexual excitement. Later perhaps they were from a woman (or a man) wearing a uniform sitting behind a desk in an office in a police station.

I am not suggesting I was set up. I think I just happened to be caught up in the ripples emanating out from some 'stone in the water' — the further the ripples spread, the weaker the waves, the less important the lone surfer caught up in them.

But I was still in the water and I had to keep my head above it. And I don't think I had helped myself during the long wait by having my solicitor contact the officers a number of times to try and reclaim my videos. At that stage I had been unaware of the kiddie porn angle of the investigation. I just assumed that porn and 'video nasties' were the items they were looking to take action on.

A year later I was charged and summons were issued. My solicitor and by now a barrister in tow had the original date of the hearing delayed by four months.

The charges related to a small number of video tapes I was accused of publishing contrary to common law. In other words, I had copied an obscene article, or articles. I was also charged with sending a postal package containing indecent or obscene written communications.

I would plead Not Guilty with the backing of my solicitor and barrister, the charges being trivial and technical they said. However, after an arranged viewing session of the named tapes at the police station, my barrister's attitude changed completely. (Not so with my solicitor.) Viewing the tapes in court, as the police intended, I was told, would influence the magistrate enough to come down heavily on me. Yes, I suppose a little oral, anal, and heavy bondage at a 10 AM sitting would be too much even for the most liberal of magistrates, as he was alluded to being.

I pleaded guilty.

A few of the written communications — the letters — were on the charge sheet along with a small number of the videos. But a large number of the tapes were left off. The child porn angle was not raised in court. The case was presented by the police prosecutor without aggression or revealed distaste. It could have been worse, I was told.

The magistrate commented on the "perverts" who get "some form of perverted pleasure from these things" and that the transactions — the tape swapping — was not commercial, but a private affair between two people. The fine was nominal.

There was a feeling that with all the work undertaken in the investigations, someone would have to carry the can at the end of the day. Almost certainly the authorities knew that I, and people like me in the same position, would plead guilty to lesser charges to save time, expense and embarrassment.

If the charges against me had not been tainted by the child porn angle (though, as mentioned, they were not part of the case), I may have pleaded Not Guilty. After all, we are part of the EC where, across the channel, pornography is legal.

In Europe, my case would not have gone to court. But sadly it will take a stronger man than me to take the fight against an injustice levelled on us all by our government, the British media, and — the biggest enemy of all — our own hypocrisy.

After the hearing I was approached by the case Detective and told I could arrange to pick up those video tapes that did not constitute part of the charges. In due course I collected a huge box containing the tapes. *Guinea Pig, Faces of Death, Snuff, Blood Sucking Freaks, Death Scenes, SS Experiment Camp* were all there, as were my movie documentaries and True Crime tapes. However, one part of the *Faces of Death* series was missing. Another cassette that had on it the title *Faces of Death IV* was, I later discovered, actually a John Wayne western. I couldn't figure that one out...

The address books and notebook listing the videos had all been returned to me much earlier.

I never learned what happened to my penpal, nor her husband, nor her other correspondences.

In a case that garnered much publicity and was the cause of some irritation and embarrassment for the police, porn historian David Flint was raided by three officers from Manchester's Obscene Publications Unit in March 1998. Having amassed material over a twelve year period, and working on *Babylon Blue*, a book about the history of sex cinema, Flint had several hundred videocassettes removed from his home, as well as VCRs, computer equipment and paperwork. He later described the operation — which was conducted at 7:30 in the morning and lasted for three hours — as like being burgled, but "having the burglars wake you up to watch, and constantly tell you that there's worse to come."[14] The police suspected Flint of possessing obscene material for gain. As noted previously, suspicion is all that the police require in order to obtain a search warrant.

Flint was told by the police that his formal arrest would take place two weeks hence, allowing them the time to examine the seized items. Said the author: "They doubtless thought that I would follow the usual pattern of behaviour: keep my head down, try to get off lightly, avoid publicity, and hire a local solicitor who had no special knowledge of the obscenity laws. That's what most people do."

A half-page report in the following morning's *Guardian* was critical of the police raid. This reaction was reciprocated by the media over the coming weeks, angry that the police would focus their time and energy on a historian involved in credible research.[15]

When the time arrived for Flint to go to the police for an interview and a formal charge, he had the leverage of the press coverage behind him as well as the services of a "heavyweight London barrister." More importantly, the police had no evidence that the accused had sold any tapes to anybody, and he was bailed until July. By which time, Flint was re-arrested on another charge: conspiracy to produce obscene material for gain (on account of the police having found a mock-up video sleeve on his computer and correspondence in which Flint had discussed the idea of shooting a porn film).

Flint was bailed until September, but at the end of August received a call from the Crown Prosecution Service telling him that there was no case to answer and all charges were dropped. What material hadn't already been handed back some weeks earlier was now returned.

"To be fair to the police," states Flint in hindsight, "they were as honest as they could be with me. Never once did they try threatening behaviour, or lie to me. They were, in the end, just doing their job. I just wish that their job had something to do with the real threats to the people of Manchester..."

Flint is adamant that it was a mean-spirited neighbour who made the initial complaint to the police, leading to a series of mysterious phone calls prior to the raid which he now believes were made by the police. The caller said he got Flint's number from a mutual acquaintance — a name not in fact familiar to Flint — and that he was in the market to buy some porn videos. Flint smelled a rat. Foolishly in hindsight, by way of some vague promises, return calls and cancelled meetings, he decided to string the police along and perhaps get a "witty article" out it all. A plan which backfired, leading to months of stress for the author as well as the other people who were raided as a consequence of material seized from his home.

On some occasions, raids are conducted by HM Customs & Excise,[16] should they intercept items which they consider to be obscene entering the country. Alas the guidelines governing this practice appear arbitrary to say the least, and in most instances the addressee to whom the items were destined will get a written "Notice of Seizure." Left uncontested the goods will be destroyed without any criminal consequence. Should the importer disagree with the forfeiture decision, he or she has one month to do so in writing, upon which Customs "are then required to institute proceedings for a court to decide the matter." Needless to say the prospect of a civil action is enough to put most people off and claims are rarely made by individuals importing videocassettes and other material for their own use (even less common is that Customs will lose a case that has gone before a court). A phonecall to Customs upon receipt of a Notice of Seizure will more often than not effectuate a reassurance of "nothing to worry about" from the officer whose signature appears on the form.

HM Customs don't take any notice of trial acquitals.[17] They draw their interpretation of 'obscenity' from Section 42 of the 1876 Customs Consolidation Act, which is no less ambiguous than that of the Obscene Publications Act. For instance, Customs Officers have on some occasions intercepted and seized the film *I Spit On Your Grave*, while on others have examined it and let it go. A perfectly innocuous film will be impounded if it is packaged together with an item that Customs believe is indecent, though on other occasions quite the reverse will happen (see below). Customs will exercise discretion and, child pornogrpahy apart, will not detain small quantities of obscene material intended for personal or professional use, yet their guide for travellers entering the UK ranks pornography amongst those prohibited goods "which are banned completely."[18]

The transit of horror films is supervised in a similarly indiscriminate and contrary manner. Apparently, Customs will call the BBFC to see whether an intercepted title already carries a certificate in Britain, although this doesn't explain why some unclassified material is examined and subsequently allowed to pass through. Customs have on occasion seized and destroyed films which an importer intends to submit to the BBFC for classification (as in the case of Screen Edge and *Shatter Dead*, see APPENDIX II). Contrary, a thirty-five minute preview copy of *The Burning Moon* was seized, designated as containing obscene imagery, but reprieved once the importer (Headpress) explained to Customs officials that, if suitable, the film would be submitted to the BBFC with a view to a release.[19]

Kevin relates his dealings with Customs & Excise:

I received a Notice of Seizure in lieu of an expected package of three videos — *Cannibal, Primitifs,* and *Night of the Devils* — which I'd ordered from a source in Holland.[20] Confident that not all of these titles could be considered obscene, I phoned the seizing officer at Mount Pleasant for some kind of explanation. I was put through to the person dealing with the case, who clarified that all the films had been watched; two of the titles were to be sent on to me, while the third was to be destroyed as it was considered obscene. I was told that the one marked for incineration was actually *Night of the Devils*, an atmospheric and stylish vampire movie made in 1972. Indeed, the woman I spoke to (she sounded middle-aged and was very pleasant, friendly, and sympathetic) said that the 'jungle films' were actually quite good — in spite of the fact that one of them was the uncut version of Ruggero Deodato's *Cannibal*, complete with animal killings, mutilations and eviscerations! If any of the three films were destined for seizure, I thought that title would have been it. Somewhat naïvely thinking it would make a difference, I explained that the films were for my personal viewing alone and I didn't find such material offensive. How then, I asked, could Customs justify preventing me from receiving my own private matter? The response I got was astonishing: "There is always the possibility that you may be burgled and the video will fall into the wrong hands." As far as I was concerned my private mail was already in the wrong hands, but I concluded from that response that there was no point in continuing arguing. I didn't push the issue any further, not wanting to jeopardise the fact that I was to get at least two of the films. A few days later *Cannibal* and *Primitifs* arrived with a note saying that *Night of the Devils* would be destroyed. A few weeks after that I got the film from a different source.

"Such cases are often not examples of people deliberately breaking the law," one Customs officer told *Sight & Sound* in May 1998. "They attempt to import the material either in good faith or in ignorance and we prevent them from doing so."

Sometimes however, items evidently intended for personal use which are intercepted

CDB4B/1117/88 LPS 3391/88.

H M CUSTOMS AND EXCISE

NOTICE OF SEIZURE UNDER THE CUSTOMS AND EXCISE ACTS 1979

Office date stamp

To: **David Kerekes**

From: THE OFFICER H M CUSTOMS & EXCISE DOVER POSTAL DEPOT 7 21 SEP 1988 CHARLTON GREEN DOVER, KENT CT16 1EH

Pursuant to Section 139(6) of the Customs and Excise Management Act, 1979, and paragraph 1 of Schedule 3 thereto, the Commissioners of Customs and Excise hereby give you notice that by virtue of the powers contained in the Customs and Excise Acts and enactments amending those Acts, certain goods namely:-

Two video tapes entitled 'Blood Cult' and 'The Gruesome Twosome' found at Dover Postal Depot, Dover on or about 25 August 1988.

have been seized as liable to forfeiture upon the grounds that the said goods are indecent or obscene articles which were imported contrary to the prohibition contained in section 42 of the Customs Consolidation Act, 1876 whereby and by force of section 49(1)(b) of the Customs and Excise Management Act, 1979 the said goods are liable to forfeiture.

If you claim that the said goods are not liable to forfeiture you must within one month from the date of this notice of seizure give notice of your claim in accordance with Schedule 3 to the Customs and Excise Management Act, 1979. In default of such notice the said goods will be deemed to have been duly condemned as forfeited and will be liable to be disposed of in such a manner as the Commissioners of Customs and Excise may direct. If you make such a claim within the time aforesaid, legal proceedings will be taken for the condemnation thereof.

MRS. M.C.O

Officer of Customs and Excise

HM CUSTOMS AND EXCISE

Parcel Post Depot

Charlton Green DOVER Kent CT16 1EH

Telephone (01304) 204678 Fax

GTN 3513

Dr Mikita Brottman
Department of Education & Community Studies
University of East London
Longbridge Road
DAGENHAM
Essex RM8 2AS

Your reference

Our reference LPS/10215/96

Date 23rd February 1996

Dear Dr Brottman

NOTICE OF SEIZURE LPS 10215/96
"CANNIBAL HOLOCAUST" AND "FACES OF DEATH"

Thank you for your letter dated 13 February 1996 concerning the above. Following your detailed explanation of the type of research project you are engaged in I have taken advice regarding any dispensation, and now request the following additional information:

(i) Written confirmation from the head of your department - J D Graham, that this is a specified research project for which the videos are an integral part, that the work is conducted under the supervision of the head of dept, and that the end product is endorsed by him/her.

(ii) A written undertaking from yourself that the videos in question will be viewed only by you, in connection with the research project, and that when your work is finished you return them to HM Customs and Excise who will dispose of them as seized material in due course.

If you wish to discuss the matter with me, please telephone 01304 224423.

Yours sincerely

CLARE
Senior Officer
Dover Postal Depot

TOP AND ABOVE: The not-so-changing face of HM Customs & Excise's "Notice of Seizure."

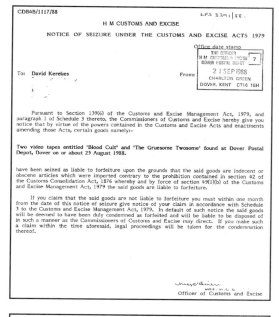

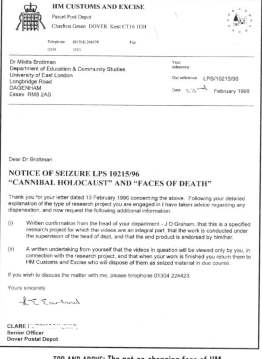

During the last few weeks. video tapes masquerading as the new James Bond film. 'THE LIVING DAYLIGHTS'. have been circulating illegally.

These low grade tapes were compiled from unedited footage which was stolen during production. ALL KEY ACTION SEQUENCES. THE MAJOR SPECIAL EFFECTS, AND ALL OF THE MUSIC IS MISSING. DON'T BE FOOLED.

The only way to see the genuine movie 'THE LIVING DAYLIGHTS' is at a Cinema.

The distributors and film-makers are advising James Bond fans and cinemagoers in general of this unscrupulous deception which in no way represents the entertainment value of their motion picture.

Albert R. Broccoli's 'THE LIVING DAYLIGHTS' will open in British Cinemas from 30th June.

ALBERT R. BROCCOLI presents
TIMOTHY DALTON
as IAN FLEMING'S
JAMES BOND 007
THE LIVING DAYLIGHTS
STARRING MARYAM d'ABO JOE DON BAKER ART MALIK AND JEROEN KRABBE
PRODUCTION DESIGNER PETER LAMONT MUSIC BY JOHN BARRY
ASSOCIATE PRODUCERS TOM PEVSNER AND BARBARA BROCCOLI
PRODUCED BY ALBERT R. BROCCOLI AND MICHAEL G. WILSON
DIRECTED BY JOHN GLEN SCREENPLAY BY RICHARD MAIBAUM AND MICHAEL G. WILSON
ORIGINAL SOUNDTRACK ALBUM AVAILABLE ON The Pretenders
WEA RECORDS, CASSETTES AND COMPACT DISC.
TECHNICOLOR PANAVISION Distributed by UNITED INTERNATIONAL PICTURES

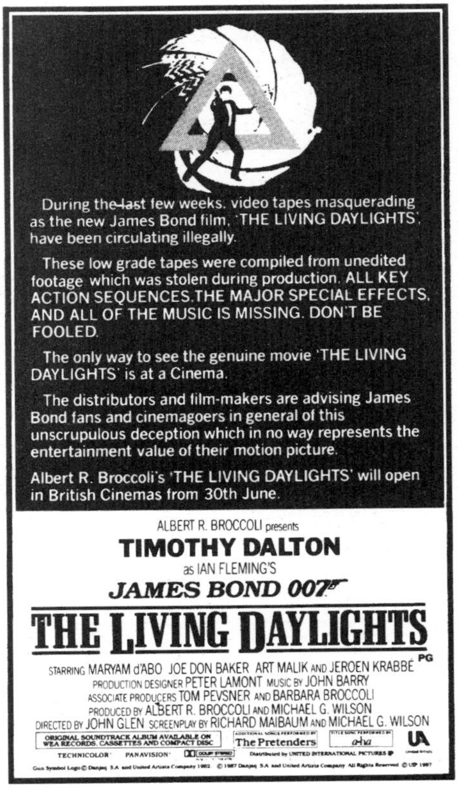

by Customs officials will not bring a straight-forward forfeiture notice but a raid. This doesn't necessarily have to be material which poses a threat to national security or is of a sexual nature involving minors, as outlined by the law,[21] but can include 'objectionable' material in general (as, say, in some recent cases involving the importation of 'squish' videos and alleged rape films[22]). Unlike a raid carried out by the police, Customs & Excise are supposedly only entitled to seize "material of foreign origin which cannot be traded lawfully in this country." This fact was pointed out to .W., raided by Customs in December 1992 following the interception of five videocassettes of an adult nature. The tapes in question — *The Story of K, Caught, You'll Love the Feeling, Top Secret* and *Bittersweet Revenge* — were sent by a fellow collector in Ireland, and had all once been legally available and obtained by mail order in London, prior to the introduction of the Video Recordings Act.

Although cleared of conspiring to import two obscene videos from France — a fact which officers would have been blissfully unaware if not for the honesty of the accused — E.W. was found guilty of the obscenity charge pertaining to the five videocassettes detailed above. In his brief summing up, the Stipendiary Magistrate made it clear that he believed both charges to be fairly trivial, and gave E.W. a two-year conditional discharge. However, E.W. maintained that the officers who dealt with the case were in abuse of their powers. Extracted in this letter of complaint dated July 1993, he outlines the reasons why.

During the search of my house Customs & Excise removed items "loosely described as 199 video tapes, twelve boxes of various documentation, magazines and books, and two computer discs." They are now claiming that most of these items are forfeit and will not be returned to me. They are in fact prepared to return sixty of the 199 tapes, and most of the magazines, but this in itself is an empty gesture. Their seizure of material during the course of the search was virtually indiscriminate. For example, amongst the seized tapes were titles like *Crystal Gale in Concert, Everyday Yoga* and a number of others, equally innocuous. These of course make up a large part of the tapes to be returned. Similarly they are prepared to return copies of such things as *Men Only* amongst the magazines, but precious little else.

I find it difficult to understand how they can seize tapes that I have made direct from films shown on public television, e.g. excerpts from films shown on the Adult Channel on cable TV. In the enclosed press cutting the statement is made that "mildly erotic scenes that have long been shown on national television and other satellite services, such as BSkyB, (which) all conform to ITC regulations." If this is true, by what right do Customs & Excise confiscate such material?

They are also seizing copies of videos that are manufactured and sold quite openly and legally in the UK [as well as] admittedly more contentious material such as videos in the *Slave Sex* series, which show scenes of whipping etc...

I have of course protested to my Solicitor about this high-haned action by Customs & Excise, but he tells me that I have no recourse to the law to recover my property. We are in the process of preparing a detailed list of those items for which there seems to be absolutely no

justification for their being confiscated, but my Solicitor tells me that, in his opinion, there is very little chance of them giving way on so much as a single item and I have absolutely no chance whatsoever of recovering any of the more contentious material. It is his view that under the terms of the Customs & Excise Management Act they are quite at liberty to confiscate anything they might find during their search of my home if in their opinion it is obscene, and I have no right of appeal. Their opinion is not subject to the law.

Nonetheless, prepared to take the case to the High Court, E.W. was notified by Customs in February 1994 that all material would ultimately be returned to him (with the exception of the five tapes seized and subsequently destroyed, and for which he had been prosecuted). It was still their belief that the material seized was liable to forfeiture, but having weighed this "against the potential costs to the taxpayers" Customs declined to take the matter further.

Following discussions with Customs, Mikita Brottman also had success in getting Customs to forward material which they had intercepted and initially found to be obscene. Mikita isn't sure if there is a lesson to be learned in the following, other than you can get your videos back so long as you've got the right kind of headed notepaper, and as long as you promise both to burn them and write a book about them afterwards...

During the whole of 1995, I'd been ordering "outlawed" videos on a regular basis from the US, all of which came through HM Customs on a regular basis, without any difficulties at all. In December, whilst working on my book *Meat is Murder*, I needed two films that the company I'd been using in the US couldn't provide — Deodato's *Cannibal Holocaust* and Conan Le Cilaire's *Faces of Death*, and so — foolishly, in retrospect — I ordered them from a European company instead (I think it was Cult Video in Amsterdam). I also ordered a copy of Kubrick's *A Clockwork Orange* in the same shipment. Sometime in the middle of January 1996, I received my copy of *Clockwork Orange*, accompanied by the familiar "Notice of Seizure" from HM Customs informing me that *Cannibal Holocaust* and *Faces of Death* had been "seized."

I thought I might have a chance of getting these videos back, since my purpose in ordering them was a "legitimate" one — they were to be used in "academic research" rather than to satisfy a voyeuristic curiosity (remember, I was trying to put myself n the mind-set of a senior officer at HM Customs & Excise). So, on the headed notepaper of my university department, I sent them a long, detailed description of my proposed research project, detailing its (admittedly somewhat minor) emphasis on censorship, accompanied by a copy of an article I wrote on Nick Bougas' *Death Scenes* for an academic film journal, *Cineaction*. I stressed that these videos had been ordered for use in a "legitimate, academic" project (rather than to be... what? enjoyed?) and would be watched by myself alone, "in the privacy of my own home."

On February 23, I received another letter from HM Customs requesting further information. They wanted "written confirmation from the head of your department... that this is a specified research project for which the videos are an integral part, that the work is conducted under the supervision of the head of department, and that the end product is endorsed by him/her", and "a written understanding from yourself that the videos in question will be viewed only by you, in connection with the research project, and that when your work is finished you will return them as seized material in due course."

So I sent them bak the further "confirmations" they needed, and they sent me my videos. They haven't been "disposed" of yet, but should I ever come to the conclusion that I've got nothing else to learn from them, they can easily be replaced. Here in the US, where I'm currently living, both *Cannibal Holocaust* and *Faces of Death* are prominently displayed on the shelves of my local video shop. The US Midwest is supposed to be a very conservative place — and in some respects, it really is. But unlike England. they don't require you to have a Ph.D. from Oxford to watch a low-budget horror film.

Global piracy costs $2bn, India, EEC are worst hit

A SURVEY of world video piracy in the International Federation of Phonogram and Videogram Producers' April IFPI Video Newsletter estimates that in 1984 piracy cost producers, distributors and retailers across the world at least $2bn.

In only a few Western countries, says the report, does piracy account for under 10% of total video industry turnover. Worst hit are India (with a pirate sector worth $300m a year) and the 10 member states of the EEC ($350-400m a year).

In Egypt, cassettes from Cairo's 40 video retailers are being copied illegally to service some 250 video clubs. IFPI has urged international video companies to find local licencees in the territory who could protect their catalogue from pirates.

Univideo, the Italian national group of IFPI, estimates that pirate copies account for 40-50% of the domestic video market with recent piracy victims including major US successes such as "Dune" and "The Woman In Red". However

• A scene from "Dune", pirated in Italy.

Dutch authors rights body, BUMA/STERMA, believes that only 10% of video retailers in The Hague carry no pirate product and has accordingly announced its intention, together with IFPI group NVPI, to carry out further raids on local dealers.

On a more optimistic note, Belgium recently saw the formation of a new anti-piracy group, the Belgian Anti-Piracy Federation (BAPF), which brings together the Belgian Video Federation and the Motion Picture Export Association of America (MPEAA).

In France, the Synd

release and its launch on video. The domestic video industry feels that the legally-sanctioned delay encourages video pirates to fill a gap in the market and has challenged it at the European Court in Strasbourg, which will decide whether the law is compatible with the legal structures of the EEC. France is the only EEC country with a legally required theatrical window and the only one with an average window of longer than nine months (although Germany and the Netherlands both operate industry agreements on the subject).

TOP: Report from *Screen International*, May 4, 1985.

In an unrelated case that occurred in April 1998, Customs officials stopped a horror video from entering Britain and called on the home to which it had been destined. They took numerous videocassettes in the raid, but later returned them all. The importer had already lost seven other packages to Customs, receiving the usual Notice of Seizure. This was his eighth offence, and the resultant raid seemed to comply with the general suspicion that Customs keep a record of individuals who repeatedly have items seized. This cannot be verified. Although interception of mail is supposedly random, Customs do admit to being familiar with the packaging that accompanies contentious material, whilst trying "to isolate the likely routes through which it would travel."[23] Any contentious material which is stopped and found to be dishonestly labelled or in some way disguised, will be viewed as smuggling and elicit rather more serious attention, possibly resulting in a raid.

The idea of a Customs blacklist doesn't really explain why some people should be raided following their first unsuccessful attempt at importing contentious material. As in the case of 'Paulo' from East London, whose tale further highlights the irregular — and some might say dubious — way in which Customs often conducts itself. Paulo ordered two magazines from a company called Nu-West in the USA, specialising in spanking and corporal punishment (CP)...

Instead of receiving the magazines, I got a knock at my door on a Sunday afternoon by three men who introduced themselves as HM Customs. They asked me my name and whether I'd bought any magazines from Nu-West. When I let them in the events went like this: I was asked whether I'd brought into the country any other similar material to which I said 'no.'

LEFT AND RIGHT: "Soon they will be banned..." As well as enabling a black market in pirate hardcore pornography to flourish, the Video Recordings Act 1984 helped pornographers to pressure-sell legitimate softcore.

> They then asked how I got hold of the address of Nu-West. I said through a UK magazine — which they then asked to see (my heart dropped!). One of the men came up to my bedroom and I showed him my collection. He looked at each magazine. If it wasn't clearly of UK origin he flicked through the contents. As all of my CP mags were from the UK he didn't bother about them. However, there were a couple of hardcore adult mags which I'd bought back from a trip to Holland. I was questioned as to where I'd got these and I said I'd bought them in London. I'm not sure he believed me, but as he decided to seize these mags as well it made no real difference.
>
> At this time I was still living at home with my mum. I made this point to the three men, and that she was likely to be back home soon. The officer who checked my magazines went and discussed something with the other two men and they decided to continue my interrogation in their car.
>
> I was told that if they had found any other imported material, or I was discovered trying to import any adult material in the future, then I would be prosecuted. They then left with my magazines.
>
> I have to say that the whole incident was a great shock, but also left me seething with rage. The material I imported was not offensive by any means — you can buy similar stuff in the UK — so what right did they have?

In this chapter we have dealt primarily with the black market which grew out of the formation of the Video Recordings Act. Keeping within the scope of this book, we have concentrated on the dealers of unclassified films for whom the VRA has made collecting not only "fun" and "exciting" — to quote one of the dealers at the opening of this chapter — but also profitable and risky.[24] All of this however, is just one side of the black market, and to the video business probably not the most contentious side either, dealing as it does with low-budget or independent films from companies that have no commercial clout and cannot afford to pursue pirates.

Whenever networks of video horror fans are infiltrated by Trading Standards and handfuls of collectors are busted, it's a "terror" or "sick film racket" that is said to have been smashed, and rarely an issue of piracy or copyright. Compare this to any new blockbuster release from Hollywood, which will invariably be preceded by a campaign in the media warning of the perils of pirates and copyright theft. One of the first and most intensive campaigns accompanied CIC Video's release of *ET—The Extraterrestrial*.[25] (Pirates still managed to get their copies on the market first.)

Video piracy is the copying and subsequent sale of feature films or any other programme without the consent of the copyright holder. A pirate might deal in material already on the market, offering cheap duplicates of desirable movies, or he may be offering copies of films that haven't yet officially been released on video. Either way, the money the pirate generates is considerable and almost pure profit, his only outlay being the price of blank cassettes on which to duplicate his master tape and perhaps the packaging.

Piracy was rife in the early days of video. The lack of quality product and high prices helped see to that. By early 1982, it was estimated that sixty-five percent of all videos sold in Britain were pirated copies, with the film industry claiming to be losing international revenue of around £100 million a year. From the earliest days of video, London was regarded as the pirate capital of the world,[26] partly stemming from the capital having such a high concentration of film facilities. "This gives the pirates very easy access to the films themselves," Peter Browne, head of the anti-piracy unit of the Motion Picture Export Association of America (MPEAA), was quoted as saying. In 1981, the MPEAA claimed there were 5,000 pirates operating in London, with virtually every West End film finding its way onto pirate videocassette within two or three weeks of its theatrical release. Unscrupulous projectionists, laboratory workers and even cinema managers were said to be responsible for bringing films onto the black market, taking the print away from the cinema overnight and allowing pirates to run a copy off using professional tele-cine converters. Unless hardcore pornography was involved — in which case the police could be brought in — it was the responsibility of the MPEAA and the Society of Film Distributors to investigate such crime in Britain.

The power and resources wielded by these organisations was considerably less formidable than the FBI, who handled piracy across the Atlantic. A report published by the Economist Intelligence Unit[27] in May 1983 stated that British video laws were "weak and toothless", resulting in the climate of piracy.

Asked what kind of material was being pirated in these early years, an anonymous source told the authors:

> The first pirate tapes that I heard of were basically all the Disney cartoons, which of course weren't officially made available on video until years later. I remember a colleague ringing me one day and saying, "There's a guy in Bolton who's got all the Disneys. Nip over and get some!" I had this old transit van at the time and I remember going over to this house and putting a hundred of these tapes in the back. *Snow White* and all that stuff. Very, very poor pirated copies of Disney films.[28]

To redress the situation, the MPEAA and the Society of Film Distributors joined forces with the British Videogram Association and formed the Federation Against Copyright Theft (FACT). The Federation comprised a large team of investigators and administrative staff, whose dedicated role it was to combat piracy and illegal public performances. By the end of 1983, FACT had seized some 30,000 illegal tapes, and supposedly reduced the pirates' share of the market to under thirty-five percent.

At a press conference, Peter Duffy of FACT revealed that most pirated films in circulation were not now being mastered in Britain, but had actually originated overseas. Evidence of US origin was demonstrated in the way some pirate tapes had flaws which were systematic with duplication between the incompatible American NTSC and the British PAL formats. One primitive way around the problem was to aim a PAL video camera at a TV screen on which an NTSC film was playing. The end product was understandably terrible, with washed-out colours, a constantly flickering screen and an unshakeable, ghostly after-image which hung onto every movement. But this eye-straining method of piracy did offer moments of unintentional amusement, as in one instance recounted by Kevin:

> This copy of Buddy Giovanni's *Combat Shock* I got from abroad — whenever the screen darkened it revealed the reflection of the person making the copy, who was sitting naked in an armchair!

London lost the stigma of being the piracy capital of the world.[29] The Federation's claim that no new films had been pirated since their formation however, were proven inaccurate when copies of *Educating Rita* and *Scarface* turned up in the hands of dealers prior to their official video release. Also erroneous was the assertion that FACT had stamped out the counterfeiting of tapes, in which videos were made and packaged to look identical to genuine releases, even down to incorporating copyright warnings. Special reflective security labels and even the introduction of Macrovision, a process causing picture deterioration in second generation copies of pre-recorded videocassettes, didn't curb the pirates.[30] (Far from being stamped out, piracy has now moved from videotape to VCD and DVD — the evolution from analogue to digital making such recordings all the more easier, quicker and cheaper to manufacture.)

"Bootleg videos are pouring into Britain," was a report in the *Daily Express* dated December 18, 1995. Illegal copies of new movies such as Disney's *Pocahontas* and the James Bond blockbuster *GoldenEye* had been found at car boot sales and market stalls. Reg Dixon, the director of FACT, said, "People think they are simply getting a video on the cheap but they are helping finance crime at its worse."

FACT had a detrimental effect on the illicit video trade, but they couldn't seriously hope to bring it to an end. Indeed, in years to come, they would be forced to change tactics and increasingly target the consumer as opposed to the pirates directly, trying to halt the trade with campaigns that pricked the public's conscience. Recently, a shocking FACT advertisement arrogated that children were put at risk by the blasé parents who purchased pirated tapes.[31] Other attempts to put consumer off buying pirate tapes were dispersed through the media, and implied that the profits accrued from illegally duplicated films — Disney in particular — funded the IRA,[32] the drug trade[33] and manufacturers of child pornography.[34] As no evidence was forthcoming to support this claim it can only be construed as a type of aversion propaganda.

But it isn't only the film industry that alleges a link between movies and criminal activity (albeit, in this instance, pirated movie revenue funding crime). The news media and politicians are the worst offenders when it comes to making these allegations. But, as we shall see in the next chapter, these supposed links are for the most part self-serving propaganda.

"IT'S HERE" THE MOVIE YOU'VE BEEN WAITING FOR!
A FILM TO AWAKEN YOUR WILDEST FANTASIES
SEX WISH
AWAKEN YOUR WILDEST FANTASI
ALL IT TAKES IS A CANE, A BRIEFC
AND A...
TAURUS PRODUCTIONS PRESENTS
SEX WISH
YOU'VE NEVER SEEN ANYTHING LIKE IT!
AWARD WINNING MOVIE Voted the most erotic film of 1981!
THE WORD WENT OUT – 'GET THE SWORDCANE KILLER'! Harry Reems (Deep Throat, etc) is a rising young attorney whose life is changed by the brutal and sadistic rape of his beautiful young wife. Bent on revenge, Harry seeks the intruder but the sexual fiend strikes again – the victim being the dazzling, elegant Terri Hall (Story of Joanna) in a scene of sexual provocation that guarantees perspiring hands. The shattering climax takes place in a magnificent supper club, where Harry catches up with the Swordcane killer.
YOU MUST SEE 'SEX WISH'. IT'S DIFFERENT!
IT'S COMPELLING! IT'S FRIGHTENING. IT'S A GLITTERING ACHIEVEMENT IN EROTIC FILM FARE.
PINK CHAMPAGNE
VISTA VALLEY
PLEASURE PALACE
Pleasure Palace
FROM CALVISTA VIDEO – the company that gave you all these fabulous Adult Blockbusters ... and many more. Our full range of 20 titles is always available from all Calvista Dealers.
...A SEXUAL MASTERPIECE... OUTRAGEOUS
V – THE HOT ONE
LESLIE BOVÉE
JOHN HOLMES
ERUPTION
AN EROTIC EXPLOSION!
NAKED AFTERNOON
EASY
Garage Girls
V – The Hot One
Eruption
Naked Afternoon
Easy
Garage Girls
LOOK FOR THIS CALVISTA WINDOW STICKER, ASK FOR A FREE! BROCHURE NOW!
CALVISTA VIDEO
Available in VHS Betamax and VCC 2000 video format
The above are available from all good video shops, or in case of difficulty, they are available by Mail Order at £39.95 each (Post Free) from:
GOLBEK SALES LTD.
27 PIRBRIGHT RD. LONDON SW18
(No callers)
PROBE VIDEO
TRADE ENQUIRIES
(Sole Distributors)
PROBE PRODUCTS LTD
15 - 17A RICH INDUSTRIAL ES
CRIMSCOTT ST., LONDON SE
01-237-4334/7

'Who supports violent films now?'

THE BIG INFLUENCE

Critics say that the coercive influence of motion pictures — its ability to make people do what they wouldn't ordinarily do — is confirmed by the fact that industry spends vast sums of money advertising its products on television. If viewers are not influenced by the commercials, then industry wouldn't waste money producing them, the argument goes. However, they fail to understand that the fundamental purpose of advertising is to make potential customers *aware* of a product — there is no *influential effect* because it doesn't cause viewers to purchase something they wouldn't normally buy. If the critics were right in their argument that advertising is influential then we would all be purchasing goods we had no use for and we wouldn't understand why we were doing it. If you haven't got a cat you won't buy a tin of cat food simply because you saw it advertised on television. (Similarly every toy advertised would become the latest craze with children. But they don't.) If you are not a violent person and have no intention of committing any violent act you do not do so just because you have seen a violent scene in a film.

The cause and effect argument was used during the debate for amendments to the Criminal Justice and Public Order Bill in the House of Commons on April 12, 1994. (See SEX & WRECKS.) The discussion was focused on videos; primarily David Alton MP's attempts to add a clause to the Video Recordings Act which would deny adults the right to purchase or hire any video work not suitable for children. Frank Cook MP stated, "I am anxious to nail the argument of those who say that such material is innocuous and does not cause harm. If that were so, what is the justification for the amount that we spend on video material to train our military, our tank and air crews, and those in industry and education? Why do we waste so much money on that if it does not have an impact on the recipients?" Alton added, "In addition, why does the advertising industry spend £1.6 billion trying to sell us its wares if such material does not have an effect on anybody? It seems an extraordinary waste of money if that is the case. The honourable gentleman is right, which is why we must take such issues very seriously." Both men are so focused on their goals that they are blind to common sense. Cook's claim that movies have the same effect as educational videos is utterly preposterous. An educational video is instructive and the viewer is aware of its nature and purpose and therefore receptive towards its content (the effect being erudition). A movie is *emotive* and the viewer is *perceptive* of its content (the effect being ephemeral entertainment).

Films have been the scapegoat for many of society's ills since they first went into production. Common sense eventually prevails but when a new format is developed, like video or computer games, the moral crusade peaks again. (See UNEASE.) The press has censured films and videos so openly and for so long that law-breakers will readily try to mitigate their own criminal acts by blaming a movie. Usually this occurs with the full co-operation, even initial prompting, of a contemporary lawyer or progressive psychologist (see *Natural Born Killers* below in particular). Parents, too, will often attribute their children's offensive behaviour to television, videos, computer games, and now the Internet. Indeed, they will blame *anything* other than themselves, totally ignorant of the fact that for the most part they have provided their children with the very things they censure.[1]

But this is not to state categorically that certain aspects of the media cannot influence the behaviour of those it is aimed at. Advertising certainly doesn't — it simply informs of a product's availability and capability; films certainly don't — they entertain through fictitious characters and events in an emotive manner be it melancholy, laughter, fear, or excitement. Though cinematic entertainment is non-influential, a good example of efficacious entertainment is sport — in particular football. Supporters ally with the players — *real* people — and their "tribal" contest. As a result we see criminal influence derive from it ranging from mindless vandalism to murder. Imagine for a moment if a cinema audience spilled onto the streets and smashed property and assaulted people as a result of the film they had just watched. The film would be banned outright. Such an event has never taken place, yet similar scenes occur regularly following football matches. Football has become so unduly revered, and is such a powerful high-finance conglomerate it is no longer accountable for its criminal — sometimes murderous — side effects.[2]

Like football, the news media can and does influence people's conduct. In a social climate where it is viewed as healthy to have a positive "role model" — in other words, to deny your own distinctive attributes and replace them with those of a successful celebrity of one form or another — imitating those in the media is the current trend. Role models do not take the form of movie characters but movie *stars*, sports personalities, successful business people, pop stars, and so on. Certain people's publicised achievements tend to emphasise other people's lack of attainment and the "underachiever" may react to that situation by trying to emulate the achiever. This is often recognised as a positive response, and indeed actively encouraged. However, it only diminishes individuality and offers generally unattainable goals for the imitators (plus ego boosts for the imitated). But, as we shall see, people do not always choose "moral" role models.

One current trend is for the media to outline real-life events as being 'film-like.'[3] A shooting incident or police pursuit will be described as 'like something out of a film.' For instance, an arsenal of illegal weapons seized by police will be outlined in the press as resembling something out of *The Terminator* movie. Hazel Savage, the Detective who had launched proceedings against Fred and Rosemary West, was likened in an *Express* article on the case to "TV's Prime Suspect Detective Jane Tennison, played by Helen Mirren." When Paul Britton's book *The Jigsaw Man*, a biographical account of his work as a criminal psychologist, was published, it was described by a press critic as being like a "real-life Cracker" (a popular television crime/psychology drama). Even in analysing the Budget report for 2000, *The Express* newspaper used pictures of soap opera characters to illustrate the types of people who would be affected by the new taxes.

It would seem that members of the public are unable to appreciate the realities of society without cinematic reference. This may be because most people have only 'experienced' shooting incidents and criminal psychology in the movies or on TV, but the immediate, off-the-cuff link paves the way for accusations of undue movie influence. So when an incident is described as being like something out of a film, the next conclusion is that maybe a film inspired the event. A typical example is a report in the *Stockport Express* on Wednesday, September 8, 1999, which described a local sword attack. Ian Morrison used an ornamental sword to break through a door of his ex-wife's house. The police were called and Morrison attacked them in the street with the sword before he was run down by the police van, overpowered and arrested. Though films had nothing to do with the incident, the headline for the page-one report was "The Shining" and it was illustrated with the famous still of Jack Nicholson grinning though a smashed bathroom door. The link was contrived simply to generate an eye-catching, though utterly irrelevant, headline.

On Saturday, March 16, 1996, in relation to Thomas Hamilton's horrifying Dunblane school massacre, a piece in *The Times* was headlined "Who Supports Violent Films Now?" The question in most people's minds however, was "who supports legalised guns now?" as Hamilton was a legitimate gun club member and a legitimate gun owner. But somehow films had been brought into the equation despite there being absolutely no link with movies and Hamilton's moment of insanity. The reporter, speaking on behalf of the population regardless of any contrary opinion, said, "This week... we would willingly burn every violent book, film and magazine that we could lay our hands on if we felt that we might be stopping another madman from tipping over the edge." Burn books, films, and magazines? Could it be simple self-righteousness that the writer did not include *newspapers* as another medium to be destroyed? Or is the writer only prepared to destroy things that don't affect his own lifestyle? It is ironic that the press reports which emblazoned Hamilton's action would themselves be the key source of inspiration for future acts of violence, as we shall see.

One of the first high-profile and effective media attacks on a contemporary movie was launched against Stanley Kubrick's groundbreaking *A Clockwork Orange*. Because Kubrick's film was original, daring, and controversial, it inevitably drew condemnation. Though it did also receive much critical acclaim, the moral crusaders vilified the movie and proceeded to ascribe virtually every criminal act that occurred during its first cinema release as a spontaneous reaction to the film.[4] The British press, with the support and encouragement of MPs, claimed that juveniles were imitating scenes from the film, dressing in a manner similar to the main characters and behaving violently. Indeed, Jill Knight MP (see multiple rapist 'The Fox' below) claimed there existed a link between the film and a murder committed by a juvenile despite there being no evidence to support the allegation. In another case, sixteen-year-old Richard Palmer assaulted a tramp and a psychiatrist said that viewing *A Clockwork Orange* was "the only possible explanation for what this boy did." Palmer's defence lawyer also asked, "what explanation can there be for this savagery other than the film?" Such conclusions suggest that no vagrant had ever been beaten up before *A Clockwork Orange* had been made.

In actual fact, Anthony Burgess' novel on which Kubrick's film was based was modelled upon the vicious street gangs who were operating in the North of England during the late 1800s. Amongst their many other nefarious preoccupations, these gangs — called 'scuttlers' — were not averse to knifing innocent people for kicks. General William Booth, founder of the Salvation Army, lamented on what he perceived were declining moral standards when he wrote in 1890:

> The lawlessness of our lads, the increased license of our girls, the general shiftlessness from the home-making point of view of the product of our factories and schools are far from reassuring. Our young people have never learned to obey. The fighting gangs of half-grown lads in Lisson Grove, and the scuttlers of Manchester are ugly symptoms of a social condition that will not grow better by being left alone.[5]

Moving pictures had yet to become a form of popular entertainment.

Kubrick withdrew his film from circulation in the UK, not because of its alleged corrupting influence (as was believed for many years) but because of anonymous death threats made against himself and his family by groups and individuals opposed to movie violence – the self-proclaimed moral crusaders. It is quite bizarre that those condemning fictional violence seemed so willing to administer real brutality.[6]

Incriminating *A Clockwork Orange* for unlawful behaviour was so well publicised that it was adopted as a mitigating defence argument in other cases. On May 15, 1972, in the USA Arthur Bremer attempted to shoot dead Alabama Governor George C Wallace. Wallace survived the public attack but was permanently paralysed. During the trial it was claimed that Bremer's diaries revealed that he decided to kill Wallace while watching *A Clockwork Orange.* This may well have been the case as he had to be doing *something* when the thought occurred to him. It would also suggest that the film had little impact on him if he were daydreaming while viewing it. Contrary to the allegations that the film influenced his actions, Bremer admitted that he had committed the crime with the desire for media attention distinctly in mind.[7] By the time of the trial, indicting Kubrick's film had become a common defence tactic. Over twenty years later Oliver Stone's *Natural Born Killers* would find itself in an identical situation.

But the story has a further twist. Screenwriter Paul Schrader used Bremer's diaries as inspiration for the *Taxi Driver* script. When Martin Scorsese directed the film he used the television footage of Bremer's attack as a blueprint for the scene when an armed and dangerous Travis Bickle (Robert DeNiro) gets close to a presidential candidate. In the news footage the casually dressed Bremer is caught on camera moments before he opens fire. He has an unusual hairstyle, dark glasses and a beaming smile, just as Bickle modelled. What is more ironic is that five years after the release of *Taxi Driver*, John Hinckley became infatuated with Jodie Foster who played the role of an underage prostitute in the film. Hinckley began stalking Foster and sending her obsessive letters, telling her that on occasion he had been close enough to kill her. She failed to respond to his letters, so Hinckley tried to assassinate President Ronald Reagan on March 31, 1981, as a means of impressing her. *Taxi Driver* was instantly indicted as the cause of the attack when letters written by Hinckley showed that he had seen the film on several occasions. Indeed, Hinckley's behaviour certainly seemed modelled on that of the Bickle character, at least according to his parents who wrote a book about their son, *Breaking Points*.[8] The book, of course, may have been a cathartic reaction or a prerequisite 'we're not to blame – Hollywood is' declaration. But Hinckley's obsession was with Foster, a *real* person, not the film nor the character of Iris whom Foster portrayed. Hinckley was nothing more than a deranged stalker, a dangerous schizophrenic who became fixated on an actress. The only way he was able to relate to Foster in writing was by reference to *Taxi Driver* – he had seen it; she was in it. It was the single common factor between them. If he was in fact influenced by Bickle, Hinckley would surely have sported a Mohican haircut and shot pimps, not the president. Moreover, in the film, Bickle doesn't open fire on the politician, so Hinckley's attack is therefore imitation of Arthur Bremer's attempted assassination of a political figure – i.e. Hinckley mimics a news media event. Bremer shot Wallace to get media attention; Hinckley shot Reagan to get Foster's attention.

When David Morrell wrote his best-selling novel *First Blood* in 1972, and Sylvester Stallone played the lead character Rambo in the movie adaptation of it in 1982, little did they imagine that their work would become associated with real life murder. But courtesy of the temporary madness of one dysfunctional gun fanatic and an over-zealous British press, that was to be the case. It was on Wednesday, August 19, 1987, that Michael Ryan re-enacted the scenario of *First Blood* for real. Or at least that is how the majority of the newspapers interpreted the Hungerford massacre. They called it the "Rambo Killings" and attempted to homogenise the fictitious John Rambo with the real-life Michael Ryan, implying that the celluloid-existence of the former was somehow responsible for the violent actions of the latter. But was this correlation by the media justified, or was it nothing more than the deliberate spreading of misinformation?

On the morning of August 19, Michael Ryan drove from his home at 4 South View in Hungerford to the Savernake Forest, a Wiltshire beauty spot some miles from his house.

There he came across Sue Godfrey and her two children who were packing their car following a picnic. Ryan parked next to Godfrey's car and approached her carrying a Beretta 9mm automatic pistol. He picked up the groundsheet the family had used and put the children back in their car. He forced their mother into the woods for about 75 yards where, it is speculated, he intended to rape Godfrey (the groundsheet was later discovered laid out on the grass). But instead of indulging in sexual activity, Ryan shot Godfrey ten times in the back. As she collapsed into a wire fence he fired three more bullets into her. The back-wounds indicate Godfrey made an attempt to escape.

Up to this point Ryan had fired his pistol only at paper targets. Human-shaped they may have been, but they were paper nonetheless. With a dead woman at his feet Michael Ryan had crossed the Rubicon. He left the scene without harming the children and drove to a petrol station, filled the car tank and a spare canister with petrol, and approached the cashier Kakoub Dean, with every intention of shooting her dead. The first shot, now from an automatic rifle he had stored in the boot of his car, missed its target. As he moved closer and re-aimed, the rifle misfired and Ryan's intended second victim survived. As Dean telephoned the police Ryan returned to the car and drove on to his home. Once there he collected his survival kit and bullet-proof vest and loaded the boot with his remaining weapons. He doused his house with petrol and set it alight. The car, however, failed to restart so he strafed it with gunfire and set off on foot. At the back of his burning house he shot dead his neighbours Ronald and Sheila Mason. Moments later seventy-seven-year-old Dorothy Smith confronted Ryan face-to-face for making such an amount of noise. For some reason he didn't open fire on her, but shot and wounded Margery Jackson instead. Ryan followed a route that eventually led him to his old school opening fire on all he encountered along the way. Those to die after the Masons were Ken Clements, PC Roger Brereton, Abdul Khan, George White, Dorothy Ryan, Francis Butler, Marcus Barnard, Douglas Wainwright, Eric Vardy, Sandra Hill, Jack and Myrtle Gibbs and Ian Playle.

There was no apparent purpose to Ryan's actions other than the destruction of his only known world. He killed his mother and his pet dog; ruined his car, and destroyed his home by fire before casually walking around the town shooting all he encountered. Sixteen people lay dead with as many injured, before Ryan finally sought refuge from the pursuing army of police in his old school. After futile negotiations, he decided the only way to outwit his potential captors was to kill himself. He placed the Beretta to his head and pulled the trigger. Then it was over. And the truth about whatever really pushed Ryan so far over the edge was blasted from his head with that single pistol round. The cause of Ryan's rampage was left open to speculation. Within hours the news media had unanimously agreed on a designated patsy: Rambo.

Whatever Michael Ryan was, he most certainly wasn't a film buff. A military fanatic, definitely; a gun obsessive, yes; a friendless loner still living with his mother, positively — all idiosyncrasies which could be indicative of some psychological instability. No available information on Ryan suggests he had any interest in either films or film characters. To purport that he allowed his reason to be overwhelmed by a movie character without any evidence to indicate he was even *aware* of that character is extravagant speculation, indeed. But something evidently did push Ryan over the edge. And there are subtle pieces of evidence that help pinpoint the most likely catalyst that transformed Ryan into a cold-blooded killer.

The most telling is when Ryan made his final purchase of stockpile ammunition. The date was August 12, seven days before he summoned the courage to put the ammunition to its intended use. He went to the Wiltshire Shooting Centre shop and bought a reconditioned M-1 Carbine rifle and fifty rounds of ammunition. Had *First Blood* aired on television on August 11, then the press would have had a piece of credible, even though only circumstantial, evidence to aggrandise their claims of movie influence. However, the BBC had shown the film only once — almost a year prior to the shootings — in September 1986.[9] If we are to believe that Ryan had watched and been influenced by the film, surely the Hungerford massacre would have occurred closer to its being aired? The theory that Ryan had a video recorder and a VHS copy of *First Blood* that he repeatedly viewed is nothing other than desperate supposition to support the argument. But even if he had seen *First Blood* — and he may well have viewed it when it toured the cinemas or was aired on television — there is absolutely nothing to suggest he was influenced by its content.

One of the staunchest partisans of the Rambo connection is journalist and author Tom Davies. Davies, a "born again Christian" wrote *The Man of Lawlessness* with the intention of establishing a link between films and real-life incidents of violence, though he failed to offer any credible evidence to substantiate his view. Indeed, one person credited in the acknowledgements is Dennis Coggan who was behind the seriously flawed *Children and Video Violence* publication, a volume from which Davies gets much of his data. To get an idea of the angle that Davies is coming from one need only read the acknowledgements where he states, "I must always try to honour the fire that God has built in me." Such pious rhetoric runs throughout the book. "We glory in the greatness of God's creation," he claims; "God spoke directly to me..."; "I knew then that God was at work in my life again,"; "...God has finally raised the curtains for the Son of Man to make his reappearance on the world's stage." Disturbing stuff, indeed. In fact, it was a "vision", which he claims took place while he was in Malaya working on a novel of violence and homosexuality, that inspired Davies to write *Man of Lawlessness*.[10]

It is evident that Davies already had decided upon the book's conclusion before embarking on any investigation to verify it. Such a stance would lead him to manipulate any evidence to fit his theory, which indeed he does. He relates an incident in Walsall, September 11, 1988 when Anthony Haskett (named by the press "Rambo Boy") shot three youths with a shotgun before turning the gun on himself. Davies claims that Haskett was influenced by the Rambo films. He makes an issue of the fact that camouflage paste was found in Haskett's bedroom and similar paste "crops up a lot in the Rambo stories." However, as Davies points out himself, Haskett was in the Territorial Army where they supply and train cadets in the use of weapons and camouflage materials. According to Davies, Haskett wasn't the only one to be corrupted by the Rambo films. So were James Huberty, James Purdy, Julian Knight (see below), Michael Ryan and Darren Fowler (see below). An exorbitant claim, indeed.

But the Rambo films aren't Davies' only cinematic targets. He states, "*Taxi Driver* is still widely available in most video shops, but after Hinckley's widely-publicised trial, the British Video Association should have known of the vital role that it played in the attack on President Reagan. Why is it still available?" Yet later he says, "Nowhere in this book — or in my mind — is there an argument — either covert or overt — for banning a film."

Davies notes an incident in which a man rammed a police roadblock following a chase. The court were told that he was re-enacting a scene from *Vanishing Point*, the 1971 Richard C Sarafian road movie starring Barry Newman. But if he *were* re-enacting a sequence from a film *then the police must also have been re-enacting the same scene*. It was either a remarkable coincidence that both parties were acting out the same film scene on the same stretch of road at the same time, or they colluded beforehand. But such an explanation is, of course, preposterous. The driver wasn't re-enacting any film scene — he was being pursued by police and he tried to evade arrest by smashing his way through a roadblock. Such things happen. After the event it may have *reminded* some people of a scene from a film, but that is all. Davies however, unreservedly accepts the claim that the incident occurred because of *Vanishing Point*, simply because this amplifies his argument. Davies even goes so far as to blame the film industry for football violence and brawls between drunken thugs!

But what is his evidence that Ryan was imitating *First Blood*? Davies asserts that together with journalist Robert Peart he found the remains of a video recorder in Michael Ryan's burned-out home. "Just standing there and looking at that charred recorder, all God's grief came flooding back to me. *Just look at what they're doing to all my babies*," he enunciates. He makes much of the following points and offers them as proof that Ryan watched *First Blood*:

- Ryan liked to wear military-style clothing
- He owned a video recorder
- He had a Second World War helmet

- He had a thin beard
- Ryan wore a black bandanna[11]
- Ryan attacked a petrol station just as Rambo had[12]
- Both were surrounded by police
- Both were shadowed by helicopters

Davies also points out that Rambo spared children, implying that this was why Ryan failed to shoot Sue Godfrey's children in Savernake Forest. But if Ryan was imitating Rambo to such a discriminatory degree, why did he shoot and seriously wound fourteen-year-old Lisa Mildenhall later that day, and why did he kill several women? To suggest that the police surrounded Ryan, and that a helicopter was put to use because it occurred in *First Blood* implies that the police, too, were mimicking the film. *Reductio ad absurdum*, perhaps, but it indicates Davies' desperation to prove, even if only to himself, that the movie is somehow to blame. He continues, "It is true that no one ever actually saw Michael Ryan watch *First Blood*, but the overwhelming body of evidence [i.e. the bulleted points above] suggests that he watched it again and again." In reality Davies offers not a single iota of evidence to prove that Ryan saw the film even once.

However, it's reasonable to suggest that Michael Ryan may have had 'Rambo' on his mind the day he stockpiled his ammunition in preparation for the massacre — but this was nothing to do with Ryan having watched the film. Rather, it was around this time that the press were reporting the killing spree of a young Australian failed soldier and gun fanatic named Julian Knight, who they predictably likened to Rambo...

On the evening of August 9, 1987, in Melbourne, Australia, Julian Knight, after drinking in the Royal Hotel, made a decision to go home "and get my guns and start shooting." Armed with two rifles — a Ruger semi-automatic and an M-14 semi-automatic — a Mossberg repeating shotgun and a ten-inch sheath knife, Knight embarked on a killing spree. He found a vantage point overlooking a busy road then randomly fired at passing motorists. By the time of his arrest later that night, following a brief shoot-out with police, six people were dead and forty-six injured. Knight claimed he intended to commit suicide rather than be arrested or shot by police, but had not done so because he ran out of ammunition and lost the single bullet he had placed in his pocket for that purpose. In custody, the day after the incident, Knight was observed in his cell searching the newspapers for reports about himself.

What is most important here is the fact that British newspapers reported the event on Monday, August 10, and Tuesday, August 11. The first report in the *Daily Mail* ran the headline "Rambo Sniper on the Loose Kills 6." The report went on

> 6 people were shot and at least 16 others injured after a sniper went berserk last night. The gunman dressed in Rambo-style clothing shot at police and motorists from bushes in a busy street. One woman was gunned down as she sat in her car at a service station... Other victims were picked off at random as the gunman walked down a suburban street in Clifford Hill, Melbourne Australia.

The next day, the *Mail* followed up the story with "The Misfit who Killed 'For Love'" suggesting that "a broken romance may have triggered the rampage..." Further details about Knight's character came from his neighbours who described him as "a weird type of boy who stalked around wearing military fatigues... He kept a library of military books and magazines." The report offered details of the shootings, the weapons and pictures of the killer and Knight's dead victims.

Knight's description fitted Michael Ryan's persona perfectly. Even he would have perceived the resemblance between Knight and himself. The fact that on August 12, Ryan went to purchase a rifle like Knight's M-14, as described in the newspaper report (he settled for an M-1), plus a stockpile of ammunition suggests a plan of action had formed in his mind. Eight days after the *Daily Mail* glorified Knight's rampage, Ryan duplicated the events almost identically. This points to a clear and direct influence by the press coverage.

Thursday March 26 1998

The Mirror

www.mirror.co.uk

30p

EXCLUSIVE: RACHEL'S TITANIC CUT

HOW TO GET THE LOOK THAT'S SWEEPING HOLLYWOOD: PAGE 3

MY RAMBO GRANDSON

PAL: Gun boy Johnson, 13

WORLD EXCLUSIVE

THE grandad of one of the two boys who carried out the Jonesboro school massacre said last night: "I don't think he knows what he's done."

FULL STORY: PAGES 4, 5, 6 & 7

"All Andrew remembers is shooting at a car, the rest is blank.. I do not think he knows what he's done. He cries and cries"

GIRLFRIEND: Shot Candace

The Mirror, March 26, 1998.

Following the Hungerford massacre the *Daily Mail* tried to concoct an unequivocal link between Ryan's actions and the plot of *First Blood*. The report pointed out that Rambo started killing deputies in a forest, ignited petrol pumps in a service station, and set a building on fire. These incidents were analogised to the killing of Sue Godfrey in Savernake forest, the attempted murder of Kakoub Dean at the petrol station, and the igniting of Ryan's own home. However, police believe Ryan intended to rape Godfrey and that it was her attempt to escape which led to her death. Such a scenario would fit more comfortably with the *Mail*'s "Misfit who Killed 'For Love'" heading. Ryan's attempt to shoot the female service station attendant doesn't correlate with anything in *First Blood* (Rambo shot the petrol pumps) but closely mimics the *Mail*'s claim that Knight shot a female in a service station. Ryan walking through the streets of Hungerford shooting innocent people at random doesn't conform to any scene in the film but reproduces identically the *Mail*'s report. It is further worth noting that on the morning that Ryan embarked on his killing spree the *Mail* had a front-page report of Rudolph Hess' suicide. It stated that by killing himself Hess was "outwitting and humiliating his allied captors." Within hours Ryan would be "outwitting and humiliating" his potential captors in a similar manner.

So similar and so adjacent are the Melbourne and Hungerford incidents that the latter is doubtless a copycat event of the former. Indeed, it is extremely unlikely that journalists at the *Mail* didn't tie the two together, but it is quite obvious why they failed to acknowledge and publicise the fact. It would seem that they deliberately chose to divert evidential blame from themselves by indicting *First Blood* as the likely cause.

It wasn't just the *Mail* that proclaimed the link — other popular tabloids were equally parochial. *The Sun* called the event the "Rambo Shootings", the *Daily Mirror* refered to it as the "Rambo Killings", while the *Daily Star* simply stated "Rambo" — all perhaps indicative of Fleet Street collusion. One year after the event, *Rambo III* was released much to the delight of the press. It gave them the opportunity to resurrect old headlines and reopen the wounds of Ryan's victim's families. "Fury as Sly's new movie revives the horror of Hungerford" shouted the *Mirror*, though the 'fury' was only provoked by the author of the piece, despite Reverend David Salt's request that "the townsfolk just want the anniversary to pass by quietly." One Hungerford resident, former Mayor Ron Tarry said, "A lot of people identify Ryan with Rambo. We don't need this film as a reminder." This was further evidence that people's perception had been influenced by the press-invented link between Ryan and Rambo. It would seem that any incident involving a gun was attributed to the Rambo films and this happened not only when the films were popular. "A fifteen-year-old boy could lose the sight in one of his eyes after it was hit by a paint-filled pellet in a Rambo-style wargame. Oliver Bennett was hit as he lifted his goggles to clean them after they misted up," reported one article illustrated with a picture of Stallone. Such a trivial accident would never have made the national press without this contrived link to the movie. As late as March 26, 1998, the *Mirror* ran the headline "MY RAMBO GRANDSON" in reference to the Jonesboro school massacre in which five people (four pupils, one teacher) were shot dead. The killers were eleven-year-old Andrew Golden and thirteen-year-old Mitchell Johnson, and the newspaper referred to them as the "Rambo Boys," claiming that Golden "thought he was Rambo." In the multiple-page article there is no direct reference to the Rambo films to suggest any causative link; indeed, the name is only used twice in the body text yet used three times as headers.

Just as the press reports on Julian Knight had stimulated Ryan to kill sixteen innocent people, the subsequent reports on Ryan would correspondingly influence others.

On Wednesday, January 6, 1988, sixteen-year-old Darren Fowler, using a shotgun, fired at and wounded people at his school in Northamptonshire. Deputy headmaster Michael Cousins and two pupils were hit in the face, neck and chest. Fowler was eventually overcome by a physical education instructor and was disarmed. Following his arrest, police discovered he had a great interest in Michael Ryan. This obsessive fascination was generated by intensive press coverage of the Hungerford massacre. An even greater link was established between the press enthusiasm with Ryan and copycat murders, one year later when Robert Sartin took up arms.

"The Satan Boy" was the ostentatious headline (used by the *Daily Mirror* on Tuesday, May 1, 1990) to describe Robert Sartin during his trial for murder and attempted murder. One year earlier, on Sunday, April 30, 1989, twenty-three-year-old Sartin had wandered around the streets of his hometown, Monkseaton, carrying his father's shotgun and shooting people at random. At one point he was confronted by an elderly resident Vera Burrows. "What the hell is going on?" she challenged him. Sartin replied that he was killing people and was going to kill her, too, but suddenly changed his mind saying, "Oh, you're old, I'm not going to kill you." Of the seventeen people he opened fire at, one died: Kenneth Mackintosh, who was shot in the chest at point blank range. The other victims received injuries that varied in severity, but this was only due to the weapon Sartin carried and not any intention of his to inflict less-serious damage. Had Sartin carried an automatic rifle then he would have likely achieved a death toll similar to that of his role model Michael Ryan. Indeed, the Monkseaton shootings virtually duplicated the Hungerford massacre, and Sartin himself admitted visiting Hungerford to tour the route of Ryan's kill-spree eight months before he decided to re-enact it. The actions of Sartin were incredibly similar to Ryan's: he commenced his attack after a car journey, his first victim was a female motorist and he even refrained from shooting an elderly lady who verbally confronted him, exactly as Ryan had done. Sartin was finally talked out of his rampage by a police officer. Unlike Ryan he didn't have the courage to take his own life.

Despite this evidence identifying the source of Sartin's influence as the news media, consultant psychiatrist Marion Swan let it be known during trial that the "Michael" he was impelled by was not Michael Ryan, but Michael Myers, a fictitious character from the popular *Halloween* series of films. Remarkably, a psychiatrist had been treating Sartin for three years before he took the gun on the streets. Quite evidently the therapy he was subjected to had failed catastrophically. Sartin had even told his psychiatrist that voices in his head were instructing him to kill. Considering the outcome it seems that little effective treatment was given to deter him from carrying out his threat.

Sartin, the *Mirror* reported, was so obsessed with everything evil — Satanism, cannibalism, murder — that he acquired the nickname "Satan." Such a claim makes good sensational copy, though the assonance between "Sartin" and "Satan" is more likely the origin of the sobriquet. Moreover, as his school peers gave him this nickname, the constant use of it could well have formulated his interest in the occult from the beginning.

When *The Sun* covered the story it made the front page under the banner "I Heard Voice Of Video Michael." It continued, "Bloodbath gunman Robert Sartin was ordered to kill by a voice from a video nasty..." The piece was illustrated with a picture of the killer that was dwarfed by the reproduction of the video sleeve of *Halloween 4*. The film was described by a journalist as having "gallons of blood flying about", and the Michael Myers character was described as a "teenage psychopath who hacks his family to pieces one by one." But, in the interest of maintaining their trite connection, they failed to reveal that the character Myers is a mute killer who had never spoken a single word in any of the Halloween instalments.

Had the accusation of influence been turned away from the dubiously indicted film character and directed at its proper source, the real-life Michael Ryan, then the question should be asked: How did Sartin become influenced by a dead killer? At that time the only readily available source of information on Ryan's methods of killing was the newspapers. It is from these publications that Sartin undoubtedly drew his inspiration.

On Friday, February 12, 1993, six years after Michael Ryan's massacre, James Bulger was tortured and murdered. In this instance there was but one fatality on a railway track, in comparison to the seventeen who perished in Hungerford. Yet this case was far more disturbing and its repercussions far more extensive. The victim was a toddler, he had been snatched in full view of the public (the event being caught on security camera), and most astonishingly, the killers were but children themselves.

Every new detail of the crime compounded the tragedy. Several members of the public admitted to seeing Bulger in tears while he was being dragged, kicked and punched by his murderers through the streets. Needless to say, no one intervened. Everyone minded their own business, aware, in the current climate of 'political correctness', of the criminal liabilities involved in accosting a juvenile — delinquent or otherwise.

Before it was known that the child had been tortured, mutilated and killed, every household in Britain was watching him being led away by his killers-to-be on television. The blurry security video was aired in the hope of leading to the safe retrieval of James. Everyone reasoned that the child must have been okay because his abductors were only kids. Once the news broke that Bulger's body had been found, that same video footage developed an even more disturbing snuff movie-like quality. All these elements combined, lifted this case into — *if not beyond* — the magnitude of the Moors Murders some thirty years previous. Brady and Hindley were deviants feeding off each other's depravity, anomalous sex being the prime motivation for the crimes. The children they assaulted and murdered were discreetly snatched off the streets, bundled into a car and driven away. Bulger was simply lured from his mother and dragged in full view of the ignorant public to be battered to death simply to alleviate boredom. It wasn't long before two ten-year-olds boys, Jon Venables and Robert Thompson, were arrested. They were subsequently tried and found guilty of the crime.[13] The general public were in a state of shock, and as any newspaper editor and politician well knows, when people are in this state they are very easy to deceive and manipulate. Such deception and manipulation of people's emotions began the day after the trial.

During Judge Morland's summing up of this perplexing case, he made the speculative comment: "It is not for me to pass judgement on their upbringing, but I suspect that exposure to violent video films may in part be an explanation." This was a very indeterminate statement that would subsequently be swallowed up and modified by the sensation-hungry press.[14] Following Morland's comments, a campaign was launched against the video industry by the tabloids, which was spearheaded by David Alton MP, a self-appointed moral crusader. The purpose of the campaign, they claimed, was to protect the nation's children. Such an emotive aspiration is guaranteed success no matter how unreliable or ludicrous its foundation. At the time, Alton (compared to Goebbels, the propaganda expert of the Third Reich, by some[15]) was a Liberal Democrat MP from Liverpool but as of writing he is Professor of Citizenship at John Moore's University and a crossbencher in the House of Lords. Like Tom Davies, Alton is unreservedly pious. He is parliamentary advisor for the Movement of Christian Democracy. Speaking in 1997 to a Christian group and referring to film director Oliver Stone and his like he stated, "Their abolition of God — and the man made in His image — has left us poor beyond belief."

The film that was unanimously held up as being causative in James Bulger's murder was *Child's Play 3*, probably because the title fitted well with the fact that the killers and victim were children and there were three in total. It was suggested that a copy of the film had been in Jon Venables' home three weeks before he and Thompson murdered Bulger though there was no evidence of this. As with *First Blood* and Hungerford, similarities were pointed out between scenes in the film and events of the incident. For instance, Bulger had been splashed with paint and the doll in the film is struck with a paintball; Bulger died on a railway line and a set-piece in the movie takes place on a ghost train ride; the killers admitted that Bulger constantly got back on his feet no matter how hard they hit him and the doll in the film shows a similar indestructibility. (The suggestion that Bulger repeatedly rose to his feet after being struck down because of a scene in the film, poses the ridiculous and outrageous notion that Bulger must have seen the film and was mimicking it himself.) So ambiguous are the supposed links that if we were to transpose *Child's Play 3* with *Home Alone 2* the results would be just the same — indeed, the latter film would be more fitting as it features a child being separated from his parents and terrorised by two older males.

THE Sun

WIN £100,000 HOUSE FREE -Page 13

I HEARD VOICE OF VIDEO MICHAEL

Killer's mad obsession

MY FOUR YEARS IN A BLINDFOLD

The Sun, May 1, 1990.

In one instance a newspaper actually printed stills from the film (including shots of the Chucky doll with half its face hacked away) and ran them next to a reconstructed photo of two young boys dragging a toddler along a railway line. They were attempting to illustrate Bulger's facial wounds with pictures from the film,[16] a tactic that surely would have caused great distress to the dead boy's parents. Because of the speculative nonsense being published in the press, many tabloid readers became convinced that the movie really was to blame for the boy's murder. The *Daily Star* claimed to have asked a "cross-section" of people to view the film and report their responses to it. "Outraged father-of-two Les Clayden", said, "The message children could draw is that murder, blood, mutilation... well, that's entertainment. It should be withdrawn from video shops immediately." Natalie Miller said, "Having seen this I am sure this is where the two boys who murdered James got their evil ideas from." Neil Carroll said, "This should really be banned. We can't risk other children copying what these boys did." Anne Naughton said, "I can imagine that certain children watching this couldn't wait to experiment afterwards." Judging by their reactions, if indeed they were genuine vox pop reactions, all were obviously influenced by the *Daily Star* and probably instructed to respond in the way they did. If anyone did have a contrary opinion the paper chose not to print it. However, any individuals retaining a degree of self determination wanting to check out the claims of the papers and actually hiring the film were cut down and branded as "ghouls" by the tabloid journalists. The hacks responsible for such accusations were ignorant of the true definition of a ghoul: a legendary creature that disinters graves in order to feed off the dead. (It is also worth noting that in the piece, the adjective "evil" was used *five times* on one page in relation to the film.) Feeding off the death of James Bulger is exactly what the tabloids were doing and Alton was, metaphorically, using his tiny coffin as a soapbox.

Proper investigation revealed that there was nothing to indicate either child had seen *Child's Play 3*. Both of Venables' parents claimed that their son had not seen the film. All who were closely involved with the case (the police, the parents of the killers and Mark Thomas, author of the detailed account *Every Mother's Nightmare: The Killing of James Bulger*), insisted that videos played no part in the events. Detective Superintendent Albert Kirby, who led the murder case from beginning to end, concluded that *no* evidence had been found to indicate that either child had access to videos any worse than would be found in many homes. Inspector Ray Simpson said, "We looked at all the videos in their houses and checked their lists of rentals from the shop. We did not find *Child's Play 3*, nor did we find anything in the list that could have encouraged them to do what they did. If you are going to link this murder to a film, you might as well link it to *The Railway Children*."

After questioning, Venables and Thompson revealed that they first tried to get Bulger to fall in the canal so he would drown. All they succeeded in doing was dropping him head first on the towpath as he struggled to keep away from the water. They then considered leaving him by the roadside in the hope that he would step in front of a moving vehicle — something they confessed to having planned to do to a child in the past.[17] The fact that they failed to get the boy drowned or run over explains why they took him to the railway line: these are the three main dangers impressed on children at school — bodies of water, roads, and railway lines. Venables and Thompson were probably hoping to see the toddler get hit by a train, but no trains passed while the boys were there because the line they chose only carried freight and was infrequently used. They made Bulger lie on the track but as he kept getting up they beat him with bricks and a discarded metal fishplate[18] until he stayed down and it was the severity of the beating, resulting in multiple fractures of the skull, that ultimately killed him. Even so, the boys laid Bulger's body across the line in the naïve hope that his death would appear to be an accident, exactly as it would have had he drowned or been hit by a car.

Psychiatric study of Venables in detention showed him to be not just uninterested in scenes of violence but positively repulsed by them. Of course, it seems somewhat peculiar that he should be disturbed by make-believe violence considering what he had done to James. It may have been that such scenes reminded him of what happened on that railway. But it is more likely that Venables really was offended by violence. The nature of the crime is such that neither boy would have committed it alone. A sadistic area of the brain was tapped into and each boy's presence spurred the other on to greater atrocities. They knew exactly what they were doing and probably thoroughly enjoyed the experience as it was occurring, but most likely regretted what they had done once it was over and they went their separate ways. Both children were misfits. Robert Thompson — who eventually admitted murdering Bulger seven years after the event — was an urban recidivist brought up in a family led by a violent, indifferent father, also named Robert. Venables by all accounts was a simple-minded tag-along. The fact that there were signs of sexual interference with James — his trousers and underpants had been removed, his foreskin had been retracted and batteries may have been inserted into his anus[19] — also points to the possibility that either one or both of the killers are victims of sexual abuse themselves. It would seem that they are simply the products of a defective upbringing rather than innocent children corrupted by the influence of a ninety-minute fantasy film. Even Susan Venables, Jon's mother, called the link to the film "rubbish", stating that her son was never allowed to watch adult films. A school friend of the killers told of how they often tortured animals and had a long-standing plan to push a child under a bus at the Strand shopping centre.

David Alton was generally unknown outside of Liverpool, but following Bulger's death he became a nationally recognised figure. Rational thinkers would conclude that he was manipulating the tragedy to enhance his political career, hoping that the attention generated for himself would guarantee he retained his seat in parliament, which, indeed, it did. To corroborate his claim that video violence did influence the action of children, Alton commissioned an investigative report on the subject. The report was supposed to be an independent inquiry into whether children were adversely affected by video imagery, but it proved to be a politically motivated piece designed to "confirm" Alton's claims. The resultant work is worth looking at in some detail as it proved widely influential, and ultimately helped lead to a strengthening of the law concerning videos (see SEX & WRECKS).

The rushed paper, titled *Video Violence and the Protection of Young Children* and eight pages long, was written by Professor Elizabeth Newson of Nottingham University and it opened by directly referring to the Bulger case: "Two-year old James Bulger was brutally murdered on February 12, 1993, by two ten-year-old children. This stark fact has prompted a long overdue focus upon what conditions in our society could precipitate such an unthinkable act." Thus, in the very first sentence Newson unequivocally sustains the myth that a video film was connected with Bulger's death. In the third paragraph she shrewdly refers to the two killers as "the two children who survive" and "victims themselves", as though they were somehow not responsible for what they did. This implies even further that some outside force was to blame for the murder. Newson goes on to detail the attack and describe the wounds suffered by Bulger. Once the child was dead and draped across the railway line she points out that the killers "wander down to the video-shop where they were known." Again she brings in an irrelevant link with video. In order to show that such a terrible crime is a new and contemporary phenomenon (this idea is the foundation of the theory), she writes:

> Shortly after this trial, children of a similar age in Paris were reported to have set upon a tramp, encouraged by another tramp, kicked him and thrown him down a well. In England an adolescent girl was tortured by her 'friends' over days, using direct quotations from a horror video (*Child's Play 3*) as part of her torment, and eventually set on fire and thus killed; while the following note appeared in a local newspaper on December 7, 1993:
>
>> Two schoolboys were today expected to appear in court accused of torturing a six-year-old on a railway line. The youngsters, aged ten and eleven, allegedly tried to force the boy to electrocute himself on a track in Newcastle upon Tyne last week. They are also accused of stabbing him in the arm with a knife.
>
> We do not have the information to be able to comment on the full background of any of these crimes at present...

Newson admits to not having proper details of the crimes yet she chooses to be selective and use what scant tabloid information promotes her/Alton's theory. The adolescent girl she refers to is Suzanne Capper (see below) who was tortured and murdered by a gang of drug-addled *adults* – something Newson fails to mention. An audio tape was found in the house where the crime took place which included a techno track containing samples of dialogue from the first *Child's Play* film. The track was played often on a local radio station. There was no videotape of the film. These important facts were available at the time Newson was writing her report but were ignored. The case of the two schoolboys assaulting a child on a railway line was accepted as being mimicry due to the excessive media coverage of the Bulger case. It had nothing to do with any movie.

Other possible causative factors are mentioned with regard to what drove Thompson and Venables to kill Bulger: emotional neglect, physical/sexual abuse, disturbed family relationships, poverty etc. But these options are swept aside because they "have been part of many children's experience over the years." Newson declares that none of these factors are relevant and ponders on what different factor "has entered the lives of countless children in recent years." This she claims must be "the easy availability to children of gross images of violence on video." But are these her own theories or is she merely writing to Alton's requirements? Alton is quoted in a newspaper in November 1993, many months before publication of Newson's paper (April 1994), stating, "I strongly believe the easy availability of videos, often containing highly explicit scenes of violence, helps to explain the level of violence today compared with fifteen years ago."[20] One point both fail to realise is that over a decade before the Bulger murder, videos were uncensored and unrated. Many contained far more violence than those available today and by the time of the killing they were certified and censored. Any that remained uncertified were withdrawn from circulation. If there was any truth in their theory that videos were to blame for serious juvenile crimes then incidents would have peaked in the early eighties.

Contrary to Newson's claims, the Bulger killing is not so special or unique, nor is it a

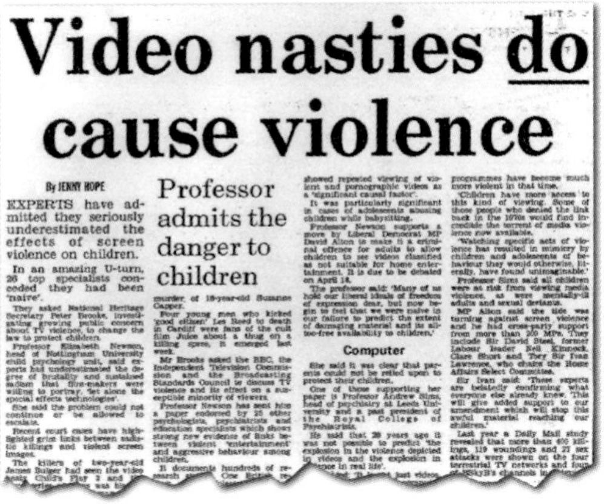

Video nasties do cause violence

Professor admits the danger to children

By JENNY HOPE

EXPERTS have admitted they seriously underestimated the effects of screen violence on children.

In an amazing U-turn, 26 top specialists conceded they had been 'naive'.

They asked National Heritage Secretary Peter Brooke, investigating growing public concern about TV violence, to change the law to protect children.

Professor Elizabeth Newson, head of Nottingham University child psychology unit, said experts had underestimated the degree of brutality and sustained sadism that film-makers were willing to portray, 'let alone the special effects technologies'.

She said the problem could not continue or be allowed to escalate.

Recent court cases have highlighted grim links between sadistic killings and violent screen images.

The killers of two-year-old James Bulger had seen the video nasty Child's Play 3 and ...

... murder of 16-year-old Suzanne Capper.

Four young men who kicked 'good citizen' Les Reed to death in Cardiff were fans of the cult film Juice about a thug on a killing spree, it emerged last week.

Mr Brooke asked the BBC, the Independent Television Commission and the Broadcasting Standards Council to discuss TV violence and its effect on a susceptible minority of viewers.

Professor Newson has sent him a paper endorsed by 25 other psychologists, psychiatrists and education specialists which shows strong new evidence of links between violent 'entertainment' and aggressive behaviour among children.

It documents hundreds of research ... One British re...

... showed repeated viewing of violent and pornographic videos as a 'significant causal factor'.

It was particularly significant in cases of adolescents abusing children while babysitting.

Professor Newson supports a move by Liberal Democrat MP David Alton to make it a criminal offence for adults to allow children to see videos classified as not suitable for home entertainment. It is due to be debated on April 12.

The professor said: 'Many of us hold our liberal ideals of freedom of expression dear, but now begin to feel that we were naive in our failure to predict the extent of damaging material and its all-too-free availability to children.'

Computer

She said it was clear that parents could not be relied upon to protect their children.

One of those supporting her paper is Professor Andrew Sims, head of psychiatry at Leeds University and a past president of the Royal College of Psychiatrists.

He said that 20 years ago it was not possible to predict 'the explosion in the violence depicted in videos and the explosion in violence in real life'.

... 'It is not just videos ...

... programmes have become much more violent in that time.

'Children have more access to this kind of viewing. Some of those people who denied the link back in the 1970s would find incredible the torrent of media violence now available.

'Watching specific acts of violence has resulted in mimicry by children and adolescents of behaviour they would otherwise, literally, have found unimaginable.'

Professor Sims said all children were at risk from viewing media violence, as were mentally-ill adults and sexual deviants.

MP Alton said the tide was turning against screen violence and he had cross-party support from more than 200 MPs. They include Sir David Steel, former Labour leader Neil Kinnock, Clare Short and Tory Sir Ivan Lawrence, who chairs the Home Affairs Select Committee.

Sir Ivan said: 'These experts are belatedly confirming what everyone else already knew. This will give added support to our amendment which will stop this awful material reaching our children.'

Last year a Daily Mail study revealed that more than 400 killings, 119 woundings and 27 sex attacks were shown on the four terrestrial TV networks and four of BSkyB's channels in ...

The Newson report as received by the *Daily Mail*, April 1, 1994.

sudden insidious development of the nineties, because children murdering children is not a new phenomenon. Rare, certainly, but a sign of the times not at all. The case of Mary Bell (post-dating the Comics Code and pre-dating the availability of domestic video) is a remarkably similar example. Mary Bell was eleven-years-old when she murdered four-year-old Martin Brown and three-year-old Brian Howe in 1968. The killings occurred on separate occasions and Howe's body was mutilated with a pair of scissors and a razor. When questioned, Mary tried to blame her friend Norma Bell (no relation) but the ploy failed. Though Norma admitted being at the scene and a witness to the murder of Howe, it was decided she was under the complete control of Mary and she was acquitted. The parallels between the two cases are plain and significant. Newson's failure to acknowledge the Bell case in her report suggests she was striving to force the Bulger killing into being unique rather than attempt to discover the true cause of child brutality. This would achieve nothing other than the apparent validation of Alton's claims. Appalling though Bulger's murder was, it was incorrectly made unique by those wishing to gain reputation or reward from it.[21]

Newson cannot resist adding to the report that "industry finds it worth while to spend millions of pounds on advertising," as though this statement (another one of Alton's favourites), in itself serves to prove her case.

Following publication of the report, Newson was quoted in one newspaper saying, "Violence may continue. The government has not addressed the question of video games, or the effect of violent videos on adults." Can she truly believe that videos and video games alone are responsible for violence in society? Does she think that if all films were erased overnight violence would *not* continue? She also added her doubts concerning another, genuinely independent report,[22] which thoroughly contradicted her own dubious findings and indicated that there was no discernible link between films and behaviour.

The false allegation that *Child's Play 3* was embroiled in the death of James Bulger has been repeated so often that it is accepted as an established fact by the ill-informed, yet it is nothing more than an urban myth. On Wednesday, April 13, 1994, the *Daily Mirror* (with its erroneous masthead claim of "Honesty, Quality, Excellence") ran the headline "Banned—Thanks To Your Daily Mirror" alongside the video sleeve of *Child's Play 3*. Needless to say the headline was dishonest — another tabloid fabrication used to justify their campaign to ban the film, "after the *Child's Play* video was linked to the murder of Merseyside toddler James Bulger." The film wasn't banned at all. *Child's Play* was given a BBFC 15 certificate on December 8, 1989, *Child's Play 2* received the same certificate on March 21, 1991, and *Child's Play 3* was given an 18 certificate on November 18, 1992. No video certificates were revoked. It would seem that the newspaper was tiring of sustaining a bogus story and so invented a conclusion to appease their beguiled readers. Indeed, that fact alone identifies the hypocrisy of the *Daily Mirror* — if they truly believe, as they claim, that the film was powerful enough to cause the death of a child, then their campaign should never have ended. They should still be demanding the banning of the video — but they have become wearied with the subject and it is no longer a lucrative theme. Instead of achieving their campaign's goal they simply lied to their readers by claiming it was successful.

On Monday, March 30, 1998, during a BBC current affairs program concerning violence among children the narrator stated, "The judge in the Bulger case said, 'video nasties played a part in the role.'" This is evidence of a hypothesis being transposed into a fact by the simple omission of the words "may have."

The case of the campaign against *Child's Play 3* is another powerful example of how the news media influences the behaviour of the public. The film languished on video shelves being regularly rented and remaining unremarked upon for months before the campaign. Following it, people were calling it "sick" and "obscene" and literally burning copies of it in the street at the behest of the press. In one of the most sinister and hypocritical moves by the tabloids *The Sun*, on November 26, 1993, ran the front page headline "For the sake of ALL our kids... BURN YOUR VIDEO NASTY." The copy ran,

> A video chain boss yesterday torched his entire £10,000 stock of tapes linked to the James Bulger murder. And last night *The Sun* launched a nation-wide campaign to get all other copies of *Child's Play 3* burned. If you own one yourself, burn it safely. If you have rented one, take it back to the shop and ask dealer to destroy it. Last night Liverpool MP David Alton praised *The Sun*'s campaign. He said burning was the answer...

Though very few members of the public followed the newspaper's dictatorial and somewhat medieval orders, readers of the paper tend to be easily influenced by its fascistic principles. (See in particular multiple murderer and *The Sun* reader Colin Ireland below.)

Even Trading Standards Officer Peter Mawdsley fell under their influence and stated, "The Bulger case brings into focus the problems of children getting hold of films." And what was most ironic was the fact that Judge Morland himself would later speak of the film and the incident as though inseparable — he, too, being influenced by the press.

Writing the introduction to an in-house article 'Television Violence', the NVALA president Revd Graham Stevens makes the following statement:

> The shocking murder of Merseyside toddler James Bulger in 1993 by two older children was seen by many observers — expert commentators and ordinary people alike — as one more piece of evidence of the link between real life violence and the violence that we see every day in TV dramas, movies and videos.
>
> But even after such an horrific event there are, of course, many others — academics and film directors, as well as broadcasters and even a number of leading politicians — who still refuse to recognise any connection between violence on our screens and violence in our society. No wonder. For them to admit a clear cause and effect would mean they would have to admit that they have been wrong about a major cause of social ill, and wrong not to take corrective action. Thankfully, there are some people in high places who have the right idea.

In the immediate aftermath of Bulger's murder, the Strand shopping centre from where he was abducted provided a crèche where mothers could safely leave their children while using the shopping facilities. It was reported recently that the crèche was to be closed due to lack of funding. Consider for a moment the amount of public attention and financial gain the likes of David Alton and the tabloid press made from Jamie's death — all claiming concern for the safety of children. None of them, it seems, were concerned enough to be benefactors of a tiny safe haven once the Bulger case was no longer valid as a means of self promotion.

On Tuesday, December 15, 1992, sixteen-year-old Suzanne Capper was found wandering naked and terribly burned near Stockport, Greater Manchester. In intensive care she lived for three days and was able to tell police of the circumstances that led to her condition and announce who her assailants were. Capper had been abducted by known associates. Investigations soon uncovered the people responsible and details of her ordeal began to filter out. She had been chained to an inverted bed, shaved of body hair, scrubbed with a yard broom and raw bleach, injected with drugs and had her teeth removed with pliers, amongst other torments. The press however, were more interested in the audio tape that had been played at full volume through headphones taped to Capper's head. It was rave music, but one particular track was composed of samples containing dialogue from *Child's Play 2*. This was enough for the press. This was the "proof" that the series of movies *were indeed* evil and caused viewers to commit murder. The *Daily Mirror* on December 18, 1993 ran the front page headline "Murdered by Chucky's Children" using a photograph of the murder victim dressed as a bridesmaid with the Chucky doll looming over her shoulder. Later in the report it claimed that her attackers, "were fascinated by the occult, practised with Tarot cards and rune stones and kept a "black library." Behind their sick obsessions lurked the demonic figure of Chucky, also mentioned in the Bulger murder trial." The report not only took the opportunity to reiterate the erroneous Bulger connection, this time claiming the film title was referred to during the trial, but went on to show what it considered to be links between the film and Capper's ordeal:

> In *Child's Play*, Chucky breaks a man's arm and leg — Suzanne's arm was battered. The doll is burned in the face with a cigarette lighter — Suzanne was burned with cigarettes. The doll kills a psychiatrist by electrocuting him with a headset — a headset was forced over Suzanne's head. Finally, the doll is apparently destroyed by fire — just like Suzanne.

If the reporter believes these acts of violence were performed on Capper solely because they were part of a film scenario, then what explains the extraction of her teeth; the shaving of her body hair; the scrubbing with bleach; the injecting with drugs? None of those real-life events occurred in the film, just as none of the cinematic attacks on Chucky were played out on Capper: she didn't have her arm and leg broken; she wasn't burned with a cigarette lighter; she wasn't electrocuted. The only similarity is that Capper was burned. The tortures she suffered were simply conjured from the minds of her sadistic captors. Despite the *Mirror*'s attempts to take some of the blame away from Capper's tormentors the report stated that, "Police said there was no video in the torture house." And as there was no film, how could it be classed as an "obsession" by the newspaper? When Capper's parents appeared on a television chat show they let known their disgust with the press for attempting to associate their daughter's death with a horror movie and attaching more blame for her terrible ordeal to a movie character rather than her real-life killers.

Les Reed was kicked to death by a gang of thugs on a Cardiff estate and during his killer's trial the attack was attributed to the film *Juice*. It was alleged that one of the thugs said, "I've got the juice," following the attack. It was revealed in court that the only "juice" the thugs had was the lager and cider they had consumed earlier. But the press concluded that it was "irrefutable evidence of the link between violent videos and crime on our streets," pointing out that that there is a scene in *Juice* in which a man is kicked to death by four youths for remonstrating about their destructive behaviour. However, according to James Ferman there is no such scene in the film – "no one is kicked to death in *Juice*, which is a serious anti-violence film." The Ely estate where the assault took place is a renowned troubled area rife with crime and violence. One area, Charteris Green, had been declared a no-go area by police well before the film *Juice* had even been made.

During David Alton's opening statement concerning proposed amendments to the Criminal Justice and Public Order Bill (see SEX & WRECKS), he said:

> ...a number of cases have come before the courts which have involved the use of videos and videos have been cited in the course of those court cases. I think particularly of the Suzanne Capper case in Manchester, where a young woman was tortured and brutally murdered while the sound tape of the movie *Child's Play 3* was transmitted to her. Quite recently, in a case in Cardiff the video *Juice* was cited as an influence on the young people who were involved in a terrible murder.[23]

On June 29, 1994, the House of Commons published a report titled *Video Violence and*

Young Offenders, paragraph nine of which states:

> As we have said, the present debate about violent videos was sparked by the grotesque murders of Jamie Bulger, Suzanne Capper, and Les Read [sic], and the allegation made, following the trials of those three cases, by some parts of the media that the videos *Child's Play 3* and *Juice* had played some part in motivating the murders. Closer analysis of these three cases has indicated that these allegations were in fact unfounded.

Memorandum 16 of the report was submitted by James Ferman, Director of the BBFC. He stated that members of the Video Consultative Council, an advisory body appointed by the Home Office, were invited to view *Child's Play 3* and *Juice* following the allegations made against the films:

> Their unanimous view was that *Child's Play 3* was 'irrelevant' to the Bulger case and that it was properly classified 18. *Juice* elicited an even stronger reaction: they considered it an excellent film, exploring moral issues in a constructive fashion.
>
> It is a pity that the issue of research should have been muddied by assumptions about the supposed link between *Child's Play 3* and the killing of James Bulger, a factor which weakened the paper circulated by Professor Elizabeth Newson and a number of distinguished academics and child carers.

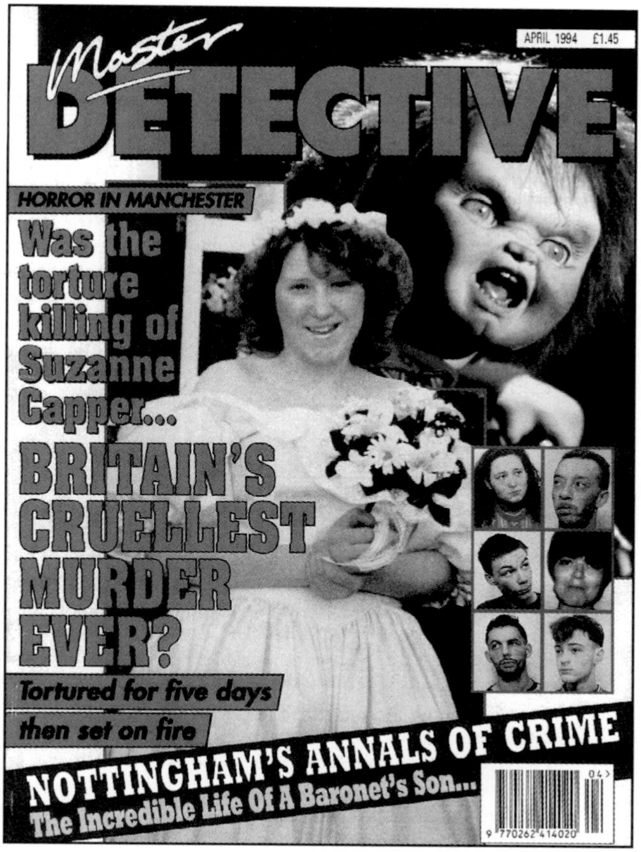

Suzanne Capper and Chucky.
***Master Detective*, April 1994.**

Yet the press persisted in ignoring the truth. Even as late as February 7, 1999, the *Sunday Telegraph* was reporting that

> A NEW horror film featuring "Chucky", the psychopathic doll blamed for inspiring the murderers of James Bulger, has been passed for relese in Britain by the British Board of Film Classification.
>
> Three previous films in the same series were removed from shops after the court case which convicted James's two killers. *The Bride of Chucky* is already a box office hit in America but Universal Pictures, distributors of the previous films *Child's Play* I, II, and III, have refused to be associated with the new movie.
>
> Denise Bulger, James's mother, refused to comment on the new film last night. But Mary Whitehouse, the anti-sex and violence campaigner, said: "It's utterly irresponsible. The Director for Public Prosecutions should have a look at it. But it is really up to the public to react.

They should write to their MPs."

The fact that the reporter actually contacted Denise Bulger in order to provoke a reaction from her is really quite appalling and identifies what little sympathy is actually felt by the press towards the loss of her son.

On March 10, 1993, forty-five-year-old Peter Walker was found dead in his flat in Battersea. He was a frequenter of gay bars and was diagnosed HIV-positive. Walker was discovered lying on his bed naked and bound with nylon cord. He had a condom in his mouth and another on his nose. Cigarette burns and small puncture wounds were visible on his body. His penis was blemished with what appeared to be a "love bite." Two small teddy bears had been placed against his body in some curious pose. Death was a result of suffocation. After the discovery of the body a man telephoned *The Sun* newspaper and took anonymous credit for the murder, promising there would be further killings.

On May 30, thirty-seven-year-old Christopher Dunn was discovered murderd in his north-west London home. He was wearing a bondage-style harness and a studded belt. Like Walker, Dunn was a homosexual and he had been strangled with some kind of ligature. A "love bite" was evident on his back. Five days later the body of Perry Bradley III was found in his west London flat. Like Dunn, he had been strangled in his bed though it wasn't commonly known that Bradley was a homosexual. A doll had been placed on his body.

Five days after the discovery of Bradley's body, thirty-three-year-old Andrew Collier was found murdered in his flat. A dead cat with a condom on its tail had been laid across his body. Like Walker, Collier was HIV-positive. It became apparent that all the victims had frequented the Coleherne pub in west London, a place frequented by sadomasochistic homosexuals. It was the same location from which Dennis Nilsen and Michael "The Wolf" Lupo had selected their victims many years earlier. Following the discovery of Collier, the police received a call from a man claiming to be the killer who threatened to kill one person every week. Later he phoned again telling the police he had killed another man, and asked if they had found his body. The fifth victim was Emanuel Spiteri — a regular of the Coleherne. The police theorised that Spiteri would be likely to use the Underground to travel from the pub to his flat, so examined the surveillance tape from Charing Cross station. A few frames identified Spiteri and the fact that he was with another man. The second man's image was made public and shortly after its broadcast Colin Ireland notified the police that he was the man on the videotape (though he claimed to know nothing of Spiteri's murder). The police took Ireland's fingerprints and checked them against a single unidentified print lifted from the windowsill in Andrew Collier's apartment. They matched, and when confronted with this evidence Ireland confessed to all five murders.

In December 1993, Colin Ireland — an ex-soldier and 'survival fanatic' — was convicted of the murder of the five men and sentenced to life imprisonment. Despite the fact that all the victims were homosexual and the killings were of a sexual nature Ireland claimed to be heterosexual. His girlfriend confirmed his sexuality and she resolutely put the blame for his conversion from a decent man into a vicious killer on "video nasties" though no particular films were identified by title. However, Ireland would have other scapegoats in mind, one of which was the diluted television police drama series *The Bill*. "They should ban *The Bill*," he declared, "it gives people ideas." It was also implied that he'd been inspired to kill by true crime books, in particular Brian Master's *Killing For Company* and Robert K Ressler's *Whoever Fights Monsters* and *Sexual Homicide: Patterns and Motives*. Ireland claimed later that the "FBI manual" he owned state a murderer was classified as a serial killr if they killed at least fou people. Recognition by *The Sun* as a serial killer of homosexuals was likely to be Ireland's goal; "I've got the book. I know how many you have to do," he told police during one of his phone calls. He apparently wanted to achieve the same kind of media fame as had Dennis Nilsen. A neighbour confirmed Ireland's obsession with such written material and claimed to have been loaned a copy of the Nilsen book, though later Ireland wanted it back to re-read. Brian Masters was taken aback by the suggestion that his work may have inspired a murder. He wrote for a

Mail on Sunday supplement, '...it cannot be stated too often that there is no evidence whatever to support the notion of a pure 'copycat' crime undertaken in emulation of a viual or literary experience.'

It is no great surprise that Colin Ireland chose *The Sun* with which to collude[24] – the tabloid is officially the most popular newspaper amongst Britain's criminal population.[25] Geraldine Bedell writing in the *Independent n Sunday* describes it as "a newspaper read widely by persistent young offenders" and Anne Nagell's research shows it to be the favourite amongst the juvenile elinquents she interviewed. During the House of Commons debate on the Criminal Justice and Public Order Bill, Angela Eagle MP stated, "...offenders are in large numbers readers of *The Sun*." David Alton, who was in league with the tabloids, responded, "I will resist the temptation to be drawn into a wider debate about the quality of our newspapers..." (As of writing, *The Sun* are sponsors of the shockingly violent and foul-mouthed TV series *Lock, Stock*...).

Peter Moore was a movie aficionado to such an extent that he started up his own small time cinema chain in Wales. Moore was an only child and an archetypal mother's boy. However, unknown to his mother he was a violent homosexual and had been carrying out random attacks on people for over twenty years. In May 1994 his mother died and Moore progressed from assaults to murder. In September 1995 he murdered fifty-six-year-old Henry Roberts, a Nazi enthusiast living on the island of Anglesey. He was found with his trousers round his ankles and almost thirty stab wounds to his body. In November, Moore attacked forty-nine-year-old Keith Randles in his caravan and stabbed him to death. The following month, thirty-five-year-old Anthony Davies was discovered stabbed to death in an area well known for being a homosexual meeting place. Traces of blood which were not from the victim were found at the scene. A hotline was set up by the police encouraging local gay men to report any violence they may have encountered. The name of Peter Moore was reported on several occasions. Police went to question Moore and search his house. They discovered items stolen from the victims and a blood test matched the samples taken from the Davies murder scene.

Moore confessed openly to the killings but would later claim that he had an accomplice and that it was this second man who had committed the murders. He said the name of this other man was Alan, then changed it to Jason. It was suggested that the Jason he spoke of was not a real person at all but the character from the *Friday the 13th* series of films. Another film implicated in his crimes was *Dirty Harry* of which Moore says (in referring to an assault on a lorry driver) – "I think I got the idea out of the Clint Eastwood film..." Because Moore was referred to as a mummy's boy the press also likened the case to Alfred Hitchcock's *Psycho*.

Thomas Hamilton had spent eight months as a Scout Master with the 4th/6th Stirling Scout Group when, in 1974, he was forced to resign from the Association after two children in his charge had suffered from hypothermia on an outing. Still wanting to work with young boys he formed a youth group called the Stirling Rovers but in 1983 he became entangled in a dispute with the Central Regional Council on how he ran the club. He complained about his treatment to a local Government Ombudsman who studied the claim and finally ruled in Hamilton's favour that the council had been unjust towards him. However, the council then refused to allow him to continue using a hall in the town's high school that he previously used for the weekly group meetings. The parents of seventy boys who attended the meetings were puzzled by the council's decision and wrote letters of complaint praising the way in which Hamilton ran the group. Meanwhile, because of the council's action and the rumours that were being circulated, his kitchen fitting business lost custom and collapsed. Hamilton was increasingly concerned about the gossip and the unsubstantiated claims that he was a child molester. He requested permission to defend himself against the allegations but the authorities refused to listen to him. In 1993 he was investigated by the police but they found nothing to confirm the rumours. On March 24 of that year he wrote to Michael Forsyth, the Scottish Secretary, extracts from which follow:

> With the horrific murder of little James Bulger, possibly by two ten-year-old boys, the whole question of juvenile crime is in greater debate across the country. The work of my group in providing sporting and leisure time activities for young boys has the effect of channelling young energies into creative and worthwhile pursuits. Sadly, having run for eight years, our two Dunfermline Boys' Sports Clubs closed last year. It is ironic the decline of these clubs was caused by the irresponsible actions of overzealous police officers from Central Scotland police, obsessed with child abuse, in carrying out their failed pervert hunt using unfair tactics. Mr Forsyth, in twenty years of operation of our lawful activity, there has never been any lawbreaking or any suggestion of sexual child abuse from any boys against either myself or any of my leaders. I know that sexual child abuse must be identified and the abusers rooted out as a matter of national priority and this, in concept, is wholeheartedly supported by the general public. Nevertheless, such a complaint against myself, claiming that I was taking photographs of the children and the purely malicious innuendos [sic] associated with this claim, should not have resulted in a full-scale pervert hunt. The officers themselves confirmed that there was no suggestion of improper or indecent photographs having been taken but that the taking of photographs of children in itself is a cause for concern. The proper and legitimate purpose of the need to take such photographs had been fully explained previously to their superiors. When senior officers had been shown these photographs in earlier years, their only comments had been that "the colours were nice." Serious and lasting damage has been caused to our work and ability by these modern day witch-hunts where ordinary everyday events are given sinister slants by police officers. In my work with children, any suggestion of child abuse, however vague, will do great damage to public and parental support. However, to have police officers suggesting to parents in Dunfermline that I am a pervert, even on a nod and a wink basis, in the hope that they will be forthcoming with information of a sinister nature, is gross injustice. There can be reams of letters of communication with Central Scotland police over a twenty-year period and still young officers appeal in a panic stating that they do not know me from Adam and have never heard of my group; hence the gross over-reaction. Such action seems to be condoned by senior police officers, the Scottish Office, etc. The officers involved are protected in an elaborate cover-up and whitewash and the officer in charge is promoted. Any legal action is ruled out, as legal aid is not available to me under Government rules and the Citizen's Charter seems ineffective. If the government is going to effectively condone the police undermining, smashing and destroying voluntary youth groups in modern day witch-hunts, it is perhaps hardly surprising that bored children with little or nothing to do turn their energies to crime from a young age.

These intelligent expressions seem hardly the ramblings of a guilty paedophile, as they do nothing other than draw further attention to himself and the allegations made against him. Paedophiles desire and require anonymity. Acting on the rumours, Doreen Hagger boasted that she and a friend confronted Hamilton outside a youth club in Linlithgow and threw a bucket of eggs, oil, shampoo and flour over him. Such puerile actions, however, achieved nothing other than further isolating Hamilton and no doubt contributed to his final actions.

In 1996, already a member of the Stirling Rifle and Pistol Club, he applied to join the Callander Rifle and Pistol Club but was refused membership. He eventually wrote directly to the Queen claiming that the Scout organisation had ruined his reputation and, as a result, he was branded a pervert. Shortly after this, it seems he made a decision to commit suicide, but not before seeking revenge on the community that he felt had persecuted him.

On March 13, 1996 at 9.30 in the morning forty-three-year-old Hamilton strode into Dunblane Primary School carrying his handguns and shot dead sixteen children and one teacher before placing a pistol in his mouth and taking his own life.

Little was known about Hamilton, so it was important for the press to demonise him, as though his crime was not enough in itself to make him a figure of hate.[26] Some papers would make clumsy attempts to link Hamilton's actions to movies. *Scotland on Sunday*, for instance, reported that he chatted to young club members about *The Terminator* "the movie which features Arnold Schwarzenegger as a crazed killing machine pursuing a young boy."

The reporter has changed the character that the futuristic robot seeks to destroy from a woman, played by Linda Hamilton, into a "young boy." The reason for this is to make it appear that there was a connection between Hamilton's viewing of the film, his interest in young boys, and his subsequent actions. The *Times*, as we have seen, also attempted to link his actions to films with the "Who Supports Violent Films Now?" article. This newspaper, however, couldn't think of any specific movie to fortify their implication and so accused violent films in general.[27]

On April 29, 1996, shortly after the international publicity given to Thomas Hamilton, a similar shooting spree occurred in Port Arthur, Tasmania. Twenty-eight-year-old Martin Bryant, dining in the Broad Arrow Café, lifted two semi-automatic rifles from his sports bag, shot dead twenty customers and wounded another eighteen. He then casually strolled around the streets and shot dead a further twelve people before coming close to losing his own life in a house fire where three other bodies were finally discovered. The short amount of time between the two similar events would suggest that this was some kind of imitative act, and that Bryant was seeking similar notoriety afforded to his ephemeral role model Hamilton.

The press however, had other ideas and in typical simplistic fashion blamed the Chucky doll, the universal scapegoat from the *Child's Play* films. On Friday, May 3, 1996, the *Daily Mirror* ran the facetious headline "Psycho surf boy mad on Chucky." The piece continued "Monster Martin Bryant was obsessed with Chucky, the evil video doll who figured in the murder of toddler James Bulger..." As we have seen, the film had nothing to do with the Bulger case other than with relation to links that tabloids like the *Mirror* had previously invented. The current story, written by Mark Dowdney and derived from foreign news sources, was composed from details supposedly given by Bryant's one-time girlfriend Janette Hoani. How much Hoani was paid for the information is not disclosed but it is unlikely she gave it for free, and if the press were to pay, then the story would have to be luridly sensational. The piece concluded with suggestions that Bryant slept with a pig, had sex with animals, and wanted sex with other men. (This suggestion that he may have had homosexual tendencies, like his counterpart Hamilton, would figure strongly in the mind of one particular reader. See Horrett Campbell, below). It wasn't just the tabloids either which promoted the film link. The *Times* on May 5, 1996, undoubtedly using the same source as the *Mirror*, reported "Renewed fears about video nasties were raised last night after it was revealed the Tasmanian mass murderer Martin Bryant was obsessed with a film that has already been linked to killings in Britain." On May 7 the *Daily Mail* ran the headline "...Chucky Doll was Killer's Inspiration" but couldn't follow up the claim with anything to suggest that that was really the case. Eager to reaffirm his position as one of the original rumourmongers in the Bulger case, David Alton asked in the same report, "How many more tragedies must occur before the world takes notice?"

Reports would go even further in an attempt to firmly implicate films as the main cause of Bryant's deranged state of mind, and would assert that he had a collection of videos depicting violence and hard-core pornography (including bestiality). "Massacre suspect's violent video hoard", headlined the *Daily Telegraph* claiming that, "more than 2000 violent and pornographic videos have been found at the home of Martin Bryant."

Understandably concerned, John Dickie, Australia's chief censor, in order to determine exactly what the contents of the films were, contacted Tasmania's Department of Justice and Perpetual Trustees which was holding the assets of Michael Bryant. What the collection proved to be was early romance and musical feature films with stars such as Clark Gable and Bette Davis. Indeed, they actually belonged to the previous owner of the house, Helen Harvey, who was Bryant's benefactor. Out of the entire collection only four videos did not fit in the romance/musical category and they were two episodes of *Blackadder*, *A Nightmare on Elm Street*, and *Taxi Driver*. The gulf between the truth and the report is quite staggering — the press declared there were 2,000 violent videos in Bryant's possession when in fact there were only *two*. Following disclosure of the true nature of the films, Dickie stated, "I have no doubt that misreporting such as this has contributed substantially to the perception that some violent incident on the television or on some video has led to this tragedy." As a result of the false and malicious press reports sixty-five percent of the community believed there was a connection between violence in films and violence in real life. Such outrageous fabrications are nothing new and we need only look at the Derek Alan Poole case from 1951. Poole, from Chatham, England, shot and killed a policeman after he was disturbed breaking into a farm building. Poole escaped to his parents' home and hid in the attic. Police surrounded the house and in the subsequent shoot-out, Poole was killed. The press claimed that when the police entered his home they discovered hundreds of crime and horror comics, implying they were the cause of his criminality. In reality there was just *one* western comic but the incident occurred at the time of the anti-horror comics campaign.

Dr Park Dietz, the FBI's leading forensic psychiatrist claimed the most likely catalyst that triggered Bryant's assault was television coverage of the Dunblane massacre. He stated, "Were it not for the experience of someone else's actions, such people would more likely just kill themselves." And added, "[Bryant] probably thought to himself, 'I am as powerful as [Hamilton] is. The world needs to know my suffering and feel my rage.'" Speculative argument, for sure, but Dietz has far greater insight, experience and understanding of psychotic behaviour than any hack journalist writing for a mass-market tabloid. Of course, if media coverage of Dunblane was indeed the catalyst that triggered Bryant, then it is something the press couldn't possibly report on as they would be implicating themselves in inducing his kill spree. Direct evidence may be currently lacking as proof of the news media's influence in the Bryant case — though future psychiatric examination of Bryant may well confirm it. Other incidents, conversely, can be exclusively associated with excessive and lurid press coverage of crimes.

Horrett Campbell fell under the influence of the tabloids and on Monday, July 8, 1996, he attempted to re-enact what he had read in the newspapers about the Dunblane and Port Arthur massacres. However, thirty-three-year-old Campbell didn't have access to a firearm so he used a machete. He entered the grounds of St Luke's nursery school in Blakenham, Wolverhampton and attacked the children and staff with the heavy blade on which was written "you filthy devil" and "666 marks the devil."[28] None of his seven victims died despite many suffering severe head wounds. When Campbell was arrested, police discovered in his flat newspaper cuttings relating to Thomas Hamilton and Michael Bryant. He had drawn a heart-shape pierced with a Cupid's arrow around the photograph of Bryant. Campbell was probably "turned-on" by the newspaper allegation that Bryant wanted sex with other men and developed an idolatry kind of sexual desire for him. He was also said to regard Thomas Hamilton as a "kindred spirit."

After serving a thirty month jail sentence for assault, fifty-year-old David Jenning told a prison chaplain that he planned to "do a Dunblane" once he was released from prison. He claimed he wanted to protest against the treatment of his children who were in council care. Because of this threat, Jenning is now banned from approaching school children, teachers, and from going near the local school. He has previous convictions for assaulting a council officer and carrying a firearm in public. Like Campbell, he had been made aware of Hamilton's attack by the media and it had inspired him enough to contemplate copying it.

The *Daily Express*, on Wednesday, June 14, 1995 reported the case of two juveniles who committed robbery at gunpoint. The sub-heading announced unambiguously "Crime Spree Caused By Reservoir Dogs," and the father of fourteen-year-old Scott Richards suggested that the film drove his drug-induced, gun-toting son to commit the crime. Using a blank-firing pistol to threaten staff, the two youths robbed local shops. Earlier, Richards had held the gun to his mother's head and threatened to kill her. Such behaviour would suggest that the Richards were a dysfunctional family. "It's outrageous that someone as young as Scott can get hold of a film like *Reservoir Dogs*," said Scott's father Chris Richards, a former soldier. Yet this statement says more about his own failure to take responsibility for his son, and conveniently omits to point out the outrageousness of a fourteen-year-old using drugs and having a gun. The fact that the two youths watched *Reservoir Dogs*, if indeed they *did*, was used as a means of drawing attention away from the failure of the parents to control their own offspring.

On March 7, 1995, in Hernando, Mississippi, Bill Savage was shot twice in the head at point blank range and robbed of $200. The following day, some 300 miles away in Ponchatoula, Louisiana, a female robber shot shop assistant Patsy Byers in the throat. The event was recorded on the shop's security camera and images of the attacker were made public. Following a tip-off from an informant, nineteen-year-old Sarah Edmondson was arrested on June 2. Her apprehension led to the arrest of her boyfriend, eighteen-year-old Ben Darras. The couple were charged with the murder of Bill Savage and the attempted murder of Patsy Byers.

It would transpire that both were regular drug abusers. Indeed, Edmondson had serious psychiatric problems from the age of thirteen and Darras' father had been an alcoholic and committed suicide. Despite such dysfunctional backgrounds, claims would be made that they were driven to commit the crimes through viewing Oliver Stone's *Natural Born Killers*. Chief promoter of this notion was novelist and one-time-lawyer John Grisham who would declare that, "The artist should be required to share the responsibility along with the nut who pulled the trigger." He claimed that there was overwhelming evidence to link the film to the crime. One such piece of evidence was that the perpetrators had no history of violence. (But that applies to everyone — no one has a history of violence until they have committed their first violent act.) Edmonson's father claimed that the two teenagers watched *Natural Born Killers* more than twenty times and, in an interview with *Vanity Fair*, said that "on one occasion they watched it six times in one night." As the movie has a running time of 118 minutes this claim is difficult to believe, no matter how drug addled the viewer may be. But it is inevitable that parents seek anything outside the family environment to blame for their children's defects, more so when there is the prospect of a multi-million dollar lawsuit. Grisham hoped to employ the product-liability laws against Oliver Stone and Warner Bros whereby manufacturers are responsible for any injury or death caused by their product. He argues that *Natural Born Killers* is an artistic product that caused the death of Bill Savage. However, if his lawsuit were successful he would leave himself in an extremely vulnerable position and open to similar claims against his own violent novels and film spin-offs. If Grisham wanted to utilise the product-liability law it would make more sense to target the manufacturers of the guns that were used in the killing, for there is no grey area in this argument. The fact that he doesn't take this practical route suggests he may just be on a personal vendetta against Oliver Stone.[29]

One tabloid tried to link murderers Eric Elliot and Lewis Gilbert to the same movie. "Sick Killers Copy Woody's New Film" claimed the headline and continued, "Two young men have murdered four people — including three pensioners — in a real-life imitation of a brutal, new Hollywood blockbuster. The actions of the sick pair, arrested in America last week, were a copy-cat of killings featured in *Natural Born Killers...*" Robert Hawk, an FBI agent speaking about the case, said, "There are a lot of movies that imitate life. Whether these two picked up on that, we don't know." A very inconclusive statement indeed, but sufficient grist for the press to get inventive. The evidence they used to back up their allegation was that there were two killers operating as a team in the film and likewise in the real-life incident.

France, too, wanted to get in on the act and when Audry Maupin and Florence Rey shot dead three policemen and a taxi driver in Paris on October 4, 1994, they were christened by the press as "France's natural born killers." Maupin and Rey had raided a police pound armed with sawn-off shotguns and pistols stolen from the policemen. They hijacked a taxi as an escape vehicle but the driver rammed a police car to attract attention. Maupin shot the driver in the back of the head and a shoot-out commenced with the two policemen, who were both shot dead. The couple hijacked another vehicle and were pursued by a police motorcyclist who was also killed in the gunfire. They were eventually forced to a standstill at a police roadblock and in the subsequent shoot-out Maupin was fatally wounded. Rey — who the *Sunday Times* described as a "Natural born killer [who] was a fool for love" — was arrested at the scene. It would later be reported that a poster for the film *Natural Born Killers* was found in the room the couple shared.

The Fox is video nasty fan

By PETER HOOLEY

THE VICIOUS rapist dubbed The Fox is a video nasty freak, police believe.

Detectives have made urgent checks on video libraries, clubs and postal outlets in their hunt for the perverted beast who has struck five times in the triangle of terror at Leighton Buzzard, Beds.

The man leading the hunt Detective Chief Superintendent Brian Prickett, said yesterday: "We think there is a link.

Identical

"There are many video nasties which depict scenes identical to some of his actions."

Meanwhile the Mayor of Leighton Buzzard, Councillor Robert Cook, hit out at police failure to catch the Fox. He said: "People's confidence is low. It's bordering on complete panic."

Yesterday police ruled out any link between the Fox and a burglary at a house in Great Gaddesden on Sunday night.

The *Daily Express* reported a "Video murder hunt" on March 6, 1996. Police were searching for seventeen-year-old Sebastien Dubois and his eighteen-year-old girlfriend Veronique Malarme after the body of a sixteen-year-old boy was found buried at Dubois' home in Gournay near Paris. Because a video copy of *Natural Born Killers* was also found in the home, investigator Jean Michot said, "This horrific video could well have inspired the boy's lust to kill." There was no mention of any other items found in the home, which indicates that attention was only drawn to the video because of previous questionable claims of its causative effects publicised in the United States. Indeed, here we have a case of police officers being influenced by press reports of what other police officers have theorised. At this time it was nothing other than *dernier cri* to blame Stone's movie for any dyadic crime that occurred.

When an eleven-year-old hooligan and his gang attacked a brother and sister on waste ground in Ipswich, Suffolk, he beat them both with a three-foot bamboo stick. He also forced the two children to put the stick in their mouths and suck on it and told them he was going to kill them. When the case came to court child psychologist David Morgan claimed that the child may have been imitating a scene in the film *The Krays*. "The film shows a gun being put into someone's mouth to humiliate and degrade. It could be this is a case of him learning behaviour from the film," he said. Despite the psychologist merely making wild guesses the *Daily Express* accepted it as a proven fact and ran the story under the headline "Bully 'copied Kray gun scene in film.'"

Sixty-four-year-old Bryn Price, a gun enthusiast from Mid Glamorgan, was shot and killed by his six-year-old granddaughter. Price had handed the girl his Magnum revolver unaware that it was loaded and she pulled the trigger firing a round into Price's throat. He died later in hospital. Newspaper coverage ran under the headline "Girl, 6, Shot Man Dead In Imitation Of Video Comedy." The film that she supposedly imitated was *Stop! Or My Mom Will Shoot*.

In November 1984, forty-one-year-old Vanessa Ballantyne went to a night-club and picked up John Parr. Unknown to Parr, Ballantyne was carrying a five-inch kitchen knife. Later in the evening when they left a snooker club and headed for a taxi rank she lured Parr into a dark alley. "I've got something for you," she said and drove the knife into his stomach. Parr survived the attack, removed the blade and went back to the snooker club for assistance. Ballantyne was arrested and while in custody told the police the film *Basic Instinct* made her attack the man. "*Basic Instinct* made mother stab stranger" and "Mrs Average turned into stab maniac after watching *Basic Instinct*" were the headlines used in the *Daily Express* following Ballantyne's trial. The report was written in a sympathetic manner towards the violent woman describing Ballantyne as a "respectable housewife", and Sharon Stone, star of *Basic Instinct*, as a "sex siren" and "knife-wielding temptress."[30] The fact that Ballantyne chose to deliberately stab an innocent man shows that she most certainly wasn't "Mrs Average." The film was no guiltier of the crime than the knife.

Sandy Charles was fourteen-years-old when he lured seven-year-old Jonathan Thimpsen into the woods near his home in La Ronge, Canada, and murdered him. Charles stabbed the youngster several times then crushed his skull with a rock. He mutilated the body by cutting away portions of flesh. After his arrest Charles told police, "There's a strong spirit in my room that gave me these thoughts... I was going to commit suicide until this thing popped into my head. I started thinking about killing someone else." However during trial Charles' defence lawyer Barry Singer claimed it was actually the film *Warlock* that drove the defendant to murder. His evidence for such an assertion was that the film showed that "if you cut the fat off a virgin or an unbaptised child, then boiled it down and drank it, it would give you the power to fly."

An incident was related in *The Sunday Post* October 18, 1987, under the headline of "Terror of Man in Silver Mask." A twelve-year-old girl had been pursued by a strangely-dressed man wielding a machete. He was described as wearing a silver mask, black cloak and spurs and had been seen by many other children in the area. The report went on, "He's nicknamed Freddy because he dresses the same way as the murderer in the horror film *Freddy's Revenge*." The report stated that the children who described the attacker were all of a similar age, i.e. twelve, a fact which controverts their knowing how Freddy in *Freddy's Revenge* dressed — the film was on general cinema release with an 18 certificate. The description of the attacker's dress is far removed from Freddy's trademark fedora and stripped pullover, yet it sounds remarkably similar to the costume worn by the Phantom of the Opera in Andrew Lloyd Webber's musical. However, it would be unseemly for the press to attribute a "copy-cat" crime to such an esteemed and popular production. It is evident that the press are very discriminating when it comes to condemning a movie — they first take account of its popularity or its "class" distinctiveness. When fourteen-year-old Imtiaz Ahmed hanged himself he left a note referring to Walt Disney's *The Lion King* saying, "I want to die, Allah. Please make me the Lion King." The press reported on the incident, but in spite of its links with the death of a child, there were no calls for the film to be banned.

Fox's rape video is still on sale

A PORNOGRAPHIC video which a judge blamed for influencing the rapist called The Fox in his depraved sex crimes was still available in Britain last night.

The 45-minute film Sex Wish, condemned by Mr Justice Caulfield last week when he sentenced Malcolm Fairley to six life sentences, was to be found on the shelves of some lending libraries and corner shops.

Sex Wish, made in America, portrays violent rape by a man carrying a shotgun and wearing a Balaclava helmet — the way The Fox operated.

Legislation could soon lead to such videos being banned, with a £20,000 fine for anyone dealing in them.

The British Board of Film Censors will begin classifying all videos after Easter, when Parliament has given formal approval to regulations piloted into law by Tory MP Mr Graham Bright.

Mr Bright, MP for Luton South, said: 'The chance of The Fox, or anyone like him, getting hold of such material if this legislation had been in force at the time would have been reduced significantly.'

Like so much on the British porn market, the cheap budget movie began in Los Angeles, at the studios of Cal Vista Inc.

They shared profits with their British distributors, *David Gold and Tommy Harris* — but both were said last night to have withdrawn the film.

Daily Mail | MAIL TODAY | 20p

He started as a petty burglar—then Malcolm Fairley discovered porn videos

THE FOX —EVIL BEYOND WORDS

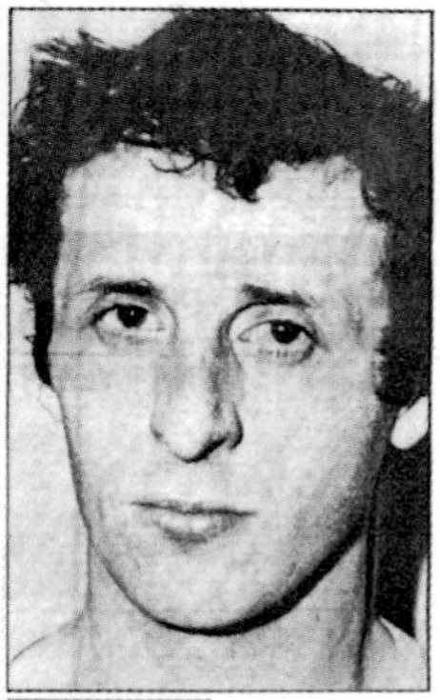

By TED OLIVER

THE man they called The Fox was behind bars for life last night for his horrific sex crimes.

Malcolm Fairley, 32, was sentenced to a total of six life sentences and 82 years for a series of rapes, burglaries and sex attacks on both men and women, mostly committed in a 'terror triangle' around Leighton Buzzard in Bedfordshire over four months last summer.

A life sentence in some cases can mean exactly that—and the judge who sentenced Fairley said he was imposing the maximum terms for his crimes.

Accent

Turn to Page 2, Col. 3

The face his victims never saw

THE real face of The Fox (above) is remarkable only for its ordinariness. But what all but the first of Malcolm Fairley's victims saw was the image of a monster (left) in a black balaclava hood with holes torn for eyes and mouth—the face of a nightmare.

PREVIOUS PAGE: *Daily Star*, July 24, 1984.
THIS PAGE, TOP: *The Mail on Sunday*, March 3, 1985.
ABOVE: *Daily Mail*, February 27, 1985.

When a ten-year-old schoolboy fought with classmates and scratched their faces his teacher, Carol Shields, stated, "He has been exposed to violent videos and is exhibiting violent behav-

EVENING MAIL, THURSDAY, JANUARY 22, 1998

PORN FILM KILLER JAILED FOR LIFE

Falklands vet raped and strangled mum after watching movie

Headlines following the arrest of Stuart Hulse.

iour." The report in *Today* April 20, 1994, claimed the youngster was copying Freddy Krueger from *A Nightmare on Elm Street*.

When two robbers poured petrol into a ticket clerk's office on a New York subway and set the clerk alight the crime was attributed to *Money Train* in which a similar incident occurs.

Thirty-six-year-old Stuart Hulse was jailed for life in 1998 after being convicted of the rape and murder of Shirley Brown in Lowton, Greater Manchester. Because Hulse had been to a party where a pornographic video had been shown Hulse's subsequent action was attributed to the viewing of the film. Roderick Carus QC defending the killer rapist claimed he had become "inflamed" by the video. Ann Winterton MP stated, "This case gives the lie to those who claim, with supposed authority, that violence on the media does not affect the behaviour of people who watch it." But it was also reported that everyone at the party paired off leaving Hulse alone. He had gone to the party hoping for sex and found himself isolated while everyone else was "at it" around the house. Despite the fact that Hulse was married such a situation would accent Hulse's inadequacy at securing a relationship by normal means and he concluded that the only way he would get a woman was by force. As his chosen victim lived only 300 yards from Hulse's home she was murdered to avoid any subsequent identification of her attacker.

Thirty-two-year-old Malcolm Fairley was a multiple rapist who was known as The Fox prior to his proper identification and arrest. Fairley showed no sexual preference during his attacks by raping both male and female victims — even a family's pet dog, it was reported. It was claimed that he was influenced by films and, before his arrest, the press ran headlines like, "The Fox is a video nasty fan." The conclusion was drawn because on one of his attacks he stole two tapes from the home he invaded: a copy of John Carpenter's *The Thing* and John Landis' *National Lampoon's Animal House*, a juvenile comedy starring John Belushi. Neither of the films have ever been classed as a "video nasty" by the DPP or any other organisation. The fact that Fairley chose to steal *The Thing* may be linked to the press reports of Christopher Meah who was sentenced to two life terms in 1983 (see also UNEASE). Meah was a violent rapist and he desperately tried to claim that the John Carpenter film had influenced him. Just months after the report, Fairley would be focusing on the same title and behaving in a similar manner to Meah. When he was finally caught, Fairley tried to blame his sex attacks on pornographic videos but Joan Fairley, his first wife, described him as "a compulsive liar." Notwithstanding, the *Daily Mail* acquiesced to Fairley and said he was just a burglar[31] who turned into a rapist after watching "pornographic video nasties." The *Daily Star* sympathetically described him as "A quiet, non-smoking tee-totaller with a wife and three children," who was, "turned into a monster by the most disgusting hard core pornography imaginable."

Pre-empting the Bulger case by a decade, the police said that too much significance had been put on the video connection. Indeed, it transpired that Fairley had been watching pornographic films for several years before any sex attack took place. The first time he had assaulted a person was on April 11, 1984, when he entered the house of a seventy-four-year-old woman. He found her in bed and had the urge to touch her so he placed his hands under her nightdress but ran from the house when she started screaming. From that point on, most of his home invasions had a sexual motive. During one of his burglaries he stole a shotgun, sawed off the barrel and removed the butt to make it easy to conceal. The weapon was used threateningly on subsequent attacks. With this new dangerous element the press tried to link his crimes directly to a film called *Sex Wish*.[32] This film included scenes of a rapist wearing a Balaclava and carrying a shotgun (Fairley wore a hood with eye and mouth holes made from a trouser leg).[33] The police didn't find a copy of the film in Fairley's collection and he denied ever having seen *Sex Wish*, even though admission to viewing it could have aided his defence. He also told police that he wore the mask when he went on his burglaries when no sex attack was planned. It transpired that most of the porn videos he had amassed had been stolen from the houses he had burgled. Fairley denied raping the dog.

Mrs Jill Knight MBE MP, wrote an article for the *Sunday Express* that was never printed. In it she states,

> Malcolm (the Fox) Fairlie [sic] had been an avid watcher of porno-videos and his particular favourite was a charming American-made seventy-minute movie called *Sex Wish*... What Fairlie saw over and over again on the screen he finally went out and re-created for himself in real life. He openly admitted to the police that watching pornographic films had turned him into a rapist. *Sex Wish*, astonishingly, does not come under Section 2 of [the Obscene Publications Act] because the sex act in the film was simulated and not real. However, it was real enough for Malcolm Fairlie and his victims.

She concludes with the nonsensical and clichéd question, "Is the freedom to see porno movies more important than the freedom from rape, murder and terror?"

The *Daily Mail* reported a case on July 7, 1983, as part of its campaign to "Ban the Sadist Videos." It related to Kevin Cooper who murdered four people in Chino north of Los Angeles. The report, under the headline "Cruel movies fan hacks four to death", stated that Cooper, after escaping from the California Institution for Men, "hacked to death a married couple and their two children after regularly watching violent video films." In a *non sequitir*, the piece reported that the film link was established because "two days after the killings inmates at the Chino Institution watched a video of the film *The Texas Chain Saw Massacre*." However, it failed to explain how people watching a film *after* a murder committed by another person could somehow be linked. Again, as is seen so often, the *Mail* was twisting facts and proffering misinformation to bolster its misguided crusade against its own definition of "evil."

3G RK THE SUN, Saturday, May 8, 1999 35

JUDGE BLAMES VIDEO NASTIES FOR MURDER

'They fuelled killing'

By MIKE SULLIVAN

A JUDGE yesterday blamed video nasties for fuelling the violent fantasies of two college students who stabbed a pal to death.

Neil Sayers, 19, and Graham Wallis, 18, burnt and dismembered Russell Crookes's body before burying his remains in a wood.

Thirty-four violent films including Scream and The Evil Dead were found in their rooms. Scream is about two murderers preying on college students.

And Evil Dead features a gang of youths who chop up their victim with an axe and bury him in woods.

Prosecutor Charles Miskin, QC, told Maidstone Crown Court: "Everybody will recognise the similarities about the mode of disposal of the body and that description."

Jailing the killers, judge Mr Justice Newman said he had little doubt the video nasties "served to fuel your fantasies."

He added: "They carried a potency which could not readily be predicted and served to desensitise and remove

Gory . . . shocking scene from Evil Dead film

Wallis . . . attacked pal

Sayers . . . planned killing

Bug shuts Chunnel

CHUNNEL bosses have scrapped passenger trains on New Year's Eve night because of fears they could be stranded by the Millennium Bug.

Services will be cancelled from 10pm until 6am on January 1.

Empty test trains will run so boffins can check computer gear. A spokesman said: "All our engineers will be on call."

SQUEEZY DOES IT

A car park designed specially for women has been built with extra wide bays in Budapest.

Own a Genuine Victorian Postage Stamp Collection for just £9.99 (+p&p)

Now you can own your own piece of Britain's postal history.

Ten genuine British postage stamps from the Victorian era.

Each stamp you'll receive is a superb, sought-after classic, including **3 different Penny Reds, the first British surface-printed Penny stamp**, the highly prized **1d Lilac**, and two desirable **1887 Jubilee Issues celebrating Queen Victoria's 50th year on the throne**.

If you want acclaimed stamps – look no further. This is a collector's dream come true!

All 10 stamps for under a tenner!

The best news is, tha… plete with **FREE deluxe Display Page** this… package can be

1841 Penny Red Imperforate

1857 Penny Red Star

On May 12, 1996, the *Mail on Sunday* was congratulating Dustin Hoffman for speaking out about movie violence. Hoffman, star of *Straw Dogs* which is currently unable to gain a certificate in the UK because of its violence, suggested that the Dunblane and Port Arthur massacres may have been sparked by violence in the movies. He failed to elaborate or give any credence to his theory but it was noted that he also failed to take any responsibility for crimes of violence that occurred in the early seventies, which, by his argument, may have been sparked by *Straw Dogs*. Indeed, James Ferman said of the film,

> *Straw Dogs* has been cited by men in prison as having turned them on to rape because of the way that the woman responded to the rape at first and therefore appears to welcome the advances of men. Now we passed that uncut on film in the early 1970s before I came to the Board. We have never passed it on video because if you cut the scene you destroy the motivation of the film and it is rather a good one. We just think it does not belong on video because certain men with certain proclivities could watch that scene selectively out of context over and over again obsessionally and turn it into masturbatory fantasy and we are not very happy with that.[34]

Ferman may have been getting a bit carried away, but Hoffman is simply speaking out against an industry in which he is no longer a major player. The report sanctimoniously stated that "if anyone is triggered into murder by a film, then the film-makers have a lot on their conscience." A reasonable statement but a disposition conveniently unspoken following the newspaper inspired Hungerford massacre and St Luke's attack.

On May 14, 1998, Graham Wallis and Neil Sayers were drinking lager and cider around a campfire in woods with their friend Russell Crookes. All three had an interest in the SAS. They were students at Hadlow agricultural college near Tonbridge in Kent and their friendship was bonded by the formation of a clique called the Brotherhood which was based on a

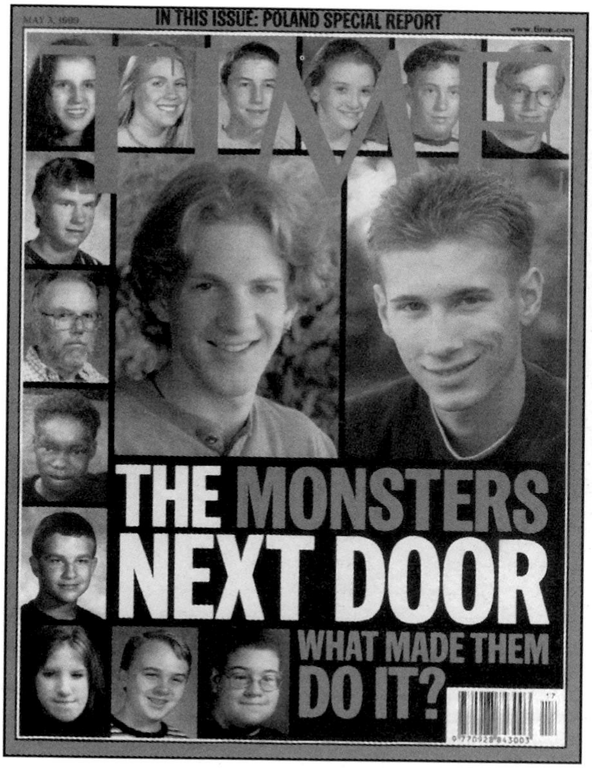

PREVIOUS PAGE: *The Sun* reports the Wallis and Sayers case. May 8, 1999.

THIS PAGE, LEFT: *Time* ponders the Columbine High School shootings. RIGHT: *Daily Express*, April 21, 1999.

military-like survivalist group. Sayers — whose father was a former army officer — was the self-styled leader of the group and called himself the Emperor. Crookes had been vying for leadership of the Brotherhood, and constantly tormented and humiliated Wallis and Sayers. For that reason Sayers and Wallis had already made plans to kill Crookes, and when he chose to return to the college they attacked and murdered him. Crookes was stabbed repeatedly in the body, neck, and head then carried onto a pre-prepared woodpile, doused in lighter fuel and set alight. The following day Wallis and Sayers returned to the scene to dismember and bury the remains of their victim. The body was discovered some weeks later and the two students were arrested. A simple and straightforward case with a trivial motive, it would seem.

When the case came to trial, the police, prosecution and judge focused much attention on the thirty-five video films owned by Wallis and Sayers. One of them was Sam Raimi's *The Evil Dead*. Prosecuting, Charles Miskin QC pointed out that in the film a zombie is chopped up with an axe, carried in a sheet into the woods and buried. Miskin implies parallels between the killers' actions and the film stating, "Everyone who has heard the evidence in this case would recognise the similarities between the mode of disposal of the body here and in that description." In a sense, Miskin is partially right, as he only mentions *disposal of the body* and that it was buried in the woods. But there the similarity ends. Crookes wasn't killed indoors, he wasn't killed with an axe, he wasn't carried into the woods in a sheet. Sober judgement dictates that Crookes was buried in the woods because he was murdered in the woods, not because such a scene happened in a zombie film. Of the thirty-five films, two others named by title were Wes Craven's *Scream* and Fritz Kiersch's *Children of the Corn*. As these where the only titles mentioned, it would seem that the others in their collection were non-violent movies. *Scream* was claimed to be influential in the crime because it depicted college students killing and being killed. *Children of the Corn* was linked to the case because it contains stabbings and corn is an agricultural product and the three students where studying agriculture.

Chief Inspector Dave Stevens said "The videos were pretty innocuous in one sense. They were not banned, they could be purchased in the shops. But I suppose it was the context in which they were watched, what they did to the minds of the defendants." So Stevens seems in no doubt that the films affected the minds of the killers. But in what context does he believe the films where watched? Though his statement is somewhat confusing, it seems he is implying they were watched with murder already in mind which absolutely invalidates the view that the films made them kill.

In summing up the case Mr Justice Newman stated, "Videos — not recognisably extreme and designed to be seen for entertainment — have, I have very little doubt from the synopses, served to fuel your fantasies and isolated you from conventional counterbalancing. They carried a potency that could not be readily predicted, and served to desensitise you and remove you from the enormity of killing another person by stabbing them." A remarkably similar statement to that made by Judge Morland in summing up the Bulger case, and which undoubtedly influenced Newman. The statement also shows that Newman based his conclusion on *synopses* of the films. Indeed, these synopses, as presented to the judge, would have been provided out of context by the police and prosecution with every intention of demonstrating their causality.

The story made front-page news in the tabloids simply because of the insignificant film link. "Murder By Video" was the ridiculous front page headline in *The Express*. "Judge Blames Video Nasties For Murder" stated *The Sun*. "Life For Horror Video Copycats" said the *Daily Star*. The *Daily Star* did a follow up piece some days later reporting that, "After being mutilated, [Crookes] was burnt then buried. It was *identical* to scenes in *The Evil Dead*, which was watched by the killers." [Our italics.] What was initially described as 'similar' has now become 'identical.' The only readers who would know it wasn't true were those who had actually seen the film. No newspaper attempted to challenge or oppose the Judge's conclusion, and even the *Guardian* ran the headline "Horror videos inspired student killers." Oddly the *Daily Mail* didn't use the story as one might expect, and relegated it to page forty-one. However, the newspaper had another crusade at this time — generating hatred towards the impending influx of Kosovan refugees who were escaping the Balkan crisis.

Ever on the tailcoats of tragedy, MPs were quick to take advantage of the judge's comments. Alan Beih a Liberal Democrat said, "This is a very distressing case and should be looked at carefully by the Home Secretary and British Board of Film Classification." Julian Brazier MP president of the Conservative Family Campaign demanded stricter control of violent videos. He said, "This case is further proof that innocent people can become victims of crime as a result of the widespread culture of violent videos and films. There has to be a mechanism whereby films which have passed the classification in the past can be reviewed in the light of new evidence." Dr Adrian Rogers director of Family Focus espousing opinions cognate to John Grisham's stated, "The makers of these films should be held responsible for the dreadful consequences of their work." Jonathan Bartley of the Movement for Christian Democracy said, "We recognise the link between what we see on the screen and how we act are complex, but this seems to be another piece in the jigsaw of cause and effect. There is little doubt now there is a relationship." Roger Gale MP said, "I believe there is a direct relationship between violence on the screen and violent behaviour." For these people, such ill-judged observations make ideal self-serving or campaign-serving propaganda. They are not interested in what the actual truth of the matter is, only whether the statements serves their purpose.

Little mention was made of the fact that Wallis and Sayers were under the influence of alcohol when they attacked Crookes. Although there is no doubt that they had intended to kill him — they had plotted the crime for months — they couldn't carry out the murder until they had consumed a necessary amount of alcohol. The same need to diminish the natural inhibitors was evident in the cases of Jeffrey Dahmer and Dennis Nilsen — they both *needed* to imbibe quantities of alcohol before being able to consummate the act of homicide. Indeed, alcohol consumption is prevalent in most acts of violence. But because of its widespread popularity, the product escapes censure by the press.

When the Columbine High School massacre occurred in Littleton, Denver and was broadcast around the world on the same day, it was only a matter of time before it would be imitated. Two students, Eric Harris and Dylan Klebold were members of a small gang known as the Trenchcoat Mafia. Subjugated over the years by the school élite – or 'jocks' as those who excel in sport are known – Harris and Klebold became increasingly segregated and viewed the glorified jocks as enemies. One pupil at the school said, "The ones who are the worst at spreading rumours and lies are the jocks and the cheerleaders." On April 20, 1999, carrying home-made bombs and guns, Harris and Klebold invaded the school premises and shot dead thirteen people before killing themselves. Some media factions chose to ignore eyewitness accounts – explaining that the killers were specifically targeting the jocks and saying it was their way of getting revenge for the torment and humiliation administered over the years – and invented their own theories as to what brought about the attack. Blaming the school massacre on films was the obvious and most simplistic route. *The Baseball Diaries* starring Leonardo DiCaprio has a dream sequence in which a character wears a long coat and shoots teachers and classmates in school. Other films postulated by the press as potential triggers are *The Faculty* in which students rebel against alien teachers, *Heathers* in which a pupil plots to eliminate despised classmates, *The Craft* in which school girls adopt the powers of black magic, and *The Matrix* simply because a character wears a long coat and carries guns. The governor of Colorado suggested TV violence may be to blame. Charlton Heston, president of the National Rifle Association, and vehemently opposed to any kind of gun control chose to blame trenchcoats and suggested such items of clothing should be banned.[35] Also targeted as a possible source of influence was Marilyn Manson and his music. Attempts were made to suggest that Manson's lyrics contained subliminal messages and that his philosophy may have inspired these and other killings. *The Express*, under the header 'Shock rocker who filled pair with a thrill to kill', quoted Manson as saying, "if someone hurts me, I'll hurt them back", which has a certain Old Testament timbre to it, and is hardly an original or provocative statement. But the quote was immediately followed by: '(one of Tuesday's gunmen had apparently spoken of his schoolmates having made his life hell)', implying there was some kind of link between the Columbine revenge shootings and Manson's words.[36]

Another element that arose was indicting computer games as causative. Shoot-em-ups, as the games are generically termed, were said to be regularly played by the two killers. *The Express* picked up on this loose contention and, under the nonsensical title "Video nasty you can't buy because it's for free," stated, "games such as Quake and Doom were alleged to have influenced US teenagers Eric Harris and Dylan Klebold who massacred thirteen of their Colorado classmates." The report was referring to a cover disc supplied free with *PC Zone* magazine that contained a demo of a new game called *Kingpin*. *The Express* claimed that, "If the game escapes a UK ban it would give manufacturers a green light to make their products as cinematic and gruesome as possible." The killers referred to Doom in a videotaped explanation of their actions made in the build up to the massacre. "It's going to be like fucking Doom," Klebold said, and Harris added: "That fucking shotgun is straight out of Doom." Klebold said of his family, "You made me what I am. You added to the rage."

However, like Dunblane and Hungerford, the foremost problem was gun accessibility. Even the motive reflected that of Thomas Hamilton, who had felt persecuted by the community and then taken revenge.

A public opinion Internet poll as to where the blame for Columbine Massacre lay brought the following results:[37]

1.06%	Drugs
9.02%	TV Violence
13.62%	Permissive Gun Laws

HELL RAISER

Horror movie drove Nazi bomber to kill

HORROR: Burned drinkers stagger from Soho pub blasted by Copeland

WARPED Nazi maniac David Copeland hatched his nailbomb plans for mass murder after watching the infamous Hellraiser horror films. His favourite was Hellraiser III: Hell On Earth.

The blood-curdling hit was one of the series of graphic movies-turned into videos—about a serial killer called Pinhead whose head and face is embedded with nails.

The monster -played by Doug Bradley-rips his victims apart with hooks. And the film's chilling slogan is: "What began in Hell will end on Earth."

Last night Copeland's brother Jonathan, 26, told the News of the World: "David would always repeat that line. There were three Hellraiser videos available then and he owned all of them." Copeland, 24, would wallow in his bedroom, festering with hatred for gays and the black, Asian and Jewish communities–then rewind the videos and watch them again, formulating his plan.

Jonathan recalled: "I once watched ... and that was ... could watch

EXCLUSIVE

BY NADIA COHEN

the grim theme of the Hellraiser videos, he boast... intention was to cause murde... damag...

FACE OF EVIL: Nailbomber Copeland blew victims apart

FACE OF EVIL: The nailed head of film villain Pinhead

round snarling all the time looking at the floor, so he always bumped into people. I think he liked the nickname, but nothing made him laugh. In all our family photos he never smiled. He lived up to his nickname and just looks angry."

Sexually David was a late developer. He ... reach puberty until he

immediately race out to meet her in a playground near our house. He told me that they used to have sex on a toy train in the playground.

"It sounded really funny to me but David said he loved doing it on that toy train."

In 1997 David left home to travel ... Thailand for six months but ... weeks ...

fore and Jonathan talked him out of it. David never managed to forge any lasting friendships with other lads either.

But he adored the pet rat he named Heinrich Himmler after Hitler's right-hand man in the Nazi party.

When he was arrested David—who slept under two Nazi fl... ble atte... for the...

Several press reports concerning nailbomber David Copeland concentrated more on the fact that he watched horror videos than on his actions or far-right associations. *News of the World*, July 2, 2000.

34.16%	Parents
42.15%	The Perpetrators Themselves

It is remarkable how low the TV violence score actually is, despite the media's impetuous attempts to influence public feeling. Interesting also is the high rating on parents. Klebold's father was a military man, and a military connection is a statistic that recurs in many of the cases (see Michael Ryan/Julian Knight/Anthony Haskett/Scott Richards/Neil Sayers/Colin Ireland).

Time magazine ran an oddly slanted article on the school shootings. There is no doubting the appalling nature of the crime, but the article went out of its way to demonise the killers and beatify the victims. So one victim "dabbled in witchcraft before she was born again", another was "an avid soccer fan", others were "into wrestling, golfing and fishing"; "writing poetry, composing songs..."; "planned to become a missionary..."; "earned a spot on the football team"; "travelled with his dad to Mexico to build a house for the poor." Survivors are quoted as saying, "God made us invisible," "God put an invisible shield around us," "God gave me an inner peace," "God told me to get out of there", and so on. The killers, however, are simply quoted as saying, "Oh, you fucking nerd. Tonight's a good time to die." The purpose of after-the-fact demonisation is to present the perpetrators as abnormal and unpleasant. But the truth is, prior to committing their crime, they appeared no different from anyone else, which is why people who knew them were totally taken aback by their actions.[38]

On Wednesday, April 28, 1999, in Taber a small farming town in Canada, a fourteen-year-old schoolboy mimicked the media reports of the Columbine school shootings. Wearing the same style clothing as detailed in the newspapers and on television he entered his local school and shot two pupils with a sawn off automatic rifle. It was reported that he wore a trenchcoat similar to those the media claimed were worn by Harris and Klebold. One of the pupils died, the other was seriously injured. The duration of time between the Columbine news flash and this event is remarkably close to that which Michael Ryan waited before mimicking the Julian Knight massacre. On the same day, a gun attack occurred at Gloucestershire College of Art and Technology. A sixteen-year-old fired three shots through an open window. However, no injuries occurred and the firearm proved to be an air pistol.

On July 22, 1999, *The Express* ran the headline, "Horror film boys left stab friend for dead." The report began, "Two teenage boys stabbed a friend after watching a horror film..." and only mentioned four paragraphs later that the attackers were actually using cocaine. The accused film was Wes Craven's *Scream*. In order to persuade readers that the movie was responsible for the attack, a very brief and selective synopsis of the film ran as follows, "some American teenagers are stabbed to death by two of their friends." This is simply another case of drug-using delinquents carrying out a violent attack. Because they had watched a movie on one occasion doesn't suggest implication.

The Express, November 14, 1999, reported that scenes from the film *Fight Club* were being re-enacted across America.

> The victim of the Seattle fight, 16-year-old Jonathan Wills, suffered convulsions and bleeding from nose, mouth and right ear. Local Sheriff John Urquhart said the teenager and his friends had been re-enacting *Fight Club* after going to see the film. The fighters wore gloves but no head gear... In another outburst linked to the film, a 24-year-old Brazilian medical student at a screening of *Fight Club* in Rio de Janeiro earlier this month opened fire in the cinema, killing three people and wounding five.

Following the trial and conviction of British neo-Nazi nail bomber David Copeland, the media couldn't resist the temptation of unnecessarily bringing movies into the final analysis. As if Copeland's warped political views were not evidently the source of his crime, Channel 4 news happened to claim that he repeatedly watched *Henry: Portrait of a Serial Killer*. The *News of the World* took a more sinister step and alleged he watched all three *Hellraiser* movies, not omitting the fact that they had been "turned into videos" – as though the transfer process from film to video tinctured them with some kind of influential evil. Following an attack, one of Copeland's victims was taken to hospital to have a six-inch nail extracted from his skull. The *News of the World* played on this and illustrated their article with a shot of Pinhead, the most prominent *Hellraiser* character, whose entire head is embedded with nails. The picture was the same size as that of the mad bomber, as though both characters were equally responsible for the atrocities. To some readers it appeared that the tenuous film link report was covertly deflecting blame from extreme right-wing factions.

Scapegoating movies is now a fundamental part of contemporary culture. From it evolves a strange vicious circle in which an accusation is made, picked up by the press, embellished, and then disseminated into the public domain. The original accuser will then utilise the press reports as independent corroboration. The charge snowballs out of all proportion, yet if all the collected clutter and nonsense is cut away the original catalyst is revealed as a tiny pea of an idea. It may only be fabricated accusation, but it makes for sensational headlines and increased newspaper sales. It also provides much needed attention for idea-redundant politicians, and stands as an easy target for self-proclaimed moral crusaders. It also offers potential lenient treatment for criminals who don't wish to take proper responsibility for crimes committed.

Even though many of the media reports are founded on prevarications they still present an influential impact on public perception and, ironically, the workings of the BBFC – as we shall see in the next chapter.

Run from this man!
MANIAC
JOE SPINELL–CAROLINE MUNRO IN "MANIAC"
ASSOCIATE PRODUCER JOHN PACKARD
MUSIC BY JAY CHATTAWAY
EXECUTIVE PRODUCERS JOE SPINELL AND JUDD HAMILTON
DIRECTED BY WILLIAM LUSTIG
DOLBY STEREO
IN SELECTED THEATRES
COLOR BY TVC A MAGNUM MOTION PICTURE
Copyright © 1980 MANIAC PRODUCTIONS
SPECIAL MAKE-UP AND EFFECTS BY TOM SAVINI
SCREENPLAY BY C.A. ROSENBERG AND JOE SPINEL
PRODUCED BY ANDREW GARRONI AND WILLIAM LU
ORIGINAL SOUNDTRACK AVAILABLE ON VARESE SARABANDE RECORDS
T.M.

'At the least provocation'

SEX & WRECKS

With the media furore that followed the murder of the infant James Bulger, and the publication of Professor Newson's *Video Violence and the Protection of Young Children* (see THE BIG INFLUENCE), Parliament bowed to pressure and supported a strengthening of the Video Recordings Act. This came in the form of amendments contained within the Criminal Justice and Public Order Act 1994.

As outlined in a press release issued in July 1994, the BBFC originally regarded these amendments as pertaining exclusively to works exempt from classification, such as music videos and videos "designed to inform, educate or instruct." Under the new law, the depiction of drug use (added to the criteria already outlined in CLAMPDOWN) would now also forfeit exemption. In actual fact, the amendments as they finally appeared were wider ranging than this, and certainly weren't restricted to exempt works. Instead — as the following excerpt indicates — they required the BBFC to consider whether a video was likely to cause harm to its potential audience, or to society through the behaviour of its audience.

> 4A. (1) The designated authority [the BBFC] shall, in making any determination as to the suitability of a video work, have special regard (among the other relevant factors) to any harm that may be caused to potential viewers or, through their behaviour, to society by the manner in which the work deals with—
>
> (a) criminal behaviour;
> (b) illegal drugs;
> (c) violent behaviour or incidents;
> (d) horrific behaviour or incidents; or
> (e) human sexual activity.

'potential viewer' means any person (including a child or young person) who is likely to view the video work in question if a classification certificate or a classification certificate of a particular description were issues;

'suitability' means suitability for the issue of a classification certificate or suitability for the issue of a certificate of a particular description;

'violent behaviour' includes any act inflicting or likely to result in the infliction of injury; and any behaviour or activity referred to in subsection (1)(a) to (e) above shall be taken to include behaviour or activity likely to stimulate or encourage it.[1]

As had happened earlier with the Video Recordings Act, this new legislation was passed quickly, rashly and was only deemed necessary because of the influence of a moral panic.

Few films are rejected outright by the BBFC. From September 1985 to April 1989, a period when film companies were still coming to terms with the Video Recordings Act, the Board refused a classification certificate to a concentration of twenty-six videos. These films ranged from the sixties drug opus *The Trip* through to the DPP casualty *Island of Death*, which was submitted to the Board under the not-so-cunning guise of *Psychic Killer II* (presumably in an attempt to have the BBFC believe the film was a follow-up to the unrelated *Psychic Killer*, which they had passed for theatrical release in 1979).[2]

Nowadays, distributors are less willing to risk submitting possibly contentious titles — the whole process being too expensive for an outcome so unpredictable — and so the BBFC can truthfully say they reject very few films. In 1998 five films were rejected on video, three in the period 1995-96, one in 1993, three in 1992, none in 1991... Rape as titillation, sexual subjugation and sexual violence are factors which feature in many rejected works — even persistent spanking between clearly consenting adults which leads to the "reddening of the buttocks"[3] will see that a work is rejected (the Law Lords state that the consent of a victim in masochistic practice is no defence to a charge of actual bodily harm). Films have been banned on other grounds, notably criminal libel (*International Guerillas*), excessive violence and dangerous combat techniques (*Kickboxer 4: The Aggressor*), schoolgirl uniforms (*Sixteen Special*), blasphemy (*Visions of Ecstasy*), and a constant focus on the details of torture (*Boy Meets Girl*). Manga cartoons have always proved problematic with the Board, and two of these were refused a certificate in 1996 (*Urotsukidoji IV Part One: The Secret Garden* and *La Blue Girl*). Several documentaries have also been banned, for including imitable weapons (*SAS Weapons & Training*) and for "promoting gross violence and selling its pleasures" (*Bare Fist: The Sport That Wouldn't Die*). In the case of at least one film (*Banned from Television*), the BBFC appear unable to offer any quantifiable reason for rejection at all[4]. (See APPENDIX I for more on these films.)

Films are rejected when the Board decides that cuts will "not make sufficient difference to the nature of the work to prevent its being found depraving and corrupting under British obscenity law." In some cases, a film has been rejected because the distributor declines to make the cuts required by the Board. But then, the fact that the Board examines a film and requests cuts is no guarantee that the work will eventually be granted a certificate anyway — as was proven recently with Jim VanBebber's *Deadbeat at Dawn*, a low-budget action thriller concerning urban warfare. After examination, the BBFC informed the distributors (Exploited) that *Deadbeat at Dawn* would need to be resubmitted with a total of fifteen cuts (2m 12s) before the proposed 18 certificate could be given. However, several weeks after making this decision, the Board informed the distributors that even in this trimmed form the work would not now be suitable for classification. A letter from James Ferman, the Board's director, outlined some of the reasons for this change of opinion:

... By requesting the cutting of all shots glamorising the use of imitable weaponry, we hoped to reduce the violence sufficiently to make the video acceptable as an '18', but this cutting merely revealed that the frequency and intensity of violent behaviour and incidents was an

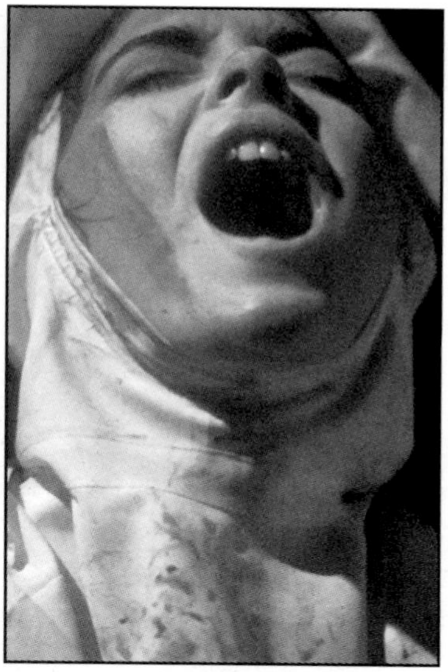

Visions of Ecstasy – rejected by the BBFC on the grounds of being "contemptuous of the divinity of Christ." This decision was upheld by the European Court of Human Rights. See also APPENDIX I.

insuperable problem in itself. All the male gang members resort to violence at the least provocation, and the violence they inflict results in maiming, mutilation and death. Violent problems provoke violent solutions, and the acting out of violent impulses provides the only pleasure on offer. Given the problem of violence by youth gangs in Britain, the Board is concerned that this video could attract viewing by young offenders whose own behaviour might be validated and confirmed by the behaviour of the characters, resulting in harm to society and members of society.

Along with Screen Edge (who presently appear to be on a hiatus with regard to releasing any new material), Exploited are one of the few British video companies of recent years dedicated to releasing obscure, low-budget cult films. (See APPENDIX II.) This kind of product doesn't sit awfully well with the BBFC, who are far more comfortable and lenient with what they perceive to be works of 'art' as opposed to works of 'commerce.'[5]

Take, for instance, the Board's defence of Lars von Trier's controversial *The Idiots* following their decision to classify it as 18 without cuts:

This challenging art film, in Danish, concerns a group of young people who have formed a commune founded on 'anti-middle class ideology.' As part of that philosophy, they pretend to be 'idiots' (i.e. people with learning difficulties) and behave accordingly in public places. The BBFC considered the possible offensiveness of this behaviour to members of the public who are disabled, and to those who are concerned with them. The view of the film, taken as a whole, is however a positive and sensitive one — particularly when real disabled characters

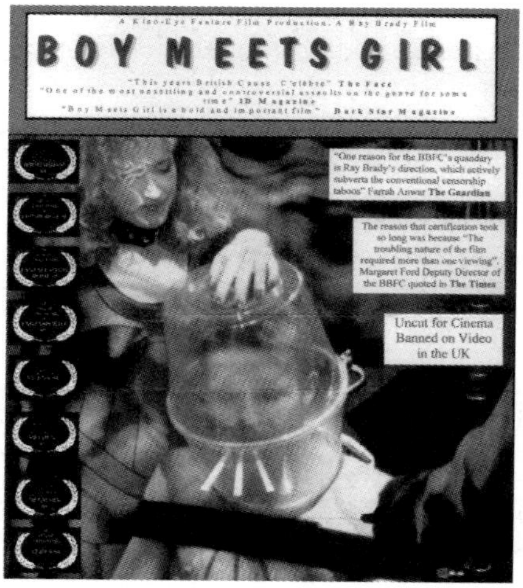

TOP: **Advertisments appeared in the press announcing the imminent release on video of *Natural Born Killers*, before Warners pulled the plug.**

ABOVE AND NEXT PAGE: **Two films recently rejected by the BBFC. See also APPENDIX I.**

are involved.

The Board can be even more patronising when it comes to ventures that fall short of their artistic yardstick. In these instances, the BBFC might request cuts or suggest some post-production tampering. This happened with *Henry: Portrait of a Serial Killer*. A sequence which appeared to show the killers murdering a family had originally pulled away to reveal that the events were actually taking place on video, watched now by the killers. In order to secure a video release, not only did the distributors (Electric Video) have to make cuts to the film, but also had to juxtapose this sequence to make it evident much earlier on that the killers were in fact watching a tape. As a result, the potency and whole point of the sequence is gone.

If this 'hands-on' approach failed to turn *Henry* into a better film (just a classifiable one), there are plenty of other instances in which the Board claim a film has benefited from their intervention.

The character played by Arnold Swarzenegger in the theatrical release of *Eraser*, for instance, is not the same as the character in the video version. In order to attain a 15 rating on video, thirty-eight cuts were made to the film (on top of the five already required to secure a theatrical 18). This change in category was at the behest of the distributor, on account of the film having flopped at the box office. The result was a less sadistic hero and, according to the Board, a film "which proved to have far greater appeal to the British audience"[6].

For *Lethal Weapon 2*, scenes were removed which showed Mel Gibson slamming a car door repeatedly into the head of a bad guy after his girlfriend has been murdered. Replacing these scenes, Gibson now carries his girlfriend's body along a beach, vowing revenge. According to James Ferman, this change didn't simply remove excessively violent footage, but allowed the Gibson character to grieve — and the film was all the better for it.

Not only is the Board "prepared to read scripts for British film-makers"[7] advising on how best to make films that accord to their own standards, they also take receipt of major international films in 'rough cut' form so that film companies can tailor the end product to the widest possible audience. This was the case with three films during the period 1995-96 — amongst them James Bond's *GoldenEye*, which was "carefully crafted to achieve a 12"[8].

The messed-up *Batman Forever* was re-edited by distributors on both sides of the Atlantic, with the BBFC requesting even more cuts in order to achieve a rating suitable for British children. This was heralded as another success for the Board when the advisory PG

enabled *Batman Forever* to top the box office charts for 1995.

"He likes the idea of being in Hollywood," one ex-examiner said of James Ferman in a TV documentary.[9] When Steven Spielberg was working on *Indiana Jones and the Temple of Doom*, Ferman flew out to the US to "help" the director with cutting the film for British audiences. Spielberg's films have met with remarkably little resistance when passing through the BBFC. At a time when the Board was exercising a stricter policy in order to — amongst other things — 'protect children from excessive fear',[10] *Jurassic Park* was only classified PG (Parental Guidance) but had children cowering in fear wherever it played.[11] *Saving Private Ryan* was another Spielberg film that was given a seemingly lenient (15) certificate and as a result met with some outcry. The film comprises some of the most brutal and realistic depictions of mutilation and carnage ever committed to celluloid — not to mention one of the most protracted stabbing scenes.

When the Board rejected Exploited's intended debut release, the stalk-and-slash movie *Maniac*, they did so on the grounds that it was "unhealthy and dangerous because of the way that the killing of women is linked with the sexual arousal of men." The Board's decision to reject *Maniac* came back-to-back with their decision to pass *Lolita* uncut for the cinema. The latter film was afforded considerably more analysis, with the BBFC explaining that Adrian Lyne's film of Nabokov's novel — concerning a middle-aged man's infatuation with a "precocious under-age girl" — was viewed by the police and distinguished experts in the fields of child psychiatry and sex abuse before any decision was reached. Ironically in light of the decision to ban *Maniac*, the BBFC determined that the confrontational *Lolita* be passed on the pretext that "adult cinemagoers have a right to judge for themselves."[12]

Exploited had acquired the rights to *Maniac* and submitted it to the BBFC in November 1997. A search made by the Board revealed that the film had never been classified and Exploited were quoted a classification fee of £941 + VAT. This figure was dropped to £535 + VAT however, when the Board subsequently discovered that *Maniac* had indeed already been submitted for theatrical release in 1981, but was rejected.[13]

The BBFC normally expect to reach a decision on a film within seventy-two hours of viewing it. They are however, under no obligation to stick to these figures and the processing period can quite often take considerably longer.

"I was obviously curious to know how long the classification process would take so I could plan my release schedule around it," Exploited's David Gregory wrote in *Samhain*.[14] "The BBFC themselves were unwilling to commit to any length of time, not even a ball park figure. In any other business paying anything like that for a service would get you all kinds of feedback, certainly including a delivery date. But what I was starting to realise was that the BBFC do not consider their work a service, it is a privilege."

Exploited finally received word on *Maniac* in a letter dated January 12, 1998. The film had been examined, but was being referred for further consideration. It was unlikely that any decision would be reached within the next five working days. Time rolled by and Exploited were once again forced to chase up the matter. When finally Gregory got through to James Ferman, he was told that *Maniac* had been rejected, and that he really should do his homework before submitting material in the future — a reference to the fact that *Maniac* had already been submitted and rejected by the Board some sixteen years earlier (even though the BBFC themselves had originally overlooked this fact). Exploited received written confirmation of the film's status on March 20, 1998, eight months after having submitted it.

The kind of low budget features that predominated prior to the Video Recordings Act are all but gone. However there has been something of a renaissance recently with *The Exorcist*, *The Texas Chain Saw Massacre* and *A Clockwork Orange* each being granted a certificate (for cinema and/or video release).[15] Indeed, the ban imposed on these three particular films has been so long and so often debated in the media that their unavailability has been absorbed as part of British culture. Even *The Driller Killer*, one of the most vilified of the video nasties and one of the first to be prosecuted under the Obscene Publications Act, suddenly found itself with a certificate in 1999, and a terrestrial television airing, after a fifteen year ban. No doubt this decision was primarily reached on account of director Abel Ferrara's subsequent credibility as a 'serious' filmmaker, with films like *King of New York* and *The*

BBFC
BRITISH BOARD OF FILM CLASSIFICATION

David Gregory
Exploited
3 Summer Court
27 Mapperley Road
Nottingham
NG3 5AG

3 Soho Square
London W1V 6HD
Telephone 0171 439 7961
Facsimile 0171 287 0141

24/08/98

Dear Mr Gregory

Title: **DEADBEAT AT DAWN** (Video)

I have to inform you that cuts, as detailed below, are required by the Board to the above Video work submitted by you. The proposed category is 18.

Should you desire to discuss the contents of this form, I shall be pleased to make an appointment for this purpose.

The following cuts are required:-

In opening credits (Music) Remove sight of throwing star in ashtray [00.01.30.15. to 00.01.33.07].

At 10 1/2 Mins After mid shot of woman in red dress, remove all sight of chainsticks hanging on wall; remove all sight of man with head scarf taking chainsticks from wall. [00.11.48.07 to 00.11.51.01] Resume on mid shot of man facing door before he removes knife sticking out of door.

At 11 Mins: After sequence in which man with head scarf has been practising martial arts in cemetery, remove all sight of him picking up and wielding chainsticks in practice.[00.12.24.09 to 00.12.52.02]Resume on mid- shot of man walking to right of screen.

At 12 Mins: Remove long shot through railings of man walking towards camera carrying chainsticks.[00.13.09.00 to 00.13.12.08] Resume on shot of man riding motor cycle.

At 12 Mins: As man with head scarf approaches man standing by motor cycle and assaults him, remove all sight of chainsticks.[00.13.32.17. to 00.13.36.13] Resume on man, hands at his waist, about to mount motor cycle.

At 57 Mins: After sequence of man jumping from roof, remove all sight of man holding and throwing combat star, and subsequent shot of star striking and sticking in neck of policeman.[00.58.10.00 to 00.58.13.15] Resume on extreme long shot of man lowering himself on rope against building.

At 59 1/2 Mins: After close up of man picking up magazines, remove all sight of two throwing stars amongst other weapons.[01.01.05.03 to 01.01.06.06] Resume on close up of hand picking up gun.

At 60 Mins: After mid shot of bare-backed man placing a knife in sash, and turning, remove all sight of him picking up throwing star and putting it in his belt. [01.01.24.21 to 01.01.28.02] Resume on close up of back of man in blue jacket.

At 72 1/2 Mins: After mid shot of man on ground with knife near his face, remove all sight of chainsticks being wielded by man in yellow shirt.[01.13.54.02 to 01.13.54.22]. Resume on mid shot of back of man beginning to stand up.

At 72 1/2 Mins: In same fight sequence, remove all sight of chainsticks as man in dark clothes struggles with man in yellow shirt. [01.13.56.04 to 01.13.58.22] Resume on mid shot of man in yellow shirt on ground, arms outstretched.

At 74 Mins: During fight sequence between man in brown jacket and man in black leather jacket, remove all sight of chainsticks being picked up and used in continuing fight. [01.15.22.16 to 01.15.31.24].Resume on close shot of face of man with beard.

At 74 Mins: After close shot of man with red head scarf holding his head, remove all sight of subsequent attack with chainsticks on man in brown jacket - striking him and throttling him; also remove subsequent sequence where man in black leather jacket is carrying chainsticks in fight with three men.[01.15.35.17 to 01.15.48.01] Resume on shot of man's shadow.

At 74 1/2 Mins: After mid shot of man in black leather jacket and beard, remove all sight of him wielding chainsticks. [01.15.53.07 to 01.15.54.08] Resume on long shot of man carrying beam.

At 75 Mins: After long shot of bearded man behind wall, remove all sight of him picking up chainsticks and using them in following fight sequence. [01.16.10.05 to 01.16.29.04] Resume on shot of underside of bridge.

At 75 Mins: In same fight sequence, after mid shot of blond man, remove all sight of man in black leather jacket removing throwing star from shirt and throwing it; also remove subsequent sight of star in man's forehead.[01.16.32.18 to 01.16.36.16]. Resume on long shot of man in black leather jacket sitting on ground.

At 75 1/2 Mins: In fight sequence on roof top, remove all clear sight of throwing star sticking in blond man's head as other man bangs his head against parapet. [01.16.49.20 to 01.16.53.23] Resume on long shot of blond man lying on wall, the other about to push him over edge.

Resubmit.

Signed..
Director / Deputy Director / Principal Examiner

The BBFC request extensive cuts to *Deadbeat at Dawn*... and then reject it altogether.

Addiction under his belt.

Following in the footsteps of *The Driller Killer* were other films that had once languished on the DPP list, including *Shogun Assassin*, *Tenebrae*, *The Toolbox Murders*, and *Axe*. The BBFC aren't about to call an amnesty on all the former nasties — and indeed have recently rejected *Last House on the Left* on account of its "explicit and sadistic sexual violence" — but it can argue that some have merit of one form or another. Or, nothing too offensive that couldn't be remedied with a few snips.

Not that any of these films are quite the same as the versions available pre-VRA. Having been tainted by inclusion on the DPP list, they're now released in a form essentially different to that which was regarded as obscene and liable to prosecution back in the eighties. In the case of *Tenebrae*, this difference is courtesy of a few seconds of gore being excised;[16] for *Axe*, nineteen seconds of cuts were made, replaced in part by other scenes played in slow motion (see APPENDIX II); in *The Driller Killer* a slight cut was made and footage of nearly six-and-a-half minutes added by the distributor, Visual Film.

This apparent relaxation in the BBFC's attitudes and emergence of formerly banned material has come with the retirement of James Ferman in December 1998. Director of the BBFC for twenty-three years, Ferman regarded himself as the last of the 'traditional' censors on account of the fact that his successor (Robin Duval) would not only have to contend with film and video as he had done, but also digital technology and the Internet. Ferman announced his retirement on the cusp of some particularly hostile press, including that which surrounded the BBFC's decision to pass several highly contentious films (see below).

Ferman ran the BBFC with a draconian hand, contractually binding those who worked there to secrecy. When one employee transgressed this rule, she received a solicitor's letter informing her of her duty and obligation to the Board. Maggie Mills, another examiner, called Ferman "a control freak" and described how he

> would sit in his office alone, late into the night, obsessively watching videos. His lack of contact with the normal human world showed; he ran the BBFC as his personal fiefdom, overriding those who disagreed with him.[17]

Another disgruntled employee told *The Guardian* in February 1994 that "censorship here is not a democratic process... in reality, James Ferman calls the shots." It was in that month Ferman proposed to

BBFC
BRITISH BOARD OF FILM CLASSIFICATION

3 Soho Square
London W1V 6HD
Telephone 0171 439 7961
Facsimile 0171 287 0141
http://www.bbfc.co.uk

From: Robin Duval *Director*

23rd September 1999

David Gregory
Exploited

Dear Mr Gregory,

SNUFF

Thank you for your letter of 16th September.

It is not the Board's policy to classify material which has been subject to successful prosecution under the Obscene Publications Act within recent history. Since 1990, I understand that there have been four such actions against **Snuff**, the most recent in 1994. I would recommend that, before you consider submitting the work for classification, you take whatever measures are necessary to remove those elements which are likely to have led to forfeiture and conviction.

You have my assurance that I will give the same advice to any other distributors who approach the Board in similar terms in the next few years.

Yours sincerely,

BBFC
BRITISH BOARD OF FILM CLASSIFICATION

3 Soho Square
London W1V 6HD
Telephone 0171 439 7961
Facsimile 0171 287 0141
http://www.bbfc.co.uk

From: Robin Duval *Director*

27th September 1999

David Gregory
Exploited

Dear Mr Gregory,

SNUFF

I honestly do not believe that preceding **Snuff** with an investigative documentary will make any difference to the acceptability of the main work.

Yours sincerely,

Exploited contact the BBFC with regard to the likelihood of *Snuff* getting passed should they submit it. The Board's new director, Robin Duval replies. See also APPENDIX II.

Daily Mail, Saturday, April 2, 1994

AFTER EXPERTS FINALLY ACCEPT THE CONNECTION BETWEEN SCREEN VIOLENCE AND YOUNGSTERS' BEHAVIOUR

Howard on fast-forward

Home Secretary will act to keep video nasties out of the home

Mr Howard: 'Deep concern'

Clare Short: 'Time to act'

THE HORRORS ON SALE IN ANY HIGH STREET

COMMENTARY

by ROY HATTERSLEY

Phoney freedom that damages us all

sack thirteen of the Board's part-time examiners, who had earlier passed a vote of no confidence in the director. It was primarily Ferman's decision that kept *The Exorcist* from seeing a video release for so long. He flatly refused to review his position on this matter until December 1991, when examiners forced a vote. But even with the majority opting to grant the film a video certificate (fifteen voted yes, one wanted to maintain the ban and three abstained), the video remained shelved.

Ferman has verified his stance with regard to *The Exorcist* many times since, offering a whole gamut of reasons why the film shouldn't be made available for video. These range from the predictable (i.e. the harm the film might inflict on impressionable young girls viewing it in their bedroom) through to the downright peculiar (i.e. the problem it raises with regard to the power of the supernatural). In 1992, principal examiner Guy Phelps offered another explanation in that the Board feared "the potential use of the film in terrifying children as a part of 'satanic' abuse. We know that videos are used in this way..."

(Although it didn't generate a video certificate for *The Exorcist*, Satanic abuse was exposed as a myth in 1994 following a three year investigation.)

The Texas Chain Saw Massacre was another film that suffered a long and meaningless ban under Ferman — this in spite of the fact that virtually all of the violence is implied and he himself considered *Texas Chain Saw* "a very good piece of craft"[18]. One of the knock-on effects of this particular ban was that *Hollywood Chainsaw Hookers* — an otherwise unrelated low-budget horror-comedy — had to have the word "chainsaw" removed from its title, replaced instead with a picture of the offending power tool. The Board conceded, when finally they passed *The Texas Chain Saw Massacre* in March 1999, that "The notoriety of the film may owe a lot to its original rejection by the BBFC in 1975."

The threat that video was said to have posed in the early days of the Video Recording Act was to return anew a decade later. Throughout the nineties pressure was on once again to curb video sex and violence — or, as some argued, any video that wasn't suitable for children. Following the massacres in Dunblane and Tasmania (see THE BIG INFLUENCE), Warner Home Video deemed their intended video release of *Natural Born Killers* as "inappropriate" and pulled the plug on it indefinitely (despite it already having obtained a video certificate). The theatrical release of the film had been preceded by substantial fuss in the media, with calls for it to be banned on account of supposed copycat crimes.[19] It was amidst this concern that the BBFC issued a press statement outlining their reason for passing *Natural Born Killers* 18 without cuts.

When Ros Hodgkiss resigned from her job as an examiner at the BBFC, she told *The*

Guardian that whenever stories condemning violent culture broke in the tabloids,

> whatever the facts, there was a reigning in [at the Board]. Decisions undoubtedly became more conservative. In such a climate it is difficult to keep your cool and remain objective.[20]

The press reported on March 4, 1993, that American TV networks were turning down BBC dramas — like *The Men's Room* and Melvyn Bragg's *A Time to Dance* — on account of their sex and violence. Home Secretary Kenneth Clarke urged programme makers to show more common sense in the battle against crime. (When in July 1994 the BBC's licence fee was confirmed for another five years, it was on the understanding that the corporation publish a statement of promises to cut back on sex and violence and deliver it to everyone who had a TV licence.)

Following a remark made by Sir Anthony Hopkins, that he may pull out of a sequel to *Silence of the Lambs* because he didn't want to contribute to a climate of violence, the onus shifted invariably from television to the BBFC. Hopkins may have been smarting from remarks made about *Silence of the Lambs* in *Hollywood vs. America*, a highly publicised and inflammatory book by US film critic Michael Medved. The book accused the entertainment industry — in particular Hollywood — of following "its own dark obsessions, rather than giving the people what it wants." Hollywood was said to ignore and assault the values of ordinary, God-fearing American families.[21]

Towards the end of 1993, the media was awash with speculative headlines concerning the death of James Bulger, with many reports linking the murder to the video *Child's Play 3*. (See THE BIG INFLUENCE.) The *Daily Express*[22] claimed that it had the list of videos which the young killers had watched in the weeks leading up to the fateful day, but admitted they weren't going to divulge it because doing so "might persuade youngsters to go out and rent copies." (If they had divulged it, readers would have seen that *Child's Play 3* wasn't listed.)

Home Secretary Michael Howard was all set to put pressure on the BBFC and introduce tougher measures for video shops who rented films to the wrong age groups. Liberal Democrat MP David Alton wanted to go further and ban for home rental any video which contained "inappropriate models." He intended this restriction to take the form of a new classification: "Unsuitable for Children." Despite the fact that Alton's madcap proposal would effectively ban anything that wasn't made for kids, the

VISIONS OF VIOLENCE

Children have grown used to scenes of simulated slaughter

SICK SCRIPT: Was James Bulger's killing a video-inspired act of brutality?

Corruption of the video generation

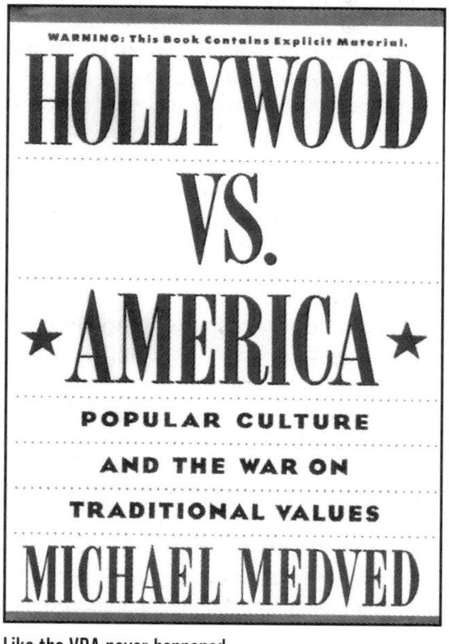

WARNING: This Book Contains Explicit Material.
HOLLYWOOD
VS.
AMERICA
POPULAR CULTURE
AND THE WAR ON
TRADITIONAL VALUES
MICHAEL MEDVED

Like the VRA never happened...

PREVIOUS PAGE: The Home Secretary is forced to tighten video legislation. *Daily Mail*, April 2, 1994.

THIS PAGE, TOP: Lost innocence. *Daily Express*, November 26, 1993. ABOVE: Michael Medved's influential book.

panic that was generating in the media enabled him to garner much support. So much support in fact — 300 MPs from all parties — that Howard had to concede to some of Alton's demands otherwise run the risk of almost certain Commons defeat. The result was a new clause to the Criminal Justice Bill (which can be found at the beginning of this chapter).

Having been faced with the daunting prospect of Alton's original proposal, an understandably relieved James Ferman told *The Times*, "From now on, we are going to have to cut more and classify higher."

However, the victory that was the 'toughest-ever crackdown on violent videos'[23] saw the BBFC fly into a panic and put on hold films they believed might be affected by the legislation. Under the new ruling the Board had a statutory obligation *and a responsibility* to protect viewers from harmful video material. One film put on hold was the British horror thriller *Beyond Bedlam*, despite it initially having been given an interim 18 certificate for video only a week earlier.[24] *Heavenly Creatures* on the other hand, the true story of two girls who murdered a parent in fifties' New Zealand, was given an 18 certificate rather than the proposed 15 for no other reason than the killers were adolescent.

Any film that associated killing and juveniles became problematic in light of the Bulger murder. "Terror is as close as the boy next door" was the tag line for *The Paperboy*, a film which remained in limbo until November 1994 when it was passed 18. Shedding his *Home Alone* persona for something more malevolent, Macauley Culkin starred in *The Good Son* which was granted an 18 with cuts in September 1995. *Mikey*, on the other hand, was rejected outright in December 1996. The furore over *Child's Play 3* even resulted in CIC withdrawing its forthcoming release *Dollman vs. Demonic Toys*.

Newspaper headlines at the end of April 1994 focused on 'lost innocence'. In a world dominated by television, computers, drugs, crime and career worries, only three percent of children considered themselves to be living the carefree lives depicted by Enid Blyton — so was the claim of psychologist Dr David Lewis.[25] More curbs on video were suggested by MPs. Amongst them the idea that adults buying or renting a film classified 18 should be handed a warning notice reminding them not to let children view it; in addition it was suggested that compulsory identity cards be necessary for all schoolchildren visiting a video shop.

Before its release in Britain, British transport police requested to view the film *Money Train* on account of scenes that had supposedly encouraged the murder of a New York Subway toll booth operator. Columbia-Tristar released a press statement in which the director, producers and employees of the studio condemned the "isolated act of senseless violence."

The screen violence debate raged on. The world and its film makers were divided. Some considered the idea of a movie inciting real life violence to be absurd (John Landis, Paul Verhoeven, Michael Winner, Quentin Tarantino), a few believed that film makers had a responsibility to society to refrain from violence (David Puttnam), while others blamed everyone but themselves (Jon Amiel).[26]

Experimental psychologist Michael Yardley counted, frame by frame, the number of guns and killings in the most popular videos of 1995, and deduced from the high figures that viewers were being given an unspoken justification to real violence. "It is time to challenge film makers who routinely peddle this pornography of violence," he determined. In August 1996, the NVALA released figures from their own poll concerning the movies of the previous year. Horrified, they called for more control in dealing with Hollywood action and thriller movies.

"Time to sack this feeble censor" opined the film critic for the *Daily Mail* on December 13, 1996. The remark was in reference to a statement made by James Ferman earlier in the week, in which the BBFC director had put the culture of violence permeating mainstream film making "beyond the reach of British law." There was, said Ferman, no scope to make further cuts because the BBFC were already rigorous in their approach. Ferman may have been "fighting a losing battle," concurred the *Mail*, "but he is losing it partly because of his own half-heartedness."[27]

DAILY Mirror

Woman GET SLIM FAST 4 PAGE EXTRA INSIDE

HONESTY, QUALITY, EXCELLENCE

Jane on a Princess in torment

BANNED

Thanks to your DAILY Mirror

CHILD'S PLAY 3

Nude Fergie photos fury

SEE PAGE 5

ONLY 25p TODAY

Anne Robinson

GET Rich £10,000 TO BE WON EVERY DAY

Maniac hacks couple to death and attacks girls

BRAINDEAD

CHILD'S PLAY

BRANDED

BODY

Now Chucky can't come out to play

Banned or 'branded' – thanks to the *Daily Mirror* or *Today*?
April 13, 1994.

As the tabloids whipped themselves into a lather over Ferman's proclamation, the government seethed. After all, the government was trying to impress upon the public (in the very same tabloids, no less) that it shared their concern over video violence, and the dangers it presented to the nation, its youth and seemingly its thugs ("Young offenders are set to be barred from watching violent videos in institutions," reported *The Express*, August 18, 1997).

The relationship between the BBFC and the new Labour government was never a particularly good one. Labour, who had promoted moral values in their party conferences, came to office in 1997 amidst the furore surrounding some particularly controversial films. No sooner had the brouhaha on one film died down (invariably after it had been passed and released), then another film jumped in to take its place. Following the violent attributes of *Reservoir Dogs*, *Pulp Fiction* and *Natural Born Killers*, the depiction of strange sex colluded to embarrass the authorities yet further in controversial films like *Kids*,[28] *Crash*,[29] *Kissed*,[30] *Lolita* and *The Idiots*. The fad that was the 'educational video' also brought its share of problems, notably with *Executions*,[31] *Hookers: Sex for Sale* and *Everyday...Operations*.[32]

In December 1997, the newly elected "people's government" intervened to block the automatic appointment of Lord Birkett as successor to Lord Harewood, the retiring president of the BBFC. This unprecedented step was taken in "a bid to make the board more accountable to Parliament and public taste"[33] and resulted in the appointment of Andreas Whittam Smith, founding editor of *The Independent* newspaper, whose knowledge of film was meagre to say the least. Whittam Smith felt that public accountability could best be achieved through these stated objectives:

> (1) to promote consistency in the classification process, (2) to encourage the Board to be as open as possible, and (3) to make sure that the Board is well informed about the public's attitude to its work.[34]

Daily Mail

SATURDAY, NOVEMBER 9, 1996 NEWSPAPER OF THE YEAR 40p

SUPPORT POPPY APPEAL 1996

Britain's very best TV guide

WEEKEND

LAURA BAILEY

7 FREE INSTANT SCRATCH CARDS PLUS WIN UP TO £50,000 INSTANT CASH EXTRA

Campaign to stop depraved movie being shown in Britain

BAN THIS CAR CRASH SEX FILM

By STEVE BUSFIELD

THE Heritage Secretary called last night for a depraved new film to be banned.

Premier concedes free vote on caning

Starring in controversy: Holly Hunter

Shocking scenes: Rosanna Arquette

INSIDE: Weather 2, Saturday Essay 8 & 9, Simon Heffer 11, Coffee Break 44 & 45, Gardening 46, Travel 56-60, City 65-68, Sport 69-80

THE EXPRESS

TUESDAY MARCH 24, 1998 35p

Whatever happened to the Tiller Girls? • PAGE 24

FURY AS CENSOR PASSES LOLITA

Concern over film's paedophile risk

JENNIFER FLIES IN WITH SOME CLOSE FRIENDS

FULL STORY • PAGE 7

WEATHER 2 • OPINION 10 • HICKEY 17 • YOUR STARS 32 • CITY 34-36 • CROSSWORDS 40 • LETTERS 42 • TV GUIDE 43-48

A couple of recent films (and BBFC decisions) unpopular with the tabloid press.
LEFT AND RIGHT: *Daily Mail*, November 9, 1996 and *Daily Express*, March 24, 1998.

The Labour Home Secretary, Jack Straw, also thought it necessary to halt the liberalisation measures the Board were undertaking with regard to the R18 category. Discussions between Tory Home Office Minister Tom Sackville and the Board back in 1996 had concluded that the R18 guidelines, as they stood, did not permit enough sex to lure purchasers away from black market hardcore. Straw however — having once described porn as "nasty, degenerate and worthless"[35] — was having none of it. When news reached him that BBFC approved sex films (in the form of *The Pyramid* and *BatBabe*) now contained erections and glimpses of penetrative and oral sex, Straw ensured that the porn breakthrough went no further.[36]

James Ferman steadfastly denied that it was the media and government backlash which had influenced (or forced) him to retire when he did. Nevertheless, as soon as he made the decision to do so, he let his views on certain matters be known — matters that he would undoubtedly have had to keep under his hat had he stayed at the BBFC. His farewell message was a call to make hardcore pornography legal. In what appeared a provocative rebuttal of Jack Straw's intervention on the matter of R18 videos, Ferman told the press that "The more you try to ban it the more it grows."

The ban on 'conventional' pornography had encouraged a black market ready to deal in far more obscene material, Ferman claimed. In his twenty-three years of office, it was the influx of violent sex videos into the country that he considered his biggest failure. And with regard to cutting sex videos in 1996, he felt that to be "the most soul-destroying use of professional expertise yet invented."

The BBFC Annual Report for 1997-98 reiterated:

In response to a steady increase in the public's tolerance of screen sex, confirmed by a wide range of research, the Board relaxed its stringent standards to allow marginally more explicitness in sex videos sold through licensed sex shops. This move was promptly curtailed when it became apparent that these standards were out of line with those of enforcement agencies such as Customs & Excise and the police and Magistrates' Courts. In October 1998, the Board reverted to its previous standards, but it is concerned that the failure to distinguish between harmful forms of pornography and those which are merely offensive will fuel the already flourishing black market which mixes pornography with obscenity. Mr Ferman says that this is one of the biggest problems he leaves for his successors and calls for a solution to be found.

Since his retirement, the BBFC has undertaken to rid itself of the stigma brought about by Ferman's directorship and craving for secrecy. For the first time, the Board has published Draft Guidelines for Classifying Films and Videos, in which are detailed "the criteria used to arrive at the decisions it makes on behalf of the public." Then there is the Public Consultation Programme, a nation-wide roadshow to which members of the public are invited. Problem scenes from recent films are screened at these events, and an insight into the process which led the Board to pass or cut them is provided. Afterwards the audience puts their questions to members of the examination team. ("Maybe it's a subjective opinion but it's mine," commented one examiner during a recent roadshow.)

As film producer Stephen Woolley points out in the documentary *The Last Days of the Board*, indeed they are "the censors who want to be loved."

The first contentious film for Robin Duval, Ferman's successor, came in the form of Gaspard Noé's *Seul Contre Tous*. Subtitled and French, it contained scenes showing a pregnant woman being beaten, hardcore footage being played in a porn cinema, and a protagonist who dreams that he rapes and murders his daughter. Given its art-house aspirations, Ferman was of the unofficial opinion that *Seul Contre Tous* should be passed uncut. Duval however, wanted the porn in the cinema scene removed before granting it an 18, leaving intact the two violent and arguably more objectionable sequences.[37] It was a telling decision for the new director, and an almost complete turnabout for the Board in light of Ferman's twenty-three year legacy.

"People are all excited that they're relaxing standards," commented one video distributor of the new BBFC,[38] "and that's completely not true."

There is something inherently ridiculous in opening a newspaper and seeing the face of Chucky, the doll from *Child's Play 3*, with the word "DANGEROUS" emblazoned beneath it.

As outlined in the previous chapter, quite often the news media is the catalyst that provokes serious criminal incidents. The reporting of Julian Knight's massacre induced the Hungerford massacre, reporting of which in turn induced the shootings in Monkseaton and Northamptonshire. Reports on the Dunblane massacre were followed by the killings in Tasmania and indubitably linked to the attempted murders by Horrett Campbell at St Luke's nursery school. Indeed, it is these facts which the newspapers fear most. It is why they generate public distaste for films and other mediums — diverting responsibility for the terrible crimes they themselves have provoked.

Not all the criminal acts that the press induces are as serious as Hungerford or St Luke's. Ram-raiding, for instance, was an isolated incident that was demonstrated to the nation's criminals by the news media and consequently became a national problem overnight. The value of computer RAM chips and the ease with which they could be stolen was demonstrated on one television news broadcast and the crime suddenly escalated. When Ayatollah Khomeni placed a fatwa on *The Satanic Verses* author Salman Rushdie, and a $2 million purse on his head, it was the news media that informed all potential assassins of the awaiting prize, thus utterly compounding Rushdie's dilemma. Los Angeles burned following the media coverage of the Rodney King beating and subsequent trial. Terrorist bomb attacks are generally carried out so that the news media can report them, thereby ensuring the organisation's cause remains in the public eye.

Does all of this mean there should be media censorship; a news blackout? It would be simplistic to paraphrase words spoken by Jill Knight MBE MP (now Dame Knight) and direct them at the news media as opposed to "porno movies", which was her original intent: "Is the freedom to *report news items* more important than the freedom from rape, murder and terror?" The difference is however, that the news media does incite imitative crime whereas films don't.

Politicians and journalists use emotive language to further their campaigns and secure public attention. They may claim to be protecting children but in truth are simply protecting their own interests and promoting themselves.[39] The tabloid press is constantly looking to invent a new menace from which to protect us, not unlike a parent warning a child there is a monster in the closet so that they can take pleasure in comforting and protecting them. Politicians and the tabloid press do the same to the general public — enthusing that some child-eating monster awaits around every corner. They did it with horror comics in the fifties, they did it with Satanic abuse, they did it with "devil dogs", they did it with horror videos, and looming on the agenda is the Internet. All of these exist only as perils on the pages of the newspapers — the only way to remain safe is to buy the next edition and await the all-clear (by which time the next threat will be upon us).

Statistics can be used and manipulated to mislead the public and advance a political career or moral crusade. The community will be temporarily deluded into believing that the reformist is campaigning for an improvement in *their* rights. It will be argued that failure to follow and offer support will result in an unprecedented danger to the children. Cuckolded public opinion will then carry the acclaimed reformer into a higher-ranking or higher-salaried position. Once this step-up in status is achieved, from MP to Lord for instance, the campaign will suddenly cease. One dubious statistic thrown around during the early days of the video controversy indicated that half the nation's children had seen a video nasty. Had this and the theorised effects of viewing such material been true, then half the country's current thirty-year-olds would be depraved and corrupt due to the viewing experience they had in their youth.

When an incident as inexplicable as the Bulger murder grips the nation the simplest form of action is to blame a movie. This way the film can be publicly pariahed, with the instigator of the bogus mitigation claiming credit for a great public service when in actual fact nothing has been accomplished at all. In the wake of the Bulger case, when the government announced its crackdown on violent videos, *Today* printed an assortment of horror video sleeves with the word "BRANDED" stamped across them. Never a newspaper to allow the facts to get in the way of a good campaign, the *Daily Mirror* went the whole hog and reproduced the sleeve to *Child's Play 3* beneath the huge fatuous claim that it was "BANNED — Thanks to your Daily Mirror." The film wasn't banned then and isn't banned now.[40]

It is clear that blame for such incidents as the Bulger murder cannot simply be laid at the door of films — the causes of crime are much more deeply rooted within social structure. To find the source would take time and absolute effort, something politicians refuse to give. For every study that determines there is a causative link between film and crime, another one appears whose findings are quite the opposite. Television violence is good for you, researchers in Germany concluded in 1994. It makes people less likely to act aggressively and more likely to identify with victims. However, this is not generally an opinion that fires the editorial imagination, and research like this is rarely afforded the space or sobriety that the counter-argument tends to receive.

In November 1990, a psychologist named Jeffrey Goldstein determined that youngsters aged six were able to spot when they were being brainwashed by commercials. By the age of ten most had become sceptical of claims made by advertisers, the research revealed. A decade later, in August 1999, the American Academy of Paediatrics was suggesting that television at too early an age could lead to irreversible brain damage or psychological impairment.

Research into juvenile crime, conducted by the BBFC no less, found that young offenders were watching very much the same films as non-offenders of the same age, with neither group showing undue interest in horror films or films about violent criminal lifestyles.[41]

It may be true to say that crime has increased since video came into the homes, but it is equally true to say that violent crime has increased since the formation of the NVALA, or since the introduction of the Video Recordings Act, or since the spread of fast-food burger chains. Likewise, actual evidence can also be used to mislead. It was noted that serial killer Jeffrey Dahmer had a copy of *Exorcist II: The Heretic* in his flat — but what did this fact actually *mean* and why was it thought so important? Right-wing Christian groups used it as evidence that malevolent films engendered malevolent people, yet the same groups chose to ignore the fact that a copy of the Bible was also found in Dahmer's flat. Dahmer openly admitted that throughout his killing spree he was "living on nothing but McDonald's." The killers of James Bulger were also fast-food consumers and burger bars are the favourite haunts of America's gun maniacs — does such evidence identify a link? Does it imply a potential peril of food additives? Should fast food products be banned for the sake of the children? The increased use of aspartame, the artificial sweetener in soft drinks, also correlates to the increase in juvenile violence.[42]

THE EXPRESS

WEDNESDAY AUGUST 12, 1998 35p

I can't forget my little dead daughter, by Cilla Black

• PAGES 28 & 29

MAKE HARD PORN LEGAL

Censor calls

Battle to ban porn is lost says censor

FROM PAGE ONE

into the country as the biggest failure of his 23-year term of office.

He argues that the ban on "conventional" pornography has encouraged the growth of a black market ready to deal in far more obscene videos involving children, animals and violence.

He also suggested a former Conservative Home Office Minister had favoured the policy of legalising hard-core pornography.

Mr Ferman admitted the report could be seen as a provocative parting shot.

"Yes, I feel strongly about it because the black market will just grow and grow," he said.

"A little of what people want is OK as long as it's on the harmless end of the spectrum. The more you try to ban it the more it grows." However Mr Ferman, who said he was aware that there were bestiality tapes circulating in Britain, stressed that anything involving violence should not be legalised.

John Beyer, director of the National Viewers' and Listeners' Association, said: "We agree entirely with Mr Ferman that violent pornography undermines a healthy society and that this problem must be tackled urgently."

But he called for harsher penalties for those trafficking in obscene videos.

"A new restrictive definition of 'obscene' is absolutely vital with more severe penalties for those found guilty," said Mr Beyer.

FERMAN: Warning over growing black market

Going in a blaze of glory... James Ferman makes a controversial announcement on his retirement. *The Express*, August 12, 1998

This does not mean of course that children should be allowed to watch any type of film, because the argument isn't about children — despite attempts by groups and individuals to put them in the line of fire. BBFC guidelines to the consumer (i.e. certification as opposed to censorship), followed by regulation of video outlets and parental control should suffice to keep children from unsuitable material. Of course some parents care little about their own children, let alone about what they watch. Should the whole adult population be subjected to prohibition because some children are unrestrained or left unsupervised?

If there was any substantial truth to the theory that screen violence influences the actions or mindset of people, then the most dangerous people in the country would not be the inmates of Broadmoor's maximum security wing but the staff at the BBFC and members of the NVALA.[43] These people watch more scenes of violence than any average member of the public. Following the Russell Crookes murder case, the NVALA was quick to use the tragedy for their own propaganda. John Beyer, the NVALA director, said that broadcasters should stop showing violent films, and asked, "How many more murders will there be before someone does something about the violence?" During a TV debate on screen violence, Beyer mentioned the fact that Channel 5 had aired Oliver Stone's *Natural Born Killers*. When asked whether it should have been shown he responded in the absolute negative. But because he is so blinded by his organisation's crusade he failed to comprehend that the film had been shown and nothing untoward had happened as a consequence. There was no increase in crime, no mass murders, no collapse into anarchy, *nothing*. The film was aired again by Channel 5 with similar non-events.

DANGEROUS: Chuckie

Members of organisations such as the NVALA, Customs & Excise, and the BBFC believe themselves to be immune to the effects of viewing violence — that is to say, the effects *they* insist exist. This they do not perceive as evidence that viewing such material inspires no imitative reaction, but rather that it identifies their own intellectual superiority and mental stability. It is everyone else who is susceptible to an adverse effect. When it comes to viewing violent imagery, BBFC examiners are said to have "ways of defending themselves."[44] While they may become, at worst, "desensitised" to certain scenes, we will become "depraved and corrupt." This distinction in the divided classes was highlighted when the controversial *Man Bites Dog* was certified for video without cuts. The BBFC argued that the film ("a savage lampoon of media complicity") would not appeal to certain social classes because it was b&w and subtitled. As a result, its excessive violence — far stronger than anything in the banned *Straw Dogs* (colour/English language) — was left intact. Conversely, the violent scenes in James Cameron's *True Lies* underwent cuts, as the movie had more of an appeal to the 'lower' social classes (the easily influenced feeble-minded) and little attraction to the art-intellectuals (the resistant secure-minded). This theory of the susceptible and easily influenced residing on the deficient side of the intellectual divide is merely self-aggrandising speculation by those believing they occupy the opposite side. The adversely affected can never be identified by example, only alluded to hypothetically — or the accuser would stand to lose support and favour from the stated group.[45]

What was really gained by the Video Recordings Act and the banning of a bunch of cheap horror movies? Everything, one suspects, that the authorities wanted to avoid. In recent years, some of these same movies have been returning with an official BBFC stamp of approval, and heralded in some quarters as renaissance pieces. Today, distributors promote films like *Axe*, *Zombie Flesh-Eaters*, *Shogun Assassin*, *The Slayer* and *The Driller Killer* on the back of their association with that most tumultuous of times.[46] If the nasties weren't a "term of art" to begin with, that's what banning them has turned them into. Almost two decades later, critics extrapolate and analyse ideas and meanings from these films. Legitimate companies publish and distribute many quality books and magazines devoted to them. A new generation of collectors — some too young to remember the controversy that sparked off the VRA in the first place — are tuning into the subject. Where once trade was conducted via the pages of fanzines and magazines, now it's on the Internet.

> WE HAVE A WIDE RANGE OF FULLY UNCUT HORROR MOVIES WHAT HAVE TAKEN US AGES TO COLLECT ALL FILMS ARE 10+++ QUALITY AND ONLY PROFESIONAL EQUIPMENT IS USED TO TRANSFER THE FILMS FROM NTSC-PAL MENNING NO QUALITY LOSS FOR FULL LIST E-MAIL ME AT ——— ALL FILMS ARE £13 INCLUDING P A P. FOR A QUICK EXAMPLE WE HAVE CANNIBAL MOVIES, ZOMBIE MOVIES, AND LOADS MORE AND ALL FILMS ARE THE TRUE UNCUT VERSIONS SO YOU WON'T BE DISSAPOINTED.

There would be no underground niche and much less interest in cannibal and zombie movies if the fad of the early eighties had been left to run its natural course. The VRA succeeded only in creating a locked groove, where the cinematic equivalent of disco plays endlessly to an ever growing crowd. Cinema has moved on. Video nasties haven't. It is almost inconceivable that terrible feature films like *Werewolf and the Yeti*, *Contamination* and *Evilspeak* could ever have been perceived as a danger, indeed nothing short of a national threat. But they were, and to a large degree still are — thanks to a news media which continues to regard every questionable celluloid experience as a video nasty.[47] The truth of the matter is that they are exploitation films, whose only mind-altering threat comes via an abundance of stilted acting, poorly dubbed dialogue, cheesy plots, cornball special effects and occasional lapses into poor taste.

Responding to questions raised by the Home Secretary concerning its responsibilities under the Video Recordings Act, a brooding BBFC stated in a report dated December 6, 1996, that "the 'video nasties' are still the most violent videos ever submitted to the Board, but they were never a part of mainstream cinema." (Not only had the Board decided in 1985 to avoid media generalisations like 'video nasties,' but very few of the films on the DPP list had been submitted for classification in the first place. Hence their 'banned' status.) That blatant self-justification tactic is made to look positively impoverished however, in light of what follows it:

> Fringe industries were created in South America, Asia, and Europe, with Italy specialising in scenes of rape, torture and mutilation, many of them played by a small American group of porn performers allegedly funded by the Mafia. In Britain such films were banned or heavily cut...

Whether or not one regards the public accountability of the new BBFC to be something of a façade, or the apparent leniency to be an empty gesture, things undoubtedly are changing. Access to the Internet and the evolution of the DVD format has globalised the film market even further — much to the chagrin of those who wish to control not only their own viewing habits but those of everyone else. Virtually any film can be imported from any country at the click of a button. When *Tenebrae* was re-released on video and DVD recently, the several seconds of footage excised at the behest of the BBFC was made available on the Internet. Consumers could watch the cut print of the film on their TV sets, and later witness on their computer monitor the bloody sight of actress Veronica Lavia getting her arm severed with an axe (but out of any context and streaming in an endless loop). It is this kind of accessibility that brings the censorial capacity of the BBFC one step closer to redundancy, and quantifies reformists like the NVALA as an even more pointless governance.

Shortly before his retirement, James Ferman conceded that with advancements in technology perhaps the future of the BBFC lay as an advisory body, not as governors of what should and shouldn't be seen. As to whether this was a prospect that bothered him much, he replied, "No, I think history moves on and standards change."[48]

Which is where we came in...

APPENDIX I: A MISCELLANY
OF REJECTED VIDEO WORKS, 1990-2000

BARE FIST: THE SPORT THAT WOULDN'T DIE

dir: David Monaghan / Rejected by the BBFC on June 21, 1999

Does this work have the potential for anti-social influence? That's one of the questions BBFC examiners have to ask themselves nowadays whenever a film comes before them. (See SEX & WRECKS.) The Board certainly considered the potential audience for *Bare Fist* a dubious one, that society was at risk as a consequence, and duly banned it.

Monaghan's film focuses upon the outlawed age-old sport of bare-knuckle fighting, and argues that its practice probably poses less health risks than the gloved boxing commonly practised today. The Board claim not to have a problem with the promotion of this belief in itself. However, they regarded a number of lengthy sequences of illegal fighting as unacceptable, as well as some scenes "giving instruction in achieving lethal effects," for example when a bandaged fist is laced with glass fragments. "These have the effect of promoting gross violence and selling its pleasures," the Board decided. "The extent of the use of the illegal fighting sequences also far outstrips any reasonable justification based on the need to make a case for legalisation."

As well as wanting Monaghan to "re-angle" the film so as "not to encourage violence," the BBFC recommended four cuts. These included the shortening of the "illegal fight footage," removal of part of a knife scene, removal of shots of bandaged hands being laced with glass, and the removal of the words "good shot" heard as a nose was broken. Monaghan said he would comply with making the cuts, but regarded them as vague and requested in writing more information. On October 8, 1998, Monaghan visited the BBFC office and was allowed to hear the reports of three examiners concerning his film. However, he wasn't allowed to look at the reports himself or take any notes, and consequently had to deal with the concerns of the Board from memory. (See also APPENDIX IV.)

The list of cuts requested by Monaghan in order to gain a certificate for *Bare Fist* weren't forthcoming, and in June 1999 the film was rejected.

Monaghan subsequently gained access to the examiners' secret reports and claimed not only did they contain "personal insults" against him but also "dishonest claims of pornographic content" about his film. With regard to the last claim, it is worth noting that Robin Duval, director of the BBFC, recently suggested to a journalist for the *Sunday Times* that R18 rated films — of which he is most certainly not fond — contained "sadistic sex." Which they don't, by law.

(There is another film on the BBFC rejected list with the title *Bare Fist: The Sport That Wouldn't Die.* This was refused a certificate on December 23, 1996, also on the grounds that it sold and demonstrated "the pleasures of gross violence." However, the stated director, production company and running time of this work do not correspond with the documentary above.)

BOY MEETS GIRL

dir: Ray Brady / Rejected by the BBFC on September 13, 1995

Boy Meets Girl was passed uncut for cinema release on February 27, 1995, but was refused a certificate for video — their reason being that in the home "scenes of torture and mutilation could lend themselves to viewing out of context by sensation seekers old and young."

Following a pick-up in a night-club, a man returns to the apartment of a young woman. The promise of a "quickie" however is curtailed when the man passes out, his drink having been spiked. He awakens to find himself strapped into a dentist's chair in a darkened basement. The rest of the film is played out in this location, the man completely at the mercy of his "one night stand," plus a shadowy film-maker. To atone for his sins (i.e. infidelity to his wife and homophobia) as well as the savagery of the world in general, the man is tortured before finally he is murdered.

A low-budget independent production, *Boy*

Meets Girl was intended by the film-makers to draw the viewer into the complex issue of "violence and the portrayal of violence" as well as to highlight inconsistencies within BBFC attitudes to violence. The usual roles of aggressor and victim are reversed, along with what is generally perceived to be gender etiquette. For instance, in the opening scenes at the woman's apartment, the man is thrilled that his latest pick-up should offer to play him some porno, but at the same time he's a little uncomfortable that she should openly do so. "Can you identify with the attitudes the male character stands for?" ask the film-makers.

> Are you guilty as he is? He is used and abused by his two dominant female captors, held up as an example of the worst kind of tabloid mentality; he is made to pay for (accepted) social attitudes and behaviour that his captors (and the film makers) believe are wrong.

The victim is sodomised with a dildo, cut with a knife (and perhaps given Aids), refused toilet facilities, and fed excrement. In *Violence and the Censors*, a Channel 4 documentary, a BBFC examiner was heard to say that they couldn't cut or tone down *Boy Meets Girl* because the film was about "torture and captivity and the horror of being in somebody else's power in a sadistic way." Another examiner was less pragmatic and pondered "whether something can be terminally boring and obscene at the same time" — but then considered why they should pass Steven Seagal movies and not *Boy Meets Girl*.

Argue the film-makers: this for once is a film which "has a totally violent subject matter *but does not glamorise it*."

INTERNATIONAL GUERILLAS

dir: Jaan Mohammed / Rejected by the BBFC on July 22, 1990
Passed 18 uncut on August 29, 1990

"If we were to pass this film," an examiner at the BBFC said of *International Guerillas*, "and Rushdie were killed, how would we ever forgive ourselves?"

This three-and-a-half epic made in Pakistan depicted Muslim revenge on the author Salman Rushdie, showing him torturing Muslims by playing tapes of his 'blasphemous' book *The Satanic Verses*, before being struck down by lightning. In July 1990, the BBFC rejected *International Guerillas* on the grounds that it presented a case of criminal libel on a British citizen, Salman Rushdie, and exposed him to public hatred. (Many people pondered that if the film was to be banned, why ban it on the grounds of criminal libel — as opposed to say, incitement to murder — as criminal libel remains, to quote *Media Law*, "an ancient offence that is now unlikely to be invoked against the media by prosecuting authorities: the Law commission has recommended its abolition.") The Board regarded it as one of the most difficult decisions they have had to make, and one of their considerations in refusing a certificate was that other films might follow which urged retribution on specific members of society. The Muslim community argued that double-standards were at work because they considered that Rushdie's book was inflammatory and should be banned. In August, the Video Appeals Committee upheld an appeal against the Board's decision to reject *International Guerillas* and the ban was lifted — no less because Rushdie himself was of the opinion that the film should be in the public domain, and in a statement said:

> ...in spite of the film's clearly abusive content, I do not wish to seek the dubious protection of censorship. Censorship is usually counter-productive, and can actually exacerbate the risks which it seeks to reduce.

LA BLUE GIRL

dir: Raizo Kitakawa

UROTSUKIDOJI IV PART ONE: THE SECRET GARDEN

dir: Not known
Both films rejected by the BBFC on December 30, 1996

Japanese cartoons — Anime or Manga cartoons being the preferred terms — have been around for many years (remember *Marine Boy*?). Only recently however, has the West come to regard these films as constituting anything other than a medium for children. With the huge success of *Akira* and *Urotsukidoji: Legend of the Overfiend* in the early nineties, English speaking audiences gradually began to unearth a wealth of hitherto unknown Anime material. Some of this dealt with adult themes and contained some incredibly brutal imagery — a favourite being monsters that captured and literally fucked their female victims to death. Other Anime elements, such as sadism, incest and a predilection for doe-eyed young-looking characters, also drew on a culture that remains impenetrable to most Westerners. British tabloids labelled all Anime as "snuff cartoons," while a perplexed BBFC (in their Annual Report for 1996-97) said of the most virulent examples:

> It is difficult to fathom where such attitudes come from. Male chauvinism is far too mild a term to describe the film-makers' psychology, since many of these cartoons drag misogyny down to the level of atrocity.

The previous year, while acknowledging the technical brilliance of Anime, the BBFC suggested a likeness with the fascistic fantasies of the Nazis, which sought to destroy "the female principle" and "'filthy softness' of female bodies."

The Board cut eight Manga cartoons in 1996-97 and rejected two more outright — these being *La Blue Girl* and *Urotsukidoji IV Part One: The Secret Garden* — because of their "pornographic treatment of sexual violence." The Board were concerned with many scenes, but primarily those that demonstrated "the art of gang rape as a marital technique," the abuse and physical mutilation of women at the hands of children, monsters with penile tentacles that "subject female captives to multiple penetration," and victims who respond "lasciviously under the influence of an aphrodisiac." The Board considered the overwhelming message to be that "rape is the ultimate source of sexual pleasure." Although some critics — such as Helen McCarthy and Jonathan Clements in *The Erotic Anime Movie Guide* — prefer to read this as "a homage to several popular motifs from Japanese legend, such as the power of the female genitals to subjugate beastly males."

The BBFC makes a "genre allowance" for the fact these films are animation. However, when the content comprises sexual violence or sexualised violence, they make no distinction between animation and live-action. As examiner Imtiaz Karim pointed out in discussing cuts made to the film *Overfiend 4* (in an interview that appeared in *Manga Mania* No 30):

> When you show somebody a scene like this [sustained anal and oral rape, mutilation and much worse in which the woman is crying repeatedly for the demons to stop] there is often very little argument whether we should censor it or not. There may well be an audience which is mature enough to watch this and appreciate and understand the scene in the way the filmmakers intended. But our concern is that this is presented in a very titillating manner which is not appropriate for an audience in their mid-teens. There is no sense of horror or disgust at what the woman is going through; the way it is shot and designed invites the audience to take pleasure from the scene…

SIXTEEN SPECIAL

dir: [not known] / Rejected by the BBFC on November 9, 1990

This sex tape begins with an actress dressed as a schoolgirl and clutching a teddy bear who is trying to fight off the amorous advances of a middle-aged man. Several minutes later she disrobes and discards her uniform. The problem with *Sixteen Special* resided in this opening section. The actress was evidently older than sixteen (apparently she was twenty-one) and therefore the film contained no actual indecent photographs of a child under sixteen which could be prosecutable under the Protection of Children Act 1978. However, it was the attempt to "glamorise and eroticise the seduction of a schoolgirl" that led the BBFC to believe *Sixteen Special* had a clear tendency to deprave and corrupt. The distributor (BPC) agreed that the film served no purpose other than to turn men onto the idea of seducing schoolgirls, but interpreted the root of the problem to be the title of the film and suggested several alternatives — *School Uniform Love*, *Miss Bennison's Older Lover* and *Dirty Ian Gets His Way* — none of which the BBFC "considered an improvement." The Board wanted the opening sequence removed or replaced, suggesting that the film company provide the actress with clothes other than a school uniform. They declined.

"Given the increasing concern in Britain about paedophilia and child sexual abuse," the BBFC said of the film in their Annual Report for 1990, "the Board has accepted the need to exercise the greatest caution in this area."

After *Sixteen Special*, the Board drew up restrictive guidelines concerning the depiction of schoolgirl attire in sex videos. The problem of uniforms was raised again several years later when another film — *Schoolgirl Fantasy* — was submitted and suffered the same fate (rejected on October 5, 1995). In this instance, the story featured two young women "dressed convincingly as schoolgirls" whose consent is systematically eroded over the course of much of the film. The Board concluded that there

> was no doubt in the minds of anyone who saw the video that it would encourage men to fantasise about seducing unwilling, and probably under-age schoolgirls… For viewers, the link between innocent schoolgirls and sexual excitation would almost certainly be reinforced.

The fact that *Schoolgirl Fantasy* was a camcorder sex video also weighed against the film. Camcorder sex — a growing trend in 'reality porn,' filmed in real-time with few edits or cutaways —

was perceived by the BBFC to be "less honest and more sexist than frank hardcore porn," in that it tended to bring "porno values into what purports to be the viewer's own neighbourhood." (The comparison here with "frank hardcore porn" is strange, as the Board would certainly not give a certificate to such material.)

The sexualisation of children arose again in the form of Adrian Lyne's controversial *Lolita*, a film which was passed uncut after the Board sought professional advice (see SEX & WRECKS). However, on March 27, 2000, the Board rejected two outtakes that were intended as bonus material for the DVD release of the film. 'The Comic Book' (2m 27s) and 'The Lake Point Cottages' (3m 41s) were both said to be "highly sexually charged," showing "images of sexual nudity and behaviour which were not present in the feature version and which are made even more problematic when presented in isolation or out of context as here." Had either scene been present in *Lolita*, the film would not have been passed.

VISIONS OF ECSTASY

dir: Nigel Wingrove / Rejected by the BBFC September 18, 1989

Incorporating self-inflicted wounds, lesbian encounters, and a climb up the cross to wrap herself around the figure of Christ — the rapture experienced by St Teresa of Avila, a sixteenth-century Carmelite nun, is interpreted in this film literally. St Teresa spends the film's eighteen minutes duration in sexual longing for the physical, crucified body of Christ. After seeking legal advice, the BBFC rejected *Visions of Ecstasy* in September 1989 on the grounds that it was "contemptuous of the divinity of Christ" — in other words, they considered it liable to prosecution for blasphemy (which well it could be: after publishing a poem in 1976 recounting a Roman's imagined homosexual acts on the crucified Christ, *Gay News* and its editor were successfully prosecuted for producing a blasphemous libel). The director of *Visions of Ecstasy*, Nigel Wingrove, argued that his film was not intended as a depiction of St Teresa partaking in any actual "overt sexual act," but was instead a fantasy projection of the nun's mind.

Martin Scorsese's *The Last Temptation of Christ* was also drawn into this argument as it had been passed for video release the previous year. This film also featured a fantasy sequence which many Christians regarded as blasphemous. The Board was of the opinion however, that Scorsese made it very clear "that the illusion was subjective" (Christ leaves the cross but nobody watching notices). Wingrove in *Visions of Ecstasy* on the other hand, didn't indicate

> that the human figure of Christ on the cross was a fantasy on the part of St Teresa, the fantasy in this case being the total film, and since this was a sex fantasy, and treated as such, it was bound to risk causing offence if the sexual elements were too blatant.

No doubt also influential in the matter was the fact that James Ferman holds Scorsese in the highest regard. When the matter of blasphemy was raised at a censorship debate at the ICA in November 1998, Ferman said that *Visions of Ecstasy* was "not on the same plane" as *Last Temptation of Christ*, and when someone remarked that Scorsese was a "decent" filmmaker, the director of the Board snapped back with uncharacteristic ire, "Decent?! He's a *great* director!"

Wingrove took *Visions of Ecstasy* to the Video Appeals Committee who upheld the ban. He then went to the European Court of Human Rights — the first time in the BBFC's eighty-four year history that anyone had challenged a decision of theirs in the courts. However, when finally the Strasbourg court returned its verdict in November 1996 it was in support of the BBFC and the ban was upheld, effectively sounding the death knell for the film in Britain.

Wingrove got the inspiration for *Visions of Ecstasy* in an ecstatic swoon, when he stood before Benini's statue of St Teresa in Rome. "The celestial orgasm is a matter of fact, not fiction," he said.

Even the tabloids seemed divided on the dredging up of a law as archaic and ancient as blasphemy: In an article entitled "Blasphemy or freedom?," *The Mail on Sunday* offered some rather half-hearted outrage, directed as much at Euro-judges as the film itself. On the other hand, while he did not mock the religious beliefs of others, Chris Peachment of *The Express* suggested that

> if your religious belief happens to be made weaker by the viewing of a rather silly video, then I would suggest that your personal faith is shaky. Rather than ban the film, would it not be better to examine your faith in the light of an argument against it...?

Wingrove may well be the man most rejected by the BBFC! As well as his own *Visions of Ecstasy*, cult European movies submitted through his company Salvation Films have also been ensnared by the Board. These include Osvaldo de Oliveira's *Bare Behind Bars* (rejected on September 20, 1994) and Jess Franco's *Demoniac* and *Sadomania* (rejected on August 10 and September 21, 1994).

APPENDIX II: INTERVIEWS
WITH TWO INDEPENDENT VIDEO DISTRIBUTORS

SCREEN EDGE

INTERVIEW WITH RICHARD KING, CO-FOUNDER AND COMPANY DIRECTOR

The Screen Edge catalogue comprises many contemporary low-budget independent films, including *Addicted To Murder* (d: Kevin Lindenmuth), *The Dead Next Door* (d: J R Bookwalter), *Der Todesking* (d: Jörg Buttgereit), *Pervirella* (d: Alex Chandon & Josh Collins), *Shatter Dead* (d: Scooter McCrae) and *Transgression* (d: Michael Dipaolo).

The following interview was conducted in November 1998, at a time when *Original Sins* (d: Howard Berger & Matthew Howe) was raising one problem after another for Screen Edge.

What effect do you think the recent shake-up at the BBFC will have on Screen Edge?

RICHARD KING: I can't see it getting any better, really. Especially since they are aware that their role is getting more and more ludicrous, with the advent of digital television and communications technology in general. What role can they actually play? Basically, it's one of the biggest and most successful scams of the last hundred years, isn't it?

You've had a lot of problems with Original Sins. When did you first submit that?

It was two and a half years ago — getting on for three years now.

And they came back to you with a list of initial objections...

Yeah, we did cut some scenes... We sent the cuts list to [co-director] Howard Berger and he told us what he didn't mind going and what he wanted us to try and save. So we made cuts and sent it back to the BBFC. But even then they said the cuts hadn't been done at one stage, because we'd put black bands across some images as opposed to taking them out altogether — obscuring blood-on-breasts which they had objected to — and so we had to re-cut it again to satisfy them that we'd done the cuts.

The version that eventually does come out, will that be missing the black bands?

Who knows? Hopefully we can keep the black bands in. We don't know the new cuts. I daresay it won't make any sense at all by the time we release it — it's a shame, you know. One of the scenes has a guy spewing up his own spine. We had to cut that down by a considerable amount. And there's a scene where the devil emerges from a *papier-mâché* vagina — we had to cut that out. It's obviously a papier-mâché model, and the devil's got his arse painted bright red for Christ's sake! They didn't even know it was comedy. Because none of them found it funny they didn't consider it a comedy. They couldn't understand it at all.

Did you have any trouble with the sleeve to Original Sins?

The BBFC haven't even looked at that yet — that's the next hurdle!

You mentioned that one of the issues brought up with regard to Original Sins was the fact that, quite out of the blue the BBFC decided the girls in it were under-age.

Yeah. That was one of the main reasons — under-age girls. But nowhere is it suggested in the whole film that they're under-age. The BBFC came back to us with that claim after they'd had the film for a number of months... and after we'd made cuts to it at their request.

So, do you think they were trying to railroad you into not releasing it?

It was during all the debate with *Crash*, with David Alton, and the moral majority, when all that sort of thing was going on. And I think there was a lot of hysteria, so James Ferman thought the best thing was to sit on it. He phoned me and explained all this and I wrote a letter of appeal, but it never got any further. So I got the impression that he was waiting till all the furore over *Crash* and various things have subsided.

And of course it's all expense to you, isn't it?
Yes. We have to pay the initial submission fee. Then there are various other charges on top of that, such as the black title card that they give you — it's £27 for a piece of black cardboard. That's gone up actually. If you put a film in that has been released previously, you have to pay for it to be watched again — to make sure it's the certified cut.

And if the BBFC do request cuts...
We have to pay somebody to do them. Basically the BBFC gives you the timecode reference, and we have to pay someone to make the cuts. Which is another big expense.

Do you ever predetermine what the BBFC might think is offensive?
We try, but it's impossible to tell really. I mean, we never cut anything before we submit it, because if we'd done that with say, *Addicted To Murder*, we'd have cut out the chainsaw scene — yet that got through completely uncut. Same with *Dead Next Door* — we'd have cut certain things from that if we'd been trying to pre-empt the BBFC. It's basically a good day/bad day scenario with them, I think.

How do you think the BBFC perceives Screen Edge?
Probably find us amusing, patronising us with a pat on the back... Relatively speaking we've had a good relationship. We get on with them because we know that it's something we have to deal with, and we can't afford to kick up a fuss. The BBFC have not actually rejected anything we've put to them. But we've had to go with the flow. In the case of *Transgression* we actually ended up with two completely different versions of the film. It was re-cut following the BBFC's initial examination and list of cuts required. We did it here in the Screen Edge office. Michael Dipaolo, the director, sent us extra footage from his cutting room floor, which we inserted over the offending scenes. He looked at the cuts list, did a re-cut in the States, and then sent us all the extra footage so we could re-cut it according to his directions.
Ironically, when he sent the Beta master with all the inserts that we had to replace, the Customs seized it and refused to let us have it. The Customs guy who phoned us up was called Officer Dibble! We had to get James Ferman to phone him back and explain the situation. Half an hour later, Customs let it through. Ferman actually phoned up Customs to say we were re-cutting the film. When we finally resubmitted *Transgression* he said, "Well done, it's a much better film."

You also had Customs trouble with Shatter Dead...?
With *Shatter Dead*, Customs seized the tape and destroyed it, along with all literature that was with it, such as biographies and stuff. Customs said I could travel to London and watch the tape under controlled circumstances — padded cell or Mogadon, perhaps? But by this time, another copy was already on its way so I passed on that little pleasure. Customs weren't interested in the slightest that I was running a legitimate company. But for a while thereafter, I managed to get stuff through via a sympathetic officer who trusted me to have the films on the condition that I sent them back when I'd finished, and showed them to no one else, not even copy them... I guaranteed this in writing. After a few months however, all of this was stopped. I was told that the officer had no right to make such an arrangement in the first place — and they were pretty pissed off with me, too! After that everything coming through Customs got opened.
Strangest of all for me though, was that Customs were more concerned with the 'shotgun abortion' sequence in *Shatter Dead* than with the 'gun fuck' sequence — which was ultimately cut by the BBFC. Customs seemed to regard the latter as far more offensive, and strictly against their secret little rules. In other words, they were upset by a plastic baby doll and some raspberry syrup — which is what the scene comprises of — as opposed to the use of a deadly weapon as a sex toy!
Like many other people, I spent a lot of time writing letters to various places about the ludicrous inconsistencies between Customs and the BBFC. I was told by Customs that I was virtually breaking the law by even submitting uncut films to the BBFC, as this was tantamount to distribution of obscene material! I wrote to the Home Office, but got no reply.

[Original Sins was passed 18 in February 1999 with 6m 14s of cuts; Richard King no longer works in the video business, with "no real desire to ever do so again."]

EXPLOITED

INTERVIEW WITH CARL DAFT, COMPANY DIRECTOR

A relatively new force in independent video distribution, Exploited have already released some notable cult titles, including *Dead of Night* (d: Bob Clark), *Deranged* (d: Alan Ormsby & Jeff Gillen), *Hated* (d: Todd Phillips) and *Axe* (d: Frederick R Friedel). Many of their tapes include bonus documentary material. One recent release has been an exclusive documentary entitled *The Texas Chain Saw Massacre: The Shocking Truth* (d: David Gregory). To date the company has had two films rejected by the BBFC: *Maniac* (d: William Lustig) and *Deadbeat at Dawn* (d: Jim VanBebber).

The following interview was conducted in May 2000.

You used to submit your video sleeves for the Video Packaging Review Committee (VPRC) seal of approval. You've stopped doing that, now. Why?

CARL DAFT: Essentially the VPRC are supposed to be independent from the BBFC, and they look at packaging to deem whether it's suitable to be out there on the video shelves. In actual fact they're not separate from the BBFC at all. When we write out the cheques, it is to the "BBFC (VPRC)". But unlike the BBFC classification service itself, the service of the VPRC is voluntary and after the problems we'd had with them over some sleeves we decided that we would elect not to use it anymore, and were within our rights to do that.

What benefits are there in submitting packaging to the VPRC in the first place?

When you first start submitting films to the BBFC, they won't release a certificate until the sleeve has been approved by the VPRC. But you're perfectly entitled to write a letter stating that you don't want to use the VPRC, and they will still release the certificate. The majority of people use it. We wouldn't have known at the start that we had a choice, but once we were aware...

If it's in writing that your sleeve won't be going through the VPRC, then your film certificate is released at the time that you get your interim clearance form.

Is the VPRC an expensive process?

It's too expensive, yeah. They charge, I think, £35 + VAT just to have a look at the packaging. It must take all of one minute. The reason we stopped comes down to the problem we had with the *Three on a Meathook* sleeve... when we first submitted it they said we should remove the gory picture of the woman hanging on a meathook on the back. Reluctantly we did so, replaced it with a far less offensive image, and resubmitted it. By the way, you have to pay again when you resubmit material to the VPRC. They looked at the sleeve again and said that the picture on the back was fine, but now they wanted to change the picture on the front – and this was exactly the same picture that was on the front the first time we submitted the sleeve. There was a lack of consistency going on here. We phoned them up and asked how the picture on the front could be OK last week, but not OK this week. Their answer to that was that different examiners sit on different weeks. The BBFC claim to be objective about things! It just shows that it is a subjective thing – who's seeing what and how they feel on the day.

Moving on to Axe/California Axe Massacre... because this film was originally on the DPP list, you had to provide a different version in order to get it released?

Yeah, and this is not actually a law or a stipulation contained anywhere in the Video Recordings Act – it actually boils down to BBFC guidelines and the codes of practice that they use. It's basically just to cover themselves and show that they're doing the right thing, so they don't get themselves in trouble with the DPP by releasing material that was once liable for prosecution. But something relatively innocuous like *Axe* gets bundled in with a load of other titles from some obscure prosecution way back in the eighties, and it's just blanketed in the same category as more controversial films like *Cannibal Holocaust* and *Snuff*. Anything that was prosecuted was all tarred with the same brush. So, if there's a record of a film actually having a successful prosecution, I suppose the BBFC have to show they are releasing a version that is different from the version that was originally prosecuted.

So, who suggested the different version? You made nineteen seconds of cuts...

It was suggested by the principal examiner, Mike Bor. As anyone who has seen the film knows, there is very little in it to cause offence. But it had been on the DPP list, and so in spite of the fact that nobody had a problem with the film, it had to now be a different version if we wanted to re-release it. Reluctantly we undertook some cuts, even though the BBFC itself didn't really deem them necessary. In other words they were just following the letter of their code and regulations, rather than what appeared to be practical and sensible.

One scene in Axe has been slowed down slightly, which I understand was also to make it a different film to the one that was originally on the DPP list.

We did something similar to that in *Hated* — the film about the shock-rocker G G Allin — in which the BBFC requested six to eight cuts. What we did to try and get around those and to keep the film as much intact as possible, was just to pan and scan on some of the images. For instance, the scene where Allin squats down on stage and defecates (as the Board so nicely put it in their letter), rather than cut the whole scene as they asked, we panned it so you don't actually see the offensive slop leave his backside even though it remains patently obvious what he's doing. We did the same thing when he had the prostitute urinating in his mouth for his birthday. We didn't cut the whole scene as they asked, we just panned away. There were no scenes that we actually cut out of that film *per se*. We got round it the best we could, being rather cheeky with it.

Evidently the Board were quite happy with that?

Strangely enough, yes. I mean, we took the risk with it and we got away with it. We tried to do the same with *My Sweet Satan* when they asked for basically the whole climax to the movie to be cut. Removing it takes away a lot of the impact, a lot of the emphasis and a lot of the point of the film. We tried the same sort of cheap thing on that, panning over a few images instead of making the eighteen seconds of cuts requested. Half we panned and half we cut. We re-submitted *My Sweet Satan* in two different versions, and told the BBFC over the phone that one version had the whole eighteen seconds cut out as per their request, while the other version, we believed, removed most of the offensive material without actually making cuts. We'd agreed with the examiners that we'd send these two prints in, but when they received them they asked why we'd sent in two different copies. Basically they completely ignored the second cut that we'd done, and went ahead with the butchered print.

They don't like being told what to do?

No, they don't. What they say goes. Which is why it's quite a result that we got away with *Hated* in the form that we did. Had we been made to cut everything exactly as their request, it would have greatly lessened the impact of the movie.

Deranged is a film that has only ever seen a theatrical release in Britain before. Did you have any problems with the video, because again that is quite a strong film?

It is quite a strong film. I think the BBFC weren't as harsh on that as they could easily have been, probably seeing that it was a well-made film and that it did have artistic points to it. They requested about a half dozen cuts in the end of only a second here and there.

You had intended to release Snuff at one point. I take it that's no longer going ahead?

It's very much on the back-burner, shall we say. We did contact the BBFC about the fact we were looking into the idea of picking up *Snuff*. Obviously at this point we were quite upset at *Deadbeat at Dawn* having been rejected — it had cost a lot of money, and had basically put the company in a lot of trouble. We'd only been trading for three months and it was a huge setback for us. We didn't have any releases after that until the following September, so essentially we lost ten months of trading. *Snuff* was a title we knew we could get the rights for if we wanted, and it was something that we'd looked at. We heard through someone in the BBFC that we know, that the very mention of *Snuff* caused a panic there. Robin Duval had a copy fetched up from the vaults especially to watch it, knowing that we were intending to submit it. Anyone who's seen the film knows that it's just a cheap movie that had this ending tagged on — pure exploitation, but not a snuff film. What we wanted to do was put it into a serious context where we could make a documentary about the legend, or the myth if you like, of snuff films. The BBFC are great ones for context; they like to look at everything in context. Hence situations like *Three on a Meathook*, where the film got through completely uncut but the trailer had to have seven or eight cuts to it, even though it contained nothing that wasn't in the film. That's the context for you. So, we told the BBFC that we'd put *Snuff* into context, that we would take the film seriously and not exploit it, and they wrote back to us saying that whether we put a documentary on the tape or not, it wouldn't alter the fact that *Snuff* was not the sort of film that was suitable for British viewing. I think those were their exact words.

Do you think that the documentaries you include on many of your releases have helped get some of the more contentious films through the Board?

I don't think so. With the market that we're in, obviously we're going to be very borderline on what does get through and what doesn't. That makes it difficult for us to plan ahead. But the special bonus footage that we put on the back of *Deranged* (*The Making of Deranged*) and on *Lemora* (*The Confessions of Lemora*), I don't think helped in any way to get the films themselves through the BBFC net. They do add something extra for the collector, however, and that's what we've always tried to do at Exploited — make things as collectable as possible and give as much value as possible, and that certainly helps in the cases where we unfortunately have to cut the films. Some films are cut so we try to add something on there to make up for that fact.

How do you think that the BBFC view Exploited?

I think they don't like us! I think they are always wary of what we're going to be doing and will keep a special lookout for whatever we send in to them. The whole thing boils down to a subjective matter; the BBFC will look at things subjectively and if it is an Exploited title or a Screen Edge title then they will look at it from that point of view. We could talk for days about the subjectivity of the examiners as well. When James Ferman left the BBFC *The Texas Chain Saw Massacre* and *The Exorcist* were suddenly deemed OK for public viewing when they hadn't been for the past twenty-five years. Is the passing of a great man like Ferman making everyone more morally aware in the country? Plus there are his great quotes as well. At the National Film Theatre at the back end of the screening of *The Texas Chain Saw Massacre* — we actually include this in our documentary *The Shocking Truth* — Ferman says that the film probably won't get a certificate in this country. It was fine playing for middle class intellectual audiences at the NFT, he said, but imagine the effect it might have on the average car worker in Birmingham. I think that sums it up really. It's the middle class conservative Christians looking out for the moral good of country. Surely that's not the way to do it?

APPENDIX III: FBI REPORT

CONCERNING THE PREMIERE OF THE FILM SNUFF IN INDIANAPOLIS

United States Department of Justice
Federal Bureau of Investigation
Indianapolis, Indiana

January 22, 1976

"SNUFF MOVIE"

Following investigation was conducted by Special Agents of the Federal Bureau of Investigation at Indianapolis, Indiana:

During mid-December, 1975, WIBC, a local Indianapolis AM radio station, telephonically interviewed one —— — Monarch Releasing Corporation, New York, concerning captioned movie. These interviews, which were aired publicly on WIBC, disclosed that Indianapolis had been selected as the site for the world premiere of captioned movie since, according to ——— a "valid test" can be made because "Indianapolis is in my opinion a typical city in the United States... with this particular type of film it will be a valid test because there is the right kind of mixture of people in Indianapolis to test the playability of this film." ——— went on to state that he knew whether or nor the murder depicted in the film was actual but that, for legal reasons, he could not say whether or not it was real.

The movie was initially scheduled to premiere at the Uptown Theatre, 4215 North College Avenue, Indianapolis, on January 14, 1976, but was subsequently postponed until January 16, 1976.

Previous investigation conducted by the FBI regarding the Uptown Theatre in an unrelated case revealed that the theatre is owned and operated by Tudor Amusement Company which in turn is owned by the Cosby Corporation, Indianapolis...

It should be noted that the disclaimer, "This is a theatrical production, no one was harmed or injured during filming," was the result of a meeting held between —— — and ——— Marion County, Indiana ———. It is further noted the a representative of the Marion County Prosecutor's Office advised that captioned movie did not constitute a violation falling within the jurisdiction of that office.

On January 16, 1976, FBI Agents, accompanied by an MD-Pathologist, attended the first showing of "Snuff" at the Uptown Theatre. Admission price was $7.50 each and the following observations were noted:

The film was in color and the beginning showed only the title, "Snuff" in capital letters which then turned red and disappeared in a dripping motion to simulate blood. No credits were listed nor were the identities of any actors or actresses reflected. The opening scene depicted a female sitting next to an abandoned railway box car snuffing cocaine. Her female associates caught her in this act and, believing that she has "held out" drugs, proceed to shoot and torture her by cutting her feet with a large knife.

The movie was approximately one and one-half hours in length and , with the exception of the final three or four minutes, English was dubbed in over, apparently, Spanish conversation.

The major portion of the movie generally consisted of a portrayal of sadism during which a male individual known as SATAN (phonetic) and a tribe of female followers travel around the countryside of, apparently, a South American country via motorcycle wantonly killing and torturing various individuals. The fifteen to twenty "murders" committed by SATAN and his tribe are obviously fake. During the sequence of these killings, there were allusions to practically every type of sexual perversion, including sodomy, beastiality and lesbianism. However, no actual scenes occurred which depict sexual intercourse or any of the above sexual aberrations. After setting the scenario for such activities, the camera always focused on the facial expression of the victims or on some inanimate object. In fact, at no time did the movie show the genitals and, on only one occasion, was pubic hair shown. Nudity was depicted only from the waist up. Some scenes were filmed at a modern airport and a Lan Chile airliner was observed in the background.

The last scene of the movie was approximately four minutes in duration and consisted of a second film crew photographing the first film crew following the last murder committed by SATAN's followers. However, with regard to this "add on" segment, English was spoken directly by the film crew turned actors. The scenery in this "add on" segment was not compatible with the scenery in the preceding final murder scene but it was an apparent attempt to recreate the preceding scene.

In the final scene, a white male member of the film crew, who is attired in slacks and a tee-shirt bearing Spanish wording on the front, approaches female member of the film crew and states to the effect, "You know that last gory scene really turned me on." He made amorous advances to the female and, pulling a knife, threw her on a bed. She then exclaimed to the effect, "They're filming this. You're not kidding, are you?" The camera then focused on her terror stricken face as the male individual straddled her with knife in hand. Both of these individuals remain fully clothed, and the female was attired in long sleeved blouse and slacks. The other members of the alleged film crew proceed to restrain the female with arms outstretched on the bed.

Next, the male proceeds to slash the female, through her blouse, on her left shoulder. What appears to be blood immediately appeared and, thereafter, a pair of wire or bolt cutters were utilized to amputate two fingers of the female's left hand. What appeared to be blood flowed from the stubs. Thereafter, the male individual used a power saw, possibly a circular or saber saw, to amputate the female's left hand at the wrist adjacent to the sleeve of her blouse. Blood spilled from her arm but did not appear to be the arterial type of bleeding. At this point, the camera focused on the dismembered, quivering hand lying on the sheet.

Thereupon, the male individual, straddling the female's legs, proceeds to stab her, through her clothing, at approximately navel level with a sweeping motion so as to open the abdominal cavity. The male individual then thrusts his hands into the cavity and extracts what, according to the accompanying pathologist, appeared to be a heart. He continued to explore the abdominal cavity and extracted what appeared to be the large intestine. The final scene depicted the male individual holding this intestine outstretched between his hands.

At this point the audio portion of the movie continued but the screen remained blank. An individual then stated to the effect, "We're out of film," to which another alleged film crew member stated to the effect, "Did you get all of that?" Another voice then stated, "Let's get out of here." At this point the movie abruptly ended.

The above "murder victim" appeared to be a white female American, approximately 18 to 22 years old, 5'6" in height, slender build, with light brown hair.

The "murderer" appeared to be a white male, 6'1", 185 pounds, dark complexion, with dark hair and mustache.

The "film crew" photographer in the final scene consisted of five or six other individuals, one of whom was a Negro female, approximately 25 years of age, who was clad in black leotards.

It is noted that, in addition to the two FBI Agents and the accompanying doctor, only approximately nine other individuals were present, including at least two local vice officers.

Subsequent to viewing the movie, the MD-Pathologist who accompanied the Agents in viewing same, advised that he doubted that an actual murder was committed during the last three or four minutes of the movie and cited the following points to substantiate that the murder was a staged theatrical production:

(1) When the alleged victim's left hand was amputated, there was no spurting of arterial blood as would be present if the radial and ulnar arteries had in fact been severed.

(2) The body organ extracted from the abdominal cavity of the victim appeared to be a heart. However, the extraction of a heart from an abdominal incision could not have been performed with the ease experienced by the alleged murderer.

(3) The heart removed from the "victim" was in too good condition for one that had been "pulled out," noting that the actual removal of a human heart has to be performed by cutting the many and various tissues and vessels that hold it in place. Furthermore, the heart in the movie appears to be too small for that of a normal adult and the heart depicted in the movie may have been from an animal.

On January 19, 1976, the facts of this matter were presented to First Assistant United States Attorney John E Hirschman, Indianapolis, who stated that he would decline prosecution since the matter lacked prosecutive merit, particularly in view of the absence of any hard core pornography and since there were no indications of any other Federal violations.

APPENDIX IV: BARE FIST: THE SPORT THAT WOULDN'T DIE

was rejected by the BBFC on June 21, 1999. Here follow letters which David Monaghan, the writer and director of the documentary, sent to the BBFC prior to that decision being formally reached

[These letters are presented as originally written, without editing — unless noted otherwise — or grammatical correction.]

September 22, 1998

Andreas Whittam Smith
President
British Board of Film Classification
3 Soho Square
London W1V 6HD

Re: Formal complaint of inequity in classification decisions, passing of Lenny Mclean's Lock Stock & Two Smoking Barrels banning of Lenny McLean documentary Bare Fist

Dear Mr Andreas Whittam Smith,
I make a formal complaint about the board's policy, specifically the decision to pass the Lenny McLean's film Lock, Stock & Two Smoking Barrels while continuing to ban the British public from seeing Lenny McLean's documentary Bare Fist: the Sport That Wouldn't Die.
These decisions breach the all three of the board "Principles of Classification Policy" as outlined on page 2 of Appendix I, 1997/98 BBFC Annual Report.
These Principles state that the principle the board follow must be:

• ***reasonable.***
It is not reasonable to ban a documentary examining violence, and condemning it, while passing murder done on screen for entertainment and for laughter.

• ***consistent with the broad intentions of Parliament.***
Parliament passed no law allowing harsher censorship of documentary films. These decisions show a system of extreme inequity of application of parliamentary law. Parliamentary law allows films to be banned to "reduce harm to individuals, or through their actions, society". The BBFC has ignored scientific studies showing ritualised bare knuckle boxing has the capacity to reduce violence in societies, and that it's long term effects on individuals are akin to, or safer than, the legal sport of gloved boxing. The BBFC ban will not reduce harm to society, but contribute to harm.

• ***in line with the Freedom of Expression provisions of the European Convention of Human Rights.***
The board is aware that the documentary written by me is a means of my freedom of expression as defined under the Convention. Further, the film contains interviews with Gypsy men and leaders, who believe is it their right under the Convention to freely express their opinion, and the evidence, about their traditional sport of bare knuckle boxing. The BBFC has ignored this principle and breached freedoms with this ban.

I make formal complaint about the breach of the BBFC own principles in the banning of Bare Fist: The Sport That Wouldn't Die.
Below I detail the further evidence of the iniquitous, unfair, and unprincipled behaviour of the board, by comparison of the Lock, Stock & Two Smoking Barrels certification and the Bare Fist ban.

Reasons given to the director why Mr Lenny McLean must be banned in films to be seen by the British public.
In a meeting at the BBFC in summer, 1997, Mr James Ferman, the boxing documentary Bare Fist had to be banned because it featured a "violent icon", Mr Lenny McLean, a former bare knuckle boxing champion. Mr Ferman said Mr McLean could become role model to young people. The board had a duty to stop the "drip, drip" of violence, so the boxing documentary featuring Mr McLean must be banned.
Mr Ferman also specifically instructed me to cut out part of the documentary he didn't like. These were Mr McLean's satirical commentary on one of the boxing match shown in Bare Fist. Mr Ferman said the BBFC had a rule that "you were allowed to laugh at violence" and that the phrase "nut him" used by Mr McLean was an encouragement to violence.
I followed faithfully the instructions of the censor Mr James Ferman, and cut out Lenny McLean taking the piss

out of two gypsy men having a boxing match. I did so in order that my film be given a certificate. I was incurring crippling losses on my investigative documentary making business, because of the ban on the film made by Mr Ferman on December 23, 1996, and the de-facto ban of the film since March 15, 1998.

How the BBFC's Decision is An Attempt to Crush Documentary Making, but Encourage Gun Killing Films for Entertainment.

The board has certified '18' the McLean movie Lock Stock and Two Smoking Barrels, while banning the documentary, Bare Fist.

Mr James Ferman banned the documentary featuring Mr Lenny McLean, which was written and directed by me. But very different treatment was given to another director who had made a film where Mr McLean was a funnyman, a murderer, and a torturer.

As a professional film maker, I am hurt and astonished by unreasonable treatment given to me by the board. I have been lied to and deceived, after making a difficult investigative documentary in good faith.

I am not a pop video maker using gang murders to get laughs.

I am a journalist and investigative documentary maker attempting to reveal the truth about British society.

The decision shows the government censor is trying to crush journalists from making documentary investigation, but encouraged pop video makers to make gun violence as entertainment. This is how BBFC principles are applied:

Mr James Ferman banned my documentary, which has Mr McLean warning against violence. Mr James Ferman passed the film where Mr McLean is forced to act as a gun-wielding torturer and murderer.

The British public is banned from seeing Mr McLean tell the history of boxing.

Mr Ferman allows the public to see Mr McLean kill and torture two men, by the imitable techniques of drowning in a barrel and throwing a hatchet into a man's back.

Mr Ferman allows Mr McLean to explain how to conduct torture in this Hollywood- style feature Lock Stock & Two Smoking Barrels but bans him from explaining the tragedy of punch drunk syndrome in the documentary Bare Fist.

Mr Ferman allows a handsome young heroes of Lock Stock & Two Smoking Barrels to boast that "knives are for pros". Mr Ferman bans Mr McLean from warning viewers that "knives are for cowards" in the documentary Bare Fist.

The biography of Mr Lenny McLean's has been the best selling book in Britain for four weeks. The book documents the world of bare fist boxing.

The BBFC has banned this sport from being examined in the documentary Bare Fist. The British public want to know about sporting men forced into illegality by a bizarre law, the prize fighting prohibition. But the public is banned from being educated about this matter by the BBFC, and instead served up with a film such as Lock Stock and Two Smoking Barrels which shows how rewards are reaped from gun murder.

To ban a British documentary that examines the history and causes of violent sporting death, while encouraging another British film to show gun and knife murder as entertainment, is more than hypocrisy.

Mr James Ferman stood up at a public meeting in July 1998, and said that the BBFC did not hold different standards of censorship for documentary films or for feature films. He had to say so, as it would be illegal under the act for the board to apply different censorship standards.

The passing of the far more brutal Smoking Barrels, while banning the documentary Bare Fist, shows that either Mr Ferman lied at that public meeting, or there is a policy in the BBFC that suppresses serious consideration of social issues, such as sporting violence, in favour of making gun violence a matter to be laughed at.

I would hope that the BBFC will begin to follow it's own principles and end it's policy of suppression of documentary films on video. I would suggest that the improper favouritism shown to gun weilding feature films end, and proper consideration be given to thoughtful documentary making.

Regards

David Monaghan
Writer & director
Bare Fist: The Sport That Wouldn't Die

November 23, 1998

Andreas Whittam Smith
President
British Board of Film Classification
3 Soho Square
London W1V 6HD

Re: The banned documentary Bare Fist

Dear Mr Whittam Smith,

Thank you for your letter of November 4. I have followed your suggestion and on November 9 asked for Mr Ferman to provide to me a cut list in writing. It has been two weeks and I have had no reply.

I had attended the meeting at your offices on October 8 because of your specific promise that there was a wish

by the board to assist me in gaining a certificate.
I informed you in writing on September 14 I would not attend such a meeting if you had no intention of issuing a certificate to my sports documentary.
I asked you to ban my film immediately so I might go to the Home Office Appeals Committee, rather than attend a pre-emptive meeting that merely told me why my film was to be banned.
I trust you will honour your promise under which I attended your meeting of October 8, and assist me in gaining a certificate for the documentary Bare Fist.

1) What I will do the change the documentary.
I would draw your attention to page 3 of the BBFC Draft Code of Practice of February 1997: "when there is a choice between banning and video and requiring cuts, the Board will always attempts cuts".
The cuts I am willing to make to Bare Fist are:

Cut 1: a further 2 minutes and 14 second from the "illegal fight footage".
Cut 2: The words "good shot" that comes prior to a nose being broken.
Cut 3: Part of the knife scene, if it is put in writing what part of this scene is breaches the Act.
Cut 4: Part of the fist & glass scene, if it is put in writing what part of this scene breaches the Act.

Below is detail from a letter to James Ferman sent on October 3. Mr Ferman had kindly told me on the telephone he felt the film could be passed if three elements were cut. I asked the Director to write to me listing those cuts to prevent confusion. Again, Mr Ferman has not written to me to tell me why my film has broken any law. This is what I wrote to Mr Ferman:

a) Cut of fight scene
I am presuming you are saying you want the boxing to 11 minutes, i.e. 2 minutes 41s cut. Please tell me if this is correct.
As discussed the "boxing" is that described as "illegal fight footage", what you incorrectly call "street fights". The fighting does not include the credits, the international fights shots (kung fu, Thai boxing, vale tudo), the Hollywood fights nor the McLean gloved match as broadcast on TV. Even with this extremely wide definition of "fighting" there is still well under 21 minutes of "fighting" in the documentary.

b) Cut of knife scene.
I list below the three cuts which include the knife. Which is the "glistening blade shot you want cut?

28.08 **First knife shot** Mclean hold's knife, v/o Geoff Thompson criticises weapons culture as problem, not bare fist culture
28.39 **2nd knife shot** - Lennie eyes knife. "This is real violence, I've seen men cut...this is filth.
29.05-29.09 **3rd knife shot** - knife thrown in puddle.

To tell you the truth, I think this is a bizarre and ridiculous cut — McLean is holding a serrated-edge bread knife, not an illegal combat knife, and is warning people against using knives. For you to cut that scene, and have certified the "Smoking Barrels" knife scene where these weapons are laughed at, while someone encourages their use, is an hypocrisy. Your suggestions of this cuts just smacks of your harassment of documentary makers as compared to violent comedy makers.

c) Cut of glass on fist
You want the scene with the "glass on the fist" cut out.
There is no shot of glass on a fist. This is the shot sequence:

43.00 glass is broken by hammer & put in tub, where glass is unseen
43.16 hand is wrapped in bandage
43.22 glue is put on bandaged hand
43.22 hand is dipped in tub, where glass is unseen.

Please tell me which of those elements you want cut, and tell me why.

2) Changes to the documentary Bare Fist
I want an adult certificate for my documentary Bare Fist.
I thank you for your assistance on October 8 in allowing me to hear the reports of three examiners during a visit to the BBFC office. Since I was forbidden to actually look at or take copies of those reports, they have been of no use in trying to work out what the board is claiming is illegal about my documentary.
However, I will deal with issues raised at the meeting. The content of the examiners reports raise serious matters about the propriety of the classification process of my film.

2.1 The Angle of the Film
The BBFC has delayed the issuing of a certificate to "Bare Fist" for so long that Lennie McLean, presenter of the documentary, is dead.
I have considered carefully your closing advice of October 8 that the documentary need "re-angling" in order that it "not to encourage violence". I cannot "re-angle" my film because:

a) You won't say it
No one from the Board will put in writing to me what

parts of my film break which laws in what ways. It is clear to me the documentary is legal. Changing the "angle" of the film would be unlawful political censorship as there is nothing illegal about current "angle" of the film anyway.

b) I can't do it.

Presenter Lennie McLean, the authorial voice of the documentary who gives the angle, is now dead.

c) I have already done it

The documentary does not encourage violence in any manner whatsoever that breaches the law. Large sections of commentary have already been removed under protest from this historical sports documentary.

d) I won't do it

I will not be politically censored by the government. The key revelation of the my film is evidence of the lethal nature of boxing gloves, and the evidence of the true nature of the original form of the sport, bare knuckle boxing. I believe the British public have the right to judge this evidence for themselves.

I, the Gypsy men and sportsmen in this film have a right to freedom of expression in any medium given to us by the United Nations Convention of Human Rights in 1948. I have been denied a certificate I am legally entitled to for two years. Now a government board tells me I may only meet to discuss the certificate if I don't bring my lawyer, I am denied copies of key documents I have paid for, and if I am forbidden from recording what is said about me in a closed door meeting. Although such actions may be done with the best intention, I find this scary authoritarianism not in line with parliaments intention for classifying videos for grown ups to watch. I am the maker of a boxing documentary. I am not a pornographer nor an urban terrorist.

3) Lies told about the documentary Bare Fist by the BBFC.

The board's technical report lists eight sections the great majority of the film as "non-contentious", and shows 33 cuts made to the fight scenes along to comply with the board's wishes. But the examiner's reports contain repeated and provable lies about the content and the intent of my documentary Bare Fist.

This even includes personal insults. The examiner say I am "insincere" for exposing the 20th century greatest sports health scandal — the imposition of boxing gloves as a safety measure that is in fact contributing to death and brain damage.

After being read out three reports written by BBFC examiners, I believe they must be made pubic for the proper running of a designated authority.

The secret examiners reports on Bare Fist are prejudiced, deceptive legally irrelevant, and offer no proper analysis of key legal concepts of the Video Recordings Act.

3.1 The Lies of the October 8

The Big Lie — "gross violence" & the claim of "promotion"

Mr James Ferman claims Bare Fist is "promotion" of "gross violence".

The Truth

The documentary Bare Fist does not show what is legally nor under common law or ordinary definition "gross violence". The documentary shows 13 minutes of consenting boxing with no gloves. The "illegality" shown is prize fighting. This is a crime of social disorder, not a crime of violence, such as bodily harm. Mr Ferman is legally wrong is describing the fight footage as "gross violence".

Secondly, by repeated precedent the BBFC has given certificates to films showing extended sequences of boxing with no gloves (3 volumes of Ultimate Fight Championship, 1995, Best of Best, Death Ring, 1995). The most serious injury shown in Bare Fist is a bloodied nose and a loosened tooth. These occurred unintentional as part of a consenting boxing match. They fall far below a reasonable legal definition of "gross violence". The House of Commons pre-amble to the 1984 act on the statutory controls of video recordings made it clear the law was designed specifically to control what had become known as "video nasties". Violence in these films featured murder, mutilation and sexual torture. This is far beyond a consenting boxing match with no gloves. The law was not passed in order to ban a documentary revealing an underground sport. The board is acting beyond the intention of Parliament.

Secondly, Mr Ferman's disingenuous use of the word "promotion" to describe the act of making a documentary is inaccurate and purposely misleading. It is specifically designed to confuse thinking away from the true nature and intention of the documentary Bare Fist. The film "promotes" historical, social and medical analysis of a key sport in British history. It is not true to say that showing evidence about, or discussion of, is promotion.

3.2 The Lie by James Ferman (1)

On October 8, Mr James Ferman told you I had "cut 30 minutes from the film, and put 36 minutes back".

The Truth

Mr Ferman's lie implies I did not make cuts Mr Ferman asked for. Yet the board's own technical report shows that 33 cuts amounting to 598 seconds were made to the documentary Bare Fist. Mr Ferman had instructed me to put in two scenes — a doctor interview and an interview with another boxer. The other "sequences put back" were a major re-ordering of the film to accommodate new sequences shot with the presenter to re-enforce the films opposition to violence. Mr Ferman was told in detail about what was "put back" in writing on June 11, 1997.

3.3 The Lie by James Ferman (2)

Mr Ferman said none of the instructions set down by the board were followed in the re-submitted version of Bare Fist.

The Truth

On December 23, 1996, Mr Ferman wrote to David Monaghan saying the board *"would support your proposal to reduce the bare fist footage, although cutting 30 per cent would be insufficient in our view and I suggest you think in terms of cutting a minimum of 50 per cent"*. Following this instruction, on March 15, 1998, ten minutes of bare fist footage was censored from 23 minutes in the original film. This was exactly in line with what was instructed by Mr Ferman, and what I felt as a film maker was sufficient to comply. Mr Ferman was told exactly what was in the re-edit in writing on June 11, 1997, and by telephone in February and March 1998. The board's refusal to supply cut lists in writing, then make accusations of not making agreed cuts, is a Catch-22 policy that is a disturbing mis-use of the board's powers.

3.4 The Lie by James Ferman (3)

On October 8, Mr James Ferman told you his board had never passed a video that had "more fighting than the documentary Bare Fist".

The Truth

A check the first two kick boxing films I saw in my local newsagents shows Mr Ferman's signature is on the BBFC certificates for "Best of the Best II" (1994) and "Death Ring" (1994). Both films contain more than 13 minutes of bare fist style fighting, the same as in the banned documentary Bare Fist. Unlike the documentary, these films show eye gouging, face punching to prostate opponents, neck breaking, choking, car chases, gun murder, and beautiful girls having sex with bare fist fighters. Feature films are regularly certified that have more bare fist fighting, and more violence than my documentary.

3.5 The Lie by the Examiners No.1

The un-named examiner claims in his report that banning film like Bare Fist was exactly what parliament had in mind with the 1994 amendments to the 1984 Video Recordings Act.

The Truth

The 1994 amendment to the Video Recording Act allows the banning of films which "may cause harm to the individual, or through their acts to society". The act followed concern about the murder of the child Jamie Bulger by two other children, and the incorrect belief these children had watched films showing multiple murder by a fantasy monster. Nothing said in parliament, or in the press, suggested banning of documentary films, nor of films showing consenting acts of boxing. Bare Fist was not what parliament had in mind in the framing of the 1994 Amendments.

3.6 The Lie by the Examiners No. 2

The unnamed examiner said that violence was encouraged by the documentary because commentary said the sport was "respectable".

The Truth

This is one of the many instances of dishonest, selective quotation in the examiners reports. Your examiner claims a statement of historical fact in a documentary is encouragement to violence. Your ban on Bare Fist will create a dangerous legal precedent that will declare historical accuracy illegal.

The documentary alleged "encouragement to harm" is commentary that describes the social status of world champion boxers 100 years ago. The quote says:

> *Boxing may not have been respectable, but the bare knuckles fighters were men of respect. Bare fist champs like Kilrain, Sullivan & Goss were international sports stars. They was savage, but there was ritual. All that violence started with a handshake. Bare fist law ran boxing for 150 years, until well after the Marquis of Queensbury wrote his glove rules in 1867.*

Not only does the BBFC wants to censor journalistic examination of the present — the underground sport of bare fist boxing. The examiners want the past re-written as well.

3.7 The Lie by the Examiners No. 3

The examiners report said the documentary contains a "money shot", a male ejaculation shown in a pornographic films.

The Truth

There is no sex at all in the documentary Bare Fist, let alone an act of ejaculation. Such pornographic, crude and puerile language used in a document from a designated authority shows remarkable impropriety which should result in censure to the examiner involved. Such language can only have been placed there to mislead on the content and intent of the documentary to be classified. Such conduct should be allowed to pass for professional behaviour in the board.

3.8 The Lie by the Examiners No. 4
The examiner said in the report the documentary "has no thesis".

The Truth
Either by incompetence or by maliciousness untruths are told about even the structure of this documentary.
The documentary has a clear, over arching thesis about how bare fist boxing has survived over 6,000 years until today.
Within that, there are three sub-sections, that posit:

1) The contemporary survival of bare fist boxing among doormen and the Gypsy race.
2) The connection between the sporting disease "punch drunk syndrome" and in the introduction of boxing gloves under Queensbury rules. Statistics, a medical report and illustrative evidence is shown to support the thesis.
3) The different cultural treatment of bare fist boxing in Hollywood, in different societies and in Britain in the past.

This claim could only have been made to mislead any reader about the true nature of the documentary Bare Fist. This act of lying within an internal report of a designated authority is of great public concern. I would again urge you to discipline the examiner involved for telling falsehoods that have great consequences to my business and my rights under the United Nations Convention.

3.9 The Lies of the Examiners No. 5
The documentary Bare Fist is an "encouragement to violence".

The Truth
There is no encouragement to violence in the documentary.
Certificates issued by the board to kick-boxing films indicate the examiners believe that the same level and greater intensity of fighting in feature films is not "encouragement to violence" that would warrant a ban. Boxing in the documentary Bare Fist is consenting, non-lethal, and part of evidence in a expose of great harm (the creation of punch drunk syndrome), and is not "encouragement to violence".

4) Failure of the examiners to apply the law of "stimulate"
It is abundantly clear the advice being given to the director and the president from examiners ignores their duty to report on how video submitted to classification actually relates to law. The claim that the documentary Bare Fist must be banned because it is "an encouragement to violence" shows the improper grasp the examiners have of the law and its intention. The examiners seem to be trying to mis-apply the Video Recordings Act of 1984. This statutory regulation uses the phrase that allows the board a power of limitation on video recordings "designed to stimulate...acts of gross violence".
There is absolutely no evidence that the documentary Bare Fist is designed to stimulate acts of gross violence. The documentary begins and ends with clear message against the use of any forms of violence — a fact ommitted by all examiners reports. The examiners have had to omit reference to key sections of the film attacking genuine "gross violence" such as knife wounding and gun use.
The examiners have repeatedly passed more violent films such "Best of the Best" (13 minutes illegal fighting with killings) and "Death Ring" (13 minutes bare illegal fighting, including weapons use). Their depiction of far greater violence have been certified as legal by the board. It is clear the mere depiction of violence is necessarily a stimulation.

5) Failure of the examiners to apply the law of "harm"
There is no consideration of the comparative level of "harm" caused by the individual, or to society, by bare fist boxing.
Any consideration of evidence put to the board would show that

1) there have been no reported deaths or serious injury from bare fist boxing in Britain in recent memory and
2) there have only been two arrests under the prize fighting laws this century, one of whom is interviewed in the film Bare Fist.

I have made a documentary that exposes a harm caused to individuals by the use of boxing gloves. 600 boxers are dead. The actions of your board to delay the release of my documentary for more than two year has caused harm.

This can not be justified under the 1984 Video Recording Act or other law or regulations that are published, and able to be read and understood by film makers like myself. Banning the documentary Bare Fist will stop harm to more individuals, such as the young boxers who had been mislead about the safety of boxing with gloves.

The ban on this documentary by the board, is far out of proportion to the potential for harm to an individual or to society by the action of bare fist boxing.

6) Research relevant to Bare Fist ignored in the ban

Your board is operating a policy to ban documentary films without the support of any research, study, or professional analysis that suggests documentary films are harming the individual or society.

The principles of classification introduced by Andreas Whittam Smith and quoted to me by letter on May 24, 1998, state the "classifications decisions must take into account public attitudes and relevant research".

"Public attitude"

I would request the president note that the presenter of Bare Fist, Lennie McLean, has now sold 75,000 copies of his auto-biography, The Guv'ner, since its release on July 1998. The books has remained in the top five selling hardback books for 15 weeks. This shows a public attitude of intense interest in Mr McLean and his lifetime of sporting involvement in bare knuckle boxing. There has been no objection to, and only adoration of, Mr McLean since the publication of this book. Bare fist fighting is now shown on cable television in matches of the Ultimate Fighting Championship with no objection.

"Relevant Research"

I would draw the president's attention to relevant research which supports the crucial thesis of the documentary Bare Fist — the bare fist boxing causes less harm than the gloved sport.

These demonstrate that censorship of Bare Fist is a breach of the 'harm' requisite of the 1994 Amendment to the 1984 Video Recordings Act. There is clear and sufficient evidence that the act of bare knuckle boxing per se is less harmful than gloved boxing, which is freely shown on video as "sport", even without classification [Space restricts us from including the numerous paragraphs taken from professional research and other sources supporting this evidence]...

7) As I have paid £595 for a classification service from your board, I want a certificate for my documentary. Please notify me of your:

7.1) list of cuts in order to gain certification as requested most recently on November 9, 1998, and repeatedly since March 3 1998.

or

7.2) your reasons for banning the video, so I might immediately apply to the Home Office Video Appeals Committee.

and

7.3) Whether you will endorse future actions by the board's new director to re-edit films in a foreign country to help a foreign film maker win UK film certificates. As a local film maker who has failed to be obtain even a cut list from the BBFC, I would like to know how I might obtain such special treatment from the board.

Regards

David Monaghan

PS I have received not reply to my correspondence of September 22, 1998.

NOTES

BEGINNINGS

1 The attempt to absorb rising production costs resulted in b&w prints of films costing the same as colour prints in Britain.

2 Although 600-foot reels were obtainable, choice in this format was limited and expensive, and the accepted standard length tended to be 200-foot and 400-foot, the latter providing approximately eighteen minutes of viewing time. A complete unabridged feature film on Super-8 could run to four or five reels, each of which would require manual change-over and feeding into a projector.

3 The royal wedding itself left retailers unable to meet the demand for blank videocassettes and hardware.

4 Narrated by Robert Lacey, author of the best-selling book of the same name.

5 The *Electric Blue* series ran to *at least* twenty-six volumes.

6 The sport section of volume one was film of the 1976 Indy 500 in which more than thirty people died, while volume two featured a compilation of motor racing pile-ups identified in the *Electric Blue* catalogue only as "carnage for the connoisseur!" Volume seven had skiing accidents.

7 *Continental Film and Video Review* June 1982.

8 Although 3-D movies had been screened on Scottish TV and Philips even demonstrated a prototype 3-D television set at around about the time of the release of *Electric Blue* volume eight, the concept of home 3-D — constantly in development — remains today nothing more than a gimmick.

9 Producer and director were a fashion photographer by the name of Ron Harris, who had worked on high-fashion magazines like *Vogue*, *Cosmopolitan* and *Harper's Bazaar*.

10 Trailers for movies could already be found on pre-recorded feature film tapes.

11 Ironically, as pre-recorded tapes were given space for advertising, a device known as the Commercial Cutter came on the market. This was an electronic box that coupled to the VCR and detected advertising breaks between programmes. It would automatically activate the pause mode during the commercials. The device was often heard about but very rarely seen.

12 Manufactured by Thorn EMI, the video jukebox played clips from a videodisc (supplied by Albion Leisure Services in the UK). The unit was available originally in a stand alone design, and later as a wall box with a 'hideaway' unit.

13 It's worth noting that according to the Department of Trade, cinema attendence in Britain has suffered something of a downslide for many years prior to video. In 1973, 142 million people went to the cinema, compared with the 107 million who went in 1976. The following year saw the figure rise. The year after that it fell again.

14 RCA's prototype video recorder Selectavision, although never making it to the marketing stage, was heralded by the manufacturer as "the most significant development since the invention of colour television."
David Johnson, chief executive of the 400-strong Rumbelow's chain of electronics shops, told the *Sunday Times* in July 1981 that "Video is the biggest household spending spree since the colour television boom of the early seventies."

15 Part of the reason for the dominance of VHS over Betamax lies with the giant Thorn EMI group, who owned many high street TV and video rental chains through which they marketed their own Ferguson brand VHS recorder.

16 Far greater sales were achieved on blank cassettes, however. Time-shift recording — the recording of television programmes for later viewing — remains to this day the most popular use for the VCR.

17 A twelve-month membership cost £85 and came with a full-length feature film which could be exchanged for anything in the Video Club catalogue direct by post. Postage not included.

18 WEA Records handled Warner Home Video, EMI Records handled Thorn EMI, PRT Records handled ITC/Precision, and CBS Records handled CIC Video and MGM.

19 The majority of mail order companies offered adult titles, and it was this type of product that kept mail order alive when video moved into the high street.
The more daring consumer of porn tapes could try the Private chain of shops which, for a while, offered a preview-before-buying option. Customers after hardcore would have been disappointed as such material was illegal and not sold in the Private shops. Customers almost certainly would have been convinced otherwise by the aggressive salesmanship employed in such places, however.

20 The voice of Patrick Allen could also be heard on releases from Hokushin, reciting the 'copyright proprietor/home use' warning typically found on videocassettes. He is perhaps best known on British television as the public face (and voice) of the Barrett Homes advertisements.

21 The BVA was the brainchild of the British Phonograph Industry (BPI), whose members had become a sizeable force in the distribution of videos for home entertainment. After some negotiation, and in a sense of fair play, it drew on representatives not only from the record industry, but also from film, publishing and the BBC. The head of Thorn EMI was elected the chairman.

22 A 'spoiler signal', which would interfere with recordings made from TV, was one alternative that was considered but dismissed on account of the 'anti-spoiler signal' devices which were sure to surface.

23 In January 1984, the US Supreme Court ruled that using a VCR to record programmes for home use was not a

violation. The decision brought to a close a near two-year battle that Walt Disney Productions and Universal Studios had fought against Sony, which contended that the manufacturer of the Betamax video recorder be held accountable under copyright law for time-shift recordings made by consumers.

UNEASE

1 As was the modus operandi of one successful video theft as related to the authors.

2 We are unable to substantiate claims that in April 1985, the Pope warned of video dependence.

3 Go Video, distributors of *SS Experiment Camp* and *Cannibal Holocaust*, had a penchant for outrageous ads. *The Demons* incorporated similarly outrageous imagery.

4 The organisation is generally referred to as National VALA — the acronym pronounced Valour.

5 Whitehouse remains within the NVALA, though frailty has considerably diminished her fervent pro-activity. She recently handed over the position of presidency to Revd Graham Stevens, herself being honoured with President Emeritus.

6 *"Who Does She Think She Is?"*, Mary Whitehouse.

7 When the BBC aired Quentin Tarantino's *Pulp Fiction*, 3.8 million viewers watched the film. Afterwards a mere forty-five complaints were received, yet the NVALA declared that it offended "good taste and decency" and should not have been shown.

8 Commander of the Order of the British Empire.

9 To give some deeper insight into what they consider to be a breach of their moral criterion, here are a few films the Association believe should never have been broadcast, on the grounds they contain "unexceptable violence": *The Color Purple, The Commitments, Four Weddings And A Funeral, Pretty Woman, Dirty Dancing, Great Balls Of Fire!, Legal Eagles, Stakeout, Last Of The Mohicans, Planes, Trains And Automobiles...*

10 The degree of restraint is exemplified in the NVALA's guideline for nudity on television, which deems that "the state of undress that we accept in the street is what is appropriate on our screens."

11 See *A Most Dangerous Woman?*, one of Whitehouse's several autobiographies, for the full story.

12 *Outsiders: Studies in the Sociology of Deviance*, Howard Becker, 1963.

13 Some reports put the figure as high as 35,000.

14 The British Humanist Association described Mary Whitehouse and the NFOL as "at the best, a music hall act, at the worst, as a well organised attempt to destroy the basis of individual freedom". The real moral pollution they argued was unemployment figures of one million, schools that had been condemned thirty years ago, the mental hospitals, inner city slums and the poverty of old age pensioners.

15 An observation made by David Tribe in his book *Questions of Censorship*.

16 Longford was the first to admit that "none of the other subjects in the House of Lords debates ever roused one-tenth of the interest" as did his debate on pornography.

17 *Questions of Censorship*, David Tribe.

18 See Gilbert Kelland's *Crime in London* for a detailed insider's account of the investigation into corrupt detectives and pornographers.

19 Some women's groups wanted men to carry licenses proving they had legitimate business being out at night, while others called for a curfew on all men. Some simply resorted to verbal and physical abuse.

20 *Midnight Marquee* No 31.

21 The tally of pornographic videocassettes seized by police rose from 125 tapes in 1979, to over 5,000 in the first three months of 1982 alone.

22 *The Times*, April 14, 1983.

23 "Rape Of Our Children's Minds," *Daily Mail*, June 30, 1983.

24 The irony of gauging someone's reaction to a film in which aversion therapy is a key theme is not recorded. What unnerving influence must the Ludovico treatment sequence in *A Clockwork Orange* have had on Dr Carruthers' volunteers, which shows the film's main character being forced to view increasingly violent and sexual imagery?

25 Often just the title of a movie would incite protestations, as in the case of *Violation of the Bitch*, a somewhat plodding piece of Spanish erotica that had even less titillation value following BBFC cuts totalling of fifteen minutes.

26 "Obscenity" for such protestors, according to John Sutherland, author of *Offensive Literature*, "was redefined in sectarian terms as "containing violence or condoning violence against women."

27 As described by the *Sunday Times*, June 13, 1982.

28 Curiously, in the case of *The Driller Killer, Death Trap* and *I Spit On Your Grave*, the courts were told that Scotland Yard had originally pressed for the more serious Section Two ruling. But Stephen Wooller, for the DPP, said that the legal papers had been marked in error. "There had been a breakdown of communication between the director's office and the court because, following consultations with the Metropolitan Police, the clear decision was that this matter would be dealt with under Section Three."

29 As described by Andrew Sims and Graham Melville-Thomas in their "Psychiatrist's Survey" chapter of the book *Video Violence and Children*.

30 The *Sunday Times*, September 5, 1982.

CLAMPDOWN

1 In the article entitled "How High Street Horror is Invading the Home," see also previous chapter.

2 Which isn't tainted with any libel or racial offensiveness.

3 A 'clean-up' campaign in Manchester during the mid seventies resulted in the removal of many books and magazines that were readily obtainable in any other city. Amongst them such relatively innocuous fare as *The Sun Book of Page 3 Girls*. While in Portsmouth, anything outside of child

porn, bestiality and torture was tolerated by police.

4 On February 3, 1970.

5 Noted by John Trevelyan, director of the BBFC, who was quick to lodge a public complaint following the police action. See Trevelyan's book, *What The Censor Saw*.

6 *The Times* described how one cinema in New York reacted to the news by allowing anyone with a British passport in to see the film for nothing, while *The Sun* parodied the raid in a cartoon that showed a theatre full of pop-eyed policemen distracted from their duties by the film playing.

7 At the suggestion of John Trevelyan.

8 Editor Richard Neville's credo was "the weapons of revolution are obscenity, blasphemy and drugs." The editorship of *Oz 28*, the offending issue, had been given over to schoolchildren, who made some appropriately rude contributions.

9 It should be noted that search and seizure of private collections is not authorised by the Act.

10 "Repulsive... filthy... loathsome... indecent... lewd..."

11 Sir Cyril Black, a lay preacher and member of the Public Morality Council. More than one of the prosecution witnesses against *Last Exit to Brooklyn* admitted in court that by reading the book they had been depraved and corrupted.
In February 1998, in court for having tried to import sexually explicit material and several video nasties into Britain, Mark Wright used the defence that he was unlikely to be corrupted by such items because he was an "experienced viewer." He was found guilty, with the two judges ruling that the law was obliged "not only to protect the innocent — but also the less innocent from further corruption."

12 Calder & Boyars refused to cease publication of *Last Exit*, forcing the DPP to proceed with Section Two proceedings. This meant that the firm stood to lose a lot more than forfeiture of goods, but granted them the right to trial by jury, who found the book guilty. This decision was overturned on appeal, on account of the judge not having instructed the jury sufficiently with regard to the Obscene Publications Act.

13 The Act had been extended to cover the public screening of feature films in 1977.

14 "The 1959 Obscene Publications Act, as amended by the 1977 Criminal Law Act, exempts from liability 'anything done in the course of television or sound broadcasting.'" Noted Robertson in his book *Obscenity*, "Video cassettes may be fed along short cables to standard television sets, tuned to standard channels, which then decode and depict obscene images, and sometimes emit obscene sounds, for the patrons of Soho's more technologically-advanced clubs. If this process amounts to 'television' or to 'sound broadcasting', such publications would fall outside the Obscene Publications Act..."

15 The pressure was certainly great. Hetherington's stock response to publishers in the seventies who came to him for assistance was: "I regret that I am unable to give you the type of advice you seek regarding the operation of the Obscene Publications Acts. I am unable to do so because of the generally recognised uncertainty in the operation of law in this field."

16 The films had been seized from Leonard Matthews' shop in Highgate over two years prior, a place in which, agreed the police, most of the videocassettes were "perfectly proper." Matthews claimed to have already removed from his stock three of the titles on account of the bad publicity they had received in the press, and while *Cannibal Apocalypse* had still been for hire, he did not suspect anything wrong with it. After viewing the films in their entirety, it took the jury just one hour to acquit Matthews of having obscene articles for publication and gain.

17 In compiling a list of 'banned' video titles for *Video Violence and Children*, researchers tellingly had to do so without access to a copy of the DPP blacklist and relied instead on 'conversations with officers at Scotland Yard... and off the Obscene Publications department of provincial forces.'

18 Ironically for Hamilton-Grant, the case brought as much publicity to him and his film as had the tasteless promotional gimmick he had created for its video release several years earlier. (See VIDEO NASTIES.)

19 Also victorious in the case against *Inside Linda Lovelace* and, much later, the Savoy novel *Lord Horror*.

20 Malcolm was also called to give evidence for *The Story of O*. "One of the most boring softcore sex films I've ever had to sit through," he would concede, although it was well photographed by Just Jaecklin. "Well photographed? Really?" queried the presiding magistrate. "I could do better myself."

21 *The Times*, May 31, 1983.

22 Including outlets which were based in laundrettes, dry cleaners, garages and the like, the total number of video dealers in Britain was anything up to 10,000.

23 Alas, at the beginning of the article, the reporter admits that the same audience who couldn't stomach the film were "feeling slightly sick from a surfeit of British wine the previous evening."

24 On the subject of context, a major grievance with politicians is that they are frequently quoted out of it — an irony which was evidently lost on Bright when he was presenting his cut-and-paste showreel.

25 The Annual Assembly of the Methodist Church fell on the same day as the meeting and thus prevented its leaders from attending. They were represented instead by a lecturer from Oxford Polytechnic.

26 It was Hill who had instigated the first meeting, having been inspired by various members of the Vice Squad he had spoken to with regard to these "horrific" and "dreadful" videos.

27 According to Hill, the secrecy which surrounded the compiling of the Report and the source of its data, was in part due to the threat of "underworld forces" on his life. A mafia-type underworld controlling the video industry was one of the concerns aired at the launch of the Enquiry.

28 *Illusions*, a film designed to warn schoolchildren of the perils of sniffing glue, was prevented from being shown in schools by the Department of Health in September 1983.

29 The Report stated that thirty-seven

per cent of children aged under-seven had seen a video nasty, but a member of Brown's staff could only recall forty-six questionnaires for this age group, in which the majority of children had never watched a video at all. Hill's *national* average appeared to have been drawn from a total of *three* children, who had claimed to have watched some seventeen video nasties each.

30 In an experiment replicating the Video Enquiry, psychologist Dr Guy Cumberbatch found that most children readily admitted to watching films that didn't exist. Indeed, *Zombie Terror*, a film cited in the Report as being one of the children's 'top ten' video nasties, *doesn't* exist.

31 Palace Video MD, Nik Powell.

32 Wrongly presented in the showreel as a factual event, the scene was actually fabricated utilising a rubber monkey head stuffed with red-dyed cauliflower. A similar scene was passed without comment in *Indiana Jones and the Temple of Doom*.

33 David Mellor MP.

34 There were some companies who volunteered works for video classification, however. These included World of Video 2000, who sought to protect their new French Label erotica line by securing a BBFC certificate, and ensuring that the content and packaging didn't contravene the Obscene Publications Act.

35 Part (a) of the 'model licensing conditions' drafted by the Home Office states that "no film, other than a current newsreel, shall be exhibited unless it has received a certificate of the British Board of Film Classification or is the subject of the licensing authority's permission."

36 This at a time when the Home Secretary was sensitive to the opinion that a "recent increase in juvenile delinquency is, to a considerable extent, due to demoralising cinematographic films."

37 It isn't often that local authority will overrule a BBFC decision, although it did happen recently in the case of the Robin Williams comedy *Mrs Doubtfire*. The film was passed with a 12 certificate (on account of some of American colloquialisms featured). Parents complained that they weren't able to take their children to see the film and as a result some local authorities changed the category to a PG (Parental Guidance).

38 Under this Act, the Board amended the existing, unsatisfactory category system, as it would again in 1970 and 1983 in keeping with the changing times and attitudes.

39 The Cinematograph Acts 1909, 1952 and 1982 were consolidated into the Cinemas Act 1985.

40 The Report was started amidst the repercussions of several high profile obscenity cases (involving *Gay News*, *Inside Linda Lovelace* and *Libertine*), the "sickening glut of blood and guts films" invading British cinemas (as highlighted by *The Sun* newspaper *et al*), and the investigation into police corruption within Scotland Yard's Vice Squad.

41 *The Times* urged "that the knowledge and instinct of the public in this matter is more important than that of the skill of a handful of committee sitters using their intellectual agility to verbalise a social problem out of existence." But in truth, the 'instinct' of an estimated four million members of the public was to read one or more pornographic magazines every month, according to research by the Williams Committee.

42 The fact that many local authorities refuse to licence sex shops or adult cinemas — thus considerably limiting the market for R18 — is one of the troubles facing films in this category. There are currently only an estimated eighty licensed sex shops in Britain.

43 Although 'Censors' has been replaced with 'Classification' the Board reject or cut (i.e. censor) about seven per cent of submitted material. The title change is more a political ploy than practical reality. The Board is offended by the notion they might be censors. When Tom Dewe Mathews's book *Censored: The Story of Film Censorship* was published, James Ferman responded with a damning article in the *Sunday Times* (July 24, 1994). At a BBFC roadshow in Manchester in March 2000, during a question and answer session, the new director of the Board Robin Duval coldly dismissed the allegation that he might be a censor, snubbed the question and quickly moved on.

44 Unlike the Obscene Publications Act, the Video Recordings Act made no provision for imprisonment.

45 *BBFC Annual Report 1985*.

46 In 1977, the BBFC were to discuss the "questionable taste" of a feature film based on a true life British murder case. Although *The Black Panther* made no attempt to glamorise or dwell either on the crime or the criminal, nor stray from the facts as they were known, the BBFC felt the film deserved an X-rating. In a bulletin, the Board gave the reason for their decision: "The idea of teenagers seeing a film about the maltreatment of a real girl of seventeen who died less than two years ago seemed sufficiently distasteful for us to prefer to restrict the film to adult audience."
Asked how the BBFC assessed public taste, its director James Ferman told a Video Consultative Council meeting in September 1985, that it was a continuing process which the Board had been trying to maintain throughout the last seventy years; one which he hoped they had got about right.

47 The BBFC's treatment of rape has often had an adverse effect, and in trimming the portrayal of the crime the Board have often been accused of sanitising it. Ironically, Sam Peckinpah's 1971 *Straw Dogs* remains unavailable in this country on account of BBFC intervention with regard to the treatment of rape. The turning point in this tale of petty-mindedness and desperation comes with the rape of the Susan George character, Amy, by two men. John Trevelyan — director of the Board at the time the film was being made — consulted with the filmmaker and advised on how the scene should be shot, in order that there should be less of a problem during the examination process. In actual fact, the editing and cut-aways during this scene have effectively 'banned' the film in this country (following its initial theatrical run and video release pre-VRA).
Straw Dogs was submitted to the BBFC in 1999 and was refused a video certificate. The press release issued by the Board outlined several reasons for its decision: "The first is the fact that the rapes are clearly effected by violence and the threat of violence. The second is the extent of the erotic content, notably Amy's forcible stripping and nudity. The third element of concern is the clear indication that Amy comes to enjoy being raped. It is

Board policy not to condone material which endorses the well-known male rape myth that "women like it really.'"

48 This is a list compiled by the Department of Trade and Industry.

49 For instance, as pointed out in the booklet, film distributors whose catalogues had been examined by the BBFC were required "to publish lists of the categories granted to their titles under the Act. In such lists they should indicate instances where the certificate awarded under the Act differs in category from a certificate which may have been granted to that title for the purposes of cinema exhibition. Similarly, such lists should indicate titles where the film and video categories are the same but where the certificated video version has been cut more extensively by the censor than was the certificated film version. Videos of the less cut film version already in circulation must not be labelled with the classification category awarded after additional cuts to the new video version."

50 Neither was it an offence under the Act, to supply video records of events like weddings and anniversaries to those who took part in them or their acquaintances (so long, of course, as those events didn't depict any sex or acts of violence).

51 Other criteria which prevented video works from qualifying as exempt were added a decade later, courtesy of the Criminal Justice and Public Order Bill 1994. (See SEX & WRECKS.)

52 Foreign language works were also entitled to a lower tariff, as were works made by charity or non-profit-making organisations. In the case of those video titles which had been voluntarily submitted for classification prior to the VRA, the BBFC were obliged to assess free-of-charge whether their certificates could be confirmed under the Act.

53 Anderton's campaign resulted in Greater Manchester joining Nottinghamshire, Devon and Cornwall in forming a local video traders' association. Between them they were set to create news bulletins and present their members and the police with a blacklist of video titles. Members of the association faced expulsion if they continued to hire out films that had been blacklisted — a deterrent that certainly didn't hold much sway with Anderton, who wasn't dissuaded from raiding any video stockist under his jurisdiction.

54 Tim Brinton, a Tory MP, went on record in July 1984 as saying that the Bill wouldn't stop the flow of nasties and that the upsurge in a black market was inevitable.

SIEGE

1 Videobox blurb for Gerardo de Leon's *Creatures of Evil.*

2 Interview with James Ferman by David Kenny.

3 Another title released by LVC was *Tiger Love*, a curious Chinese production in which a woman gets intimate with a tiger after she urinates on it. The synopsis on the sleeve ran: "Warning — Some scenes in this film actually happened."

4 Evidently the distributors were unable to obtain original publicity materials for the films and so resorted to producing their own artwork — but who painted those terrible sleeves?!

5 The slip-cases were very fragile and quite often rental outlets would cut them apart to place them inside sturdier plastic cases. Original, intact boxes have become collectors' items in themselves.

6 Palace released all John Waters' early movies. The titles included the Divine-free, "XXX rated" *Desperate Living*, and, under the banner "The Divine Collection," *Mondo Trasho* (doubled with *Sex Madness*), *Female Trouble* and *Pink Flamingos*. Arcade Video released Waters' *Polyester* and included a scratch-and-sniff card so viewers could participate in the 'Odorama' effect.

7 This somewhat tedious movie about a witch resurrected from a shipwreck was filmed in the Philippines. Remarkably, the opening credits are still popping up almost fifteen minutes into the film.

8 These days it would cost £1005.57 to get a video certificate for an eighty minute English language film. With manufacturing costs and duplication fees on top of this, few obscure low-budget features could hope to make much of a profit.

9 It was submitted yet again in 1999 with a longer running time of 84m 59s and passed without cuts.

10 James Ferman during a debate on Film Censorship and British Social History, at the Institute of Contemporary Arts, November 20, 1998.

VIDEO NASTIES

1 According to Massaccesi, he plucked the name Joe D'Amato off a calender, at a time when Italian-American sounding directors were very much in vogue. At least one of the other names in *Absurd*'s technical credits is also a pseudonym for Massaccesi: Richard Haller (photography). "That's for legal reasons," claimed Massaccesi in an interview that appeared in *European Trash Cinema* (No 12). "You can't have too many jobs on one project because of the unions."

2 In *Anthopophagous*, Eastman wore lumpy makeup on his face. In this film he wears nothing more sinister than a beard — but a nurse still refers to him as being "strange" looking.

3 *The DarkSide* April 1992.

4 *Filmfax* No 8.

5 Suggested by Lucas Balbo in *Shock Xpress* (Vol 2 No 1), but a sentiment reiterated by many other film critics, generally through plagiarism and critical mimicry rather than true opinion. There are many other directors who would be better suited to this citation — the generally unwatchable Jesús Franco, for example, whose *Bloody Moon*, *Devil Hunter* and *Women Behind Bars* can also be found on the DPP list.

6 As Massaccessi reported in *European Trash Cinema* (No 12), although earlier in the same interview he claims "every film is like a son to me."

7 If you include the several cutaway shots of Katya trying to free herself from traction and Willie running through the house, Emily's death actually seems to go on for much longer.

8 *Flesh & Blood* No 7.

9 There is a trifling bone of contention as to whether the title is actually *The Anthropophagous Beast* [our emphasis] which makes more grammatical sense.

As it appears on screen the order of the wording is somewhat ambiguous.

10 D'Amato claims that of all the films he's directed, *Anthropophagous* is one of his favourites. "*Anthropophagous* for horror," he said in an interview with *Flesh & Blood* (No 7), "and *11 Days, 11 Nights* for softcore, erotic movie."

11 The foetus of a sheep still encased in its amnion was supposedly used for the scene.

12 It looks for a moment like the girl derives sexual pleasure from the dead body on top of her.

13 "She" could infer that Lisa told the cops the gang was holed up in the house several days ago (whilst Steele was holding a gun to grandpa's head), in which case they've waited a long time to do anything about it. Or it could be that the cops have been talking to the shop cashier.

14 It also sounds remarkably similar to a keyboard solo in The Blues Project's 1967 garage favourite, 'No Time Like The Right Time.'

15 A review of the US print of the film that appeared in *The House of Hammer* (No 18), back in 1978, also stated that Lisa's age is thirteen.

16 *Sleazoid Express* Vol 3 No 1.

17 *Date with a Kidnapper* was the British video title. Original title was *The Kidnapper*, aka *House of Terror*, aka *Kidnapped Coed*.

18 A company called Lynx distributed *Date with a Kidnapper*. It isn't known what other titles they had to their name.

19 More people have a credit for 'Radio and Television Shows' than there are people who appear in the movie itself.

20 The limited acting capacity of the woman who plays the cashier — who appears to have been told to emote as little as possible as a result — does indeed elevate the sequence to a plane far greater than the sum of its parts.

21 This scream and parts of the electronic score — along with a soundbite from Lee Frost's *Love Camp 7* — were utilised in Jörg Buttgereit's *Der Todesking*, in a segment that pastiched Nazi camp exploitation films.

22 One suspects that a more substantial credits list was conceived, but for reasons unknown failed to materialise or was cut short in this print. A French release on the Assault label omitted the opening Swastika altogether, but retitled the film *Holocauste Nazi...*

23 *Ilsa, She-Wolf of the SS* (d: Don Edmonds), *Ilsa, Harem-Keeper of the Oil Shieks* (d: Don Edmonds), *Ilsa, Tigress of Siberia* (d: Jean Lafleur).

24 The original title is *Kaput Lager: Gli Ultimi Giorni Delle SS*, whose translation bears a confusing similarity to *Horrifing Experiments of S.S.Last Days*: 'Kaput Camp: The Last Days of the SS.'

25 This still managed to be "boring and insipid" according to the Italian journal *Nocturno*. It starred Gordon Mitchell and was again comprised of excerpts from at least one other film.

26 Gianni Vernuccio's *Frankenstein's Castle of Freaks* amongst them.

27 The idea of a blind girl watching over the gates of Hell is used in *The Sentinel*. The blind girl's dog being suddenly possessed and tearing out her throat is derivative of a very similar scene in *Suspiria*. The concept of houses being constructed over doorways to Hell is the basis of *Inferno*.

28 *Fangoria* No 17.

29 All but a handful of the titles on the DPP list — notably *Blood Feast*, *Blood Rites*, *Cain's Cutthroats* and *Night of the Bloody Apes* — are films from the seventies or the eighties.

30 *The Monster Times* No 24.

31 *Nostalgia* No 4.

32 Producer David Friedman parted ways with Lewis on completing *Color Me Blood Red* after arguing about the quality of their product. Friedman compared their own work with other low-budget film-makers (like Lee Frost and Bob Cresse), telling the director that audiences were getting more sophisticated. Hershell didn't make comparisons and didn't think the pictures had to improve.

33 Having appeared in fifteen of Milligan's movies, Hal Borske, the actor who played Colin in *Blood Rites*, told *Video Watchdog* No 54 that "an Andy Milligan credit list should read: '*Everything* by Andy Milligan.' Period."

34 *Video Watchdog* No 52.

35 *Castle of Frankenstein* No 16.

36 *Demonique* No 4.

37 *Blood*, which was less than an hour long, was released in the UK on the Iver Film Services label.

38 The three films Milligan made for J.E.R. were *Depraved!*, *The Degenerates* and *Blood Rites*.

39 Craig Ledbetter in *Hi-Tech Terror* No 25.

40 For instance, the painting out of mirrors and Willy being startled by his own reflection (he's possessed by the bogeyman at the time and is strangling a girl) draws on folklore which is closely linked and has several variants. Some of these include it being unlucky for a sick person to see his own reflection, mirrors having to be turned to the wall when death enters the room, death being able to steal your soul through your reflection, etc.

41 Interview with Ulli Lommel by Stephen Thrower, *Eyeball* No 5.

42 Many critics believed that Fassbinder would restore German cinema to the status it had enjoyed before the war. Fassbinder worked with a closely knit unit of actors and technicians, of which Lommel was a part.

43 Lommel's other genre films as director include *Brainwaves*, *The Devonsville Terror*, and *Vampire Club*. His 1983 *Strangers in Paradise* is a sci-fi musical in which Lommel plays Hitler and a band called Moonlight Drive provide the music. This same band also released an eponymously titled mini-album featuring covers of songs The Doors made famous (Agara Records).

44 Actually, she only *snips* at her T-shirt, allowing a mere glimpse of her blood-covered nipples as she lies into the bathtub. (There is no other instance of bare breasts in the movie.) The 'coyness' with which this sequence is constructed is curious.

45 *Monthly Film Bulletin*.

46 Although Jason Alexander has little to work on in *The Burning*, he established for himself a varied career in film and

television, later to appear in *Brighton Beach Memoirs*, *Pretty Woman*, *Jacob's Ladder*, *North*, and *Love! Valor! Compassion!*. Holly Hunter went on to win an Oscar in *The Piano*.

47 Neither version however has cutaways to "a modern day biker gang," as stated in reviews of *Cain's Way* that appeared in *The DarkSide* (No 40) and *The Psychotronic Encyclopedia of Film*.

48 Made the same year as *Cannibal Apocalypse*, Dawson's *The Last Hunter* was a fully-fledged copy of *Apocalypse Now*.

49 The young actress, Cinzia de Carolis, also played a vampire child in Giorgio Ferroni's *Night of the Devils*. In this film she tore open the blouse of her mother and clawed into her naked breast.

50 *Uncut* No 8.

51 *Video Watchdog* (No 8) accuses the director's bland direction for "killing the fun and the potent metaphor inherent in the screenplay."

52 In which an albino outlaw by the name of Bad Bob is shot in the back, resulting in a gaping bloody hole the size of a football which frames the assassin in the distance.

53 Ferox is latin, but like the film's title, its usage here is a bastardisation and its meaning ambiguous. In a good sense ferox is *courageous*, *high-spirited*, *warlike*, *brave*; in a bad sense, *wild*, *unbridled*, *arrogant*.

54 The use of large bugs as a means to elicit horror and disgust reaches absurd proportions later in the film: Watching as the cannibals are about to castrate Mike, Pat screams at the sight of a giant leech on her arm.

55 "We did everything we could at that time to bring people into the cinemas," Lenzi told *European Trash Cinema*. "Life for directors was very hard and we had to eat, you know."

56 Maybe this is a joke: One of the cannibals holds Gloria's American Express card up to the camera. Accepted all over the world, as the advertising campaign says, the card is quite meaningless here in the jungle.

57 Although it should be noted that at least one animal was spared — the small pig trapped with Gloria in a hole — when actor John Morghen refused to stab it, and the scene had to be implied via sharp edits and special effects. Just like a real movie.

58 *Fangoria* No 53... But not an opinion shared by everyone. When *Cannibal Ferox* opened on New York's 42nd Street, it played directly opposite a theatre showing another Lenzi movie, *Nightmare City*. Wrote Tim Ferrante in *The Splatter Times* (No 4): "What a luxury to have a choice between two shockers by this occassionally brilliant director."

59 This was the boast by Continental Inc, the US company who released Lenzi's third and final cannibal picture as *Doomed To Die!* 'The Most Violent Human Sacrifices You'll Ever See!' promised the poster.

60 Typically, the ad for a screening of *Cannibal Holocaust* at Detroit's Adams Theater declared: "SAVAGE! TERRIFYING! TRUE! THOSE WHO FILMED IT WERE ACTUALLY DEVOURED BY CANNIBALS!"

61 Critics of *Cannibal Holocaust* often paraphrase Monroe's outrage about the atrocities in *The Green Hell* footage and throw them back at Deodato, calling him a hypocrite for showing us the footage in the first place.

62 In *Spaghetti Nightmares*, Deodato claims that all through filmming *Cannibal Holocaust* he had the Animal Protection League "breathing down my neck," and defends the animal slaughter depicted on-screen as simply being a document of the natives hunting and killing for food in their natural habitat. Presumably the Animal Protection League were up-river on the days that the white men kicked and shot a tethered pig, stomped on a giant spider, gutted alive a turtle and muskrat, hacked a snake to pieces...

63 *Photo* Januray, 1981.

64 "... and *eaten alive*!" Jean-Paul Lacmant, *Fantasy Film Memory* No 1.

65 *The Independent*, April 6 1993.

66 *Spaghetti Nightmares*, Palmerini & Mistretta.

67 ibid.

68 A title which translates as 'Week of the Killer' and throws up a blackly humorous slant on the subject matter: Marcos commits six murders over the course of a week and on the seventh he gives himself up. If this idea was presented blatantly, it could have been perceived as blasphemous by the Spanish authorities and no doubt have spelled trouble for de la Iglesia.

69 Vincent Aranda's *The Blood-Spattered Bride*, Javier Aquirre's *Count Dracula's Great Love*, and Amando de Ossorio's *The Night of the Sorcerors*, to name but a few of the other Spanish films that appeared alongside *The Cannibal Man*, mixing a dash of sex with their horror.

70 Following the evening swim they take together, Marcos sets off to work the following morning a new man: he wears a brand new colourful shirt, we first discover that he's been promoted, and there's a certain skip in his step.

71 The lenthy sex scene with Paola is particularly unerotic with some bizarre close-ups and the *frisson* of loud extraneous noises throughout. When it's over, the post coital cigarette that Marcos offers to Paola looks like a joke.

72 An effeminate store-keeper later furnishes the film with some tired comic relief, advising Marcos, after he has asked for ten bottles of strong perfume (to mask the odor in his home), "You know, that's enough to supply a whole navy."

73 TV ads and consumerism are elements that reappear in de la Iglesia's peculiar science fiction movie, *Murder in a Blue World*.

74 *Hi-Tech Terror* No 40.

75 *Cannibal Terror* runs a gamut of wildly different musical styles, from what sounds like something by The Nice to a virtual reprise of 'La Bamba' at the film's end when Florence is reunited with her mother. In between tribal drums underpin pan pipes and perhaps a mellotron.

76 But it's Franco's *Cannibals* that is actual deserving of the accolade 'single most terrible dubbing scene ever commited to celluloid': Having lost his arm to cannibals, actor Al Cliver lies in a delirious fever in a hospital bed. Tossing and turning, he mutters things like "Get away... foul creatures..." in a tone which suggests that somebody in the dubbing plant isn't taking their job at all seriously.

77 Their differences are later resolved with a slap, as Hubbard strikes the Colonel across the face and tells her "That's just so we understand one another."

78 Rather than see an unrealised film script go to waste, Cozzi turned them into novels. The unmade sequel(s) to *Starcrash* became *Star Riders*, a book he co-wrote with A E Van Vogt.

79 In the US, *Contamination* was titled *Alien Contamination*.

80 Spectacular is not a word one could use to describe the Cyclops however. In spite of the special credit awarded its makers at the beginning of the picture, the *papier-mâché* creature is lame even in half-shadow and supposedly took an exasperated Cozzi "over ninety-six cuts and countless shifts in camera position" to get it looking this good. *Spaghetti Nightmares*.

81 Interview with Luigi Cozzi, *Delirium* No 4.

82 ibid.

83 *The DarkSide* No 66.

84 *Contamination* was shot in the US, Italy and South America. The week's worth of exteriors shot in New York are an attempt to lend to the film a certain cedibility overseas (as was Cozzi's anglicised pseudonym 'Lewis Coates'), while the South American location — Columbia to be precise — was worked into the story for cost-cutting reasons and the fact one of the film's investors was South American. Interiors were filmed in Italy.

85 Ian McCulloch interview, *Fangoria* No 52.

86 "The original script," says McCulloch of *Zombie Holocaust*, "was called *Queen of the Cannibals*, which I didn't like because everyone thought it referred to me!" *Fangoria* No 52.

87 One of the murdered woman's breasts poking through her shallow grave, for instance, and the police who for reasons unknown search for clues in the dead of night. The *Monthly Film Bulletin* of February 1982 accredits Christian Marnham as director.

88 Donald Farmer, *The Splatter Times* No 3.

89 One of the few such scenes in *Deep River Savages* — that depicting the cannibalisation of a woman — was edited into Lenzi's later cannibal picture, *Eaten Alive*. Again it was a revolted civilised Caucasian who watched the act from a distance.

90 *European Trash Cinema* Vol 2 No 3.

91 Interview with Umberto Lenzi, *Necronomicon* No 5.

92 A tinkling musical piece is familiar to anyone who has ever watched a cops and robbers show, usually used in a dramatic capacity but here accompanying Charlie as he swaggers across open fields. The rather pompous piece that plays during the clandestine meetings and over the end credits is equally ill-fitting, but more unfortunately will be associated by British viewers with the long-running quiz show *Mastermind*.

93 Their names in the film don't correspond with the character names in the end credits.

94 *Tombs of the Blind Dead*, *Return of the Evil Dead*, *Horror of the Zombies*, and *Night of the Seagulls*.

95 Franco, originally a jazz trumpet player, has suggested in interviews that he is "a jazz musician that makes films." There can be little coincidence that Clifford Brown, the pseudonym he uses for *The Devil Hunter*, was also the name of a jazz trumpeter (1930–1956).

96 "Of about 150 films or so that I have made," Franco told Gerard Alexander in an as yet unpublished interview, "I'd say sixty were done using sync sound and the rest were shot without sound."

97 *Ungawa* No 1.

98 Franco also states that the alien creature's point-of-view in *Predator* adopts the same bizarre colours as the monster in *Devil Hunter*. This isn't true (and if it was, it's a cheap and familiar cinematic device anyway): the monster in *Devil Hunter* sees the world with a little blurring round the edge of the screen.

99 *Eyeball* No 5.

100 *Fangoria* No 27.

101 The scene has a parallel in another, earlier low-budget horror yarn, Michael Findlay's *Shriek of the Mutilated*, in which observers spied the approach — from a great distance — of a killer abominable snowman, but were unable to get free in time.

102 *Don't Go in the Woods* had "a budget apparently culled from the refunds on bottles found beside the road during filming," writes L A Morse in his book *Video Trash & Treasures*.

103 Incredibly this might not be the case! A director bearing the name James Bryan is also responsible it seems for *Hellriders*, *I Love You, I Love You Not* and *The Dirtiest Game*. Watching *Don't Go In the Woods*, however, it's nigh impossible to accept that it's made by someone with three pictures already under his belt and with at least thirteen years directorial experience!

104 *Don't Go In the Woods* was released in most areas of the US in 1980, and became a second-feature at drive-ins everywhere else the following year. In 1983 it was re-released in the New York area.

105 *The Splatter Times* No 2.

106 Suspended and powerless is obviously a pet fear for Bryan. Before Joanne is caught in the skylight, she finds herself in a smiliar predicament, dangling in a sleeping bag as the wild man attacks below. "Everyone has nightmares about the ugliest way to die," is the byline on the videobox. Could the film be an exorcising of demons for Bryan?

107 According to *Halls of Horror* (No 30), the original title of the movie was *Don't Go Into the Woods* [our emphasis], until its re-release in 1983 when it became *Don't Go in the Woods*. We have been unable to verify this information.

108 Linnea Quigley interviewed by Jewel Shepard, *Invasion of the B-Girls*.

109 If this is the case, it would be the film's only twist on Roy Ward Baker's similarly themed *Asylum* of the previous year. Legend has it that the working title for *Don't Look in the Basement* was *Asylum*.

110 Outside of her thoroughly unprofessional look of disgust and horror on first meeting into the old lady in the corridor.

111 *Draculina* No 13.

112 *Demonique* magazine, reviewing *Don't Look In The Basement* in their first issue, claimed that Brownrigg wasn't the first choice of director. "It is rumoured," wrote Barry Kaufman, "the first director who worked on *Don't Look in the Basement* died."

113 Writing in *Shock Xpress* (Vol 3 No 1), Steve Thrower suggests that Gene Ross, who plays the Judge in *Basement*, could well be the elusive Brownrigg under a pseudonym. Ross appears in each of Brownrigg's four movies, playing a judge again in his 1979 picture, *Don't Open the Door*.

114 Hallmark also acquired Jorge Grau's *Living Dead at Manchester Morgue* and released it as *Don't Open the Window*.

115 *Demonique* No 2.

116 Some of the material excised from the British release (and which can be found in VCI's 1999 DVD release) includes Allyson, the nymphomaniac, showing her breasts to the Judge and later to Danny. Much exposition is also gone with these passages. The night time attack on Mrs Callingham reveals, via closeup, that the old woman has had her tongue cut out. Nurse Charlotte screams in affirmation, "Your tongue has been cut out!" The closing scenes of carnage are also considerably protracted in their original form. The pummeling of Dr Masters by the other patients comes with plenty of flesh rending, as axe, knives and even Harriett's doll (!) are brought down on the screaming woman. There is more bloodshed when Sam enters the scene and kills the Judge before turning the axe on everybody else. Some of the cuts in these final scenes show up in the end credits of the British print.
A review of *Basement* which appeared in *Demonique* (No 1) refers to offal being thrown onto walls in the closing massacre, but this seems unlikely. As does the idea of there being a sequence where the body of a woman dead for seven months is exhumed by for the benefit of her widow, resulting in "a three minute scene of husband and mutilated corpse making love."

117 Like *Basement*, this film also has a pre-credit axe murder.

118 According to Kim Newman in *Nightmare Movies*, all these films bear out Brownrigg's "*auteur* status by concentrating on heroines driven insane by exposure to grottily staged violence."

119 McCormick — who also interviewed Brownrigg for *Draculina* — is the director of many straight-to-video movies, like *The Abomination*, *Macon County War* (shot with Brownrigg's "old 16mm Éclair"), and *Fatal Justice*. His inspiration as a director appears to be Brownrigg's *Don't Look in the Basement*.

120 Reviewing the film for *The Splatter Times* No 1, Donald Farmer warned "For those hoping for plenty of gross-out effects, the 'driller-killer' of the title doesn't begin unleasing [sic] pandemonium until about halfway through the picture..."

121 Abel Ferrara interviewed by Kim Newman, *Shock Xpress* No 1.

122 ibid.

123 The wonky camera angles of Ashley with the shotgun are similar to those in Damiano Damiani's *Amityville II: The Possession* — released a few months prior to *The Evil Dead* — wherein another young man (wonkily) clutches a shotgun.

124 To bring things full circle — and beyond — when Craven made *A Nightmare on Elm Street*, he showed a clip of *The Evil Dead* playing on a TV set. When Raimi made *Evil Dead II* he supposedly incorporated a Freddy Krueger glove..

125 Fans of the *The Evil Dead* were up in arms recenly when Raimi saw to it that a new cut for an American distributor was missing the shot of lighning striking a tree. He considered the poor effect to cheapen the movie.

126 *Starburst* No 57.

127 *The Evil Dead* also inspired a succesful Commodore 64 video game and a 7-inch single ('Another Half Hour Till Sunrise' by The Tall Boys).

128 Bruce Campbell explained in an interview in *Video—The Magazine* (September 1987) that it was the video nasties issue surrounding *The Evil Dead* that led the film-makers to play part II more for laughs.

129 Guy Phelps interviewed by Alex J Low, *Killing Moon* No 2.

130 *Psychotronic* No 23.

131 Refered to in the final credits as 'Big Youth' and 'Small Youth.' Small Youth is wearing a T-shirt inscribed 'I am a vampire,' a nod to the previous year's *Vampyres*, a film on which Clarke — and several of the *Exposé* crew — also worked.

132 Another seemingly paranormal aspect that remains unexplored is the strange noise the telephone makes when Paul picks it up — strange enough for him to look quizzically at the receiver, anyway.

133 Which suggests that Intervision acquired a US print of the film for video release in Britain; *The House On Straw Hill* has always been known by that, its original title, stateside.

134 "Linda [Hayden] was hired purely on her strength as a very good young actress," claimed producer Brian Smedley-Aston in an interview with *Gore Creatures* (No 25). Acting abilities to one side, having already appeared in *Baby Love*, *Blood on Satan's Claw* and *Confessions of a Window Cleaner*, Linda's name on a film almost certainly guranteed sexual titilation and a flash of bare flesh.

135 "They wanted a punchy, one-word title with vaguely sexual connotations," producer Brian Smedley-Aston told Tim Greaves in *Flesh & Blood* No 8.

136 If only in the local bully boys attempting to gang rape the beautiful outsider.

137 Clarke would produce *Paul Raymond's Erotica* in 1980, a feature film in which the publishing magnate was able to air his philosophies on life. It was directed by Brian Smedley-Aston.

138 See 'Jolly Hockey Sticks!' by David Kerekes (in Jack Stevenson's book *Fleshpot*) for more on Taboo.

139 Some of which are labelled 'Mary Millington Classics.' These include *Come Play with Me*, *The Playbirds*, *Confessions from the David Galaxy Affair*, *Queen of the Blues*, and the bio-pic *Mary Millington's True Blue Confessions*. These films were awful and — given the restrictions of the BBFC — sexless, but turned a tidy profit thanks to the fervent ad campaigning of producer David Sullivan. He ran reviews and photo-

spreads which promised much more than any of the films actually delivered. Eventually the hyperbole landed him in bother with the Trading Standards Office, and Sullivan pulled out of making films.

140 *Psychotronic* No 8.

141 Tim Greaves, *Flesh & Blood* No 8.

142 Michael Carr, an actor who one source has claimed made guest appearances in TV shows like *Hunter* and *Alias Smith and Jones*, although we are unable to confirm this.

143 The sequence is probably influenced by a scene in Umberto Lenzi's *Deep River Savages*, where native tribesmen hack off the top of monkey's head and dine on the exposed brain.

144 Part of this monologue and other pearls of wisdom spoken by Gröss were sampled by techno industrialists New Mind for 'Life In Hell,' a track on their 1993 CD *Fractured*.

145 The clapperboard identifies the movie as *Hell Raisin'* or *Hell Raisers*, directed by one Emile Scott. Gröss claims it was released shortly after the stunt was filmed, but no record of a movie or director by those names can be traced.

146 The missing footage includes film of various state executions, all evidently bogus. In the first of these clips the coughs of a man dying in a gas chamber can be clearly heard emenating from the air-tight chamber. Next is the death by electrocution of one Larry DeSilva. A mournful harmonica plays as the condemned man is escorted from his cell, but once strapped in the chair the music takes on a merry, slapstick timbre. As the electricity surges, blood leaks from under the tape covering DeSilva's eyes and white goo rolls from his mouth. A third execution is said to have been secretly shot by a tourist in the Middle East (which fails to explain the variety of camera angles and close-ups used). A man is led from a tent, forced to kneel at a chopping block and is beheaded with the single stroke of a sword. The headless body topples to the sand and refuses to bleed, such is the shabbiness of the economical effect.
A Satanic cult performing a cannibalistic ritual is next. Set "on the outskirts of San Francisco" with a leader who resembles Charles Manson, the cult feast on organs sliced effortlessly from a fresh cadaver. Gröss claims to have gained the trust of the cult's leader and thus been granted the privilege of filming the ritual, which culminates in a bloody orgy.
No deaths occur in film of serpent handlers in a Kentucky church. Newsreel footage of a woman throwing herself to her death from an apartment block is real, but again the choice of music is desperately insensitive. The intro to the Dixieland jazz piece ("One, two, ah-one, two, three, four...") is timed to coincide with the woman's leap. After a brief look at cryogenic suspension, the same musical insensitivity accompanies the bloated, washed-up victim of a drowning.
Concocted footage resumes with supposed randomly shot tourist film set in a national park, in which a man exits his car to feed a grizzly bear and is promptly killed. The final shot has the bear ambling into the woods with a rubbery severed limb hanging from its jaws.
An anti-nuclear protestor douses himself in petrol and sets himself alight, much to the horror of his fellow campaigners. This bogus set-piece marks the end of the footage excised from the British print of *Faces of Death*.

147 In their review of the film, *Magick Theatre* (No 7) state that "wildlife film-maker Bill Burryd" is amongst the *Faces of Death* crew, but that's not a name that appears anywhere in the credits.

148 In these sequels, the spelling of Frances Gröss' name was gender-corrected to Francis.

149 Flellis first appeared in Gorgon Video's compilation *Worst of Faces of Death*, where he admited to being a surgeon and that Gröss had died under his knife undergoing a simple operation. He seems to be playing his role for laughs, fidgeting, staring wide-eyed into the camera, and even offering the viewers of Part IV one of his own compositions as a musical backdrop to a scene of unconvincing carnage.

150 Schier's *Faces of Death 5*, for example, takes much of its atrocity footage from Nick Bougas' *Death Scenes*. While *Faces of Death 6* incorporates Fred Warshofsky's *Days of Fury* — a mondo film with Vincent Price as the host — almost in its entirety.

151 Tellingly, the film concludes on the following admonition: "Exigious scenes within this motion picture have been reconstructed to document and further clarify their factual origin."

152 It features as a bonus on a recent DVD release of the original film.

153 As told in soft focus flashback, it transpires that Karen had a thing going with the Turner's eldest son, but that he was killed in a car crash. Mrs Turner holds Karen responsible for his death. It's an insignificant and misleading revelation in an otherwise clear-cut script.

154 The slurs don't only volley between Kane and the Turner family, but also between the rest of the convicts. "Nigger." "Spade." "Turd." "Uncle Remus." "Coon." "Black Ass Coon." "Booger." "Monkey Face." "Chink." "Spic." "Boy." "Poor White Trash." "Brown Dirtball." "Darky." "Jive Ass Coon." "Martin Luther Coon." "Jungle Bunny." "Pink Pig." "Honky." "White Trash Faggot."

155 A sequence filmed in a way that attempts to show each blow in a realistic manner, but only succeeds in looking 'clipped' and curiously inanimate. Not unlike the blows reigned down on Aubrey at the beginning of *Axe*.

156 Directed by Jackson St Louis, it features a prison break that results in three cons taking refuge in a house shared by four beautiful women. "Bet you fucked a lot of assholes in prison," one of the hostages says to Joey Silvera. "Bet you really know how to do it." In no time at all everybody is enjoying sex, some of it anal.

157 Which featured a cancer ravaged Humphrey Bogart in his last gangster role. He was to die two years later.

158 One of its alternative titles — *I Hate Your Guts* — even borrows from Roger Corman's 1962 film *The Intruder*, which deals with racism in a Mississippi town and which became *I Hate Your Guts!* on its re-release some years later.

159 The ad with this byline also makes use of the familiar *Fight For Your Life* artwork, which depicts Kane and Turner, face-to-face, locked in mortal combat. However, it rotates the image

slightly in Turner's favour, making it look as if he's got more of the upper hand, bearing down on the white trash.

160 Played by William Sanderson, whose penchant for playing cinematic villians prompted him to remark in *Empire* magazine, "I'd rather be typecast than not cast at all." Sanderson also appears in *Coal Miner's Daughter*, *Blade Runner*, *Last Man Standing*, amongst others.

161 *Shock Cinema* No 6.

162 Ten minutes of film was cut by the distributors prior to submission to the BBFC, who then went on to remove a further thirty-one sections totalling half-an-hour.

163 As *Uncle Tom* was an imported film, charges could not have been brought against the film-makers anyway, but only the distributor or exhibitor.

164 The release of *Uncle Tom* saw no race riots erupting around theatres. In fact, not much controversy of any kind, with the exception of a solitary protest from Mrs Mary Whitehouse.

165 More than one source has erroneously stated that *Fight For Your Life* received a theatrical release in Britain.

166 In removing this final reel, the BBFC also deprived black audiences of the 'joy of total revenge,' and effectively stacked the film in the white man's favour. Making *Uncle Tom* 'more racist' in other words.

167 As noted in the *BBFC Annual Report 1993*.

168 It happened in a (now closed down) cinema in Manchester city centre, which was showing a a late-night Romero double-bill. The character of Peter in *Dawn of the Dead* — wearing full military garb and gasmask — is portrayed first as a hero and then revealed to be black. This other film on the bill that night had been *Night of the Living Dead*, whose central character is also a black man.

169 Cinema licenses in London, however, do carry a condition which prohibits the screening of a film that may stir up hatred "on grounds of colour, race or ethnic or national origins."

170 Film Censorship and British Social History, Institute of Contemporary Arts, November 20, 1998.

171 *Forest of Fear* was also shot in Pennsylvania, Romero's home state.

172 Indeed most of the cast are murdered off-screen, including the crop pilot and his wife, the two hippies who drink from the stream, the hermit, the pickup truck driver...

173 This incestuous relationship doesn't come as quite the surprise one suspects is intended. Incestuous innuendoes are littered throughout the film, i.e. the Baron refering to his sister's beautiful body on more than one occasion.

174 No one is actually addressed or refered to as Frankenstein in the picture.

175 *Castle of Frankenstein* (No 20) announced in the news column of their Summer 1973 issue that "Andy Warhol is adapting *Frankenstein* in Rome, with Udo Kier..."

176 Given the highly publicised case in which police seized a print of *Flesh* being shown in London (see CLAMPDOWN), it can be no coincidence that the first of Morrissey's two horror pictures is called *Flesh for Frankenstein.*

177 *DarkSide* No 48.

178 "I shot a lot of the special effects scenes with the blood and intestines bursting in the direction of the audience," Margheriti told *Video Watchdog* (No 28). "Of course," he added, "it has to be seen in 3-D, otherwise it is just vulgar and dirty."

179 Vipco's video packaging in Britain sported the titles *Andy Warhol's Frankenstein* and *Andy Warhol's Dracula*.

180 Aided by his physical appearance and the fact that he lost ten pounds over the weekend break between filming *Flesh for Frankenstein* and *Blood for Dracula*. "That's why in *Dracula* I had to sit in a wheelchair," Kier told *San Francisco Bay Guardian* in 1998. "I had no more power. I was sweating all over because I had to wear that fur coat, and it was so heavy and I was so weak that I could hardly walk."

181 The Aurum Encyclopedia of Horror states that this famous remark is often misquoted... and then go on to misquote it. Notably, Aurum was one of the first sources to attribute *Flesh for Frankenstein* to Antonio Margheriti. The print under review is evidently Italian and Aurum's woefully po-faced interpretation of the film suggests that much of the humour in Morrissey's original has been lost in the translation.

182 In the gloriously eccentric tradition of supporting features, the other short film was *Our Cissy*, the tale of a Northern lass moving down to London and finding misery.

183 Directed by Georgie Miller in 1972, this satrical piece runs for only thirteen minutes. *Violence in the Cinema Part 1* is presented as a lecture whose topic is illustrated with violent actions meted out first on the speaker himself and later to a female victim in a torture chamber. These comprise shotgun blasts, a bottle being smashed in a face, immolation, falling from a window, being struck by a car, and disembowelment. The *Monthly Film Bulletin* described it as 'unusually detailed stunts and effects, floating like sadistic daydreams in a slough of trivilaity.' The doctor-lecturing-the-viewer hook was utilised in another Australian film, Richard Franklin's 1976 *Fantasm*. The topic in this instance was sex.

184 *Psychotronic Video* No 6.

185 You can spot the real reanimated dead because they have a reflective cat's eye stuck onto the side of their neck.

186 The hooded figures look to be modelled on Ray Dennis Steckler's Cash Flagg persona, particularly as he appears in *The Incredibly Strange Creatures who Stopped Living and Became Mixed-Up Zombies!!?*

187 A set-piece that would resurface in John Dahl's *Red Rock West*.

188 With a good old fashioned, pasty faced monster, courtesy of a not-very-convincing makeup design from the usually resilient Rick Baker.

189 Most of these references are to films released by Universal, the company also behind *The Funhouse*.

190 In Larry Block's originally screenplay, the barker and owner of the Funhouse does have a name: 'Conrad Straker.' Another facet which failed to make the transition to the screen is the fact that Amy's mother — virtually a non-

entity in the movie — is strictly religious.

191 She is also the only girl in the film whose breasts are exposed for the audience — twice. There is probably something deeply telling in that.

192 Which stipulates that after a day's shooting, actors must not be back on set until a period of twelve hours has elapsed. Going overtime on one day may mean you lose several hours the next day.

193 The director's chair on *Venom* was given over to Piers Haggard, a film whose cast is described by Leonard Maltin as appearing to be drunk or looking as though it wishes it were in equal measures.

194 Although disappointed with *The Funhouse*, Hooper was evidentally impressed enough by the spooky attributes of a carnival-after-dark to feature one at the core of his eagerly awaited *The Texas Chain Saw Massacre 2*.

195 "When the superman wishes to amuse himself he must do so even at the cost of the life of others."

196 To be fair he doesn't actually call them rats, but that is obviously the implication. Unless of course the Germans had a strain of gerbils excited by blood or interested in eating flesh as opposed to feeding on seeds, grasses and roots? Rat-substitutes can also be found in *Beast in Heat* and no doubt many other cheap Italian exploitation vehicles.

197 The scene appears to have been shot in a functioning industrial brick kiln.

198 And no doubt inspired by Kubrick's *The Shining* with a dash of Stuart Rosenberg's *The Amityville Horror* thrown into the mix.

199 Ann's decapitation is foreseen by May (a showroom dummy bearing the babysitter's face falls off and oozes blood), inferring that they share a supernatural link.

200 Steve Thrower in his book *Beyond Terror: The Films of Lucio Fulci* makes the observation that, after the attack, as Gittelson is being dragged away, "we get a glimpse of *further* injuries to the head that seem to have been omitted... As it turns out, they are all that is left of an effects sequence that was filmed but failed to meet with Fulci's requirements."

201 Riz Ortolani wrote the film's horribly sickly, wildly inappropriate main theme, a typical verse of which goes: 'Sweetly, oh sweetly / Summertime is coming / Happy and carefree / Waiting just for you.' One can only assume Riz had yet to view the film when he penned those lines.

202 The theme of rape is a relatively common one in porn loops of the seventies, though it also featured in a feature-length hardcore production by the name of *Expensive Tastes* at the tail end of the decade. Here a man brings his dates back to his apartment only to orchestrate their rape at the hands of some friends dressed in ski-masks who 'break-in.'

203 *Gore Gazette* No 73.

204 Sullivan is the first person to have gone on record as admitting in print that this elusive version of *House on the Edge of the Park* exists.

205 The videobox claims it to be based on the "notorious recent Canadian murder trial of one, Peter Demeter."

206 During the rape, he keeps on manouevering her skirt so that the viewer can see a lot of flesh, but not quite enough to be technically 'indecent.'

207 Christianity and religion has hitherto played no part in Jennifer's life or in the film.

208 A good and insightful film critic, Ebert has also written screenplays for Russ Meyer, including his smash hit *Beyond the Valley of the Dolls*.

209 *Los Angeles Times*, March 21, 1982.

210 According to an interview with Zarchi in *Fangoria* (No 39), the director himself made these cuts

211 *Sleazoid Express* Vol 2 No 3.

212 Camille Keaton — Buster Keaton's grand-niece — married director Meir Zarchi shortly after completing *I Spit On Your Grave*, her first American film. Prior to that she had worked in Italy and appeared in Massimo Dallamano's *What Have They Done To Solange?*, Mino Guerrini's *Decameron II* and Elo Pannaccio's *Sex of the Witch*. Christian Kessler in *ETC* (No 16) suggests that Keaton went on to appear in "sex movies."

213 *Draculina* No 7.

214 In *Elliot's Guide to Films on Video*, there are no details listed under 'Wizard,' but instead a cross-reference to Video Programme Distrubtors Ltd, based in Middlesex. Could it be that VPD — or some other UK company — simply utilised the American distributor's name and logo for an unofficial release of the film?

215 It's an image that Zarchi "duplicated exactly" in the film. The one where Jennifer, after being sodomised over a rock, stands before the summerhouse in a daze. It's also a scene that conjures the familiar image of the Vietman war where a burned little girl runs slowly from her napalmed village.

216 *Fangoria* No 39.

217 *No Time For Pranksters* and *No Love on the River* were potential titles that Zarchi considered for *I Spit On Your Grave*.

218 "The idea that a rape victim would seduce her attackers to lure them to their deaths," deliberated Michael Gingold in *Fangoria* No 179, "is almost more offensive than the rapes themselselves."

219 *Demonique* No 4.

220 'Sola Perduta Abandonatto' from *Manon Lescaut* by Giacomo Puccini. (Which roughly translates as 'Alone Lost Abandoned.')

221 Incidentally, the harmonica provides the film with its very own 'Duelling Banjos' — another 'nod' to *Deliverance*.

222 According to Zarchi, he is also responsible for *producing* the film — in spite of what the credits say.

223 He has a co-writer credit on Shlomo Suriano's *Nini*.

224 *Fangoria* No 179.

225 Though the title *The Rape and Revenge of Jennifer Hill* appears to predate this.

226 In his article for *Is it... Uncut?* (No 3), Nigel Burrell states the missing dialogue comes from an early scene in which the gang discuss how women

are full of shit and that California is the place to get laid. Later, further small talk (in the scene where the men consider why no one has yet discovered Jennifer's body) is also removed. The cuts appear to have been made to bring the running time down from an initial 101 minutes.

227 Apparently, some of the material eventually surfaced in the guise of Farmer's *Snuff All Bitches/Ms. Maniac*.

228 Lorenzo Battagua is credited with the "Underwater Sequence," although it is somewhat common knowledge that the aging Mario Bava had a considerable part to play. Bava's son, Lamberto, is credited with assistant director on *Inferno*.

229 *Psychotronic Video* No 18

230 Oddly enough, there is a sequence in *Inferno* which looks like it belongs in the murder-mystery setting of *Tenebrae* – that of black gloved hands cutting the heads off paper figures.

231 The realistic, throwaway banter between the gang members also brings to the film an almost documentary quality.

232 *Wes Craven's Last House on the Left*, David A Szulkin.

233 The original draft for the story was apparently even more extreme, both in terms of sex and violence.

234 Wes Craven interviewed by Kim Newman, *Shock Xpress* Vol 2 No 4.

235 Craven's next film *The Hills Have Eyes* would similarly focus upon middle-class characters seeking over-the-top, cartoon-like revenge on the degenerates who have wronged them.

236 Music in the film was by David Hess (and an uncredited Steve Chapin). Hess, a former A&R man at Mercury Records in New York, had completed two albums prior to *Last House*, as well as having written songs that would become hits for Elvis Presley, Pat Boone and Andy Williams.

237 A remnant of the sequence can be seen at the end of the Replay Video print, in the flashback moments that one supposes should have credits running over the top. (The film has no end credits.)

238 The intestine shot as it appears in *Last House* lasts only a few brief seconds.

239 Extra footage concerning the switchblade attack can be found in the Dutch Best Video release of the film.

240 Rather, George is *one* of the proprietors. There are two names scribed onto the door of the ('Antiques Modern') shop: George Meaning and Tony Gordon.

241 It's a little unclear as to what business George actually has in Windermere. According to his various conversations, he has a weekend retreat there, is working on a house with some people he knows, and/or has an appointment to sell some antiques to a dealer. Whatever the reason, a phonecall he later makes, notifying an anonymous friend/associate of his delay, takes on a sinister, desperate edge.

242 He actually says, accusingly, "Up from London then?" George neither agrees nor disagrees. But then, the film makes no actual reference to the rush-hour montage of the opening credits being scenes of Manchester (David Pirie, in *The Vampire Cinema*, assumes it's London); it's just a major city from which George must travel. And the Lakes – where "Saturday to Monday I can hear the grass grow," so George tells Edna early on in their journey together – is just a place that is removed from it. It's this lack of any real definition of time or place that helps to create the ethereal, other-worldly quality which permeates the film. (The only mention of Manchester in *The Living Dead* comes when a doctor at the hospital in Southgate explains to George that Manchester is where they ship bodies for pathological tests.)

243 McCormick calls Katie "Mrs West." When asking for directions, George refers to Katie and Martin's house as "the Madison place."

244 The owner of the garage has a daughter with Downs Syndrome, in whose face Edna sees a vision of Martin – a 'subtle' insinuation that she is amongst those whose makeup includes a 'primitive nervous system' affected by the pest-control device. In case you don't get it, the last we see of the girl, she is reaching for a piece of broken glass, the soundtrack playing its menacing refrain.

245 The name of the hotel is inscribed on a glass pane on a door. We only get to see it from its reverse side but more astute viewers may realise there is a spelling error (perhaps a set-designer's prank?). From the correct side the inscription would actually read: 'THE OLD OLW HOTEL.'

246 The clumsy grammar can't be attributed to a poor or literal translation of the original Spanish title – *No Profanar el Sueño de los Muertos* – as the two bear no relation whatsoever. (A literal translation would be 'Don't Disturb the Sleep of the Dead.') One US retitle of the film – *Breakfast at Manchester Morgue* – also suffers from being similarly clipped.

247 The way having been paved by Jonas Cornell's *Hugs and Kisses* and Lindsay Anderson's *If....*, both films which showed pubic hair and were passed without cuts. With this, the maxim that "the difference between art and pornography is bodily hair" to which the BBFC had always adhered, was finally laid to rest.

248 Alberto de Martino's *The Tempter*, Ovidio G Assonitis' *Beyond the Door*, Juan Bosch's *Exorcismo*, and Amando de Ossorio's *Demon Witch Child*.

249 The posters and other illustrations in *Monster Mag* – which ran for fourteen issues – were for the most part scenes lifted from Hammer films. Relatively innocuous fare like *Dracula A.D. 1972* and *The Reptile*, which might only have had a split-second of on-screen viscera, looked like complete bloodbaths courtesy of *Monster Mag*'s choice selection. Hammer 'full-gloss gore' later found its way into the completely lacklustre and short-lived *Legend Horror Classics* series of poster-magazines.

250 Romero's own follow-up to *Night of the Living Dead*, the more 'upbeat' *Dawn of the Dead*, would exert an incredible influence on the Italian horror film. See *Zombie Creeping Flesh* and *Zombie Flesh-Eaters*.

251 The British print of *The Living Dead* opens with Guthrie's face popping up in a painting in George's antique shop, suggesting that his part in the film might have at some earlier stage been a greater one.

252 The X-certificated theatrical print of *The Living Dead at the Manchester Morgue* is missing much of the footage of the zombies devouring the

policeman in the churchyard, and the entirety of the sequence where zombies tear apart the telephone receptionist. Here it cuts from them closing in on the receptionist, to them munching on something and then to the bloody aftermath.

253 *Don't Open the Window* was a heavily truncated US version of *The Living Dead*, also made available in Britain in the days before the VRA. This version wasn't classed as a nasty.

254 *The Living Dead at the Manchester Morgue* was the first major work for de Rossi, who went on to handle effects on *Fellini's Casanova*, and countless Italian horror films through the rest of the seventies and eighties.

255 Against the envy of less happier lands,
This blesséd plot, this earth, this realm, this England...

—*Richard II*

256 Look to José Larraz' *Vampyres* for a similar sense of English-countryside-as-alien-landscape, and a film which utilises even fewer characters than those to be had in *The Living Dead*. The two films also have a curious link in that one of them closes with a murder set in a hotel bedroom, and the other one opens with a murder set in a hotel bedroom.

257 Music composed, arranged and conducted by Giuliano Sorgini. The soundtrack album was originally released on the Manchester-based Eurobeat label in 1974 (this is now hard to find — more accessible are the recent CD incarnations). Other tracks on it include 'Mysterious Country' and 'Drowned Guthrie.'

258 *Fandom's Film Gallery* July 1978. Quoted in *Let Sleeping Corpses Lie*, by Nigel Burrell.

259 Latham is evidently the "one who lived it" stated in the opening title. Though there is no way of knowing whether the story is fact or not, the film-makers pin the unfolding events down with plenty of uneccessarily accurate references to time, as if this alone authenticates matters.

260 The entire Love Camp outdoor set consists of a single wall in the courtyard, painted blue.

261 Godhardt says to one girl, "I personally don't agree with any of this." To which she replies "Do you mean the war or this concentration camp?" There is an uncertainty in the way she delivers this line and for a fleeting moment it seems that her response is going to be: "Do you mean the war or this film?"

262 Curiously there is a single fleeting glimpse of pubis near the beginning of the film but this seems almost an accident, or a crafty insinuation that the film is going to deliver a lot more than it actually does. Which is no doubt what made experts in these Adults Only pictures so expert; as authors Turan and Zito point out in their book *Sinema*, "although [these directors] did not show the viewer what he wanted to see, the audience kept coming back."

263 The lesbian orgy is filmed in exactly the same way, with women wrestling against the pawing of fellow prisoners.

264 His gun was his undoing: Brandishing his revolver and rushing to aid a woman he believed was in distress, Cresse was shot twice in the belly by — the story goes — two police officers, who then opened fire on Cresse's dog.

265 According to Muller & Faris in their book *That's Sexploitation!!*

266 And whilst on the subject... there can be no doubting that the rather ridiculous *nom de plume*, Captain Calais, belongs to a French man.

267 Including what is probably the first US nudie documenatry, *Hollywood's World of Flesh*.

268 Jack Starrett took his place.

269 *That's Sexploitation!!*, Muller & Faris.

270 The relationship between Frost and Cresse hadn't been helped by the fact Friedman had called on Frost to direct one of his films, *The Defilers*, which proved a smash hit. The revalry deepened when Cresse invested more time and money than usual in promoting a western called *Hot Spur*, only to have Friedman ride his coattails and pip him at the post with *Brand of Shame*, a western of his own.

271 It would be many years before Friedman came clean and admitted his involvement in the picture.

272 Dr Lewis is probably a tip of the hat to H G Lewis, director of *Blood Feast*.

273 'Perception and presentation of Mesoamerican groups by the film industry,' a talk by Dr Richard Shupp, Lafayette College, to The Pre-Columbian Society on February 14, 1998. Among the other films excerpted or discussed in the lecture were Larry Cohen's *Q*, Tobe Hooper's *I'm Dangerous Tonight* and numerous Aztec Mummy films from Mexico.

274 *Psychotronic Video* No 28.

275 *Video Watchdog* Special Edition No 2.

276 Played by José Elias Moreno, "South of the Border's answer to George Kennedy" according to a review in *Dreadful Pleasures* No 3.

277 But the fun doesn't stop there — later the same elderly woman runs into a cop and explains, "There around the corner is a man and he's dead!"

278 *Monster Mag* No13.

279 Some sources suggest that a more sexually explicit version of *Bloody Apes* was released under the title *Horror y Sexo*. Although 'Horror and Sex' is possibly the finest title ever to grace an exploitation film, it is highly unlikely that it would have contained additional Cardona footage not present in the IFS version.

280 Patterson was a onetime rodeo rider, inventor and promoter, who spent what free time he had roaming the Pacific Northwest woods with a 16mm camera, shooting footage which he hoped to turn into a documentary on the mystery of the Bigfoot. On October 20, 1967, whilst travelling the woods with a companion, Patterson caught on twenty-eight feet of film what is arguably a female Bigfoot.

281 It doesn't explain how Cheryl had been raising Billy prior to this for the last three years.

282 *Psychotronic Video* No 6.

283 The camera makes an issue of religious upbringing only once, in the latter part of the film, when it lingers over a familiar sketch of Jesus Christ that looks to have its eyes both open and closed at the same time.

284 Asher directed all five of AIP's dedicated beach movies: *Beach Party*, *Muscle Beach Party*, *Bikini Beach*, *Beach Blanket Bingo*, and *How To Stuff a Wild Bikini*. (AIP's *Pajama*

Party and *Ski Party*, not set on a beach, and not directed by Asher, were banded beach movies nonetheless.)

285 Bo Svenson (Lieutenant Carlson) played no-nonesense Tennessee sheriff Buford Pusser in a NBC-TV series in 1981, a reprise of the role he had in two of the *Walking Tall* hit movies of the Seventies. (He played cops in a lot of other movies, too.) Julia Duffy, who plays Billy's girlfriend Julie, was a regular on the *Newhart* TV show.

286 Which begs the question that if the DPP doesn't consider a film to be obscene or liable to be prosecuted, how can the Board justify their decision to reject it?

287 In between which is a peculiar trailer for Tom McLoughlin's *One Dark Night* that has no narration, virtually no dialogue, and looks unfinished.

288 Lester Lorraine committed suicide a year or so after *Nightmares* was released. His name is nowhere in evidence in the British print of the film.

289 Although in his *Spaghetti Nightmares* interview Scavolini does appropriate some truly cringe-inducing significance on C J's pranks and, because they were encouraged to improvise their dialogue, the actors spoke "sincerely" and from the "inside."

290 Made of plastic, according to a reporter for the *Sunday Times*.

291 Reporting on the trial, *The Daily Telegraph* noted how Hamilton-Grant had a previous conviction for indecently exposing himself in a sex cinema.

292 *Spaghetti Nightmares*, Palmerini & Mistretta.

293 *Continental Film and Video Review* Vol 29 No 4. The unaccredited article is systematic of the eclectic mix that constituted *Continental Film and Video Review*. The high-brow analysis of *Possession* is followed by photospreads from Michael Winner's *Death Wish 2*, something from Jay Jay Film Distributors that appears to be called *Swedish Erotic Sexations*, and an advertisement for *Bog* starring Aldo Ray.

294 *Eyeball* No 5.

295 Zulawski points to the scene in the kitchen as an example. Indeed, the exchange that takes place here between Marc and Anna — she deflecting each of his pleas and questions with a pointed "Excuse Me!" — is so skewered that it has no place in the realm of fiction; it could only have been drawn from reality.

296 Interview with Zulawski, *Eyeball* No 5.

297 ibid.

298 This being the result of a French law at the time of *Possession*'s release, which meant that the screening of a foreign language picture had to be met with the screening of a French language print on another screen, elsewhere in the country.

299 Also known as *The Lorelei's Grasp*.

300 *Fangoria* No 17.

301 It does seem that the film-makers originally intended to have a lot of gore in *Pranks*. "The effects are almost the most important part of this film," Obrow told *Fangoria*. When New Image Releasing picked up the film for distribution in the US, they did so on the understanding that cuts may be necessary, "because the effects are so very strong, and because it's so very realistic." Of course, such remarks may simply have been down to Obrow trying to generate horror-fan interest prior to the release of the film.

302 The British print looks to contain the original credits, being written in dripping 'blood' on a series of title cards (modified credits of this era usually appear over a freeze frame or on a plain background insert). Fingertips holding the cards fall into shot with alarming regularity. In America the film was also known as *Boogeyman II*.

303 It's a name that crops up in other Lommel films. *The Devonsville Terror*, a film Lommel directed the same year as *Revenge of the Bogeyman* (and quite possibly back-to-back with it) is sometimes credited to Starr.

304 Review of *Double Jeopardy* (under its US title, *A Taste of Sin*), Donald Farmer, *The Splatter Times* No 4.

305 Some sources credit *Revenge of the Bogeyman* as being made in 1980. The reference to de Palma's *Blow Out* — a film made in 1981 — irrefutably contradicts this however.

306 None according to the critic in *Fangoria* (No 31), who claims that the dialogue in *Revenge of the Bogeyman* "is so off-the-beam that the actors seem like they are reciting words learned phonetically without any knowledge of what they mean."

307 The blurb on the video jacket even states as much: "There's black humour all the way to the graveyard ending which is strongly reminiscent of de Palma's *Carrie*."

308 The girl who stabs herself in the bathroom is shown lifting the scissors to her throat. But the bloody point of entry is removed and the next we see of her she is falling over, the scissors sticking out of her neck. The sequence depicting the young man who gets a knife driven out his mouth whilst seated in a car is similarly truncated.

309 In the third film in the Baby Cart series (*Lightning Swords of Death*), Lone Wolf faces an entire army and reveals the cart to be fitted with primitive machine guns. It's a ridiculous moment.

310 The films appear to exist under a multitude of different titles, largely thanks to reference works citing anglicised translations of the original Japanese titles.

311 For more information concerning *Shogun Assassin*, the original Japanese film series and the manga comic that inspired it, see *Asian Trash Cinema* Vol 1 No 2, No 5 and No 6.

312 Actually Tybee Island, off the coast of Georgia.

313 Not to mention one of the more poetic — Brooke makes it so far as a window and dies in its frame, with the rain coming down outside.

314 In the cut version, all visual references to the woman being stabbed with the fork are gone. As Brooke struggles to exit the boarded window, the pitchfork is seen looming closer. With a close-up of Brooke's hand on the window frame, bleeding from the broken glass, the scene cuts to the pitchfork. Cut back to hand, relaxing in death. Cut to Brooke's face, blood coming out of her mouth (and a very noticeable jump in the musical soundtrack). Cut to the following day.

315 Antonio Climati and Mario Morra's *Savage Man... Savage Beast*, a big hit

in Times Square and pre-dating *Snuff* by several months, was a mondo film which featured highly dubious home cine footage of a man being eaten alive by lions in a safari park. Scenarios like this were incorporated into mondo films spanning two decades, and surruptiotiously passed off as depicting actual fatalities.

316 See Kerekes & Slater's *Killing For Culture* for the full story.

317 The Findlay's were no strangers to exploitation. Prior to *Slaughter*, they had made low-budget efforts like *Body of a Female*, *The Sin Syndicate*, and *Ultimate Degenerate*.

318 These figures have been contradicted a number of times by Roberta Findlay herself. She told *Fangoria* (No 52) in 1986 that the shoot lasted three months and the budget was $50,000 (even though she didn't get paid and they were able to hire a bus and driver to carry their "large crew" for "about 30¢ a day"). Given the look of the film, and — by Roberta's admission — the gung-ho approach to making it, it's impossible to believe it might have taken three straight months to shoot.

319 Others included Frank Howard's *The Other Side of Madness*, David Durston's *I Drink your Blood*, Lee Madden's *The Night God Screamed*, and Ray Danton's *The Deathmaster*. The June 25, 1970, edition of *Rolling Stone* made a reference to a porn movie by the name of *Love in the Commune* which it claimed had a "Manson-type balling a headless chicken." Al Adamson's *Angels Wild Women* features a hippy cult and a girl-biker gang, and has the added distinction of being the last film to be shot at the Spahn ranch — the home of the Family at the time of Manson's arrest. It also had actual Family members appearing as extras.

320 Roberta Findlay, in conversation with the French magazine *Mad Movies* (issue No not known), defended the film by calling it an "impressionist" movie. In another interview, she dismissed it as making no sense.

321 Shackleton, who had previously been employed as a research engineer and consultant to the Department of Defence, started The Monarch Releasing Corp in 1969 (under the name of A L Shackleton Films). His catalogue generally comprised of watered-down X-rated sex films, but in the mid-seventies he experimented with other genres, acquiring the rock concert film *Get Down, Grand Funk*, Arch Oboler's 3-D sci-fi movie *Fantastic Invasion of Planet Earth*, and of course the Findlays' *Slaughter*.

322 *CCVL* No 2.

323 The FBI launched an investigation following the allegation made by the *National Decency Reporter*, but were unable to uncover any further information pertaining to the films mentioned in the piece.

324 Shackleton was involved with another director of porno, Chuck Vincent. Indeed he supposedly produced Vincent's first adult picture in 1973 (*Blue Summer*) and announced that Vincent was set to direct for Monarch in 1975 a film called *Vanilla Odyssey* — "a sexy sci-fi comedy about a lovable vistor from outer space."

325 Liam T Sanford, *Video Viewer*, July 1983.

326 "Everywhere had a copy of *Snuff*," recalls Steve Ellison. When pressed who might have been distributing the film, he replied "It was on the Astra label... I'm not sure who was the head honcho at Astra [Mike Behr, by all accounts] — that was always kept a little bit secret. But some of the big players in the early days were incredible characters, and if you could get hold of some of them now... if they're not at the bottom of a river or whatever..."

327 The film doesn't so much end as just stops: during the gun battle in which Helmut is shot, the sound goes dead, Helmut falls to the floor and the words 'The End' flash up on the screen.

328 *Le Amanti del mostro* and *La Mano che nutre la morte*.

329 Sources credit him with either being the owner of a pizzeria or working as a jeweller.

330 *Shock Xpress* Vol 2 No 3.

331 At least this is the case with the English language print.

332 Goblin's slapstick zombie tune from Romero's *Dawn of the Dead* is the muzak that plays in the store where the shoplifter at the beginning of *Tenebrae* is caught.

333 Ronny Svensson in Fantasy Film Memory's *Directed By Dario Argento*.

334 Dario Argento interview, *Spaghetti Nightmares*, Palmerini & Mistretta.

335 *Halls of Horror* No 23.

336 These films being *The Bird with the Crystal Plumage*, *Cat O'Nine Tails* and *Four Flies on Grey Velvet*.

337 The title can also be interpreted as a reference to the matins and lauds of Holy Week in which candles are extinquished.

338 Millett seems ill at ease spreading the preserve over Eleanor's body, particularly as the further down he goes the more it begins to look like heavy menstrual discharge.

339 Cheesy easy listening music plays throughout the film's first half-hour, courtesy of a radio in the room of each of the victims, or — as in the case of Mrs Andrews — a record player. A nice touch is when the record player, left unchecked following the death of Mrs Andrews, begins to start playing over again as the killer leaves.

340 An anecdote told by David Konow in his book *Schlock-O-Rama*.

341 Courtesy of the Pamelyn Ferdin Web Page Fan Mail.

342 Whose presence flagrantly contradicts Edith's statement of refusing to allow a man in the house.

343 *Unhinged* also beat *Psycho II* into the cinemas by a few months, which may simply have been fortuitous for the film-makers or a pre-emptive bid at the bandwagon.

344 Like the heavy breathing she later encounters, the location of the muted radio playing during these opening minutes can't be sourced. It appears to be eminating from Terry's apartment, even after she has left it. When her friends arrive to collect her in their car it appears to be eminating from that too.

345 Deborah owes her life to a man who appears in the basement after her fall, who is never refered to at all and whose identity remains a mystery.

346 Nurse Shiela has the curious habit of addressing the camera directly in several of her dialogues with Deborah

Ballin. No other character in the film does this.

347 Where would a hospital-based drama such as this be without a few curtains being ripped off their rails? *Visiting Hours* keeps them all until the end.

348 A brief cycle of films probably influenced by Michael Crichton's *Coma*.

349 Snapshots of homicide victims featured in another film made the same year, Gary Sherman's *Dead and Buried* — which happens to have a scene where a nurse kills a patient in a hospital.

350 Paul Naschy, interviewed by José Luis González and Michael Secula, *Videooze* No 6/7.

351 Michael Secula, from his introduction to a Paul Naschy interview, *Videooze* No 6/7.

352 As already stated, Naschy's films often turned up on the export market with specially shot, gorier scenes — material that couldn't be shown in his homeland. The US zine *Demonique* (No 1) ran a review of *The Werewolf and the Yeti* in 1980 and stated of the climactic battle: "Until now, the violence and gore was well-handled and restrained, so it is both good and bad that some explicit, bloody scenes take place at this point in the narrative." Should this be true, it would suggest that the print released in Britain was the tamer version intended for the Spanish market as it contains nothing approximating "explicit, bloody scenes."

353 *Absurd* No 3.

354 Zadora returned for a starring role in Cimber's next picture, *Fake-Out*, a remake of his own *Lady Cocoa*.

355 Turan & Zito, *Sinema*.

356 If it isn't influenced by Carlino's movie, then Cimber chose to do an unofficial adaptation of the same book (by Mishima Yukio) on which Carlino's movie was based.

357 According to *Video Watchdog* (No 1), *Visa pour mourir* — the French release title of *Women Behind Bars* — not only features extra footage of the robbers, but also utilises a "slightly different Daniel White score."

358 The original title of which, according to *Video Watchdog* (No 1), is *Un Secondina in un carcere femminila* (trans. 'Wardeness at a Women's Prison').

359 *Condemned*, *The Big House*, *The Criminal Code*, *I Am a Fugitive From a Chain Gang*, *Escape From Devil's Island*, *Jailbreak*, *Alcatraz Island*, and *Convicted* represent a mere handful of the prison films released by major studios at the dawn of the Talkies era. Some of the recent entries include *Penetentiary III*, *Lock Up*, *Against the Wall* and *Dead Man Walking*. James Robert Parish, in his book *Prison Pictures from Hollywood*, lists close on 300 American movies alone for which prison plays an integral part.

360 An hierachy of stereotyped characters which, as Jim Morton points out in his essay for *RE/Search #10: Incredibly Strange Films*, consists of "The Queen Bee: dominant female prisoner who lords it over the others. The New Fish: usually the lead actress, in jail for the first time. The Sadistic Warden: more often than not the one who proves to be the root of all evil and unrest in prison. The Hooker with the Heart of Gold: a street-smart dame who knows the ropes and befriends the New Fish, for better or worse. The Dyke Guard: sometimes named 'Ruby'..."

361 One scene that does make something of a 'subliminal' impact is the curiously framed head and breast shot. Completely forced and unnatural, it looks almost like one of Ingres' nudes. A similarly staged shot is utilised in another of Franco's WIP film, *Women For Cellblock Nine*. Graf Haufen, in his review for *Film Extremes* (No 1), says of the sequence (in which a prisoner on the run has a bullet removed with some grass!): "There is an unintentionally funny moment during the operation, where a single breast is dangling in the picture, right next to the face of the wounded girl. Is there a hidden message in this poetic moment?"

362 All of which are known by several alternate titles. To make matters even more confusing, *Women For Cellblock Nine* has a character called Milton and another called Maria (who, crying for water, is forced to perform cunnilingus on the female warden, then given salted champagne to drink).

363 *Fangoria* No 19.

364 Two of the working titles for *Xtro* were *Monstromo* and *Monstro*, which have a certain resonance with the name of the mother ship in *Alien* — *Nostromo*.

365 *Fangoria* No 24.

366 The PolyGram Video release of *Xtro* also carries a couple of names for characters who don't appear in the film.

367 *Monthly Film Bulletin*.

368 *Flesh & Blood* No 7.

369 *Starburst* No 57 — a review which carries a publicity still that some *Starburst* office wag has evidently seen fit to doctor. What should be Sam sucking on his son's distended shoulder has been altered to show Sam sucking on what looks uncannily like an erect penis!

370 *The DarkSide* No 81.

371 The living dead ouevre reached its nadir with Umberto Lenzi's *Nightmare City*, A M Frank's *Oasis of the Zombies* and Jean Rollin's *Zombie Lake*.

372 Established in the precursor to *Dawn of the Dead* and the first film of Romero's 'Dead' trilogy: *Night of the Living Dead*.

373 Mattei has used several pseudonyms during his career, such as Jordan B Matthews, Jimmy Matheus and Stefan Oblowsky. Though he would credit himself as Vincent Dawn on several subsequent productions, *Zombie Creeping Flesh* was the first instance in which he utilised that particular name.

374 *European Trash Cinema* Vol 2 No 5.

375 Other films by Bruno Mattei released in Briatin include *SS Girls* (Nazi exploitation), *The Other Hell* (nunsploitation), *Rats: Night of Terror* (horror), *Strike Commando* (action) and *The Seven Magnificent Gladiators* (sword-and-sorcery).

376 As was common in the days before the multiplex, cinemas in some smaller towns didn't always have official posters to promote the films they were screening. As a rough-and-ready alternative they often made their own. Sometimes these impromtu posters comprised of plain text — black marker pen on a brightly coloured sheet of

paper; other times a member of staff with an artistic bent would include a picture of a zombie with fangs — as happened with *Zombie Creeping Flesh* on its run at one long-gone cinema in the north.

377 In his review for *Imaginator* No 6, Ken Miller pondered whether the shark bitten by the zombie would "become an undead shark?"

378 Some time in the early nineties, the scene was actually broadcast uncut on British cable TV as part of Ken Dixon's undead compilation movie, *Zombiethon*.

379 *Absurd, Blood Feast, Blood Rites, The Bogey Man, Cannibal Ferox, Dead and Buried, Forest of Fear, Frozen Scream* and *Night of the Bloody Apes*.

380 Randall Larson, *CineFan* No 3.

381 Interview with Lucio Fulci by Robert Schlockoff, *Starburst* No 48.

382 BBFC press statement.

BLACK MARKET & PIRATES

1 From an article by Andrew Allard found at DVD Nightmare (but which no longer appears to be available).

2 *News of the World*, March 5, 2000.

3 There has been a serious decline in the apprehension of true criminals and in order to keep the books balanced police in general are hitting soft targets — minor motoring offences, litter dropping etc. In this case the police hoped they would find evidence of illegal activity and use it as proof of their crime busting vigilance.

4 Needless to say, most everybody who was interviewed or contributed to this chapter wished to remain anonymous or supplied the authors with an assumed name.

5 Sandwiched between a section on apparel as worn by the cast of *Star Trek*, and lobby cards from the thirties and forties, *Film & Rock'n'Roll Collectables* offers a price guide to a random selection of video titles. For the most part these are pre-certificated video tapes, and regarded as "banned" (though some are clearly foreign imports). Not only is the guide occasionally erroneous and the monetary values misleading, but the whole concept of the video section is lawfully suspect — Lyles or not, you simply cannot evaluate an illegal item in terms of collectability.

6 Nowadays pre-VRA copies of virtually any kind of film are considered collectible and can command relatively high prices.

7 Invariably it was a male. During the course of their research, the authors heard of no instances of females dealing in illicit tapes back in the eighties.

8 The Scala had been the location for an anti-Video Recordings Act festival back on March 10, 1984. Ten films cited by the DPP as video nasties (but all passed for cinema release) were screened: *Don't Go in the House, The Beyond, The Burning, The Evil Dead, Zombie Creeping Flesh, Zombie Flesh-Eaters, House by the Cemetery, The Living Dead at the Manchester Morgue, The Toolbox Murders* and *Dead and Buried*.

9 The police evidently hadn't yet seen the film, as the article concluded with a police spokesperson requesting that the tape be handed over for investigation. And while the newspaper didn't allow the law to get in the way of a good story, they did excite David Alton MP into giving them some knee-jerk copy. Alton said he dreaded to think what the psychological effects of viewing the film might be on children.

10 Reprinted from *Fandamania: It's Only a Movie!* No 1, with the kind permission of editors Tristan Thompson and Carl Nolan.

11 Another tactic that Trading Standards hoped would bust video crime was announced in March 1994. Officers in the North West town of Bury intended to send children into video shops to try and hire 18-certificate films. These "baby-faced snoopers" — in the words of *The Journal* newspaper — were an attempt to weed out dealers who broke the law, supplying adult material indiscriminately. The scheme had proven successful in helping to stop newsagents selling cigarettes and fireworks to those under-age. Video dealers who swallowed the bait were said to face a £5,000 fine.

12 Figures vary. Some press reports claimed that "more than 3,500 videos" had been seized, while thirty people had been held for questioning.

13 Not improbable: Police and Customs were already doing it in their search for porn and fraudsters. According to an article in *The Observer* (April 29, 1990), "disguised as a Jones or a Smith," they peruse the likes of *Video World*, "looking in particular at the classified ads, where a two-line entry may lead them to a trader in bizarre material."

14 This and the other quotes attributed to David Flint are taken from "Busted!," Flint's own reminiscence on the case which appears on the Melon Farmers' Video Hits web site.

15 Not dissimilar to the furore that surrounded a raid of a few days earlier, in which Midlands police took from a student's flat a book by photographer Robert Mapplethorpe on the grounds that it was obscene. Containing images of homosexuality and bondage, the book belonged to the University of Central England and was being used for a thesis on 'Fine Art versus Pornography.' In this instance, the police were alerted by a chemist to whom the student had taken photos from the book to be developed.

16 They describe themselves as "a front-line organisation responsible for protecting society against the growing threat of illicit drugs, firearms and paedophile material."

17 *Obscenity*, Geoffrey Robertson.

18 Right along side other items such as unlicensed drugs (such as heroin, morphine, cocaine, cannabis, amphetamines, barbiturates and LSD), offensive weapons (such as flick knives, swordsticks, knuckle-dusters and some martial arts equipment), indecent and obscene material featuring children (such as books, magazines, films, videotapes, laser discs and software), and counterfeit and pirated goods and goods that infringe patents (such as watches, clocks and CDs and any goods with false marks of their origin).

19 The plan to release the film was abandoned due to its explicitly violent content.

20 *Cannibal* was available in a cut version in the UK. It was never banned but disappeared from shelves due to its

association with other banned cannibal titles. *Primitifs* was released in the UK as *Savage Terror*; *Night of the Devils* never came out officially on video in Britain, though it did have a cinema release in the seventies.

21 Official Secrets Act 1989 and Protection of Children Act 1978.

22 'Squish' is the name given to a brand of fetishism which focuses upon women — often in high heel shoes — trampling to death insects and small animals. A man in Shropshire was fined £2,000 in 1998 for the importation of squish films, following a joint RSPCA and Customs & Excise investigation... A man from Edinburgh was fined £1,000 in 1999 after Customs intercepted films with titles like *Debased Dolly* and *Pain 32* which, according to *The Scotsman* newspaper, "portrayed horrific sex scenes, including footage of women being raped."

23 Customs Officer Mark Thompson. *Sight & Sound*, May 1998.

24 It isn't accurate to state that the VRA was also responsible for creating a black market in hardcore pornography. Despite claims made by some journalists, there has always been a trade in under-the-counter porn in Britain. Indeed, it was porno that helped to galvanise interest and shape video in the first place — as it tends to do with any new technology. A Home Video Show sponsored by the *Daily Mirror* in the early eighties, was raided by police who removed videocassettes on the Swedish Erotica label. And while films like *Debbie Does Dallas*, *A Dirty Western* and *Deep Throat* were being released legitimately by companies in Britain in specially trimmed formats — albeit in a form stronger than would be tolerated by the BBFC today — full uncut versions of the same titles were always available to those who sought them out.

25 The *ET* anti-piracy task force was in operation a full six months before the film made it onto video. Anti-piracy screenings of *ET* were held for team personnel; master tapes were coded and their transportation closely supervised and logged as they made their way into the eight major territories.

26 In the first months of 1980, many of the 10,000 owners of VCRs in Israel were watching illegal copies of new films like *The Deer Hunter* and *Kramer Vs. Kramer*. Israeli police sourced them back to London.

27 *The Home Video Revolution in Western Europe*, Economist Intelligence Unit, London, 1983.

28 Another source recalls that many of the pirated Disney films in circulation had Arabic subtitles.

29 Nowadays Southeast Asia is largely considered the piracy epicentre, with illicit copies of films being sold quite openly mere days after they have opened theatrically in the US. Some shops deal exclusively in pirated product. In order to try and combat the problem, major films have occasionally played in Malaysia and Singapore ahead of their US dates.

30 Marcrovision worked by confusing the automatic gain control in the copying recorder. The process was the result of research that had started in 1983. Embassy Home Entertainment, involved in its development, launched Macrovision with their massively hyped, commercial flop *The Cotton Club*.

31 The ad, shown on TV and in cinemas, starts with the parent of a small boy buying a pirate tape. Instead of watching an innocent cartoon, the child is subjected to a terrifying onslaught of brutally horrific and violent sexual imagery.

32 The claims were made prior to the current IRA ceasefire when acts of terrorism on mainland Britain were still a serious threat.

33 In *Film 95* (September 25), following a report concerning pirate copies of Disney's *The Lion King*, Barry Norman advised viewers that "Each pirate video you buy could contribute to your child shooting up in the school lavatory." Two years later, in *Film 97* (September 29), he offered viewers another salutory warning: "If you're tempted to buy a pirate copy of — I dunno — *Titantic* at the local car boot sale, do remember that the money you hand over may well be laundered back into the drug trade."

34 The threat of child pornography is a common tactic used to generate support for any campaign. Indeed, most people would be happy to help stamp out the production and distribution of such material. (What's the alternative? To be seen *not* endorsing a campaign that claims to be fighting child porn?) Take the NVALA — although child pornography has never been legal in the UK, the NVALA claims to act for "Securing effective legislation to *outlaw child pornography*, video nasties and indecent displays," [*our emphasis*] and to curtail "media obscenity pervading our country and endangering our children."
The same scare tactic is now being used by ELSPA (European Leisure Software Publishers Association) in their crackdown on software piracy. They claim that eighty per cent of organised piracy rings are also involved in drugs, prostitution and funding paramilitary organisations in Northern Ireland.

THE BIG INFLUENCE

1 One of the authors of this book assisted late one Sunday night in the local search for a missing child. As people were drawn by the sight of flashlights, sounds of commotion, and a helicopter overhead providing information via a loudspeaker, the search party grew. In the end the child turned out not to be lost, but with his father who had collected him earlier in the day. The mother expressed in the local paper her relief that the child had not been abducted, dreading to think what might have happened if he had. Speculation which, of course, side-stepped the real issue of lack of parental communication and perhaps even negligence.

2 On April 5, 2000 (the eve of a UEFA cup semi-final match between Leeds United and Turkish club Galatasaray), two Leeds supporters were stabbed to death following clashes between rival fans. Despite the incident and the threat of further violence, the match was considered too important to postpone and went ahead the following evening.

3 A television series depicting footage of accidents and disasters entitled *The World's Most Amazing Videos* opens with the statement that what the viewer will see is "so startling, so awesome, so unbelievable, you might think you're watching a movie." Incongruously, it prefaced footage of a sinking ship with the remark "like a real-life Titanic," as though the viewer is unaware that Titanic is only the title

of a movie and not an historical event.

4 *A Clockwork Orange* was "put on the 'black list' by the Festival of Light although one of the festival's most prominent members stated that it was the best film he had ever seen" – John Trevelyan, *What the Censor Saw*.

5 *In Darkest England and The Way Out*, General Booth, pub: The Salvation Army, 1890.

6 Reminiscing in the pages of *Sight and Sound*, a journalist recalled trying to rent a 16mm copy of *A Clockwork Orange* as part of a film course, in the days when its ban in the UK was less widely publicised. Although it featured in the Columbia-Warner-EMI 16mm catalogue, they were told that rental of the film was restricted to "prisons, hospitals and borstals."
Following Kubrick's death *A Clockwork Orange* was re-released to British cinemas and certified for video.

7 The *Daily News* (philly.com) reported on February 15, 2000, that a man exposing himself to staff at a McDonald's drive-through restaurant, masturbating and hurling his semen at them, may have been committing the acts for publicity. Psychologist Dr James Pedigo said "the publicity may be encouraging the man."

8 *Breaking Points*, Hodder & Stoughton 1985.

9 Following the furore and bogus accusations, the BBC would never air the film again despite having paid for multiple showings. Channel 5 picked up the film and aired it on several occasions. No violent incidents followed the broadcasts.

10 Davies wrote in a *Sunday Telegraph* article (September 18, 1988) that he "wept and felt a little less lonely" on hearing Prince Charles condemn the television, film and video industry for their menu of violence. Earlier in the same article he mentions the Clint Eastwood western *The Outlaw Josey Wales*, and how the world is "heading for a bitter and dead harvest" – which, without any explanation, he claims is already evident "in the valleys of South Wales, where I went to live recently for two years with the miners." Josey Wales... South Wales...?

11 A claim supposedly related to Davies by a "local teenager" but disputed by everyone else.

12 Untrue. Ryan attempted to murder a cashier, Rambo set fire to petrol pumps.

13 In 1999 the European Court of Human Rights declared the two killers had been given an unfair trial.

14 The tabloid editors were on familiar territory using misinformation and propaganda to worry the nation. Several years earlier they spread the bogus satanic child abuse scares across the country. That campaign resulted in the break-up of families, the arrest of innocent people, burning of homes, and worst of all, the sexual abuse of children by those claiming to be *examining them* for signs of abuse. One method used to assess whether a child had been sexually abused is to insert a finger into the child's anus. The reaction of the sphincter muscle determined whether penetration had occurred prior to that moment. At least that is what the examiners claimed.

15 See *Independent on Sunday*, April 17, 1994

16 The press had often reported on the fact that James Bulger had part of his face mutilated during his attack. In what appears to be in-house twisted black humour from the *Daily Star* part of the page describing the Bulger killing was given over to an ad for the film *The Man Without a Face* in which Mel Gibson played a man with half his face mutilated. See *Daily Star* November 26, 1993, p5.

17 Had either of these contrivances succeeded, what film would the press have then chosen to indict as causative? No such scenes were played out in *Child's Play 3*.

18 A metal fixing about two feet long used to bolt lengths of rail track together.

19 Some would attempt to link the insertion of the batteries to *Child's Play 3* suggesting that dolls often contain batteries. This is a further futile, straw-grasping claim. Even at ten-years-of-age the two killers were fully aware of the fact that humans are not battery-operated.

20 "Why Sick Videos Must Be Banned," *The Star*, November 26, 1993.

21 Representing the DPP and instructing counsel for the Crown, Brian Blacklock attended Mary Bell's trial in 1968. In an article published in *Mensa Magazine* in August 1998, he recalls that the facts in the case "were simple, and all the more horrific for being so, but clearly not horrific enough for [today's tastes]." Referencing Gitta Sereny's controversial book *Cries Unheard: The Story of Mary Bell*, he states that a new demonised Mary Bell has been created, thanks to witnesses adding fanciful details over the years, and writers misinterpreting the facts of the case. "How soon," he asks, "before Ms Sereny and others register "Mary Bell plc"? There are, after all, marketing opportunities..."

22 *Young Offenders and the Media,* Hagell & Newburn.

23 It is curious that Alton fails to mention the Bulger case at this point as it was the foundation of his campaign. It is possible that he realised, or was told, that he was over-exploiting the toddler's death.

24 Ireland may have targeted homosexuals to fit with the newspaper's homophobic stance. *The Sun* did, after all, reach its nadir of homophobia when reporting on a so-called "gay-Mafia" running the British government in November 1998.

25 See *Scapegoat* No 1.

26 Similarly, some tabloids are in the habit of doctoring photos of murderers, making the sometimes innocuous looking perpetrators appear as sinister and wicked as their actions. This happened with Hamilton's familiar visage in at least one instance and it also happened with Fred West.

27 A week after the massacre, the *News of the World* turned its attention to the Internet and launched a campaign to "Fight The Filth." The article claimed that Hamilton "could have been tipped over the edge by the stream of paedophile filth available on his computer." By way of illustration, a picture of a child in a bikini with her face blanked out was utilised, dwarfing that of mugshots of Hamilton himself and Sir Cliff Richard, who had sent a heart-felt prayer to the victims of Dunblane. In an unrelated feature the previous December, the *News of the World* ran a double-page story concerning two schoolgirl sisters who aspired to be models. Following the

publication of a topless photo of them in a rival ("sleazy") newspaper, the report stated that the girls had been "hounded by perverts." Not only did the *News of the World* reproduce the "sleazy" shot (albeit with a bold "censored" over their breasts), but ran their own 'tasteful' stocking-tops picture of the two schoolgirl sisters in uniform beside it.

28 Use of the numbers 666 indicate an element of biblical influence. Indeed, the Bible can be attributed to more crimes against humanity than any other single publication and those who act under the book's influence strongly believe it to be a factual record.

29 Grisham predicted that victory in such a case would "come from the heartland, far away from Southern California, in some small courtroom with no cameras."

30 Take the castration of John Wayne Bobbitt by his wife Lorena in 1993. Far from being viewed as a terrible crime, the case was often handled by the media in a light-hearted and humorous way. Lorena had suffered escalating abuse at the hand of her husband. Not only did this lead her to ultimately seek her revenge, but also brought sympathetic votes from women world-wide, who regarded Lorena as the innocent victim. Reverse the situation for a moment: If he had cut off one of her breasts, who would dare to raise a sympathetic voice and what news report would regard the case with anything but the utmost gravity?

31 In their attempt to lay the blame for criminal activity on video, the press will often play down the felon's criminal record, presenting house-breaking and burglary as slight, inoffensive activities with little bearing on the bigger picture.

32 Directed by Tim McCoy starring porn actor Harry Reems and released on video by Cal Vista.

33 How differently would the press have reacted to Edward Paisnel (who donned a hideous mask and ghoulish apparel to commit sex offences against children) had his reign of terror been post-*Texas Chain Saw Massacre*, rather than during the sixties?

34 From Minutes of Evidence taken efore the Home Affairs Committee, Wednesday, June 22, 1994.

35 Some schools took Heston's advice and did just that. The coats were described by officials as intimidating and inappropriate and could be used to hide weapons. Susan Carlson, spokeswoman for schools in Adams County said wearing such coats was "alarming enough to others that it disrupts the educational environment..."

36 Far from being the unique, sign-of-the-times monster the press make him out to be, Marilyn Manson is nothing more than a contemporary Alice Cooper. Like Manson, Cooper was androgynously named, sang rebellious songs, and had a wild and violent stage show. Indeed, the press would have had no trouble implicating Cooper's 1972 No 1 single 'School's Out' — in particular its final line "*school's been blown to pieces...*" — as the inspiration for the Columbine massacre.

37 Results taken from an ongoing poll at apbonline.com on May 11, 1999.

38 In the Spring months of 2000 there came the curious news that one of the emergency services who arrived at the Columbine High School following the massacre, had set to music video footage taken of the devastated classrooms and were selling copies. The report was unclear about the details surrounding the video or indeed who was benefiting from its sales. Time Warner gained access to the security camera footage of the killings and published stills from the video, much to the fury of relatives of the dead who were themselves denied the opportunity to view the film.
An independent no-budget comedy-dramatisation of the massacre entitled *Duck! The Carbine High Massacre*, resulted in the film-makers being arrested because they had carried guns on school property (regardless of the school being closed at the time).

SEX & WRECKS

1 Although amendments had already been made to the 1984 Act in the form of the Criminal Justice Act 1988 and Video Recordings Act 1993, these comprised only of minor tweaks and clarifications. The Criminal Justice and Public Order Act 1994 remains the only significant update.

2 The complete list of films rejected in this period is as follows: *Angel of Vengeance* (a woman studying survivalist techniques is abducted by a group of men in the wilderness but uses her skills to escape and kill them all; this film was effectively remade as *Savage Instinct* which was passed 18 for video); *Caligula: The Untold Story* (Italian cash-in that was denied a certificate in spite of the removal of a hardcore sex scene involving a horse); *Chained*; *Class of 1984* (high school punks take over the classrooms, before a teacher decides to stand up and fight); *A Coming of Angels*; *Curfew*; *The Evil Protégé* (aka *Nightmare Maker*, which had initially formed part of the DPP banned list but was dropped); *Game of Survival* (hoodlums take over a tenement block before the residents mete out their revenge); *Head Girl at St Winifreds*; *Hidden Rage* (Aids victim seeks retribution by transmitting the disease to as many women as he can rape); *Hotline*; *House of Hookers*; *Possession (Until Death Do You Part)*; *Precious Jewels*; *Psychic Killer II*; *Savage Streets* (rape-revenge movie starring Linda Blair armed with a crossbow; an abridged version was eventually classified 18 with some thirteen-and-a-half minutes missing), *Silent Night Deadly Night Part 2* (serial killer dressed as Santa Claus); *Sixth Form at St Winifreds*; *Slumber Party Massacre II*; *Story of O Part 2*; *Target Massacre*; *The Trip*; *Violators*; *War Victims*; *Warden's End*; and *Wild Riders* (biker movie which is a cinematic first in that it features a death by cello).

3 *BBFC Annual Report 1993*.

4 "The Board is conscious that a particular genre that has always been identified as entirely unacceptable is that of so-called 'snuff movies'. Their main identifying feature is that at least one of the participants is actually killed. *Banned from Television* is only different in that, instead of a death being created for the work, actual death and injury is collated from a wide range of pre-existing sources to create the work..." — was one justification the BBFC gave for rejecting this mondo compilation.

5 This was a pet phrase of Ferman's and used to somehow rationalise the role of the censor — Bond movies, for instance, were said to be "not a work of art [but] a work of commerce." When one of the authors of this book contacted the BBFC in 1988 with relation to banned films and censorship, the response from Guy

Phelps — then principal examiner — contained the statement: "I would be most surprised to find many films likely to be of interest to a *serious* collector that have been changed in any way by us." [*Our emphasis.*]

6 *BBFC Annual Report 1996-97.*

7 *BBFC Annual Report 1985.*

8 *BBFC Annual Report 1995-96.*

9 *The Last Days of the Board*, d: Claire Lasko, Channel 4.

10 *BBFC Annual Report 1993.*

11 So great was the concern of parents that the BBFC drew up a form letter to respond to all the complaints (allaying fears by offering statistics and quoting from the glowing review given to the film by the *Daily Mail*). The follow-up to *Jurassic Park, The Lost World*, was the first theatrical release to carry consumer advice. Regarded by the BBFC as a "major initiative", this comprised the following warning: "Passed PG (Parental Guidance) for scary scenes of violence that may be unsuitable for sensitive children or those under 8."

12 BBFC press statement, dated March 20, 1998.

13 *Maniac* was available on video in Britain prior to the Video Recordings Act, in a cut form on the Intervision label.

14 *Samhain* No 69.

15 It should be noted that *A Clockwork Orange* was denied a certificate because its director Stanley Kubrick withdrew the film in 1972. However, it is debatable whether Ferman would have allowed the film to pass intact if it had gone before him: *A Clockwork Orange* is undoubtedly one of the films to which he was referring when lamenting on the tirade of movies from the seventies which featured unacceptable scenes of rape.

16 The video sleeve of *Tenebrae* is also notably different. The trickle of blood on a victim's throat is now transformed into a red ribbon and bow.

17 "Sinful Days in Soho" by Maggie Mills, *The Sunday Times*, courtesy Melon Farmers' Video Hits web site.

18 James Ferman interviewed by David Kenny.

19 Before it had been granted a certificate and the likelihood that it would ever see a British release was still debatable, *Natural Born Killers* played the 1994 London Film Festival to a packed house of 850 people. Tickets were exchanging hands for £100 each outside the theatre. One ticket holder told a reporter for *The Daily Telegraph*: "If something is going to be kept from our eyes, and this is the our one and only chance to see it, I'm not going to miss out."

20 "Confessions of a Censor," Ros Hodgkiss, *The Guardian*, November 20, 1998.

21 Absent from the biographical notes in *Hollywood vs. America* — and indeed the book as a whole — is Medved's former championing of grade-Z horror fare like *Plan 9 From Outer Space* and *The Thing with Two Heads*. Through his *Golden Turkey* books and even his own television show, Medved made a career out of bringing obscure schlock to a new audience. During a screening of *Blood Feast* in London, he ran up and down the aisle howling with demented glee at the gore on screen. To paraphrase one of the chapters in *Hollywood vs. America*: 'What went wrong?'

22 *Daily Express*, November 26, 1993.

23 *The Times*, April 13, 1994.

24 It was eventually passed with seventeen seconds of cuts in November 8, 1994. The full version was submitted in January 1995 and passed without cuts.

25 Although it wasn't mentioned in the reports, Political Correctness probably played its part in robbing kids of their innocence. In 1987, the golliwogs of Enid Blyton's original Noddy books were considered inappropriate and were forever changed to gnomes.

26 Amiel is the director of *Copycat*, a film in which a serial killer utilises the modus operandi of several infamous murderers. In an episode of *Film 96* (transmitted January 1), Amiel said that the films "most likely to create copycat violence are the ones in which our heroes — the Bruce Willises and Sylvester Stallones and Jean-Claude Van Dammes of this world — go out and, during the course of the movie, waste a good twenty to fifty bad guys on the basis they're so bad they deserve everything they get."

27 Almost a year to the day after calling for Ferman to be sacked, the *Mail* travelled a rather tired full circle and on December 14, 1997, pledged "It's time to censor the Censor."

28 The depressing plight of tearaway American teenagers, *Kids* was called child porn by the tabloids on account of some simulated sex scenes (but involving actors over the age of consent).

29 In the case of David Cronenberg's *Crash*, the idea of a 'car crash sex film' was enough to stir the tabloids into near orgasmic frenzy at the end of 1996. Barely a day seemed to go by when the film wasn't the focus of some outraged reporter, critic, or letter-writer. The *Daily Mail* — who spearheaded the campaign to try and ban the film — even went so far as to 'doorstep' BBFC examiners and dig into their personal lives. The newspaper also requested that readers boycott the film (despite the fact that it was not yet on general release) and attacked the managing director of its distributor, Columbia Tristar UK, for being "single, 40, Belgian...and bringing 'depravity' to Britain." (Several days earlier, the film critic for the *Mail* expressed his disgust that *Crash* included people having sex with "cripples.")
When asked what film stood out most in his twenty-three years at the BBFC, James Ferman without hesitation cited *Crash*.

30 The story of a female necrophile, loosely based on the real life case of Karen Greenlee.

31 See *Killing for Culture*, Kerekes & Slater.

32 Courtesy of hidden cameras, *Hookers: Sex for Sale* shows an Australian model by the name of Peter Benedict having sex with a series of prostitutes and giving them marks out of ten. The film makers claimed it made a serious point and helped to expose the inner world of prostitution.
Everyday...Operations featured in close-up a selection of the most common surgical procedures performed in British hospitals. In a press release, the BBFC stated that they had given the film an 18 certificate because it demystified remedial practices and demonstrated "the skills of the

surgeons involved." However, there is something of an apologia in the sentence: "When this tape was submitted for classification, the BBFC considered that the material contained in it was presented in a factual and informative way with no attempt to sensationalise or exploit"... It could be that the BBFC, having passed the film, got wise to the fact that *Everyday... Operations* came from the same team as *Police Stop!* and *Caught in the Act*, the latter masquerading as a serious look at surveillance but which was found to contain fabricated footage of a couple having sex in a lift.

33 Bruce Gyngell, a fore-runner for the position of BBFC president, writing in *The Mail on Sunday*, December 14, 1997.

34 *BBFC Annual Report 1997-98*.

35 "More Sex Please, We're British," Laurence O'Toole writing in the *New Statesman*, August 30, 1999.

36 Consequently, the BBFC refused to pass uncut *Makin' Whoopee*, which contained material no more pornographic than either *The Pyramid* or *BatBabe*. Its distributor went to the Video Appeals Committee (VAC), who conceded unanimously that the film was not obscene within the terms of the Obscene Publications Acts and should be granted an R18 certificate. Regarding this as a benchmark, seven other videos to which the Board had denied R18 certificates were also taken before the VAC and found not obscene: *Horny Catbabe*, *Nympho Nurse Nancy*, *TV Sex*, *Office Tart*, a trailer for *Carnival (International Version)*, *Wet Nurses 2 (Continental Version)* and *Miss Nude International (Continental Version)*. The Board announced they would be seeking a Judicial Review. In May 2000, the High Court ruled that the videos could be legally sold in Britain.

37 The film's distributor, Alliance, actually left the forty second scene in but blurred it to remove the offensive detail. They wanted the viewer to be aware that censorship had been imposed.

38 David Gregory interviewed by Simon Collins, *Headpress 20*.

39 Following the Dunblane massacre, there was a move to bring a ban on all handguns above single shot types. The bill was met with strong criticism from gun enthusiasts, as well as many politicians. One Tory MP went so far as to say that the family of those killed at Dunblane were reacting "emotively." The gun owners were subsequently portrayed as victims and, when their weapons had to be handed in, were financially compensated with public money. Suddenly the emphasis switched from guns and back onto film and TV violence.

40 *Today* and *Daily Mirror*, April 13, 1994.

41 *BBFC Annual Report 1993*.

42 Equally we could argue that television gameshows and the National Lottery have encouraged a something-for-nothing generation. But we diversify into an endless spiral of potential blame.
To lift a quote from John Waters' *Pecker:* "Pubic hair causes crime."

43 Members of the NVALA spend their viewing time specifically watching violence — over an unspecified duration they collated 107 incidents of arson and bomb attacks, 340 stabbings, and forty-four scenes depicting illegal drugs.

44 James Ferman interviewed by David Kenny.

45 "The vice hunter declares that most adults are mentally deficient and need protection..." This was a statement made back in 1929 (by Morris L Ernst and William Seagle in their book *To The Pure...*). It wasn't that many years ago when selling or exhibiting books to negroes was a punishable offence.

46 Vipco, a distributor from the early eighties, revitalised themselves in the nineties by exhuming former nasties. Although these BBFC certified versions were cut, each re-release carried a bold disclaimer on the box notifying the consumer of the film's former banned status. Similarly, the recent reissue of *Axe* remains for Exploited a "commercial decision, because it had been a video nasty."

47 "The Street's video nasty" (Granada television are said to face a heavy fine for broadcasting a special episode of the soap *Coronation Street* which had hitherto been marketed as exclusive to video)... "Tintin takes on the video nasties" (Herge's famous cartoon creation is set to make a comeback)... "Video shock for parents" (Scarborough police intend to crack hooliganism with security cameras and "asking parents to watch video 'nasties' starring their own children")...

48 James Ferman interviewed by David Kenny.

BIBLIOGRAPHY / PERIODICALS / WWW

Barker, Martin (ed). *The Video Nasties: Freedom and Censorship in the Media*. London: Pluto Press, 1984.

Barlow, Geoffrey and Hill, Alison. *Video Violence and Children*. London: Hodder and Stoughton, 1985.

Bertrock, Alan. *The I Was A Teenage Juvenile Delinquent Rock'n'Roll Horror Beach Party Movie Book! A Complete Guide to the Teen Exploitation Film, 1954–1969*. London: Plexus, 1986.

British Videogram Association. *A Trade Guide to the Video Recordings Act*. UK: HMSO, 1985.

Brottman, Mikita. *Offensive Films: Towards an Anthropology of Cinéma Vomitif*. CT: Greenwood Press, 1997.

Buchanan, Larry. *It Came From Hunger! Tales of a Cinema Schlockmeister*. North Carolina: McFarland, 1996.

Burrell, Nigel J. *Knights of Terror: The Blind Dead Films of Amando de Ossorio*. Cambs: Midnight Media, 1995.

Burrell, Nigel J. *Let Sleeping Corpses Lie: The Living Dead at the Manchester Morgue — A Critical Dissection*. Cambs: Midnight Media Publishing, 1996.

Davies, Tom. *Man of Lawlessness*. London: Hodder & Stoughton, 1989.

Fenton, Harvey; Grainger, Julian & Castoldi, Gian Luca. *Cannibal Holocaust and the Savage Cinema of Ruggero Deodato*. Surrey: FAB Press, 1999.

Caputi, Jane. *The Age of Sex Crime*. London: The Women's Press, 1988.

Chester, Graham. *Berserk! Motiveless Random Massacres*. London: Michael O'Mara Books, 1993.

Clover, Carol J. *Men, Women, and Chainsaws: Gender in the Modern Horror Film*. London: BFI Publishing, 1992.

Cohen, Stanley. *Folk Devils & Moral Panics: The Creation of the Mods and Rockers*. Oxford: Blackwell, 1987.

Curtis, Tony. *Lyle Price Guide: Film & Rock'n'Roll Collectables*. Scotland: Lyle Publications, 1994.

Davies, Tom. *The Man of Lawlessness*. London: Hodder & Stoughton, 1989.

Dhavan, Rajeev & Davies, Christie. *Censorship and Obscenity*. London: Martin Robertson & Co., 1978.

Elliot, John. *Elliot's Guide to Films on Video*. London: Boxtree, 1990.

Ernst, Morris L. & Seagle, William. *To the Pure... A Study of Obscenity and the Censor*. London: Jonathan Cape, 1929.
Ferguson, Michael. *Little Joe Superstar: The Films of Joe Dallesandro*. California: Companion Press, 1998.
French, Karl (ed). *Screen Violence*. London: Bloomsbury, 1996.
Fountain, Nigel. *Underground: The London Alternative Press 1966–74*. London: Routledge, 1988.
Green, Jonathon. *The Encyclopedia of Censorship*. New York: Facts on File, 1990.
Hagell, Ann & Newburn, Tim. *Young Offenders and the Media*. London: PSI, 1994.
Hardy, Phil (ed). *The Aurum Film Encyclopedia: Horror*. London: Aurum Press, 1985.
Hardy, Phil (ed). *The Encyclopedia of Science Fiction Movies*. London: Octopus, 1986.
Hebditch, David & Nick Anning. *Porn Gold: Inside the Pornography Business*. London: Faber and Faber, 1988.
Hoberman, J. & Rosenbaum, Jonathan. *Midnight Movies*. NY: Harper & Row, 1983.
Jaworzyn, Stefan (ed). *Shock Xpress 2: The Essential Guide to Exploitation Cinema*. London: Titan, 1994.
Josephs, Jeremy. *Hungerford: One Man's Massacre*. London: Smith Gryphon, 1993.
Jouis, Pierre (ed). *Directed By Dario Argento*. Maisons-Alfort: Fantasy Film Memory, 1991.
Kelland, Gilbert. *Crime In London*. London: HarperCollins, 1993.
Kerekes, David & Slater, David. *Killing for Culture: An Illustrated History of Death Film from Mondo to Snuff*. London: Creation Books, 1995.
Killick, Mark. *The Sultan of Sleaze: The Story of David Sullivan's Sex and Media Empire*. London: Penguin, 1994.
Kinnard, Roy & Davis, Tim. *Divine Images: A History of Jesus on the Screen*. NY: Citadel Press, 1992.
Koch, Stephen. *Stargazer: The Life, World & Films of Andy Warhol, Revised and updated*. London: Marion Boyars, 1991.
Konow, David. *Schlock-O-Rama: The Films of Al Adamson*. Los Angeles: Lone Eagle, 1998.
Lee, Walt. *Reference Guide to Fantastic Films: Science Fiction, Fantasy & Horror, Vols 1, 2 & 3*. CA: Chelsea-Lee Books, 1975
Longford Committee Investigating Pornography, The. *Pornography: The Longford Report*. London: Coronet, 1972.
Luther-Smith, Adrian (ed). *Delirium: A Guide To Italian Exploitation Cinema 1975–1979*. London: Media Publication, 1979.
McCarty, John. *The Sleaze Merchants: Adventures in Exploitation Filmmaking*. New York: St Martin's Griffin, 1995.
McCarty, Helen & Clements, Jonathan. *The Erotic Anime Movie Guide*. London: Titan, 1998.
Mathews, Tom Dewe. *Censored: What They Didn't Allow You To See and Why—The Story of Film Censorship in Britain*. London: Chatto, 1994.
Medved, Michael. *Hollywood vs. America: Popular Culture and the War on Traditional Values*. NY: HarperCollins, 1992.
Michael, Richard (ed). *The ABZ of Pornography*. London: Granada, 1972.
Michel, Jean-Claude. *Lucio Fulci: Italy's Gore Master*. Maisons-Alfort: Fantasy Film Memory, 1990.
Muller, Eddie & Faris, Daniel. *That's Sexploitation!!: The Forbidden World of "Adults Only" Cinema*. London: Titan Books, 1997.
Newman, Kim. *Nightmare Movies: A Critical History of the Horror Film, 1968–88*. London: Bloomsbury, 1988.
O'Toole, Laurence. *Pornocopia: Porn, Sex, Technology and Desire*. London: Serpent's Tale,1998.
Opie, Iona & Moira Tatem (ed). *A Dictionary of Superstitions*. Oxford: Oxford University Press, 1993.
Palmerini, Luca M. & Mistretta, Gaetano. *Spaghetti Nightmares: Italian Fantasy—Horrors as Seen Through the Eyes of Their Protagonists*. Florida: Fantasma Books, 1996.
Parish, James Robert. *Prison Pictures from Hollywood: Plots, Critiques, Casts and Credits for 293 Theatrical and Made-for-Television Releases*. North Carolina: McFarland & Co, 1991.
Phelps, Guy. *Film Censorship*. London: Victor Gollancz, 1975.
Pirie, David. *The Vampire Cinema*. Middlesex: Hamlyn, 1977.
Puchalski, Steven. *Slimetime: A Guide to Sleazy, Mindless, Movie Entertainment*. Manchester: Critical Vision, 1996.
Ray, Fred Olen. *The New Poverty Row: Independent Filmmakers as Distributors*. North Carolina: McFarland, 1991.
Riley, Patrick. *The X-Rated Videotape Star Index*. NY: Prometheus, 1994.
Rimmer, Patrick H. *The X-Rated Videotape Guide I*. NY: Prometheus, 1993.
Robertson, Geoffrey. *Obscenity: An Account of Censorship Laws and their Enforcement in England and Wales*. London: Weidenfeld and Nicolson, 1979.
Robertson, Geoffrey & Andrew Nicol. *Media Law*. London: Penguin, 1992.
Robertson, James C. *The Hidden Cinema: British Film Censorship in Action, 1913–1972*. London: Routledge, 1989.
Ross, Jonathan. *The Incredibly Strange Film Book*. London: Simon & Schuster, 1993.
Shepard, Jewel. *Invasion of the B-Girls*. CA: Eclipse, 1992.
Smith, Tim. *The Complete Video Guide*. London: Virgin Books, 1981.
Springhall, John. *Youth, Popular Culture and Moral Panics: Penny Gaffs to Gansta-Rap, 1830–1996*. Hampshire: Macmillan, 1998.
Stanley, John. *Creature Features: The Science Fiction, Fantasy, and Horror Movie Guide*. NY: Boulevard, 1997.
Stern, Chester. *Dr Iain West's Casebook*. London: Little Brown, 1996.
Stevenson, Jack (ed). *Fleshpot: Cinema's Sexual Myth Makers & Taboo Breakers*. Manchester: Critical Vision, 2000.
Sutherland, John. *Offensive Literature: Decensorship in Britain, 1960–1982*. London: Junction Books, 1982.
Szulkin, David A. *Wes Craven's Last House on the Left: The Making of a Cult Classic*. Surrey: FAB Press, 1997.
Taylor, Laurie & Mullan, Bob. *Uninvited Guests: The Intimate Secrets of Television and Radio*. London: Chatto & Windus, 1986.
Thomas, Mark. *Every Mother's Nightmare: The Killing of James Bulger*. London: Pan, 1993.
Thompson, Bill. *Soft Core: Moral Crusades Against Pornography in Britain and America*. London: Cassell, 1994.
Thompson, David & Christie, Ian (ed). *Scorsese on Scorsese*. London: Faber and Faber, 1989.
Thrower, Stephen. *Beyond Terror: The Films of Lucio Fulci*. Surrey: FAB Press, 1999.
Trevelyan, John. *What the Censor Saw*. London: Michael Joseph, 1973.
Tribe, David. *Questions of Censorship*. London: George Allen & Unwin, 1973.
Turan, Kenneth & Zito, Stephen F. *Sinema: American Pornographic Films and the People Who Make Them*. NY: Praeger, 1974.
Vogel, Amos. *Film as a Subversive Art*. London: Weidenfeld and Nicolson, 1974.
Weaver, Tom. *Attack of the Monster Movie Makers: Interviews with 20 Genre Giants*. North Carolina: McFarland, 1994.
Weldon, Michael J. *The Psychotronic Encyclopedia of Film*. New York: Ballantine, 1983.
———. *The Psychotronic Video Guide*. New York: St Martin's Press, 1996.
Whitehouse, Mary. *"Who Does She Think She Is?"* London: New English Library, 1971.
———. *Whatever Happened To Sex?* East Sussex: Wayland, 1977.
———. *A Most Dangerous Woman?* Herts: Lion, 1982.
Williams, Bernard (ed). *Obscenity and Film Censorship: An Abridgement of The Williams Report*. Cambridge: University Press, 1981.
Wingrove, Nigel & Morris, Marc. *The Art of the Nasty*. London: Salvation Films, 1998.
Yallop, David. *Deliver Us From Evil*. London: Corgi, 1993.
Zalcock, Bev. *Renegade Sisters: Girl Gangs on Film*. London: Creation, 1998.

Absurd (UK); Asian Trash Cinema (USA) BBFC Annual Report (UK); Broadcast (UK); Castle of Frankenstein (USA); CineFan (USA); Continental Film and Video Review (UK); DarkSide, The (UK); Deep Red (USA); Delirium (UK); Demonique (USA); Diabolik (UK); Draculina (USA); Dreadful Pleasures (USA); Eerie (USA); European Trash Cinema (USA); Empire (UK); Eyeball (UK); Fangoria (USA); Film Extremes (UK); Film Threat (USA); Filmfax (USA); Flesh & Blood (UK); Gore Gazette (USA); Headpress (UK); Hi-Tech Terror (USA); House of Hammer, The / Halls of Horror (UK); Imaginator (UK); Is it... Uncut? (UK); Killbaby (Canada); Killing Moon (UK); Magick Theatre (USA); Manga Mania (UK); Master Detective (UK); Men Only (UK); Midnight Marquee (USA); Monster! International (USA); Monster Times, The (USA); Monthly Film Bulletin (UK); Nocturno (Italy); Nostalgia (France); Outré (USA); Panicos!! (Canada); Photoplay (UK); Psychotronic Video (USA); Samhain (UK); Scapegoat (UK); Screen International (UK); Shock Cinema (USA); Shock Xpress (UK); Sight and Sound (UK); Sleazoid Express (USA); Splatter Times, The (USA); Sub Human (USA); Video—The Magazine (UK); Video Watchdog (USA); Video Viewer (UK); Videooze (USA); World of Horror (UK)

APBnews.com
http://www.apbnews.com/
British Board of Film Classification
http://www.bbfc.co.uk
DVD Nightmare
http://www.dvdnightmare.com/
Headpress
http://www.headpress.com/
Internet Movie Database (IMDb)
http://www.imdb.com
Melon Farmers' Video Hits
http://www.dtaylor.demon.co.uk/index.htm
Total Rewind
http://www.popadom.demon.co.uk/vidhist/enquiry.htm

INDEX

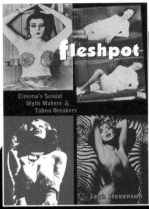

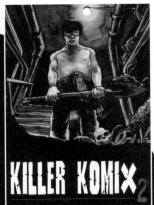

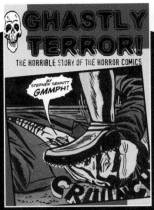

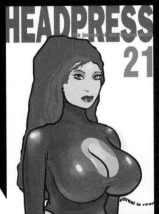